T0321929

Integrating Machine Learning Into HPC–Based Simulations and Analytics

Belgacem Ben Youssef
King Saud University, Saudi Arabia

Mohamed Maher Ben Ismail
King Saud University, Saudi Arabia

IGI Global
Scientific Publishing
Publishing Tomorrow's Research Today

Vice President of Editorial   Melissa Wagner
Managing Editor of Acquisitions   Mikaela Felty
Managing Editor of Book Development   Jocelynn Hessler
Production Manager   Mike Brehm
Cover Design   Phillip Shickler

Published in the United States of America by
  IGI Global Scientific Publishing
  701 East Chocolate Avenue
  Hershey, PA, 17033, USA
  Tel: 717-533-8845
  Fax: 717-533-8661
. E-mail: cust@igi-global.com
  Website: https://www.igi-global.com

Library of Congress Cataloging-in-Publication Data

Names: Ben Youssef, Belgacem, 1965- editor. | Ben Ismail, Mohamed Maher Ben, 1979- editor.
Title: Handbook of research on integrating machine learning into HPC-based simulations and analytics / edited by Belgacem Ben Youssef, Mohamed Maher Ben Ben Ismail.
Description: Hershey, PA : Engineering Science Reference, [2025] | Includes bibliographical references and index. | Summary: "This edited book aims to present to the reader recent research efforts in designing and using ML techniques on HPC systems, discuss some of the results achieved thus far by cutting-edge relevant contributions. Another objective is to identify research challenges and opportunities in the area spanning the intersection of HPC and ML. In fact, further collaboration between the HPC and ML communities is encouraged for rapid and seamless progress toward an ecosystem that effectively serves both of these communities.
  Furthermore, new tools and benchmarks are required to overcome the common challenges across HPC and ML applications. The goals of this form of convergence are fourfold: 1. Obtain optimized solutions that show discernible reduction in compute requirements. 2. Facilitate having a more dynamic view of domain sciences. 3. Develop integrated knowledge through interdisciplinary collaboration. 4. Stimulate innovations with deep societal impact through the provisioning of new advances in scientific research spanning many application areas"-- Provided by publisher.
Identifiers: LCCN 2022057598 (print) | LCCN 2022057599 (ebook) | ISBN 9781668437957 (h/c) | ISBN 9781668437964 (eISBN)
Subjects: LCSH: High performance computing. | Machine learning. | Computer simulation.
Classification: LCC QA76.88 .H353 2023 (print) | LCC QA76.88 (ebook) | DDC 004.1/1--dc23/eng/20230123
LC record available at https://lccn.loc.gov/2022057598
LC ebook record available at https://lccn.loc.gov/2022057599

British Cataloguing in Publication Data
A Cataloguing in Publication record for this book is available from the British Library.

To all our parents and our respective families.

Editorial Advisory Board

Table of Contents

C. Indhumathi, Department of Computer and Business Systems, Sri Sairam Engineering
College, Chennai, India

Shaik Abdul Hameed, Department of Computer Science and Engineering, VNR VJIET,
Hyderabad, India

R. Jothilakshmi, Department of Information Technology, R.M.D. Engineering College,
Chennai, India

Syed Musthafa A., Department of Information Technology, M. Kumarasamy College of
Engineering, Karur, India

M. Ramesh Babu, Department of Electrical and Electronics Engineering, St. Joseph's
College of Engineering, Chennai, India

S. Muthuvel, Kalasalingam Academy of Research and Education, Srivilliputhur, India

E. Afreen Banu, Department of Computer Engineering, Shah and Anchor Kutchhi
Engineering College, Mumbai, India

Chalumuru Suresh, Department of Computer Science and Engineering, VNRVJIET,
Hyderabad, India

V. Nyemeesha, Department of Computer Science and Engineering, VNRVJIET, Hyderabad,
India

Mannepalli Venkata Krishna Rao, Department of Computer Science and Engineering,
VNRVJIET, Hyderabad, India

B. Muthuraj, Department of Electrical and Electronics Engineering, Panimalar Engineering
College, Chennai, India

S. Muthuvel, Kalasalingam Academy of Research and Education, Srivilliputhur, India

Prachi Rajendra Salve, Department of Computer Engineering, MKSSS's Cummins College of
Engineering for Women, Pune, India

M. R. Mano Jemila, Department of Biomedical Engineering, Dr. NGP Institute of
Technology, Coimbatore, India

S. Sridharan, Department of Electrical and Electronics Engineering, St. Joseph's College of
Engineering, Chennai, India

Vinod Kumar V. Meti, Department of Automation and Robotics, KLE Technological
University, Hubballi, India

Bhaskar Roy, Department of Computer Science and Engineering, Asansol Engineering
College, India

Detailed Table of Contents

Chapter 1

Belgacem Ben Youssef, King Saud University, Saudi Arabia
Mohamed Maher Ben Ismail, King Saud University, Saudi Arabia
Ouiem Bchir, King Saud University, Saudi Arabia

Social network platforms ought to be a place where no user gets insulted via verbal abuse. Cyberbullying and online abusive language is becoming a major concern for all stakeholders. Research on insult detection has seen a surge in interest over the last few years to address this problem. The emergence of deep learning techniques and their promising achievements in various fields have promoted their use as a natural alternative to tackle the many challenges related to insult detection. The authors describe in this chapter a supervised deep learning model to capture the online comments' semantics and detect insults. The proposed approach relies on two main components: (i) Text pre-processing and representation, and (ii) A Transformer-based deep learning model trained to classify the comments submitted on social media platforms as an insult or insult free based on the BERT method. The obtained results indicate that the proposed model outperforms CNNs and RNNs in the detection of insults for the same OLID benchmark yielding a macro F1-score of 0.83 and an accuracy of 86%.

Chapter 2

Jan Kalina, Institute of Computer Science, The Czech Academy of Sciences, Czech Republic

Artificial intelligence is nowadays equipped with a plethora of tools for obtaining relevant knowledge from (possibly big) data in a variety of tasks. While habitually used methods of machine learning applicable within artificial intelligence tools can be characterized as black boxes, practical applications often require to understand why a particular conclusion (e.g. decision) was made, which arouses interest in explainable machine learning. This chapter is devoted to variable selection methods for finding the most relevant variables for the given task. If statistically robust variable selection methods are exploited, the harmful influence of data contamination by outlying values on the results is typically eliminated or downweighted. Principles of prior, intrinsic, and posterior variable selection approaches are recalled and compared on three real datasets related to gene expression measurements, neighborhood crime rate, and tourism infrastructure. These examples reveal robust approaches to machine learning that outperform non-robust ones if the data are contaminated by outliers.

Tariq Lasloum, King Saud University, Saudi Arabia
Belgacem Ben Youssef, King Saud University, Saudi Arabia
Haikel Alhichri, King Saud University, Saudi Arabia

Deep neural networks and in particular Convolutional Neural Networks (CNNs) are considered to be the state-of-the-art tools for scene classification. However, training deep CNN models requires huge amounts of labeled data to achieve excellent classification accuracy. Thus, an important goal in deep learning is how to reduce the data labelling burden. Domain Adaptation (DA) is the main technique in this regard. The goal is to classify the target domain correctly by learning from the source domain. This chapter examines the basic concepts required to understand RS. Then, it proceeds to describe in detail a method for multi-source semi-supervised domain adaptation in remote sensing scene classification called Semi-Supervised Domain Adaptation Network (SSDAN). Performance results in terms of overall accuracy and Kappa coefficient values obtained when conducting experiments using single-source, two-source, and three-source scenarios are also provided. The achieved results of these two metrics reached values of more than 99%, demonstrating the efficacy of the SSDAN method.

Mohamed Maher Ben Ismail, King Saud University, Saudi Arabia
Yasser Al-Ali, King Saud University, Saudi Arabia
Ouiem Bchir, King Saud University, Saudi Arabia

In today's world of technological advancement, smartphones have become akin to a cybernetic implant for most people. Those phones that we carry everywhere are capable of doing things from taking pictures to tracking the number of steps we take. Fitness activities can be recognized using the smartphone's inertial sensors. Moreover, machine learning can be exploited to design predictive or descriptive models able to discover and/or predict fitness activity patterns with better accuracy. As different fitness activities exhibit different patterns and characteristics, classifying them would allow the users to better track their performance, endurance and calories burned. This chapter introduces a ML-based system that can accurately recognize the user's fitness activity. Specifically, deep learning models were investigated to automatically map the signals captured by the sensors of the user's smart device into some pre-defined classes of fitness activities. The designed models were implemented, validated, and tested using standard benchmark datasets and appropriate performance measures.

Chapter 5

Ibtihal Ferwana, University of Illinios at Urbana-Champaign, USA
Soumaya Chaffar, University of Prince Mugrin, Saudi Arabia
Samir Brahim Belhaouari, Hamad Bin Khalifa University, Qatar

Mobile applications have been ubiquitous in our daily life. Given the success of Deep Neural Networks (DNNs) in image recognition tasks, DNNs are widely implemented on mobile phone applications. Due to the limited memory and energy on mobile phones, DNNs size and execution time are still roadblocks for efficient processing and instant inferences. Many transformative efforts were able to compress DNNs to the desired size for efficient speed, energy, and memory consumption. In this chapter, two areas of compression: pruning and redesigning efficient neural architectures were discussed. For each, recent advancements and highlight their strengths and limitations are discussed along with showing the improvements brought up by each selected methods and compare them. Comparisons are based on evaluating compression rate, inference time, and accuracy. The aim of this chapter would help practitioners who are implementing DNN based mobile applications to choose a compression approach that satisfies their requirements.

Chapter 6

Abdullah Alsalemi, De Montfort University, UK
Abbes Amira, University of Sharjah, UAE
Hossein Malekmohamadi, De Montfort University, UK
Kegong Diao, De Montfort University, UK

With varying applications of Artificial Intelligence (AI) on an expanding global scale, performance metrics and standards of platforms have steadily elevated. High-Performance Edge Computing (HPEC) plays an instrumental role in lifting a substantial load on cloud computing for Deep Learning (DL). Notwithstanding, the collection, pre-and-post processing of big data engenders many challenges and opportunities for optimizing HPEC performance for data classification and, in turn, yields better outcomes. This is where the concept of data lakes is employed, which are raw-formatted large masses of data that are plausibly more compatible with many algorithms than structured data stores. Therefore, in this work, we carry out a comparative study that examines the merits, performance and efficiency metrics, and limitations of two notable HPEC platforms centered around a DL data lake framework. With classification accuracy of ~90%, results show that adequate performance and impressive computational efficiency, as fast as 8.19 msec per classified GAF image is achieved on the Jetson Nano.

Vladyslav Pliuhin, O.M. Beketov National University of Urban Economy in Kharkiv, Ukraine
Yevgen Tsegelnyk, O.M. Beketov National University of Urban Economy in Kharkiv, Ukraine
Maria Sukhonos, O.M. Beketov National University of Urban Economy in Kharkiv, Ukraine
Ihor Biletskyi, O.M. Beketov National University of Urban Economy in Kharkiv, Ukraine
Sergiy Plankovskyy, O.M. Beketov National University of Urban Economy in Kharkiv, Ukraine
Vitaliy Tietieriev, O.M. Beketov National University of Urban Economy in Kharkiv, Ukraine

The current approach to designing electric machines is carried out using a 'cascade' algorithm, wherein sequential calculations are performed according to formulas derived from electromagnetic theory. However, this approach is tailored to each specific type of electric machine, making modification of projects difficult and not always feasible. One promising solution to address this issue is to leverage HPC (High-Performance Computing) calculations in conjunction with machine learning capabilities. This chapter examines established methodologies for designing and optimizing electric machines, ultimately advocating for the integration of machine learning and modern optimization algorithms.

Aswathy Ravikumar, Vellore Institute of Technology, India
Harini Sriraman, Vellore Institute of Technology, India

Optimal high-performance computing (HPC) use for deep learning is a difficult task that requires progress in a variety of research domains. Complex systems and events are represented using a combination of science-based and data-driven models. Additionally, there is a growing demand for real-time data analytics, that necessitates the relocation of large-scale computations nearer to data and data infrastructures, as well as the adaptation of HPC-like modes. Parallel deep learning tries to maximize the performance of complex neural network models by executing them concurrently on recent hardware platforms. Considerable time has been invested in integrating HPC technology into deep learning frameworks that are both reliable and highly functional. In this chapter, distributed deep neural network model designing using parsl, tensor flow, Keras, Horovod libraries, and the implementation of these models using Hadoop, SPARK clusters on local-area networks (LAN) as well as on cloud services like Amazon web services (AWS) and Google cloud platform (GCP) are discussed.

An integration of machine learning (ML) with high-performance computing (HPC) is radically transforming research in the scientific field. ML algorithms can span large-scale simulations and predict a great deal in materials science, climate modeling, and drug discovery by optimizing resource allocation and finding novel insights. HPC has accelerated complex data-sets processing, and ML models allow automation in pattern recognition and advanced analytics. The synergy of these technologies accelerates the experimentation rate, shortens time-to-discovery, and improves the scalability to tackle complex scientific challenges. It explores different key methodologies, case studies, and directions with future impacts that illustrate how advances in ML and HPC can revolutionize scientific innovation across disciplines. It demonstrates improved problem-solving capacity and accuracy in prediction as it addresses some of the most profound global challenges.

This chapter explores how high-performance computing (HPC) can be a transformative force towards further acceleration of AI-driven energy harvesting and environmental monitoring systems. With increasing demand for sustainable energy solutions and effective environmental management, this affords a golden opportunity through the integration of HPC and AI, which can largely optimize the processing of large datasets with respect to energy collection and increase monitoring precision. The methods used in harvesting renewable energy, such as solar and wind-based methods using AI algorithms, that analyze the energy output to optimize system efficiencies, are discussed. The chapter also discusses how HPC allows real-time analysis of environmental data that can be used in decision-making and in being proactive when there are changes in ecosystems. Case studies that focus on successful implementations show the synergistic benefits of this integration, which may directly contribute to the global sustainability agenda.

Chapter 11

S. Subashree, Department of Computer Science and Engineering, E G.S. Pillay Engineering
College, Nagapattinam, India

T. Akila, Department of Information Technology, Mahendra College of Engineering, Salem,
India

Pravin A Dwaramwar, Department of Electronic and Computer Science, Ramdeobaba
University, Nagpur, India

Saurabh Chandra, School of Law, Bennett University, Greater Noida, India

Ketki P. Kshirsagar, Department of Electronics and Telecommunication, Vishwakarma
Institute of Technology, Pune, India

The rapid digital transformation in this era has led to the rise of high-performance computing (HPC) systems as a hub for addressing computationally intensive requirements, but their energy consumption is also a growing concern due to sustainability efforts. This chapter surveys the potential transformative impact of Artificial Intelligence (AI) in optimizing energy management in the context of HPC systems. With machine learning algorithms and predictive analytics, an AI system can dynamically adapt to power use levels, optimize workload distributions, and reduce energy consumption without compromising computational performance. The techniques discussed in this chapter include AI-driven techniques founded on computational methods such as reinforcement learning and neural network models that change HPC workloads appropriately to support real-time decision-making and energy-efficient operations. This chapter presents successful AI-based system implementations while highlighting high performance and energy savings.

Chapter 12

C. Indhumathi, Department of Computer and Business Systems, Sri Sairam Engineering College, Chennai, India

Shaik Abdul Hameed, Department of Computer Science and Engineering, VNR VJIET, Hyderabad, India

R. Jothilakshmi, Department of Information Technology, R.M.D. Engineering College, Chennai, India

Syed Musthafa A., Department of Information Technology, M. Kumarasamy College of Engineering, Karur, India

M. Ramesh Babu, Department of Electrical and Electronics Engineering, St. Joseph's College of Engineering, Chennai, India

S. Muthuvel, Kalasalingam Academy of Research and Education, Srivilliputhur, India

This chapter explores the integration of federated learning and gestural technology in the healthcare sector, aiming to enhance patient care, diagnostics, and treatment. Federated learning allows decentralized machine learning models to train on patient data from multiple healthcare institutions while maintaining privacy, making it ideal for protecting sensitive medical data. Gestural technology is mainly utilized in human-computer interaction to assist healthcare professionals in the management of accessibility and usability of healthcare systems, especially during remote diagnostics and rehabilitation. The integration of these two technologies ensures that individualized care can be achieved, workflow operations streamlined, and outcomes improved without compromising data security. It also explores use cases of telemedicine, rehabilitation, and clinical decision support, addressing challenges like data privacy, model accuracy, and technical integration.

Chapter 13

Advances in Computational Visual Information Processing for Neuroscience and Healthcare
Applications 329

E. Afreen Banu, Department of Computer Engineering, Shah and Anchor Kutchhi
Engineering College, Mumbai, India

Chalumuru Suresh, Department of Computer Science and Engineering, VNRVJIET,
Hyderabad, India

V. Nyemeesha, Department of Computer Science and Engineering, VNRVJIET, Hyderabad,
India

Mannepalli Venkata Krishna Rao, Department of Computer Science and Engineering,
VNRVJIET, Hyderabad, India

B. Muthuraj, Department of Electrical and Electronics Engineering, Panimalar Engineering
College, Chennai, India

S. Muthuvel, Kalasalingam Academy of Research and Education, Srivilliputhur, India

Advances in visual information processing have revolutionized computational neuroscience and healthcare by enhancing our understanding of neural mechanisms and developing new medical solutions. Techniques like deep learning algorithms, convolutional neural networks, and computer vision applications have provided unprecedented insights into brain activity and visual organ function. These technologies also enhance our ability to model and simulate cognitive processes, making them crucial in understanding and improving medical outcomes. Visual information processing enhances healthcare diagnostics, medical imaging, and treatment personalization, ranging from radiology to pathology. It integrates advanced technology with neural interfaces and AI, revolutionizing patient care and neurological research. Further, ethical considerations, data privacy, and the challenge of transforming complex visual data into actionable insights for healthcare professionals and neuroscientists are discussed in this chapter.

Chapter 14

*Prachi Rajendra Salve, Department of Computer Engineering, MKSSS's Cummins College of
Engineering for Women, Pune, India*

*M. R. Mano Jemila, Department of Biomedical Engineering, Dr. NGP Institute of
Technology, Coimbatore, India*

*S. Sridharan, Department of Electrical and Electronics Engineering, St. Joseph's College of
Engineering, Chennai, India*

*Vinod Kumar V. Meti, Department of Automation and Robotics, KLE Technological
University, Hubballi, India*

*Bhaskar Roy, Department of Computer Science and Engineering, Asansol Engineering
College, India*

Application of high-performance computer systems and microcontrollers in food quality monitoring pays extra attention to their improvements in accuracy, efficiency, and real-time analysis. Advanced microcontrollers allow the accomplishment of more precise monitoring of critical parameters such as temperature, humidity, and gas composition in order to ensure food safety and quality from supply chain outlets. Innovations in sensor technology, data processing, and wireless communication gave birth to smart systems for detecting contamination, spoilage, or adulteration. These systems feed real-time data that enables instantaneous decisions and reduces food waste. Microcontroller-based solutions allow for IoT connectivity and machine learning algorithms with a better possibility of predictive analytics and automation in the management of food quality. The chapter is focused on the key technologies, applications, and challenges, giving insight into the future regarding food quality monitoring in this very connected world, particularly about food industries.

Chapter 15

R. Muthukumar, Department of Electrical and Electronics Engineering, Erode Sengunthar Engineering College, India

Divakar Harekal, Department of Information Science and Engineering, Jyothy Institute of Technology, Bengaluru, India

Sk. Mastan Sharif, Department of Advanced Computer Science Engineering, Vignan's Foundation for Science, Technology, and Research, Vadlamudi, India

Dhivakar Poosapadi, Quest Global North America, Windsor, USA

P. Suresh Kumar, Department of Mechanical Engineering, R.V.R. & J.C. College of Engineering, Guntur, India

M. Sudhakar, Mechanical Engineering, Sri Sai Ram Engineering College, Chennai, India

The integration of Internet of Things (IoT) and Machine Learning (ML) technologies presents groundbreaking advancements in nuclear structure analysis. This chapter explores how IoT devices and sensors, combined with ML algorithms, can enhance the precision and efficiency of nuclear research. IoT enables real-time data collection from various sensors distributed across nuclear facilities, providing a comprehensive view of nuclear reactions and structural parameters. ML algorithms then process and analyze this vast amount of data, identifying patterns and anomalies that traditional methods might miss. The chapter discusses the implementation of advanced ML techniques such as neural networks and ensemble methods for predictive modeling and anomaly detection in nuclear systems. It also highlights the challenges and potential solutions related to data integration, security, and computational demands. The convergence of IoT and ML in nuclear structure analysis promises significant improvements in safety, operational efficiency, and research capabilities.

Chapter 16

D. Venkata Srihari Babu, Department of Electronics and Communication Engineering, G. Pulla Reddy Engineering College, India

Ramaprasad Maharana, Department of Electronics and Communication Engineering, Sri Sai Ram Institute of Technology, Chennai, India

M. Ponrekha, Department of Electrical and Electronics Engineering, Karpagam Academy of Higher Education, Coimbatore, India

S. Ramesh, Department of Electrical and Electronics Engineering, K.S.R. College of Engineering, Tiruchengode, India

D. Kirubakaran, Department of Electrical and Electronics Engineering, St. Joseph's Institute of Technology, Chennai, India

High Performance Computing (HPC) has established an important place in the performance analysis and simulation of electric vehicles. An enhanced study built on HPC answers to the high computational requirements of performance evaluation of electric vehicles, namely battery management, energy efficiency, and thermal dynamics. HPC, with parallel processing and improved algorithms, can intensively simulate powertrain systems, aerodynamics, and vehicle dynamics, keeping a stream of avenues to improve the design and functionality of electric vehicles. Further, it optimizes battery life and energy consumption as well as charging systems. This is useful for manufacturers and researchers to work toward enhancing the efficiency of EVs. The current chapter also deals with real-time simulations of HPC that allow prototyping, reduce development costs, and enable sustaining innovations in the electric vehicle business.

    M. Raju, Department of Software Systems, Sri Krishna Arts and Science College,
       Kuniamuthur, India
    Kimsy Gulhane, School of Management, Ramdeobaba University, Nagpur, India
    Gulshan Banu A., Department of Artificial Intelligence and Data Science, SNS College of
       Engineering, Coimbatore, India
    Saurabh Chandra, School of Law, Bennett University, Greater Noida, India
    Pravin A. Dwaramwar, Department of Electronics and Computer Science, Ramdeobaba
       University, Nagpur, India
    Sampath Boopathi, Department of Mechanical Engineering, Muthayammal Engineering
       College, Namakkal, India

This chapter explores the architectures of high-performance computing (HPC) systems designed for machine learning (ML) workloads with special attention paid to advanced hardware and software optimizations intended to accelerate computational efficiency. It discusses the state-of-the-art use of GPUs, TPUs, and FPGAs in parallelizing operations, optimizing deep learning models during training and inference periods. The final section covers distributed computing frameworks, such as Apache Spark and Hadoop, that also provide support for big data processing in clusters. It also examines the challenges arising from the handling of data, distribution of resources, and scalability aspects as well as emerging solutions, such as memory-centric architectures and quantum computing, respectively. This chapter provides a comprehensive understanding of the evolution of HPC systems to meet the requirements of modern ML workloads, faster model development, reduced energy consumption, and better scalability, along with some of the trends and future research directions in HPC for ML.

Preface

The rapid advancements in Machine Learning (ML) and High Performance Computing (HPC) have catalyzed a transformative era in scientific research and technology. As editors of the "Handbook of Research on Integrating Machine Learning Into HPC-Based Simulations and Analytics," we are honored to present a comprehensive collection that bridges these two powerful domains, showcasing innovative research and pioneering applications.

The impetus for this handbook arises from a significant challenge in contemporary research: the limitations of small-scale computing systems in handling the vast and rapidly growing datasets characteristic of grand-challenge problems. Traditional ML models, while effective in many domains, are often constrained by the memory and processing resources available. This has led to an urgent need for integrating ML with HPC environments to not only enhance scalability but also to improve the performance and efficiency of predictive models.

In recent years, the remarkable strides in ML, particularly deep learning, have underscored the necessity for substantial computational power. HPC systems, with their superior processing capabilities, provide an ideal platform to meet this demand. The synergy between ML and HPC promises to accelerate progress in various research areas by enabling faster data processing, more complex simulations, and ultimately, more profound insights.

This book is a response to the evolving technological landscape and the growing interdependence of ML and HPC. It is designed to serve as a repository of cutting-edge research, practical solutions, and insightful discussions on the intersection of these fields. Our aim is to highlight the sustained and broad efforts invested by the research community, illustrating how ML and HPC can complement and enhance each other.

This collection of chapters in the book delves into cutting-edge advancements in artificial intelligence, machine learning, and high-performance computing, exploring their applications across diverse domains. From innovative insult detection on social media and explainable AI techniques to domain adaptation in scene classification and fitness activity recognition, the chapters highlight the transformative potential of these technologies. Further discussions include optimizing deep learning for mobile applications, leveraging edge computing for data lakes, and integrating AI with IoT for energy management, healthcare, and nuclear research.

Chapter 1 addresses the growing issue of cyberbullying and online abusive language, presenting a Transformer-based deep learning model for insult detection on social media platforms. Leveraging the BERT method, the approach focuses on text pre-processing, representation, and supervised classification, achieving superior results compared to traditional CNN and RNN models, with a macro F1-score of 0.83 and an accuracy of 86%.

Exploring the intersection of machine learning and explainability, this Chapter 2 examines robust variable selection methods to minimize the influence of data outliers. It compares prior, intrinsic, and posterior approaches using datasets from gene expression, crime rates, and tourism infrastructure, showcasing how explainable models improve decision-making in contaminated datasets.

Chapter 3 introduces the Semi-Supervised Domain Adaptation Network (SSDAN) for remote sensing scene classification, highlighting its ability to reduce data labeling requirements. With over 99% accuracy and Kappa coefficient values in various domain scenarios, the method demonstrates its efficiency in leveraging multi-source data for improved classification performance.

Focusing on fitness activity tracking, chapter 4 explores deep learning models that map smartphone sensor data into predefined activity classes. Using benchmark datasets, the models deliver high accuracy in recognizing patterns, aiding users in monitoring performance and calorie expenditure with enhanced precision.

To address memory and energy constraints in mobile applications, chapter 5 examines DNN compression techniques, such as pruning and redesigning neural architectures. It evaluates these methods on metrics like compression rate, inference time, and accuracy, offering guidance for practitioners to optimize mobile DNN performance.

Chapter 6 evaluates the role of High-Performance Edge Computing (HPEC) in processing big data for deep learning applications. By employing data lake frameworks and platforms like Jetson Nano, it highlights advancements in efficiency and computational performance, achieving classification speeds as fast as 8.19 ms per image with 90% accuracy.

Chapter 7 advocates integrating machine learning and high-performance computing into electric machine design. It reviews traditional cascade algorithms and demonstrates the potential of ML and optimization techniques to overcome design challenges, paving the way for adaptable and efficient methodologies.

Exploring the integration of HPC and distributed deep learning frameworks, chapter 8 delves into designing scalable models using libraries like TensorFlow, Keras, and Horovod. It examines their deployment on platforms like AWS and GCP, optimizing real-time data analytics for reliable and functional neural networks.

Chapter 9 explores how ML and HPC collaboration accelerates discoveries in fields like materials science, climate modeling, and drug discovery. Case studies highlight the ability of these technologies to automate analytics, optimize resource use, and solve global scientific challenges with unprecedented accuracy.

Focusing on renewable energy and environmental monitoring, chapter 10 explores the integration of HPC and AI for optimizing energy systems and analyzing environmental data. It showcases case studies demonstrating enhanced precision and efficiency in sustainable energy harvesting and ecosystem management.

Chapter 11 surveys AI techniques like reinforcement learning for optimizing energy consumption in HPC systems. By dynamically adapting workloads, these methods achieve energy efficiency without compromising computational performance, contributing to sustainability goals in high-demand environments.

Integrating federated learning and gestural technology, chapter 12 demonstrates advancements in patient care and diagnostics. Use cases in telemedicine and rehabilitation illustrate how decentralized ML models and human-computer interaction technologies streamline workflows while maintaining data privacy.

Chapter 13 highlights the transformative role of advanced visual information processing technologies in neuroscience and healthcare. By enhancing diagnostics and treatment personalization, it demonstrates how deep learning and computer vision revolutionize neural and cognitive research while addressing ethical and data challenges.

Focusing on food safety and waste reduction, chapter 14 examines the application of microcontrollers and IoT-enabled systems for real-time food quality monitoring. Innovations in sensor technology and predictive analytics ensure precision in managing temperature, humidity, and contamination in supply chains.

Chapter 15 explores the application of IoT devices and ML algorithms in nuclear research. It discusses how real-time data collection and predictive modeling enhance precision in analyzing nuclear reactions, addressing challenges related to data security and computational demands.

By integrating HPC into electric vehicle design, chapter 16 examines battery management, energy efficiency, and thermal dynamics. It discusses real-time simulations and prototyping that optimize EV systems, reduce development costs, and advance sustainability in the automotive industry.

Chapter 17 reviews cutting-edge HPC architectures for ML workloads, emphasizing GPU, TPU, and FPGA technologies. It discusses distributed computing frameworks like Apache Spark and future trends like quantum computing, offering insights into improving scalability, energy efficiency, and computational performance.

The book's objectives are multifaceted: to present recent advancements in ML techniques applied on HPC systems, to discuss significant results achieved, and to identify ongoing challenges and future opportunities at this intersection. By fostering collaboration between the ML and HPC communities, we hope to promote rapid and seamless advancements towards an ecosystem that benefits both disciplines.

The convergence of ML and HPC is not merely a technical endeavor but a strategic move to overcome existing barriers related to application complexity and machine cost. To this end, this handbook sets four primary goals:

1. To develop optimized solutions that significantly reduce computational requirements.
2. To provide a dynamic and comprehensive view of domain sciences.
3. To foster interdisciplinary collaboration for integrated knowledge development.
4. To stimulate innovations with deep societal impact through advancements in scientific research.

Our target audience includes academics, researchers, computer scientists, and engineers, as well as experts in ML, HPC, and data analytics. Practitioners in computational science, artificial intelligence, and data science, along with graduate and undergraduate students interested in these fields, will find this book particularly valuable.

The topics covered are diverse, reflecting the broad scope of this interdisciplinary field:

*   High Performance Computing systems
*   Machine Learning paradigms
*   Parallelization and scaling of ML techniques/algorithms
*   ML applications on HPC systems
*   HPC system design and optimization for ML workloads
*   Convergence of HPC and deep learning
*   Data analytics using ML on HPC systems

- Networking and storage solutions for ML on HPC systems
- Libraries, tools, and workflows for ML on HPC systems
- Emerging trends in HPC and ML

We are grateful to the contributors whose expertise and dedication have made this handbook possible. Their collective efforts provide a rich source of knowledge and inspiration for anyone engaged in the fascinating journey of integrating ML into HPC-based simulations and analytics.

With great anticipation, we present this handbook, confident that it will serve as an essential resource for advancing research and practice at the confluence of ML and HPC.

Belgacem Ben Youssef
King Saud University, Saudi Arabia

Mohamed Maher Ben Ismail
King Saud University, Saudi Arabia

Acknowledgments

We would like to express our sincere gratitude to all the reviewers for their invaluable feedback, thoughtful suggestions, and constructive criticism, which have greatly enhanced the quality of the chapters. Their expertise and dedication to the field have been essential in shaping the revised submissions. We also extend our heartfelt thanks to the publisher, IGI Global, for their continued support, professionalism, and commitment to bringing this project to fruition. Additionally, we are deeply grateful to King Saud University for providing the time, resources, and encouragement to undertake this work. Without the support from all these stakeholders, this edited book would not have been possible.

Chapter 1
Detecting Insults on Social Network Platforms Using a Deep Learning Transformer–Based Model

Belgacem Ben Youssef
https://orcid.org/0000-0002-6618-3845
King Saud University, Saudi Arabia

Mohamed Maher Ben Ismail
https://orcid.org/0000-0001-7770-5752
King Saud University, Saudi Arabia

Ouiem Bchir
King Saud University, Saudi Arabia

ABSTRACT

Social network platforms ought to be a place where no user gets insulted via verbal abuse. Cyberbullying and online abusive language is becoming a major concern for all stakeholders. Research on insult detection has seen a surge in interest over the last few years to address this problem. The emergence of deep learning techniques and their promising achievements in various fields have promoted their use as a natural alternative to tackle the many challenges related to insult detection. The authors describe in this chapter a supervised deep learning model to capture the online comments' semantics and detect insults. The proposed approach relies on two main components: (i) Text pre-processing and representation, and (ii) A Transformer-based deep learning model trained to classify the comments submitted on social media platforms as an insult or insult free based on the BERT method. The obtained results indicate that the proposed model outperforms CNNs and RNNs in the detection of insults for the same OLID benchmark yielding a macro F1-score of 0.83 and an accuracy of 86%.

DOI: 10.4018/978-1-6684-3795-7.ch001

INTRODUCTION

Social network platforms play a significant role in the daily life of many people. In addition, the expanding smartphones market has made these platforms even more popular, leading to a drastic increase in the number of users exceeding 4.2 billion in 2021 (Kemp, 2022). This represents nearly 53.6% of the world population with an annual growth rate of 13% (Kemp, 2022). Social media platforms have kept users more informed and opened paths for them to connect with people from all over the world. However, the afforded anonymity in these platforms has yielded an increasing number of cyberbullying incidents. One of the most common cyberbullying types reported by social media users is name-calling or the use of abusive language such as insults (Waseem et al., 2017).

The widespread occurrence of insult incidents in social media networks has triggered many companies and community interest groups to develop solutions to confront this phenomenon. One of the earliest efforts consisted in appointing moderators to either approve user comments prior to publication, or review the comments reported by peer users. However, these approaches proved to be limited for real-world applications because they create a bottleneck effect on the network platform. In other words, the post-approval system could get overwhelmed by the number of user posts. Furthermore, mental harm could have occurred due to the insults reported to the moderator. The users who reported the insult would have already read the content without any form of warning or protection. Additionally, for a daily duty, reading and filtering insults may place a psychological toll on the moderators of these platforms, possibly engendering a Post-Traumatic Stress Disorder (PTSD) (Anderson, 2018). Such a manual and human-led effort is obviously tedious and even counter-productive. It is also inadequate for certain application domains whereby early intervention would be a more effective alternative.

Later solutions have relied on algorithms to automatically detect insults in social media platforms. These solutions have formulated insult detection as a string-matching problem (Khatri, 2018). Here, the system flags a given post as insulting based on a list of prohibited or blacklisted words. However, such solutions proved to be inaccurate because they neither consider context nor the alternative spelling of keywords. Moreover, they require frequent updates of the considered blacklist. For instance, the comment *"I hate people of a given nationality"* does not contain an insulting word per se. Nevertheless, the context of the sentence is insulting. Thus, one can state that naïve string-matching solutions are insufficient to solve the insult detection problem adequately (Khatri, 2018). Recent research works based on machine learning techniques, have achieved better results, particularly via the use of deep learning models (Vaswani et al., 2017; Pitsilis et al., 2018).

In this chapter, we formulate the challenge of online insult detection as a combined text mining and supervised learning problem. In particular, we consider one of the recent and cutting-edge deep neural network paradigms, namely Transformer models, which have proved to be efficient for various natural language processing (NLP) applications (Raza et al., 2020; Sak et al., 2014). We propose herein an online insult detection system that maps unseen user comments into two pre-defined classes: insult or insult-free, where the Transformer model is used to capture the semantics of user comments and recognize insulting posts. Further, two pre-trained models are investigated to transfer their "knowledge" into the insult detection domain. We summarize our main contributions through this work as follows:

1. Provide an investigation and a brief overview of the problem of insult detection using deep learning techniques.
2. Present the design of a transformer model-based insult detection system.

3. Describe the model's performance using standard evaluation metrics based on a widely available benchmark dataset.
4. Compare the model's performance with the results obtained from typical deep learning models, such as Convolutional Neural Networks (CNNs) and Recurrent Neural Networks (RNNs).

The rest of the chapter is structured as follows: In the Background Section, we elaborate on the concepts related to cyberbullying, give a brief overview of text mining techniques, and review relevant machine learning techniques and deep learning models including the Transformer model. Next, Section 3 discloses some of the pertinent works in the area of abusive language detection using deep learning models. Afterwards, we elaborate on the proposed system and report on the experimental settings and results in Section 4 and Section 5, respectively. Finally, in Section 6, we present our conclusions and ideas for future work.

BACKGROUND

Cyberbullying

According to the United Nations Children's Fund (UNICEF), cyberbullying can be defined as the repeated behavior of scaring, angering, or shaming targeted to individuals using digital technologies (UNICEF, 2022). A dominant example would be sending hurtful or threatening text through a messaging platform. In particular, most teenagers in the United States of America (USA) have experienced some forms of cyberbullying. Specifically, 42% of those teenagers have been a target of cyberbullying through name calling (Waseem et al., 2017). Although cyberbullying is alarming among adolescents, it is not limited to this age group. For instance, 27% of Saudi's higher-education students reported having committed cyberbullying at least once (Al-Zahrani, 2015). Moreover, cyberbullying has a negative psychological impact on the bullied person. Studies show that the level of psychological symptoms related to depression positively correlates with the frequency of being bullied (Perren et al., 2010), which could lead to self-harming tendencies (Corcoran & McGuckin, 2014). This highlights the importance of creating a safe virtual environment, devoid of negative and harmful experiences, for everyone.

Text Mining

Text mining is the process of extracting interesting and meaningful patterns from an unstructured text in order to acquire new knowledge and support decision making processes (Maheswari & Sathiaseelan, 2017). The term text can be defined as a collection of words or letters that are recognizable by the reader. Particularly, unstructured text does not have a predefined data format like in social media or news (IBM, 2021).

In general, unstructured text is easy for people to understand but may be complicated for a computer program to make sense of. In fact, difficulties with automated text comprehension are caused by the nature of human language, which includes ambiguous terms and phrases, with some meanings being highly dependent on the context (Maheswari & Sathiaseelan, 2017). To address these challenges, the adoption of text mining techniques, such as information retrieval, natural language processing, information extraction, and data mining has attracted considerable interest from many researchers recently.

The goal is to extract non-trivial and valuable patterns from a large volume of textual documents, thus allowing for the discovery of interesting information that can be used for decision making and future prediction (Zhou, 2021; Heidenreich, 2021).

As it can be seen in Figure 1, text mining can be defined as the intersection of five computing domains along with five additional practice areas. Namely, these domains consist of databases, data mining, artificial intelligence and machine learning, computational linguistics, and information sciences. Although they enclose distinctive properties, they exhibit considerable interrelated tasks. Actually, a typical text mining task requires the use of techniques from multiple domains. On the other hand, the five practice areas enclose information retrieval, document clustering, document classification, information extraction, and Natural Language Processing (NLP). In this regard, the document clustering area aims at grouping terms and/or documents into homogeneous clusters, while the document classification area adopts classification techniques to categorize terms and/or documents. Besides, Information Extraction is intended to identify and extract the correlated evidence and relations from unstructured data. On the other hand, Information Retrieval (IR)l is understood as the process of extracting relevant and associated patterns according to a given set of words or phrases. Typically, IR relies on two main pre-processing tasks:

- Tokenization: This task consists of dividing the text into sentences and words known as tokens. The representation of tokens has several methods in text mining. One of them is achieved by turning arbitrary text into fixed-length vectors via counting how many times each word appears, known as the bag-of-words model (Zhou, 2021).
- Stemming: This task involves separating the prefixes and suffixes from words to derive the root word form and its meaning. For example, in the case of the word "studying", we get the root word "study" by removing the suffix "ing" (Heidenreich, 2021).

Figure 1. Computing domains related to text mining and its applications

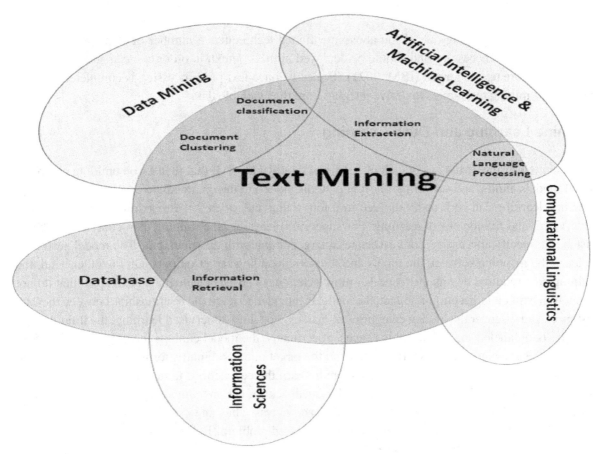

Natural Language Processing (NLP) represents the process that makes the human language in both written and verbal form understandable by the computer (Bengfort et al., 2018). Typical NLP tasks can be categorized into three main categories:

- Sentiment analysis: It involves the detection of positive or negative sentiment from internal or external text data sources.
- Summarization: It provides a synopsis of long text pieces to create a concise and coherent summary of a document's main points.
- Text categorization: It deals with analyzing text documents and classifying them based on predefined topics or categories.

The process employed in information extraction uses textual sources to extract specific information and is based on two subtasks (Marquez, 2022):

- Feature selection: It consists of selecting the important features that contribute the most output of a predictive analytics model.

- Feature extraction: This subtask represents the process of selecting a subset of features to improve the accuracy of a classification task.

In addition to applying one of the above-mentioned techniques, a number of steps involving text pre-processing are necessary and should be deployed in this context, in order to clean and convert text data into a more usable format (IBM, 2021). Typically, once text pre-processing is completed, we can deploy text mining techniques to derive insights from the available data.

Machine Learning and Deep Learning

Machine learning (ML) is a branch of Artificial Intelligence (AI) that focuses on building computational models aiming at discovering relevant patterns hidden in the data with no explicit programming. Machine learning can be broadly divided into four main categories: supervised, unsupervised, semi-supervised, and reinforcement learning. For supervised learning, the training data consists of labeled instances. Specifically, each record associates a target output with the input data. The model aims then to learn the mapping between the inputs and the corresponding target outputs. On the other hand, the training data required by unsupervised learning techniques consists of unlabeled examples that do not include an explicit target output. In fact, the model is intended to learn the relationships between the data instances and discover the hidden categories or classes. For semi-supervised learning, the training data includes both labeled and unlabeled instances. Specifically, the model exploits the unlabeled records to optimize the association between the inputs and the target outputs. Finally, for reinforcement learning, the model operates in an uncertain environment to learn the best actions to take in each state based on the current state and the information received as feedback for actions previously taken. Such feedback informs the machine on how appropriate the taken action was. Thus, the model relies on a trial and error approach to achieve an optimal solution to the considered problem (Burkov, 2019).

Deep learning (DL) involves the use of models and algorithms initially designed to imitate the human brain by utilizing Artificial Neural Networks (ANNs) (Skansi, 2018). In particular, a feed-forward neural network with one hidden layer can be considered as the simplest type of an artificial neural network. ANNs consist of multiple connected layers that contain a number of nodes. Each node is connected with all nodes in the previous layer, and a weight is associated with each one of those connections. As depicted in Figure 2, the first layer of the network is typically the input layer. The last one represents the output layer, while the layer(s) in between is (are) called hidden layer(s). The model learns through tuning the weights of the entire network (Quiza & Davim, 2011).

Figure 2. Architecture of a simple deep learning model, that of a feed-forward neural network with two hidden layers

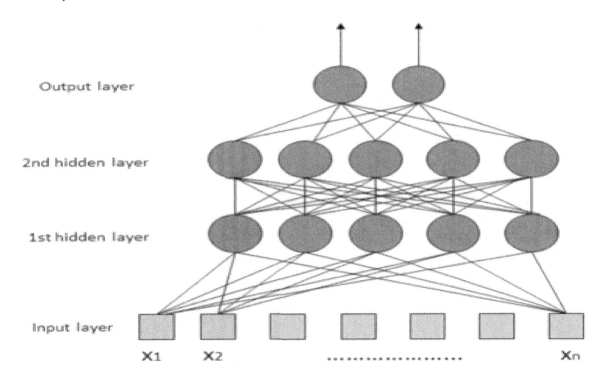

Convolutional Neural Networks (CNNs) are an example of a deep neural network that consists of an input layer, a set of hidden layers, and an output layer. In particular, the hidden layers usually consist of convolution layers, pooling layers, and fully-connected layers. The convolution and pooling layers work collectively to select the features using the procedure illustrated in Figure 3. Afterwards, the fully connected layer processes the features extracted by the previous layer. CNNs were initially designed for computer vision and image classification applications (Georgakopoulos et al., 2018). When CNNs are used for text classification, the input is transformed into a dense vector before it is fed into the network. Such transformation is accomplished by utilizing a particular layer called the "Embedding Layer" (Valueva et al., 2020).

Figure 3. Illustration of the convolution operation in CNNs

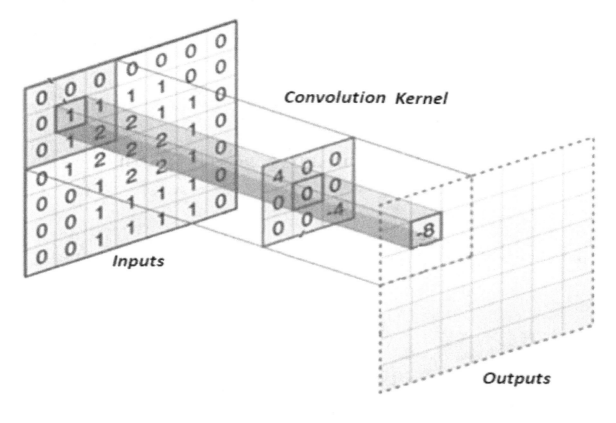

The wide-spread use of CNNs to address image classification problems can be attributed to the model's ability to exploit two important and valuable statistical properties: *(i)* Local stationarity, and *(ii)* Multi-scale compositional structure (Henaff et al., 2015). These properties allow the network to capture the long-range interactions between the image patterns, thus enabling the network to have more depth with lesser computation requirements. In other words, this yields a reduction in the number of the network's learnable parameters.

A Recurrent Neural Network (RNN) is another type of deep learning model and can be defined as a neural network that includes recurrent connections between the hidden units (Miljanovic, 2012). As a matter of fact, it was designed to overcome text classification challenges by capturing sequentially the semantic information through fixed-length hidden layer vectors that process words in consecutive time steps (Ben Ismail, 2020). Particularly, RNNs rely on their feedback connections to store representations of recent input events in the form of activations through short-term memory (Schmidhuber & Hochreiter, 1997). Further, adding feedback to a network can be done through different methods including: *(i)* Propagation from the hidden layers to the context portion of the input layer, which pays attention to the sequence of input variables; *(ii)* Propagation from the output layer to the context portion of the input layer, which is meant to focus more on the arrangement of output values (Miljanovic, 2012).

A basic RNN adopting the first method is depicted in Figure 4. We should mention that the output of the network is impacted by the outputs of the hidden layer in addition to the input layer (Aggarwal, 2018). Specifically, the overall effect is achieved using a nonlinear function, such as the hyperbolic tangent (denoted by *tanh)*, whose range is from -1 to 1 and can thus, model positive and negative values.

Figure 4. Illustration of: (a) a simple RNN node, and (b) connected RNN cells where cell A represents the abstraction of the node in (a)

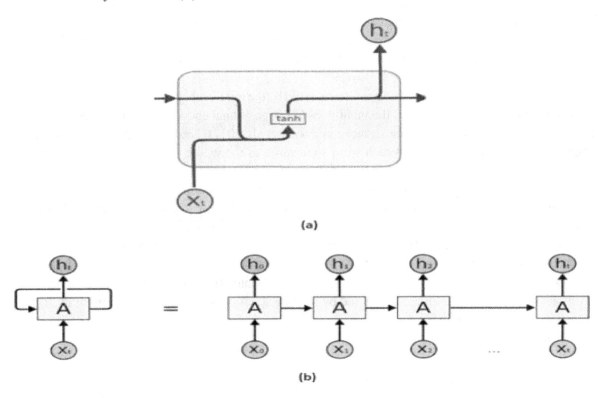

Recurrent Neural Networks operate by capturing the long and short-term dependencies between data instances (Georgakopoulos et al., 2018). One should note that such statistical properties are also present in the context of text classification. In fact, the words that exist in a given sentence depend on one another to convey the intended semantic meaning (Georgakopoulos et al., 2018). While raw images are simply represented as matrices storing the intensity of the image pixels, textual data need to be encoded in such a way that preserves the stationarity and the compositionality properties discussed above. Such encoding is normally achieved using a vocabulary that maps the indexed words into some integer values *[1, 2, ..., d],* where *d* represents the vocabulary size. Next, the encoded text is transformed into a matrix, where each row represents a word in the text. Afterwards, the matrix goes through the embedding layer and gets passed into the network (Georgakopoulos et al., 2018). However, RNNs fail to capture the dependency between data instances in case an output depends on an input processed far back in time. This limitation is overcome using Long Short-Term Memory (LSTM) cells (Miljanovic, 2012). In fact, LSTM bridges the long temporal lags and deals with long-term dependencies and generalizes well for many problems. It also exhibits low computational complexity per each time step (Schmidhuber & Hochreiter, 1997).

Transformers

Some of the limitations of neural network paradigms such as CNNs, RNNs, and LSTMs are manifest in their inherent sequential computations. This inhibits the need for parallelism. Transformers were introduced as a deep learning network built solely on attention mechanisms with no incorporation of convolutions and recurrent connections (Vaswani et al., 2017). In this regard, Transformers exploit the available data parallelism by allowing the input to be fed in parallel leading to fast processing time and a concomitant reduction in training cost (Vaswani et al., 2017). Like other transduction models, Transformers use an encoder-decoder architecture. The decoder is located to the right of the encoder. The latter is comprised of two main components: A multi-head attention mechanism followed by a feed-forward network. Moreover, the decoder has a masked multi-head attention connected to similar components of the encoder.

Starting with the encoder part, the input is processed by the input embedding process, which converts the given words into vectors. Then, the input goes to the positional encoding in order to add information about the word's position in the sentence (Vaswani et al., 2017). Next, the input is conveyed to an attention module, which calculates each word's relevance to the whole sentence. This layer is called multi-head attention because the parallelization takes place there. That is, instead of passing one word at a time, all words in a given sentence are processed at once. In addition to this special attention layer, the input is conveyed to a feed-forward network, which is applied to each position. Finally, the output of the encoder is fed into the decoder. The decoder encloses layers similar to those in the encoder plus a masked multi-head attention layer, whose role is to mask the tokens in the sequence not intended to be the attention token (Vaswani et al., 2017). An important advantage of using a multi-head attention is the ability to simultaneously consider information represented from different subspaces at different positions without the inhibiting effect caused by a single attention head. The architecture of the Transformer model is depicted in Figure 5 below.

Figure 5. Architecture of the Transformer model, as originally presented in (Vaswani et al., 2017)

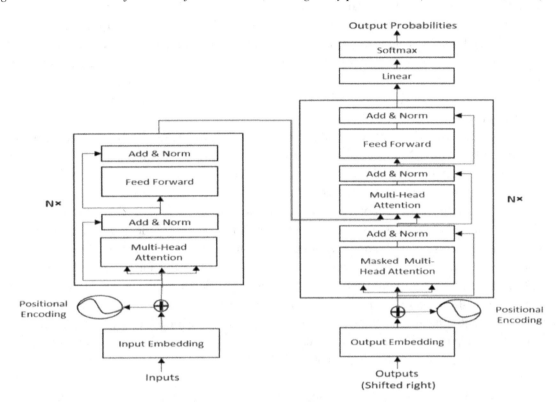

RELATED WORK ON INSULT DETECTION

In this section, we survey some of the recent research works that used deep learning models for the purpose of detecting insults, abusive language, and hate speech (Aggarwal, 2018).

Research Based on Recurrent Neural Networks

In (Sax, 2016), the author investigated the performance of a number of recurrent networks used for the detection of abusive comments. The evaluated models include linear models with Bag-of-Ngrams features, word vector averaging, a character-level LSTM, a bi-directional LSTM, a multi-layer LSTM, and a character Gated Recurrent Unit (GRU). The results showed that the character-level LSTM out-performed all other models in terms of the F1-score by yielding a value of 0.721. Some drawbacks of using character-level LSTM include the inability of the model to neglect negation words, such as "not", and capture dependencies in the later parts of comments. The author suggested the use of a bidirectional RNN coupled with a large dataset to overcome some of these shortcomings. Researchers in (Founta et al., 2019) proposed a system that integrates metadata in addition to textual data to help classify abusive behavior on social media platforms using a deep learning architecture. The system consists of two paths, namely, a text classification path and a metadata network path. Specifically, the text classification path relies on a GRU model while the metadata network comprises six fully connected dense layers. Then, both of these paths are connected to a concatenation layer and a classification layer. We should note that the training of both paths of the model is conducted in an alternating way, where in each mini-batch only one path is updated. According to the study's findings, the deep learning model outperformed other models when a metadata is used along with text data. An F1-score and an Area Under the Receiver Operating Characteristic (ROC) Curve (AUC) of 0.85 and 0.93, respectively were achieved using the "abusive dataset" (Founta et al., 2019).

The work described in (Pavlopoulos et al., 2017) deals with online moderation of user comments. It showed that, in general, RNN models outperform CNN and Logistic Regression (LR) models, when associated with character and word n-grams features. By adding an attention mechanism to the RNN model, the resulting model's performance reached an AUC of 98% for datasets containing comments from Wikipedia talk pages and a Greek sports news portal (Pavlopoulos et al., 2017). The work in (Zinovyeva et al., 2020) evaluated the success of automatic content monitoring using deep machine learning and natural language processing. The authors conducted a comparison between different models in terms of performance and feasibility for malicious content detection. In their findings, they showed that the accuracy of detection slightly improved when adding a bidirectional recurrent layer to RNN models. Additionally, a relatively simple GRU and Bidirectional-GRU outperformed more complex models. Although RNNs outperformed most other models, with the exception of pre-trained Transformer-based language models, CNNs can achieve in some cases comparable results. This demonstrates that RNNs are not the only viable and suitable models that can be used in the detection of antisocial online behavior (Zinovyeva et al., 2020).

In the paper by Iwendi et al. (2023), the authors explore various deep learning methods for detecting cyberbullying in online content. The study focuses on improving the accuracy and efficiency of detection algorithms using advanced neural network architectures. The authors present a detailed review of existing cyberbullying detection techniques, highlighting the challenges associated with accurately identifying harmful content in social media and online interactions. The proposed deep learning models comprise RNNs, LSTMs, and BiLSTMs. The obtained results indicate that the proposed models outperform traditional methods in terms of accuracy and F1-score, showcasing their effectiveness in distinguishing between cyberbullying and non-cyberbullying content. The authors also emphasize the importance of feature extraction and data preprocessing in enhancing model performance. The study utilizes multiple datasets for training and evaluation, including a Twitter dataset containing tweets labeled for cyberbullying and Kaggle datasets specifically organized and prepared for detecting cyberbullying incidents. The models are trained on the selected datasets, with a focus on optimizing hyperparameters and employing techniques like dropout and batch normalization to prevent overfitting. The authors evaluate the models using metrics such as precision, recall, and F1-score, where the achieved values range from 0.80 to 0.93, 0.75 to 0.90, and 0.78 to 0.91, respectively. It was found that the BiLSTM model generally outperformed both the RNN and LSTM models across all metrics, indicating its effectiveness in capturing context in text data for cyberbullying detection.

Research Based on Convolutional Neural Networks

Recent research works in (Plum et al., 2019; Zaheri et al., 2020) showed that CNNs performed better than other deep learning models in this task. This confirms the findings in (Zinovyeva et al., 2020), where CNNs were presented as accurate models for antisocial behavior classification. In particular, the work in (Plum et al., 2019) studied five different neural network architectures for the classification of Tweets in the context of preventing offensive language. In this regard, a two-Dimensional convolution model with pooling layers surpassed the other four models achieving 77.96% and 0.733 as accuracy and $F1$-score values, respectively. Similarly, the authors in (Zaheri et al., 2020) outlined a CNN model that slightly outperformed, in terms of the $F1$-score metric, a pre-trained Transformer-based model called Bidirectional Encoder Representations from Transformers (BERT). This performance can be attributed to the fact that the data set used to train BERT was small and unbalanced. Nevertheless, the work proved that using a less complex model, such as a CNN, can achieve results comparable to those obtained using more complex models (BERT).

We should mention that CNNs rely on employing embedding layers to encode text so that it can be processed by the deep network. The work in (Kumari & Singh, 2019) showed that the association of fastText, which is a pre-trained word embedder, with a CNN model achieves the highest performance compared to GolVe embedding and one-hot embedding. A group of researchers participated in the SemVal-2019 Challenge and presented their work dealing with identifying and categorizing offensive language in social media (Zhang et al., 2019). CNN performed better compared to a variety of RNN models, which included Bidirectional LSTM with Attention and Bidirectional LSTM followed by Bidirectional GRU, achieving a macro F1-score of 0.802. However, it was slightly overtaken by an ensemble of CNN and RNN models. The latter reaching a value of 0.807 for the same metric and a fifth place ranking out of 103 participants in the said Challenge (Zhang et al., 2019).

The 2022 paper by Elbasani and Kim propose a novel approach combining Abstract Meaning Representation (AMR) with Convolutional Neural Networks (CNNs) to enhance the detection of toxic content in online communications (Elbasani & Kim, 2022). The authors argue that traditional methods often struggle to capture the subtle meanings in text, which is crucial for effectively identifying toxic language. The AMR-CNN model integrates AMR parsing, representing the meaning of sentences in a structured form, with CNNs that can learn hierarchical features from this representation. This approach allows the model to focus on the semantic content of sentences, improving its sensitivity to the context of the language used. The authors evaluated their model on several well-known datasets for toxic content detection, including the Jigsaw Toxic Comment Classification Challenge Dataset featuring user comments labeled for toxicity, encompassing various forms of hate speech and abusive language and a Toxicity Dataset from the Wikipedia Talk Pages. The latter contains comments from Wikipedia discussions, categorized by different levels of toxicity. The results demonstrate that the AMR-CNN model outperforms several baseline models, achieving higher accuracy, precision, recall, and F1 scores on the benchmark datasets. The paper reports an accuracy improvement of over 5% when compared to others. The study illustrates the potential of combining semantic representations with advanced deep learning models for more accurate detection of online toxic language.

Research Based on Transformer Models

We review herein some of the previous work based on pre-trained Transformer models. To the best of our knowledge, no vanilla Transformer model was designed and developed to address the insult detection problem. When comparing the pre-trained Transformer models with other deep learning models, it was reported that the former achieved the highest scores and outperformed all other models in all the datasets employed in (Zinovyeva et al., 2020). The research in (Wiedemann et al., 2020) compared a number of different pre-trained Transformer models, namely, BERT, Robustly Optimized BERT Pretraining Approach (RoBERTa), Cross-lingual Language Model (XLM)-RoBERTa, and A Lite BERT (ALBERT) for self-supervised Learning of Language Representations were used in the reported experiments. These models were pre-trained using the Masked Language Model (MLM) task for further fine-tuning. The results showed that the averaged-macro $F1$-score did not vary significantly for the considered models. Additional experiments in (Wiedemann et al., 2020) indicated also that the use of ensembles of pre-trained Transformers did not yield noticeable improvements. This finding was confirmed by the results obtained in (Das et al., 2020) where the authors used a checkpoint ensemble of transformers with no enhancement in performance. Specifically, they used a system, which was a combination of the same Generative Pre-Trained Transformer 2 (GPT-2) saved at different checkpoints. This level of performance was attributed to the fact that the considered models did not fulfill the critical conditions of independence and diversity, required for a successful ensemble model.

The research results reported in (Wang et al., 2020; Pant & Dadu, 2020) showed that the capabilities of the Transformer models, such as the Cross-Lingual Language Model with RoBERTa (XLM-R) and XLM-R Large (XLMR-Large), can be promising multilingual offensive language detectors. Both of these two models were tested on the same dataset, and yielded nearly the same $F1$-score of 0.846 (Wang et al., 2020; Pant & Dadu, 2020). In addition, when tested on a language without any fine tuning (that is, with zero-shot learning), the XLMR-Large model achieved an $F1$-score of 0.7 (Pant & Dadu, 2020). The authors in (Roy et al., 2021) showed that XLM-R outperformed the other pre-trained multilingual models. Further, they disclosed that the use of emojis as features helps the models to achieve better performance. In this case, emojis can be incorporated using a pre-trained embedding such as emoji2vec (Eisner et al., 2016).

Although, for most of the time, pre-trained Transformer models outperform other models in detecting insults, there were some cases in which they were overtaken by other non-transformer-based models. For instance, BERT-based solutions achieved a macro-averaged $F1$-score of 0.7705. On the other hand, the macro-averaged $F1$-score attained by CNN-based solutions was 0.7933 and 0.7964 in (Pavlopoulos et al. 2019) and (Zhang et al., 2019), respectively. Moreover, an ensemble model combining RNN and CNN achieved an $F1$-score of 0.8066 (Zhang et al., 2019). Besides, the results of the BERT-based solution outlined in (Pavlopoulos et al., 2019) might have been compromised by the fine-tuning stage of the model. In fact, the results achieved in (Liu et al., 2019) prove clearly that BERT-based solutions achieved the highest performance on SemEval-2019 test set, with a macro-averaged $F1$-score of 0.8286. The results in (Pavlopoulos et al., 2019) and its apparent contradiction in (Liu et al., 2019) show the clear importance of the fine-tuning stage of a pre-trained model and its impact on performance.

Kumbale, Singh, Poornalatha, and Singh present in their 2023 paper a novel model designed to detect threats and harmful content on Twitter using Transformer-based architectures (Kumbale et al., 2023). The authors recognize the critical need for effective monitoring of social media platforms to mitigate the spread of harmful information and protect users from potential threats. The proposed model, called

BREE-HD for Bert inspiRed machinE lEarning model for automatic tHreat Detection, employs a Transformer architecture to analyze tweet content and classify it based on the potential threat level. By leveraging attention mechanisms inherent in Transformers, the model can focus on relevant parts of the text, thereby improving its understanding of context and subtleties in the language used. To enable the model to learn from a range of examples as well as to enhance the model's generalization capabilities, the authors utilize several datasets for model training and evaluation. The results demonstrate that BREE-HD significantly outperforms baseline models in threat detection accuracy. The authors report an F1-score exceeding 92%, indicating the model's strong capability to identify threats in real-time on social media. Additionally, the paper highlights improvements in precision and recall compared to traditional machine learning approaches, suggesting that the Transformer architecture effectively captures the complexities of online communication and thus can be used to enhance online safety.

The recent work by Liu, Wang, and Catlin (2024) focuses on the application of large Transformer-based language models for the specific task of identifying anti-Semitic hate speech (Liu et al., 2024). The authors highlight the growing prevalence of hate speech online, particularly targeting specific communities, and aim to leverage advanced NLP techniques to improve detection accuracy. The authors employ several state-of-the-art Transformer models, including BERT and its variants, to analyze and classify instances of anti-Semitic speech. They fine-tune these models on datasets specifically prepared for the detection of hate speech, emphasizing the importance of contextual understanding in distinguishing subtle forms of hate speech from benign content. The study utilizes a combination of publicly available and newly prepared datasets, including an anti-Semitic hate speech dataset, comprising annotated examples of anti-Semitic comments sourced from social media platforms and online forums as well as general hate speech datasets including a broader spectrum of hate speech, thus enabling the model to learn from various contexts and forms of abusive language. Reported results show significant improvements in detection performance, with the employed Transformer-based models achieving high precision, recall, and F1 scores. Specifically, the models demonstrated an F1-score above 90% on the Anti-Semitic Hate Speech Dataset, indicating a robust capability to identify various instances of hate speech.

Research Based on Hybrid Deep Learning Architectures

An interesting aspect of using deep learning models is the ability to combine different architectures in order to achieve better performance. The system proposed in (Ben Ismail, 2020) represented a partitional CNN-LSTM, where instead of using the whole document as input to the CNN layer, the document is divided into parts, called partitions. That way local information is captured through the CNN layer. Then, it is conveyed to the LSTM to sequentially exploit the information across partitions. The model allows for the integration of local information and long-distance correlation across comments. The obtained results show that the system outperforms Support Vector Machines (SVM) and typical CNN models.

The system outlined in (Wang et al., 2020) relies on a combination of deep learning architectures to build a generic abusive language detection model. As components of this model, a multi-aspect features embedding, a Graph Convolutional Network (GCN), a cross-attention gate flow model, CNNs, and a Multi-Layer Perceptron (MLP) were utilized for this classification task. Researchers in (Mozafari et al., 2020) used the BERT model with different fine-tuning strategies to detect hate speech. Particularly, three different deep learning layers were added to the pre-trained transformer to classify text instances. This was achieved by inserting nonlinear (hidden), bidirectional recurrent neural network (Bi-LSTM), and convolutional layers, respectively. The experiments showed that the BERT model, with the inserted convolutional layer, achieved the best performance in terms of precision, recall, and *F1*-score.

A robust hybrid approach to detect cyberbullying on social media platforms is proposed by Muneer, Alwadain, Ragab, and Alqushaibi (2023). The authors focus on enhancing the performance of BERT (Bidirectional Encoder Representations from Transformers) by employing a stacking ensemble learning methos, which combines multiple models to improve overall accuracy. BERT is enhanced with additional layers to capture more nuanced features of text data. They then implement a stacking ensemble model, which combines the outputs of various classifiers, including decision trees, logistic regression, and other machine learning algorithms. This ensemble technique helps in leveraging the strengths of different models, ultimately boosting detection performance. The authors report an F1 score exceeding 93% while utilizing Kaggle's cyberbullying detection dataset for training and testing. The study highlights the effectiveness of using ensemble learning strategies with transformer models, such as BERT, to promote the detection of harmful content in social media and address the complexities of social media language.

In the recent work by Chen, Wang, and He (2024), the authors propose a hybrid approach for detecting cyberbullying in Chinese online content by combining XLNet, a transformer model, with a Deep Bidirectional Long Short-Term Memory (Bi-LSTM) network (Chen et al., 2024). The authors aim to address the challenges posed by the linguistic and cultural nuances of the Chinese language in identifying online harmful behavior. The proposed hybrid model integrates XLNet for effective feature extraction, leveraging its ability to capture contextual dependencies in language, while the Bi-LSTM component is used to enhance the model's understanding of sequential data. This combination allows the model to effectively identify patterns indicative of cyberbullying in the Chinese language. This work used a dataset containing labeled instances of cyberbullying in Chinese taken from online forums and social media. The dataset was further supplemented by other datasets that include general online interactions, allowing the model to learn from a broader context. The hybrid model achieved an F1-score of over 90% as well as high precision and recall rates. These results illustrate the potential of combining transformer models with recurrent architectures to enhance the detection of harmful online content in a linguistically and culturally diverse context.

PROPOSED INSULT DETECTION SOLUTION

The proposed system relies on pre-trained models, such as BERT, to address the insult detection problem. Figure 6 exhibits an overview of the designed system and illustrates the data flow through its different components. As it can be seen, the proposed solution starts with a text pre-processing step where user comments are handled using typical text mining-relevant techniques. Specifically, stop words removal, tokenization, and stemming are performed to prepare the considered text dataset. Next, a text embedding approach is deployed to learn the appropriate representations of the text, where words with the same meaning exhibit a similar representation. Specifically, the transformer paradigm is exploited to optimize this embedding task. Additionally, the insult detection problem is formulated as a supervised learning task, where the output of the text embedding stage is fed into a classification model for training. Besides, a testing phase is dedicated to categorize new comments into the two predefined classes: insult and insult free.

Figure 6. Overview of the proposed insult detection system

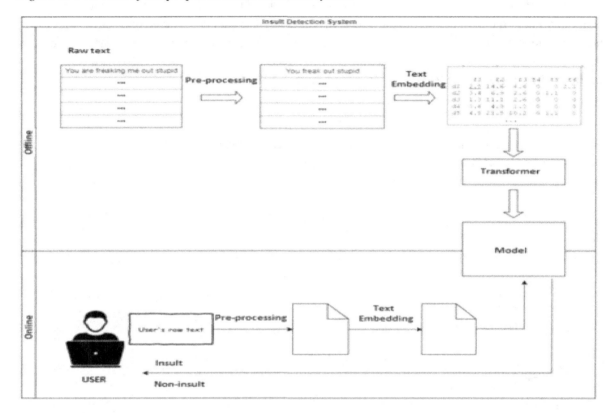

The employed Transformer model is a DL model whose architecture relies on an encoder-decoder structure. Actually, as it can be seen in Figure 5, both the encoder and decoder share the same embedding and positional encoding. The input first comes to the embedding as a text, and the embedding changes it into a vector with similar words having similar vectors. Then, the vectors go to a positional encoding component of the model. Since the transformer model takes the entire input at the same time, there is no information about each word's position. The positional encoding adds the positional information to the vector, and finally the input goes to the encoder and decoder parts, respectively.

In order to depict the transformer further, one should first explain the attention concept. In this regard, the attention mechanism captures the relevance of a particular word with respect to the other words in the sentence. The transformer uses this mechanism in two main sub-layers. The first one is the multi-head attention sub-layer, which applies the attention mechanism simultaneously to all words in the sentence. The second sub-layer is the masked multi-head attention sub-layer, which is similar to the multi-head attention sub-layer, except that for each word in the output, the next words are hidden. Thus, the attention mechanism considers the previous output words only.

On the other hand, the encoder is made of a stack of identical layers. As shown in Figure 7(a), each layer has a multi-head attention sub-layer connected with a normalization layer which adds the first input processed by the encoder layer and the input after going through the multi-head attention. Then, the input is fed into a feed-forward network. Next, it is normalized for the second time before being conveyed to the decoder, as depicted in Figure 7(b). Similar to the encoder, the decoder associates a stack of identical layers with an extra sub-layer that precedes the multi-head attention and the feed-forward network sub-layers. Such sub-layer is called masked multi-head attention sub-layer. Actually, the output is initially fed to the masked multi-head attention sub-layer, and then normalized and sent to the multi-head attention sub-layer. This process holds for the input provided by the encoder. Afterwards, the output gets normalized a second time before getting sent to a feed-forward network. Finally, as it can be seen in Figure 7(c), it gets normalized a third time before it exits the decoder.

(a) (b) (c)

Figure 7. (a) The multi-head attention sub-layer within the transformer model. (b) The layers of the encoder part of the employed Transformer model. (c) The layers of the decoder part of the Transformer model

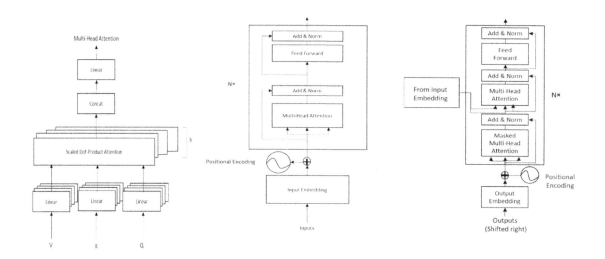

COMPUTATONAL EXPERIMENTS

Our research experiments were conducted using a standard benchmark dataset, called the Offensive Language Identification Dataset (OLID), to assess the detection capabilities of the proposed system (Zampieri et al., 2019; Zampieri, 2021). This dataset, contains 14,100 annotated tweets. It exhibits a clear imbalance of the class distribution with 33% representing insulting tweets. In addition, OLID encloses 13,240 tweets reserved for training and the remaining 860 tweets are dedicated for testing. One should mention that the dataset was annotated using crowdsourcing involving three annotators. Besides, no revision was conducted on the annotations. In other words, the risk of having noisy and incorrectly labeled instances is not excluded. As part of pre-processing, the mentions of twitter users were changed to "@ USER" and the URLs were replaced by the acronym "URL". Further, we dedicated 90% of the training subset to train the models and the remaining 10% for validation. Note that the testing set was unchanged in order to ensure objective comparison with the state-of-the-art works. Moreover, data augmentation techniques were deployed on the training subset only.

Performance Measures

The main evaluation metric used in this work is the *F1*-score. It is equal to the harmonic mean of precision and recall. It is used as a statistical measure to rate classification performance. When computed for a single class, this performance measure is obtained using the equation below:

$$F1 - score = \frac{2*(precision * recall)}{(precision + recall)}, (1)$$

$$F1 = \frac{2*(precision * recall)}{(precision + recall)} (2)$$

where the precision, also known as Positive Predictive Value (PPV), is calculated as follows:

$$Precision = \frac{\sum True\ Positive}{\sum True\ Positive + \sum False\ Positive} (3)$$

and the recall, or sensitivity, is computed using the following formula:

$$Recall = \frac{\sum True\ Positive}{\sum True\ Positive + \sum False\ Negative} (4)$$

Moreover, we use two *F1*-score variants for classification problems with multiple classes. Specifically, we consider the macro-averaged *F1*-score (denoted by macro-*F1* score):

$$Macro\ F1 - score = \frac{1}{N} \sum_{i=1}^{N} F1 - score_i (5)$$

where *N* represents the number of classes. On the other hand, the weighted *F1*-score is calculated as:

$$Weighted\ F1 - score = F1_{class_1} * W_1 + F1_{class_2} * W_2 + ... + F1_{class_N} * W_N, (5)$$

with W_i being equal to the weight of class *i*. The term false positive is defined as a tweet that was classified as an insult by the model, but was in fact an insult-free tweet. False negative denotes a tweet that was classified as insult-free by the model, but in fact its content included some form of insult. True negative stands for a tweet that was classified as insult-free, without any offensive language, and was in fact a normal, or acceptable, and thus insult-free tweet. A true positive means that a tweet that was classified as abusive speech containing insult(s) and its ground truth is in fact enclosing abusive content in the form of insult(s).

Data Pre-Processing

Further pre-processing was performed on the OLID dataset. The obtained accuracy and macro $F1$-scores using the proposed model with different pre-processing scenarios are reported in Table 1. As it can be seen, replacing the URLs with "HTTP" as well as hashtags and word segmentation yielded an improvement of the model performance. In particular, URL handling enhanced the performance because the word "URL" is an out-of-vocabulary (OOV) word for the model. In fact, replacing OOV words with synonyms improves the model performance. On the other hand, using word segmentation helped with the tokenization of the tweets. In order to investigate this effect further, we took the strings "#HelloWorld!" and "# Hello World !" as an example. The mapped values of the first string are [101, 1001, 7592, 11108, 999, 102] while those corresponding to the second string are [101, 1001, 7592, 2088, 999, 102]. This discrepancy helped the model achieve better results. However, removing the "@user" and replacing emojis with text yielded no noticeable improvements for the model as it can be seen in Table 1.

Table 1. Data pre-processing steps applied to OLID dataset and their corresponding performance results

Pre-Processing Step	Accuracy	Macro F1-Scores
No preprocessing	85%	0.81
Remove all @user instances from text	84%	0.79
Hashtag and word segmentation	85%	0.80
Representing emojis as text	85%	0.80
Replacing the word URL with HTTP	86%	0.82
Replacing HTML tags with their symbols	86%	0.82

Tuning of Hyperparameters

In the following, we outline the set of experiments conducted to fine-tune the model's hyperparameters:

- Input maximum length: The input maximum length dictates at which length the model truncates and pads the input. We varied the range for this parameter from 1 to 512 tokens. In fact, a large maximum length slows down the model but helps it to process a larger text. On the other hand, a lower value for this hyperparameter speeds up the model training. However, it truncates a large text to fit the input requirement. One should note that the length represents the number of tokens, not characters. Our experiments showed that a maximum length of 300 tokens, which is around 1500 characters, represents the optimal value for this hyperparameter.
- Learning rate: The learning rate is a highly important parameter that affects the speed at which the model learns. It impacts the model's convergence and its prediction performance. In Figure 8, we plot the training loss functions recorded for various number of epochs and learning rate values. As it can be seen, a learning rate value of 2e-5 (= 2×10^{-5}) yielded the best learning performance.

Figure 8. Training loss functions obtained, using the OLID dataset, as the number of epochs is varied for different learning rate (lr) values

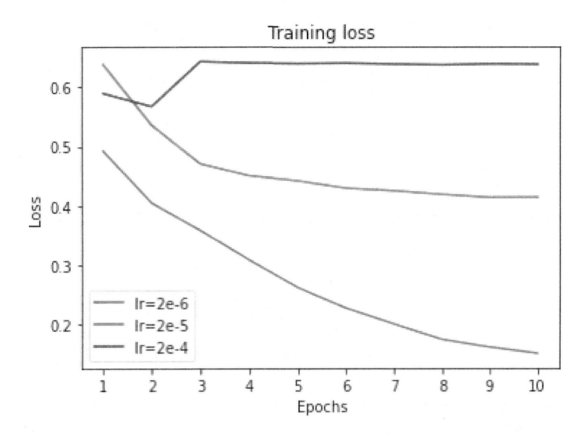

- Number of epochs: As it can be seen in Figure 9, the best validation loss was obtained for a number of epochs equal to 1. Then, it increased as the model over-fitted the training set. We can conclude that the model over-trains, especially when the number of epochs exceeds three.

Figure 9. Validation loss and training loss of the model obtained using OLID dataset for different number of epochs and a fixed learning rate of 2e-5 (= 2×10⁻⁵)

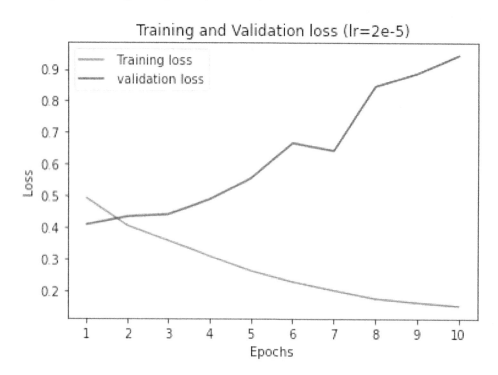

- Classifier head: In the proposed model, only the base Transformer was pre-trained while the classifier head was trained from scratch. In addition to employing BERT models, the used classifier in most of the NLP tasks is the feed-forward network (or a dense layer)-based model. In this research, we experimented with four classifiers. Each one of them includes an additional dense layer. Figure 10 depicts the training and validation loss curves recorded over five validation epochs. One can observe that using two- and three-layered classifiers yielded the best performance. Additionally, Table 2 reports the corresponding macro $F1$-scores. These scores clearly confirm the advantage of using two- and three-layered classifiers whose respective values for this metric reach 0.82.

(a) (b)

Figure 10. (a) Validation loss and (b) training loss curves obtained using the OLID dataset and different number of layers for the employed classifier as the number of epochs is varied

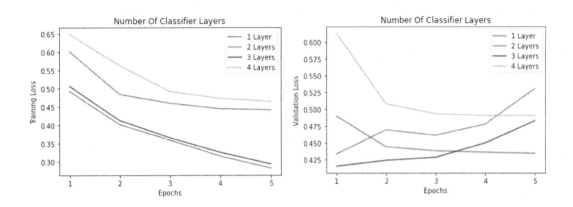

Table 2. Best macro F1-scores obtained for different classifier types by varying the number of dense layers using the OLID dataset

Classifier Type Used with the Model	Macro F1-Scores
One dense layer at 5 epochs	0.81
Two dense layers at 1 epoch	0.82
Three dense layers at 2 epochs	0.82
Four dense layers at 5 epochs	0.79

- Solo-training of the classifier: Here, we experimented with freezing all network layers besides the classification layers to investigate if further training of the classifier yields better performance. The resulting training and validation losses over five epochs are shown in Figure 11. As it can be seen, further training of the classifiers does not improve the performance of the model.

Figure 11. Training and validation loss curves over five epochs obtained after freezing all the other layers of the model, except the ones used for classification while utilizing the OLID dataset

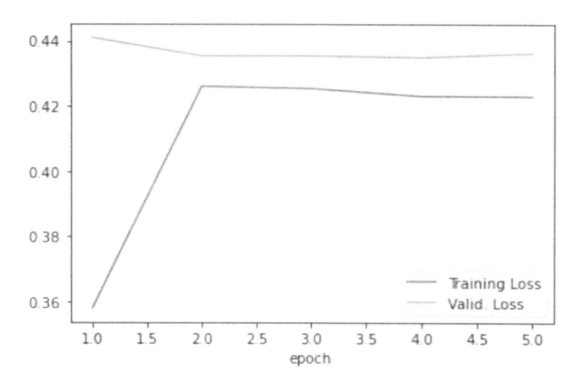

Data Augmentation

In terms of experiments related to data augmentation, we expanded the original training set by 30%. In this regard, three data augmentation techniques have been investigated. First, synonym augmentation was conducted. Specifically, words in given comments were randomly replaced by their synonyms. This technique was deployed using WordNet (Mikolov et al., 2013) and Easy Data Augmentation (EDA) datasets (Wei & Zou, 2019). As reported in Table 3, the use of WordNet has negatively affected the classification performance by decreasing the macro $F1$-score. On the other hand, EDA-based augmentation yielded comparable results to those obtained with no data augmentation.

Table 3. Results obtained using the proposed model along with synonym based data augmentation techniques on the OLID dataset

Synonym Augmentation Method	Macro F1-Scores
WordNet	0.80
EDA	0.82
Base model	0.82

The second data augmentation technique considered in our experiments involved back translation. Specifically, the text was translated into French. Then, it was translated back to English using Google Translate Application Programming interface (API) (Pavlopoulos et al., 2017). This technique decreased the macro $F1$-score for the considered model from 0.82 to 0.80. This process of "double" translation is illustrated in Figure 12.

Figure 12. An example of the translation of an original text to French and then back to English used as data augmentation

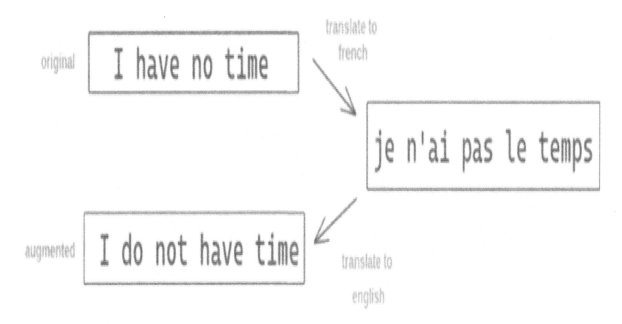

Finally, the third data augmentation method consisted in random alteration of the text. Particularly, we randomly deleted and inserted words in the considered comments. The experiments showed that random insertion improved the performance. This is in contrast to the use of random deletion, which did not impact the classification performance. Table 4 reports the obtained performance results after applying random alteration to the dataset. After augmenting the dataset, the model achieved a macro F1-score of 0.81. The employed data augmentations introduced variations to the model, which we postulate may enhance the generalizability of the model to examples outside the dataset.

Table 4. Results obtained after applying random alteration to the OLID dataset

Random Alteration of Text	Macro F1-Scores
Random deletion	0.82
Random insertion	0.83
Base model	0.82

Comparing BERT and Distilled BERT

In Figure 13 below, we plot the training and validation loss functions obtained using BERT and distilled BERT models. We can deduce that while both exhibit similar learning curves, BERT did not over-fit the training set as much as the distilled version did. The respective macro *F1*-scores obtained using both models confirmed this finding. Specifically, distilled BERT yielded a value of 0.81 compared to 0.83 for BERT-based model. Therefore, BERT ought to be selected as the preferred pre-trained model for our insult detection system.

(a) (b)

Figure 13. Training and validation loss curves obtained using (a) BERT and (b) distilled BERT models with OLID dataset

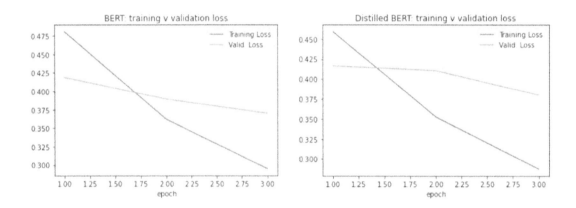

Overall, our experiments showed that the best performance was achieved by adopting the following configuration:

1. Pre-processing the data using word segmentation, representing the emoji as text, replacing URL with HTTP, and replacing html tags with their corresponding symbols.
2. Setting the learning rate to 2e-5, the input maximum length to 300 tokens, and the number of training epochs to 2.
3. Adding two stacked dense layers for classification.
4. Using BERT over distilled BERT as the pre-trained model of choice.

Testing Results and Comparison with State-of-the-Art Models

By applying the above configuration, the best model achieved a macro *F1*-score of 0.83, a weighted *F1* score of 0.86, and an accuracy of 86%. The corresponding confusion matrix obtained using OLID dataset is depicted in Figure 14. Further, the performance of the model for each of the two classes is presented in Table 5. We observe that the model's exhibits some limitation in correctly detecting insult cases. This limitation can be attributed to the severity of the data imbalance in the OLID dataset. Moreover, the dataset is extremely small and the proportion of examples containing insults is even smaller.

Figure 14. Confusion matrix obtained after testing the proposed insult detection model on the OLID dataset

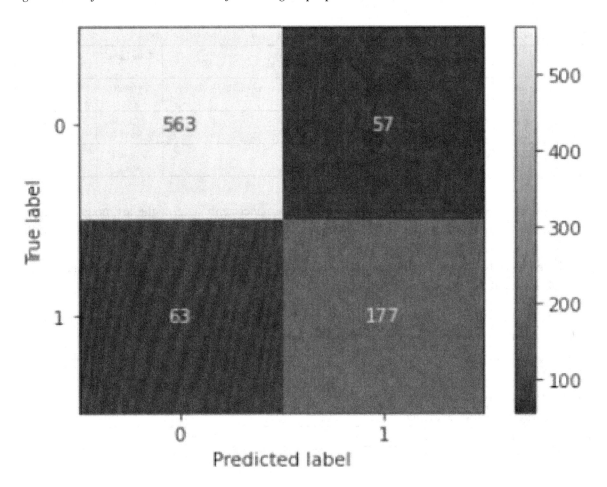

Table 5. Performance results of our insult detection model for each prediction class using the OLID dataset

Prediction Class	Precision	Recall	F1-Score
0 (Insult free)	0.90	0.91	0.90
1 (Insult)	0.76	0.74	0.75

Below, we provide a sample of three comments from the OLID dataset and the corresponding misclassification outcomes generated by the proposed model. As it can be seen in Table 6, some of the obtained false positives include accusations, vulgar language, and talking about crimes such as rape and murder. On the other hand, false negative samples include sarcasm, and some were not really an insult but rather they were critical of someone or something. For example, the comment *"#Antifa: Take note of how to protest with civility. This is why socialism (aka communism) will never win. It is inherently evil and unsustainable. URL"* did not insult anyone but instead included the word *"evil"* and thus, was labeled as an insult in the dataset.

Table 6. Sample test comments illustrating false negative and false positive cases

Text Message	True Label	Predicted Label
"#Antifa: Take note of how to protest with civility. This is why socialism (aka communism) will never win. It is inherently evil and unsustainable. URL".	1 (Insult)	0 (Insult free)
*"Are you f***ng serious? URL".*	0 (Insult free)	1 (Insult)
"@USER She Is A ChiCom Spy... #ClubGITMO".	0 (Insult free)	1 (Insult)

Moreover, we compared the proposed model's performance with state-of-the-art models using the OLID dataset as a benchmark. The obtained results are reported in Table 7. As it can be seen, our insult detection system yields better performance in terms of the macro F1-score (0.83) than other CNN and RNN-based models adopted for the insult detection problem (Kumari & Singh, 2019; Ranasinghe et al., 2019; Das et al., 2020).

Table 7. Comparison of the proposed model's performance with state-of-the-art models using OLID dataset

Insult Prediction Model, Ref.	Macro F1-Score
CNN- based method, (Das et al., 2020)	0.80
RNN-based method (Kumari & Singh, 2019)	0.79
LSTM-GRU model, (Ranasinghe et al., 2019)	0.72
Proposed Transformer-based model (BERT)	0.83

CONCLUSION AND FUTURE RESEARCH DIRECTIONS

In this chapter, we described a deep learning system based on the Transformer model to study the insult detection problem. The presented model relies on two main components: First, text pre-processing and representation are employed. Second, a Transformer-based deep learning model is trained to classify the comments from social media platforms as an insult or insult free. The obtained results indicate that performance of the proposed Transformer model exceeded the results obtained using the best performing CNN and RNN-based models on the same OLID dataset adopted for insult detection, with a macro *F1*-score of 0.83 and an accuracy of 86%.

As part of our future research work, we plan to investigate additional transformer-based models such as BERT-Large, which has 24 layers of encoders stacked on top of each other, RoBERTa, GPT-3, and cross-lingual models (Liu et al., 2019; Mann et al., 2020; Aluru et al. 2020; Chaudhari et al., 2021;

Kumbale et al., 2023; Liu et al., 2024). Moreover, having access to larger and more balanced datasets could potentially improve the realized, yet promising performance results obtained thus far. The ability to handle long sequences of text efficiently will be investigated in light of the large memory footprint and computational requirements of the Transformer models. The Reformer model described in (Kitaev et al., 2020) could be an interesting candidate in this regard as well as other hybrid models (Muneer et al., 2023). Further, we call for the development of multimodal datasets that include other formats of data. Future studies will need to develop methods that integrate both textual and image data for the detection of online insults and other forms of cyberbullying, including hate speech.

ACKNOWLEDGMENT

This research project was supported by a grant from the "Research Center of College of Computer and Information Sciences", Deanship of Scientific Research, King Saud University, Riyadh, Saudi Arabia.

REFERENCES

Aggarwal, C. C. (2018). *Neural networks and deep learning* (Vol. 10, No. 978, p. 3). Cham: springer.

Al-Zahrani, A. M. (2015). Cyberbullying among Saudi's Higher-Education Students: Implications for Educators and Policymakers. *World Journal of Education*, 5(3), 15–26. DOI: 10.5430/wje.v5n3p15

Aluru, S. S., Mathew, B., Saha, P., & Mukherjee, A. (2020). Deep learning models for multilingual hate speech detection. *arXiv preprint arXiv:2004.06465*.

Anderson, M. (2018). *A majority of teens have experienced some form of cyberbullying*. Pew Research Center.

Ben Ismail, M. M. (2020). Insult detection using a partitional CNN-LSTM model. *Computer Science and Information Technology*, 1(2), 84–92.

Bengfort, B., Bilbro, R., & Ojeda, T. (2018). *Applied text analysis with Python: Enabling language-aware data products with machine learning*. O'Reilly Media, Inc.

Burkov, A. (2019). *The hundred-page machine learning book* (Vol. 1). Andriy Burkov.

Chaudhari, S., Mithal, V., Polatkan, G., & Ramanath, R. (2021). An attentive survey of attention models. [TIST]. *ACM Transactions on Intelligent Systems and Technology*, 12(5), 1–32. DOI: 10.1145/3465055

Chen, S., Wang, J., & He, K. (2024). Chinese Cyberbullying Detection Using XLNet and Deep Bi-LSTM Hybrid Model. *Information (Basel)*, 15(2), 93. DOI: 10.3390/info15020093

Corcoran, L., & McGuckin, C. (2014). Addressing bullying problems in Irish schools and in cyberspace: A challenge for school management. *Educational Research*, 56(1), 48–64. DOI: 10.1080/00131881.2013.874150

Das, K. A., Baruah, A., Barbhuiya, F. A., & Dey, K. (2020, December). Checkpoint ensemble of transformers for hate speech classification. In *Proceedings of the fourteenth workshop on semantic evaluation* (pp. 2023-2029). DOI: 10.18653/v1/2020.semeval-1.267

Eisner, B., Rocktäschel, T., Augenstein, I., Bošnjak, M., & Riedel, S. (2016). emoji2vec: Learning emoji representations from their description. *arXiv preprint arXiv:1609.08359*. DOI: 10.18653/v1/W16-6208

Elbasani, E., & Kim, J. D. (2022). AMR-CNN: Abstract meaning representation with convolution neural network for toxic content detection. *Journal of Web Engineering*, 21(3), 677–692. DOI: 10.13052/jwe1540-9589.2135

Founta, A. M., Chatzakou, D., Kourtellis, N., Blackburn, J., Vakali, A., & Leontiadis, I. (2019, June). A unified deep learning architecture for abuse detection. In *Proceedings of the 10th ACM conference on web science* (pp. 105-114). DOI: 10.1145/3292522.3326028

Georgakopoulos, S. V., Tasoulis, S. K., Vrahatis, A. G., & Plagianakos, V. P. (2018, July). Convolutional neural networks for toxic comment classification. In *Proceedings of the 10th hellenic conference on artificial intelligence* (pp. 1-6). DOI: 10.1145/3200947.3208069

Heidenreich, H. (2021, Dec. 21). *Stemming? Lemmatization? What?* [Available online] https://towardsdatascience.com/stemming-lemmatization-what-ba782b7c0bd8

Henaff, M., Bruna, J., & LeCun, Y. (2015). Deep convolutional networks on graph-structured data. *arXiv preprint arXiv:1506.05163.*

IBM. (2021, Dec. 15). *Text mining.* [Available online] https://www.ibm.com/cloud/learn/text-mining

Iwendi, C., Srivastava, G., Khan, S., & Maddikunta, P. K. R. (2023). Cyberbullying detection solutions based on deep learning architectures. *Multimedia Systems*, 29(3), 1839–1852. DOI: 10.1007/s00530-020-00701-5

Kemp, S. (2022, Feb. 26). *Digital 21: Global overview report.* [Available online] https://datareportal.com/reports/digital-2021-global-overview-report

Khatri, A. (2018, June). *Detecting offensive messages using deep learning: A micro-service based approach.* Pycon APAC Conference Presentation. [Available online] https://www.youtube.com/watch?v=6ciGTSrL-l4

Kitaev, N., Kaiser, Ł., & Levskaya, A. (2020). Reformer: The efficient transformer. *arXiv preprint arXiv:2001.04451.*

Kumari, K., & Singh, J. P. (2019). Deep learning approach for identification of abusive content. In *Proceedings of forum for information retrieval evaluation* (FIRE) (pp. 328-335), vol. 2517.

Kumbale, S., Singh, S., Poornalatha, G., & Singh, S. (2023). BREE-HD: A Transformer-Based Model to Identify Threats on Twitter. *IEEE Access : Practical Innovations, Open Solutions*, 11, 67180–67190. DOI: 10.1109/ACCESS.2023.3291072

Liu, D., Wang, M., & Catlin, A. G. (2024). Detecting Anti-Semitic Hate Speech using Transformer-based Large Language Models. *arXiv preprint arXiv:2405.03794.*

Liu, P., Li, W., & Zou, L. (2019, June). NULI at SemEval-2019 task 6: Transfer learning for offensive language detection using bidirectional transformers. In *Proceedings of the 13th international workshop on semantic evaluation* (pp. 87-91). DOI: 10.18653/v1/S19-2011

Liu, Y., Ott, M., Goyal, N., Du, J., Joshi, M., Chen, D., Levy, O., Lewis, M., Zettlemoyer, L., & Stoyanov, V. (2019). RoBERTa: A robustly optimized BERT pretraining approach. *arXiv preprint arXiv:1907.11692.*

Maheswari, M. U., & Sathiaseelan, J. G. R. (2017). Text mining: Survey on techniques and applications. *International Journal of Scientific Research*, 6(6), 1660–1664.

Mann, B., Ryder, N., Subbiah, M., Kaplan, J., Dhariwal, P., Neelakantan, A., Shyam, P., Sastry, G., Askell, A., Agarwal, S., Herbert-Voss, A., Krueger, G., Henighan, T., Child, R., Ramesh, A., Ziegler, D. M., Wu, J., Winter, C., . . . Amodei, D. (2020). Language models are few-shot learners. *arXiv preprint arXiv:2005.14165, 1.*

Marquez, M. (2022, Dec. 18). *What is information extraction?* [Available online] https://www.ontotext.com/knowledgehub/fundamentals/information-extraction/

Mikolov, T., Sutskever, I., Chen, K., Corrado, G. S., & Dean, J. (2013). Distributed representations of words and phrases and their compositionality. *Advances in Neural Information Processing Systems*, ●●●, 26.

Miljanovic, M. (2012). Comparative analysis of recurrent and finite impulse response neural networks in time series prediction. *Indian Journal of Computer Science and Engineering*, 3(1), 180–191.

Mozafari, M., Farahbakhsh, R., & Crespi, N. (2020). A BERT-based transfer learning approach for hate speech detection in online social media. In *Complex Networks and Their Applications VIII: Volume 1 Proceedings of the Eighth International Conference on Complex Networks and Their Applications COMPLEX NETWORKS 2019 8* (pp. 928-940). Springer International Publishing. DOI: 10.1007/978-3-030-36687-2_77

Muneer, A., Alwadain, A., Ragab, M. G., & Alqushaibi, A. (2023). Cyberbullying detection on social media using stacking ensemble learning and enhanced BERT. *Information (Basel)*, 14(8), 467. DOI: 10.3390/info14080467

Pant, K., & Dadu, T. (2020). Cross-lingual inductive transfer to detect offensive language. *arXiv preprint arXiv:2007.03771*.

Pavlopoulos, J., Malakasiotis, P., & Androutsopoulos, I. (2017). Deep learning for user comment moderation. *arXiv preprint arXiv:1705.09993*. DOI: 10.18653/v1/W17-3004

Pavlopoulos, J., Thain, N., Dixon, L., & Androutsopoulos, I. (2019, June). Convai at semeval-2019 task 6: Offensive language identification and categorization with perspective and bert. In *Proceedings of the 13th international Workshop on Semantic Evaluation* (pp. 571-576). DOI: 10.18653/v1/S19-2102

Perren, S., Dooley, J., Shaw, T., & Cross, D. (2010). Bullying in school and cyberspace: Associations with depressive symptoms in Swiss and Australian adolescents. *Child and Adolescent Psychiatry and Mental Health*, 4(1), 1–10. DOI: 10.1186/1753-2000-4-28 PMID: 21092266

Pitsilis, G. K., Ramampiaro, H., & Langseth, H. (2018). Detecting offensive language in tweets using deep learning. *arXiv preprint arXiv:1801.04433*.

Plum, A., Ranasinghe, T., Orasan, C., & Mitkov, R. (2019). Offensive language detection with deep learning. In *Proceedings of 15th conference on natural language processing* (KONVENS) (pp. 421-426).

Quiza, R., & Davim, J. P. (2011). Computational methods and optimization. In Davim, J. P. (Ed.), *Machining of hard materials* (pp. 177–208). Springer Science & Business Media. DOI: 10.1007/978-1-84996-450-0_6

Ranasinghe, T., Zampieri, M., & Hettiarachchi, H. (2019, December). Deep learning models for multilingual hate speech and offensive language identification. In *Proceedings of forum for information retrieval evaluation* (FIRE) (pp. 199-207).

Raza, M. O., Memon, M., Bhatti, S., & Bux, R. (2020). Detecting cyberbullying in social commentary using supervised machine learning. In *Advances in Information and Communication: Proceedings of the 2020 Future of Information and Communication Conference (FICC)*, Volume 2 (pp. 621-630). Springer International Publishing. DOI: 10.1007/978-3-030-39442-4_45

Roy, S. G., Narayan, U., Raha, T., Abid, Z., & Varma, V. (2021). Leveraging multilingual transformers for hate speech detection. *arXiv preprint arXiv:2101.03207.*

Sak, H., Senior, A., & Beaufays, F. (2014). Long short-term memory recurrent neural network architectures for large scale acoustic modeling. In *Fifteenth annual conference of the international speech communication association.* DOI: 10.21437/Interspeech.2014-80

Sax, S. (2016). *Flame wars: Automatic insult detection.* Technical Report, Stanford University, California, USA.

Schmidhuber, J., & Hochreiter, S. (1997). Long short-term memory. *Neural Computation,* 9(8), 1735–1780. DOI: 10.1162/neco.1997.9.8.1735 PMID: 9377276

Skansi, S. (2018). *Introduction to Deep Learning: from logical calculus to artificial intelligence.* Springer. DOI: 10.1007/978-3-319-73004-2

UNICEF. (2022, Jan. 24). *Cyberbullying: What is it and how to stop it.* [Available online] https://www .unicef.org/end-violence/how-to-stop-cyberbullying

Valueva, M. V., Nagornov, N. N., Lyakhov, P. A., Valuev, G. V., & Chervyakov, N. I. (2020). Application of the residue number system to reduce hardware costs of the convolutional neural network implementation. *Mathematics and Computers in Simulation,* 177, 232–243. DOI: 10.1016/j.matcom.2020.04.031

Vaswani, A., Shazeer, N., Parmar, N., Uszkoreit, J., Jones, L., Gomez, A. N., Kaiser, L., & Polosukhin, I. (2017). Attention is all you need. *Advances in Neural Information Processing Systems,* ●●●, 30.

Wang, K., Lu, D., Han, S. C., Long, S., & Poon, J. (2020). Detect all abuse! toward universal abusive language detection models. *arXiv preprint arXiv:2010.03776.* DOI: 10.18653/v1/2020.coling-main.560

Wang, S., Liu, J., Ouyang, X., & Sun, Y. (2020). Galileo at SemEval-2020 task 12: Multi-lingual learning for offensive language identification using pre-trained language models. *arXiv preprint arXiv:2010.03542.* DOI: 10.18653/v1/2020.semeval-1.189

Waseem, Z., Davidson, T., Warmsley, D., & Weber, I. (2017). Understanding abuse: A typology of abusive language detection subtasks. *arXiv preprint arXiv:1705.09899.* DOI: 10.18653/v1/W17-3012

Wei, J., & Zou, K. (2019). Eda: Easy data augmentation techniques for boosting performance on text classification tasks. *arXiv preprint arXiv:1901.11196.* DOI: 10.18653/v1/D19-1670

Wiedemann, G., Yimam, S. M., & Biemann, C. (2020). UHH-LT at SemEval-2020 task 12: Fine-tuning of pre-trained transformer networks for offensive language detection. *arXiv preprint arXiv:2004.11493.* DOI: 10.18653/v1/2020.semeval-1.213

Zaheri, S., Leath, J., & Stroud, D. (2020). Toxic comment classification. *SMU Data Science Review,* 3(1), 13.

Zampieri, M. (2021, August 4). *OLID* [Data set]. https://sites.google.com/site/offensevalsharedtask/olid

Zampieri, M., Malmasi, S., Nakov, P., Rosenthal, S., Farra, N., & Kumar, R. (2019). Predicting the type and target of offensive posts in social media. *arXiv preprint arXiv:1902.09666.* DOI: 10.18653/v1/N19-1144

Zhang, H., Mahata, D., Shahid, S., Mehnaz, L., Anand, S., Singla, Y., Shah, R. R., & Uppal, K. (2019). Identifying offensive posts and targeted offense from twitter. *arXiv preprint arXiv:1904.09072*.

Zhou, V. (2021, Dec. 11). *A simple explanation of the bag-of-words model*. [Available online] https://towardsdatascience.com/a-simple-explanation-of-the-bag-of-words-model-b88fc4f4971

Zinovyeva, E., Härdle, W. K., & Lessmann, S. (2020). Antisocial online behavior detection using deep learning. *Decision Support Systems*, 138, 113362. DOI: 10.1016/j.dss.2020.113362

ADDITIONAL READING

Alatawi, H. S., Alhothali, A. M., & Moria, K. M. (2021). Detecting white supremacist hate speech using domain specific word embedding with deep learning and BERT. *IEEE Access : Practical Innovations, Open Solutions*, 9, 106363–106374. DOI: 10.1109/ACCESS.2021.3100435

Davidson, T., Warmsley, D., Macy, M., & Weber, I. (2017, May). Automated hate speech detection and the problem of offensive language. In *Proceedings of the international AAAI conference on web and social media* (Vol. 11, No. 1, pp. 512-515). DOI: 10.1609/icwsm.v11i1.14955

Jahan, M. S., & Oussalah, M. (2023). A systematic review of hate speech automatic detection using natural language processing. *Neurocomputing*, 546, 126232. DOI: 10.1016/j.neucom.2023.126232

Li, L., Fan, L., Atreja, S., & Hemphill, L. (2024). "HOT" ChatGPT: The promise of ChatGPT in detecting and discriminating hateful, offensive, and toxic comments on social media. *ACM Transactions on the Web*, 18(2), 1–36. DOI: 10.1145/3643829

Pozzi, F. A., Fersini, E., Messina, E., & Liu, B. (2016). *Sentiment analysis in social networks*. Morgan Kaufmann.

Ranasinghe, T., & Zampieri, M. (2020). Multilingual offensive language identification with cross-lingual embeddings. *arXiv preprint arXiv:2010.05324*. DOI: 10.18653/v1/2020.emnlp-main.470

Risch, J., & Krestel, R. (2018, August). Aggression identification using deep learning and data augmentation. In *Proceedings of the first workshop on trolling, aggression and cyberbullying (TRAC-2018)* (pp. 150-158).

Sultan, D., Mendes, M., Kassenkhan, A., & Akylbekov, O. (2023). Hybrid CNN-LSTM Network for Cyberbullying Detection on Social Networks using Textual Contents. *International Journal of Advanced Computer Science and Applications*, 14(9). Advance online publication. DOI: 10.14569/IJACSA.2023.0140978

Toxic Comment Classification Challenge. (2019). Kaggle [Data set]. https://www.kaggle.com/c/jigsaw-toxic-comment-classification-challenge/data

Zampieri, M., Malmasi, S., Nakov, P., Rosenthal, S., Farra, N., & Kumar, R. (2019). Semeval-2019 task 6: Identifying and categorizing offensive language in social media (offenseval). *arXiv preprint arXiv:1903.08983*. DOI: 10.18653/v1/S19-2010

KEY TERMS AND DEFINITIONS

Confusion Matrix: A confusion matrix is a table, used in machine learning, specifically for classification tasks. It provides a clear visualization of how well a model performs at distinguishing between different categories or classes. By analyzing the confusion matrix, the user can obtain correct predictions, known as true positives and true negatives, when reading the diagonal entries while incorrect predictions appear outside it. The latter are summarized by false positives and false negatives.

Cyberbullying: Broadly speaking, cyberbullying is using electronic devices to bully someone. It involves repeated, aggressive behavior meant to hurt, insult, or embarrass. This can include sending mean messages, posting rumors online, or sharing private information about someone. Cyberbullying can happen anonymously, making it harder to stop.

Deep Learning (DL): DL is a subfield of machine learning inspired by the brain's structure and function. It utilizes artificial neural networks with multiple layers to process information and extract intricate patterns. These layered networks can learn from vast amounts of data, allowing them to tackle a multitude of tasks like image recognition, speech translation, and natural language processing. DL models achieve high accuracy by iteratively refining the connections between their layers based on the data they are trained on.

F1-Score: The F1 score is a metric used in machine learning for classification tasks. It takes the harmonic mean of precision and recall, giving a single value that considers both aspects. A high F1 score indicates a good balance between the model's ability to identify true positives and avoid false positives. This makes it a valuable metric for evaluating the effectiveness of a classification model, especially when dealing with imbalanced datasets.

Hyperparameter: In ML, a hyperparameter is a setting that the user defines before training that controls the learning process itself, not the model itself. Unlike regular parameters that the model learns from data, hyperparameters are set manually and influence how the model learns. Examples include the learning rate, the optimizer, or the number of layers in a neural network.

Machine Learning (ML): ML is a subfield of artificial intelligence that equips computers to learn without explicit programming. It involves algorithms that can analyze data, identify patterns, and make predictions. Over time, these algorithms can improve their performance, essentially enabling machines to learn and act like humans while being able to process massive amounts of information.

Transformer Model: This is a DL architecture initially developed for natural language processing (NLP). Unlike traditional models, it depends on using a self-attention mechanism, thus allowing it to analyze all parts of a text input simultaneously. This makes Transformers very effective at capturing long-range dependencies in textual input. Recent breakthroughs in tasks like machine translation, text summarization, and question answering have been largely facilitated by Transformers.

Chapter 2
Robust Dimensionality Reduction:
How to Increase Efficiency of Machine Learning Computations

Jan Kalina

https://orcid.org/0000-0002-8491-0364

Institute of Computer Science, The Czech Academy of Sciences, Czech Republic

ABSTRACT

Artificial intelligence is nowadays equipped with a plethora of tools for obtaining relevant knowledge from (possibly big) data in a variety of tasks. While habitually used methods of machine learning applicable within artificial intelligence tools can be characterized as black boxes, practical applications often require to understand why a particular conclusion (e.g. decision) was made, which arouses interest in explainable machine learning. This chapter is devoted to variable selection methods for finding the most relevant variables for the given task. If statistically robust variable selection methods are exploited, the harmful influence of data contamination by outlying values on the results is typically eliminated or downweighted. Principles of prior, intrinsic, and posterior variable selection approaches are recalled and compared on three real datasets related to gene expression measurements, neighborhood crime rate, and tourism infrastructure. These examples reveal robust approaches to machine learning that outperform non-robust ones if the data are contaminated by outliers.

INTRODUCTION

Although grand futuristic visions of artificial intelligence contributing to the transformation of the humankind towards the ideals of the knowledge society (Tegmark, 2017) may remain to represent a science fiction at least for some time, artificial intelligence can be agreed to have the potential to dramatically influence the society worldwide already soon. When artificial intelligence needs to obtain practically useful knowledge from available information while accounting for uncertainty, machine learning with its statistical algorithms comes into play. A great number of innovative machine learning tools are nowadays available for obtaining relevant knowledge from (possibly big) data in a variety of tasks. The adoption of high-performance computing (HPC) could enhance the computational feasibility of very demanding

DOI: 10.4018/978-1-6684-3795-7.ch002

algorithms even further. To present an illustrative example, several promising artificial intelligence tools have been engaged in the fight against the COVID-19 pandemic (Lalmuanawma et al., 2020). The quickly growing field of scientific computations, exploiting advanced computing for analyzing scientific problems, has also been denoted as computational science (Holder & Eichholz, 2019). At the same time, the role of scientific computations has acquired increasing attention from practitioners (Quarteroni, 2018).

While habitually used methods of machine learning applicable within scientific computations can be characterized as black boxes, practical applications often require understanding why a particular conclusion (e.g. decision) was made. This motivates the need for explainable artificial intelligence and at the same time clarifies the increasing interest in explainable machine learning, which is designed to analyze the available data in an interpretable way. Naturally, understanding the limitations of artificial intelligence belongs to ethical issues and the impossibility to explain rigorously why given algorithms yield particular results represents an important ethical issue as such (Jacobson et al., 2020). Two approaches (or in fact aims) for improving the explainability of machine learning tools, which may be used at the same time, are dimensionality reduction and robustness to outlying values (outliers), where the latter makes it possible to reduce the influence of individual outliers and actually to evaluate the influence of individual observations.

Various types and formats of available data require a broad spectrum of sophisticated machine learning methods for their analysis. A correct analysis of data with a large number of available variables (features) therefore becomes an emerging issue. Together with the increasing complexity of available data, data analysts begin to realize the importance of methods of complexity reduction for their reliable and effective analysis (Fordellone, 2019). The amount of data observed in various fields grows very rapidly, while complex data are commonly agreed to have a big potential to influence research or everyday routine activities (López-Robles et al., 2019). Complexity reduction is a general concept including any approach to simplifying data analysis and may include finding suitable relevant features from images (e.g. using images of the brain as in Bučková et al. (2020)), voice records, narrative text (e.g. in health reports), etc. We understand dimensionality reduction (dimension reduction) to represent a special case of complexity reduction for the situation with numerical data, i.e. when dealing with data in the form of numbers. Naturally, dimensionality reduction methods are suitable also for Big Data, which can be described as a valuable capital with an underutilized opportunity for decision making and relevance to the society (cf. Bradlow et al., 2017).

The objective of this chapter is to explain principles of robust dimensionality reduction, recall some promising methods, and present illustrations of real data revealing that the methods work reliably. Throughout the chapter, robust approaches to reducing dimensionality are explained to represent a unique methodology for an explainable (comprehensible) data analysis by machine learning. Particularly, reducing the dimensionality improves the interpretation of the knowledge acquired from the data by reducing the focus on the most important variables. While outliers can be too influential and thus misleading for standard data analysis, robust statistical tools can eliminate their influence. At the same time, the relationship between dimensionality reduction and low-energy approximate computation is discussed. Robust approaches suitable for contaminated data will be illustrated on classification and regression tasks in three real datasets related to gene expression measurements, neighborhood crime rate, and tourism infrastructure.

PRINCIPLES OF DIMENSIONALITY REDUCTION

To simplify the analysis of complex multivariate data in various applications, dimensionality reduction is generally recommended to eliminate the influence of redundant variables (Wilson, 2018). Throughout the whole chapter, we will consider having the total number of n observations (measurements) available. Dimensionality reduction is popular in machine learning in general and is unavoidable for Big Data (Blazques & Domenech, 2018) or high-dimensional data, where the latter are defined as data with the number of variables exceeding (perhaps largely) the value of n. If the data are big and dimensionality reduction is not performed at all, one would have to resort to computationally very demanding methods. We stress however that dimensionality reduction may be beneficial also for data with a relatively small number of variables (Martinez et al., 2017).

In general, dimensionality reduction may bring remarkable benefits including a simplification of subsequent computations. Parsimonious models, i.e. simple models with a small set of relevant variables, may enable good comprehensibility of the results e.g. by dividing the variables into homogeneous clusters. Some of the methods reduce or remove correlation among variables. Dimensionality reduction may even improve the results of the subsequent analysis (e.g. decision making) compared to those obtained with full data. On the other hand, dimensionality reduction may lead to a loss of some relevant information if the set of variables is reduced to a very small number of relevant ones, and the results may be severely biased.

We distinguish between supervised and unsupervised dimensionality reduction methods. Supervised ones are tailor-made for data coming from two or more groups, while the information about the group membership is taken into account. Unsupervised methods consider data only in one group. If the data are in groups but the group labeling is not known even for the training dataset, unsupervised methods must be used. It is namely suboptimal to use an unsupervised approach for data coming from several known groups.

Further, we distinguish between feature extraction, which replaces the data by combinations of variables, and variable selection (also feature selection), which selects a smaller set of important variables and ignores all remaining ones.

Feature extraction methods search for the most relevant (linear or nonlinear) combinations of the measurements and replace the original data with a small number of such combinations. Feature extraction is performed always as a prior step, i.e. before the actual data analysis. Popular methods include principal component analysis (PCA), factor analysis, correspondence analysis, independent component analysis, partial least squares regression, multivariate scaling (Greene, 2017), or methods based on information theory. Usually, feature extraction (unlike variable selection) ensures decorrelation, yields reliable predictions (at least if there are not contaminated by outliers), and its results have good local robustness (stability). It deserves to be recalled that PCA as the most common dimensionality reduction method is an unsupervised method and thus is not suitable for data coming from two or more different groups (i.e. for a mixture of populations). Although PCA is commonly appraised for finding decorrelated components (Kalina & Rensová, 2015), numerous machine learning methods do not need the data to be uncorrelated.

Variable selection procedures can be distinguished as:

- Prior (a priori, preliminary), i.e. before the data analysis of interest (regression, classification, clustering, instrumental variables estimation, etc.),
- Intrinsic (sparse), using a suitable regularization within the data analysis of interest,

- Posterior (post hoc analysis), i.e. after the data analysis of interest.

Some methods may be performed as a prior approach and also as a posterior approach. This is true e.g. for hypothesis testing and various methods of backward elimination, which may be used either before the analysis of interest or after it. Nevertheless, hypothesis testing for reducing the dimensionality cannot be used directly, because using the same procedure repeatedly may increase the probability of type I error.

Prior variable selection represents a preliminary or assistive step before the particular analysis task (e.g. regression modeling or learning a classification rule). Prior variable selection allows to analyze only a small set of relevant variables and to give comprehensible answers to various questions, e.g. how to interpret values of individual parameters or which variables are the most important ones for predicting the response. If the relevant variables are selected before the data analysis as such, future measurements in the same situation can be performed on a smaller set of variables. This may reduce the financial or organizational demands of the experiments (or measurements). Numerous variable selection methods with the ability to ignore redundant variables include wrappers, filters, embedded methods, the minimum redundancy maximum relevance approach, or methods based on information theory. An important class of tools includes hypothesis testing; this either requires distributional assumptions (such as in specific regression models) or may be performed without them (e.g. by nonparametric bootstrap).

Intrinsic variable selection (sparse variable selection) may be performed within regression or classification tasks through regularization (Fan et al., 2020). Recently proposed methods of this type typically yield sparse solutions. These method exploit information only from some variables while ignoring the remaining observations. Although regularization may ensure local robustness to small changes in the data, we can say in general that regularized methods may suffer from the presence of outliers in the data.

Posterior variable selection is commonly performed utilizing hypothesis tests or methods of information theory. Often, hypothesis testing is used in a supervised approach for data observed in two or more groups. In such context, the tests aim to order the variables in order of evidence against the null hypothesis rather than to assess the significance of a particular variable using p-values. The problem of multiple testing is commonly solved by the false discovery rate (FDR), requiring the percentage of false-positive tests among all significant tests not to exceed 5%. The most popular procedure for keeping the false discovery rate (FDR), defined as the percentage of false-positive tests (incorrectly rejecting the null hypothesis) among all significant tests, is the approach of Benjamini & Hochberg (1995) for independent tests. An extension of Benjamini & Yekutieli (2001) is suitable for (potentially) dependent statistics, even if the structure of the dependence is not known. Nevertheless, posterior variable selection used in the model selection (model choice) task has been criticized for its lack of stability (Heinze et al., 2017).

In general, it is not possible to describe a general approach for finding the best dimensionality reduction method for a particular dataset. The recent paper of Heinze et al. (2017) attempted to perform at least some systematic comparisons of various dimensionality reduction methods and formulate some practical recommendations related to this problem. Choosing the appropriate method for Big Data nevertheless contains many open problems. Of course, each method has its own set of assumptions. In addition, some methods are more suitable in the context of economic data analysis, others would be often exploited in biomedicine, etc. We can thus say that dimensionality reduction should be tailored for the particular task/problem within the given field of expertise (medicine, economics, engineering, etc.) as well as the statistical task of the analysis (regression or classification). If the data analysis requires a clear interpretation, a prior or sparse variable selection should be preferable to feature extraction (Olson, 2017).

SOME ROBUST METHODS APPLICABLE TO DIMENSIONALITY REDUCTION

Principles

Numerous commonly used machine learning methods are vulnerable to the presence of outliers in the data, which has motivated the development of robust statistical methodology in the last decades (Huber, 2009). Also, standard dimensionality reduction methods suffer from the presence of outliers in the data and there is a need for robust counterparts, i.e. methods insensitive to outliers (Filzmoser & Todorov, 2011). This is naturally true also for common variable selection methods. Therefore, their robust versions are highly desirable. Our main focus is on methods that are insensitive to the presence of outliers, i.e. globally robust in terms of the breakdown point. The users prefer reliable methods that are computationally stable and well-posed also for high-dimensional data. So far, however, only small attention has been paid to local robustness to small changes in the data, especially near the center of gravity of the bulk of the data (Jurečková et al., 2019); we can say that locally robust methods have been available only for some of the simplest statistical models.

Robust Centroid-Based Classification

In numerous applications, classification based on centroids (prototypes, templates) is known to be powerful but at the same time simple and comprehensible. Centroids are commonly used in image processing but work well also for other data, such as for high-dimensional data not in the form of images (Hall & Pham, 2010; Delaigle & Hall, 2012). We assume now two groups of p-dimensional continuous observations. Most commonly, if the task is to classify data into two groups, the centroid is obtained as the mean of the first group, and Pearson correlation coefficient is used as the measure of similarity between the centroid and a given observation. The observation is classified to belong to the first group if the correlation coefficient exceeds a given threshold; we use here the threshold of Kalina & Matonoha (2020).

A method for optimization of centroids was recently proposed by Kalina & Matonoha (2020). This supervised learning method exploits the weighted correlation coefficient r_w, i.e. weighted extension of Pearson correlation coefficient. Let us consider weights $w_1, \ldots, w_n$ and denote the weighted mean of a vector x by $\bar{x}_w$. We may recall r_w between two vectors x and y to be defined as

$$r_w(x,y) = \frac{\sum_{i=1}^{n} w_i \left(x_i - \bar{x}_w \right) \left(y_i - \bar{y}_w \right)}{\sqrt{\sum_{i=1}^{n} \left[w_i (x_i - \bar{x}_w)^2 \right] \sum_{i=1}^{n} \left[w_i (y_i - \bar{y}_w)^2 \right]}}.$$

The optimization tasks require minimizing a nonlinear loss function corresponding to a regularized margin-like distance inspired by Vapnik (2000). Such distance is evaluated for the worst pair over the training database. Kalina & Matonoha (2020) compared the results of two optimization approaches: [I] linear (i.e. approximate) approach to solving the optimization task, and [II] nonlinear approach employing the interior point method. The comparison of these two types of optimization revealed both approaches to be computationally stable and the linear approximation to the optimization yielded solutions very close to those of the nonlinear approach. Additionally, optimization of the weights may be also performed, ensuring that many pixels obtain zero weights and thus yield a sparse solution. The optimization of the weights can be described as an analogy to the optimization of the centroid, and again the linear (approximate) approach turns out to be reliable and stable. The optimal centroid may be used as such, even without any weights at all; still, optimization of the weights leads to a further improvement of the classification performance. So far, the robustness of the method has not been investigated and is revealed empirically later in this chapter. Figure 1 shows the results of the optimization procedures applied in the context of mouth localization in facial images.

Figure 1. Left: a mouth centroid suitable for mouth localization obtained by the optimization procedure proposed in Kalina & Matonoha (2020). Right: weights corresponding to this centroid.

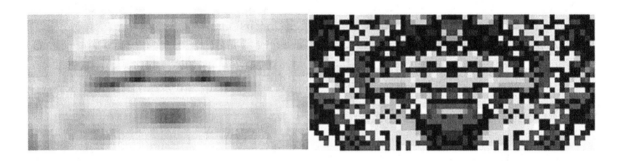

Robust Regression and Correlation

In the linear regression model, the classical least squares estimator is notoriously well known to be too vulnerable to the presence of outliers in the data (Jurečková et al., 2019). We now recall the least weighted squares (LWS) estimator (Víšek, 2011; Kalina, 2015) of parameters of linear regression, which will be later exploited as an inspiration or basis for several robust approaches to dimensionality reduction. We consider the standard linear regression model

$$Y_i = \beta_1 X_{i1} + \ldots + \beta_p X_{ip} + e_i, i = 1, \ldots, n,$$

which may be expressed in the matrix notation as $Y = X\beta + e$. Here, $\beta = \left(\beta_1, \ldots, \beta_p \right)^T$ is the vector of parameters and the i-th row of X will be denoted as $X_i = \left(X_{i1}, \ldots, X_{ip} \right)^T$ for $i = 1, \ldots, n$. If we consider a fixed estimate $b = \left(b_1, \ldots, b_p \right)^T \in \mathbb{R}^p$, it will be useful to denote the residual corresponding to the i-th observation as

$$u_i(b) = Y_i - b_1 X_{i1} - \ldots - b_p X_{ip}, i = 1, \ldots, n.$$

Ordering squared residuals as

$$u_{(1)}^2(b) \leq u_{(2)}^2(b) \leq \ldots \leq u_{(n)}^2(b),$$

the LWS estimator is formally defined by

$$\underset{b \in \mathbb{R}^p}{\operatorname{argmin}} \sum_{i=1}^{n} w_i u^2_{(i)}(b).$$

The properties of the LWS estimator, i.e. high global robustness (if suitable weights are chosen), high local robustness, and high efficiency for non-contaminated data make the estimator to be an appealing choice for practical data analysis. The LWS estimator belongs to highly robust methods, i.e. methods with a high value of the breakdown point. Let us recal the breakdown point to be defined as a measure of the minimal fraction of data that can drive an estimator beyond all bounds when set to arbitrary values (cf. Statti et al., 2017). The LWS estimator is based on implicit weights assigned to individual observations and does not require any prior outlier detection; it does not even provide outlier detection automatically, although its adaptation for outlier detection is available (Kalina, 2018). The LWS estimator has appealing properties also in the nonlinear regression model. An illustration of the LWS estimator in comparison with the least squares is shown in Figure 2.

The LWS estimator is defined for the standard linear regression model, where the response Y is explained by p independent variables (regressors, predictors). The formal definition of the LWS estimators of the parameters of the linear regression model requires the user to specify a sequence of magnitudes of non-increasing weights, which are assigned to individual observations only after the optimal permutation. Particularly, the most reliable observations (with the smallest absolute residuals) obtain the largest weight, while the outliers (with the largest absolute residuals) obtain the smallest weights (possibly zero). The LWS estimator remains consistent for any non-increasing weights (Víšek, 2011). The computation of the LWS estimator may exploit a reliable approximate algorithm of Rousseeuw & van Driessen (2006). All computations within this chapter consider LWS with weights with magnitudes equal to *1, 1-1/n, ..., n/4,0,...0,* where 25% of observations obtain exactly zero weights. These weights will be called trimmed linear weights (Kalina & Tichavský, 2020). Formally, these are defined using the weight function

$$\psi(t) = \left(1 - \frac{t}{\tau}\right) 1[t < \tau], t \in [0,1], \tau = 3/4.$$

The least trimmed squares (LTS) estimator is a special case with weights only equal to 1 or 0; the user has to specify the trimming constant h so that e.g. specifying $h=0.75$ means that 75% of the observations obtain the weight 1 and the remaining 25% are trimmed away completely.

While Pearson correlation coefficient is well known to be highly vulnerable to the presence of outliers in the data, its various robust versions have been available (Shevlyakov & Oja, 2016). Let us recall the implicitly weighted robust correlation coefficient denoted here as r_{LWS}, which is based on the LWS estimator. Formally, r_{LWS} proposed and investigated in Kalina (2018) is obtained as the weighted Pearson correlation coefficient with the weights that are found as optimal by the LWS estimator in the linear regression model $Y{\sim}X$. This symbolic notation denotes the model, where Y plays the role of the response explained by X. Known properties of r_{LWS} include its high breakdown point and asymptotic normality (Kalina & Schlenker, 2015).

Figure 2. Illustration of robust regression on a contaminated dataset from Rousseeuw & Leroy (1987). The least squares fit is heavily influenced by the cluster of 6 outliers and the LWS fit estimates very well the non-outlying data points.

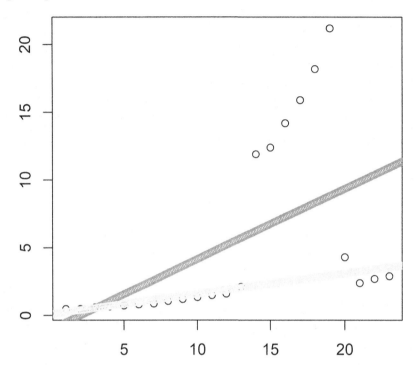

Robust Approches to Training Regularized Neural Networks

In the nonlinear regression model, where the response is explained as an unknown function of the total number of p regressors, neural networks represent a nonlinear extension of linear regression estimators. The most commonly used methods for training regression neural networks based on the least squares are biased under contaminated data and also vulnerable to adversarial examples. This non-robustness becomes especially apparent for data with a large number of regressors. This is true also for two important types of multilayer feedforward networks, namely multilayer perceptrons (denoted as MLPs) and radial basis function (RBF) networks (Haykin, 2009).

Researchers have recently become increasingly interested in proposing alternative robust (resistant) methods for training neural networks (Luo et al., 2020). Still, only a few robust approaches for training for MLPs have been introduced. Some of them become computationally infeasible for a larger p and thus were presented only on simple examples with a very small p. Their training is usually based on cmputing

$$\min \sum_{i=1}^{n} u_i^2$$

across all values of parameters, where $u_1, \ldots, u_n$ are residuals as above. The first robust alternatives were proposed by replacing the sum of squared residuals with the loss functions corresponding to the median (Aladag et al., 2014) or LTS estimator. A robust version of MLP based on the LTS estimator, denoted here as LTS-MLP, was proposed by Rusiecki (2013). Because of the appealing properties of the LWS estimator in linear regression as recalled above, we focus now on the robust loss corresponding to the LWS estimator also in the context of regression neural networks. We consider LWS-MLP with trimmed linear weights investigated in Kalina & Vidnerová (2020). This is formally defined as the LWS estimator above with minimizing across all parameters of the network. We can say that the robust networks LTS-MLP and LWS-MLP differ from MLP only by using the loss functions of the LTS or LWS estimators, respectively. An illustration of the non-robustness of a plain MLP in comparison with the robust LWS-MLP is shown on a contaminated dataset in Figure 3.

Regularized neural networks exploiting the L1-regularization are popular extensions of plain networks, which ensure some of the parameters to be equal exactly to 0. The L1-regularized MLP is defined by

$$\min \sum_{i=1}^{n} u_i^2 + \lambda \sum_{j=1}^{d} |\theta_j|,$$

where $\theta = \left(\theta_1, \ldots, \theta_d \right)^T$ is the vector of all (estimated) parameters of the network; this will be denoted here as MLP-L1. Regularized versions of LTS-MLP and LWS-MLP will be denoted here as LTS-MLP-L1 and LWS-MLP-L1; to the best of our knowledge, they have not been used in the literature. Their computations uses a back-propagation algorithm exploiting a stochastic gradient descent method. The loss function of LWS-MLP-L1 is the loss of the LWS estimator plus a penalization equal to the sum of absolute values of all parameters of the MLP multiplied by a regularization (penalization) parameter. We use 10-fold cross-validation for finding the most suitable value of the regularization parameter.

Figure 3. Illustration of non-robust MLP (left) and robust LWS-MLP (right) evaluated for a contaminated artificial dataset. The architecture was selected to contain 2 hidden layers containing 16 and 2 neurons, respectively. A sigmoid activation function is used in the hidden layers, and a linear output layer with a single neuron is used.

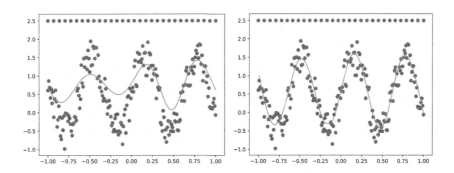

Robust Regularized Regression

Let us now consider once more the standard linear model with the task to estimate the regression parameters. The lasso estimator represents the L1-regularized (and thus sparse) version of the least squares. It performs an intrinsic variable selection and ignores the redundant variables completely, which makes the lasso a popular method for regression modeling of high-dimensional data. However, the lasso is not robust to outliers and the same is true for the ridge regression estimator (Hastie et al., 2015). A robustification of these regularized estimates can be only achieved with the help of principles of robust statistics.

The LTS-lasso estimator of Alfons et al. (2013) represents a robust regularized estimator for linear regression and can be described as a regularized (or penalized) version of the LTS estimator, which trims away a certain percentage of observations, i.e. those with the largest squared residuals. Using $h = 3n/4$ and denoting the estimated parameters by $b = \left(b_1, \ldots, b_p \right)^T$, LTS-lasso is defined by

$$\min\left[\sum_{i=1}^{h} u_{(i)}^2 + \lambda \sum_{j=1}^{p} |b_j| \right].$$

It is natural to consider an L1-regularized version of the LWS estimator denoted here as LWS-lasso.

The loss of the LWS-lasso estimator is the loss of the LWS plus a penalization equal to the sum of absolute values of all parameters multiplied by a regularization (penalization) parameter, i.e.

$$\min\left[\sum_{i=1}^{n} w_i u_{(i)}^2 + \lambda \sum_{j=1}^{p} |b_j| \right]$$

with given magnitudes of the weights. An adaptation of the algorithm for computing LTS may be used for computing both LTS-lasso and LWS-lasso. Because Alfons et al. (2013) suggested using cross-validation for finding a suitable value of the regularization parameter for LTS-lasso, we use 10-fold cross-validation here to find suitable regularization parameters of both LTS-lasso and LWS-lasso. To overview the various approaches of this methodological section, Table 1 recalls once more the important available works that are used in the following applications.

Table 1. Overview of the methodological references that are exploited in the applications.

Method	References
Centroid-based classification	Hall & Pham (2010); Delaigle & Hall (2012); Kalina & Matonoha (2020)
Robust regression	Rousseeuw & Van Driessen (2006); Víšek (2011)
Robust correlation	Shevlyakov & Oja (2016)
Robust neural networks	Aladag et al. (2014); Rusiecki (2013); Kalina & Vidnerová (2020)
Robust regularized regression	Alfons et al. (2013)

APPLICATION 1: GENE EXPRESSION MEASUREMENTS

The dataset of gene expression (GE) measurements coming from the cerebrovascular stroke study of the Center of Biomedical Informatics, Prague, was analyzed by hypothesis testing by Marozzi et al. (2020). The dataset contains 38 950 GE values measured as continuous variables in a paired design on 24 pairs of individuals. These include 24 individuals after a cerebrovascular stroke and 24 control persons without a manifested cardiovascular disease. Measurements in patients with stroke were performed as soon after the stroke as possible. Each GE measurement corresponds to a particular gene transcript. To reduce the computational demands, we consider only the first *p=3000* genes from the available dataset. The task is to learn a classification method into 2 groups, allowing to assign a set of GE measurements of a new (possibly independent) individual to the group of patients or the group of control persons. The optimization of the centroid and the weights was performed in C++ and R software was used for all remaining computations.

The centroid-based classifier is used here in various forms, while the initial centroid is obtained as the average of the measurements of the 24 patients (i.e. without the control persons). Equal weights are considered as the initial ones, i.e. each variable obtains the same weight 1/3000 so that their sum is naturally equal to 1. For the parameters of the optimization of the centroids and weights, we use here the same values as in Kalina & Matonoha (2020). We use here two improvements of available centroid-based classification approaches, which are both motivated by a need for explainability of the results. These tools denoted as thresholded optimal centroid and binarized optimal weights have not been considered before in the context of centroid-based classification.

Thresholded optimal centroid. Starting with the initial centroid (say c), a new centroid is constructed. If the value of c for a particular gene is below a given threshold, the value of the new centroid for such gene is enforced to be 0. For all remaining genes, the new centroid coincides with the initial centroid. Particularly, when normalizing the centroid to have the sum of all values equal to 1, we use the threshold equal to 0.000 05. This thresholded optimal centroid is used together with equal weights.

Binarized optimal weights. When the optimal centroid with optimal weights is computed, it is natural to ask the question of how much information would be lost by binarizing the optimal weights. Thus, we modify the optimal weights (say w) to become binary using a simple idea. If the value of w for a particular gene is below a given threshold (in our case 0.0001), the weight is enforced to be 0. For all remaining genes, the new weights are equal to a constant (the same for all genes); this constant is determined so that the sum of all the weights is equal to 1.

For comparisons, we also use PCA over the whole dataset (i.e. combining data of both groups). Linear discriminant analysis (LDA) is used to construct the classification rule only over the first 10 principal components. Using PCA makes it possible to compute LDA in a standard form without the need for using one of the numerous available regularized versions (Kalina & Duintjer Tebbens, 2015).

Apart from the raw data, we also consider 3 contaminated versions to investigate the robustness of the methods. Three different contamination levels are considered, namely we contaminate 4%, 8%, or 12% of the values for every observation (every individual) by severe outliers. For each particular individual, the variables (genes) to be contaminated are randomly chosen and independent random variables from the normal distribution with expectation 0 and standard deviation 1 are generated and added to the true values. When working with the contaminated data, the centroids and weights use only contaminated data so that the methods do not have access to raw (non-contaminated) data at all.

The results of the analysis of the GE measurements presented in Table 2 have the form of classification accuracies defined as the ratios of the properly classified samples divided by the total number of samples. The table also shows the number of genes used within the classification rule of every particular method. Comparisons with standard machine learning are not presented here, because these were already thoroughly studied by Kalina & Matonoha (2020). First, let us interpret the results obtained from raw data. Results of the optimized centroid with optimized weights much outperform those obtained with the initial centroid. The centroid-based approach exploiting r_{LWS} yields better results compared to Pearson correlation coefficient but is outperformed by the method based on the optimized centroid.

The binarized optimal weights, which were proposed here as a novel extension of the approach based on optimal centroids, yield the same result here as the optimal (and much more complex) weights. Thus, we can say that binary weights carry practically the same information as the optimal weights. In other words, although the optimization is delicate and focuses on subtle nuances of the weights, the binarization as a quite rough transformation does not lose much of the classification ability of the centroid. The thresholded optimal centroid loses the classification ability and cannot be recommended.

These computations reveal that optimizing the centroid yields very promising results and that simplifying the optimal centroid (and improving its explainability) is also possible. This can be achieved by additional optimization of the weights, i.e. by a posterior variable selection. A small set of variables turns out to carry the majority of the information relevant for the classification. Thus, it is possible to use comprehensible classification methods only at the price of a negligible reduction of the classification performance and (at least for some methods) to improve the interpretation of subsequent data analysis. Further, let us interpret the results of Table 2 obtained for contaminated data. Centroid-based approaches with initial (non-optimal) choices are influenced by outliers to a large extent. On the other hand, centroid-based classification using the optimal centroid with optimal weights turns out to be more robust and able to outperform all other approaches.

PCA turns out not to be suitable here, which follows from the fact that it represents an unsupervised dimensionality reduction method. We already explained that PCA is not intended to be used for data in two different groups (from two different populations), as it attempts to explain the variability of the response but not the separation between the groups. The vulnerability of PCA to outliers is revealed here as another disadvantage.

On the whole, the presented analysis reveals the ability of centroid-based classifiers to solve the classification task for the GE dataset well. The classification based on centroids (with or without weights assigned to the centroid) can be perceived as an explainable method yielding much improved results compared to those obtained with a simple (initial, naïve) centroid. The optimization of the weights performs a posterior variable selection. The optimal centroid with optimal weights can be interpreted as a classifier with a sparse (intrinsic) variable selection, which is based on about 1000 genes. The classification rule of the optimal centroid with binarized weights is based on about 200 relevant genes. In this context, forgetting the information much improves the explainability and does not lead to any loss of classification performance.

Table 2. *Results of Application 1 (gene expression dataset) for raw and contaminated data.*

Centroid	Weights	Classification accuracy	Number of used genes
Raw data (no contamination)			
Initial	Initial	0.73	3000
Optimal	Initial	0.81	3000
Thresholded optimal	Initial	0.77	986
Optimal	Optimal	0.85	247
Optimal	Binarized optimal	0.85	196
Initial centroid using r_{LWS}		0.77	3000
PCA⇒LDA		0.69	3000
Contamination level 0.04			
Initial	Initial	0.69	3000
Optimal	Initial	0.81	3000
Thresholded optimal	Initial	0.77	1034
Optimal	Optimal	0.85	261
Optimal	Binarized optimal	0.85	213
Initial centroid using r_{LWS}		0.77	3000
PCA⇒LDA		0.65	3000
Contamination level 0.08			
Initial	Initial	0.67	3000
Optimal	Initial	0.79	3000
Thresholded optimal	Initial	0.75	1095
Optimal	Optimal	0.83	259
Optimal	Binarized optimal	0.83	202
Initial centroid using r_{LWS}		0.73	3000
PCA⇒LDA		0.63	3000
Contamination level 0.12			
Initial	Initial	0.63	3000
Optimal	Initial	0.77	3000
Thresholded optimal	Initial	0.73	1215
Optimal	Optimal	0.81	283
Optimal	Binarized optimal	0.81	220
Initial centroid using r_{LWS}		0.69	3000
PCA⇒LDA		0.58	3000

APPLICATION 2: BOSTON HOUSING DATASET

The Boston Housing dataset is publicly available e.g. in the UCI repository (Frank & Asuncion, 2010). It was previously analyzed by standard machine learning e.g. in Chapter 3 of Chollet (2018). There are no missing values in the dataset so that we can work with all $n=506$ cases corresponding to individual pieces of real estate in the larger urban agglomeration of Boston. The task of the analysis is to model (predict) the per capita crime rate in different locations (neighborhoods) as the response of the available regressors. While the original dataset contains 14 variables, we consider only $p=11$ continuous ones omitting features 4, 7, and 9 from the original dataset. Some of the regressors available for the neighborhood of every individual piece of real estate include the average number of rooms per dwelling, median value of owner-occupied homes, percentage of the population with a lower status, or nitrogen oxide concentration in the air. We implemented the computed methods in Keras (Chollet, 2015).

We aim to compare standard and robust neural networks with a special focus on comparing regularized and non-regularized versions. An MLP with 2 hidden layers is used here, which contain 16 and 8 neurons, respectively. We use a sigmoid activation function in every hidden layer and a linear output layer. All other networks use the same architecture here. For regularized tools, the regularization parameter is found in 10-fold cross-validation. For LTS-MLP and related networks based on the LTS loss function, we use $h=0.75$.

We also perform a backward elimination for selecting variables for the standard MLP; let us recall that backward elimination represents a popular tool for model selection in linear regression. Such posterior variable selection, denoted here as Back-MLP, is used here to find the 5 most relevant variables. Starting with the full model with all regressors, we trim away one of the regressors and compute MSE (or TMSE) in it; we take such of the regressors, for which the given prediction error (MSE or TMSE) is the smallest. These measures are formally defined as

$$MSE = \frac{1}{n}\sum_{i=1}^{n} u_i^2 \text{ and } TMSE = \frac{1}{h}\sum_{i=1}^{h} u_{(i)}^2.$$

We proceed by trimming away another regressor from the model. In this way, we continue until obtaining a model with 5 regressors; the prediction error is reported for a standard MLP for such a resulting model. The same approach is used for LTS-MLP or LWS-MLP; such novel approaches are denoted as Back-LTS-MLP and Back-LWS-MLP, respectively. The results are overviewed in Table 3, which was computed in 10-fold cross-validation. Values of the mean square error are presented there together with values of its robust counterpart, namely the trimmed mean square error (TMSE). The latter is defined for a given percentage h of observations; here we use $h=0.75$ so that TMSE is defined as the sum of squared residuals computed only over such 75% of the observations with the smallest squared residuals.

Table 3. Results of Application 2 (Boston Housing dataset): comparison of MSE and TMSE for different versions of multilayer perceptrons.

Method	MSE	TMSE
MLP	57.9	5.3
MLP-L1	59.2	5.4
Back-MLP	59.3	5.4
LTS-MLP	67.2	4.3
LTS-MLP-L1	68.2	4.3
Back-LTS-MLP	68.1	4.4
LWS-MLP	70.8	4.5
LWS-MLP-L1	71.9	4.5
Back-LWS-MLP	72.0	4.6

Standard versions of neural networks turn out to be superior in terms of conventional MSE. This does not mean that the robust methods are less suitable because MSE itself is vulnerable to the presence of outliers. On the other hand, only robust versions of MSE are meaningful for data contaminated with outliers. If TMSE is used, the methods LTS-MLP-L1 and LWS-MLP-L1 outperform the remaining methods. The better ability of robust methods can be explained by the presence of outliers in the dataset; a robustness analysis not presented here reveals that the dataset contains about 10% of severe outliers. We can say that the well-known L1-regularization prunes the networks at the cost of a slight decrease in prediction ability. Back-LTS-MLP and Back-LWS-MLP greatly improve the explainability at the cost of only a slight decrease in prediction ability. We stress that regularization within LTS-MLP-L1 and LWS-MLP-L1 trims away some parameters, but does not trim away any of the variables completely from the model. Thus, L1-regularization does not perform a true variable selection here but would do this only in a linear regression model, which will be considered in Application 3.

APPLICATION 3: TRAVEL AND TOURISM COMPETITIVENESS

As the third application, the Travel and Tourism Competitiveness Index (TTCI) dataset is considered. This publicly available dataset reported by the World Economic Forum for the year 2015 is available on the website of Crotti & Misrahi (2015). The tourist service infrastructure measured across $n=141$ countries of the world is modeled as a response of $p=12$ characteristics (pillars) of TTCI. All the 12 regressors are continuous; the examples of individual regressors reported for individual countries include e.g. indicators of the business environment, international openness, air transport infrastructure, health, or hygiene. We used R software for the computations.

The methods used here for the analysis of the TTCI dataset include the least squares, lasso, LTS-lasso, and the novel LWS-lasso. For LTS-lasso, we trim away 25% of the data values (countries). For regularized methods, we use 10-fold cross-validation to find a suitable value of the regularization parameter. Table 4 presents values of MSE and TMSE (using $h=0.85$) computed by various regression methods. The values were obtained in 10-fold cross-validation. Only TMSE as a robust version of MSE should be considered for these data because they contain severe outliers. A detailed analysis namely reveals that the dataset contains 5 outliers (France, the United States, Spain, China, and Italy), which have a high influence on the resulting estimates. Robust sparse estimators (LTS-lasso and the novel LWS-lasso) outperform other methods in terms of TMSE. The approach with PCA using 4 principal components does not reveal any interesting structure in the data. We can say that the contribution of all regressors to the first principal components is approximately equal and the other principal components are too difficult to interpret.

The left part of Table 5 presents the ordering of all the 12 variables according to their importance (relevance) for the regression task, i.e. for explaining the response. To explain this, let us recall that the lasso is commonly used for such an automatic ordering of the variables as described in Hastie et al. (2015). The ordering is based on the following property of the estimator: as the value of the regularization parameter increases, the influence of individual regressors changes, and one regressor after another drops away from the model completely. We use such an approach for all the regularized methods here. Only for the least squares, we ordered the variables utilizing a backward selection performed by t-tests. Robust regularized methods yield the best results and it turns out not to be so important whether the loss of the LTS is used or the loss of the LWS; both these two robust approaches are better than least squares or standard lasso.

If using regularized methods with the optimal regularization parameters obtained by 10-fold cross-validation, the methods do not depend on all the 12 variables but only on some of them, as the methods perform a sparse variable selection. These are presented in the right part of Table 5. For the least squares, we have to use another approach; we performed a backward selection using t-tests instead. To interpret the results, we can say that the number of relevant variables turns out to be different for different methods.

Table 4. Results of Application 3 (TTCI dataset): prediction error measures MSE and TMSE.

Method	MSE	TMSE
Least squares	0.449	0.363
Lasso	0.461	0.366
LTS-lasso	0.453	0.327
LWS-lasso	0.451	0.334
PCA⇒ least squares	0.510	0.398

Table 5. Results of Application 3 (TTCI dataset): analysis of the role of individual variables in the model. Left: ordering of all variables according to their relevance for explaining the variability of the response, starting from the most relevant to the least relevant. Right: ordering only for the variables that are found as relevant (by using the optimal regularization parameter or by t-tests).

Method	Ordering of all variables	Ordering only for relevant variables
Least squares	6, 5, 9, 1, 10, 3, 4, 2, 7, 8, 12, 11	6, 5, 9, 1, 10
Lasso	6, 5, 9, 1, 3, 10, 4, 7, 2, 11, 12, 8	6, 5, 9, 1, 3
LTS-lasso	5, 6, 3, 10, 9, 7, 1, 8, 11, 2, 12, 4	5, 6, 3, 10, 9, 7
LWS-lasso	5, 6, 3, 10, 9, 7, 8, 11, 1, 12, 4, 2	5, 6, 3, 10, 9, 7

Figure 4. Horizontal axis: regularization parameter with values between 0 and 1. Vertical axis: LWS-lasso estimates of regression parameters for all 12 regressors evaluated for individual values of the regularization parameters.

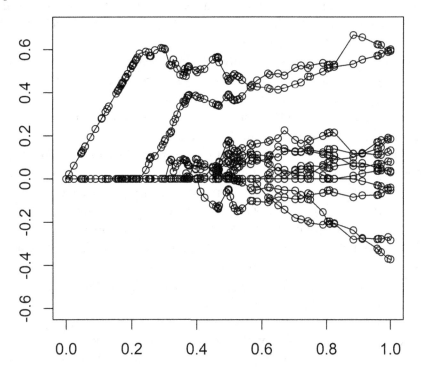

We can see that the most relevant variables detected by robust approaches are different from those detected by non-standard tools. This seems to be a consequence of the presence of outliers. Thus, we consider the sparse robust variable selection tools (LTS-lasso, LWS-lasso) to be more trustworthy in this dataset. We understand these methods to be resistant and reliable tools ensuring the explainability of the resulting regression model by ignoring all the redundant variables. Figure 4 shows the estimated parameters of the individual 12 regressors in dependence on the value of the regularization parameter. All the regressors are considered in the case without regularization and the dimensionality reduction comes into play together with an increasing level of regularization.

DIMENSIONALITY REDUCTION AND ENERGY COMPLEXITY

Methods described in this chapter can be interpreted within a broader framework of low-energy approximate computation. In the presented experiments, robustness, sparsity, and energy-efficient computation turn out not to contradict the requirement on the optimal performance. Let us now discuss the relationship between dimensionality reduction and energy complexity, particularly in the context of deep neural networks.

Shallow neural networks represent important tools of machine learning, which are however unsuitable for data with a very large number of observations possibly exceeding the number of observations. Current machine learning is therefore unimaginable without deep neural networks. While shallow networks are not suitable for data contaminated by outliers (Dey et al., 2019), deep neural networks are usually equipped with tools for more robust training. Deep learning methods with a plethora of various forms of neural networks are typically black boxes without the possibility to explain why a particular result is obtained. The architecture is either chosen to be fixed by the user, or is optimized to yield the best performance over independent data (e.g. in cross-validation). Some forms of commonly used deep networks are obtained simply as standard multilayer perceptrons only with a larger number of hidden layers. Such deep networks that do not conceptually differ from their shallow counterparts only need more sophisticated algorithms for their training. Convolutional neural networks (CNN) represent an important special case of deep networks with enormous popularity for image processing.

As was already mentioned above, one of the usual motivations for dimensionality reduction is an attempt to reduce the complexity of computations of machine learning methods. This is very useful because many intensive computations are run on mobile devices with limited memory and powered by a battery. Nevertheless, reducing computational complexity can be achieved also by other approaches than by reducing the data dimensionality, especially if modifying the computations to consider smaller and energy-efficient architectures. A trade-off between performance (approximation accuracy) and network size may be achieved if the search for the optimal architecture is accompanied by other criteria. These may be defined to control the network size or complexity in general. Available regularization approaches (weight decay, activity regularization, or dropout) or other tools (weight binarization, data quantization) may typically reduce the computational demands. Sparsity may ensure a more efficient computation of machine learning methods as well as an improved explainability and it is for this reason that regularization belongs to important tools exploited within the field of approximate computing.

With the progress of supercomputing, energy savings have been repeatedly recommended to improve the training of deep learning methods over Big Data. Li et al. (2018) studied models for energetically demanding (energy-hungry) services for internet-of-things (IoT) platforms. Mahmoud et al. (2018) investigated energy-efficient architectures in the context of CoT (cloud of things). Lakshmanaprabu et al. (2019) described a clinical decision support system for diagnosing chronic kidney disease. This system uses a deep neural network to be trained over Big Data acquired by wearable devices as well as by publicly available data downloaded from the UCI repository. The paper focused on reaching energy efficiency by considering energy models suitable for operating in a cloud-based IoT platform.

As this chapter was created in a broader framework of approximate neurocomputing research, let us consider some open problems related to energy complexity. It is desirable to perform basic research related to approximate neurocomputing and decreasing the energetic complexity of neural networks, especially for training convolutional neural networks. Neural architecture search (NAS) may be accompanied by reducing the number of variables and the number of parameters, possibly employing multi-objective Bayesian optimization. In the same way, objectives evaluating the energetic demands of the computations may be taken into account (Mrázek et al., 2016). Possible applications on mobile phones would allow energy savings and the work could thus contribute to the development of "green machine learning" (Xu et al., 2021). It is also desirable to propose specific methods for robust neural networks; here, the idea may be to combine the robust loss function with penalization on energetic demands.

CONCLUSION

Artificial intelligence, with its great potential for transforming the current society towards the ideals of the knowledge society, has to rely on machine learning methods and algorithms with the ability to extract useful knowledge from available information. For example in complex tasks of decision making under uncertainty, humans seem not to be evolutionarily prepared for rational and successful solutions (Kahneman, 2013) and can be outperformed by artificial intelligence tools. Decision support systems as promising artificial intelligence tools have already been successfully applied to complex decision-making tasks (Kalina et al., 2013; Bridge & Dodds, 2019). Such tools require machine learning methods to be accompanied by dimensionality reduction. Only machine learning performed on appropriately selected relevant variables may transform complex multivariate information into useful knowledge.

This chapter is devoted to procedures for reducing the data dimensionality that are resistant to contamination of the data by (possibly severe) outliers. The chapter does not (and cannot) bring an overview of a plethora of available variable selection methods. Particular attention is paid to intrinsic or posterior variable selection methods. Without focusing on technical details, principles of selected robust variable selection methods are recalled and some novel methods (including LWS-lasso) are proposed. Reducing the dimensionality of data always requires solving the trade-off between simplicity and retaining relevant information.

The real-life examples of this chapter are motivated by our attempt to persuade the reader about the potential of reducing the dimensionality of multivariate data. In all the three applications presented here related to classification or regression tasks, robust variable selection methods yield the best results. When appropriately performed robustly, i.e. not being misled by outliers in the data, variable selection (unlike feature extraction) is also appealing for practitioners as it can ensure explainability. Robust variable selection methods turn out to separate signal from noise, i.e. to find order in chaotically arranged multivariate information.

In the future, the authors of this chapter would like to perform basic research related to the performance and robustness of the presented tools together with extensions to more complex tasks of scientific computation, especially in the context of deep learning (Goodfellow et al., 2016). This will contribute to more intensive usage of robust estimation techniques within machine learning and thus to a rise of robust statistical learning (robust machine learning). Robust methods have not been investigated in various machine learning tasks so far, e.g. for deep fake detection by centroids, robust template matching by CNNs (Sun et al., 2021), or applying filters in convolutional layers of CNNs. Additional future research topics related to dimensionality reduction include a search for methods for combining diverse data types, e.g. by combining several dimensionality reduction techniques. So far, available results in this respect (Ayesha et al., 2020) have not focused on the robustness of the methods. A small number of available systematic comparisons of various dimensionality reduction methods e.g. to Big Data (cf. Sadiq et al., 2021) can also be explained by the difficulty to find suitable publicly available big datasets.

ACKNOWLEDGEMENT

The work was supported by the grant 22-02067S ("Approximate Neurocomputing") of the Czech Science Foundation. Eva Litavcová and Petra Vašaničová provided the TTCI dataset. The results were acquired using implementations provided by Tomáš Jurica. Figure 3 was prepared by Petra Vidnerová.

REFERENCES

Aladag, C. H., Egrioglu, E., & Yolcu, U. (2014). Robust multilayer neural network based on median neuron model. *Neural Computing & Applications*, 24(3-4), 945–956. DOI: 10.1007/s00521-012-1315-5

Alfons, A., Croux, C., & Gelper, S. (2013). Sparse least trimmed squares regression for analyzing high-dimensional large data sets. *The Annals of Applied Statistics*, 7(1), 226–248. DOI: 10.1214/12-AOAS575

Ayesha, S., Hanif, M. K., & Talib, R. (2020). Overview and comparative study of dimensionality reduction techniques for high dimensional data. *Information Fusion*, 59, 44–58. DOI: 10.1016/j.inffus.2020.01.005

Benjamini, Y., & Hochberg, Y. (1995). Controlling the false discovery rate: A practical and powerful approach to multiple testing. *Journal of the Royal Statistical Society. Series B, Statistical Methodology*, 57(1), 289–300. DOI: 10.1111/j.2517-6161.1995.tb02031.x

Benjamini, Y., & Yekutieli, D. (2001). The control of the false discovery rate in multiple testing under dependency. *Annals of Statistics*, 29(4), 1165–1188. DOI: 10.1214/aos/1013699998

Blazques, D., & Domenech, J. (2018). Big Data sources and methods for social and economic analyses. *Technological Forecasting and Social Change*, 130, 99–113. DOI: 10.1016/j.techfore.2017.07.027

Bradlow, E. T., Gangwar, M., Kopalle, P., & Voleti, S. (2017). The role of Big Data and predictive analytics in retailing. *Journal of Retailing*, 93(1), 79–95. DOI: 10.1016/j.jretai.2016.12.004

Bridge, J. & Dodds, J.C. (2019). Managerial decision making. Routledge, Abingdon-on-Thames.

Bučková, B., Brunovský, M., Bareš, M., & Hlinka, J. (2020). Predicting sex from EEG: Validity and generalizability of deep-learning-based interpretable classifier. *Frontiers in Neuroscience*, 14, 589303. DOI: 10.3389/fnins.2020.589303 PMID: 33192274

Chollet, F. (2015). Keras. Github repository. [https://github.com/fchollet/keras]

Chollet, F. (2018). *Deep learning with Python*. Manning Publications Co.

Crotti, R., & Misrahi, T. (2015). The Travel & Tourism Competitiveness Report 2015. Growth Through Shocks. World Economic Forum, Geneva. [http://www3.weforum.org/docs/TT15/WEF_ Global_Travel&Tourism_Report_2015.pdf]

Delaigle, A., & Hall, P. (2012). Achieving near perfect classification for functional data. *Journal of the Royal Statistical Society. Series A, (Statistics in Society)*, 74, 267–286.

Dey, P., Gopal, M., Pradhan, P., & Pal, T. (2019). On robustness of radial basis function network with input perturbation. *Neural Computing & Applications*, 31(2), 523–537. DOI: 10.1007/s00521-017-3086-5

Fan, J., Ke, Y., & Wang, K. (2020). Factor-adjusted regularized model selection. *Journal of Econometrics*, 216(1), 71–85. DOI: 10.1016/j.jeconom.2020.01.006 PMID: 32269406

Filzmoser, P., & Todorov, V. (2011). Review of robust multivariate statistical methods in high dimension. *Analytica Chimica Acta*, 705(1-2), 2–14. DOI: 10.1016/j.aca.2011.03.055 PMID: 21962341

Fordellone, M. (2019). *Statistical analysis of complex data. Dimensionality reduction and classification methods.* LAP LAMBERT Academic Publishing.

Frank, A., & Asuncion, A. (2010). *UCI Machine Learning Repository.* University of California. [http://archive.ics.uci.edu/ml]

Goodfellow, I., Bengio, Y., & Courville, A. (2016). *Deep learning.* MIT Press.

Greene, W. H. (2017). *Econometric analysis* (8th ed.). Pearson.

Hall, P., & Pham, T. (2010). Optimal properties of centroid-based classifiers for very high-dimensional data. *Annals of Statistics*, 38(2), 1071–1093. DOI: 10.1214/09-AOS736

Hastie, T., Tibshirani, R., & Wainwright, M. (2015). *Statistical learning with sparsity: The lasso and generalizations.* CRC Press. DOI: 10.1201/b18401

Haykin, S. O. (2009). *Neural networks and learning machines: A comprehensive foundation* (2nd ed.). Prentice Hall.

Heinze, G., Wallisch, C., & Dunkler, D. (2017). Variable selection–A review and recommendations for the practicing statistician. *Biometrical Journal. Biometrische Zeitschrift*, 60(3), 431–449. DOI: 10.1002/bimj.201700067 PMID: 29292533

Holder, A., & Eichholz, J. (2019). *An introduction to computational science.* Springer. DOI: 10.1007/978-3-030-15679-4

Huber, P. J. (2009). *Robust statistics* (2nd ed.). Wiley. DOI: 10.1002/9780470434697

Jacobson, N. J., Bentley, K. H., Walton, A., Wang, S. B., Fortgang, R. G., Millner, A. J., Coombs, G.III, Rodman, A. M., & Coppersmith, D. D. L. (2020). Ethical dilemmas posed by mobile health and machine learning in psychiatry research. *Bulletin of the World Health Organization*, 98(4), 270–276. DOI: 10.2471/BLT.19.237107 PMID: 32284651

Jurečková, J., Picek, J., & Schindler, M. (2019). *Robust statistical methods with R* (2nd ed.). CRC Press. DOI: 10.1201/b21993

Kahneman, D. (2013). *Thinking, fast and slow.* Farrar, Straus and Giroux.

Kalina, J. (2015). Three contributions to robust regression diagnostics. Journal of Applied Mathematics. *Statistics and Informatics*, 11(2), 69–78.

Kalina, J. (2018). A robust pre-processing of BeadChip microarray images. *Biocybernetics and Biomedical Engineering*, 38(3), 556–563. DOI: 10.1016/j.bbe.2018.04.005

Kalina, J., & Duintjer Tebbens, J. (2015). Algorithms for regularized linear discriminant analysis. Proceedings of the 6th International Conference on Bioinformatics Models Methods, and Algorithms (BIOINFORMATICS '15), Scitepress, Lisbon, 128-133. DOI: 10.5220/0005234901280133

Kalina, J., & Matonoha, C. (2020). A sparse pair-preserving centroid-based supervised learning method for high-dimensional biomedical data or images. *Biocybernetics and Biomedical Engineering*, 40(2), 774–786. DOI: 10.1016/j.bbe.2020.03.008

Kalina, J., & Rensová, D. (2015). How to reduce dimensionality of data: Robustness point of view. *Serbian Journal of Management*, 10(1), 131–140. DOI: 10.5937/sjm10-6531

Kalina, J., & Schlenker, A. (2015). A robust supervised variable selection for noisy high-dimensional data. *BioMed Research International*, 2015, 320385. DOI: 10.1155/2015/320385 PMID: 26137474

Kalina, J., Seidl, L., Zvára, K., Grünfeldová, H., Slovák, D., & Zvárová, J. (2013). System for selecting relevant information for decision support. *Studies in Health Technology and Informatics*, 186, 83–87. PMID: 23542973

Kalina, J., & Tichavský, J. (2020). On robust estimation of error variance in (highly) robust regression. *Measurement Science Review*, 20(1), 6–14. DOI: 10.2478/msr-2020-0002

Kalina, J., & Vidnerová, P. (2020). On robust training of regression neural networks. In Aneiros, G., Horová, I., Hušková, M., & Vieu, P. (Eds.), *Functional and high-dimensional statistics and related fields. IWFOS 2020. Contributions to Statistics* (pp. 145–152). Springer. DOI: 10.1007/978-3-030-47756-1_20

Lakshmanaprabu, S. K., Mohanty, S. N., Krishnamoorthy, S., Uthayakumar, J., & Shankar, K. (2019). Online clinical decision support system using optimal deep neural networks. *Applied Soft Computing*, 81, 105487. DOI: 10.1016/j.asoc.2019.105487

Lalmuanawma, S., Hussain, J., & Chhaakchhuak, L. (2020). Applications of machine learning and artificial intelligence for Covid-19 (SARS-CoV-2) pandemic: A review. *Chaos, Solitons, and Fractals*, 139, 110059. DOI: 10.1016/j.chaos.2020.110059 PMID: 32834612

Li, Y., Orgerie, A.C., Rodero, I., Amersho, B.L., Parashar, M. et al. (2018). End-to-end models for edge cloud-based IoT platforms: Application to data stream analysis in IoT. [https://hal.archives-ouvertes.fr/hal-01673501]

López-Robles, J. R., Rodríguez-Salvador, M., Gamboa-Rosales, N. K., Ramirez-Rosales, S., & Cobo, M. J. (2019). The last five years of Big Data Research in economics, econometrics and finance: Identification and conceptual analysis. *Procedia Computer Science*, 162, 729–736. DOI: 10.1016/j.procs.2019.12.044

Luo, X., Li, Y., Wang, W., Ban, X., Wang, J. H., & Zhao, W. (2020). A robust multilayer extreme learning machine using kernel risk-sensitive loss criterion. *International Journal of Machine Learning and Cybernetics*, 11(1), 197–216. DOI: 10.1007/s13042-019-00967-w

Mahmoud, M. M. E., Rodrigues, J. J. P. C., Ahmed, S. H., Shah, S. C., Al-Muhtadi, J. F., Korotaev, V. V., & De Albuquerque, V. H. C. (2018). Enabling technologies on cloud of things for smart healthcare. *IEEE Access : Practical Innovations, Open Solutions*, 6, 31950–31967. DOI: 10.1109/ACCESS.2018.2845399

Marozzi, M., Mukherjee, A., & Kalina, J. (2020). Interpoint distance tests for high-dimensional comparison studies. *Journal of Applied Statistics*, 47(4), 653–665. DOI: 10.1080/02664763.2019.1649374 PMID: 35707487

Martinez, W. L., Martinez, A. R., & Solka, J. L. (2017). *Exploratory data analysis with MATLAB* (3rd ed.). Chapman & Hall/CRC.

Mrázek, V., Sarwar, S. S., Sekanina, L., Vašíček, Z., & Roy, K. (2016). Design of power-efficient approximate multipliers for approximate artificial neural networks. *2016 IEEE/ACM International Conference on Computer-Aided Design (ICCAD)*, 1-7. DOI: 10.1145/2966986.2967021

Olson, D. L. (2017). *Descriptive data mining*. Springer. DOI: 10.1007/978-981-10-3340-7

Quarteroni, A. (2018). The role of statistics in the era of big data: A computational scientist' perspective. *Statistics & Probability Letters*, 136, 63–67. DOI: 10.1016/j.spl.2018.02.047

Rousseeuw, P. J., & Leroy, A. M. (1987). *Robust regression and outlier detection*. Wiley. DOI: 10.1002/0471725382

Rousseeuw, P. J., & Van Driessen, K. (2006). Computing LTS regression for large data sets. *Data Mining and Knowledge Discovery*, 12(1), 29–45. DOI: 10.1007/s10618-005-0024-4

Rusiecki, A. (2013). Robust learning algorithm based on LTA estimator. *Neurocomputing*, 120, 624–632. DOI: 10.1016/j.neucom.2013.04.008

Sadiq, M. T., Yu, X., & Yuan, Z. (2021). Exploiting dimensionality reduction and neural network techniques for the development of expert brain-computer interfaces. *Expert Systems with Applications*, 164, 114031. DOI: 10.1016/j.eswa.2020.114031

Shevlyakov, G. L., & Oja, H. (2016). *Robust correlation. Theory and applications*. Wiley. DOI: 10.1002/9781119264507

Statti, F., Sued, M., & Yohai, V. J. (2018). High breakdown point robust estimators with missing data. *Communications in Statistics. Theory and Methods*, 47(21), 5145–5162. DOI: 10.1080/03610926.2017.1388396

Sun, L., Sun, H., Wang, J., Wu, S., Zhao, Y., & Xu, Y. (2021). Breast mass detection in mammography based on image template matching and CNN. *Sensors (Basel)*, 2021(8), 2855. DOI: 10.3390/s21082855 PMID: 33919623

Tegmark, M. (2017). *Life 3.0: Being human in the age of artificial intelligence*. Alfred A. Knopf.

Vapnik, V. N. (2000). *The nature of statistical learning theory* (2nd ed.). Springer. DOI: 10.1007/978-1-4757-3264-1

Víšek, J. Á. (2011). Consistency of the least weighted squares under heteroscedasticity. *Kybernetika*, 47, 179–206.

Wilson, P. W. (2018). Dimension reduction in nonparametric models of production. *European Journal of Operational Research*, 267(1), 349–367. DOI: 10.1016/j.ejor.2017.11.020

Xu, J., Zhou, W., Fu, Z., Zhou, H., & Li, L. (2021). A survey on green deep learning. ArXiv:2111.05193.

KEY TERMS

Centroid: a template, prototype, mean shape, typical form, image model, or an ideal virtual object with ideal appearance, commonly considered as the average of observations of a given group of data.

Explainability: interpretability of machine learning tools. When using and interpreting an explainable method, it is possible to exactly state why the method yields the particular results.

Gene Expression: a numerical value proportional to the concentration of a given gene transcript product (protein) measured in tissues employing the available microarray technology.

Machine Learning: a subfield of artificial intelligence devoted to methods and algorithms for analyzing data under uncertainty, typically without specific distributional assumptions.

Regularization: a general concept embracing various tools of statistics or numerical mathematics for solving ill-posed or insoluble high-dimensional problems by employing additional available information, assumptions, or penalization.

Robustness: resistance of a statistical method with respect to the presence of outlying values (outliers) in the data.

Sparsity: a sparse model exploits only a small number of relevant parameters and trims away the remaining ones. A sparse method can typically yield sparse models over a broad class of input data.

Travel and Tourism Competitiveness Index (TTCI): a yearly evaluated economic index reported by the World Economic Forum. It is motivated by a desire to contribute to achieving a strong and sustainable travel and tourism industry worldwide.

Variable Selection: a type of dimensionality reduction based on selecting a small set of the variables that are the most relevant ones for the given task.

Chapter 3
Domain Adaptation for Performance Enhancement of Deep Learning Models for Remote Sensing Scenes Classification

Tariq Lasloum
https://orcid.org/0000-0001-5457-1042
King Saud University, Saudi Arabia

Belgacem Ben Youssef
https://orcid.org/0000-0002-6618-3845
King Saud University, Saudi Arabia

Haikel Alhichri
https://orcid.org/0000-0003-2164-043X
King Saud University, Saudi Arabia

ABSTRACT

Deep neural networks and in particular Convolutional Neural Networks (CNNs) are considered to be the state-of-the-art tools for scene classification. However, training deep CNN models requires huge amounts of labeled data to achieve excellent classification accuracy. Thus, an important goal in deep learning is how to reduce the data labelling burden. Domain Adaptation (DA) is the main technique in this regard. The goal is to classify the target domain correctly by learning from the source domain. This chapter examines the basic concepts required to understand RS. Then, it proceeds to describe in detail a method for multi-source semi-supervised domain adaptation in remote sensing scene classification called Semi-Supervised Domain Adaptation Network (SSDAN). Performance results in terms of overall accuracy and Kappa coefficient values obtained when conducting experiments using single-source, two-source, and three-source scenarios are also provided. The achieved results of these two metrics reached values of more than 99%, demonstrating the efficacy of the SSDAN method.

DOI: 10.4018/978-1-6684-3795-7.ch003

INTRODUCTION

The practice of identifying and monitoring an area's physical features by measuring its reflected and emitted radiation from a distance is known as Remote Sensing (RS), usually done from satellites or aircrafts. Aerial photographs of the earth could be used to optimize land usage and remote sensing plays a vital role in obtaining geographical data on very large scales. The scene classification task involves accurately classifying aerial scenes or images into the correct category or class (e.g., aircrafts, rivers, bridges, and farms). Classification of RS scenes is challenging because these scenes may have small target entities or many target orientations. They may also possess dense distributions as well as greater image resolutions than regular camera photos. For example, an airport region contains a variety of physical structures such as planes of various orientations and types, airstrips, and terminals, all of which can cause these photos to be classified differently (Zhang et al., 2021). In RS, new images of the earth are acquired at an ever increasing rate (Chi et al., 2016). Such new images need to be processed to perform useful tasks. Scene classification is an important processing step in many real-world applications of RS like environmental monitoring, residential design, and natural resource planning (Cheng et al., 2017). The goal of RS scene classification is to effectively label new images with pre-characterized semantic classes. Figure 1 shows how to separate different images and classify them (Cheng et al., 2020).

Figure 1. Remote sensing scene classification

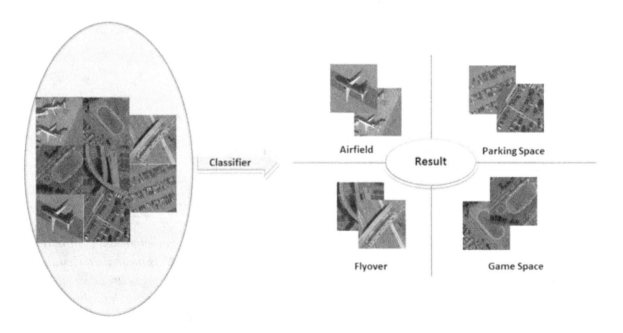

Based on the automatic extraction of high-level features from images and their great abstraction abilities, deep learning (DL) algorithms have recently achieved substantial gains and state-of-the-art accuracy in several disciplines, including image classification, image synthesis, and object recognition.

In RS image classification, DL approaches also get a lot of attention. CNNs are one of the most prominent deep learning algorithms, with unparalleled superiority on various benchmark image datasets such as ImageNet (Deng et al., 2009). They have been often used in classification, detection, and recognition applications, with excellent results (Gong et al., 2018).

However, we are still far from a seamless solution which works for any given set of images without major expert manual intervention. Given a machine learning (ML) model that has been trained on an old RS dataset while achieving excellent classification accuracy, it may still fail significantly when tested on a new dataset of images even though it has the same group of categories or classes. Researchers have shown that this is due to the shift between the statistical distributions of the data. Thus, the challenge with DL is that it is data driven. This means that we constantly need to label new images for training. This training data needs to be labeled manually, which is a tedious and costly task. Domain adaptation (DA) is one possible solution explored in the machine learning (ML) literature towards this enhanced solution. Therefore, DA aims at adapting a ML solution, which has been trained on an old manually-labeled data, to a new dataset without the need for more manual labeling.

BACKGROUND

In this section, we present an overview of important concepts needed to understand the research work presented in this chapter. In the first part, we briefly describe deep learning with a particular focus on convolutional neural networks, including its component layers and types such as the EfficientNet family of related models. Then, we explain domain adaptation in the context of machine learning used to lessen the impact of the data distribution shift between domains. We also discuss some of the relevant datasets employed in remote sensing scene classification.

Deep Learning

Deep Learning is a type of Machine Learning (ML) that is based on Artificial Neural Networks (ANNs). The latter belong under the broad umbrella of Artificial Intelligence (AI). The ANN design is inspired by the structure of the human brain. ANN can be taught to perform the same tasks on data that our brains do when they are identifying patterns and classifying different sorts of information. Individual layers of ANN can also be thought of as some kind of filter that can work from the most obvious of ways to the subtlest ones in order to improve the probability of detecting and producing the right result. The human brain operates in a similar manner.

ANNs have been introduced in the nineteen fifties, but for decades there was not much interest in them. This changed when in 1986, David Rumelhart, Geoffrey Hinton, and Ronald Williams, in their work titled "Learning representations by back-propagating errors", clearly explained how to train multi-layer neural networks through the use of back propagation of errors from the output layers to the inner layers; thus, learning the weights of the network along the way. Later on in 1989, Yann LeCun et al. (LeCun et al., 1989) at the AT&T Bell Labs applied the ANN together with the back propagation algorithm and a few other improvements to a real-world application involving handwritten digits' recognition on American checks. By the late 1990s, computer systems using ANNs were capable of reading 10 to 20% of all the checks in the US.

One of the main modification introduced by Yann LeCun et al. (LeCun et al., 1989) is to make each neuron in the first inner layer to only have a small set of weights instead of having a different weight for each pixel of the input image, making these neurons effectively convolutional. Their work is considered the birth of deep learning and Convolutional Neural Networks (CNNs). In the early 2000s, interest in ANN dwindled again because of the long training times required and the popularization of the Support Vector Machine (SVM) algorithm, which produced similar results with faster running times. However, Geoffrey Hinton, Yoshua Bengio, and Yann LeCun continued their belief in the capabilities of ANNs and with the help of funding from the Canadian Institute for Advanced Research (CIFAR) persevered in their research in the field. They were able to show the effectiveness of CNNs in different complex machine learning tasks such as speech recognition (Hinton et al., 2012) and image classification (Krizhevsky et al., 2017). Likewise, the development and improvement of digital images taken from aircraft or satellites, which cover practically every angle of the earth's surface, has significantly increased in the field of RS. The RS and geoscience community has been forced by this increase in data to use deep learning algorithms to complete various remote sensing tasks (Khelifi & Mignotte, 2020).

Convolutional Neural Networks

In deep learning, a Convolutional Neural Network (CNN) is a neural network model which consists of many layers. These layers include the input layer, the convolutional layers, the pooling layers, the fully connected layers, and the output layer. CNN can be trained to extract features and do classification at the same time. Many types and variants of CNNs are developed for the classification of images starting from the earliest LeNet-5 (Wei et al., 2019) to the many recent advanced families of CNNs such as ResNet, InceptionNet, and EfficientNet (Tan & Le, 2019). The main layers of the CNN model are shown in Figure 2. The use of convolutional neural networks is widespread. Below, we list some frequent instances of how they have been utilized in practical situations:

- Image classification.
- Object detection.
- Audio visual matching.
- Object reconstruction.
- Speech recognition.

Figure 2. Architecture of a typical CNN model

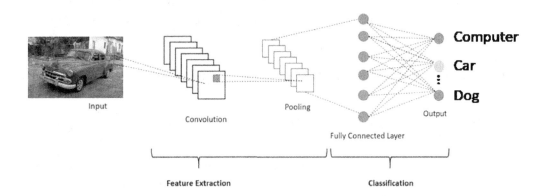

Convolutional Layer

The central portion of a CNN is the convolutional layer (conv layer). In nature, the images are usually static. Generally, all parts in the image are the same of one part which is a formation of the image. As a result, a feature learned in one location can be used to match a pattern in another. We take a small 2D filter (also denoted as Kernel) and pass it on to all points in the image (Input). We convolve this filter with the image at all pixel locations and get one single value (Output). Then, the back propagation algorithm is used to learn the weights (parameters) of the filters. Figure 3 illustrates a typical convolutional operation (Sultana et al., 2018).

Figure 3. Illustration of the operation performed by the convolutional layer on a sample input

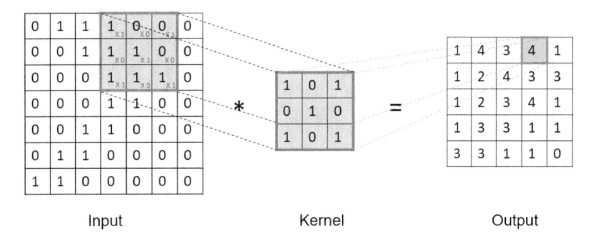

Pooling Layer

Reducing the sampling of an image is referred to as pooling. The convolutional output is sub-sampled as input to form a single output. There are various pooling techniques available such as max pooling and average pooling. Figure 4 depicts a max pooling that takes the greatest values of pixels in a 2 × 2 region. The use of pooling decreases the number of parameters that must be calculated while making the network insensitive to image changes in shape, scale, and size (Gholamalinezhad & Khosravi, 2020).

Figure 4. A max pooling example

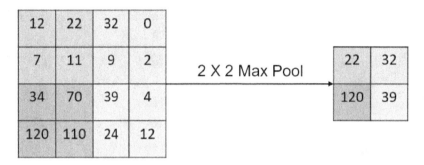

Fully-Connected Layer (FC Layer)

Figure 5 below shows the final component of CNN, which is made up of fully connected layers (FC). FC is a layer that collects the input from all neurons in the preceding layer and generates the output by performing a weighted linear combination of its inputs followed by applying a non-linear activation function (A. Zhang et al., 2021). The FC layer is displayed as a hidden layer in Figure 5.

Figure 5. A fully-connected layer shown as a hidden layer

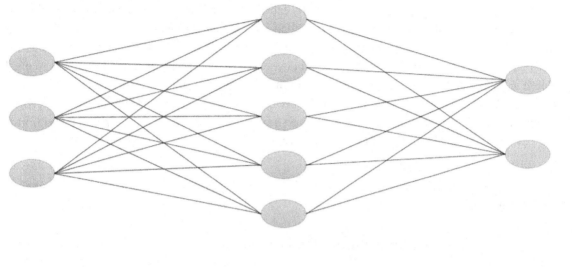

Input Layer   Hidden Layer   Output Layer

Domain Adaptation

Deep learning and CNN models have achieved tremendous success in RS scene classification, but only under a supervised classification setting, where the network is trained on a large amount of labeled examples. For computer vision applications, a large dataset of labeled images, called ImageNet, is built over the years. Subsequently, many CNN models have been trained on this dataset and made publically available to the research community. These CNN models are known as pre-trained models, and they have impressive performance in recognizing many day-to-day objects from their images. In remote sensing, these pre-trained CNN models cannot be used directly because we are interested in recognizing a different set of objects. To use these pre-trained CNN models, we first need to change the output layer which should include the objects we are interested in. The second change is that the CNN model should be retrained on our dataset of labeled images. In remote sensing, we still do not have a large labeled dataset similar to the ImageNet dataset, thus retraining the CNN model from scratch with random weights will not achieve excellent results as in many computer vision applications. Luckily, researchers have developed a fine tuning approach, where we take a CNN model with weights pre-trained on the ImageNet dataset, change its output layer to focus on the objects we are interested to recognize, and then apply a few steps or epochs of training that would fine tune the model and adapt it to our dataset.

However, this approach still does not provide a universal solution for all RS datasets even if they contain exactly the same object classes. For excellent classification results, the training and test data must come from the same source and have similar joint probability distributions (S. Chen et al., 2020). But, if we fine-tune a pre-trained model on one RS dataset, known as the source dataset, and use it to predict the object classes of another dataset of RS images (known as the target dataset), the model often fails significantly. As Figure 6 illustrates, given a CNN model that achieves excellent classification accuracy on a labeled source dataset, if we test it on a target dataset without any labeled samples, the performance is usually quite low. In order to achieve performance similar to the source dataset, a large portion of the target dataset need to be manually labelled, which is exactly what we need to avoid. It turns out, even though the two datasets contain images of the same objects from the RS field, they still represent different data domains because of the many differences related to data acquisition conditions, such as different sensors, different lighting conditions, different atmospheric conditions, and so on. The problem is known as the data shift problem between data domains, and the subfield of research to deal with this problem is known as domain adaptation (DA). DA aims to adapt a CNN model pre-trained on labeled data from a source domain so that it has a similar performance on a target domain with limited or no extra manual labeling as illustrated by Figure 6.

Figure 6. The target dataset needs a high ratio of labelled samples for training to achieve the same level of classification accuracy as the source dataset

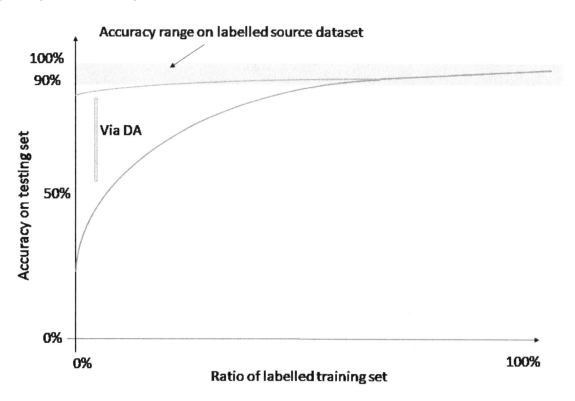

The domain shift problem can be illustrated by the diagram in Figure 7. We use a simple example of datasets with three object classes only. The three shapes used, namely the square, the star, and triangle shapes illustrate the features extracted by a CNN model and hence the figure shows the distribution of the data in feature space. Obviously, the two dimensions shown in the figure are only for illustrative purposes because the feature space has high-dimensionality and cannot be visualized fully. The distribution of the source domain is shown in blue color while the distribution of the target domain is shown in red color. The class boundaries shown in the figure are learned by a CNN model, which was fine-tuned on the source dataset. This is the main reason why the figure shows that it can separate the source domain distributions very well. The data shift between the two domains, illustrated by the blue and red distributions, caused errors in the target domain. The CNN model while fine-tuned on the source dataset is not able to separate the three object classes in the target domain. DA solutions aim to reduce the domain shift difference by aligning the distributions of the two domains, which leads to the target dataset being classified correctly (Farahani et al., 2021).

Figure 7. Domain adaptation illustration: (left) The distribution of the data in feature space for a three-class dataset. The data distribution's shift between the features of the source dataset (in blue) and the target dataset (in red) causes classification errors in the target dataset. (right) DA techniques attempt to align the data distributions of the source and target datasets and improve classification accuracy

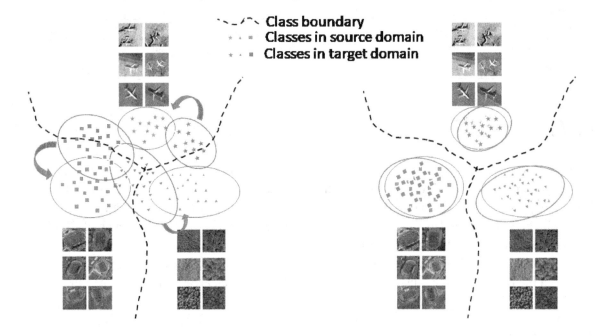

Generally, we can group DA techniques into unsupervised and supervised types. In unsupervised DA techniques, we assume that the target domain has no labeled samples, whereas in supervised DA, we assume that some labeled samples in the target dataset are available. In typical DA techniques, we need to learn how to classify images and at the same time remove the data distribution shift between domains. In past research works in RS, DA methods used two main approaches to remove the data distribution shift. The first approach minimizes the Maximum Mean Discrepancy (MMD) metric (Othman et al., 2017). Such CNN models add a second term to the standard cross entropy loss, which computes a distance between the distributions of the source and target training batches. The second approach is to use adversarial techniques, where another sub-model is added as a domain discriminator that learns domain invariant features (Liu & Tuzel, 2016). Then, the two sub-models or branches are trained in an alternating fashion so that the whole model learns to differentiate between classes and learn domain invariant features at the same time.

Datasets for Remote Sensing Images

The top view in remote sensing depends on the appropriate use of images. These images are collected from different sensors, which results in images of different types and sizes. Four common datasets are used in RS scene classification, namely, the University of California, Merced (UCMerced) dataset, the Aerial Image Dataset (AID), the Northwestern Polytechnical University RS Image Scene Classification (NWPU-RESISC45) dataset, and the PatternNet dataset. Table 1 presents details about all these four datasets, which are heavily used in remote sensing.

Table 1. Details of remote sensing datasets used in scene classification

Dataset	No. of Images	No. of Classes	Image per Class	Resolution (m)	Image Size (pixels)
UCMerced	2,100	21	100	0.3	256 x 256
AID	10,000	30	220 to 420	0.5 to 8	600 x 600
NWPU-RESISC45	31,500	45	700	0.2 to 30	256 x 256
PatternNet	30,400	38	800	0.062 to 4.693	256 x 256

UCMerced Dataset

The UCMerced dataset collection comprises 21 classes of earth scenes, such as airplanes, beaches, buildings, forests, rivers, and runways, with each class made out of 100 images. The size of each image is 256×256 pixels and the ground resolution is equal to 0.3 m. These images are gathered from the United States Geological Survey (USGS) National Map over different U.S. districts (Chen et al., 2022). Due to the abundance of similar land use classifications, including sparse residential, medium residential, and dense residential, the UC-Merced dataset is challenging to categorize. It is commonly used as a public dataset in the field of remote sensing to assess scene categorization algorithms (Alem & Kumar, 2022; Ben Youssef et al., 2024).

AID Dataset

The AID dataset is a collection that incorporates 10,000 RGB images with 30 scene classifications (Xia et al., 2017). These images are gathered from Google Earth from different places on earth, primarily in China, England, the United States, Italy, France, Germany, and Japan (Pires de Lima & Marfurt, 2019). The number of scene images in each class varies from 220 to 420. Additional details regarding this dataset are listed in Table 2. The scenes include airports, beaches, bridges, forests, parks, and parking lots (Huang & Xu, 2019). The diversity of the interclass of the AID is quickly growing as a result of the AID being collected from various sensors in different countries at various times and throughout various seasons. The images have a large size of 600×600 pixels with a ground resolution ranging from 0.5 m to 8 m.

Table 2. Detailed information about the AID dataset

Class No.	Class Name	No. of Images	Class No.	Class Name	No. of Images
1	Airport	360	16	Farmland	370
2	Bare land	310	17	Forest	250
3	Baseball field	220	18	Industrial	390
4	Beach	400	19	Meadow	280
5	Bridge	360	20	Medium residential	290
6	Center	260	21	Mountain	340
7	Church	240	22	Park	250
8	Commercial dense	350	23	Parking	390
9	Residential	410	24	Playground	370
10	Desert	300	25	Pond	420
11	Port	380	26	Sparse residential	300
12	Railway station	260	27	Square	300
13	Resort	290	28	Stadium	290
14	River	410	29	Storage tanks	360
15	School	300	30	Viaduct	420

NWPU-RESISC45 Dataset

The NWPU-RESISC45 dataset, or NWPU dataset for short, is created by Northwestern Polytechnical University. The number of images in this dataset is 31,500 images. This dataset is composed of 45 classes such as airplanes, airports, beaches, bridges, forests, and deserts. Each class includes 700 RGB images extracted from Google Earth imagery with a size equal to 256 × 256 pixels (Guo et al., 2022). Within the classes, the spatial resolution decreases from 30.0 m to 0.2 m per pixel. The dataset is somewhat difficult to handle because of the image variations, specific variances within the classes, and specific commonalities between the classes.

PatternNet Dataset

The PatternNet dataset is a collection from Wuhan University from Google Map Application Programming Interface (API) and Google Earth (Zhou et al., 2018). The number of images in this dataset is 30,400 images. This dataset has 38 classes that includes airplanes, beaches, bridges, farms, forests, oil wells, and rivers. Each class includes 800 RGB images of size 256 × 256 pixels with a spatial resolution of 0.062 m to 4.693 m (Shen et al., 2022).

LITERATURE REVIEW

In this chapter, we categorize our literature review into single-source versus multi-source DA methods. We observe that most of the works deal with single-source to a single-target dataset for domain adaptation. Very few works deal with DA using multi-source datasets, leaving a large research gap in this area. Also, these methods are not efficient, which leads to a poor performance with some datasets (average accuracy values between 80% and 90%). In addition, in some datasets, the related studies generate ambiguous features near the task decision boundary, which cause them to fail drastically. This means that more work can be done to improve the results obtained thus far by these studies.

Single-Source Domain Adaptation

Different domain adaptation strategies have been developed to decrease the spread of disparity between source and target domains. Ganin et al. (Ganin & Lempitsky, 2015) in an early work propose a method to deal with domain variation in deep structures that can be trained on large amount of labeled data from the source domain and large amount of unlabeled data from the target domain, that is no labeled target-domain data are necessary. As the training progresses, the approach promotes the emergence of "deep" features that are (i) discriminative for the main learning task on the source domain and (ii) invariant with respect to the shift between the domains.

Another work by Othman et al. (Othman et al., 2017) subjected classification scenarios to the data shift problem using a domain adaptation network. They generated an initial feature representation of images by relying on the power of pre-trained CNNs. After that, they improve learning by using outcome features on the top of pre-trained CNNs. Then, they minimize the regularization terms within the fine tuning phase to learn the weights of the created network. These regularization terms include the cross entropy error on the labeled source data, the maximum mean between the target and source data distribution, and the geometrical structure of the target data. In addition, they propose a mini-batch gradient based optimization method with a dynamic batch size for the alignment of the target and source distributions to obtain robust hidden representations. The experimental results for one source domain yield the best accuracy after comparison with other methods. The obtained results are 93.55% and 87.95% for KSA to Merced and Merced to KSA, respectively.

Another work by Tzeng et al. (Tzeng et al., 2017) lays out a novel generalized adaptation framework based on the new concept of adversarial learning. The new framework combines discriminative modeling, untied weight sharing, and a generative adversarial networks-based (GAN) loss, which they call Adversarial Discriminative Domain Adaptation (ADDA). They show that ADDA is more effective, yet considerably simpler than competing domain-adversarial methods, and demonstrate the promise of the approach by exceeding state-of-the-art unsupervised adaptation results on standard cross-domain digit classification tasks and a new more difficult cross-modality object classification task, where the accuracy average of the results increased from 13.9% to 21.1%.

In (Shen et al., 2018), a novel method is presented, based on Wasserstein Distance Guided Representation Learning (WDGRL), for learning domain invariant feature representations. WDGRL works in two ways: 1) estimate empirical Wasserstein distance between the source and target samples by utilizing the neural network, denoted by the domain expert, and 2) minimize the estimated Wasserstein distance in an adversarial manner by optimizing the feature extractor network. The domain adaptation lies in its gradient property and the promising generalization bound, which are considered as advantages of the Wasserstein distance.

For cross-domain classification in aerial vehicle images, the authors in (Bashmal et al., 2018) proposed a new algorithm dependent on GANs, which is called Siamese-GAN. It studies invariant component depictions for both marked and unmarked images, which come from two distinct domains. In order to achieve this aim in an adversarial way, they train a Siamese encoder-decoder design joined with a discriminator association. The encoder-decoder network has the errand of organizing the spread of the two domains in a typical space regularized by the propagation limit, while the discriminator hopes to remember them. After this stage, they feed the ensuing encoded marked and unmarked highlights to other features made out of two completely associated layers for classification and training. The achieved average accuracy is equal to 90.34%.

Zhang, Liu, Pan, and Shi in (Zhang et al., 2020) propose a domain adaptation method called Correlation Subspace Dynamic Distribution Alignment (CS-DDA). They made two strategies to assess the sources and target domains' effects based on the characteristics of RS scenes. They include Subspace Correlation Maximization (SCM) and Dynamic Statistical Distribution Alignment (DSDA). In particular, SCM would ensure source domain mapping to a common subspace to keep the source domain information. Also, DSDA is aimed to minimize the distribution discrepancy between the aligned target and source domains. Precisely, DSDA is a dynamic adjustment process, where the objective is to learn an adaptive factor to stabilize the inter-class and intra-class distributions between domains. In addition, the authors converted the optimal solution to the generalized Eigen-decomposition problem using derivation and they integrated SCM and DSDA into a uniform optimization framework.

The authors of (Ammour et al., 2018) present an asymmetric adaptation neural network (AANN) method. Before the variation cycle, they feed the features obtained from a pre-trained CNN to a denoising autoencoder (DAE) to perform dimensionality reduction. At that point, the first hidden layer of AANN maps the labeled source information to the target space, while the resulting layers control the partition between the land-cover classes. To get familiar with its weights, the model limits a target work made out of two misfortunes identified with the distance between the source and target information dispersions and class partition.

The authors of (Shi et al., 2022) made three changes and a compact modular network paradigm was suggested. The initial suggestion was a simple self-compensated convolution (SCC). Although classical convolution may successfully extract features, the method is time-consuming when there are many filters, such as 512 or 1024 common filters. They suggested a SCC to speed up the network without adding to the computational load. This convolution's fundamental premise is to conduct the conventional convolution while using fewer filters and to use input information to balance out the convolved channels. Additionally, based on the SCC, they suggested the self-compensating bottleneck module (SCBM). This module's broader channel shortcut makes it easier to transport more shallow data to the deeper layer and enhances the model's capacity for feature extraction. Finally, they built a compact unit for remote sensing scene image classification modular self-compensation convolution neural network (SCCNN) using the suggested self-compensation bottleneck module. By recycling bottleneck modules with the same structure, the network is constructed. They used six datasets of remote sensing image scenes, which include UCM21, NWPU-RESISC45, AID, WHU-RS19, among others. The experimental results demonstrate that the suggested method outperforms some of the state-of-the-art classification methods with less parameters in terms of classification performance. The achieved overall accuracy is 97.21%.

Cross-Domain Adaptive Clustering (CDAC) was proposed by Li et al. (Li et al., 2021). They first develop an adversarial adaptive clustering loss function to aggregate features of unnamed target data into clusters and carry out cluster-wise feature alignment across the source domain and target domain in order to accomplish both intra-domain and inter-domain adaptation. They continue to use fake labeling on unlabeled data in the target domain and maintain highly confident fake labels. In order to support adversarial learning, fake labeling increases the number of labeled samples in each class in the target domain. This results in a more reliable and potent cluster core for each class. In the experiments, they used Office3, Office-Home2 and DomainNet1 datasets. They also selected Resnet34 and Alexnet as a backbone network. In the results, they compute the accuracy with 1-shot and 3-shot scenarios. When using Alexnet with DomainNet1, the mean of accuracy is 52.1% and 56.1% with 1-shot and 3-shot, respectively. While the mean accuracy with Resnet34 is 73.6% for 1-shot and 76% for 3-shot cases. The mean accuracy values on Office-Home2 for 3-shot when using Resnet34 and Alexnet are 74.2% and 56.8%, respectively. On the Office3 dataset, when using Alexnet backbone, the mean of accuracy is 63.1% under the 1-shot scenario while it is 70% under the 3-shot variation.

Multi-Source Domain Adaptation

Recently, researchers started to focus on domain adaptation from multiple source domains to one target domain. For example, the author in (Adayel et al., 2020) proposed a methodology dependent on adversarial learning and Pareto-based ranking. Specifically, the technique aligns the distribution discrepancy between the source and target areas utilizing entropy optimization. During the alignment cycle, the method identifies candidate samples of the ambiguous class from the target domain through a Pareto-based ranking strategy.

The work by Y. Yin et al. (Yin et al., 2022) proposed a method called universal multi-source adaptation network (UMAN) that fixes domain adaptation issues. They used Office-31, Caltech-256 (Yang et al., 2021), Office-Home, VisDA2017 (Y. Zhang & Davison, 2021) and Image CLEF-DA (Meng et al., 2022) datasets. They compared their method with the state of the art approaches. The results of UMAN experiments in Office-31 yields a 92.73% average accuracy, while on Office-Home the average accuracy is equal to 79.44%, and on VisDA2017+ImageCLEF-DA, the average accuracy is equal to 92.73%.

The authors of (Elshamli et al., 2019) proposed a framework called adaptive multisource domain adaptation (AMDA). It is a framework to address the problem of DA, when there is a change in the distributions of the data on the source domain. Additionally, AMDA can handle uneven data distributions between the sources more successfully than the current baselines. These distributions use four cities for testing (Chicago, Amsterdam, Xi'an, and Madrid), where others use five different cities for training (Hong Kong, Berlin, Rome, Sao Paulo, and Paris). They computed accuracies in the experiments, when they use targets form all cities that were used in the training. Also, they compared their obtained average accuracy to the average accuracy of other state-of-art methods. They found that it was 82.4% better than the other methods used in the comparison.

RESEARCH METHODOLOGY

We have recently proposed in (Lasloum et al., 2021) a method called Multi-Source Semi-Supervised Domain Adaptation Network (SSDAN) for multi-source domain adaptation applied in semi-supervised learning. This is further described in the following section.

SSDAN Method

In semi-supervised DA, the labeled source domain and target domain are achieved with few labeled samples per class. Every source dataset is made out of a set of images and their corresponding labels. Also, the rest of the samples make up the unlabeled set. Semi-supervised DA aims to assemble a machine learning model that can move the information from the domain of the source to the domain of the target and achieve high classification accuracy on the target dataset. DA learning models need to learn how to classify images and at the same time remove the data distribution shift between domains. We proposed in (Lasloum et al., 2021) the use of an entropy-based loss function to address the data shift problem. The SSDAN method is based on a pre-trained model for extracting features, and a fully connected layer that is responsible for the classification task.

The architecture of SSDAN is shown in Figure 8. It is composed of two main parts; a pre-trained EfficientNet-B3 model denoted by G, which acts as a feature extractor, and a classifier module composed of a fully connected layer with C neurons followed by a softmax activation function to predict the class probabilities. The connected layer also uses a temperature parameter T, which controls the magnitude of its output. The idea of using a temperature parameter to scale and adjust the softmax was discussed by Hinton et al. (Hinton et al., 2015) in the context of model distillation. Then, it was used in the context of the few-shot learning scenario. The latter means that the information in the training dataset is limited. It was shown to provide positive effects on classification performance (Alajaji et al., 2020).

Figure 8. Overview of the architecture of the SSDAN model

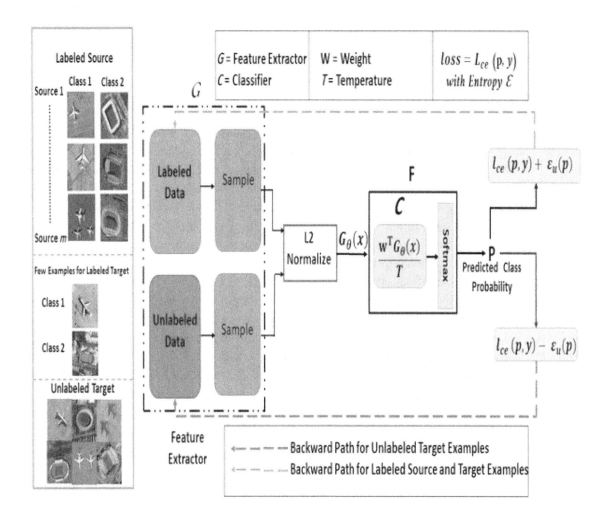

Model Optimization

Recall that DA techniques need to learn how to classify images and at the same time remove the data distribution shift between domains. In the past, DA methods used two main approaches to remove the data distribution shift. The first approach is to add a second term to the cross entropy loss which computes a distance between means of the source and target training batches. The second approach is to use adversarial techniques, where another sub-model is added that learns to differentiate between domains. Then, the two sub-models or branches are trained in an adversarial fashion. Here, we use another approach denoted as MiniMax entropy, where we minimize two types of loss functions based on the entropy of unlabeled target data. First, in order to train the model for classification, we need to minimize the standard cross entropy loss between predicted class probabilities and true class labels. To compute this loss, we use the labeled data from both source and target domains as follows:

$$l_{ce} = -\frac{1}{N_s + N_t} \sum_{i=1}^{N_s + N_t} \sum_{k=1}^{C} 1(y_{ik} = k) \ln \left(\text{Softmax} \left(\frac{1}{T} \frac{W^T G_\theta(x)}{\|G_\theta(x)\|} \right) \right) \tag{1}$$

where N_s and N_t are the number of labeled samples from the source and target sets, respectively, C is the number of classes, y_{ik} is the true label, and $1()$ is an indicator function that returns one if the included statement is true, otherwise, it returns zero. The formula inside the $ln()$ function contains a scaled result with the temperature parameter and is passed through the softmax activation function to compute the class predictions. It represents the output of the softmax layer of the pre-trained feature extractor model G.

Minimizing this L_{ce} ensures that the model learns discriminative features for the source dataset and the few labeled target samples. However, because of the dataset shift problem, this does not mean that these features will be discriminative for the whole target dataset. To solve this problem, the semi-supervised approach exploits the set of unlabeled data to align the distributions of the target domain and source domain. As mentioned earlier, we also use entropy to measure domain invariance of the learned class prototypes, which is computed over the unlabeled dataset as follows:

$$\varepsilon_u = -\frac{1}{N_u} \sum_{i=1}^{N_u} \sum_{k=1}^{C} P(y = k|x) \ln [P(y = k|x)] \tag{2}$$

where N_u is the number of unlabeled samples and $p\,(y = k \mid x)$ is the prediction probability in class k for unlabeled element x. More precisely, $p\,(y = k \mid x)$ is the kth probability vector of $p(x)$.

As information theory predicts, higher entropy values mean a more uniform distribution of probabilities. Thus, when we maximize the entropy ε_u, we are actually encouraging the model to learn more uniformly distributed probabilities for the unlabeled data, thus making the learned prototypes more domain invariant. On the other hand, to obtain discriminative features on unlabeled target samples, we cluster unlabeled target features around the learned prototypes. The features should be assigned to one of the prototypes with higher confidence probability, resulting in the desired discriminative features. To achieve this objective, we need to decrease the entropy ε_u, which is in some sense a contradiction. But, by using adversarial training, we can solve this problem by alternating the maximization and minimization steps. Repeating this entropy maximization and entropy minimization process should yield discriminative features that are at the same time domain invariant. Therefore, to learn domain invariant class prototypes for the target dataset, the classifier layer needs to maximize the entropy of the learned prototypes ε_u. In addition, to increase intra-class variance, the feature extractor G needs to minimize entropy ε_u. In other words, the prototype entropy ε_u should be simultaneously minimized by G and maximized by the classification layer. This can be accomplished by conducting the training in an adversarial fashion. At the same time, both the feature extractor G and the classification layer must also minimize cross entropy loss L_{ce} to learn discriminative features for classes. Thus, the two adversarial loss functions for the feature extractor G and the classification layer are defined as:

$$l_1 = l_{ce} + \alpha \varepsilon_u \tag{3}$$

and

$$l_2 = l_{ce} - \beta \varepsilon_u \tag{4}$$

where α and β are two parameters to control a trade-off between classification on labeled samples and MiniMax entropy loss for unlabeled target samples. To simplify the model further, the two hyperparameters can have the same value, that is $\alpha = \beta$. In other words, one could investigate one parameter only: α. The two loss functions, L_1 and L_2, are both minimized in an alternating fashion. Note that minimizing L_2 effectively maximizes ε_u. We next present the steps used to implement the model:

Input: Multi-source domain images, target domain images.

Output: Labeled target images.

Step 1: Load the pre-trained CNN model (EfficientNet-B3), which acts as a feature extractor.

Step 2: Select batch size samples randomly from the target domain and add them to the current batch.

Step 3: Compute the loss on the batch of labeled data.

Step 4: Compute the entropy loss.

Step 5: Compute the loss and apply backpropagation.

Step 6: Minimize the loss and apply backpropagation.

Step 7: Compute the loss on the validation set.

Step 8: Test the model on the target test data.

Experiments

For the pre-trained model used for feature extraction, we selected the EfficientNet-B3 model in these experiments. We remove the last output layer of the EfficientNet-B3 and use the output of the previous layer as the feature vector. In the case of EfficientNet-B3, it has a size of 1 x 1 x 1536. As for the added classification layer, its weight matrix is initialized randomly. We selected $K = 3$ labeled samples randomly per class to be samples of labeled target data. We used the whole source dataset with its labels in addition to the labeled target data to train the model. Another $K = 3$ labeled samples from the target dataset were used as a validation set to decide the early stopping of the training process. Thus, a total of six labeled samples per class from the target dataset were required in our experiments. We monitored the accuracy of the validation set, and if there was no improvement for five consecutive epochs, we stopped the training. The remaining target samples are considered as the unlabeled target set and were used in the algorithm during training to compute the entropy loss, ε_u. During testing, we used this unlabeled set to evaluate the algorithm, by comparing the predicted labels with the true ones.

To evaluate the overall performance of the proposed method, the overall accuracy (OA) metric is used, which is the fraction of correctly classified samples in relation to all samples for testing:

$$OA = \frac{\sum_{i=0}^{C} n_{ii}}{T} \tag{5}$$

where C is the number of classes, n_{ii} is the number of correctly classified test samples for class i, which is found in the diagonal of the confusion matrix, and T is the total number of test samples.

Besides the main overall accuracy (OA) metric, other metrics can be used for evaluation including, the Kappa coefficient, number of model parameters, Giga Floating-point Operations Per Second (GFLOPS), and algorithm execution time in seconds. In particular, the Kappa coefficient measures the agreement between two classifiers, where each one classifies N items into C mutually exclusive categories. In the traditional 2×2 confusion matrix employed in machine learning and statistics to evaluate binary classifications, the Cohen's Kappa formula can be written as:

$$k = \frac{2 \times (TP \times TN - FN \times FP)}{(TP + FP) \times (FP + TN) + (TP + FN) \times (FN + TN)} \tag{6}$$

where *TP* are the true positives, *FP* are the false positives, *TN* are the true negatives, and *FN* are the false negatives. If the classifiers are in complete agreement, then $k = 1$. If there is no agreement among the classifiers other than what would be expected by chance, $k = 0$. It is possible for the statistic to be negative, which can occur by chance if there is no relationship between the predictions of the two classifiers, or it may reflect a real tendency of the classifiers to give differing predictions.

To determine the effects of the loss function on the method's classification performance, we conducted experiments while changing the values of the parameter α between 0.2 and 1.4 on the single source domain and one target domain. We selected the four datasets: UC Merced, AID, NWPU-RESISC45, and, PatternNet for these experiments. For brevity and compactness, we denote these datasets as M, A, N and P, respectively. The results of all possible experiments are shown in Table 3. They provide, among others, the accuracy values for the 12 possible scenarios.

Table 3. Overall accuracy results for the twelve one-source scenarios with different α (alpha) values

Datasets		α						
		0.2	0.4	0.6	0.8	1	1.2	1.4
M → A	Acc	95.069	91.717	92.538	92.560	93.122	95.609	92.257
	Time (s)	3572	1851	2485	3257	3468	**878**	1381
	Epoch	3400	1700	2300	1800	1800	**600**	1000
M → N	Acc	84.792	85.243	85.119	86.415	**88.277**	85.061	86.971
	Time (s)	4583	5952	1710	1410	1360	2045	1861
	Epoch	600	**600**	800	800	**500**	1100	700
M → P	Acc	98.149	94.079	95.242	98.003	93.866	**98.362**	96.036
	Time (s)	2992	2640	2203	2314	1904	1507	3781
	Epoch	900	1300	800	1100	700	**500**	600
A → M	Acc	97.537	98.200	98.484	96.875	97.537	98.390	**98.579**
	Time (s)	882	870	833	1638	2203	542	**493**
	Epoch	1400	1300	1100	2700	1900	700	500
A → N	Acc	91.205	90.044	**92.309**	90.841	88.191	91.628	89.967
	Time (s)	1399	5365	2736	2321	1898	1180	4403
	Epoch	800	1500	1600	1300	1100	**500**	600

continued on following page

Table 3. Continued

Datasets		α						
		0.2	0.4	0.6	0.8	1	1.2	1.4
A → P	Acc	97.926	97.248	98.352	98.275	98.449	97.810	**98.546**
	Time (s)	2011	4976	5286	2055	**1219**	3493	2274
	Epoch	**500**	1800	1400	1100	600	2300	1400
N → A	Acc	94.356	95.242	**96.302**	92.734	93.880	92.734	93.426
	Time (s)	2910	1256	**423**	600	1088	441	842
	Epoch	1300	2000	**500**	700	1600	500	1300
N → M	Acc	98.958	98.485	**99.527**	96.117	97.727	97.064	96.875
	Time (s)	1238	543	**319**	1460	977	1118	2061
	Epoch	2400	1100	**600**	3400	2300	2600	4900
N → P	Acc	92.452	93.246	93.595	**94.641**	92.607	93.469	94.225
	Time (s)	2544	1364	1015	806	4381	777	**577**
	Epoch	700	1300	700	700	2600	700	**400**
P → A	Acc	91.133	96.324	**96.691**	95.761	92.842	86.613	94.312
	Time (s)	4051	2710	1828	**1306**	1806	1727	1989
	Epoch	900	2000	1900	1300	3100	**900**	3400
P → M	Acc	97.822	**98.390**	97.633	97.917	97.917	98.201	96.402
	Time (s)	442	1461	880	395	511	**322**	730
	Epoch	**600**	3900	2200	900	1200	700	1800
P → N	Acc	82.767	83.266	86.377	**86.731**	85.273	84.169	84.101
	Time (s)	7498	2399	1675	1540	1390	1842	1259
	Epoch	600	700	700	700	600	900	500
Average	Acc	93.514	93.457	**94.348**	93.906	93.308	93.259	93.475
	Time (s)	2844	2616	1783	1592	1851	**1322**	1805
	Epoch	1175	1600	1216	1375	1500	**1000**	1425

The best overall accuracy of 99.52% is obtained for N → M when α equals 0.6, while the lowest overall accuracy is obtained with 82.76% when α equal 0.2 for P → N. The best average accuracy on the 12 scenarios is generated when the value of α is equal to 0.6 with 94.34%, while the lowest average accuracy is equal to 93.25% when α equals 1.2.

We applied the best value of α (= 0.6) on all multi-source domain adaptation scenarios. First, we present the results of experiments with two source domains and one target domain, Table 4 shows some of the obtained accuracy results. The average accuracy is 94.586%. The best accuracy with the target domain of {A} is realized at 96.84% when the two source domains are {M, P}. On the other hand, when the target domain is {M}, the best accuracy is 99.71% with the employed source domains being the two datasets {N, P}. When the target is the dataset {N}, the best accuracy on this part of the experiments is 91.12% with the two source domains being {A, P}. Finally, when the target domain is {P}, the best accuracy is 98.26% with the utilized source domains being equal to the two datasets {M, A}.

Table 4. Overall accuracy results for selected two-source scenarios

Datasets	Results		Datasets	Results	
M, N → A	Acc.	94.096	A, P → N	Acc.	91.129
	Time (s)	3798		Time (s)	4512
	Epoch	1100		Epoch	500
M, P → A	Acc.	96.842	M, A → N	Acc.	90.61
	Time (s)	6894		Time (s)	2917
	Epoch	500		Epoch	1200
N, P → A	Acc.	95.177	M, P → N	Acc.	85.464
	Time (s)	6743		Time (s)	3418
	Epoch	3600		Epoch	1300
A, P → M	Acc.	99.053	N, A → P	Acc.	95.261
	Time (s)	1645		Time (s)	4421
	Epoch	1800		Epoch	300
N, P → M	Acc.	99.715	M, N → P	Acc.	92.645
	Time (s)	1400		Time (s)	1980
	Epoch	1400		Epoch	600
A, N → M	Acc.	96.78	M, A → P	Acc.	98.265
	Time (s)	3633		Time (s)	2452
	Epoch	1500		Epoch	900

Overall Accuracy Average 94.586%

We also computed the Kappa coefficient values whose results are presented in Table 5. The highest Kappa coefficient value of 0.994 is obtained when the target domain is {M} and the two source domains are represented by the two datasets {N, P}.

Table 5. Kappa coefficient values obtained for the different two-source scenarios

Datasets (Two-Source Scenario)	Kappa Coefficient	Datasets (Two-Source Scenario)	Kappa Coefficient
M, N → A	0.935	A, P → N	0.902
M, P → A	0.963	M, A → N	0.894
N, P → A	0.945	M, P → N	0.842
A, P → M	0.990	N, A → P	0.945
N, P → M	**0.994**	M, N → P	0.920
A, N → M	0.960	M, A → P	0.982
Average Kappa Coefficient	**0.939**		

Next, we present the results of our experiments using three source domains and one target domain. Table 6 shows the obtained accuracy results for all these possible scenarios. The best accuracy of 99.24% is generated when the three source domains are {N, P, A} and the target domain is {M} while the average overall accuracy is equal to 96.25%.

Table 6. Overall accuracy results for the three-source scenarios

Datasets (Three-Source Scenario)	Performance Results	
M, N, P → A	Acc.	97.794%
	Time (s)	9139
	Epoch	8000
N, P, A→ M	Acc.	**99.242%**
	Time (s)	**2152**
	Epoch	1600
M, P, A → N	Acc.	90.495%
	Time (s)	6370
	Epoch	**1400**
A, M, N → P	Acc.	97.5%
	Time (s)	7442
	Epoch	2800

Average of Overall Accuracy 96.257%

Finally, we computed the Kappa coefficient when utilizing three source domains and one target domain. The results are provided in Table 7. The average Kappa coefficient is equal to 0.959 and the highest Kappa coefficient value is obtained when the target domain is {M} and the source domains are the {N, P, A} datasets. In this case, the Kappa coefficient is equal to 0.993.

Table 7. Kappa coefficient results for the three-source scenarios

Datasets (Three-Source Scenarios)	Kappa Coefficient
M, N, P → A	0.975
N, P, A→ M	**0.993**
M, P, A → N	0.895
A, M, N → P	0.972
Average of Kappa Coefficient	**0.959**

CONCLUSION

In this chapter, some basic concepts related to domain adaptation in remote sensing were reviewed, including recent studies dealing with RS scene classification. Moreover, we describe different types of CNN models and discuss the datasets used in RS research. We elaborate on one of the models utilized for semi-supervised domain adaptation of remote sensing scene classification, called SSDAN. In addition, we explain how the standard cross-entropy loss was computed over the labeled samples from both the source and the target domains in the model. We also show how the novel minimax entropy loss was computed over the unlabeled target samples in the model. The combined loss function was optimized in an adversarial fashion, where it alternated between maximizing and minimizing the minimax entropy loss. Experimental work is conducted on four datasets with many single-source scenarios, two-source scenarios, and three-source scenarios for domain adaptation. The method was evaluated by using the overall accuracy and kappa coefficient as the two metrics of choice, with the highest achieved values being equal to 99.71% and 0.994, respectively.

ACKNOWLEDGMENT

This work was supported by the Deanship of Scientific Research at King Saud University, Riyadh, Saudi Arabia, through the Local Research Group Program under Project RG-1435-055.

REFERENCES

Adayel, R., Bazi, Y., Alhichri, H., & Alajlan, N. (2020). Deep Open-Set Domain Adaptation for Cross-Scene Classification based on Adversarial Learning and Pareto Ranking. *Remote Sensing (Basel)*, 12(11), 11. Advance online publication. DOI: 10.3390/rs12111716

Alajaji, D., Alhichri, H. S., Ammour, N., & Alajlan, N. (2020). Few-Shot Learning For Remote Sensing Scene Classification. *2020 Mediterranean and Middle-East Geoscience and Remote Sensing Symposium (M2GARSS)*, 81–84. DOI: 10.1109/M2GARSS47143.2020.9105154

Alem, A., & Kumar, S. (2022). End-to-End Convolutional Neural Network Feature Extraction for Remote Sensed Images Classification. *Applied Artificial Intelligence*, 36(1), 2137650. DOI: 10.1080/08839514.2022.2137650

Ammour, N., Bashmal, L., Bazi, Y., Al Rahhal, M. M., & Zuair, M. (2018). Asymmetric Adaptation of Deep Features for Cross-Domain Classification in Remote Sensing Imagery. *IEEE Geoscience and Remote Sensing Letters*, 15(4), 597–601. DOI: 10.1109/LGRS.2018.2800642

Bashmal, L., Bazi, Y., AlHichri, H., AlRahhal, M. M., Ammour, N., & Alajlan, N. (2018). Siamese-GAN: Learning Invariant Representations for Aerial Vehicle Image Categorization. *Remote Sensing (Basel)*, 10(2), 2. Advance online publication. DOI: 10.3390/rs10020351

Ben Youssef, B., Alhmidi, L., Bazi, Y., & Zuair, M. (2024). Federated Learning Approach for Remote Sensing Scene Classification. *Remote Sensing (Basel)*, 16(12), 2194. DOI: 10.3390/rs16122194

Chen, W., Ouyang, S., Tong, W., Li, X., Zheng, X., & Wang, L. (2022). GCSANet: A global context spatial attention deep learning network for remote sensing scene classification. *IEEE Journal of Selected Topics in Applied Earth Observations and Remote Sensing*, 15, 1150–1162. DOI: 10.1109/JSTARS.2022.3141826

Cheng, G., Han, J., & Lu, X. (2017). Remote sensing image scene classification: Benchmark and state of the art. *Proceedings of the IEEE*, 105(10), 1865–1883. DOI: 10.1109/JPROC.2017.2675998

Cheng, G., Xie, X., Han, J., Guo, L., & Xia, G.-S. (2020). Remote Sensing Image Scene Classification Meets Deep Learning: Challenges, Methods, Benchmarks, and Opportunities. *IEEE Journal of Selected Topics in Applied Earth Observations and Remote Sensing*, 13, 3735–3756. DOI: 10.1109/JSTARS.2020.3005403

Chi, M., Plaza, A., Benediktsson, J. A., Sun, Z., Shen, J., & Zhu, Y. (2016). Big Data for Remote Sensing: Challenges and Opportunities. *Proceedings of the IEEE*, 104(11), 2207–2219. DOI: 10.1109/JPROC.2016.2598228

Deng, J., Dong, W., Socher, R., Li, L.-J., Li, K., & Fei-Fei, L. (2009). Imagenet: A large-scale hierarchical image database. *2009 IEEE Conference on Computer Vision and Pattern Recognition*, 248–255. DOI: 10.1109/CVPR.2009.5206848

Elshamli, A., Taylor, G. W., & Areibi, S. (2019). Multisource domain adaptation for remote sensing using deep neural networks. *IEEE Transactions on Geoscience and Remote Sensing*, 58(5), 3328–3340. DOI: 10.1109/TGRS.2019.2953328

Farahani, A., Voghoei, S., Rasheed, K., & Arabnia, H. R. (2021). A brief review of domain adaptation. *Advances in Data Science and Information Engineering: Proceedings from ICDATA 2020 and IKE 2020*, 877–894.

Ganin, Y., & Lempitsky, V. (2015). Unsupervised domain adaptation by backpropagation. *Proceedings of the 32nd International Conference on International Conference on Machine Learning-* Volume 37, 1180–1189.

Gholamalinezhad, H., & Khosravi, H. (2020). *Pooling Methods in Deep Neural Networks, a Review* (arXiv:2009.07485). arXiv. https://doi.org//arXiv.2009.07485DOI: 10.48550

Gong, X., Xie, Z., Liu, Y., Shi, X., & Zheng, Z. (2018). Deep salient feature based anti-noise transfer network for scene classification of remote sensing imagery. *Remote Sensing (Basel)*, 10(3), 410. DOI: 10.3390/rs10030410

Guo, W., Li, S., Yang, J., Zhou, Z., Liu, Y., Lu, J., Kou, L., & Zhao, M. (2022). Remote Sensing Image Scene Classification by Multiple Granularity Semantic Learning. *IEEE Journal of Selected Topics in Applied Earth Observations and Remote Sensing*, 15, 2546–2562. DOI: 10.1109/JSTARS.2022.3158703

Hinton, G., Deng, L., Yu, D., Dahl, G. E., Mohamed, A., Jaitly, N., Senior, A., Vanhoucke, V., Nguyen, P., Sainath, T. N., & Kingsbury, B. (2012). Deep neural networks for acoustic modeling in speech recognition: The shared views of four research groups. *IEEE Signal Processing Magazine*, 29(6), 82–97. DOI: 10.1109/MSP.2012.2205597

Hinton, G., Vinyals, O., & Dean, J. (2015). Distilling the Knowledge in a Neural Network. *CiteArxiv:1503.02531Comment: NIPS 2014 Deep Learning Workshop.* https://arxiv.org/abs/1503.02531

Huang, H., & Xu, K. (2019). Combing triple-part features of convolutional neural networks for scene classification in remote sensing. *Remote Sensing (Basel)*, 11(14), 1687. DOI: 10.3390/rs11141687

Khelifi, L., & Mignotte, M. (2020). Deep learning for change detection in remote sensing images: Comprehensive review and meta-analysis. *IEEE Access : Practical Innovations, Open Solutions*, 8, 126385–126400. DOI: 10.1109/ACCESS.2020.3008036

Krizhevsky, A., Sutskever, I., & Hinton, G. E. (2017). Imagenet classification with deep convolutional neural networks. *Communications of the ACM*, 60(6), 84–90. DOI: 10.1145/3065386

Lasloum, T., Alhichri, H., Bazi, Y., & Alajlan, N. (2021). SSDAN: Multi-source semi-supervised domain adaptation network for remote sensing scene classification. *Remote Sensing (Basel)*, 13(19), 3861. DOI: 10.3390/rs13193861

LeCun, Y., Boser, B., Denker, J. S., Henderson, D., Howard, R. E., Hubbard, W., & Jackel, L. D. (1989). Backpropagation applied to handwritten zip code recognition. *Neural Computation*, 1(4), 541–551. DOI: 10.1162/neco.1989.1.4.541

Li, J., Li, G., Shi, Y., & Yu, Y. (2021). Cross-domain adaptive clustering for semi-supervised domain adaptation. *Proceedings of the IEEE/CVF Conference on Computer Vision and Pattern Recognition*, 2505–2514. DOI: 10.1109/CVPR46437.2021.00253

Meng, R., Chen, W., Yang, S., Song, J., Lin, L., Xie, D., Pu, S., Wang, X., Song, M., & Zhuang, Y. (2022). Slimmable domain adaptation. *Proceedings of the IEEE/CVF Conference on Computer Vision and Pattern Recognition*, 7141–7150.

Othman, E., Bazi, Y., Melgani, F., Alhichri, H., Alajlan, N., & Zuair, M. (2017). Domain Adaptation Network for Cross-Scene Classification. *IEEE Transactions on Geoscience and Remote Sensing*, 55(8), 4441–4456. DOI: 10.1109/TGRS.2017.2692281

Pires de Lima, R., & Marfurt, K. (2019). Convolutional neural network for remote-sensing scene classification: Transfer learning analysis. *Remote Sensing (Basel)*, 12(1), 86. DOI: 10.3390/rs12010086

Shen, J., Qu, Y., Zhang, W., & Yu, Y. (2018). Wasserstein distance guided representation learning for domain adaptation. *32nd AAAI Conference on Artificial Intelligence, AAAI 2018*, 4058–4065. DOI: 10.1609/aaai.v32i1.11784

Shen, J., Yu, T., Yang, H., Wang, R., & Wang, Q. (2022). An Attention Cascade Global–Local Network for Remote Sensing Scene Classification. *Remote Sensing (Basel)*, 14(9), 2042. DOI: 10.3390/rs14092042

Shi, C., Zhang, X., Sun, J., & Wang, L. (2022). Remote sensing scene image classification based on self-compensating convolution neural network. *Remote Sensing (Basel)*, 14(3), 545. DOI: 10.3390/rs14030545

Sultana, F., Sufian, A., & Dutta, P. (2018). Advancements in image classification using convolutional neural network. *2018 Fourth International Conference on Research in Computational Intelligence and Communication Networks (ICRCICN)*, 122–129. DOI: 10.1109/ICRCICN.2018.8718718

Tan, M., & Le, Q. (2019). EfficientNet: Rethinking Model Scaling for Convolutional Neural Networks. *International Conference on Machine Learning*, 6105–6114. http://proceedings.mlr.press/v97/tan19a.html

Tzeng, E., Hoffman, J., Saenko, K., & Darrell, T. (2017). Adversarial discriminative domain adaptation. *Proceedings of the IEEE Conference on Computer Vision and Pattern Recognition*, 7167–7176.

Wei, G., Li, G., Zhao, J., & He, A. (2019). Development of a LeNet-5 gas identification CNN structure for electronic noses. *Sensors (Basel)*, 19(1), 217. DOI: 10.3390/s19010217 PMID: 30626158

Xia, G.-S., Hu, J., Hu, F., Shi, B., Bai, X., Zhong, Y., Zhang, L., & Lu, X. (2017). AID: A Benchmark Data Set for Performance Evaluation of Aerial Scene Classification. *IEEE Transactions on Geoscience and Remote Sensing*, 55(7), 3965–3981. DOI: 10.1109/TGRS.2017.2685945

Yang, F., Ma, Z., & Xie, M. (2021). Image classification with superpixels and feature fusion method. *Journal of Electronic Science and Technology*, 19(1), 100096. DOI: 10.1016/j.jnlest.2021.100096

Yin, Y., Yang, Z., Hu, H., & Wu, X. (2022). Universal multi-Source domain adaptation for image classification. *Pattern Recognition*, 121, 108238. DOI: 10.1016/j.patcog.2021.108238

Zhang, A., Tay, Y., Zhang, S., Chan, A., Luu, A. T., Hui, S. C., & Fu, J. (2021). *Beyond Fully-Connected Layers with Quaternions: Parameterization of Hypercomplex Multiplications with $1/n$ Parameters* (arXiv:2102.08597). arXiv. https://doi.org//arXiv.2102.08597DOI: 10.48550

Zhang, J., Liu, J., Pan, B., & Shi, Z. (2020). Domain Adaptation Based on Correlation Subspace Dynamic Distribution Alignment for Remote Sensing Image Scene Classification. *IEEE Transactions on Geoscience and Remote Sensing*, 58(11), 7920–7930. DOI: 10.1109/TGRS.2020.2985072

Zhang, Y., & Davison, B. D. (2021). Deep spherical manifold gaussian kernel for unsupervised domain adaptation. *Proceedings of the IEEE/CVF Conference on Computer Vision and Pattern Recognition*, 4443–4452. DOI: 10.1109/CVPRW53098.2021.00501

Zhang, Z., Liu, S., Zhang, Y., & Chen, W. (2021). RS-DARTS: A convolutional neural architecture search for remote sensing image scene classification. *Remote Sensing (Basel)*, 14(1), 141. DOI: 10.3390/rs14010141

Zhou, W., Newsam, S., Li, C., & Shao, Z. (2018). PatternNet: A benchmark dataset for performance evaluation of remote sensing image retrieval. *ISPRS Journal of Photogrammetry and Remote Sensing*, 145, 197–209. DOI: 10.1016/j.isprsjprs.2018.01.004

ADDITIONAL READING

Alhichri, H., Alswayed, A. S., Bazi, Y., Ammour, N., & Alajlan, N. A. (2021). Classification of Remote Sensing Images Using EfficientNet-B3 CNN Model with Attention. *IEEE Access : Practical Innovations, Open Solutions*, 9, 14078–14094. DOI: 10.1109/ACCESS.2021.3051085

Chen, W.-Y., Liu, Y.-C., Kira, Z., Wang, Y.-C. F., & Huang, J.-B. (2019). A closer look at few-shot classification. ArXiv Preprint ArXiv:1904.04232.

Chicco, D., Warrens, M. J., & Jurman, G. (2021). The Matthews correlation coefficient (MCC) is more informative than Cohen's Kappa and Brier score in binary classification assessment. *IEEE Access : Practical Innovations, Open Solutions*, 9, 78368–78381. DOI: 10.1109/ACCESS.2021.3084050

Fan, R., Wang, L., Feng, R., & Zhu, Y. (2019). Attention based residual network for high-resolution remote sensing imagery scene classification. IGARSS 2019-2019 IEEE International Geoscience and Remote Sensing Symposium, 1346–1349. DOI: 10.1109/IGARSS.2019.8900199

Gómez-Chova, L., Tuia, D., Moser, G., & Camps-Valls, G. (2015). Multimodal classification of remote sensing images: A review and future directions. *Proceedings of the IEEE*, 103(9), 1560–1584. DOI: 10.1109/JPROC.2015.2449668

Lv, Z. Y., Shi, W., Zhang, X., & Benediktsson, J. A. (2018). Landslide inventory mapping from bitemporal high-resolution remote sensing images using change detection and multiscale segmentation. *IEEE Journal of Selected Topics in Applied Earth Observations and Remote Sensing*, 11(5), 1520–1532. DOI: 10.1109/JSTARS.2018.2803784

Sharma, N., Sharma, R., & Jindal, N. (2021). Machine learning and deep learning applications-a vision. *Global Transitions Proceedings*, 2(1), 24–28. DOI: 10.1016/j.gltp.2021.01.004

Wang, M., & Deng, W. (2018). Deep visual domain adaptation: A survey. *Neurocomputing*, 312, 135–153. DOI: 10.1016/j.neucom.2018.05.083

KEY TERMS AND DEFINITIONS

Convolutional Neural Networks (CNNs): They represent a type of artificial neural networks that are typically employed for image recognition and processing. CNNs are comprised of many layers. These layers include the input layer, the convolutional layers, the pooling layers, the fully connected layers, and the output layer. CNNs can be trained to extract features and perform classification tasks at the same time.

Dataset: A dataset is the information that is used as inputs to a machine learning model. It is a collection of data samples. Samples can be in the form of text, images, or audio.

Domain Adaptation (DA): This is a technique that enables a model trained on one domain, called the source domain, to perform well on another related but different domain, called the target domain. It involves transferring knowledge learned from the source domain to the target domain, typically when labeled data is scarce in the target domain. This helps improve model performance without requiring a large amount of labeled data from the target domain.

EfficientNet-B3: This is a convolutional neural network architecture that belongs to the EfficientNet family. The latter includes a baseline model, called EfficientNet-B0, and seven larger models known as EfficientNet-B1 to EfficientNet-B7. EfficientNet-B3 has 12 million weights and top-1 accuracy on the ImageNet dataset of 81.7%.

Entropy: The entropy is a metric in machine learning that measures unpredictability in the system. It is often used in the context of the **cross-entropy loss function**, which quantifies the difference between the predicted probability distribution and the actual distribution. Lower entropy indicates more confident and accurate predictions, while higher entropy suggests more uncertainty.

Kappa Coefficient: The Kappa coefficient measures the agreement between two classifiers that classify items into mutually exclusive categories. It ranges from -1 (complete disagreement) to 1 (perfect agreement), with 0 indicating no better agreement than random chance. In deep learning, it is often used to evaluate classification performance.

Overall Accuracy (OA): This is one metric for evaluating classification accuracy in machine learning models. It refers to the proportion of correct predictions made by the model out of all predictions. It is calculated by dividing the number of correct predictions by the total number of samples in the dataset.

Semi-Supervised Scene Classification: Semi-supervised learning is one of the techniques of machine learning that uses both labeled and unlabeled data.

Chapter 4
Fitness Activity Recognition Using Machine Learning Techniques

Mohamed Maher Ben Ismail
https://orcid.org/0000-0001-7770-5752
King Saud University, Saudi Arabia

Yasser Al-Ali
King Saud University, Saudi Arabia

Ouiem Bchir
King Saud University, Saudi Arabia

ABSTRACT

In today's world of technological advancement, smartphones have become akin to a cybernetic implant for most people. Those phones that we carry everywhere are capable of doing things from taking pictures to tracking the number of steps we take. Fitness activities can be recognized using the smartphone's inertial sensors. Moreover, machine learning can be exploited to design predictive or descriptive models able to discover and/or predict fitness activity patterns with better accuracy. As different fitness activities exhibit different patterns and characteristics, classifying them would allow the users to better track their performance, endurance and calories burned. This chapter introduces a ML-based system that can accurately recognize the user's fitness activity. Specifically, deep learning models were investigated to automatically map the signals captured by the sensors of the user's smart device into some pre-defined classes of fitness activities. The designed models were implemented, validated, and tested using standard benchmark datasets and appropriate performance measures.

INTRODUCTION

Fitness refers to someone's optimal health and overall well-being. Being fit does not only relate to physical health alone but mental health too as detailed in (What is Fitness?, 2019). Fitness can be achieved through a lot of means like eating healthy, exercising, and getting good rest. Whether be it gaining or

DOI: 10.4018/978-1-6684-3795-7.ch004

losing weight, both can be done with a healthy diet and doing more exercise, weight gain and loss are essentially your caloric intake vs caloric outtake. Health and fitness are intertwined and the importance of fitness to health is undeniable, measuring how fitness impacts health is quite a challenging task and not very intuitive. Throughout history humans always strived to accomplish their daily needs through simple means, this caused big leaps in the advancement of technology. Smartphones are now organ-like in the sense that if we forgot our smartphones it feels like a part of us is missing. The capabilities of smartphones nowadays are limitless from organizing our schedules, sending emails, to counting steps, and from that limitless capability, artificial intelligence became an essential part of smartphones.

Artificial intelligence can be defined as the ability of a machine to think like humans, leveraging a computer's hardware to mimic the problem-solving and decision-making capabilities of the human mind (IBM, 2020). When it became more integrated in-to societies, a lot of tasks that seemed impossible using traditional programming paradigms are now a breeze to solve, such as natural language processing, autonomous driving, image recognition, and much more.

Machine learning can be introduced as an artificial intelligence sub-field that uses algorithms and statistical models to learn from data and make predictions without any human interference. It can use the data gathered from a smartphone's inertial sensors to recognize what fitness activity the user is currently doing, such as running, walking, or cycling. Each fitness activity has its own unique traits recognizing that activity by using these traits allows the machine learning algorithm to make ac-curate predictions that can accurately explain the impact of fitness on health. By using state-of-the-art machine learning algorithms, the problematic nature of fitness activity recognition may be accurately recorded and measured.

Nowadays, staying healthy and fit is a difficult task due to an enormous number of reasons, and the lack of fitness activity can lead to many health issues, one of which is obesity. The World Health Organization (WHO) reports that 1.4 billion adults worldwide are obese, and the Saudi ministry of health reports that 28.7% of adults are obese (MOH, 2020). This is a huge cause for concern since the consequences of obesity are dangerous and serious like type 2 diabetes, strokes and all-causes of death (CDCP, 2021). Other health issues that can be the result of lack of fitness are heart conditions. The heart is a vital organ for human health, and aerobic exercise can drastically improve heart health. The American Heart Association recommends a minimum of 30 minutes of cardiovascular exercise such as running, five to seven days per week (Cleveland clinic, 2019).

One should note that applications that can track user activity such as steps taken and distance walked are available. However, none can accurately classify the activity of a user such as running or cycling. With the ability to correctly classify user activity we can more accurately measure calories burned, allowing us to better monitor our health. Fitness classification is an area that's sorely missing in today's world, and machine learning is the most optimal solution for such a task. Creating a machine learning model with high accuracy will allow us to more accurately classify fitness activity and measure calories burned.

The main goal of this work is the design of a machine learning based system that can accurately recognize the user's fitness activity. Specifically, deep learning models will be investigated to automatically map the signals captured by the sensors of the user's smart device into some pre-defined classes of fitness activities such as running, cycling and speed walking.

The objectives of this research can be summarized as follows:

- Increasing the awareness about the benefits of fitness through, if possible, integration of the model into some device or application.
- Making people healthier by tracking their performance measures intuitively.

- Accurately recognizing the user's current activity by using a fitting machine learning model.
- Encouraging consistent workouts and motivating users by showing them the accurate progress they have made with a good machine learning model.
- Helping the integration of Artificial Intelligence in everyday use by starting with things such as fitness activities.

RELATED WORK

In this section, we survey the most prevalent studies relevant to fitness activity recognition.

Activity Recognition using Smartphones

(Xing et al., 2014) proposed a process for activity recognition. The sensors would stream both the training and testing data then the classification model processes the collected data in order to recognize the user's activity. A research on activity recognition was outlined by (Voicu et al., 2019). Specifically, it aimed at recognizing the activity of older people. In particular, the goal was to use activity recognition to recognize if something abnormal is occurring and recommend exercise when necessary, to make living at home even safer. The researchers used two datasets; The first one was collected during the study by five participants using Androids data collection application. Note hat three smartphone sensors were used in order to record the data. Namely, the accelerometer, gyroscope, and gravity sensors were used for the data collection. The android application recorded hundreds of reading in 0.5ms intervals and 10s segments. The second dataset was recorded in a previous study using four sensors; gyroscope, gravity sensor, linear acceleration, and magnetometer sensors (Shoaib et al., 2014). Using these datasets, the researchers used a multi-layer perceptron to make a classification model for six different activities. Specifically, the considered activities were running, sitting, standing, walking upstairs, and walking downstairs. The experiments results were deployed using an android application.

The researchers found the first dataset to be significantly more accurate than the second. This can be attributed to the difference in the sensors used. In particular, the activities involving stairs were not classified accurately enough, only achieving 75% accuracy in the best-case scenario. This may be explained by the fact that the 10s segments in which the data was recorded added noise to the activities involving stairs and that lasted less than 10s. Other activities were much more accurate, all achieving an accuracy above 90% for the first dataset. For instance, walking instances were classified with an accuracy of 93% while running records classification yielded an accuracy of 91%. The researchers concluded that activity recognition is viable, but the activity recognition on a smartphone limited the machine learning model they were able to produce. Besides, the use of a remote server to process the data was considered in order to create a more accurate and powerful model.

(Kwapisz et al., 2021) stated that cell phones contain many sensors including the accelerometer. They labeled accelerometer data was collected by twenty-nine users as they performed daily activities. The time series data was also aggregated into examples that summarize the user activity over 10-second intervals. One should note that the data collected by the researches was monitored using an application that controls which sensor to be used, the accelerometer in this case. In addition, three ML techniques, namely J48 decision trees, logistic regression, and multilayer neural networks were investigated by (Kwapisz et al., 2021). The reported results demonstrated that for walking, the logistic regression yielded the highest accuracy of 93.6%. For jogging, the neural networks achieved the highest accuracy of 98.3%. In conclusion, the activity recognition task can be conducted with an accuracy exceeding 90% using a simple cell phone and conventional ML techniques/algorithms.

Similarly, (Sefen et al., 2016) investigated Human Activity Recognition using sensor data of smartphones and smartwatches, with machine learning algorithms. In particular, they proposed a platform to combine sensors of smartphones and smartwatches, to recognize human activity in real time. Several evaluations were carried out to determine which classification algorithm and features should be used to achieve the best tradeoff between recognition accuracy and the system's computational complexity. For data collection, they collected multivariate time series data from the smartphones and smartwatches sensors. The researchers mentioned that sampling frequency impacts the system resources, lowering it could reduce the number of operations and computation done in feature extraction stage, and decrease the memory usage of the system (Sefen et al., 2016). Therefore, in their experiment sensors were sampled at 30 Hz to collect data sets, from 16 participants that wore the smartwatch in the left hand and the smartphone placed in the front right pocket. Several daily and fitness activities were selected, including walking, running, rope jumping, pushups, crunches, and squats. Each activity was recorded multiple times. After data collection, Preprocessing, Feature Extraction, and Standardization were used.

The classification algorithms that were evaluated in their work, are: Support Vector Machine: linear and polynomial kernels, One-Vs-All method, Decision Tree (Gini index as a split criteria), Naive Bayes, Discriminant Analysis: linear and quadratic, and K-Nearest Neighbors.

The researchers concluded that there is no obvious winner based on the findings. However, naïve Bayes performed best in their experiment in both the classification accuracy and efficiency. Overall classification accuracy lied between 84.6% and 89.4% where performance differences are negligible. Also, researchers proved that adding smartwatches' sensor data to the recognition system improves the accuracy. Particularly, the naïve Bayes classifier yielded average accuracies of 82.1% and 89.4% without using smartwatch's sensor and using smartwatch and smartphone sensors, respectively.

Activity Recognition using Smartwatches

(Saeedi, et al. 2022) addressed the human activity recognition that is challenging due to the large variability and heterogeneity of data. In particular, supervised machine learning algorithms form the core intelligence of embedded software in such wearable systems. However, they proved to be limited due to the challenging nature of human activity. Moreover, changing the system's structure by adding new sensors would harm the performance of the algorithm. The authors proved that deep learning can address these challenges and handle efficiently the complexity of human activity recognition. The rationale behind this is that deep learning can uncover features tied to the dynamics of human movement. Moreover, the complexity of deep neural networks can help mitigate the effects of variations in the data such as walking with different paces. Furthermore, the softmax layer can be used to measure the confidence of the prediction.

(Chawla et al., 2016) stated that an activity recognition model can be used for several reasons, such as medicine and sport. They evaluated four machine learning algorithms, including; K Nearest Neighbor, SVM, Neural Networks, Classification and Regression Tree (CART). Their research relied on four steps; (i) Data collection, (ii) Feature extraction from the raw data, (iii) Features selection using a correlation based subset filter, and (iv) Machine learning algorithms investigation. The prototype consisted of a 3 axis sensor and a Bluetooth module. In the data collection process, the users wore the sensor in their non-dominant hand and sent the data to a smartphone via Bluetooth. Afterwards, necessary preprocessing steps were taken, such as feature extraction. The evaluated models scored impressive accuracies where none of them scored below 90%. KNN scored an average of 96.16%, CART scored an average of 95.31%, Neural Networks scored an average of 96.77%, and SVM scored an average of 94.4%. Neural Networks are the obvious winner here, however, they are all close to each other. The author(s) then concluded the research by stating that with proper hardware it is possible to implement a reliable and accurate human activity recognition system.

Deep Learning VS. Standard Machine Learning

(Gjoreski et al., 2016) compared deep learning and classical machine learning methods for human activity recognition. In their research, they stated that recognition of daily activities can potentially lead to proper management of preventable diseases such as obesity. They measured activities using wrist accelerometers. Nowadays most smartphones contain built-in accelerometers, which can be utilized for activity recognition. They compared deep learning methods, mainly convolutional neural networks (CNNs) and standard machine learning methods on two different datasets. The first dataset is a laboratory recorded dataset, and the other dataset is the Opportunity dataset, which is a commonly used benchmark dataset for activity recognition. For the first dataset, they used a six-layer CNN with max pooling. The first three layers are convolution-pooling layers followed by two fully connected layers, the last layer consists of SoftMax regression to capture the probability of the input window belonging to a possible class. On the other hand, for the classical machine learning methods, they tested five algorithms (j48 decision tree, Random Forest, Naïve Bayes, SVM, and KNN) with standard classification pipeline; data segmentation, data filtering, feature extraction, feature selection and building a classification model. Cross-validation was also used in the training process, which means the model was trained on the whole dataset except for one person and tested on the remaining people. This process was repeated on the whole dataset. The accuracies of both approaches on the first datasets were very similar. For the classical approach, the Random Forest scored the highest accuracy with 74.5% while CNNs achieved an average accuracy of 76%. Both approaches were close, however, deep learning has the power of automatically extracting relevant features and to achieve slightly better performance.

For the Opportunity dataset, the analysis was done for both wrists, left and right. The result shows that the left sensor placement achieved better accuracy compared to the right one for both methods. Moreover, CNN achieved higher accuracy for all test subjects for the left wrist, but the standard machine learning approach had better accuracy on the right wrist.

In conclusion, both approaches had similar results on the first dataset, and on the second dataset, CNNs performed better on the left wrist, while standard machine learning performed better on the right wrist. This shows that deep learning (CNNs in this case) has better performance than standard machine learning, however, it requires a large amount of data in order to learn.

Discussion

Based on all related works outlined above, one can see that the most challenging aspect was data gathering and data manipulation. If the sensors used to gather the data differed, it could negatively affect the final model. While on the other hand, some datasets require extensive preprocessing and cross-validation

(Gjoreski et al., 2016). Due to the natural difference in how people exercise, the data captured would have minor difference on certain features that could affect the model's accuracy.

The activity recognition can be done using smartphones and smartwatches. However, one research concluded that if a smartwatch's sensor works together with a smartphone's sensors, the model accuracy would increase (Sefen, 2016). Smartphones were limiting in terms of processing power to the overall Machine Learning model.

The choice of algorithm was competitive in most cases. A lot of machine learning models scored accuracies of over 90%. However, Neural Networks took the lead in terms of accuracy. One downside of using Neural Networks is that they require a large dataset to train, and that can be challenging (Gjoreski et al., 2016). Ultimately, the approach should be deep learning methods as they score better accuracies.

In conclusion, the surveyed related works demonstrated the importance of activity recognition in real-world scenarios. It can be helpful in medicine and in fitness. The most challenging aspect in fitness activity recognition would be data gathering. All related works showed that the deep learning approach had better performance than other approaches, however, deep learning requires large datasets.

PROPOSED ML-BASED FITNESS ACTIVITY RECOGNITION

The investigated related work showed the capabilities of different machine learning models to recognize fitness activity. As it can be noticed, the performance of such state-of-the-art systems depends considerably on the machine learning technique considered to model the fitness activity features and map into a set of pre-defined set of classes. In particular, the highest accuracy was achieved by related works that adapted deep learning techniques. However, as reported by (Gjoreski et al., 2016), the difference in accuracy between deep learning and shallow learning is not great and both can be used for an accurate classification. In this project, two models will be investigated to address the considered classification problem. Then, the most accurate model will be adopted for the proposed fitness activity classification system. Specifically, we intend to use CNN based architectures and typical multi-layer perceptron as baseline classification techniques. Figure 1 depicts the proposed system with its flow. We begin by processing the dataset, then choose the appropriate hyperparameters for the model. The model is then trained on the data and tested to compare with our previous models.

Figure 1. Proposed system

As one can see, the user will start an activity, then the sensor data will be sent to be preprocessed before it is sent to the model and classified. This allows us to see the model's real world performance.

CNN vs. Multi-Layer Perceptron

Multilayer perceptron is a feed forward neural network often referred to as the vanilla neural network. It has 3 or more fully connected layers where each node in one layer connects to every node in the next layer. Great results were achieved using a MLP that consists of 3 layers: an input layer, a hidden layer, and an output layer. In fact, convolutional neural networks are a more advanced type of neural network that add 2 types of layers, convolutional and pooling layers. The convolutional layer applies a filter to a part of the input features and the dot product is computed between the features and the filter. This gives different weights to different parts of the input. The pooling layer performs dimensionality reduction on the input by finding the max value or the average value in different parts of the input. In (Gjoreski et al., 2016), great results were achieved with a 6 layered CNN. Three convolutional-pooling layers followed by two fully connected layers and an output layer of SoftMax regression.

One should note that both neural networks often use an input layer with nodes equal to the number of features in the dataset, and an output layer with nodes equal to the number of classes in the dataset. The activation function most commonly used in the output layer for multiclass classification is SoftMax, as it gives the input a score for each class between 0 and 1, where the highest score is chosen as the final classification. Though CNN is a more advance version of MLP its performance depends heavily on the type of data received. Given that both models achieved great results in human activity recognition, we believe they are both viable for fitness recognition and further testing is required to identify the better algorithm for our task.

EXPERIMENTS

In this research experiments, two datasets were considered to validate and assess the proposed fitness activity recognition models. In fact, when recognizing fitness activity, one could use special motion sensors that can be attached to various body parts. Those sensors would increase the cost of the system and force the user to wear them on their body. In particular, the first dataset (Kaggle, 2022) relies on built-in sensors found in average quality smartphones. The data was collected in a one-hour period for each activity to achieve an even distribution of data. The dataset contains several files; each file represents an activity. In addition, the collections were aggregated into one large dataset containing relevant activities. Accordingly, the chosen activities are cycling, jogging, walking, swimming, jump ropes, pushups, tennis, and football.

On the other hand, the second dataset (Shoaib et al., 2022) also utilizes the built-in sensors in the average smartphone. The dataset was created using 10 participants with smartphones attached to multiple places on their body. The smartphones were placed in their right and left pockets and on their wrist, upper arm, and belt. The relevant classes to our model in this dataset are walking, jogging, and cycling.

Both datasets were split into two parts; the first one consists of 80% of the instances for training, the second part dedicates 20% of the records for testing. One should mention that both datasets include similar activities. Besides, standard performance metrics were used to assess the considered machine learning models. Namely, we used the F1-score, precision, recall, and accuracy.

The accuracy is obtained using:

$$Accuracy = \frac{\sum TP + TN}{\sum TP + TN + FP + FN} \qquad (1)$$

where *TP*, *TN*, *FP* and *FN* represent the true positive, true negative, false positive, and false negative cases, respectively.

On the other hand, the precision is obtained as follows:

$$Precision = \frac{\sum True\ Positive}{\sum True\ Positive + False\ Positive} \qquad (2)$$

Also, the recall is calculated as follows:

$$Recall = \frac{\sum True\ Positive}{\sum True\ Positive + False\ Negative} \qquad (3)$$

Finally, the F1-score measure is expressed using:

$$F1 = \frac{2*(precision*recall)}{(precision + recall)} \qquad (4)$$

The proposed solution as well as the considered machine learning models were implemented using Python3 (Python, 2019) and TensorFlow (Tensorflow, 2019). The code was written using Jupyter Notebooks. In order to assess the performance of the two mentioned algorithms, all testing was conducted using Google Collab (Google Colaboratory, 2019).

The two neural networks considered for this research were designed implemented and experimented on fitness activity recognition Kaggle dataset (Kaggle, 2022). Data handling, preparation and preprocessing were achieved on Pandas and NumPy. Particularly, both models were deployed with 100 epochs. In order to avoid overfitting and improve the model generalization capability, we investigated several hyper-parameters settings. The obtained results are reported in the Table 1.

Table 1. Results obtained using MLP with different hyperparameters settings

Experiment	Accuracy	Precision	Recall	F1-score
Baseline	88.63%	89.26%	88.22%	88.68%
L1 Kernel Regularization	87.46%	89.75%	85.25%	86.87%
L2 Kernel Regularization	89.57%	91.23%	88.18%	89.41%
Dropout layer	89.67%	91.53%	87.91%	89.36%
Heavy Model (Extra layers)	87.99%	88.42%	87.63%	87.87%
Learning rate decay	88.63%	89.26%	88.22%	88.68%
Oversampling	86.66%	87.07%	86.40%	86.86%
Final Model	90.76%	91.62%	89.84%	90.60%

As it can be seen, Table 1 shows the experiments done on our MLP model, with the baseline being a model with an input layer, 2 hidden layers, and an output layer. Notice that L2 regularization is better than L1 across all metrics. We can also see that adding more layers to the model did not increase performance, however, adding a dropout layer slightly increased performance. Moreover, learning rate decay had little to no effect on the model's performance, and oversampling decreased performance as the imbalance in the dataset was too great. Our final model was created by a combination of L2 regularization, dropout layer, and 2 layers more than the baseline.

Table 2. Final MLP model classification report

Class	Precision	Recall	F1
Cycling	94%	92%	93%
Football	94%	94%	94%
Jogging	62%	46%	53%
Jumping Rope	85%	82%	84%
Pushups	79%	56%	65%
Swimming	92%	91%	92%
Walking	83%	84%	84%

Table 2 shows the classification report of the final model on each class in the dataset. Notice that the cycling and football classes had the best results across all metrics whereas jogging and push ups had the worst results. The difference in the results between all classes comes from the number of examples the model was trained on. Cycling and football had the highest number of examples, 13,015 examples to be precise while the rest of the classes had a combined total of 6,434 examples. Figure 2 shows the training progression of the final MLP model with performance measures on every epoch. Notice that after 40 epochs there are diminishing returns on the model's performance. We can also notice that after 80 epochs the progress stabilizes, and more epochs could cause the model to overfit.

Table 3. Results obtained using CNN model

Experiment	Accuracy	Precision	Recall	F1 Score
Baseline	89.61%	90.73%	88.47%	89.36%
L1 Kernel Regularization	89.26%	90.53%	88.18%	89.07%
L2 Kernel Regularization	89.08%	90.40%	88.18%	89.11%
Dropout layer	89.18%	91.27%	86.93%	88.60%
Heavy Model (Extra layers)	88.90%	89.24%	88.55%	88.83%
Learning rate decay	88.67%	90.24%	87.67%	88.74%
Oversampling	85.23%	85.72%	84.86%	85.94
Final Model	89.78%	91.49%	88.16%	89.55%

.Table 3 shows all the experiments done on the CNN algorithm, with the baseline being a model with an input layer, convolutional layer, maxpooling layer, one hidden layer, and an output layer. Notice that L1 and L2 regularization had similar results, L1 was slightly better for accuracy and precision while L2 was slightly better in F1 score. As opposed to MLP, we can see that for CNN adding extra layers improved recall and F1 scores. Similar to MLP, learning rate decay had little to no effect on the model's performance, and oversampling decreased the performance. The final model was a combination of L2 regularization, dropout layer, and one hidden layer more than the baseline.

Table 4. Final classification results achieved using CNN model

Class	Precision	Recall	F1
Cycling	94%	90%	92%
Football	92%	94%	93%
Jogging	88%	43%	57%
Jumping Rope	93%	75%	83%
Pushups	73%	53%	62%
Swimming	90%	92%	91%
Walking	80%	77%	79%

Table 4 shows the classification report on the final CNN model on each class. Comparing to the MLP classification report, notice that MLP performed slightly better across all classes in the dataset.

Figure 2. Training loss and performance metrics obtained using CNN model

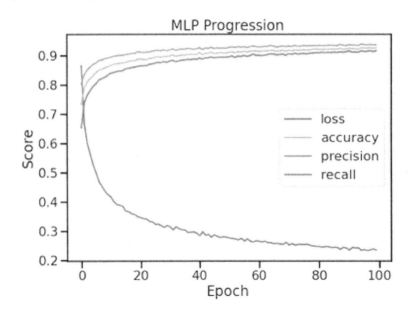

Figure 3 shows the training progression of the final CNN model with performance measures on every epoch. Similar to the MLP's progression, we can notice that after 40 epochs there are diminishing returns. After 50 epochs the performance slightly decreases then increases again after 60 epochs. After determining the optimal model, we investigated various values for the model hyperparameters. This was intended to enhance its overall performance. Figure 4 reports the results obtained using different hyperparameters settings.

Figure 3. MLP Hyperparameter Tuning Results

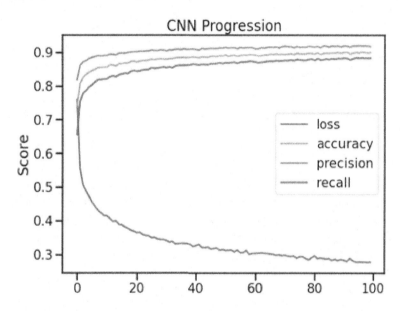

Figure 5 shows all the hyperparameter tuning techniques that we investigated for the considered MLP model. As it can be noticed the ReLu activation function yielded the best results. On the other hand, the batch size had little impact on the model performance. Figure 6 shows all the hyperparameter tuning techniques associated with the proposed CNN model. Similarly, to the MLP hyperparameter tuning, the ReLu activation function had the best result., and batch size had little impact.

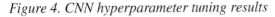

Figure 4. CNN hyperparameter tuning results

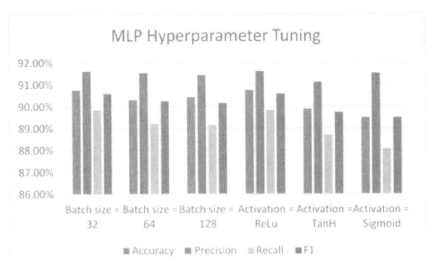

To make the datasets compatible, we trained the final model on the Kaggle dataset (Kaggle, 2022) by dropping 3 features: gravity X, gravity Y, and gravity Z, instead of data imputation techniques. We then used this trained model to predict examples from the Research Gate dataset. Table 5 reports the results obtained using our novel generalized MLP model.

Table 5. Results achieved using the proposed Generalized MLP model

Experiment	Accuracy	Precision	Recall	F1 Score
Testing on Kaggle	87.42%	89.61%	85.70%	87.33%
Testing on Research Gate	52.82%	57.14%	49.55%	56.53%

Similarly, we improved the generalization capability of our CNN model. Table 6 depicts the obtained results.

Table 6. Results achieved using the proposed Generalized CNN model

Experiment	Accuracy	Precision	Recall	F1 Score
Testing on Kaggle	86.97%	89.88%	84.39%	86.64%
Testing on Research Gate	53.87%	60.74%	49.58%	55.10%

As it can be seen, Table 5 and Table 6 show the generalization capabilities of both; MLP and CNN models. Due to the wide distribution of the datasets, we believe that in order to produce a general model, a much larger dataset would be required. It is also possible to make a specific model for every different device, however, that would be impractical. For both MLP and CNN, one can also notice the improved generalization for cycling as it exhibits a larger number of training examples. On the other hand, the model performance was affected for the walking and jogging classes as they enclose less examples.

In order to demonstrate further the improvements achieved by the proposed models, we merged the two considered datasets. Table 7 and Table 8 show the classification report obtained using the MLP and CNN models, respectively.

Table 7. Merged datasets MLP classification report

Class	Precision	Recall	F1
Cycling	97%	95%	96%
Football	94%	86%	89%
Jogging	98%	94%	96%
Jumping Rope	83%	63%	72%
Pushups	82%	43%	57%
Swimming	86%	93%	89%
Walking	95%	94%	94%

Table 8. Merged datasets CNN classification report

Class	Precision	Recall	F1
Cycling	96%	95%	95%
Football	93%	86%	89%
Jogging	97%	92%	95%
Jumping Rope	90%	58%	70%
Pushups	81%	40%	54%
Swimming	88%	91%	90%
Walking	93%	95%	94%

As it can be seen, when training on a larger dataset, such as the merged datasets, the models performance improved substantially. Compared to Table 2 and Table 4, one can see that cycling performance improved slightly and the performance of the model on walking and jogging improved substantially, whereas the performance of the model decreased on other labels. Table 9 also confirms that due to the increase in the imbalance of the dataset, the model had a stronger bias towards the more frequent classes in the dataset.

Table 9. Merged datasets overall performance

Experiment	Accuracy	Precision	Recall	F1 Score
MLP	92.35%	94.58%	90.47%	92.30%
CNN	91.69%	93.95%	90.14%	91.71%

CONCLUSION AND FUTURE RESEARCH DIRECTIONS

Fitness describes health, and for someone to achieve a fit body they must go through a vigorous process of working out, dieting well and being consistent. How far to-day's technology has gone is unfathomable, and smartphones are now capable of capturing photos, streaming TV shows, connecting with family and friends regard-less of distance and most relevant is its computational ability and sensors. Using these two features the smartphone can recognize what fitness activity the user is currently doing with great accuracy and a lot of details. The use of machine learning can allow us to achieve such accuracy by building predictive models that are able to understand the current state of the user and predict the activity.

In this research, we investigated different ML techniques to recognize fitness activities, such as supervised machine learning, unsupervised machine learning and deep learning. The conducted experiments demonstrated that the MLP model outperformed slightly CNN model in the considered activity recognition task. One should also conclude that with a large enough dataset, a conventional ML model can classify with a promising accuracy different fitness activities using smartphone sensors.

REFERENCES

CDCP. (2021), "Adult Obesity Causes & Consequenc-es," Centers for Disease control and prevention, Mar. 22, 2021. https://www.cdc.gov/obesity/adult/causes.html

Chawla J and M. Wagner, (2016), "Using Machine Learning Techniques for User Specific Ac-tivity Recognition," Frankfurt University of Applied Science, May 2016, Accessed: Mar. 28, 2022. [Online].

Cleveland clinic. (2019), "Aerobic Exercise Health Information | Cleveland Clinic," Cleveland Clinic, Jul. 16, 2019. https://my.clevelandclinic.org/health/articles/7050-aerobic-exercise

Gjoreski, H., Bizjak, J., Gjoreski, M., & Gams, M. (2016), "Comparing Deep and Classical Ma-chine Learning Methods for Human Activity Recognition using Wrist Accelerometer," Jozef Stefan International Postgraduate School, Jan. 2016.

"Google Colaboratory", (2019), Google.com. https://colab.research.google.com/

IBM Cloud Education. (2020), "What is artificial intelligence (AI)?" IBM, Jun. 03, 2020. https://www.ibm.com/cloud/learn/what-is-artificial-intelligence

Kaggle (2022), "Inertia Sensors for Human Activity Recognition", www.kaggle.com. https://www.kaggle.com/datasets/owenagius/inertia-sensors-for-human-activity-recognition (accessed May 08, 2022).

Kwapisz, J. R., Weiss, G. M., & Moore, S. A. (2021, March). Activity recognition using cell phone accelerometers. *SIGKDD Explorations*, 12(2), 74–82. DOI: 10.1145/1964897.1964918

MOH. (2020). www.moh.gov.sa. https://www.moh.gov.sa/Ministry/About/Health (accessed Mar. 22, 2022).

Python (2019), "Welcome to Python.org," Python.org, May 29, 2019. https://www.python.org/

Saeedi, R., S. Norgaard, and A. Gebremedhin, (2022), "A Closed-loop Deep Learning Architec-ture for Robust Activity Recognition using Wearable Sensors." Accessed: Mar. 28, 2022.

Sefen, B., Baumbach, S., Dengel, A., & Abdennadher, S. (2016), "Human Activity Recognition - Using Sensor Data of Smartphones and Smartwatches," *Proceedings of the 8th International Conference on Agents and Artificial Intelligence*, 2016, DOI: 10.5220/0005816004880493

Shoaib, M., Bosch, S., Incel, O., Scholten, H., & Havinga, P. (2014, June). Fusion of Smartphone Motion Sensors for Physical Activity Recognition. *Sensors (Basel)*, 14(6), 10146–10176. DOI: 10.3390/s140610146 PMID: 24919015

Shoaib, M., Bosch, S., Incel, O. D., Scholten, H., & Havinga, P. J. (2022). Fusion of smartphone motion sensors for physical activity recognition. *Sensors (Basel)*, 14(6), 10146–10176. DOI: 10.3390/s140610146 PMID: 24919015

Su, X., Tong, H., & Ji, P. (2014, June). Activity recognition with smartphone sensors. *Tsinghua Science and Technology*, 19(3), 235–249. DOI: 10.1109/TST.2014.6838194

TensorFlow. (2019), "TensorFlow," TensorFlow, 2019. https://www.tensorflow.org/

Voicu, R.-A., Dobre, C., Bajenaru, L., & Ciobanu, R.-I. (2019, January). Human Physical Activity Recognition Using Smartphone Sensors. *Sensors (Basel)*, 19(3), 458. DOI: 10.3390/s19030458 PMID: 30678039

"What is fitness? (2019) I Fitness," Sharecare. https://www.sharecare.com/health/fitness-exercise/what -is-fitness

ADDITIONAL READING

Baldominos, , Cervantes, A., Saez, Y., & Isasi, P. (2019). A Comparison of Machine Learning and Deep Learning Techniques for Activity Recognition using Mobile Devices. *Sensors (Basel)*, 19(3), 521. DOI: 10.3390/s19030521 PMID: 30691177

Bulling, A., Blanke, U., & Schiele, B. (2014). A tutorial on human activity recognition using body-worn inertial sensors. *ACM Computing Surveys*, 46(3), 1–33. DOI: 10.1145/2499621

Kulsoom, F., Narejo, S., Mehmood, Z., Chaudhry, H. N., Butt, A., & Bashir, A. K. (2022). A Review of Machine Learning-Based Human Activity Recognition for Diverse Applications. *Neural Computing & Applications*, 34(19), 18289–18324. DOI: 10.1007/s00521-022-07665-9

Li, F., Shirahama, K., Nisar, M. A., Köping, L., & Grzegorzek, M. (2018). Comparison of feature learning methods for human activity recognition using wearable aensors. *Sensors (Basel)*, 18(2), 679. DOI: 10.3390/s18020679 PMID: 29495310

Lin, L., Wu, J., An, R., Ma, S., Zhao, K., & Ding, H. (2024). LIMUNet: A Lightweight Neural Network for Human Activity Recognition Using Smartwatches. *Applied Sciences (Basel, Switzerland)*, 14(22), 10515. DOI: 10.3390/app142210515

Saez, Y., Baldominos, A., & Isasi, P. (2017). A comparison study of classifier algorithms for cross-person physical activity recognition. *Sensors (Basel)*, 17(1), 66. DOI: 10.3390/s17010066 PMID: 28042838

Zhang, S., Li, Y., Zhang, S., Shahabi, F., Xia, S., Deng, Y., & Alshurafa, N. (2022). Deep Learning in Human Activity Recognition with Wearable Sensors: A Review on Advances. *Sensors (Basel)*, 22(4), 1476. DOI: 10.3390/s22041476 PMID: 35214377

Zhao, J., Deng, F., He, H., & Chen, J. (2020). Local domain adaptation for cross-domain activity recognition. *IEEE Transactions on Human-Machine Systems*, 51(1), 12–21. DOI: 10.1109/THMS.2020.3039196

Zhou, B., Yang, J., & Li, Q. (2019). Smartphone-Based Activity Recognition for Indoor Localization Using a Convolutional Neural Network. *Sensors (Basel)*, 19(3), 621. DOI: 10.3390/s19030621 PMID: 30717199

KEY TERMS AND DEFINITIONS

Classification Accuracy: It is a metric used to evaluate the performance of a classification model. It is defined as the ratio of the number of correct predictions to the total number of predictions made. It measures how often the classifier is correct. While accuracy is a useful metric, it may not always be the best measure of performance, especially in cases where the data is imbalanced (i.e., when one class is much more frequent than the others). In such cases, other metrics like precision, recall, and F1-score might provide a more comprehensive evaluation of the model's performance.

Confusion Matrix: A confusion matrix is a table, used in machine learning, specifically for classification tasks. It provides a clear visualization of how well a model performs at distinguishing between different categories or classes. By analyzing the confusion matrix, the user can obtain correct predictions, known as true positives and true negatives, when reading the diagonal entries while incorrect predictions appear outside it. The latter are summarized by false positives and false negatives.

Convolutional Neural Network: It is a type of deep learning algorithm that is particularly effective for tasks involving image and video recognition. The convolutional layers apply a convolution operation to the input, passing the result to the next layer. This helps in detecting features such as edges, textures, and patterns in images. The pooling layers reduce the spatial dimensions of the data, which helps in reducing the computational load and controlling overfitting. The fully connected layers are typically placed after several convolutional and pooling layers. The network usually ends with one or more fully connected layers that output the final classification or prediction. CNNs are widely used in various applications, including image classification, object detection, and even natural language processing tasks. They have been instrumental in advancing the field of computer vision.

Deep Learning (DL): DL is a subfield of machine learning inspired by the brain's structure and function. It utilizes artificial neural networks with multiple layers to process information and extract intricate patterns. These layered networks can learn from vast amounts of data, allowing them to tackle a multitude of tasks like image recognition, speech translation, and natural language processing. DL models achieve high accuracy by iteratively refining the connections between their layers based on the data they are trained on.

Fitness Activity: Refers to any physical exercise or movement that is performed to improve or maintain physical health and well-being. This can include a wide range of activities such as: (i) Cardiovascular exercises: Running, cycling, swimming, and aerobics. (ii) Strength training: Weightlifting, resistance band exercises, and bodyweight exercises like push-ups and squats. (iii) Flexibility exercises: Yoga, stretching, and Pilates. (iv) Balance exercises: Tai chi, balance drills, and certain types of yoga. Typically, these activities help in enhancing cardiovascular health, building muscle strength, improving flexibility, and maintaining overall physical fitness.

Hyperparameter: In ML, a hyperparameter is a setting that the user defines before training that controls the learning process itself, not the model itself. Unlike regular parameters that the model learns from data, hyperparameters are set manually and influence how the model learns. Examples include the learning rate, the optimizer, or the number of layers in a neural network.

Machine Learning (ML): ML is a subfield of artificial intelligence that equips computers to learn without explicit programming. It involves algorithms that can analyze data, identify patterns, and make predictions. Over time, these algorithms can improve their performance, essentially enabling machines to learn and act like humans while being able to process massive amounts of information.

YOLO: "You Only Look Once" is a state-of-the-art, real-time object detection system that is widely used in computer vision tasks. It processes images in real-time, making it highly efficient for applications that require quick detection. Unlike other object detection systems that apply the model to an image at multiple locations and scales, YOLO applies a single neural network to the full image. YOLO divides the image into a grid and predicts bounding boxes and probabilities for each region, which helps in identifying and localizing objects within the image.

Chapter 5
Pruning and Neural Architectures Redesigning for Deep Neural Networks Compression in Mobiles:
A Review

Ibtihal Ferwana

University of Illinios at Urbana-Champaign, USA

Soumaya Chaffar

University of Prince Mugrin, Saudi Arabia

Samir Brahim Belhaouari

Hamad Bin Khalifa University, Qatar

ABSTRACT

Mobile applications have been ubiquitous in our daily life. Given the success of Deep Neural Networks (DNNs) in image recognition tasks, DNNs are widely implemented on mobile phone applications. Due to the limited memory and energy on mobile phones, DNNs size and execution time are still roadblocks for efficient processing and instant inferences. Many transformative efforts were able to compress DNNs to the desired size for efficient speed, energy, and memory consumption. In this chapter, two areas of compression: pruning and redesigning efficient neural architectures were discussed. For each, recent advancements and highlight their strengths and limitations are discussed along with showing the improvements brought up by each selected methods and compare them. Comparisons are based on evaluating compression rate, inference time, and accuracy. The aim of this chapter would help practitioners who are implementing DNN based mobile applications to choose a compression approach that satisfies their requirements.

DOI: 10.4018/978-1-6684-3795-7.ch005

INTRODUCTION

In recent years, Deep Neural Networks (DNNs) have been widely applied in different disciplines and achieved accuracy and performance breakthroughs tackling complicated tasks e.g. image recognition (Krizhevsky et al., 2017) and semantic segmentation (Redmon et al., 2016). The achievements of deep learning was a result of the huge number of parameters included in the learning process with efficiently running GPUs (Cheng et al., 2017). DNNs were not only kept in supercomputer labs but also were embedded in a wide range of user-friendly mobile applications in different areas such as health wellness (Bui et al., 2017) and object detection (Eichelberger et al., 2017). Due to the high demand for storage size and high energy consumption of deep models, incorporating them in mobile systems has been challenging especially for real-time applications (Han, Mao, et al., 2016a).

To achieve a real-time inference of deep learning models on mobile phones, some hardware accelerators (Y. H. Chen et al., 2019), (Y. H. Chen et al., 2017), and (Yin et al., 2019) using reconfigurable processor (Tessier et al., 2015) were able to execute DNNs efficiently and faster. However, due to the limited memory of proposed hardware solutions (Guo et al., 2019), they fail to store DNNs weights and parameters (Shawahna et al., 2019). DNNs consist of a high number of processing layers and therefore a huge number of weights (Shrestha & Mahmood, 2019) which requires a different approach, such as compression, to tackle excessive computations. DNN compression is a solution that takes into consideration the model itself, its parameters, and its neural network architecture while preserving a baseline accuracy.

Compressing DNNs methodologies can be classified under two general approaches, either compressing existing architectures or designing new efficient architectures (Hoang & Jo, 2018). Examples of compressing existing architectures methods are parameter pruning (Han et al., 2015) which removes redundant parameters, quantization (Gong et al., 2014) which reduces bit representations of a parameter, low-rank factorization (Jaderberg et al., 2014) which decomposes layers to have a more chance for ranking informative parameters. While the concept of designing efficient architectures is based on using transferred layers (Zeng et al., 2016), which builds a special structure to save parameters information, or knowledge distillation (Ba & Caruana, 2014), where a smaller network learns the distribution of a larger network output through a SoftMax for the smaller network to mimic the larger functionalities.

Quantization: One of the leading information-theoretic approaches to compress nueral networks is vector quantization (Gong et al., 2014). One way is that it uses a binary representation of the parameters to reduce the data by 32 times since each neuron is represented by one bit. Another way is the use of scalar quantization by cluster the parameters, then each parameter is assigned to one cluster, given the k centers of the clustering, only $\log_2(k)$ bits are stored.

Low-Rank Factorization: Another lienar algebraic approach to compress neural networks is the use of low-rank factorization (Jaderberg et al., 2014). The main idea is to approximate the neural networks using a low-rank basis of filters that are separable in the spatial domain. Each basis filter is decomposed into vertical and horizontal filters to create separable filters which are of rank-1. Then the final filter is approximated as a linear combination of smaller bases. This removes the reduduncy in filter channles and only keeps the informative ones.

Knowledge distillation: One method that is not model-agnostic and needs training of a separate new model is the use of shallow networks (Ba & Caruana, 2014). This way, a shallow model mimics an accurate deep model with the same number of parameters using knowledge distillation. Specifically, a deep model is trained and it is considered as the teacher model. Then, a shallow model of a single fully-connected layer, considered as the student model, trained on the predicted logits of the deep model to mimic the performance of the teacher model. Training on logits, the logarithms of predicted probabilities, makes learning easier for the student model by placing equal emphasis on the relationships learned by the teacher model across all of the classes in a classification task. This creates a less complex models that perform as well as deep models.

Deep compression had brought several desirable features while incorporating embedded systems. Compression can reduce storage used in devices, e.g. MobileNets (Howard et al., 2017) was able to reduce memory consumption by 85%. Eventually, compression leads to a higher inference rate, for instance, VGG-Net (Simonyan & Zisserman, 2015) was executed by 0.04% of its original execution time using MobileNets architecture (Howard et al., 2017). Besides, it is proved that compression not only preserved original model accuracy but also, it was able to achieve higher accuracy scores in comparison with their original models. PydMobileNets (Hoang & Jo, 2018) achieved 36% better accuracy while compressing MobileNets. Also, another powerful advantage of deep compression is the defense against adversarial examples that are injected in images producing noisy model networks (Kurakin et al., 2017). Such noises fool the model and tremendously degrades the performance. According to (Kurakin et al., 2017), noisy information in models can be perceived as redundant. Therefore, the ComDefend framework (X. Jia et al., 2019) detects adversarial examples through compressing ResNet (K. He et al., 2016) and achieves higher accuracy than ResNet baseline accuracy.

This paper presents recent trends in two specific areas of compression: pruning and neural architectures redesign. According to (Tung & Mori, 2018), effective network architectures with successful pruning can lead, complementary, to better desirable results that take into consideration hardware limited resources. Both, pruning and neural architectures redesign, are orthogonal, hence, both can be used jointly or individually in one application (Cheng et al., 2017). As far as our knowledge, the work of (Cheng et al., 2017) was the first work to produce a thorough review of all published compression algorithms. Since the work considered only papers in 2017 and earlier with a lack focus on mobile environments; therefore, we aim to extend the work and discuss recent compression approaches highlighting their advantages and limitations in mobile or mobile-like settings.

The paper is organized as follows. Section Pruning discusses pruning: pruning criterion, selected pruning variations, and a discussion section. Section Redesigned Efficient Neural Architectures discusses the neural architecture, the redesigning selected approaches and a discussion to compare between the discussed architectures. Section Performance Evaluation shows the performance evaluation that researchers depended on to evaluate their compression work, then we conclude the review.

PRUNING

To mitigate a model's complexity and overfitting, a prominent approach is pruning. Since pruning reduces the size of the model, recent studies, e.g. (Han et al., 2015)(Salama et al., 2019)(Ma et al., 2020) (Ullrich et al., 2019) and (Han, Mao, et al., 2016b), utilized pruning for compressing models to achieve fewer resource consumptions, yet, with baseline accuracy. Pruning is responsible for removing redundant elements (Han et al., 2015) as shown in Figure 1. Such redundant elements might be less impactful on the performance of a deep neural model (Cheng et al., 2017).

Figure 1. A network before and after pruning, neurons, and channels were pruned (Han et al., 2015)

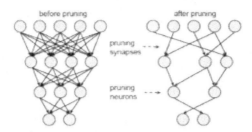

For example, consider a model architecture of 1000 input features and three hidden layers each of 1024 hidden features and a total of 2,000,000 parameters. Many of the parameters might be redundant and not useful. Thereofre, applying pruning can reduce the parameters into 100,000 parameters with the same loss convergance rate.

Pruning Criterion

To determine what to prune, different heuristics are used to determine the pruning criterion. Han and his colleagues proposed to prune any low-weight connections from the entire network (Han et al., 2015). Chen et al. in 2015, proposed a low-cost hash function that randomly groups weights into hash buckets to share one single parameter value for each bucket (W. Chen et al., 2015), in this way redundant values are eliminated. Han et al. in 2016 pruned low-weight connections (Han, Mao, et al., 2016a), then quantized the remaining weights to reduce the bits representing each weight and finally applied Huffman encoding. While Salama and his colleagues in 2019 proposed to calculate L1-norm for each layer based on the L1-norm of a layer's weights and then prune based on a global L1-norm threshold relative to all layers (Salama et al., 2019). Building on top of (Han et al., 2015), (Ko et al., 2019) proposed to consider the uncertainty of weights to evaluate their importance.

Pruning Variations

Pruning is categorized into two main classes: non-structured/fine-grained pruning and structured/coarse-grained pruning. Based on the two main abstractions, several approaches are derived and have proven successful compression rates. We will define the two categories and discuss approaches that have taken into consideration the specifications of mobile devices.

Non-Structured Pruning

Non-structured pruning removes unimportant individual elements, irregularly, from different parts of a network layer (Han et al., 2015). The irregular pruning manner creates sparse networks while achieving high compression rates with high accuracy (Y. He et al., 2018). The removed redundant connections from different locations result in a sparse model stored in either compressed sparse column format (Ma et al., 2019) or compressed sparse row format (Y. He et al., 2018).

Han et, 2015 proposed to train a network model that learns which connections are important (Han et al., 2015). Therefore, connections that are below a threshold are pruned and neurons that are connected to pruned connections are pruned as well. Finally, the networks are retrained based on the new weights. (Han et al., 2015) found that the final retraining step is crucial for a higher accuracy rate and achieved about 90% of weight reduction for AlexNet (Krizhevsky et al., 2017). (Niu, Ma, Wang, et al., 2019) achieved high compression rates, e.g. 99% of LeNet-5 (LeCun, 2015) was pruned using non-structured pruning without accuracy loss.

Although the compression rate of unstructured pruning was very promising; however, sparse models do not fulfill hardware design requirements. The compressed sparse storage makes localization much more irregular and therefore does not optimize for inference time (Niu, Ma, Wang, et al., 2019). To accelerate the processing of irregularly pruned networks, researchers are using specialized hardware such as EIE (Han, Liu, et al., 2016) or assistant compiler (Ma et al., 2019).

Structured Pruning

To overcome model sparsity produced by non-structured weight pruning, structured pruning is introduced. Structured pruning removes the entire element such as channels, rows, columns in a systematic way that does not create random gaps (Y. He et al., 2018). It is more hardware-friendly since it preserves locality with fewer memory requirements (Ma et al., 2019). As shown in Figure 2, filter and channel pruning (structured pruning) are more regular than non-structured pruning.

Figure 2. Differences between pruning levels (structured and unstructured pruning) (Ma et al., 2019)

In addition, Salama and his colleagues in 2019 proposed an approach that reserves a structured network. Their heuristic is based on calculating the L1-norm of neurons for each layer and normalizing them. Then, they stack, sort the normalized values, and then prune them based on a global threshold (Salama et al., 2019). Sorting the normalized values was a key contribution that accelerated pruning on hardware settings with fewer memory operations. In the final step, the model alternates between retraining and pruning until a minimum compression rate is reached. Active deep neurons are more pruned than shallower ones, and unpruned neurons become more active to compensate for loss (Salama et al., 2019). Although structured pruning allows for optimized localization; however, the resulting model achieves accuracy less than baseline models (Ma et al., 2019).

Pattern Pruning

To overcome accuracy degradation that results from structured pruning while preserving hardware-friendliness which is exploited by unstructured pruning, (Niu, Ma, Lin, et al., 2019), (Ma et al., 2019) and (Ma et al., 2020) proposed *pattern pruning* that combines both structured and unstructured pruning strengths and avoids both weaknesses with compiler assistance. Pattern-based pruning has two main techniques: kernel pattern pruning and connectivity pruning (Niu, Ma, Lin, et al., 2019). At *Kernel Pattern Pruning,* the remaining unpruned weights form the selected patterns, where the highly expensive convolution layers are considered for pruning and only a fixed number of weights are pruned at each kernel (Ma et al., 2019). Predefining a fixed number of weights limits the weight-pruning rate. To speed up pruning and overcome the limited rate, *Connectivity Pruning* is introduced to omit connections between input and output channels. In other words, it removes the whole kernel (Niu, Ma, Lin, et al., 2019) as shown in Figure 3.

Figure 3. Differences of kernel pattern pruning (assigning patterns for each kernel) and connectivity pruning (removing the whole kernel) (Ma et al., 2019)

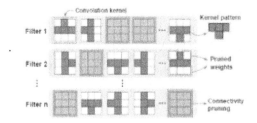

To design the pattern set for selection, (Niu, Ma, Lin, et al., 2019) depended on finding the top four weights with highest magnitudes, accordingly, they created 56 possible patterns, and therefore selected patterns that satisfied any pattern shape in the set. While (Ma et al., 2019) took advantage of Sparse Convolution Patterns (SCP) which are known to improve image processing through convolution operations, e.g. edge detection, image smoothing. Applying SCP to each kernel extracts patterns that have more detailed information about an image (information generated by saliency maps) (Ma et al., 2019). Therefore, it is easier to detect important kernels and channels. (Ma et al., 2020) had extended (Ma et al., 2019) work by adding a feature of simultaneously pruning weights, and training unpruned weights while updating the set at each iteration.

After pattern selections, kernels are reordered and organized based on their similarities, to optimize for a regularly-shaped model (Niu, Ma, Lin, et al., 2019). Accordingly, redundant kernels are eliminated through pruning the whole kernel (connectivity pruning) or through pruning selective patterns in each kernel (kernel pattern pruning) (Niu, Ma, Lin, et al., 2019).

To speed up deep neural inferences on mobile settings, a compilation platform is introduced to support pruning operations done on algorithmic levels (Ma et al., 2019). For example, researchers (Niu, Ma, Lin, et al., 2019) extended the framework of the alternating direction method of multipliers (ADMM) (Boyd et al., 2010) to extract patterns from each kernel. ADMM is a mathematical optimization for structured weight pruning (Niu, Ma, Lin, et al., 2019). It assigns patterns to kernels and performs training for unpruned weights.

Experiments of (Ma et al., 2019) and (Niu, Ma, Lin, et al., 2019) are done on Samsung Galaxy S10, using a Qualcomm Snapdragon 855 on VGGNet, ResNet, and MobileNets. The final speed of their approaches while compared with state-of-the-art frameworks outperformed TensorFlow Lite (Google, 2019). There is negligible accuracy loss but a high compression rate (See Table 1).

Table 1. Comparison of Different Pruning Approaches On Imagenet Dataset

Baseline Model	Approach	Compression rate	Speed (%)	Accuracy (%)	Study
AlexNet	Unstructured	9	33	0	(Han et al., 2015)
VGGNet	Unstructured	13	-	0	(Han et al., 2015)
VGG-16	Kernel	8	42	-0.1	(Niu, Ma, Lin, et al., 2019)
MobileNet	Structured	34	50	-0.06	(Y. He et al., 2018)

Automatic Pruning

Even though previous approaches are robust in determining parameter compression at each layer; however, they are time-consuming. According to (Y. He et al., 2018), sparsity selection has been rule-based in recent studies; which therefore limits the generalization ability of compression approaches. Therefore automatic pruning aims to find an accurate pruning rate that preserves accuracy with less memory and time consuming which can be applied to different neural network architectures (Y. He et al., 2018). (N. Liu et al., 2018) and (Z. Li et al., 2020) proposed an automatic determination of the pruning rate for each layer. (N. Liu et al., 2018) depended on a heuristic search (e.g. simulated annealing) for an optimal sample selection of hyper-parameters for each layer. The selected sample is evaluated based on accuracy loss and a decision is taken iteratively based on the evaluations. Based on a threshold (determined automatically for each layer), filters and channels are pruned (N. Liu et al., 2018). While (Y. He et al., 2018) depended on reinforcement learning for detecting redundant elements in a network. A model is trained to predict a sparsity ratio given a layer sparsity, accuracy is evaluated, and the model is updated iteratively. By the final step, (Y. He et al., 2018) a reward is calculated for any objective incentive: model size reduction, mobile inference speedup, or accuracy increase. The reward is returned back to the model to limit the search space, which therefore allows the model to reach the optimal compression ratio.

Compared with baseline accuracy and performance conducted on Google Pixel-1 phone, (Y. He et al., 2018) reached high pruning rates with higher speed and higher accuracy on ResNet (K. He et al., 2016) while slight accuracy degradation on MobileNets. Also (5) observed some slight accuracy degradations on VGGNet (Simonyan & Zisserman, 2015), but no loss on ResNet (See Table 1 & Table 2).

Table 2. Comparison of Different Pruning Approaches On Cifar Dataset

Baseline Model	Approach	Compression rate	Speed (%)	Accuracy (%)	Study
ResNet-50	Structured	60	50	0.7	(Y. He et al., 2018)
VGG-16	Automatic	33	80	-0.5	(N. Liu et al., 2018)

Discussion

Pruning algorithms proved their power in compressing DNNs; however, some pruning schemes are proved to be more efficient than others. Table 3 and Table 4 summarize all pruning variations discussed in this paper. In general, structured pruning is the most preferred compression technique for hardware platforms, e.g. mobiles and embedded systems with little sacrifice of accuracy. Kernel pattern pruning and connectivity pruning both optimize for memory size and allocation. However, for specific applications where speed is a major objective, automatic pruning reduces the required speed for model training and testing unlike other pruning schemas. VGGNet and ResNet were accelerated by 80% and 50% respectively (See Table 2) with minimal accuracy degradation using automatic pruning.

Table 3. Main Pruning Approaches

Pruning Type	Advantages	Limitations
Non-Structured	High accuracy	High sparsity and hardware inefficiency
Structured	Hardware-friendliness	Low accuracy
Automatic Pruning	High speed	Accuracy degradation

Table 4. Summarization of Multiple Pruning Schemes

Pruning Scheme	Advantages	Limitations
Kernel Pattern Pruning	Sparsity Elimination	Limits pruning rate
Connectivity Pruning	Compression size maximization	Time-consuming and rule-based sparsities selection

REDESIGNED EFFICIENT NEURAL ARCHITECTURES

The change of network architecture design of DNNs can have an impact on the inference speed and size of models (Tung & Mori, 2018). Using transferred layers, where network layers are multiplied by a transformation matrix can be one of the efficient architecture changes for optimized size and dimensions (Cheng et al., 2017). We will discuss several operations performed on neural network layers that aim to reduce computational costs such as Depth wise Separable Convolutions (DSC) and Layer Slimming.

Suggested Architecture Designs

Depthwise Separable Convolutions

A Convolution layer usually consists of three dimensions, two spatial dimensions e.g. width and height, and one channel dimension (Chollet, 2017). Convolution layers apply filters for input data to extract spatial features and then combine them to generate one output (Howard et al., 2017). Therefore, output channels and kernels are correlated and have the same size (Howard et al., 2017). Extracting features and combining them are joined in one step (Howard et al., 2017). Depthwise Separable Convolutions (DSC) aim to separate the filtering step from the combination step into two steps to eliminate correlations (Chollet, 2017). DSC factorizes spatial and channel correlations into a series of operations to reduce speed and size (Hoang & Jo, 2018). Each convolution layer is replaced with two layers that perform depthwise and pointwise convolutions (Hoang & Jo, 2018). The first layer performs a depthwise operator on input channels to only extract spatial information of images (Hoang & Jo, 2018). While the second layer performs pointwise, a 1x1 convolution that combines channel outputs and projects them into a new dimension space (Hoang & Jo, 2018). Compared with full convolutions shown in Figure 4 (a), depthwise separable convolutions on MobileNets only lost 1% of accuracy while reducing the number of parameters by 85% and the computational cost by 88% (Howard et al., 2017). In the following parts we will discuss several variations for the depthwise separable convolutions.

Figure 4. (a) Standard convolution block. (b) Depthwise separable layer. (c) Quantized friendly depthwise separable layer. (d) Concatenation of full convolution with depthwise separable

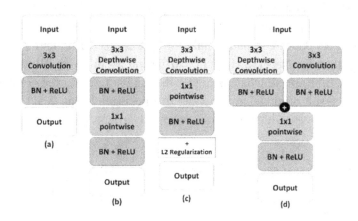

Depthwise Separable Architecture Variations

One of the very first few pioneering architectures that used depthwise separable convolution was MobileNets (Howard et al., 2017). MobileNets architecture (Howard et al., 2017) aims to build lightweight neural networks that trade-off between accuracies and latencies while introducing two hyper-parameters. (Howard et al., 2017) kept the first layer to be fully connected, and then used depthwise separable to split convolution tasks into two layers: depthwise convolution and pointwise layers. In addition, batchnorm (Ioffe & Szegedy, 2015) and non-linearity activation (Glorot et al., 2011) (e.g. ReLU or ReLU6, etc.) were added after each layer (See Figure 4b). This structure produced an optimized ordering of layers that does not require any re-ordering in memory, hence; it saves computation time (Howard et al., 2017). The two hyper-parameters that MobileNets introduced were the width multiplier to thin the network, and the resolution multiplier to reduce the spatial resolution (the final representation of the output) (Howard et al., 2017). While evaluating the width multiplier, thinner networks preserve accuracy more than shallower ones (Howard et al., 2017). Compared with GoogleNet (Zeng et al., 2016) and VGG-16 (Simonyan &

Zisserman, 2015), MobileNets is more accurate than GoogleNets and almost similar accuracy of VGG-16 with smaller size and less computational cost, as detailed in Table 5.

Table 5. Comparison of Efficient Neural Architectures on ImageNet Dataset

Baseline Model	Approach	Compression rate (%)	Speed (%)	Accuracy (%)	Study
GoogleNet	DSC	38	63	1	(Howard et al., 2017)
VGG-16	DSC	96	96	-1	(Howard et al., 2017)
MobileNets	Slimming	34	3	3	(D. Li et al., 2018)
SqueezeNet	Slimming	60	13	6	(D. Li et al., 2018)

PydMobileNets (Hoang & Jo, 2018) is a framework that suggests an enhancement to MobileNets. It used a *pyramid* of kernel sizes, which means instead of having one size e.g. 3x3, to have several sizes e.g. {3x3, 5x5, 7x7} of input channels (Hoang & Jo, 2018). PydMobileNets used a width multiplier to change channels sizes and therefore to allow for more spatial features extractions (Hoang & Jo, 2018). Before performing the pointwise operation, they combine input channels using a concatenation operation that has no cost aiming to reduce computational cost. It was able to achieve better accuracy with less number of parameters than ResNets (K. He et al., 2016) and MobileNets. However, they were not able to control the inference time speed, which is higher than the baseline speeds (Hoang & Jo, 2018) (See Table 6). This can be a result of model nonlinearity that occurred because of the continuous change of input and output channels sizes, which therefore, harmfully affects execution time (Yao et al., 2018).

Table 6. Comparison of Efficient Neural Architectures on CIFAR Dataset

Baseline Model	Approach	Compression rate (%)	Speed (%)	Accuracy (%)	Study
ResNets	PydMobileNets	75	-3	18	(Hoang & Jo, 2018)
MobileNets	PydMobileNets	27	-17	36	(Hoang & Jo, 2018)

MobileNets is very efficient when used on mobiles or in IoT environments since it is optimized for float-point processing. However, MobileNets fails to keep up the accuracy of fixed-point operations (Sheng et al., 2018). Why should we care about fixed-point operations, in other words, 8-bit quantization? Hardware platforms often depend on fixed-point operations to achieve optimal and minimal resource consumption (Jacob et al., 2018). (Sheng et al., 2018) observed the signal-to-quantization-noise ratio (SQNR) values of MobileNets layers to measure the quantization loss. They found that introducing batch-norm and the ReLU after the depthwise layer is responsible for the degradation of the SQNR. Therefore, (Sheng et al., 2018) proposed to remove the batchnorm and the ReLU activations from the depthwise layer and keep them after the pointwise layer. Besides, L2 regularization was enabled on depthwise convolution weights as shown in Figure 4(c). The accuracy of the quantized-friendly MobileNets was increased dramatically from 1.8% to 69% for fixed-point processing while preserving the same accuracy for float-point processing (Sheng et al., 2018).

Another proposed variation of depthwise separable convolutions was done by (Miles & Mikolajczyk, 2020). They aimed to avoid any loss in baseline accuracy of compressed models. (Miles & Mikolajczyk, 2020) proposed to integrate fully connected convolution output with depthwise convolutions output, as this will preserve some features from the full dense spatial and channel correlations as illustrated in Figure 4(d). Both output features are then concatenated via a 1x1 pointwise convolution. They included a Tucker Decomposition (Kim et al., 2016), that have fewer neurons to compress output channel size. (Miles & Mikolajczyk, 2020) proposed approach was able to compress L2Net (Tian et al., 2017) by a rate of 8x and less computation cost with less than 1% of accuracy loss on Liberty, Yosemite, and Notredame datasets.

Layer Slimming

According to (Yao et al., 2018) the change of network architecture due to change of size often leads to expanded nonlinearities that do not optimize for execution time. (Yao et al., 2018) suggests that compression algorithms must concentrate more on layers that need more time than other layers. Deep neural architectures usually contain two types of layers, tensor, and non-tensor layers. The difference between tensor and non-tensor layers is based on whether they contain matrix-like, tensor-type weight parameters, or not (D. Li et al., 2018). For example, convolution layers are tensor layers, while pooling, which reduces the spatial size of feature maps (Mishkin et al., 2017), and normalization (e.g. LRN) are non-tensor layers (D. Li et al., 2018). According to (Y. Jia et al., 2014), non-tensor layers slow down the execution time of the model inference. For example, AlexNet removed the LRN layer and replaced it by batch-normalization (Ioffe & Szegedy, 2015) to get rid of overwhelmed execution time, and still AlexNet spends 25% of its time on the batchnorm layer (Y. Jia et al., 2014).

Li and his colleagues in 2018 proposed the DeePrebirth architecture framework that aims to optimize inference time for deep networks in real-time mobile applications by optimizing the execution time of non-tensor layers (D. Li et al., 2018). Their approach is to merge non-tensor layers vertically or horizontally with neighboring tensor layers and then retrain the newly produced layers to not lose their original functionalities (D. Li et al., 2018). They proposed two types of slimming: first, the streamline slimming, where they merge the non-tensor layer with the previous layer; second, the branch slimming where they fuse nontensor layer with a convolution layer on the same level (D. Li et al., 2018), as illustrated in Figure 5.

Figure 5. A simplified illustration of the DeePrebirth proposed architecture. Both slimming techniques, the horizontal and the vertical slimming, are illustrated

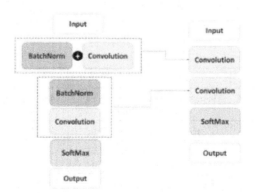

Compared with GoogLeNet, DeePrebirth (D. Li et al., 2018) achieved 5x of speed-up for image processing with only a 0.4% loss of accuracy on ImageNet and less memory occupied. DeePrebirth (D. Li et al., 2018) also conducted experiments on a Samsung 6S cell phone along with MobileNets and SqueezeNets, DeePrebirth stands to be an optimized option for real-time inference (See Table 5).

Discussion

Deep compression using efficient architectures has proved a success on several platforms. Table 7 summarizes all architectures discussed in this paper. MobileNets (Howard et al., 2017) is one of the pioneering architectures, that improves the speed of the DNN model in a mobile platform. MobileNets accelerated GoogleNets and VGGNets by 63% and 96% respectively with limited applicability on all hardware platforms e.g. 8-bit quantized. MobileNets quantized limitation was

Figure 6. A summary of reviewed architectures (a) SqueezeNet as porposed in (Iandola et al., 2016). (b) A simplification of ResNet. (c) A simplification of VGG-Net. (d) MobileNets Architecture. (e) DeepBirth Framework. (f) A simplification of GoogleNet.

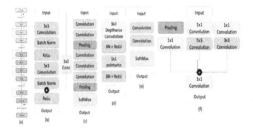

eliminated with recent research of (Miles & Mikolajczyk, 2020). PydMobileNets (Hoang & Jo, 2018) is another enhancement for MobileNets and it is a very good choice for scarce memory applications since it compresses MobileNets and ResNets by 27% and 75% respectively with a significantly increased accuracy. However, PydMobileNets does not optimize for speed. Nonetheless, layer slimming technique optimizes for speed and it is implemented through DeePrebirth (D. Li et al., 2018) architecture framework. DeePrebirth accelerates MobileNets and SqueezeNet 3% and 13%, respectively with increased accuracy. Figure 6 summarizes the architecture frameworks mentioned in the report.

Table 7. Summary of Efficient Architectures

Network Architecture	Advantages	Selected Limitations
MobileNets (Howard et al., 2017)	Thinner networks with optimized memory allocation	Accuracy degradation for 8-bit quantized models
PydMobileNets (Hoang & Jo, 2018)	High compression rate	Slow inference time
DeePrebirth (D. Li et al., 2018)	High inference time for real-time applications	Not generalized to different mobile processors such as GPU
Quantized MobileNets (Miles & Mikolajczyk, 2020)	High accuracy for fixed-point operations	Not generalized for different architectures and not fully verified on devices

PERFORMANCE EVALUATION

Execution Performance

Compression techniques have been widely used to optimize inference time on limited-resources platforms e.g. mobiles. As our review has shown, many architectures have been occasionally used as baseline models to evaluate the performance of newly proposed approaches. Baseline compressed architectures such as MobileNets (Howard et al., 2017), ResNet (K. He et al., 2016), GoogleNet (Zeng et al., 2016), AlexNet (Krizhevsky et al., 2017), VGG Net (Simonyan & Zisserman, 2015), and many more, have been thoroughly experimented and enhanced throughout the literature.

A robust compression algorithm is the one that preserves a baseline accuracy with fewer parameters and less computational cost (Cheng et al., 2017). Throughout our review, we evaluated models and compared architectures based on three factors: compression rate, inference time, and accuracy (Canziani et al., n.d.). The compression rate is calculated comparing the number of parameters of the new model and the original model (Miles & Mikolajczyk, 2020). The speed rate is measured by the running time of training or/and testing stages of a model in comparison to the running time of the original one (Cheng et al., 2017).

Some frameworks such as MobileNets (Jacob et al., 2018) and SqueezeNet (Iandola et al., 2016) use floating points operations (FLOPs) as an estimation of the model's running time. FLOPs and parameter count are widely used to evaluate the success of compression techniques and they are highly correlated with optimized latency (Miles & Mikolajczyk, 2020) (Canziani et al., n.d.). However, in some cases, the relationship between FLOPs and parameters count with model inference time may differ and turns to be not proportional and this is due to the design of the model architecture (Cheng et al., 2017). For example, fully connected layers have more parameters than convolution layers, while convolution layers take more time to execute (Cheng et al., 2017). Also, according to an experiment done by (Yao et al., 2018), two models had the same FLOPs but one was slower by a factor of 3 than the other. Since execution time is affected by other factors like memory access, caching effects, and compilation, some researchers added the memory operations to the evaluation metric besides FLOPs and compression rate (Yao et al., 2018) and others considered only intensive layers (D. Li et al., 2018).

Hardware Setup

To assess compression methods, some researchers conduct experiments on phones with supported hardware integration. For example, (Ma et al., 2019), (Niu, Ma, Lin, et al., 2019), (Z. Li et al., 2020), (Ma et al., 2020) and (N. Liu et al., 2018) used Samsung Galaxy S10 phone with a Qualcomm Snapdragon 855 integration (Qualcomm, 2018). The Qualcomm platform is built originally for gamers who seek high speed of image rendering and it consists of an octal-core CPU and a GPU (Qualcomm, 2018). (Niu, Ma, Wang, et al., 2019) and (J. Liu et al., 2020) integrated Qualcomm Snapdragon into Xiaomi 6 and Xiaomi 8 cell phones. While (D. Li et al., 2018) used Caffe, (Y. Jia et al., 2014), a deep learning framework and compiled it using Android NDK for optimization on Samsung Galaxy S5 cell phone. (Yao et al., 2018) conducted experiments on Nexus 5 and Galaxy Nexus phones incorporating TensorFlow Lite (Google, 2019), a deep learning framework for mobile devices. While (Y. He et al., 2018) and (Cai et al., 2019) used Google Pixel 1 cell phone without mentioning any other setups.

CONCLUSION

This review aims to provide a comprehensive overview of recent trends of deep compression techniques that take into consideration mobile specifications of limited energy and memory. The review sheds light on two main categories of compression, pruning, and efficient neural network designs which both made a huge transformation in the state-of-the-art compression frameworks.

Based on our review, we conclude that structured/regular pruning is the optimal type of pruning, especially, if aided with an automatic heuristic search for determining a weight threshold for pruning channels and kernels. This type produces the highest compression rate of 33, and fastest inference time improvement at 80%, with minimal accuracy degradation when compared to other pruning approaches. While architectures that induce depthwise separable convolutions (DSC) can minimize inference time in time-intensive applications, especially if aided with layer slimming, as observed in DeePrebirth (D. Li et al., 2018). DSC can compress a neural architecture by a rate of 96% while DeePrebith compressed DSC by 27%.

We observed that there is no one rule that proposes the ultimate best compression algorithm to be implemented in an application. Usually, the application's requirements determine the optimality of a compression technique. For a stable accuracy, we found that structured pruning is recommended since it showed the least accuracy degradation unlike the redesigned neural architectures. However, for optimized memory size and storage, redesigned efficient architectures are recommended, as we found that higher compression rates were produced by redesigned neural networks. Notably, pruning and modified efficient architecture can be implemented together in one application since compression techniques are usually orthogonal.

In future work, we aim to further explore and compare different compression appraoches of deep layers for mobile phone settings. For example, we aim to discuss knowledge distillation, which distills knolwedge from another model, and low-rank factorization, which decomposes tensors to extract important parameters.

REFERENCES

Ba, L. J., & Caruana, R. (2014). Do deep nets really need to be deep? *Advances in Neural Information Processing Systems.*

Boyd, S., Parikh, N., Chu, E., Peleato, B., & Eckstein, J. (2010). Distributed optimization and statistical learning via the alternating direction method of multipliers. In *Foundations and Trends in Machine Learning* (Vol. 3, Issue 1, pp. 1–122). DOI: 10.1561/9781601984616

Bui, N., Truong, H., Nguyen, A., Ashok, A., Nguyen, P., Dinh, T., Deterding, R., & Vu, T. (2017). PhO2: Smartphone based Blood Oxygen Level Measurement Systems using Near-IR and RED Wave-guided Light. *SenSys 2017 - Proceedings of the 15th ACM Conference on Embedded Networked Sensor Systems.* DOI: 10.1145/3131672.3131696

Cai, H., Zhu, L., & Han, S. (2019). Proxylessnas: Direct neural architecture search on target task and hardware. *7th International Conference on Learning Representations, ICLR 2019*, 1–13.

Canziani, A., Culurciello, E., & Paszke, A. (n.d.). *AN ANALYSIS OF DEEP NEURAL NETWORK MODELS FOR PRACTICAL APPLICATIONS.*

Chen, W., Wilson, J. T., Tyree, S., Weinberger, K. Q., & Chen, Y. (2015). Compressing neural networks with the hashing trick. *32nd International Conference on Machine Learning, ICML 2015, 3*, 2275–2284.

Chen, Y. H., Krishna, T., Emer, J. S., & Sze, V. (2017). Eyeriss: An Energy-Efficient Reconfigurable Accelerator for Deep Convolutional Neural Networks. *IEEE Journal of Solid-State Circuits*, 52(1), 127–138. Advance online publication. DOI: 10.1109/JSSC.2016.2616357

Chen, Y. H., Yang, T. J., Emer, J. S., & Sze, V. (2019). Eyeriss v2: A Flexible Accelerator for Emerging Deep Neural Networks on Mobile Devices. *IEEE Journal on Emerging and Selected Topics in Circuits and Systems*, 9(2), 292–308. Advance online publication. DOI: 10.1109/JETCAS.2019.2910232

Cheng, Y., Wang, D., Zhou, P., & Zhang, T. (2017). *A Survey of Model Compression and Acceleration for Deep Neural Networks.* 1–10.

Chollet, F. (2017). Xception: Deep learning with depthwise separable convolutions. *Proceedings - 30th IEEE Conference on Computer Vision and Pattern Recognition, CVPR 2017, 2017-Janua*, 1800–1807. DOI: 10.1109/CVPR.2017.195

Eichelberger, M., Tanner, S., Luchsinger, K., & Wattenhofer, R. (2017). Indoor localization with aircraft signals. *SenSys 2017 - Proceedings of the 15th ACM Conference on Embedded Networked Sensor Systems.* DOI: 10.1145/3131672.3131698

Glorot, X., Bordes, A., & Bengio, Y. (2011). Deep sparse rectifier neural networks. *Journal of Machine Learning Research.*

Gong, Y., Liu, L., Yang, M., & Bourdev, L. (2014). *Compressing Deep Convolutional Networks using Vector Quantization.* 1–10.

Google. (2019). *TensorFlow Lite | TensorFlow.* Tensorflow.Org. https://www.tensorflow.org/lite

Guo, K., Zeng, S., Yu, J., Wang, Y., & Yang, H. (2019). [DL] A survey of FPGA-based neural network inference accelerators. In *ACM Transactions on Reconfigurable Technology and Systems*. DOI: 10.1145/3289185

Han, S., Liu, X., Mao, H., Pu, J., Pedram, A., Horowitz, M. A., & Dally, W. J. (2016). EIE: Efficient Inference Engine on Compressed Deep Neural Network. *Proceedings - 2016 43rd International Symposium on Computer Architecture, ISCA 2016*. DOI: 10.1109/ISCA.2016.30

Han, S., Mao, H., & Dally, W. J. (2016a). Deep compression: Compressing deep neural networks with pruning, trained quantization and Huffman coding. *4th International Conference on Learning Representations, ICLR 2016 - Conference Track Proceedings*, 1–14.

Han, S., Mao, H., & Dally, W. J. (2016b). Deep compression: Compressing deep neural networks with pruning, trained quantization and Huffman coding. *4th International Conference on Learning Representations, ICLR 2016 - Conference Track Proceedings*.

Han, S., Pool, J., Tran, J., & Dally, W. J. (2015). Learning both weights and connections for efficient neural networks. *Advances in Neural Information Processing Systems, 2015-Janua*, 1135–1143.

He, K., Zhang, X., Ren, S., & Sun, J. (2016). Deep residual learning for image recognition. *Proceedings of the IEEE Computer Society Conference on Computer Vision and Pattern Recognition*. DOI: 10.1109/CVPR.2016.90

He, Y., Lin, J., Liu, Z., Wang, H., Li, L. J., & Han, S. (2018). AMC: AutoML for model compression and acceleration on mobile devices. *Lecture Notes in Computer Science (Including Subseries Lecture Notes in Artificial Intelligence and Lecture Notes in Bioinformatics), 11211 LNCS*, 815–832. DOI: 10.1007/978-3-030-01234-2_48

Hoang, V.-T., & Jo, K. (2018). *PydMobileNet: Improved Version of MobileNets with Pyramid Depthwise Separable Convolution*.

Howard, A. G., Zhu, M., Chen, B., Kalenichenko, D., Wang, W., Weyand, T., Andreetto, M., & Adam, H. (2017). *MobileNets: Efficient Convolutional Neural Networks for Mobile Vision Applications*.

Iandola, F. N., Moskewicz, M. W., Ashraf, K., Han, S., Dally, W. J., & Keutzer, K. (2016). *Squeezenet: alexnet-level accuracy with 50x fewer parameters and < 0.5mb model size*. ArXiv.

Ioffe, S., & Szegedy, C. (2015). Batch normalization: Accelerating deep network training by reducing internal covariate shift. *32nd International Conference on Machine Learning, ICML 2015, 1*, 448–456.

Jacob, B., Kligys, S., Chen, B., Zhu, M., Tang, M., Howard, A., Adam, H., & Kalenichenko, D. (2018). Quantization and Training of Neural Networks for Efficient Integer-Arithmetic-Only Inference. *Proceedings of the IEEE Computer Society Conference on Computer Vision and Pattern Recognition*, 2704–2713. DOI: 10.1109/CVPR.2018.00286

Jaderberg, M., Vedaldi, A., & Zisserman, A. (2014). Speeding up convolutional neural networks with low rank expansions. *BMVC 2014 - Proceedings of the British Machine Vision Conference 2014*. DOI: 10.5244/C.28.88

Jia, X., Wei, X., Cao, X., & Foroosh, H. (2019). Comdefend: An efficient image compression model to defend adversarial examples. *Proceedings of the IEEE Computer Society Conference on Computer Vision and Pattern Recognition, 2019-June*, 6077–6085. DOI: 10.1109/CVPR.2019.00624

Jia, Y., Shelhamer, E., Donahue, J., Karayev, S., Long, J., Girshick, R., Guadarrama, S., & Darrell, T. (2014). Caffe: Convolutional architecture for fast feature embedding. *MM 2014 - Proceedings of the 2014 ACM Conference on Multimedia*, 675–678. DOI: 10.1145/2647868.2654889

Kim, Y. D., Park, E., Yoo, S., Choi, T., Yang, L., & Shin, D. (2016). Compression of deep convolutional neural networks for fast and low power mobile applications. *4th International Conference on Learning Representations, ICLR 2016 - Conference Track Proceedings*, 1–16.

Ko, V., Oehmcke, S., & Gieseke, F. (2019). Magnitude and Uncertainty Pruning Criterion for Neural Networks. *Proceedings - 2019 IEEE International Conference on Big Data, Big Data 2019*. DOI: 10.1109/BigData47090.2019.9005692

Krizhevsky, A., Sutskever, I., & Hinton, G. E. (2017). ImageNet classification with deep convolutional neural networks. *Communications of the ACM*, 60(6), 84–90. Advance online publication. DOI: 10.1145/3065386

Kurakin, A., Goodfellow, I. J., & Bengio, S. (2017). Adversarial machine learning at scale. *5th International Conference on Learning Representations, ICLR 2017 - Conference Track Proceedings*.

LeCun, Y. (2015). *MNIST Demos on Yann LeCun's website*. https://yann.lecun.com/exdb/lenet/

Li, D., Wang, X., & Kong, D. (2018). DeePrebirth: Accelerating deep neural network execution on mobile devices. *32nd AAAI Conference on Artificial Intelligence, AAAI 2018*, 2322–2330. DOI: 10.1609/aaai.v32i1.11876

Li, Z., Gong, Y., Ma, X., Liu, S., Sun, M., Zhan, Z., Kong, Z., Yuan, G., & Wang, Y. (2020). *SS-Auto: A Single-Shot, Automatic Structured Weight Pruning Framework of DNNs with Ultra-High Efficiency*.

Liu, J., Zhuang, B., Zhuang, Z., Guo, Y., Huang, J., Zhu, J., & Tan, M. (2020). *Discrimination-aware Network Pruning for Deep Model Compression*. 1–14.

Liu, N., Xu, Z., Wang, Y., Tang, J., & Ye, J. (2018). *Ultra-High Compression Rates*.

Ma, X., Guo, F., Niu, W., Lin, X., Tang, J., Ma, K., Ren, B., & Wang, Y. (2019). *PCONV: The Missing but Desirable Sparsity in DNN Weight Pruning for Real-time Execution on Mobile Devices*.

Ma, X., Niu, W., Zhang, T., Liu, S., Guo, F., Lin, S., Li, H., Chen, X., Tang, J., Ma, K., Ren, B., & Wang, Y. (2020). *An Image Enhancing Pattern-based Sparsity for Real-time Inference on Mobile Devices*.

Miles, R., & Mikolajczyk, K. (2020). *Compression of convolutional neural networks for high performance imagematching tasks on mobile devices. c.*

Mishkin, D., Sergievskiy, N., & Matas, J. (2017). Systematic evaluation of convolution neural network advances on the Imagenet. *Computer Vision and Image Understanding*, 161, 11–19. Advance online publication. DOI: 10.1016/j.cviu.2017.05.007

Niu, W., Ma, X., Lin, S., Wang, S., Qian, X., Lin, X., Wang, Y., & Ren, B. (2019). *PatDNN: Achieving Real-Time DNN Execution on Mobile Devices with Pattern-based Weight Pruning.* DOI: 10.1145/3373376.3378534

Niu, W., Ma, X., Wang, Y., & Ren, B. (2019). 26ms Inference [*Towards Real-Time Execution of all DNNs on Smartphone.*]. *Time,* ●●●, ResNet–50.

Qualcomm. (2018). *Qualcomm Snapdragon 855 Plus Mobile Platform | Snapdragon 855+ Processor for Mobile Gaming.* https://www.qualcomm.com/products/snapdragon-855-plus-mobile-platform

Redmon, J., Divvala, S., Girshick, R., & Farhadi, A. (2016). You only look once: Unified, real-time object detection. *Proceedings of the IEEE Computer Society Conference on Computer Vision and Pattern Recognition.* DOI: 10.1109/CVPR.2016.91

Salama, A., Ostapenko, O., Klein, T., & Nabi, M. (2019). *Pruning at a Glance: Global Neural Pruning for Model Compression.*

Shawahna, A., Sait, S. M., & El-Maleh, A. (2019). FPGA-Based accelerators of deep learning networks for learning and classification: A review. In *IEEEAccess.* DOI: 10.1109/ACCESS.2018.2890150

Sheng, T., Feng, C., Zhuo, S., Zhang, X., Shen, L., & Aleksic, M. (2018). A Quantization-Friendly Separable Convolution for MobileNets. *Proceedings - 1st Workshop on Energy Efficient Machine Learning and Cognitive Computing for Embedded Applications, EMC2 2018,* 14–18. DOI: 10.1109/EMC2.2018.00011

Shrestha, A., & Mahmood, A. (2019). Review of deep learning algorithms and architectures. In *IEEE Access* (Vol. 7, pp. 53040–53065). DOI: 10.1109/ACCESS.2019.2912200

Simonyan, K., & Zisserman, A. (2015). Very deep convolutional networks for large-scale image recognition. *3rd International Conference on Learning Representations, ICLR 2015 - Conference Track Proceedings.*

Tessier, R., Pocek, K., & DeHon, A. (2015). Reconfigurable computing architectures. *Proceedings of the IEEE.* DOI: 10.1109/JPROC.2014.2386883

Tian, Y., Fan, B., & Wu, F. (2017). L2-Net: Deep learning of discriminative patch descriptor in Euclidean space. *Proceedings - 30th IEEE Conference on Computer Vision and Pattern Recognition, CVPR 2017, 2017-Janua,* 6128–6136. DOI: 10.1109/CVPR.2017.649

Tung, F., & Mori, G. (2018). Deep Neural Network Compression by In-Parallel Pruning-Quantization. *IEEE Transactions on Pattern Analysis and Machine Intelligence, PP*(c), 1. DOI: 10.1109/TPAMI.2018.2886192

Ullrich, K., Welling, M., & Meeds, E. (2019). Soft weight-sharing for neural network compression. *5th International Conference on Learning Representations, ICLR 2017 - Conference Track Proceedings.*

Yao, S., Zhao, Y., Shao, H., Liu, S. Z., Liu, D., Su, L., & Abdelzaher, T. (2018). FastDeepIoT: Towards understanding and optimizing neural network execution time on mobile and embedded devices. *SenSys 2018 - Proceedings of the 16th Conference on Embedded Networked Sensor Systems,* 278–291. DOI: 10.1145/3274783.3274840

Yin, S., Ouyang, P., Yang, J., Lu, T., Li, X., Liu, L., & Wei, S. (2019). An Energy-Efficient Reconfigurable Processor for Binary-and Ternary-Weight Neural Networks with Flexible Data Bit Width. *IEEE Journal of Solid-State Circuits*, 54(4), 1120–1136. Advance online publication. DOI: 10.1109/JSSC.2018.2881913

Zeng, G., He, Y., Yu, Z., Yang, X., Yang, R., & Zhang, L. (2016). *InceptionNet/GoogLeNet - Going Deeper with Convolutions*. Cvpr., DOI: 10.1002/jctb.4820

ADDITIONAL READING

Cheng, Y., Wang, D., Zhou, P., & Zhang, T. (2017). *A Survey of Model Compression and Acceleration for Deep Neural Networks*. 1–10.

Glorot, X., Bordes, A., & Bengio, Y. (2011). Deep sparse rectifier neural networks. *Journal of Machine Learning Research*.

Gong, Y., Liu, L., Yang, M., & Bourdev, L. (2014). *Compressing Deep Convolutional Networks using Vector Quantization*. 1–10.

Guo, K., Zeng, S., Yu, J., Wang, Y., & Yang, H. (2019). [DL] A survey of FPGA-based neural network inference accelerators. In *ACM Transactions on Reconfigurable Technology and Systems*. DOI: 10.1145/3289185

Han, S., Mao, H., & Dally, W. J. (2016a). Deep compression: Compressing deep neural networks with pruning, trained quantization and Huffman coding. *4th International Conference on Learning Representations, ICLR 2016 - Conference Track Proceedings*, 1–14.

Han, S., Mao, H., & Dally, W. J. (2016b). Deep compression: Compressing deep neural networks with pruning, trained quantization and Huffman coding. *4th International Conference on Learning Representations, ICLR 2016 - Conference Track Proceedings*.

Kurakin, A., Goodfellow, I. J., & Bengio, S. (2017). Adversarial machine learning at scale. *5th International Conference on Learning Representations, ICLR 2017 - Conference Track Proceedings*.

Zeng, G., He, Y., Yu, Z., Yang, X., Yang, R., & Zhang, L. (2016). *InceptionNet/GoogLeNet - Going Deeper with Convolutions*. Cvpr., DOI: 10.1002/jctb.4820

KEY TERMS AND DEFINITIONS

Convolution: A mathemtatical process to combine two functions to produce a third function.

Deep Compression: A complete pipeline that combines several processes for reducing the deep model size and complexity.

Deep Neural Networks: A class of machine learning algorithms similar to the artificial neural networks that aim to mimic the information processing of the brain.

Embedded System: A system in which the computer, specifically, a microcontroller is included as an integeral part of the system.

Huffman Code: A particular type of optimal prefix code that is commonly used for lossless data compression.

Pruning: A process that reduces the model size and complexity.

Quantization: A process of mapping continuous infinite values to a smaller set of discrete finite values.

Chapter 6
High–Performance Edge Computing:
An Energy Data Lakes Case Study

Abdullah Alsalemi
De Montfort University, UK

Abbes Amira
University of Sharjah, UAE

Hossein Malekmohamadi
De Montfort University, UK

Kegong Diao
De Montfort University, UK

ABSTRACT

With varying applications of Artificial Intelligence (AI) on an expanding global scale, performance metrics and standards of platforms have steadily elevated. High-Performance Edge Computing (HPEC) plays an instrumental role in lifting a substantial load on cloud computing for Deep Learning (DL). Notwithstanding, the collection, pre-and-post processing of big data engenders many challenges and opportunities for optimizing HPEC performance for data classification and, in turn, yields better outcomes. This is where the concept of data lakes is employed, which are raw-formatted large masses of data that are plausibly more compatible with many algorithms than structured data stores. Therefore, in this work, we carry out a comparative study that examines the merits, performance and efficiency metrics, and limitations of two notable HPEC platforms centered around a DL data lake framework. With classification accuracy of ~90%, results show that adequate performance and impressive computational efficiency, as fast as 8.19 msec per classified GAF image is achieved on the Jetson Nano.

DOI: 10.4018/978-1-6684-3795-7.ch006

INTRODUCTION AND BACKGROUND

With varying applications of Artificial Intelligence (AI) on an ever expanding global scale, performance metrics and standards of computing platforms have steadily elevated (Alsalemi et al., 2019). Also, a number of High-Performance Computing (HPC) paradigms emerged in conjunction with Internet of Things (IoT) including cloud computing, fog computing, edge computing, hybrid edge-cloud computing among others. Each with their own merits and drawbacks, they respectively excel in their own specific applications. Edge computing, particularly, triumphs in computing intensive operations while keeping data privacy and energy efficiency in check (Greco et al., 2020).

High-Performance Edge Computing (HPEC) can play an instrumental role in lifting a substantial load on cloud computing solutions when it comes to deploying Deep Learning (DL) algorithms for classifying big data. This can be explained by the unique architectures of HPEC platforms that employ parallel computing, tensor processing units (TPU), and even Field-Programmable Gate Array (FPGA) processors (Li & Liewig, 2020; Sittón-Candanedo et al., 2020; Y. Zhang et al., 2021). Also, edge computing boards possess specialized Graphical Processing Units (GPU) that enables faster processing of DL systems, not to mention specialized software packages that enables such processing powers. Despite its compelling performance, HPEC platforms behold limitations that prevent mainstream adoption compared to alternative solutions, such cloud computing (Merenda et al., 2020).

Notwithstanding, the collection, pre-processing, and post-processing of big data engenders many challenges and opportunities for optimizing HPEC performance for data classification and, in turn, yield better outcomes (Alsalemi et al., 2020). This is where the concept of data lakes in adopted: raw-formatted large masses of data that are plausibly more compatible with many ML algorithms than structured data stores. Data lakes help speed up the classification of big data with real-time or near-real-time performance, which is especially applicable in HPEC use cases (Sawadogo & Darmont, 2021). With an energy data classification theme, in this book chapter, we aim to carry out a comparative study that examines the merits, performance and efficiency metrics, and limitations of notable HPEC platforms centered around a DL data lake classification framework. Namely, we intend to analyze the computing performance of two common edge computing boards and shed light on their computing performance, cost, and features integrated with a brief performance comparison of cloud-based alternatives.

In the literature, there are several contributions in the field of data classification via time-series transformation. Wang and Chen present a load signature creation approach for load identification tasks in household situations (CHEN & WANG, 2022). The load signature is based on the Gramian Angular Field (GAF) encoding theory, which is simple to implement and dramatically decreases the network's data transmission volume. Furthermore, edge computing design may make good use of computational resources while relieving server strain. The experimental findings using NILM datasets show that the suggested technique outperforms other methods in the identification of household appliances when resources are limited.

Furthermore, a related study on sensor data classification is overviewed, where the authors introduce a method for sensor categorization that makes use of multivariate time series sensor data as inputs (Yang et al., 2020). The framework encodes multivariate time series data into two-dimensional colored images and concatenates the images into a larger image for classification using three transformation methods: Gramian Angular Summation Field (GASF), Gramian Angular Difference Field (GADF), and Markov Transition Field. Two open multivariate datasets were utilized to assess the effect of alternative transformation methods, picture sequences, and the complexity of ConvNet topologies on classification accuracy. The results reveal that the choice of transformation techniques and the order of concatenation have no meaningful effect on the prediction outcome.

Also, edge computing can play an imperative role in accelerating adoption of DL systems in resource-constrained applications. Zhu et al. propose the use of edge computing to mitigate power consumption in computing AI program, contributing towards a "green" manifesto for Industrial Internet of Things (IIoT) (Zhu et al., 2022). We first propose a heterogeneous intelligent edge computing framework to offload most AI workloads from servers. A unique technique to optimize scheduling for diverse AI activities is presented to improve the energy efficiency of various computer resources. In the performance evaluation, the authors built a tiny testbed to demonstrate the energy efficiency of AI-driven IIoT applications using intelligent edge computing. Meanwhile, detailed simulation findings demonstrate that in most cases, the suggested online scheduling technique uses less than 80% of the energy of static scheduling. Speaking of IIoT, the concept of data lakes is depicted in (Yu et al., 2022), where an efficient IoT big data ecosystem is developed on a three-layer architecture that includes an edge layer, a cloud layer, and an application layer. To increase both performance and efficiency, data lakes in the cloud layer are incorporated with an edge computing aided autoencoder is presented and enabled by being deployed in a distributed way. Results are collected on a real-world case study from the industry is used to show the performance increase of edge computing-based IoT systems in conjunction with the employed AI approach.

In terms of the nature of the algorithms employed in the literature, a combination of ML algorithms are utilized such as K-Nearest Neighbor (KNN), Random Forest (RF), and Decision Trees as well as DL algorithms including Convolutional Neural Network (CNN), Deep Neural Network (DNN), 2D Convolutional Neural Networks (2D-CNNs), and Transfer Learning, among others.

MAIN FOCUS OF THE CHAPTER

In terms of notable contributions, this book chapter aims to achieve the following objectives:

1. Present a unified framework of HPEC that encapsulates hardware specifications, relevant software compatibility, common research and industry applications, as well as performance and efficiency metrics; and
2. Compile a comparative performance study on two common HPEC platforms: the ODROID-XU4, and Jetson Nano running classification task of an aggregated energy consumption dataset.

The remainder of this book chapter is organized as follows Section 2 introduces data lakes for HPECs. Section 3 describes the HPEC platforms used in this study where Section 4 describes the algorithms used in evaluating the aforementioned platforms. The study results are reported and discussed in Section 5, and the book chapter is concluded in Section 6.

DATA LAKES FOR HPEC

Conventionally, data comes in three main representations: structured, semi-structured, and unstructured. Also, big data is used to identify datasets that are so large in entries that exceed traditional computation capabilities of managing it (Miloslavskaya & Tolstoy, 2016). Correspondingly, data lakes are repositories of raw-formatted data, stored as their natural file types, whether binary, blob, JavaScript Object Notation (JSON), Comma-Separated Values (CSV), Structured Query Language (SQL), etc. As less-organized data representations, data lakes allow for facilitated processing using ML and visualization purposes. As the names hints, data lakes are designed to hold big data repositories that are usually unstructured (Miloslavskaya & Tolstoy, 2016). In a data lake, a flat structure dominates the repository, where raw values are semantically identified using a unique identifier (e.g., a timestamp) coupled with metadata tags. In spirit, data lakes support real-time or near real-time data acquisition speed and is quite cost-effective in preliminary analysis of raw data using ML algorithms.

In this context, we follow a similar approach to collecting contextual appliance-level energy data. Using *energy data lakes*, power consumption information coupled with ambient conditions of the environment can be conveniently accumulated into an ever expanding raw-formatted dataset. Specifically, Figure 1 illustrates the edge computing platform role and the hybrid edge-cloud approach employed for creating the energy data lake.

Figure 1. Hybrid-edge cloud for creating an energy data lake.

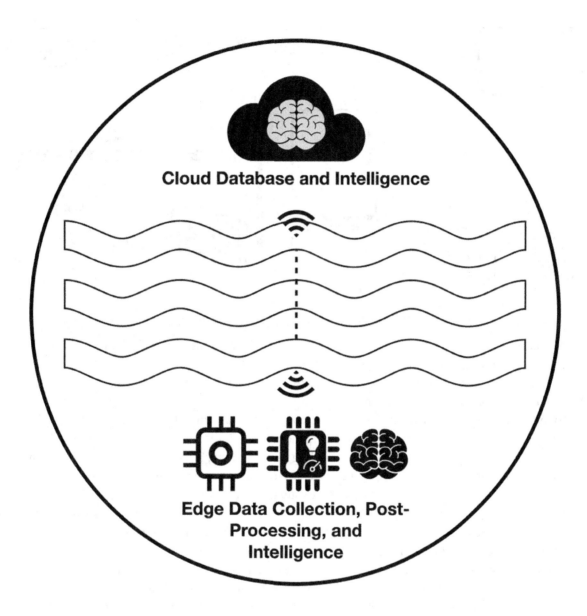

In a testbed developed by authors, it is aimed to build a novel appliance level dataset with contextual ambient environmental data. Power consumption data is collected via smart plugs that transfer the data locally to the HPEC board. The HPEC platform, on the other hand, accumulates temperature, humidity, luminosity, and barometric pressure via an externally connected to a sensing board. After the HPEC platform performs edge AI computations on the collected data, to clean it, summarize it, anonymize it, and classify it, and transmits it to a cloud server for further deep processing and storage. Figure 2 illustrates the heterogeneous sensing setup.

Figure 2. Proposed heterogeneous sensing setup.

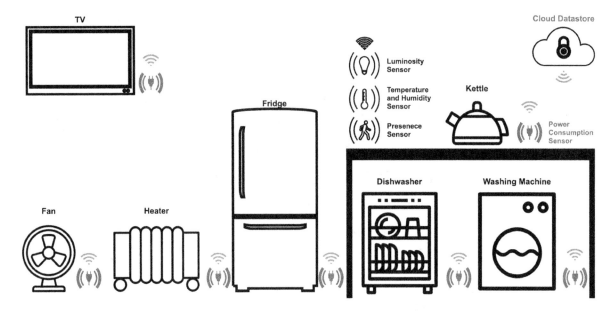

Collected energy and ambient environmental data are stored both in the HPEC platform and in a backup cloud server (i.e. Google Firebase Database). This allows for both local processing and cloud offloading of selected classification tasks. It is worthy to mention that when running deep ML algorithms the data may be converted to CSV format via a script.

To understand the contents of the energy data lake, proper labeling of data is essential for effective classification, and in turn, recommendations. Another critical building block is the concept of micro-moments. Pioneered by Google for online marketing (Ramaswamy, 2015), micro-moments are considered as short, contextual events, comprising a specific end-user behavior. Building upon the empirical work of (Alsalemi et al., 2019) for the energy context, we describe the five Energy Micro-Moment (EMM) indices, from healthy (EMM 0) to extremely excessive (EMM 5). They range from normal consumption, to identifying appliance status change, and also classifying unhealthy consumption into environment-based (i.e. consuming unnecessary power because of ambient environment), no-presence based consumption (e.g., leaving heating on while outside room or house), and extreme consumption levels in terms power magnitude. In this work, a basic EMM scheme is suggested, known as the Binary Energy Micro-Moments (BEMMs), which simplifies micro-moments into only two classes: abnormal consumption, and normal consumption. The BEMM scheme is best used for abnormality detection applications and is used in this study.

On that account, elevating dimensions to a higher level can unravel new possibilities for classifying time series data. Enter GAFs: when classifying 2D GAF representations, not only novel insights can be revealed but in potentially faster and more efficient manner. For example, new power consumption patterns can be discerned from a pictorial representation of a 24-hour consumption summary over a 12-month period indicating periods of excessive consumption. Accordingly, a GAF conversion scheme is employed to turn a large number of time series data points to several thousand images, which considerably accelerates processing time. Further information on the GAF creation process is detailed in (Alsalemi et al., 2021).

In this context, we follow a similar approach to collecting contextual appliance-level energy data. Using *energy data lakes*, power consumption information coupled with ambient conditions of the environment can be conveniently accumulated into an ever expanding raw-formatted dataset. Specifically, Table 1 describes an energy data lake created by the authors.

Table 1. Energy data lake overview.

Formatting	JSON
Geolocation	De Montfort University AI Lab and Energy Lab (stored in both edge computing device and cloud datastore)
Acquisition Frequency	5 sec – 2 min
Size	Minimum 3-6 months (100-500 MB)
Data Contents	• Power consumption data (V, A, W), • Temperature (°C), • Humidity (%), • Barometric pressure (Pa), • Light level (lux), • Carbon dioxide (CO_2) level (PPM), • Room occupancy (binary) • Outdoor conditions (e.g., temperature, humidity, Ultraviolet Index (UV) index)

Accordingly, such energy data lake is created to facilitate knowledge extraction via ML algorithms as well as effective data visualization. Therefore, the hardware aspects of the data generation and storage are described next.

Building upon the empirical work of [1], Table 2 lists the five Energy Micro-Moment (EMM) indexes, from healthy (EMM 0) to extremely excessive (EMM 5). They range from normal consumption, to identifying appliance status change, and also classifying unhealthy consumption into environment-based (i.e. consuming unnecessary power because of ambient environment), no-presence based consumption (e.g., leaving heating on while outside room or house), and extreme consumption levels in terms power magnitude.

Table 2. Data classes.

Classes	Description
0	Normal consumption
1	Switch appliance on/off
2	No-presence normal consumption
3	Context-based excessive consumption
4	Extremely excessive consumption

To illustrate the EMM index further, let us take a case study of Adam living in an urban apartment. During the morning, Adam turned on the kettle (EMM 1) to make tea and retrieved milk from the fridge (EMM 0). Then Adam went for errands and forgot the heater on (EMM 2). Later in the afternoon, Adam returned, turned off the heater (EMM 2), and switched on the lights (EMM 3) despite the fact that there was bright daytime light. In the evening, Adam fetched a meal from the fridge and cooked it in the microwave (switch on: EMM 1), although he forgot to close the fridge door, which increased its power consumption beyond normal levels (EMM 4). This example, despite its simplicity, reflect common healthy and unhealthy end-user energy habits. Thus, the EMM Index can be used as a powerful tool to classify energy data lakes into meaningful cluster for further analysis. It is noteworthy to mention that this example involves a specific case study of a domestic end-user using a specific set of appliances in a given indoor and outdoor environment. In order to scale the example to span more case studies for a variety of appliances, behaviors, and environments, a large, rich dataset is required to train ML classifiers to be able to adapt accordingly. In this article, a basic EMM scheme is suggested, known as the Binary Energy Micro-Moments (BEMMs), which simplifies micro-moments into only two classes: abnormal consumption, and normal consumption. The BEMM scheme is best used for abnormality detection applications and is used in this study.

HPEC PLATFORMS OVERVIEW

Before delving into the sensory testbed used to fill up the energy data lake, we provide a brief introduction to the single-board multicore edge platforms employed in this study.

Starting with ODROID-XU4 (Fernandes & Bala, 2016), it is a single-board computing platform that has low power usage and has a rather compact form factor relative to most other built-in ARM units. It houses the combination of an ARM Cortex-A15 and Cortex-A7 big.LITTLE CPU, and an ARM Mali-T628 GPU, which is advantageous when running deep ML algorithms locally in terms processing time.

Next, the Jetson Nano board, developed by NVIDIA, is a popular HPEC used for various computer vision, real-time image and video processing, and ML applications. It runs on a Quad-core ARM A57 @1.43 GHz CPU with a 128-core Max-well GPU with 2 GB standard RAM. Compared with boards described earlier, the Jetson Nano is the most affordable despite its comparatively competitive specifications as well as well documented installation and ML setup guides. The HPEC platforms are depicted in Figure 3. The aforementioned boards are summarized and compared in Table 3.

Figure 3. HPEC hardware platforms.

Jetson Nano

ODROID-XU4

Table 3. HPEC hardware platforms overview.

#	Board Name	CPU	GPU/TPU	Floating-Point Operations Per Second (FLOPs)	Memory (RAM)	Selling Price (USD)	ML Support
1	Jetson Nano	Quad-core ARM A57 @1.43 GHz	128-core Maxwell™ GPU	8	2 GB	59	TensorFlow, PyTorch
2	ODROID-XU4	ARM® Cortex™-A15 Quad + 2.0GHz/Cortex™-A7 Quad 1.4GHz	Mali™-T628 MP	8/8	2 GB	80.49	TensorFlow Lite, PyTorch

INTELLIGENCE OVERVIEW

To provide a concise exposition of the data processing employed in this work. In this section, classification model selection, training, validation, and testing on the cloud and on the edge are described.

Firstly, the TensorFlow (TF) Python library is employed for ML and DL model development. The library includes a lightweight counterpart, known as TensorFlow Lite (TFLite), designed to import and compute TFLite models in a process known as inference. Using TF, a model is created and trained on the provided data. It is then validated and exported as a TFLite model to be imported and executed on a compatible edge computing device.

Secondly, the TFLite Model Maker companion library is utilized for creating and exporting the TFLite model (*TensorFlow Lite Model Maker*, n.d.). It is a recently developed library by the TF team and is currently undergoing Beta testing. In this work, a modified version of the EfficientNet-B0 model is utilized (Tan & Le, 2019), which is a computationally efficient model based on CNNs with the ability to carry out transfer learning to a variety of image datasets, capturing prominent features and building a mature model accordingly. The EfficientNet-B0 is a member of the EfficientNet model family and one of the most computationally efficient versions. The EfficientNet-B0 model has been employed in this study due to (a) its well-documented implementation for image classification and (b) its edge-compatible architecture that can used be for edge-based classification. Other models can be used for this study; however, they may require elaborate programmatic changes in order to be compatible with the edge computing platform used in this work.

The model spans seven blocks that carry out a different number of operations including convolution, normalization, zero padding, rescaling, addition, etc. Also, the EfficientNet-B0 model has been employed in this study due to (a) its well-documented implementation for image classification and (b) its edge-compatible architecture that can used be for edge-based classification. Other models can be used for this study; however, they may require elaborate programmatic changes in order to be compatible with the edge computing platform used in this work. Figure. 4 shows the network architecture. In terms of model parameters, the default model configuration is used (hub_keras_layer_v1v2 (0, 1280), dropout (0, 1280), and dense (0, 2)).

Figure 4. Classification model architecture.

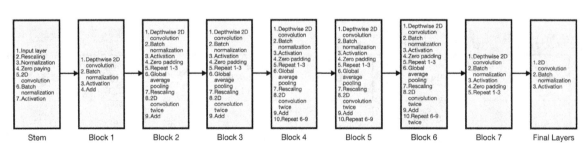

It is noteworthy to mention that the model training, validation, and export are carried out on a cloud server in order to train large sums of time series data economically with sufficient speed.

After the model is chosen and configured, data is supplied to the model instance for training. Data is split into three sub-datasets: the training, validation, and test datasets split as 80%, 10%, and 10% respectively. The model is fitted for a specified number of epochs. During training, high consumption snapshots are classified as abnormal and otherwise classified is normal. Following training, the model is validated using the validation dataset for a specified number of epochs. Then the model is exported as a TFLite model, which is downloaded to the computing edge device for inference. On the edge side, the TFLite model is downloaded, imported into a Python interface, where the test dataset is run through the imported lightweight model and classified accordingly.

RESULTS AND DISCUSSION

In this section, HPEC platform comparison in terms of computational performance, model classification, and cost are reported and discussed.

In this implementation, for the purposes of illustrating the performance of the model on a large scale, the UK Domestic Appliance-Level Electricity (UK-DALE) dataset is employed due to its large size and multi-year duration (Kelly & Knottenbelt, 2015). All data generated or analyzed during this study are included in (Kelly & Knottenbelt, 2015). However, the dataset described in Section 3 is richer in parameters yet is still under construction. The UK-DALE dataset keeps record of the power consumption data from five houses in the UK, where in each household, aggregated power consumption is collected along with appliance-level data every six seconds. In our implementation, we have used aggregated power consumption data from one house. It is important to note that the BEMM scheme has been utilized to classify the input data either as abnormal or normal.

Table 4 summarizes the HPEC platforms performance comparison. Starting, 70 million data points are converted into 1,630 GAF images with 1D-to-2D ratio of 42,945. Each image has the resolution of 648 by 648 pixels. In this implementation, the TensorFlow 2.7.0 library is employed in cloud operations run on Google Colab (with a GPU) and edge operations on the HPEC boards. After multiple tests, 35 epochs was chosen as the optimum number of epochs for the EfficientNet-B0 model, as overfitting is observed for higher number of epochs. It can be commonly noted that training accuracy is higher than the evaluation's, due to the use of a Dropout layer in the model, which is automatically deactivated in evaluation, resulting a minor accuracy drop. Model accuracy and loss curves are plotted in Figure 5.

Figure 5. Model accuracy and loss over number of epochs.

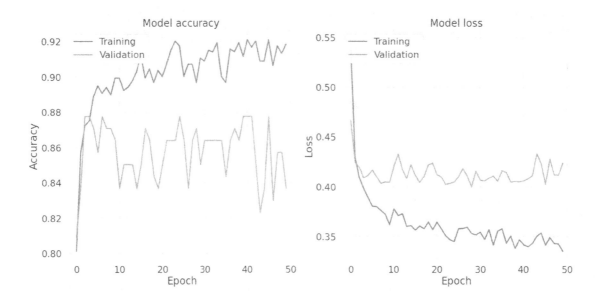

Following training and validation on the cloud, the model is exported, downloaded, imported, and tested on the each HPEC platform. It also noteworthy to mention that the TFLite model is also tested on the cloud for accuracy and computation performance benchmarking purposes. It is noteworthy to mention that in terms of classification accuracy, precision, recall, and F1 score, the performance of the four HPEC platforms are comparable, between 89% and 91%.

In terms of computational speed, the cloud implementation excels given its high performance GPU. However, the performance of the ODROID-XU4 is considerably high with 28.5 sec using 8 cores, which is approximately 6.9 times faster the cloud TFLite implementation. In terms of accuracy, the model scores evenly with an average of 89.4%. To provide more perspective, the ODROID-XU4 can classify a GAF image that represents ~42 thousand data points in less than 17.5 msec, which is very close to real-time performance.

However, when compared with the performance of the Jetson Nano, its model performance is considered the highest, with a 19.90 sec classification speed using four cores. It is almost comparable with the cloud performance, which sheds light on the potential of edge computing in enabling novel ML opportunities on the network edge.

Emphasizing on Jetson Nano classification performance, Table 5 show the model evaluation metrics. As indicated in the data, the model is providing adequate classification accuracy without risking overfitting, thanks to the evaluating the model over multiple epochs. It is worthy to mention that the edge implementation excels in terms of power consumption, with an average of less than 10 W, which is considerably lower than most conventional cloud clusters (e.g., a minimum of 350 W per GPU) (A. Zhang et al., 2021).

Table 4. HPEC platforms classification performance compared with conventional cloud ML.

	ODROID XU4 (HPEC, TFLite)	Jetson Nano (HPEC, TFLite)	Cloud (Google Colab, TF)	Cloud (Google Colab, TFLite)
Model performance (sec)	28.51	19.90	19.10	196.62
Model accuracy	89.57%	90.80%	89.65%	89.08%

Table 5. Edge micro-moment classification model metrics on Jetson Nano using TFLite.

Metric	Average Score
Precision	90.53%
Recall	93.48%
F1 score	91.98%
Accuracy	90.80%

FUTURE RESEARCH DIRECTIONS

As part of future work, the output of the presented classifier can be used as input to a recommender system to be able to produce personalized, context-driven suggestion that motivate sustainable energy behavior along with using the data for novel and meaningful visualizations that signify consumption patterns and abnormalities. The source code of the proposed system is uploaded on GitHub[1].

CONCLUSION

In the pursuit of advancing HPEC research on AI with a particular focus on IoE, a comparative study is conducted to analyze the computation performance, cost, and features of common platforms. Specifically, a specialized performance study is reported on the two common HPEC platforms: the ODROID-XU4 and the Jetson Nano using an edge GAF transfer learning based classifier as the reference algorithm.

In this implementation, a novel customizable 1D-to-2D GAF generator is presented and run on the UK-DALE dataset to convert 70 million datapoints into 1,630 GAF images. A DL classifier based on the EfficientNet-B0 model is developed on TF and exported into a lightweight version for execution on the ODROID-XU4, showcasing adequate performance and impressive computational efficiency, as fast as 8.19 msec per classified GAF image using Jetson Nano.

To conclude, unlocking HPEC potential for AI can release vast opportunities for optimizing existing use cases through cost-effectiveness, data privacy, and energy efficiency as well as create new applications that were not possible without the innovative use of Edge AI.

ACKNOWLEDGMENT

This research received no specific grant from any funding agency in the public, commercial, or not-for-profit sectors.

REFERENCES

Alsalemi, A., Amira, A., Malekmohamadi, H., Diao, K., & Bensaali, F. (2021). *Elevating Energy Data Analysis with M2GAF: Micro-Moment Driven Gramian Angular Field Visualizations.* International Conference on Applied Energy. https://dora.dmu.ac.uk/handle/2086/21303

Alsalemi, A., Himeur, Y., Bensaali, F., Amira, A., Sardianos, C., Chronis, C., Varlamis, I., & Dimitra-kopoulos, G. (2020). A Micro-Moment System for Domestic Energy Efficiency Analysis. *IEEE Systems Journal*, ●●●, 1–8. DOI: 10.1109/JSYST.2020.2997773

Alsalemi, A., Ramadan, M., Bensaali, F., Amira, A., Sardianos, C., Varlamis, I., & Dimitrakopoulos, G. (2019). Endorsing domestic energy saving behavior using micro-moment classification. *Applied Energy*, 250, 1302–1311. DOI: 10.1016/j.apenergy.2019.05.089

CHEN, J., & WANG, X. (2022). Non-intrusive Load Monitoring Using Gramian Angular Field Color Encoding in Edge Computing. *Chinese Journal of Electronics*, 31(4), 1–9.

Fernandes, S. L., & Bala, G. J. (2016). ODROID XU4 based implementation of decision level fusion approach for matching computer generated sketches. *Journal of Computational Science*, 16, 217–224. DOI: 10.1016/j.jocs.2016.07.013

Greco, L., Percannella, G., Ritrovato, P., Tortorella, F., & Vento, M. (2020). Trends in IoT based solu-tions for health care: Moving AI to the edge. *Pattern Recognition Letters*, 135, 346–353. DOI: 10.1016/j.patrec.2020.05.016 PMID: 32406416

Kelly, J., & Knottenbelt, W. (2015). The UK-DALE dataset, domestic appliance-level electricity demand and whole-house demand from five UK homes. *Scientific Data*, 2(1), 150007. DOI: 10.1038/sdata.2015.7 PMID: 25984347

Li, W., & Liewig, M. (2020). A Survey of AI Accelerators for Edge Environment. In Rocha, Á., Adeli, H., Reis, L. P., Costanzo, S., Orovic, I., & Moreira, F. (Eds.), *Trends and Innovations in Information Systems and Technologies* (pp. 35–44). Springer International Publishing., DOI: 10.1007/978-3-030-45691-7_4

Merenda, M., Porcaro, C., & Iero, D. (2020). Edge Machine Learning for AI-Enabled IoT Devices: A Review. *Sensors (Basel)*, 20(9), 2533. DOI: 10.3390/s20092533 PMID: 32365645

Miloslavskaya, N., & Tolstoy, A. (2016). Big Data, Fast Data and Data Lake Concepts. *Procedia Com-puter Science*, 88, 300–305. DOI: 10.1016/j.procs.2016.07.439

Ramaswamy, S. (2015, April). *How micro-moments are changing the rules.* Think with Google. https://www.thinkwithgoogle.com/marketing-resources/micro-moments/how-micromoments-are-changing-rules/

Sawadogo, P., & Darmont, J. (2021). On data lake architectures and metadata management. *Journal of Intelligent Information Systems*, 56(1), 97–120. DOI: 10.1007/s10844-020-00608-7

Sittón-Candanedo, I., Alonso, R. S., García, Ó., Gil, A. B., & Rodríguez-González, S. (2020). A Review on Edge Computing in Smart Energy by means of a Systematic Mapping Study. *Electronics (Basel)*, 9(1), 48. DOI: 10.3390/electronics9010048

Tan, M., & Le, Q. V. (2019). *EfficientNet: Rethinking Model Scaling for Convolutional Neural Networks.* https://arxiv.org/abs/1905.11946v5

TensorFlow Lite Model Maker. (n.d.). TensorFlow. Retrieved December 27, 2021, from https://www.tensorflow.org/lite/guide/model_maker

Yang, C.-L., Chen, Z.-X., & Yang, C.-Y. (2020). Sensor Classification Using Convolutional Neural Network by Encoding Multivariate Time Series as Two-Dimensional Colored Images. *Sensors (Basel)*, 20(1), 168. DOI: 10.3390/s20010168 PMID: 31892141

Yu, W., Liu, Y., Dillon, T. S., & Rahayu, W. (2022). Edge computing-assisted IoT framework with an autoencoder for fault detection in manufacturing predictive maintenance. *IEEE Transactions on Industrial Informatics*, ●●●, 1–1. DOI: 10.1109/TII.2022.3178732

Zhang, A., Lipton, Z. C., Li, M., & Smola, A. J. (2021). *Dive into Deep Learning.* https://arxiv.org/abs/2106.11342v2

Zhang, Y., Li, B., & Tan, Y. (2021). Making AI available for everyone at anywhere: A Survey about Edge Intelligence. *Journal of Physics: Conference Series*, 1757(1), 012076. DOI: 10.1088/1742-6596/1757/1/012076

Zhu, S., Ota, K., & Dong, M. (2022). Green AI for IIoT: Energy Efficient Intelligent Edge Computing for Industrial Internet of Things. *IEEE Transactions on Green Communications and Networking*, 6(1), 79–88. DOI: 10.1109/TGCN.2021.3100622

ADDITIONAL READING

Alsalemi, A., Amira, A., Malekmohamadi, H., Diao, K., & Bensaali, F. (2021). *Elevating Energy Data Analysis with M2GAF: Micro-Moment Driven Gramian Angular Field Visualizations.* International Conference on Applied Energy. https://dora.dmu.ac.uk/handle/2086/21303

Alsalemi, A., Himeur, Y., Bensaali, F., & Amira, A. (2022). An innovative edge-based Internet of Energy solution for promoting energy saving in buildings. *Sustainable Cities and Society*, 78, 103571. DOI: 10.1016/j.scs.2021.103571

Campolo, C., Genovese, G., Iera, A., & Molinaro, A. (2021). Virtualizing AI at the Distributed Edge Towards Intelligent IoT Applications. *Journal of Sensor and Actuator Networks*, 10(1), 13. DOI: 10.3390/jsan10010013

Imran, H. A., Mujahid, U., Wazir, S., Latif, U., & Mehmood, K. (2020). Embedded Development Boards for Edge-AI: A Comprehensive Report. *ArXiv:2009.00803[Cs].* http://arxiv.org/abs/2009.00803

Lee, H., Yang, K., Kim, N., & Ahn, C. R. (2020). Detecting excessive load-carrying tasks using a deep learning network with a Gramian Angular Field. *Automation in Construction*, 120, 103390. DOI: 10.1016/j.autcon.2020.103390

Merenda, M., Porcaro, C., & Iero, D. (2020). Edge Machine Learning for AI-Enabled IoT Devices: A Review. *Sensors (Basel)*, 20(9), 2533. DOI: 10.3390/s20092533 PMID: 32365645

Sawadogo, P., & Darmont, J. (2021). On data lake architectures and metadata management. *Journal of Intelligent Information Systems*, 56(1), 97–120. DOI: 10.1007/s10844-020-00608-7

Seon, J.-H., Sun, Y.-G., Kim, S.-H., Kyeong, C., Sim, I., Lee, H.-J., & Kim, J.-Y. (2021). Classification Method of Multi-State Appliances in Non-intrusive Load Monitoring Environment based on Gramian Angular Field. *The Journal of The Institute of Internet. Broadcasting and Communication*, 21(3), 183–191. DOI: 10.7236/JIIBC.2021.21.3.183

Shakarami, A., Ghobaei-Arani, M., & Shahidinejad, A. (2020). A survey on the computation offloading approaches in mobile edge computing: A machine learning-based perspective. *Computer Networks*, 182, 107496. DOI: 10.1016/j.comnet.2020.107496

KEY TERMS AND DEFINITIONS

Computational Efficiency: The measure of how much time a given computational task needs to run on a given computational device.

Data Lake: Repositories of raw-formatted data, stored as their natural file types, whether binary, blob, JavaScript Object Notation (JSON), Comma-Separated Values (CSV), Structured Query Language (SQL), etc.

Deep Learning: a subset of machine learning methods that employs neural networks.

Edge Artificial Intelligence: The distributed implementation of machine learning systems on resource-constrained devices with specialized hardware that optimizes for computational performance and efficiency for specific purposes. The name 'edge' is used to illustrate that the computations are conducted on the network's edge, i.e., on a local level near the data collection site.

Energy Efficiency: The study of the reduction of electric power consumption usage used to achieve a specific goal or goals.

Floating-Point Operations Per Second (FLOPs): A term used to quantify the computational performance of a given computational device.

Gramian Angular Field (GAF): A mathematical tool used to convert one-dimensional, cartesian time-series based data to two-dimensional polar counterparts.

High Performance Edge Computing (HPEC): A group of edge computing devices that are capable of running complex computational tasks, such as deep learning, by the use of advanced graphical processing units.

Endnote

[1]   https://github.com/Abdol/GAF-Energy

Chapter 7
Machine Learning and HPC in Computer–Aided Design of Electric Machines

Vladyslav Pliuhin

O.M. Beketov National University of Urban Economy in Kharkiv, Ukraine

Yevgen Tsegelnyk

https://orcid.org/0000-0003-1261-9890

O.M. Beketov National University of Urban Economy in Kharkiv, Ukraine

Maria Sukhonos

O.M. Beketov National University of Urban Economy in Kharkiv, Ukraine

Ihor Biletskyi

O.M. Beketov National University of Urban Economy in Kharkiv, Ukraine

Sergiy Plankovskyy

O.M. Beketov National University of Urban Economy in Kharkiv, Ukraine

Vitaliy Tietieriev

O.M. Beketov National University of Urban Economy in Kharkiv, Ukraine

ABSTRACT

The current approach to designing electric machines is carried out using a 'cascade' algorithm, wherein sequential calculations are performed according to formulas derived from electromagnetic theory. However, this approach is tailored to each specific type of electric machine, making modification of projects difficult and not always feasible. One promising solution to address this issue is to leverage HPC (High-Performance Computing) calculations in conjunction with machine learning capabilities. This chapter examines established methodologies for designing and optimizing electric machines, ultimately advocating for the integration of machine learning and modern optimization algorithms.

INTRODUCTION

Machine Learning (ML) is the use of mathematical data models that help a computer learn without instructions. It is considered a form of Artificial Intelligence (AI). At ML by means of algorithms regularities of data come to light. Based on these patterns, a data model is created for forecasting. The more data such a model processes and the longer it is used, the more accurate the results become. This is very

DOI: 10.4018/978-1-6684-3795-7.ch007

similar to how a person improve their skills in practice (Dimiduk et al., 2018; Cioffi et al., 2020; Sarker, 2021). Due to the adaptive nature of ML, it is ideal for scenarios in which data is constantly changing, the properties of queries or tasks are unstable or it is virtually impossible to write code to solve (Gaudio et al., 2019; Balachandran, 2020).

In its simplest form, ML uses programmed algorithms that obtain and analyze input data and predict output values from the allowable range. As new data becomes available, these algorithms learn and optimize their performance, increasing productivity and subsequently developing "intelligence".

The concepts of Data Science (DS) and ML should not be confused. These tools intersect in many ways, but still they are different and each with its own tasks. This work will also show how not to confuse such concepts, ML, AI and DS. Artificial intelligence is a variety of technological and scientific solutions and methods that help make programs like human intelligence. Artificial intelligence includes many tools, algorithms and systems, including all components of DS and ML (Raschka et al., 2020).

Data science – the science of methods of data analysis and extraction of valuable information and knowledge. It intersects with areas such as ML and cognitive science, as well as technology for working with Big Data. The result of DS is the analyzed data and finding the right approach for further processing, sorting, sampling, data retrieval. For example, there are simple data on financial transactions of enterprise costs and data of counterparties. These data are linked only through intermediate bank data or dates and times of transactions. As a result of in-depth machine analysis, it is possible to determine through intermediate data which counterparty is the most costly (Zhang et al., 2018; Aksonov et al., 2021).

Finally, ML is one of the sections of AI, algorithms that allow a computer to draw conclusions based on data without following strict rules. That is, the machine can find patterns in complex and multiparameter problems (which the human brain cannot solve), thus finding more accurate answers. The result is correct forecasting.

What is needed for ML:

- *Data* – basic information that we usually ask the client to provide. This includes any data samples that the system needs to be trained to work with;
- *Signs* – this part of the work is carried out in close cooperation with the client. We identify key business needs and jointly decide what characteristics and properties the system should track as a result of training;
- *Algorithm* – the choice of method for solving the business problem. We solve this task without the participation of the client by our employees.

Choosing the right ML algorithm depends on several factors, including the size of the data, its quality and variety, and the understanding of which answers based on this data the business needs. It is also need to pay attention to accuracy, training time, parameters, data and more. Therefore, choosing the right algorithm is a combination of business needs, specifications, experimental work and accounting for available time. Quote from the Microsoft manual (Microsoft, 2021): *"The machine learning algorithm cheat sheet helps you to choose from a variety of machine learning algorithms to find the appropriate algorithm for your specific problems"* (Figure 1). Machine learning is widely used in business intelligence, business, advertising, medicine, antivirus software, security and many others. However, there is no information on the use of ML and AI capabilities in the field of electrical engineering. However, there is a need to find a better, optimal version of the electric machine, but these problems are solved by other means, which lag far behind the current level of scientific progress.

Figure 1. Machine learning algorithms selection sheet (Microsoft, 2021)

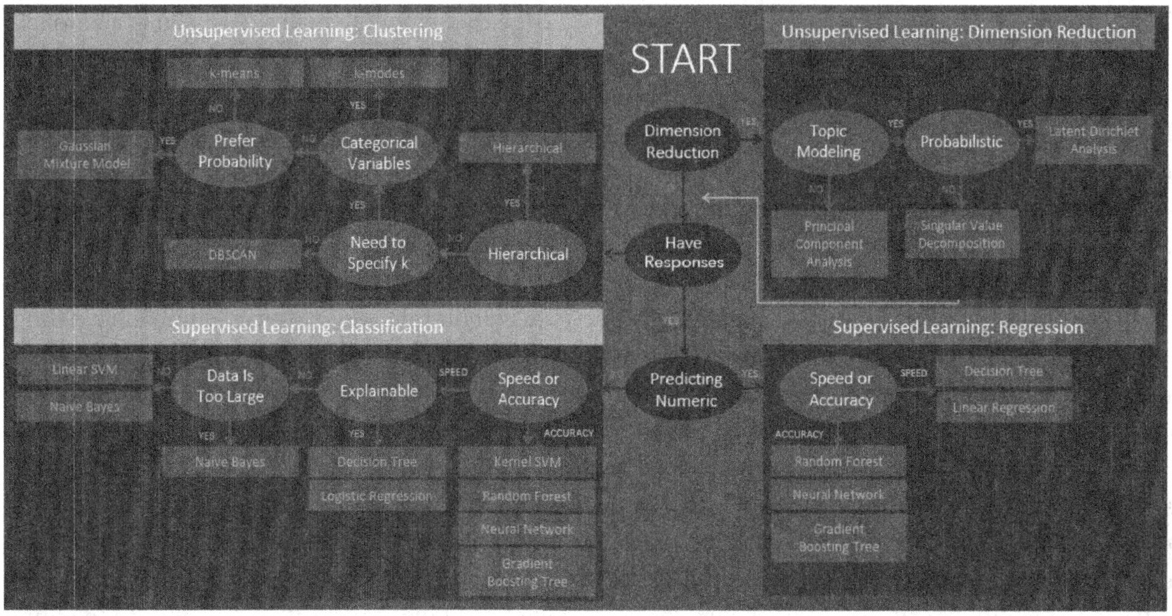

In this regard, the aim is to understand what ML offers, what is the current state of CAD programs for the design of electrical machines and how ML and HPC technology can improve the speed and quality of optimization tasks in the technical field. In addition, it will be shown how to implement a different design and optimization approach in electrical engineering, based on personal attention to customer requirements. In this case, the intelligent design system will find the best solution based on the conditions of use of the electric machine and its desired output, considering technological and economic constraints.

BACKGROUND

Currently, one of the main trends in the development of electrical engineering is the improvement of methods for designing electrical machines, which helps to reduce the weight and dimensions of machines, improve their technical and economic indicators (Liubarskyi et al., 2017; Lei et al., 2017; Aksonov et al., 2019; Iegorov et al., 2020; Kombarov et al., 2021; Okhrimenko and Zbitnieva, 2021; Tsegelnyk et al., 2022). For example, we can single out the model-based design method developed at the Fraunhofer Research Institute (Magdeburg, Germany), which makes it possible to simplify and systematize the work of an motorer, as well as reduce the time required for project development (Fraunhofer IFF, 2015).

The operational properties of EM are provided by the appropriate selection of the main dimensions and electromagnetic calculation, which includes the calculation of windings, magnetic circuit, parameters, and performance characteristics. Among the methods for finding the parameters, electromagnetic loads and losses of EM, one can note the method of conductivities of toothed contours (Okhrimenko and Zbitnieva, 2021), the wave theory of electrical machines (Mukerji et al., 2018), graphic-analytical methods (Awwad et al., 2021), equations of the theory of electrical circuits (Cheng et al., 2017).

An analysis of the numerous scientific and technical literature makes it possible to single out the currently formed methods for designing EMs (Cathey, 2001; Sen, 2006; Deshpande, 2011; Upadhyay, 2011; Aravind et al., 2012; Favi et al., 2012; Stojkovic, 2012; Benamimour et al., 2013; Duan and Ionel, 2013; Pyrhönen et al., 2014; Tsai et al., 2016; Daukaev et al., 2017; Bonneel et al., 2018; Jastrzebski et al., 2018; Kallaste et al., 2018; Ghorbanian et al., 2019; Schwarz and Moeckel, 2019; Ulu et al., 2019; Finkelshtein et al., 2020; Rivière et al., 2020; Choi and Kim, 2021; Digă et al., 2021; Lupu et al., 2021; Pliuhin et al., 2021; Shevkunova, 2021).

There is a known method for designing an EM based on the use of a calculation form with formulas that represent the parameters of the machine, and the design is carried out according to a sequential (cascade) scheme (Pyrhönen et al., 2014; Lei et al., 2017). This design method includes setting the initial data, calculating the geometric dimensions, magnetic circuit, winding data, electromagnetic loads, winding parameters (their active and inductive resistances), operating and starting characteristics, determining the power factor, efficiency, thermal ventilation calculation, mechanical calculation of individual machine components, evaluation of reliability indicators, calculation of vibroacoustic indicators, economic calculation with the definition of economic efficiency.

However, this design method is inefficient for recursive calculations, as a result of which it becomes practically impossible to organize optimization algorithms. This method is focused on the use of a standard design methodology, which is clearly stated. As a result, it is difficult to modify the project and reuse it. In addition, any structural change in the designed machine leads to the revision of the entire project, since in sequential design, the calculation formulas are rigidly connected to each other by input and output data, and each subsequent formula (lower level formulas) depends on the variables names of the previous formulas (upper level formulas). This design method does not involve the calculation of transient processes, as well as field calculations (electromagnetic, thermal, etc.). Also, this design method is focused on the choice of averaged optimal geometric dimensions according to empirical graphs and tables, and optimization according to any criteria is not provided. In addition, the design is individual for a particular type of electrical machine, and the results of the design, as well as the finished parts of the project, are almost impossible to use for other purposes, for example, for a new project that has both common components with the previous project and its own.

There is a known method for designing an EM, which consists in the sequential use of pre-written subroutines, each of which calculates one of the stages of the project (Sen, 2006; Favi et al., 2012; Bonneel et al., 2018; Lupu et al., 2021). Each subroutine includes a set of formulas. The subroutines are interconnected by serial links organized in a cascade scheme so that the data of the lower-level subroutines depend on the results of the calculation of the upper-level subroutines. Software implementation is made in procedural programming languages. This design method reduces design time through the use of computer technology and facilitates the design process and allows to optimize EM according to one or more optimality criteria.

However, this design method is also individual for a particular type of EM. In addition, the design results, as well as the finished parts of the project, are practically impossible to use for other purposes, for example, for a new project that has both components common with the previous project and its own. At the same time, the consistent scheme of the project organization makes it difficult to modify the project and reuse it. In addition, the orientation of the project towards procedural programming languages does not allow the use of modern optimization algorithms, such as the Cartesian product and the genetic algorithm, in which all variable variables can be changed simultaneously.

There is a known method for designing EM, in which the calculation of EM is implemented, the data of which are refined after the calculation of electromagnetic transients (Tsai et al., 2016; Ghorbanian et al., 2019; Ulu et al., 2019). At the same time, the variable parameters of dynamic calculations refine the design of the base machine.

However, since this design method is organized in a sequential pattern, it is difficult to modify the design and reuse it. In addition, such a design method is individual for a particular type of EM, and the design results, or its individual parts, are problematic to use for a new project that has both common components with the previous project and its own. Also, this method does not provide optimization of the underlying machine.

There is a known method for designing EM, which implements the calculation of EM, the data of which are refined after the calculation of the distribution of the electromagnetic field (Stojkovic, 2012; Miller and Staton, 2013; Bramerdorfer et al., 2018; Rivière et al., 2020). In this case, the variable parameters in the calculation of the electromagnetic field refine the design of the prototype machine.

However, this design method has the same disadvantages as the previous method, in which the data obtained as a result of the calculation are refined after the calculation of electromagnetic transients.

There is a known method for designing EM based on the use of software (Benamimour et al., 2013; Rosu et al., 2018; Kitagawa et al., 2019; Schwarz and Moeckel, 2019; Pliuhin et al., 2021). With this design method, the initial data, geometric dimensions, winding data, electromagnetic loads are set, and the power losses and characteristics of the electric machine are obtained from the calculation results. Also, this design method allows to perform parametric optimization according to the selected optimality criterion when varying the initial geometric dimensions of the machine. This design method allows to calculate the distribution of the electromagnetic field and electromagnetic transients.

However, this design method is limited by the types of EM provided by the software. In this method, there is no possibility of choosing the geometric dimensions of the EM, winding data, choosing electromagnetic loads, but they must be known in advance. In addition, this method is individual and does not involve the use and transfer of calculation results to other types of machines. At the same time, it is not possible to make changes to the calculation formulas embedded in the software.

An important problem is the correspondence of the accepted design methods to the level of software on which these methods are implemented. Existing techniques were developed in the era of procedural programming languages, the nature of which is subject to the so-called "cascade" or "waterfall" scheme. Subsequent work improved design techniques in terms of improving the quality of parameter determination, but not in the direction of their software implementation.

Currently, the designer is inextricably linked with a computer, independently solves design problems or uses third-party software. However, software has come a long way in its development and moved from a procedural to an object-oriented (OO) level a long time ago. As a result, the problem of adapting the existing procedural "book" methodology to the OO software environment constantly arises (Pliugin et al., 2015; Zablodskiy et al., 2018).

The existing design methods based on the "waterfall" organization of the calculation stages and the procedural representation of the project do not allow to implement the tasks associated with the following:

1) there is no possibility of automated transfer of the entire project or part of it to create a new one, which has both common features with the base one and its own (for example, replacing a squirrel-cage rotor in an induction motor (IM) with a winding rotor involves a complete redesign of the project from start to finish);

2) there is no mechanism for including data and dependencies of other projects into the existing project (for example, including the methodology for calculating reliability indicators in a project where they were not determined or modifying the calculation of reliability when replacing machine components);

3) it is impossible to apply modern methods of intellectual optimization, such as the Cartesian product and genetic algorithms;

4) the classification of EM, in addition to being ambiguous, is not related to the organization of design and therefore does not allow, even at the stage of forming the representation of EM as a type, to synthesize design methods and give evaluation results of the obtained modifications in scientific research;

5) the quality of development, the cost of human and material resources, the design time, which are especially relevant in the conditions of market relations and competition, with the traditional approach, are significantly inferior to object-oriented systems;

6) there is no synthesis of modern information technologies and design methodology, which would improve the efficiency of modern projects.

In computer-aided design (CAD) systems, the design of an EM consists in multiple calculation of the dependencies between the main indicators specified in the form of a system of formulas, empirical coefficients, graphical dependencies, which can be considered as design equations (Ansys, 2011). Optimal design of EM can be represented as a search for optimal parameters by solving this system of equations. The complexity of the calculation algorithm complicates the optimization problem. Despite the widespread use of computers, the optimal options for EM are sometimes chosen based on the experience and intuition of the designer.

Reducing the number of independent variables by increasing the number of stages in solving the design problem greatly facilitates the search for the best option. The main difficulty of the stated strategy for finding the maximum is to obtain optimal functional dependencies between physical variables. For most complex problems, which also include the problem of optimal design of electrical machines, these relationships cannot be obtained analytically in a general form. However, it is possible to construct multi-stage logical structures and corresponding computational algorithms for finding the maximum of a function of many variables (Pliuhin et al., 2020).

Methods for searching for options for calculating an object, such as the method of coordinate descent, Nelder-Mead, the deformable polyhedron method, etc., do not allow performing calculations with a simultaneous change in all variable variables. As a rule, many methods allow alternate variation of variables with subsequent adjustment of the region of convergence of calculations.

Even simultaneous variation of all variables does not give acceptable results: a machine that has received the status of optimal at the found optimal value, for example, the length of the stator core, does not guarantee that this length will give the best result when varying another variable, for example, the diameter of the stator core. There is a possibility that a machine that is optimal for a given diameter will be even better for a length different from that fixed in the previous step.

Obviously, the most acceptable optimization method would be one that would allow to perform machine calculations for all possible combinations of variable variables within given limits and with a given step (Pliuhin et al., 2023).

In this chapter, optimization methods for the Cartesian product (CP) and a genetic algorithm (GA) are considered, which make it possible to search for the best variant of computer-aided design of EM with a given optimality criterion, and to select the best one from the set of calculated variants (Petrushin and

Yenoktaiev, 2019). Obtaining an acceptable area of design decisions involves the simultaneous change of all variable variables.

It should be noted that the optimization algorithms under consideration are currently leading in terms of performance and accuracy of the resulting optimum and are involved in neural networks and artificial intelligence theory. Meanwhile, such algorithms have not yet been involved in the design of EMs. Their use in procedural projects is technically impossible.

TRADITIONAL ELECTRICAL MACHINE DESIGN APPROACH

Let's consider the design of an induction motor without optimization. The calculation procedure contains a set of about 180 formulas and covers about 300 motor parameters. The main stages of motor design are as follows:

1) determination of the main geometric dimensions (diameter, length, linear load, induction in the air gap, preliminary values of the efficiency factor and power factor);
2) calculation of the parameters of the stator tooth zone (number of stator teeth, number of turns in the winding, current density, number and size of conductors);
3) calculation of stator groove filling (groove dimensions, groove filling factor);
4) calculation of the rotor;
5) determination of operating mode parameters (active and inductive resistances of stator and rotor windings);
6) calculation of losses;
7) construction of starting and mechanical characteristics, determination of the final values of the coefficient of useful action and the coefficient of power;
8) assessment of the thermal condition and ventilation calculation;
9) calculation of shaft not mechanical strength.

The ANSYS RMxprt software forms clearly show parameters that significantly affect motor performance (Figures 2–5). However, it should be noted, that this software does not design the motor, but its verification calculation, because the geometric dimensions and winding data must be known in advance.

Figure 2. Induction motor settings page in ANSYS RMxprt

General | IndM3 |

	Name	Value	Unit	Evaluated ...	Description
	Name	Setup1			
	Enabled	✔			
	Operation Type	Motor			Motor or generator
	Load Type	Const Power			Mechanical load type
	Rated Output ...	1500	W	1500W	Rated mechanical or electrical output power
	Rated Voltage	380	V	380V	Applied or output rated line-to-line AC (RMS) or DC voltage
	Rated Speed	1410	rpm	1410rpm	Given rated speed
	Operating Tem...	75	cel	75cel	Operating temperature

Figure 3. Stator settings page in ANSYS RMxprt

Stator |

	Name	Value	Unit	Evaluated Value	Description
	Outer Diameter	131	mm	131mm	Outer diameter of the stator core
	Inner Diameter	ds		86mm	Inner diameter of the stator core
	Length	L		105mm	Length of the stator core
	Stacking Factor	0.95			Stacking factor of the stator core
	Steel Type	steel_2212			Steel type of the stator core
	Number of Slots	36			Number of slots of the stator core
	Slot Type	1			Slot type of the stator core
	Lamination Se...	0			Number of lamination sectors
	Press Board T...	0	mm		Magnetic press board thickness, 0 for non-magnetic press board
	Skew Width	0		0	Skew width measured in slot number

At each of the specified stages, the developer has to use tables or graphs with recommended ranges for selecting motor parameters. The extent to which such a choice will be correct depends on the qualification of the researcher and the correspondence of the type of motor projected to the available empirical data.

Usually, the design of an electric motor is divided into two stages: the first consists in the initial calculation of the base machine based on assumptions based on the recommended values of the input parameters, and the second – in the optimization of the base machine according to the selected optimality criteria.

Figure 4. Rotor settings page in ANSYS RMxprt

Rotor

Name	Value	Unit	Evaluated Value	Description
Stacking Factor	0.95			Stacking factor of the rotor core
Number of Slots	34			Number of slots of the rotor core
Slot Type	1			Slot type of the rotor core
Outer Diameter	dr		85.5mm	Outer diameter of the rotor core
Inner Diameter	dri		30mm	Inner diameter of the rotor core
Length	L		105mm	Length of the rotor core
Steel Type	steel_22...			Steel type of the rotor core
Skew Width	1.3		1.3	Skew width measured in slot number
Cast Rotor	✔			Rotor squirrel-cage winding is cast
Half Slot	☐			Half-shaped slot (un-symmetric)
Double Cage	☐			Double-squirrel-cage winding

Figure 5. Example of output data page in ANSYS RMxprt

Performance | Design Sheet | Curves

Data: Rated Performance ▼

	Name	Value	Units	Description
1	Stator Ohmic Loss	268.84	W	
2	Rotor Ohmic Loss	48.606	W	
3	Iron-Core Loss	42.138	W	
4	Frictional and Windage Loss	20.618	W	
5	Stray Loss	15	W	
6	Total Loss	395.2	W	
7	Output Power	1500.1	W	
8	Input Power	1895.3	W	
9	Efficiency	79.1486	%	
10	Power Factor	0.812097		
11	Rated Torque	9.85538	NewtonMeter	
12	Rated Speed	1453.54	rpm	
13	Rated Slip	0.0309718		

OPTIMIZATION OF ELECTRIC MACHINES USING MODERN ALGORITHMS

Cartesian Product

The problem of finding combinations in several sets is solved using the theory of Cartesian Product (CP) (Zablodskiy et al., 2013a). The simplest data structure occurs when there are no relationships between separate isolated data. The totality of such data is a set that does not have an internal structure.

A set can be represented as a collection of elements that have some common property. For a certain set of elements to be called a set, the following conditions must be met (Petrushin and Yenoktaiev, 2019; Pliuhin et al., 2023):

1) there must be a rule that allows to determine whether the specified element belongs to this population;
2) there must be a rule that allows to distinguish elements from each other (this, in particular, means that a set cannot contain two identical elements).

Sets are usually denoted by capital Latin letters. If the element x belongs to the set A, then this is denoted $x \in A$.

If every element of set B is also an element of set A, then set B is said to be a subset of set A: $B \subset A$.

A subset B of a set A is called a proper subset if $B \neq A$. Using the concept of a set, one can build more complex and meaningful objects.

The CP is the set $A \times B$ of all ordered pairs of elements (a, b), of which a belongs to set A, b belongs to set B. The order of the pairs can be any, but the arrangement of elements in each pair (vector) is determined by the order of the elements to be multiplied. So

$A \times B \neq B \times A$, if $B \neq A$.

If we generalize what has been said to any number of sets A_1, A_2, ..., A_n, то CP written as:

.

Degree of the CP $A_1 \times A_2 \times ... \times A_n$ will be the number of sets n, included in this CP. If all sets A_i are the same, then use the notation

$A^n = A \times A \times ... \times A$.

Cartesian product of a finite number of sets $A_1 \times A_2 \times ... \times A_n$ is defined as the set of all possible sets (tuples) of length n (composed of the elements of these sets), in which each element a_i belongs to the corresponding set A_i. In particular, for zero sets, the result is a set containing a single element, the empty tuple. For a family of sets $\{X_i\}_{i \in I}$ with possibly infinite index set I Cartesian product can be defined as a function that maps each element $i \in I$ set element X_i.

Let's consider a simple example. Let the length of the active part L, the internal D and external Da diameters of the stator vary in the EM. The task is to determine such a combination of variable parameters at which the maximum efficiency is achieved, subject to the restrictions imposed on the design solution. Combinations of variable project variables are presented in Table 1.

Table 1. Set of project variables

D, mm	100	105	110	115
D_a, mm	150	200	-	-
L, mm	95	99	103	-

The Table 1 is deliberately containing an unequal number of variable variables so as not to reduce the problem to a simple enumeration. In contrast, for example, to the coordinate descent method, where we would first obtain a set of solutions when varying one variable (the rest are fixed), we set the task of finding all possible non-repeating combinations of variable variables.

As a result of the calculation, when using such a data set, there really is a real opportunity to assess the adequacy of choosing the optimal option, without any simplifying assumptions, based on all possible combinations of variables.

Let's compose tuples (sets) of data sets for D, D_a and L:

$$D = \{100, 105, 110, 115\},$$

$$D_a = \{150, 200\},$$

$$L = \{95, 99, 103\}.$$

Then we get 24 tuples in CP $D \times D_a \times L =$
{(100, 150, 95), (100, 150, 99), (100, 150, 103), (100, 200, 95), (100, 200, 99), (100, 200, 103),
(105, 150, 95), (105, 150, 99), (105, 150, 103), (105, 200, 95), (105, 200, 99), (105, 200, 103),
(110, 150, 95), (110, 150, 99), (110, 150, 103), (110, 200, 95), (110, 200, 99), (110, 200, 103),
(115, 150, 95), (115, 150, 99), (115, 150, 103), (115, 200, 95), (115, 200, 99), (115, 200, 103)}.

Thus, the set of all ordered pairs of integers considered by Descartes is an example of the product of a set by itself. An example of a practical application of CP is the Optimetrics library used in the optimization of the ANSYS Maxwell software. Consider the practical implementation of CP based on the tuples presented in Table. 1. The set product algorithm is implemented on a recursive call of the function to enumerate data in tuples (Buhr et al., 2014). The result of the program for searching for non-repeating combinations, written by the authors in Java, is shown in Figure 6. As can be seen from Figure 6, the resulting combinations are fully consistent with those that were obtained manually.

Figure 6. The output window of the Java program for searching combinations using the CP algorithm

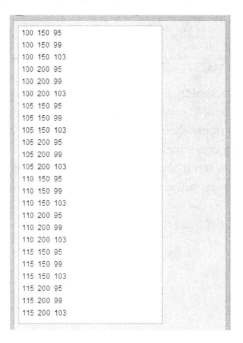

Consider optimizing the underlying machine using the CP (Petrushin and Yenoktaiev, 2019) and the Pareto preference rule (Duan and Ionel, 2013). In this example, in order to simplify the presentation of the material, the length of the active part L, the inner D and outer D_a diameters of the EM stator vary. The task is to determine such a combination of variable parameters at which the maximum efficiency is achieved, subject to the restrictions imposed on the design solution.

In contrast, for example, to the coordinate-wise descent method (Pliuhin et al., 2023), where we would first obtain a set of solutions by varying one variable (the rest are fixed), we pose the problem of finding all possible non-repeating combinations of variable variables.

As a result of the calculation, when using such a data set, there really is a real opportunity to assess the adequacy of choosing the optimal option, without any simplifying assumptions, based on all possible combinations of variables (Back, 1996).

The problem of finding combinations in several sets is reduced to the CP problem.

In order to reduce the calculation time, we perform optimization by varying two variables: the inner diameter of the stator package and the length of the stator package. As optimality criteria, the maximum efficiency and the minimum multiplicity of the starting current were chosen.

The optimization order is as follows (see Appendix A):

1) set the range of variable variables;
2) we set restrictions;
3) choose the optimality criteria and set the weight coefficients for each of them;
4) call the CP function to search for possible combinations of variable variables in a given range;
5) open a loop with the number of iterations equal to the number of previously found CP combinations;

6) in the cycle we call the function of automatic calculation of the electric motor and the function of control of restrictions; the variant that passed the constraint check is saved to a vector; if the specified restrictions are not observed, the current selection from the found combinations is eliminated as inefficient.

7) after the end of the calculation cycle, we call the function of searching for the best version of the machine among those that have passed the restrictions and have been entered into the vector; we take into account the selected optimality criteria and their weight in the calculation of Pareto optimality;

8) for the found best option (with the optimal combination of variable variables), we call the function of automatic calculation of the electric motor for the last time.

The known order of the internal organization of the CP algorithm (Zablodskiy et al., 2013a) is usually as follows (Figure 7):

1) all possible combinations of variable values are found;
2) found combinations are stored in a vector (RAM);
3) the function of recalculating the machine is performed;
4) constraints are checked and options that do not pass the test are eliminated;
5) choosing the best option among those who passed the test.

If the CP optimization algorithm is used in this way, then if there are more than four variable variables, the computer memory overflows, and the number of available combinations increases to several million.

To increase the efficiency of the algorithm under consideration, the procedure for selecting combinations that passed the check for restrictions was modified by the authors. It was decided not to store all combinations in memory, but to implement them in the constraint check function at the stage of tuple formation. The critical point in this order of operations is Point 2. The program closes with a memory overflow error.

If the found combinations are saved to a file, and not to RAM, then the program works, but the sampling process is delayed for a long time (for four variable values up to 15 hours), which is unacceptable.

Figure 7. Classical optimization algorithm using CP

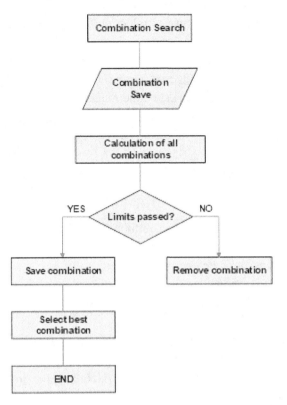

The CP algorithm (Pliuhin et al., 2023) modified by the authors is proposed in the following form (Figure 8):

1. the next combination is searched;
2. an automated calculation of the machine for the current combination is performed;
3. checking the current version for restrictions;
4. a combination of variable variables that has passed the check for restrictions, as well as an object of the calculated machine, are stored in a vector (RAM);
5. choosing the best option among the saved objects.

The result of the work of this modified algorithm exceeded expectations: the memory does not over-flow, the operating time is reduced from several hours to several seconds. Point 2, in which the automated calculation of the machine is performed, is performed in thousandths of a second due to the use of the object-oriented structure of the program.

The results of the optimization of the base machine based on the CP set algorithm are shown in Figure 9 in the form of a diagram of the average Pareto optimality criterion and in Figure 10 with variants that have passed the test (see Appendix B).

The length and inner diameter of the stator core were chosen as variable parameters. The maximum efficiency was set as the optimization optimality criterion. However, the optimization program also supports multi-criteria optimization.

According to the results of the CP calculation in the example under consideration, 710000 sets (combinations) of lengths and diameters were found, and only 128 of them passed all the specified restrictions. The basic EM variant in the diagram is represented by the last column (No. 128 on the variant number axis). 118 sets of combinations turned out to be the most optimal, 27 were the worst.

Figure 8. Modified optimization algorithm using CP

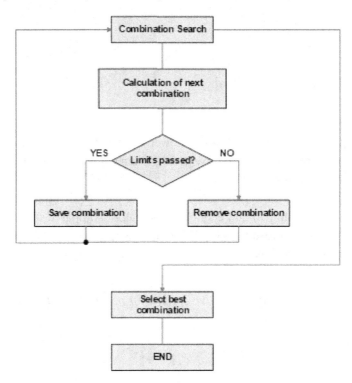

Figure 9. Results of multi-criteria optimization using the modified CP algorithm

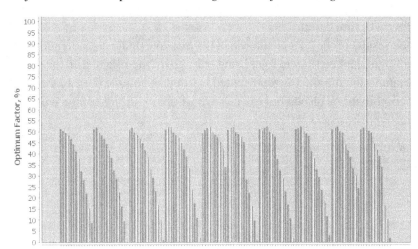

Even though the optimal option has a slightly lower efficiency than some calculation options, it wins in terms of the starting current multiplicity, which, when calculating the average Pareto criterion, brought this option to the forefront.

As a result of the optimization, the parameters of the IM with squirrel-cage rotor (SCR) were obtained, which have improved technical and economic indicators compared to the base case. Based on the obtained positive optimization results of the IM with SCR, improved EM design methodology was implemented in "Ukrelectromash" electrical machines building factory.

Figure 10. The results of the selection of effective options for multi-criteria optimization

№ в.	Bd, Тл	D, мм	Ld, мм	КПД	cos Φ	Iп/Iн	Mп/Mн	Mmax/Mн	J1, А/мм...	t1, град	Опт., %
0	0.812	140.0	190.0	0.7782	0.8213	4.38	2.06	2.35	8.47	94.6	99.24
1	0.833	141.0	184.0	0.7798	0.8178	4.46	2.11	2.41	8.47	96.4	99.74
2	0.828	141.0	185.0	0.7799	0.8196	4.45	2.1	2.4	8.47	95.9	99.76
3	0.824	141.0	186.0	0.7799	0.8214	4.44	2.09	2.38	8.47	95.5	99.77
4	0.85	142.0	179.0	0.7803	0.8124	4.51	2.15	2.46	8.47	98.2	99.89
5	0.845	142.0	180.0	0.7804	0.8144	4.5	2.14	2.45	8.47	97.7	99.93
6	0.841	142.0	181.0	0.7805	0.8164	4.49	2.13	2.43	8.47	97.2	99.96
7	0.836	142.0	182.0	0.7806	0.8184	4.48	2.12	2.42	8.47	96.7	99.98
8	0.831	142.0	183.0	0.7807	0.8202	4.48	2.11	2.41	8.47	96.2	100.0
9	0.854	143.0	177.0	0.7799	0.8096	4.52	2.16	2.47	8.47	98.9	99.76
10	0.849	143.0	178.0	0.78	0.8117	4.51	2.15	2.46	8.47	98.4	99.8
11	0.844	143.0	179.0	0.7802	0.8138	4.5	2.14	2.45	8.47	97.9	99.84
12	0.839	143.0	180.0	0.7803	0.8159	4.5	2.13	2.44	8.47	97.4	99.88
13	0.857	144.0	175.0	0.7802	0.8089	4.54	2.17	2.49	8.47	99.5	99.85
14	0.852	144.0	176.0	0.7804	0.8112	4.54	2.16	2.48	8.47	98.9	99.91
15	0.848	144.0	177.0	0.7805	0.8131	4.53	2.15	2.47	8.47	98.4	99.94
16	0.715	151.0	200.0	0.7774	0.8631	4.27	1.87	2.15	8.47	88.0	99.0

Based on the analysis of the obtained results, the following conclusions can be drawn:

1. In the CP algorithm, with a range of variation of variable variables ±1% of the base value (15 combinations), the calculation time was 14 s. With a variation range ±10% (1200 combinations), the calculation time increased to 12 min, which is quite acceptable. With a variation range ±20% (3976 combinations), the calculation time has already approached 48 min. If we change the number of

variable variables to 4 and accept the range of their variation ±20% relative to the base value, then we get about 1.5 million combinations and 8 hours of calculation. This consumes up to 1.5 GB of computer RAM.

2. A further increase in the number of variable variables is not advisable, since memory consumption increases sharply, and the resources of a personal computer become insufficient to process a huge number of variables. A preliminary estimate of the calculation time leads to several days of optimization.

3. The CP algorithm is expedient with a small number of variable parameters (2–3) and a range of their deviation relative to the base value up to ±10%.

4. The CP algorithm, in comparison with the genetic algorithm, allows you to perform multi-criteria optimization, which is its undoubted advantage. In addition, CP always gives an unambiguous single best option (absolute extremum value) among existing ones.

Genetic Optimization Algorithms

Neural networks, which are one of the promising areas of research in the field of AI, were created as a result of observing the processes occurring in the human nervous system. Approximately the same genetic algorithms were "invented", but they were no longer observing the human nervous system, but the process of evolution of living organisms (Goldberg, 1989).

Genetic algorithms (GA) is one of the areas of research in the field of AI, which is engaged in the creation of simplified models of the evolution of living organisms for solving optimization problems (Owatchaiphong and Fuengwarodsakul, 2009; Zablodskiy et al., 2013b).

Classic GA consists of the following steps (Figure 11):

1) initialization, or selection of the initial population of chromosomes;
2) assessment of the fitness of chromosomes in a population – the calculation of the fitness function for each chromosome;
3) checking the stopping condition of the algorithm;
4) selection of chromosomes – the choice of those chromosomes that will participate in the creation of descendants for the next population;
5) the use of genetic operators – mutations and crossings;
6) formation of a new population;
7) selection of the "best" chromosome.

Figure 11. Classical genetic algorithm

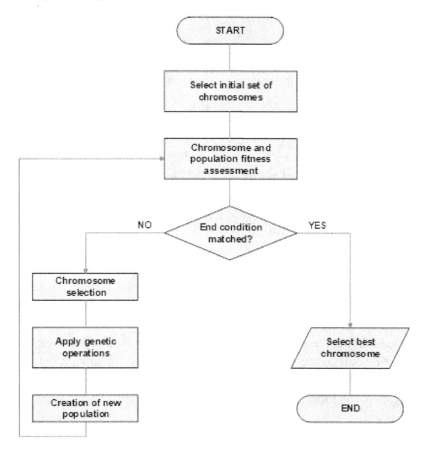

Simple GA randomly generates an initial population. The operation of GA is an iterative process that continues until a given number of generations or some other stopping criterion is met. At each generation, proportional selection for fitness, crossing and mutation is realized. Chromosomes obtained as a result of applying genetic operators to the chromosomes of the temporary parental population are included in the new population. It becomes the so-called current population for this GA iteration.

The order of optimization when using GA is different from that which was considered for CP, and is as follows (see Appendix C):

1) set the range of variable variables;
2) we set restrictions;
3) choose the optimality criterion;
4) we call the GA optimization function and obtain the optimal set of variable variables;
5) for the found set, we call the function of automatic calculation of EM.

At each next iteration, the values of the fitness function for all chromosomes of this population are calculated, after which the condition for stopping the algorithm is checked and either the result is fixed in the form of a chromosome with the highest value of the fitness function, or a transition is made to the next step of the genetic algorithm, i.e. to the selection.

Consider, using the example of optimizing an asynchronous motor, the software implementation of a genetic algorithm in the Java language in the NetBeans environment (Murach and Urban, 2015). To solve this problem, we use the freely distributed Java library EvoJ (eng. Evolution Java) (EvoJ, 2002).

The EvoJ project is conceived as an extensible Java class framework for solving various optimization problems using evolutionary (genetic) algorithms. To use EvoJ, the programmer needs to implement only one simple interface, consisting of one method. All other steps of the algorithm are taken over by EvoJ.

To solve a problem with EvoJ, it is need to:

1) create an interface with variables;
2) implement the fitness function interface;
3) create a population of solutions and perform the required number of GA iterations on them using the code above.

The example will consider two variable variables: the inside diameter of the stator pack and the length of the stator pack (Petrushin and Yenoktaiev, 2019). EvoJ allows to change variables without setting the range of variables. However, if you need to implement your own mutation strategy, then you will have to declare the setters – otherwise you will not be able to change the variables.

If the solution is not satisfactory, GA iterations can be continued (increasing the number of populations and iterations) until the desired quality of the solution is achieved. The results of the GA implementation when choosing the maximum efficiency as an optimality criterion showed that the efficiency in the optimal machine is higher than that of the base machine, and the other parameters do not go beyond the allowable redistribution.

The previously considered CP algorithm, in comparison with GA, allows you to perform multi-objective optimization, which is its undoubted advantage. In addition, CP always (!) gives an unambiguous single best option among existing ones. However, in CP, when only two variables are varied with a deviation of ±20% from the base value, the calculation time approaches 48 min.

Using GA with the same variable parameters and a deviation of ±100% (!) relative to the base value, the calculation time was only 40 s! However, GA, at least in the minimization setting given in this paper, does not allow performing multi-criteria optimization.

In GA, the number of variable parameters and the range of their change is not critical in terms of performance, because the set of variable variables is created dynamically, and not in advance, as in the CP combination method. In addition, all combinations with variables and values of the objective function are carried out in binary form. However, the running time of GA is very critical to the number of created populations and the number of iterations in populations.

The choice of the number of populations and iterations is carried out empirically and increased until an acceptable result is obtained. The result of optimization using GA will always be the best according to the selected criterion, but there is no guarantee that there is no better option than the one obtained. Actually, this is the logic of genetic selection – we get a result that approaches the best among randomly generated populations. The more of them, the more reliable the result. At the same time, the degree of reliability can be assessed by how large the spread of the results of repeated calculations for a given number of populations is.

GA performance is determined not by the number and range of variable variables, but only by the size of populations of efficient options, and the optimization result is ambiguous and close to the best. If you need to make estimated calculations as soon as possible, and the quality of the results obtained fits into the permissible error, then the use of GA optimization can become an indispensable tool for the designer.

Which algorithm to choose is up to the designer. If the importance of obtaining the optimal result outweighs the cost of obtaining it, then often the calculation time is not taken into account, and a complex optimization algorithm can be applied. When it is necessary to make estimated calculations in the shortest possible time, and the quality of the results obtained fits into the permissible error, then you can use high-speed, but less accurate algorithms.

USING MACHINE LEARNING TO OPTIMIZE ELECTRICAL MACHINES

The problem of optimal design of an EM or a series of EM can be represented as a general non-linear mathematical problem, which boils down to finding the minimum or maximum of the optimality criterion in the presence of a certain number of independent variables and limiter functions, which are technical or technological requirements-limitations to the project (Arnoux et al., 2015; Erricolo et al., 2019; Yao et al., 2019; Khan and Lowther, 2020; Romeo et al., 2020; Jackson et al., 2021; Li et al., 2021).

In computer-aided design systems, the optimization of an EM consists in multiple calculation of the dependencies between the main indicators specified in the form of a system of formulas, empirical coefficients, graphical dependencies, which can be considered as design equations (Papalambros and Wilde, 2017). Optimal design of EM can be represented as a search for optimal parameters by solving this system of equations. The complexity of the calculation algorithm complicates the optimization problem.

Reducing the number of independent variables by increasing the number of stages in solving the design problem greatly facilitates the search for the best option. However, in this case, the accuracy of determining the optimal value of the objective function is lost.

The disadvantage of the existing method is that the total development time for a Java project was about 3 days (72 hours). In addition, the operating time of the calculated algorithm increases significantly with a change in the range and number of varied values. In Figure 12 shown a comparative chart of the obtained results. As can be seen from Figure 12, already at 4 variable variables and the range of their variation $\pm$ 20% of the base value, the calculation time was about 8 h.

Figure 12. Comparative chart of time spent on optimization calculations

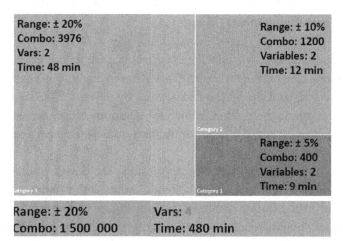

In real projects of optimization of electric cars, it is necessary to vary about 32 parameters, with a range from ± 10% to ± 100% of the base value. It is easy to assume that the resources of the local PC are not enough to solve such problems, and the debugging time of the project becomes unattainable.

The solution to the problem of operations with large amounts of data and computational operations is the parallelization of calculations and the organization of high-performance cluster computing. However, parallel computing will inevitably entail both changes to the code of an existing program (and an inevitable increase in the debugging time of the program), and will require the presence of the cluster itself. One solution to this problem is to use the computing power of the Microsoft cloud cluster and machine learning technology based on the Microsoft Azure service (Pliuhin et al., 2018).

The solution to the problem of operations with a large amount of data and computational operations is the parallelization of calculations and the organization of high-performance cluster computing. However, parallel computing will inevitably entail both changes in the code of the existing program (and an inevitable increase in the debugging time of the program), and will require the presence of the cluster itself.

Azure Machine Learning enables computers to learn from data and experiences and to act without being explicitly programmed. Customers can build Artificial Intelligence (AI) applications that intelligently sense, process, and act on information – augmenting human capabilities, increasing speed and efficiency, and helping organizations achieve more (Microsoft, 2022).

Machine Learning finds patterns in large volumes of data and uses those patterns to perform predictive analysis. Microsoft offers Azure Machine Learning, while Amazon offers Amazon Machine Learning and Google offers the Google Prediction API. Software products such as MATLAB support traditional, non-cloud-based ML modeling.

There are four steps in the process of finding the best parameter set (Figure 13):

1) define the parameter space: For the algorithm, first decide the exact parameter values you want to consider;
2) define the cross-validation settings: Decide how to choose cross-validation folds for the dataset;
3) define the metric: Decide what metric to use for determining the best set of parameters, such as accuracy, root mean squared error, precision, recall, or f-score;

4) train, evaluate and compare: For each unique combination of the parameter values, cross-validation is carried out by and based on the error metric you define. After evaluation and comparison, you can choose the best-performing model (Figure 14).

To iterate on your model design, you edit the experiment, save a copy if desired, and run it again. When you're ready, you can convert your training experiment to a predictive experiment, and then publish it as a web service so that your model can be accessed by others (Hayakawa and Hayashi, 2017).

Elastic cloud infrastructure is the optimal choice for solutions requiring large design capacities in short periods of time. It allows you not to wait for training models for weeks and at the same time not to keep "supercomputers" on balance.

Machine learning opens a fundamentally new approach to the design of electric motors of various types. The conducted studies were tested on an induction motor with a short-circuited rotor. And there is a certain justification for this. On the one hand, we can say in advance that machine learning gives stunning results and is not similar to design in the usual sense. On the other hand, the new approach requires significant preparatory work.

The main prerequisite is a database with data from experimental tests of motors of different sizes in different operating modes and different performance within the same power line. Here we are talking about thousands of data series, preferably, as practice has shown, more than 2000.

What is experimental data? It is an imprint of an electric motor with its unique geometric dimensions, winding data, applied materials, etc. Thus, it is possible to formulate the principle of feedback between the parameters of the electric machine and its initial characteristics.

Figure 13. Azure Machine Learning model optimization block diagram (Chappel, 2015)

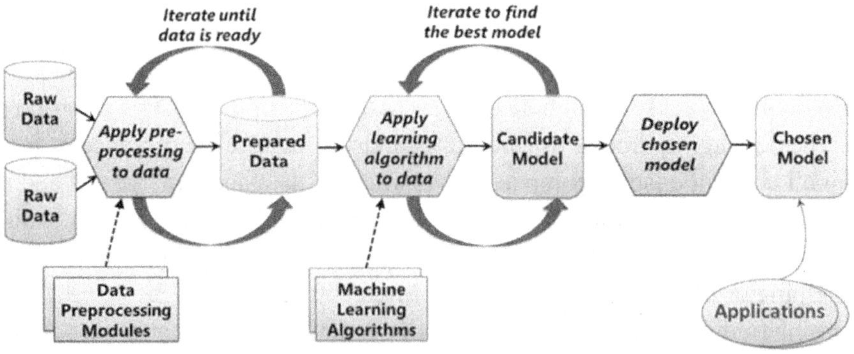

Figure 14. Microsoft Azure ML optimization options

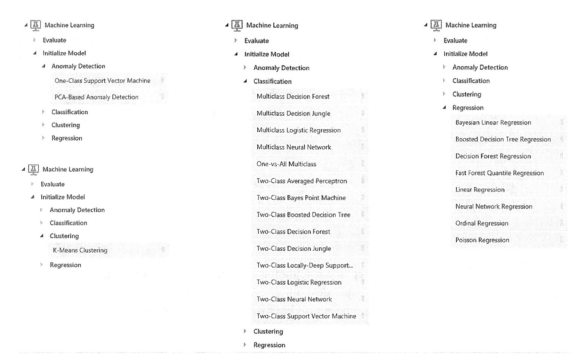

Certain parameters of the motor give strictly defined values of efficiency, power factor, mass, cost of materials, operating and starting characteristics. Similarly, the named output parameters lead to a well-defined electric machine with its geometric and winding data. This is logical, because before the machine was tested, it was manufactured according to calculations using specific formulas. So, in the results of the experiment, along with the geometric dimensions of the machines, there are hidden formulas, input data, operating conditions and technical limitations. In traditional design, there are formulas between these groups of data (Figure 15).

Figure 15. Connection between initial data and output data in traditional design

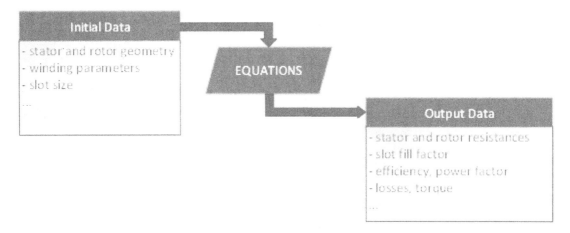

The task of machine learning is to replace calculations based on formulas by finding the optimal match between input and output data. Thus, designing "without formulas" is implemented: the user specifies the desired output machine parameters and constraints and as a result of the search receives reference input data (Figure 16).

Figure 16. Formation of machine learning datasets

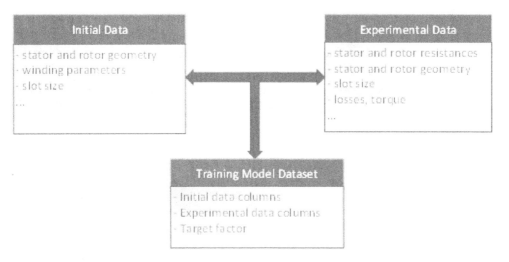

It is not necessary to find all 200–300 machine data. It is enough to find only you of them, which are parents of derived parameters. For this, there is a separate Python module that performs post-processing functions: on the basis of limited parameters, it finds the rest according to known relationships, which are linear and unambiguous, and do not require the user's participation in making decisions regarding the selection of associated parameters. The process of such design is shown in the Figure 17.

Figure 17. Data dependencies in machine learning approach

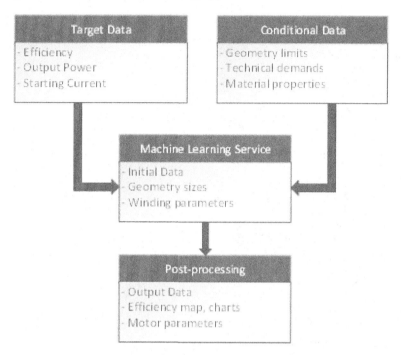

For the EM under study, the initial data vector (with the parameters of the base machine and its non-repeating combinations) was saved in a .csv file (comma-separated data) and imported into the Microsoft Azure model block (Figure 18). In this table (Figure 19) there were 10 variables (columns) and 442 combinations (rows) for the test task.

Figure 18. Initial IM with SCR dataset in .csv format

Q21

	A
1	Combination,Diameter,Length,Efficiency,PowerFactor,Induction,StartCurrent,StartTorque,MaxTorque,Temperature
2	0,175.0,120.0,0.8824,0.8618,0.857,6.16,1.57,2.88,101.8
3	1,175.0,121.0,0.8831,0.8679,0.85,6.16,1.55,2.86,100.8
4	2,175.0,122.0,0.8838,0.8739,0.843,6.15,1.54,2.84,99.9
5	3,175.0,123.0,0.8844,0.8787,0.836,6.14,1.53,2.82,99.1
6	4,175.0,124.0,0.8848,0.8828,0.829,6.13,1.52,2.8,98.4
7	5,175.0,125.0,0.8852,0.8866,0.823,6.11,1.51,2.78,97.7
8	6,175.0,126.0,0.8855,0.8896,0.816,6.09,1.5,2.76,97.1
9	7,175.0,127.0,0.8858,0.8923,0.81,6.07,1.49,2.75,96.5
10	8,175.0,128.0,0.886,0.895,0.803,6.05,1.48,2.73,96.0
11	9,175.0,129.0,0.8862,0.8973,0.797,6.03,1.47,2.71,95.5
12	10,175.0,130.0,0.8864,0.8994,0.791,6.01,1.46,2.7,95.0
13	11,175.0,131.0,0.8865,0.9014,0.785,5.98,1.45,2.68,94.5
14	12,175.0,132.0,0.8766,0.8285,0.779,5.62,1.5,2.78,100.5
15	13,175.0,133.0,0.8777,0.8364,0.773,5.63,1.49,2.76,99.3
16	14,175.0,134.0,0.8787,0.8439,0.767,5.63,1.47,2.73,98.2
17	15,175.0,135.0,0.8796,0.8505,0.762,5.64,1.46,2.71,97.3
18	16,175.0,136.0,0.8803,0.8567,0.756,5.64,1.45,2.69,96.4
19	17,175.0,137.0,0.881,0.8621,0.751,5.63,1.44,2.67,95.6
20	18,175.0,138.0,0.8796,0.8537,0.745,5.57,1.43,2.66,96.0
21	19,175.0,139.0,0.8802,0.8589,0.74,5.57,1.42,2.64,95.2
22	20,175.0,140.0,0.8807,0.8635,0.735,5.56,1.41,2.62,94.5
23	21,176.0,120.0,0.8838,0.872,0.852,6.19,1.55,2.86,100.5
24	22,176.0,121.0,0.8844,0.8772,0.845,6.18,1.54,2.84,99.6
25	23,176.0,122.0,0.8848,0.8814,0.838,6.17,1.53,2.82,98.9
26	24,176.0,123.0,0.8852,0.8854,0.831,6.15,1.52,2.8,98.2
27	25,176.0,124.0,0.8856,0.8885,0.825,6.13,1.51,2.78,97.6
28	26,176.0,125.0,0.8858,0.8914,0.818,6.11,1.5,2.76,97.0
29	27,176.0,126.0,0.8861,0.8941,0.812,6.09,1.49,2.75,96.4

Figure 19. EM parameters after import in Azure data sheet

Electric Motors Optimization › IM_Data › dataset

rows 442 columns 10

Combination	Diameter	Length	Efficiency	PowerFactor	Induction	StartCurrent	StartTorque	MaxTorque	Temperature
0	175	120	0.8824	0.8618	0.857	6.16	1.57	2.88	101.8
1	175	121	0.8831	0.8679	0.85	6.16	1.55	2.86	100.8
2	175	122	0.8838	0.8739	0.843	6.15	1.54	2.84	99.9
3	175	123	0.8844	0.8787	0.836	6.14	1.53	2.82	99.1
4	175	124	0.8848	0.8828	0.829	6.13	1.52	2.8	98.4
5	175	125	0.8852	0.8866	0.823	6.11	1.51	2.78	97.7
6	175	126	0.8855	0.8896	0.816	6.09	1.5	2.76	97.1
7	175	127	0.8858	0.8923	0.81	6.07	1.49	2.75	96.5
8	175	128	0.886	0.895	0.803	6.05	1.48	2.73	96
9	175	129	0.8862	0.8973	0.797	6.03	1.47	2.71	95.5
10	175	130	0.8864	0.8994	0.791	6.01	1.46	2.7	95
11	175	131	0.8865	0.9014	0.785	5.98	1.45	2.68	94.5
12	175	132	0.8766	0.8285	0.779	5.62	1.5	2.78	100.5

Statistical analysis according to the selected optimality criterion (COP) is performed automatically after importing the source data table into the Microsoft Azure workspace (Figure 19). The Microsoft Azure database contains hundreds of computational blocks, from which it is possible to compose a research task, the complexity of which is limited by the skill of the designer (Collier and Shahan, 2015). Numerous examples of already completed work available in the Azure cloud allow you to choose as a basis for developing your own (Pliuhin et al., 2019b).

In this example, the Microsoft Azure project contained the following elements:

- IM_Data – table of parameters;
- Clean Missing Data – deleting of empty rows;
- Select Columns in Dataset – selection of columns of variable parameters;
- Split Data – initial dataset dividing (70% for model teaching in left port and 30% for model analyses using original data in right port);
- Algorithm (Boosted Decision Tree, Multiclass Neural Network);
- Train Model – blocks for model teaching;
- Score Model – block of selection and analysis of the optimality criterion;
- Evaluate Model – block for calculating of statistical information.

The block diagram of the project is shown in Figure 20.

Figure 20. Electric Machine Optimization Project in Microsoft Azure

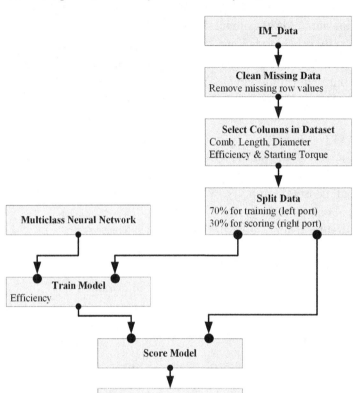

After performing the calculations related to the training of the system, testing the sampling algorithm and searching for the optimum, results were obtained that can be used to obtain various reports. An example of sampling by efficiency is shown in Figure 21.

In Figure 22 shown the report obtained after analyzing the built model in Microsoft Azure using the multiclass neural networks method.

The generated report in a tabular format (Figure 23) presents sets of initial data, accompanied by columns with calculated indicators of deviation from the optimum, as well as statistical indicators (the figure shows one column (far right) out of 10 available for analysis).

Figure 21. MS Azure ML results: optimization of EM diameter, length and efficiency

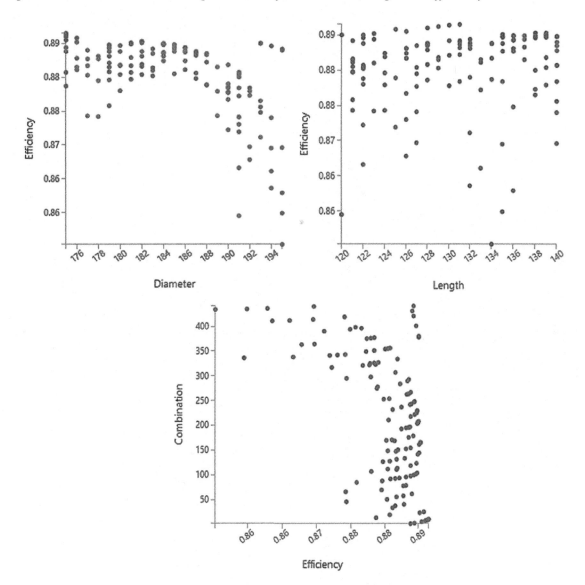

Figure 22. Summary of efficiency distribution

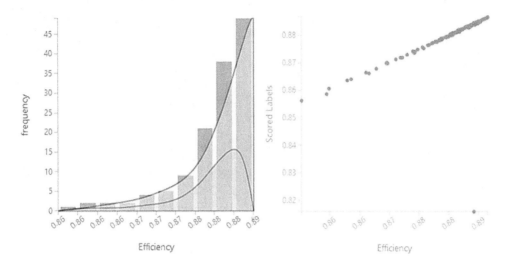

Figure 23. Results of the sampling algorithm using the neural networks method in the Microsoft Azure report

rows 133 columns 11

Efficiency	PowerFactor	Induction	StartCurrent	StartTorque	MaxTorque	Temperature	Scored Labels
0.8849	0.9052	0.709	5.65	1.35	2.53	90.6	0.884643
0.8828	0.8793	0.73	5.61	1.39	2.59	92.9	0.883075
0.8778	0.8582	0.729	5.61	1.42	2.66	96.2	0.877819
0.8696	0.8256	0.659	5.12	1.36	2.57	95.9	0.870004
0.8779	0.8524	0.768	5.76	1.48	2.76	98.9	0.877824
0.8811	0.8598	0.769	5.72	1.46	2.72	96.8	0.881201
0.8835	0.9042	0.684	5.54	1.32	2.49	89.7	0.88304
0.8765	0.8627	0.676	5.36	1.35	2.55	93.1	0.87646
0.88	0.8829	0.683	5.48	1.34	2.53	91.6	0.8797
0.8831	0.8805	0.743	5.7	1.41	2.63	93.8	0.8832
0.8787	0.8439	0.767	5.63	1.47	2.73	98.2	0.878945
0.8829	0.8756	0.777	5.86	1.45	2.71	96.2	0.883164

Statistics

Mean	0.8801
Median	0.8817
Min	0.8553
Max	0.8865
Standard Deviation	0.0059
Unique Values	87
Missing Values	0
Feature Type	Numeric Label

Visualizations

Efficiency
Histogram

compare to None

In Figure 24 shown the appearance of the project in the Microsoft Azure user workspace, where, in addition to the neural network method, the decision tree algorithm, Poisson regression analysis were connected to the analysis of the initial data sample, and the calculation was performed using the linear regression method. According to the calculation results, the optimal combination No. 420 was selected with the following parameters: stator core length (L) 120 mm, stator core diameter 195 mm, efficiency 0.884.

Figure 24. Full project tree in Microsoft Azure

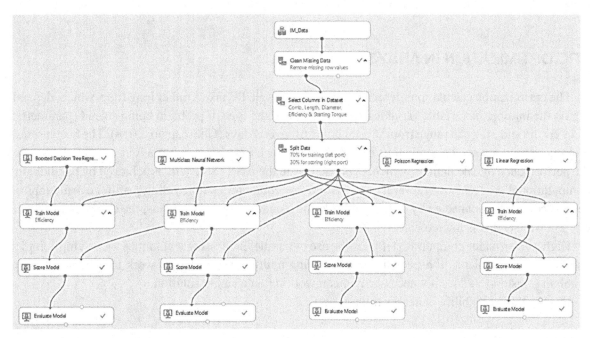

The computation time was only 1 min 45 s. The metric evaluation module built into Microsoft Azure (Figure 25) made it possible to determine the quality of the calculations performed: absolute error 0.000702, standard deviation 0.005926, relative absolute error 0.164582 and relative square error 1.011483 (the lower the value, the better).

Figure 25. MS Azure optimization error metrics

◢ Metrics

Mean Absolute Error	0.000702
Root Mean Squared Error	0.005926
Relative Absolute Error	0.164582
Relative Squared Error	1.011483
Coefficient of Determination	-0.011483

Thus, the process of designing an induction motor with a squirrel-cage rotor without using the traditional "formula" approach has been implemented. As with artificial intelligence, the Chat GPT service, the accuracy of predicting machine parameters using the machine learning service depends on the amount and variety of input data. This is the future of intelligent design. The described approach will make it possible to obtain configurations of electric motors with specified parameters and maximum efficiency in a matter of seconds, and the accuracy of such a choice will be based on tens of thousands of verified experimental studies of previously manufactured electric machines.

HPC OPTIMIZATION IN ANSYS

The optimization calculations described above on a single PC take a rather long time, which, depending on the number of variable variables, their range, and the type of problem being solved (parametric, field 2D or field 3D), can range from several hours to several days (Ghorbanian, 2018). The heaviest task took more than a week of continuous calculations. In such cases, it is extremely necessary to increase the performance of calculations, which, in particular, in the ANSYS system, is achieved by parallelizing computational processes into several cores within one computer and providing parallel calculations on several computers connected by a local network into a computing cluster. Thus, the computing technology known as HPC is implemented.

High-performance computing (HPC) is the use of parallel processing techniques for solving complex computational problems. It especially refers to using multiple computers to work together on a single problem (clusters). It does not necessarily mean working on a single solution.

Having HPC capability increases throughput:

- faster results;
- more design iteration;
- hit hard deadlines;
- greater engineering efficiency;
- parametric analysis & optimization.

HPC enables more thorough design and analysis on a tighter deadline.

With the ANSYS HPC software suite, you can use today's multicore computers to perform more simulations in less time. These simulations can be bigger, more complex and more accurate than ever using HPC. The various ANSYS HPC licensing options let you scale to whatever computational level of simulation you require, from single-user or small user group options for entry-level parallel processing up to virtually unlimited parallel capacity.

Taking advantage of HPC can dramatically speed up solutions for electronics simulations. Depending on whether you have ANSYS HPC licenses or ANSYS HPC Pack licenses, a different setting needs to be made in the HPC options.

In Electronics Desktop, we click Tools > Options > HPC and Analysis Options (Figure 26).

Figure 26. Selection of HPC ANSYS module

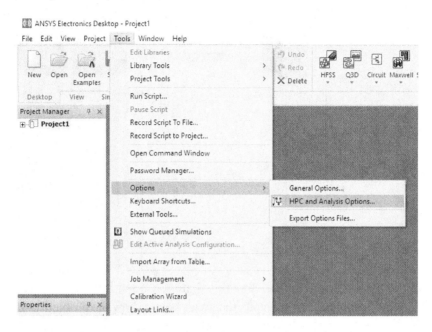

Maxwell HPC supports all steps being parallelized:

- meshing, matrix assembly, solving, post processing. In its classic matrix decomposition mode early performance saturation is achieved (around 8 cores). Other parallelization techniques are needed to utilize more resources efficiently;
- Time Domain Decomposition;
- Distributed Solve Options (parameterization).

Submitting project to RSM (Figure 27) via GUI is easier than batch submission:

- control over which subsystems are solved, and resource usage;
- project must be stored in a shared location, accessible to both submission workstation and cluster;
- relative path translation is available.

Figure 27. Configuration of remote solver manager

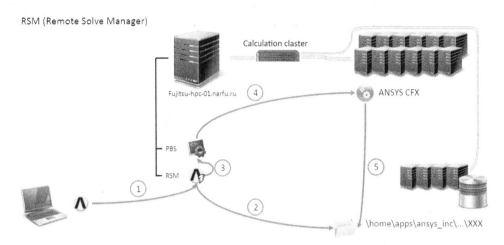

One can select the "High Performance Computing Setup" – to make the job run faster by using my CPU resource to solve the problem. For example, the image below show the problem being solved across 8 CPU's (Figure 28).

Figure 28. HPC settings in ANSYS

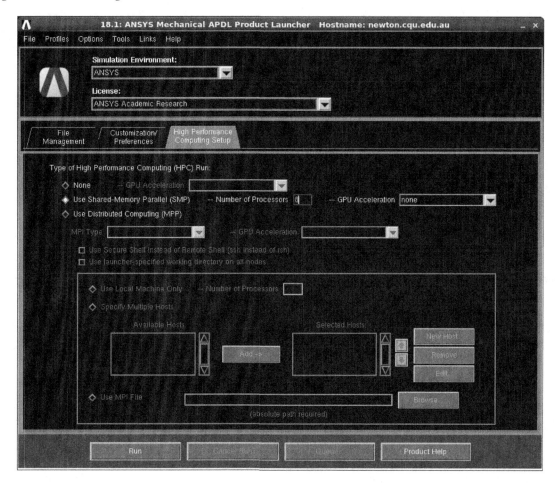

Once you are ready, click on the Run button to fire off your job to be solved (Figure 29). The progress of your program in a XTERM window shown on Figure 30. After the time required, the problem will be solved. Then one can use the workbench interface to look at the solved model.

Figure 29. ANSYS HPC calculation report (message window 1)

Figure 30. ANSYS HPC calculation report (message window 2)

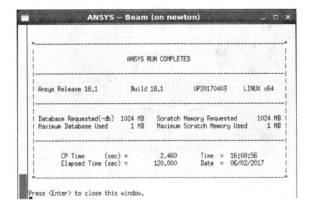

FUTURE RESEARCH DIRECTIONS

It should be noted that if the functionality of the built-in Microsoft Azure tools is not enough for some reason, researchers can write and execute scripts in R and Python (Müller and Guido, 2016; Pliuhin et al., 2019a; Liang et al., 2021).

Thus, the use of Microsoft Azure in the optimization of electrical machines was demonstrated. In the example shown, only one data vector was used and there were no modules for intermediate processing and data transfer between modules.

Further research is aimed at creating our own computational blocks in the Python language and R scripts in order to transfer to the Microsoft Azure platform not only the optimization of the finished sample, but also the creation of a population of initial data based on the vector of parameters of the base machine.

CONCLUSION

The aim was to replace the classical approach to the design and optimization of electrical machines, based on formulas and mathematical modeling, to obtain optimal geometric dimensions and parameters based on machine learning, in particular using Microsoft Azure ML Studio with HPC support. The task will be successfully completed and the ability to use machine learning in the optimal design of electric machines has been proven.

The chapter substantiates and shows a customer-oriented approach to design, in which the user-user sets the required targets for future electric machines and the necessary restrictions, and the output receives the full range of parameters of the finished optimized machine. Thus, the use of powerful cloud cluster technologies and HPC not only significantly reduces the time of design work, but also gradually improves the quality of the results obtained by improving artificial intelligence, which is self-learning.

This approach has objective difficulties in creating an initial database of parameters of electric machines that have already been manufactured and tested, but this is not a problem, but rather a one-time task. In the future, the system starts running on the web service instantly in a fully automatic mode. Work on this approach is still ongoing and constantly improving, but the results have already embodied a firm hope that the work is going in the right direction.

ACKNOWLEDGMENT

The research was supported by the National Research Foundation of Ukraine (Grant Agreement No. 2023.03/0131), and partially by the European Union Assistance Instrument for the Fulfilment of Ukraine's Commitments under the Horizon 2020 Framework Program for Research and Innovation (Research Project No. 0123U102775), by the Ministry of Education and Science of Ukraine (Research Project No. 0123U101805).

REFERENCES

Aksonov, Y., Kombarov, V., Fojtů, O., Sorokin, V., & Kryzhyvets, Y. (2019). Investigation of processes in high-speed equipment using CNC capabilities. *MM Science Journal*, 2019(04), 3271–3276. DOI: 10.17973/MMSJ.2019_11_2019081

Aksonov, Y., Kombarov, V., Tsegelnyk, Y., Plankovskyy, S., Fojtů, O., & Piddubna, L. (2021). Visualization and analysis of technological systems experimental operating results. In *2021 IEEE 16th International Conference on Computer Sciences and Information Technologies (CSIT)* (Vol. 2, pp. 141–146). IEEE. DOI: 10.1109/CSIT52700.2021.9648592

Ansys. (2011). *User's Guide – Maxwell 2D*. Ansys Inc.

Aravind, C. V., Grace, I., Rozita, T., Rajparthiban, R., Rajprasad, R., & Wong, Y. V. (2012). Universal computer aided design for electrical machines. In *2012 IEEE 8th International Colloquium on Signal Processing and its Applications* (pp. 99–104). IEEE. DOI: 10.1109/CSPA.2012.6194699

Arnoux, P. H., Caillard, P., & Gillon, F. (2015). Modeling finite-element constraint to run an electrical machine design optimization using machine learning. *IEEE Transactions on Magnetics*, 51(3), 7402504. DOI: 10.1109/TMAG.2014.2364031

Awwad, A. E., Al-Quteimat, A., Al-Suod, M., Ushkarenko, O. O., & AlHawamleh, A. (2021). Improving the accuracy of the active power load sharing in paralleled generators in the presence of drive motors shaft speed instability. *International Journal of Electronics and Telecommunications*, 67(3), 371–377. DOI: 10.24425/ijet.2021.137822

Back, T. (1996). *Evolutionary Algorithms in Theory and Practice: Evolution Strategies, Evolutionary Programming, Genetic Algorithms*. Oxford University Press. DOI: 10.1093/oso/9780195099713.001.0001

Balachandran, P. V. (2020). Adaptive machine learning for efficient materials design. *MRS Bulletin*, 45(7), 579–586. DOI: 10.1557/mrs.2020.163

Benamimour, T., Bentounsi, A., & Djeghloud, H. (2013). CAD of electrical machines using coupled FEMM-MATLAB softwares. In *2013 3rd International Conference on Electric Power and Energy Conversion Systems* (pp. 1–6). IEEE. DOI: 10.1109/EPECS.2013.6712995

Bonneel, P., Le Besnerais, J., Pile, R., & Devillers, E. (2018). Pyleecan: an open-source Python object-oriented software for the multiphysic design optimization of electrical machines. In *2018 XIII International Conference on Electrical Machines (ICEM)* (pp. 948–954). IEEE. DOI: 10.1109/ICEL-MACH.2018.8506884

Bramerdorfer, G., Tapia, J. A., Pyrhönen, J. J., & Cavagnino, A. (2018). Modern electrical machine design optimization: Techniques, trends, and best practices. *IEEE Transactions on Industrial Electronics*, 65(10), 7672–7684. DOI: 10.1109/TIE.2018.2801805

Buhr, K., Fajtl, R., Lettl, J., & Plyugin, V. (2014). Electromobile drive diagnostics and property prediction. In *XX International Symposium on Electric Machinery* (pp. 38–44).

Cathey, J. J. (2001). *Electric Machines: Analysis and Design Applying Mathlab*. McGraw-Hil.

Chappel, D. (2015). *Introduction Azure Machine Learning: a Guide for Technical Professionals*. Chappel & Associates.

Cheng, M., Han, P., & Hua, W. (2017). General airgap field modulation theory for electrical machines. *IEEE Transactions on Industrial Electronics*, 64(8), 6063–6074. DOI: 10.1109/TIE.2017.2682792

Choi, B., & Kim, Y. S. (2021). New structure design of ferrite cores for wireless EV charging by machine learning. *IEEE Transactions on Industrial Electronics*, 68(12), 12162–12172. DOI: 10.1109/TIE.2020.3047041

Cioffi, R., Travaglioni, M., Piscitelli, G., Petrillo, A., & De Felice, F. (2020). Artificial intelligence and machine learning applications in smart production: Progress, trends, and directions. *Sustainability (Basel)*, 12(2), 492. DOI: 10.3390/su12020492

Collier, M., & Shahan, R. (2015). *Microsoft Azure Essentials – Fundamentals of Azure*. Microsoft Press.

Daukaev, K., Rassõlkin, A., Kallaste, A., Vaimann, T., & Belahcen, A. (2017). A review of electrical machine design processes from the standpoint of software selection. In *2017 IEEE 58th International Scientific Conference on Power and Electrical Engineering of Riga Technical University (RTUCON)* (pp. 1–6). IEEE. DOI: 10.1109/RTUCON.2017.8124818

Deshpande, M. V. (2011). *Electrical Machines*. PHI Learning Private Limited.

Digă, S. M., Năvrăpescu, V., Digă, N., & Dina, C. (2021). Considerations on the optimal computer-aided design of induction motors from the turbomachines drive systems in power plants. In *2021 12th International Symposium on Advanced Topics in Electrical Engineering (ATEE)* (pp. 1–6). IEEE. DOI: 10.1109/ATEE52255.2021.9425259

Dimiduk, D. M., Holm, E. A., & Niezgoda, S. R. (2018). Perspectives on the impact of machine learning, deep learning, and artificial intelligence on materials, processes, and structures engineering. *Integrating Materials and Manufacturing Innovation*, 7(3), 157–172. DOI: 10.1007/s40192-018-0117-8

Duan, Y., & Ionel, D. M. (2013). A review of recent developments in electrical machine design optimization methods with a permanent-magnet synchronous motor benchmark study. *IEEE Transactions on Industry Applications*, 49(3), 1268–1275. DOI: 10.1109/TIA.2013.2252597

Erricolo, D., Chen, P. Y., Rozhkova, A., Torabi, E., Bagci, H., Shamim, A., & Zhang, X. (2019). Machine learning in electromagnetics: A review and some perspectives for future research. In *2019 International Conference on Electromagnetics in Advanced Applications (ICEAA)* (pp. 1377–1380). IEEE. DOI: 10.1109/ICEAA.2019.8879110

Evo, J. (2002). *EvoJ – Evolutionary Computations Framework*. http://evoj-frmw.appspot.com

Favi, C., Germani, M., Marconi, M., & Mengoni, M. (2012). Innovative software platform for eco-design of efficient electric motors. *Journal of Cleaner Production*, 37, 125–134. DOI: 10.1016/j.jclepro.2012.06.019

Finkelshtein, V., Iegorov, O., Petrenko, O., & Koliada, O. (2020). The analytic-field method for calculating the squirrel-cage induction motor parameters. *Naukovyi Visnyk Natsionalnoho Hirnychoho Universytetu*, 2020(3), 67–72. DOI: 10.33271/nvngu/2020-3/067

Fraunhofer, I. F. F. (2015). *Expediting and Validating Development.* https://www.iff.fraunhofer.de/ content/ dam/iff/en/documents/publications/expediting-and-validating-development-fraunhofer-iff.pdf

Gaudio, J. E., Gibson, T. E., Annaswamy, A. M., Bolender, M. A., & Lavretsky, E. (2019). Connections between adaptive control and optimization in machine learning. In *2019 IEEE 58th Conference on Decision and Control (CDC)* (pp. 4563–4568). IEEE. DOI: 10.1109/CDC40024.2019.9029197

Ghorbanian, V. (2018). *An HPC-based data-driven approach to system-level design process for integrated motor-drive systems* [Doctoral dissertation, McGill University]. McGill University's institutional digital repository. https://escholarship.mcgill.ca/concern/theses/t722hc204

Ghorbanian, V., Mohammadi, M.H., & Lowther, D. (2019). Design concepts of low-frequency electromagnetic devices based on a data-driven approach. *COMPEL – The International Journal for Computation and Mathematics in Electrical and Electronic Engineering, 38*(5), 1374–1385. DOI: 10.1108/ COMPEL-12-2018-0524

Goldberg, D. E. (1989). *Genetic Algorithms in Search, Optimization and Machine Learning.* Addison-Wesley Longman Publishing., DOI: 10.5555/534133

Hayakawa, S., & Hayashi, H. (2017). Using Azure machine learning for estimating indoor locations. In *2017 International Conference on Platform Technology and Service (PlatCon)* (pp. 1–4). IEEE. DOI: 10.1109/PlatCon.2017.7883736

Iegorov, O., Iegorova, O., Kundenko, M., & Potryvaieva, N. (2020). Ripple torque synchronous reluctance motor with different rotor designs. In *2020 IEEE Problems of Automated Electrodrive. Theory and Practice (PAEP)* (pp. 1–4). IEEE. DOI: 10.1109/PAEP49887.2020.9240820

Jackson, D., Belakaria, S., Cao, Y., Doppa, J. R., & Lu, X. (2021). Machine learning enabled design automation and multi-objective optimization for electric transportation power systems. *IEEE Transactions on Transportation Electrification*, 8(1), 1467–1481. DOI: 10.1109/TTE.2021.3113958

Jastrzebski, R. P., Jaatinen, P., Pyrhönen, O., & Chiba, A. (2018). Design optimization of permanent magnet bearingless motor using differential evolution. In *2018 IEEE Energy Conversion Congress and Exposition (ECCE)* (pp. 2327–2334). IEEE. DOI: 10.1109/ECCE.2018.8557878

Kallaste, A., Vaimann, T., & Rassālkin, A. (2018). Additive design possibilities of electrical machines. In *2018 IEEE 59th International Scientific Conference on Power and Electrical Engineering of Riga Technical University (RTUCON)* (pp. 1–5). IEEE. DOI: 10.1109/RTUCON.2018.8659828

Khan, A., & Lowther, D. A. (2020). Machine learning applied to the design and analysis of low frequency electromagnetic devices. In *2020 21st International Symposium on Electrical Apparatus & Technologies (SIELA)* (pp. 1–4). IEEE. DOI: 10.1109/SIELA49118.2020.9167158

Kitagawa, W., Inaba, A., & Takeshita, T. (2019). Objective function optimization for electrical machine by using multi-objective genetic programming and display method of its results. *IEEJ Transactions on Electronics. Information Systems*, 139(7), 796–801. DOI: 10.1541/ieejeiss.139.796

Kombarov, V., Sorokin, V., Tsegelnyk, Y., Plankovskyy, S., Aksonov, Y., & Fojtů, O. (2021). Numerical control of machining parts from aluminum alloys with sticking minimization. *International Journal of Mechatronics and Applied Mechanics*, I(9), 209–216. DOI: 10.17683/ijomam/issue9.30

Lei, G., Zhu, J., Guo, Y., Liu, C., & Ma, B. (2017). A review of design optimization methods for electrical machines. *Energies*, 10(12), 1962. DOI: 10.3390/en10121962

Li, Y., Lei, G., Bramerdorfer, G., Peng, S., Sun, X., & Zhu, J. (2021). Machine learning for design optimization of electromagnetic devices: Recent developments and future directions. *Applied Sciences (Basel, Switzerland)*, 11(4), 1627. DOI: 10.3390/app11041627 PMID: 34671486

Liang, Z., Liang, Z., Zheng, Y., Liang, B., & Zheng, L. (2021). Data analysis and visualization platform design for batteries using flask-based Python web service. *World Electric Vehicle Journal*, 12(4), 187. DOI: 10.3390/wevj12040187

Liubarskyi, B., Petrenko, O., Iakunin, D., & Dubinina, O. (2017). Optimization of thermal modes and cooling systems of the induction traction motors of trams. *Eastern-European Journal of Enterprise Technologies*, 3(9-87), 59–67. DOI: 10.15587/1729-4061.2017.102236

Lupu, T., Marţiş, R. A., Nicu, A. I., & Marţiş, C. S. (2021). Open source software based design and optimization tool for electrical machines. In *2021 9th International Conference on Modern Power Systems (MPS)* (pp. 1–5). IEEE. DOI: 10.1109/MPS52805.2021.9492624

Microsoft. (2021). *Cheat sheet: How to choose a MicrosoftML algorithm.* https://docs.microsoft.com/en-us/machine-learning-server/r/how-to-choose-microsoftml-algorithms-cheatsheet

Microsoft. (2022). *What is Azure Machine Learning studio?*https://docs.microsoft.com/en-us/azure/machine-learning/overview-what-is-machine-learning-studio

Miller, T. J., & Staton, D. A. (2013). *Electric Machine Design using SPEED and Motor-CAD.* Motor Design.

Mukerji, S. K., Khan, A. S., & Singh, Y. P. (2018). *Electromagnetics for Electrical Machines.* CRC Press., DOI: 10.1201/9781315222523

Müller, A. C., & Guido, S. (2016). *Introduction to Machine Learning with Python: a Guide for Data Scientists.* O'Reilly Media, Inc.

Murach, J., & Urban, M. (2015). *Murach's Beginning Java with NetBeans.* Mike Murach & Associates.

Okhrimenko, V., & Zbitnieva, M. (2021). Mathematical model of tubular linear induction motor. *Mathematical Modelling of Engineering Problems*, 8(1), 103–109. DOI: 10.18280/mmep.080113

Owatchaiphong, S., & Fuengwarodsakul, N. H. (2009). Multi-objective based optimization for switched reluctance machines using fuzzy and genetic algorithms. In *2009 International Conference on Power Electronics and Drive Systems (PEDS)* (pp. 1530–1533). IEEE. DOI: 10.1109/PEDS.2009.5385926

Papalambros, P. Y., & Wilde, D. J. (2017). *Principles of Optimal Design: Modeling and Computation* (3rd ed.). Cambridge University Press., DOI: 10.1017/9781316451038

Petrushin, V. S., & Yenoktaiev, R. N. (2019). Modification of the criterion of the present expenses for the design of energy-saving induction motors. *Technical Electrodynamics*, 2019(2), 19–22. DOI: 10.15407/techned2019.02.019

Pliugin, V., Shilkova, L., Lettl, J., Buhr, K., & Fajtl, R. (2015). Analysis of the electromagnetic field of electric machines based on object-oriented design principles. In *Progress in Electromagnetics Research Symposium Proceedings* (pp. 2522–2527). https://ssrn.com/abstract=3201920

Pliuhin, V., Aksonov, O., Tsegelnyk, Y., Plankovskyy, S., Kombarov, V., & Piddubna, L. (2021). Design and simulation of a servo-drive motor using ANSYS Electromagnetics. *Lighting Engineering & Power Engineering*, 60(3), 112–123. DOI: 10.33042/2079-424X.2021.60.3.04

Pliuhin, V., Korobka, V., Karyuk, A., Pan, M., & Sukhonos, M. (2019a). Using Azure Machine Learning Studio with python scripts for induction motors optimization web-deploy project. In *2019 IEEE International Scientific-Practical Conference Problems of Infocommunications, Science and Technology (PIC S&T)* (pp. 631–634). IEEE. DOI: 10.1109/PICST47496.2019.9061447

Pliuhin, V., Pan, M., Yesina, V., & Sukhonos, M. (2018). Using Azure maching learning cloud technology for electric machines optimization. In *2018 International Scientific-Practical Conference Problems of Infocommunications. Science and Technology (PIC S&T)* (pp. 55–58). IEEE. DOI: 10.1109/INFOCOMMST.2018.8632093

Pliuhin, V., Plankovskyy, S., Zablodskiy, M., Biletskyi, I., Tsegelnyk, Y., & Kombarov, V. (2023). Novel features of special purpose induction electrical machines object-oriented design. In Cioboată, D.D. (Eds.) *International Conference on Reliable Systems Engineering (ICoRSE) – 2022* (pp. 265–283). Springer. DOI: 10.1007/978-3-031-15944-2_25

Pliuhin, V., Sukhonos, M., & Bileckiy, I. (2020). Object oriented mathematical modeling of electrical machines. In *2020 IEEE 4th International Conference on Intelligent Energy and Power Systems (IEPS)* (pp. 267-272). IEEE. DOI: 10.1109/IEPS51250.2020.9263158

Pliuhin, V., Sukhonos, M., Pan, M., Petrenko, O., & Petrenko, M. (2019b). Implementing of Microsoft Azure machine learning technology for electric machines optimization. *Electrical Engineering & Electromechanics*, 0(1), 23–28. DOI: 10.20998/2074-272X.2019.1.04

Pyrhönen, J., Jokinen, T., & Hrabovcová, V. (2014). *Design of Rotating Electrical Machines* (2nd ed.). John Wiley & Sons., DOI: 10.1002/9780470740095

Raschka, S., Patterson, J., & Nolet, C. (2020). Machine learning in python: Main developments and technology trends in data science, machine learning, and artificial intelligence. *Information (Basel)*, 11(4), 193. DOI: 10.3390/info11040193

Rivière, N., Stokmaier, M., & Goss, J. (2020). An innovative multi-objective optimization approach for the multiphysics design of electrical machines. In *2020 IEEE Transportation Electrification Conference & Expo (ITEC)* (pp. 691–696). IEEE. DOI: 10.1109/ITEC48692.2020.9161650

Romeo, L., Loncarski, J., Paolanti, M., Bocchini, G., Mancini, A., & Frontoni, E. (2020). Machine learning-based design support system for the prediction of heterogeneous machine parameters in Industry 4.0. *Expert Systems with Applications*, 140, 112869. DOI: 10.1016/j.eswa.2019.112869

Rosu, M., Zhou, P., Lin, D., Ionel, D. M., Popescu, M., Blaabjerg, F., & Staton, D. (2018). *Multiphysics Simulation by Design for Electrical Machines, Power Electronics, and Drives*. John Wiley & Sons., DOI: 10.1002/9781119103462

Sarker, I. H. (2021). Machine learning: Algorithms, real-world applications and research directions. *SN Computer Science*, 2(3), 160. DOI: 10.1007/s42979-021-00592-x PMID: 33778771

Schwarz, P., & Moeckel, A. (2019). Electric machine design automation with Python and ANSYS Maxwell. In IKMT *2019: Innovative Small Drives and Micro-Motor Systems – 12. ETG/GMM-Fachtagung* (pp. 46–52). VDE.

Sen, S. K. (2006). *Principles of Electrical Machine Design with Computer Programs* (2nd ed.). Oxford and IBH Publishing.

Shevkunova, A.V. (2021). Optimization algorithms in the design of switched-reluctance machines. *E3S Web of Conferences, 258*, 11007. DOI: 10.1051/e3sconf/202125811007

Stojkovic, Z. (2012). *Computer-Aided Design in Power Engineering: Application of Software Tools*. Springer., DOI: 10.1007/978-3-642-30206-0

Tsai, M. C., Wu, Y. C., Chan, C. T., Cai, P. Y., Huang, P. W., & Tsai, M. H. (2016). Integrated design of magnetic gear and electric motor for electric vehicles. In *2016 International Conference of Asian Union of Magnetics Societies (ICAUMS)* (pp. 1–4). IEEE. DOI: 10.1109/ICAUMS.2016.8479780

Tsegelnyk, Y., Kombarov, V., Plankovskyy, S., Aksonov, Y., Pliuhin, V., & Aksonov, O. (2022). Investigation of the portal-type machine tool gear-belt gearbox. *International Journal of Mechatronics and Applied Mechanics*, 2022(11), 295–302. DOI: 10.17683/ijomam/issue11.41

Ulu, C., Korman, O., & Kömürgöz, G. (2019). Electromagnetic and thermal design/analysis of an induction motor for electric vehicles. *International Journal of Mechanical Engineering and Robotics Research*, 8(2), 239–245. DOI: 10.18178/ijmerr.8.2.239-245

Upadhyay, K. G. (2011). *Design of Electrical Machines*. New Age International Ltd.

Yao, H. M., Jiang, L., Zhang, H. H., & Wei, E. I. (2019). Machine learning methodology review for computational electromagnetics. In *2019 International Applied Computational Electromagnetics Society Symposium-China (ACES)* (Vol. 1, pp. 1–4). IEEE. DOI: 10.23919/ACES48530.2019.9060439

Zablodskiy, M., Pliuhin, V., & Chuenko, R. (2018). Simulation of induction machines with common solid rotor. *Technical Electrodynamics*, 2018(6), 42–45. DOI: 10.15407/techned2018.06.042

Zablodskiy, N., Lettl, J., Pliugin, V., Buhr, K., & Khomitskiy, S. (2013a). Induction motor optimal design by use of cartesian product. *Transactions on Electrical Engineering*, 2(2), 54–58.

Zablodskiy, N., Lettl, J., Pliugin, V., Buhr, K., & Khomitskiy, S. (2013b). Induction motor design by use of genetic optimization algorithms. *Transactions on Electrical Engineering*, 2(3), 65–69.

Zhang, Y., Huang, T., & Bompard, E. F. (2018). Big data analytics in smart grids: A review. *Energy Informatics*, 1(1), 8. DOI: 10.1186/s42162-018-0007-5

ADDITIONAL READING

Barnes, J. (2015). *Azure Machine Learning: Microsoft Azure Essentials*. Microsoft Press.

Campesato, O. (2020). *Artificial Intelligence, Machine Learning, and Deep Learning*. Mercury Learning and Information. DOI: 10.1515/9781683924654

Elston, S. F. (2015). *Data Science in the Cloud with Microsoft Azure Machine Learning and R*. O'Reilly Media Inc.

Etaati, L. (2019). *Machine Learning with Microsoft Technologies*. Apress., DOI: 10.1007/978-1-4842-3658-1

Hwang, K. (2017). *Cloud Computing for Machine Learning and Cognitive Applications*. MIT Press.

Khanuja, M., Sabir, F., Subramanian, S., & Potgieter, T. (2022). *Applied Machine Learning and High-Performance Computing on AWS*. Packt Publishing.

Nielsen, F. (2016). *Introduction to HPC with MPI for Data Science*. Springer., DOI: 10.1007/978-3-319-21903-5

Robey, R., & Zamora, Y. (2021). *Parallel and High Performance Computing*. Manning.

Terzo, O., & Martinovič, J. (Eds.). (2022). *HPC, Big Data, and AI Convergence Towards Exascale: Challenge and Vision*. CRC Press. DOI: 10.1201/9781003176664

Vetter, J. S. (Ed.). (2017). *Contemporary High Performance Computing*. CRC Press.

KEY TERMS AND DEFINITIONS

Artificial intelligence (AI): the intelligence of machines or software, as opposed to the intelligence of humans or animals. It is a field of study in computer science which develops and studies intelligent machines. Such machines may be called AIs.

Big Data: refers to data sets that are too large or complex to be dealt with by traditional data-processing application software. Data with many entries (rows) offer greater statistical power, while data with higher complexity (more attributes or columns) may lead to a higher false discovery rate.

Computer-Aided Design (CAD): is the use of computers (or workstations) to aid in the creation, modification, analysis, or optimization of a design. This software is used to increase the productivity of the designer, improve the quality of design, improve communications through documentation, and to create a database for manufacturing. Designs made through CAD software help protect products and inventions when used in patent applications. CAD output is often in the form of electronic files for print, machining, or other manufacturing operations.

Cartesian Product: in mathematics, specifically set theory, the Cartesian product of two sets A and B, denoted $A \times B$, is the set of all ordered pairs (a, b) where a is in A and b is in B. A table can be created by taking the Cartesian product of a set of rows and a set of columns. If the Cartesian product rows $\times$ columns is taken, the cells of the table contain ordered pairs of the form (row value, column value).

Data Science: is an interdisciplinary academic field that uses statistics, scientific computing, scientific methods, processes, algorithms and systems to extract or extrapolate knowledge and insights from potentially noisy, structured, or unstructured data. Data science also integrates domain knowledge from the underlying application domain (e.g., natural sciences, information technology, and medicine). Data science is multifaceted and can be described as a science, a research paradigm, a research method, a discipline, a workflow, and a profession.

Data Set (or dataset): is a collection of data. In the case of tabular data, a data set corresponds to one or more database tables, where every column of a table represents a particular variable, and each row corresponds to a given record of the data set in question. The data set lists values for each of the variables, such as for example height and weight of an object, for each member of the data set. Data sets can also consist of a collection of documents or files.

Deep Learning: is a class of machine learning algorithms that uses multiple layers to progressively extract higher-level features from the raw input. For example, in image processing, lower layers may identify edges, while higher layers may identify the concepts relevant to a human such as digits or letters or faces.

High-performance computing (HPC): uses supercomputers and computer clusters to solve advanced computation problems. HPC integrates systems administration (including network and security knowledge) and parallel programming into a multidisciplinary field that combines digital electronics, computer architecture, system software, programming languages, algorithms and computational techniques. HPC technologies are the tools and systems used to implement and create high performance computing systems.

Machine Learning: is a field of study in AI concerned with the development and study of statistical algorithms that can effectively generalize and thus perform tasks without explicit instructions. Recently, generative artificial neural networks have been able to surpass many previous approaches in performance. Machine learning approaches have been applied to large language models, computer vision, speech recognition, email filtering, agriculture, and medicine, where it is too costly to develop algorithms to perform the needed tasks.

Microsoft Azure (or Azure): is a cloud computing platform run by Microsoft. It offers access, management, and the development of applications and services through global data centers. It also provides a range of capabilities, including software as a service (SaaS), platform as a service (PaaS), and infrastructure as a service (IaaS). Microsoft Azure supports many programming languages, tools, and frameworks, including Microsoft-specific and third-party software and systems.

APPENDIX A

Program Implementation of the Carsten Product Algorithm in Java

```java
// ALGORITHM FOR THE CARTEES PRODUCT OF SETS
public void CartesianProduct(int var, int crit){
//Range and number of variable variables
//Diameter D
double D_min = stator.get_LD_min();
double D_max = stator.get_LD_max();
int N1 = (int)((D_max - D_min)/0.001)+1;
//Air gap length ld
double ld_min = stator.get_Lld_min();
double ld_max = stator.get_Lld_max();
int N2 = (int)((ld_max - ld_min)/0.001)+1;
int[] dim1 = new int[N1];
int[] dim2 = new int[N2];
//Fill arrays
dim1[0] = (int)(D_min*1000);
for (int i = 1; i < N1; ++i){dim1[i] = dim1[i-1]+1;}
dim2[0] = (int)(ld_min*1000);
for (int i = 1; i < N2; ++i){dim2[i] = dim2[i-1]+1;}
//Formation of the initial data vector
Vector srs = new Vector();
srs.add(dim1);
srs.add(dim2);
//array storing the size of arrays of variable parameters
number_elem = srs.size();
int[] size = new int[number_elem];
size[0] = dim1.length;
size[1] = dim2.length;
//vector of found combinations
dest = new Vector();
Vector curr = new Vector();
combinations(srs, size, curr, 0);
}//End of DPM module
//Search for non-repeating combinations for the DPM algorithm
public Vector dest;//vector with possible combinations
public int number_elem;//number of parameters to be combined
public Vector get_comb(){return dest;}
public int get_number_elem(){return number_elem;}
public void combinations(Vector srs, int[] size, Vector curr, int index){
if (index == srs.size()){
```

```
int s = curr.size();
Integer[] d = new Integer[s];
curr.toArray(d);
dest.add(d);
}
else{
for (int i = 0; i < size[index]; i++){
int n = size[index];
int[] dim = new int[n];
dim = (int[])srs.get(index);
curr.add(dim[i]);
index++;
combinations(srs, size, curr, index);
index--;
curr.remove(curr.lastElement());
}
}
}//End of the module for searching for non-repeating combinations
```

APPENDIX B

Software Implementation of the Pareto Rule in Java

```
//Selecting the best candidate according to the Pareto rule
public static int Pareto(Vector eff, int[] crit){
int Nopt = 0;//optimal variant index
//vector of optimal solutions (index and sample Fw Pareto)
opt_pareto = new Vector();
int Ni = eff.size();//number of efficient options
int Nj = krit.length;//number of weights
//comparative values of the current variant with the record one
double[][] W = new double[Ni][Nj];
double[][] W1 = new double[Ni][Nj];//normalization array W
double[] Wmax = new double[Nj];//array of worst values W
double[] Fmax = new double[Nj];//array of record values
double[] Fw = new double[Ni];//generalized optimality criterion
double[] Fwp = new double[Ni];//generalized optimality criterion in %
for (int i = 0; i < Nj;i++){
Fmax[i] = Double.POSITIVE_INFINITY;
}
//Search for record numbers
for (int i = 0; i < Ni; ++i){
double[] temp = new double[Nj];
temp = (double[])eff.get(i);
```

```
for (int j = 0; j < Nj; ++j){
if (temp[j] < Fmax[j]){
fmax[j] = temp[j];
}
}
}


//Calculation of comparative indicators
for (int i = 0; i < Ni; ++i){
double[] temp = new double[Nj];
temp = (double[])eff.get(i);
for (int j = 0; j < Nj; ++j){
W[i][j] = (temp[j] - Fmax[j])/Fmax[j];
}
}
//Search for the worst value in array W
//The worst value is the maximum discrepancy with the record
for (int i = 0; i < Nj; i++){
Wmax[i] = W[0][i];
}
for (int i = 1; i < Ni; ++i){
for (int j = 0; j < Nj; ++j){
if (W[i][j] > W[i-1][j]){Wmax[j] = W[i][j];}
}
}
//Normalization
//Worst case would have W1 greater than 1.0
for (int i = 0; i < Ni; ++i){
for (int j = 0; j < Nj; ++j){
W1[i][j] = W[i][j]/Wmax[j];
}
}
//Calculation of the generalized optimality criterion
//The best indicator will have a lower Fw value
//The current indicator is improved (decreased) by a weighting factor
//Weight range:
//from 1 (no correction) to 100 (max. correction)
for (int i = 0; i < Ni; ++i){
for (int j = 0; j < Nj; j++){
Fw[i] += W1[i][j]/((double)crit[j]);
}
Fw[i]/=Nj;
}
//Choosing the best option
```

```
double Fpmin = Double.POSITIVE_INFINITY;
double Fpmax = Double.NEGATIVE_INFINITY;
for (int i = 1; i < Ni; ++i){
if (Fw[i] < Fpmin){
Fpmin = Fw[i];
nopt=i;
}
if (Fw[i] > Fpmax){Fpmax = Fw[i];}
}
//Translate array Fw to %
for (int i = 0; i < Ni; ++i){
if (Fw[i] == Fpmin){
Fwp[i] = 100 - (Fw[i] - Fpmin)*100/Fpmax;
}
else{
Fwp[i] = 100 - Fw[i]*100/Fpmax;
}
}

opt_pareto.add(Fwp);//Pareto array Fw in %
opt_pareto.add(Nopt);//number of the best option
//Return the index of the optimal variant
return nopt;
```

APPENDIX C

Program Implementation of the Genetic Algorithm in Java

```
//GA - main module
public void GeneAlgorithm(int var, int crit){
DefaultPoolFactory pf = new DefaultPoolFactory();
GenePool<Solution> pool = pf.createPool(populations, Solution.class, null);
Rating rtg = new Rating();
rtg.set_motor(this, crit);
DefaultHandler handler = new DefaultHandler(rtg, null, null, null);
handler.iterate(pool, iterations);
Solution solution = pool.getBestSolution();
double x = solution.getX();
double y = solution.getY();
int iter = rtg.get_iter();
opt_pareto = new Vector();
opt_pareto.add(x/1000);
opt_pareto.add(y/1000);
opt_pareto.add(iter);
```

} //End of main GA module

//GA - implementation
```
public class Rating extends AbstractSimpleRating <Solution> {
static Reactor;
static int crit;
static int iter_numb;
static boolean flag;

public void set_reactor(Reactor react, int crit){
this.reactor = react;
this.crit = crit;
this.iter_numb = 0;
this.flag = false;
}
public int get_iter(){return this.iter_numb;};

public static double calcFunction(Solution solution) {
flag = true;
iter_numb++;
doubleDi = (double)solution.getInnerDiameter();
double Dw = (double)solution.getWireDiameter();
int nt = solution.getTurns();
int np = solution.getNumParallelWires();
reactor.set_innerDiameter((double)Di);
((RoundReactor)reactor).set_diameter(Dw/1000);
reactor.set_numTurns(nt);
reactor.set_numParallelWire(np);
((RoundReactor)reactor).ControlGA();//wire
double fn = ((RoundReactor)reactor).CalculationGA(crit);
//Last control
flag = reactor.Control();
return fn;
}
@Override
public Comparable doCalcRating(Solution solution) {
double fn = calcFunction(solution);
if (Double.isNaN(fn) | flag == false) {
return null;
} else {
return -fn;
}
}
}
```

```java
//GA - interface of variable variables
public interface solution {
//Inner Diameter
String smin1 = "20";
String smax1 = "1000";
//Wire Diameter (x1000)
String smin2 = "50";
String smax2 = "4000";
//Number of Turns
String smin3 = "1";
String smax3 = "1000";
//Number of Parallel Wires
String smin4 = "1";
String smax4 = "3";
@MutationRange("10")
@Range(min = smin1, max = smax1, strict = "true")
int getInnerDiameter();
@MutationRange("1")
@Range(min = smin2, max = smax2, strict = "true")
int getWireDiameter();
@MutationRange("1")
@Range(min = smin3, max = smax3, strict = "true")
int getTurns();
@MutationRange("1")
@Range(min = smin4, max = smax4, strict = "true")
int getNumParallelWires();
```

Chapter 8
Parallelization and Scaling of Deep Learning and HPC:
Libraries, Tools, and Future Directions

Aswathy Ravikumar
https://orcid.org/0000-0003-0897-6991
Vellore Institute of Technology, India

Harini Sriraman
https://orcid.org/0000-0002-2192-8153
Vellore Institute of Technology, India

ABSTRACT

Optimal high-performance computing (HPC) use for deep learning is a difficult task that requires progress in a variety of research domains. Complex systems and events are represented using a combination of science-based and data-driven models. Additionally, there is a growing demand for real-time data analytics, that necessitates the relocation of large-scale computations nearer to data and data infrastructures, as well as the adaptation of HPC-like modes. Parallel deep learning tries to maximize the performance of complex neural network models by executing them concurrently on recent hardware platforms. Considerable time has been invested in integrating HPC technology into deep learning frameworks that are both reliable and highly functional. In this chapter, distributed deep neural network model designing using parsl, tensor flow, Keras, Horovod libraries, and the implementation of these models using Hadoop, SPARK clusters on local-area networks (LAN) as well as on cloud services like Amazon web services (AWS) and Google cloud platform (GCP) are discussed.

INTRODUCTION

In the present era, Neural Networks have become a vital tool for performing complicated tasks ranging from Picture Categorization, Voice detection, and medical diagnosis to the recommender system and sophisticated video games. Developing a Convolutional network needs a significant amount of data, which is both data and computing-intensive, resulting in higher training time. Many parallels and distributed computation strategies are developed to significantly increase the DNN models to give fast

DOI: 10.4018/978-1-6684-3795-7.ch008

and efficient learning methods to tackle this difficulty. Fundamentally, it is separated into data-parallel, model parallel, pipeline parallel and hybrid parallel processing (a blend of data and model parallel processing). Data parallelism is a parallelization approach that utilizes a different set of data, referred to as mini-batches, to train clones of the same model on various devices. In data parallelized training, each computer node or worker maintains a neural network replication and a subset of data and calculates gradients distributed with the other workers and utilized by the parameter server to update the model parameters (Kim et al., 2019). Data parallelization is quite simple to implement and is provided for all major frameworks, including Mxnet (Chen et al., 2015a), PyTorch, and TensorFlow (Abadi et al., n.d.).

When the size of a DNN model is too large, it cannot be executed on a single machine. As a result, data parallelization is not feasible. Model parallelism is a technique for parallelizing large models by partitioning them and performing concurrent operations using the same mini-batch across several devices. In model parallelism, each node or worker has its own set of parameters and computations for each layer in the neural network model and the ability to change the weights allocated to the model levels. There is no necessity for parameter values to be synchronized between employees; communication often occurs when transferring training results across employees (Ono et al., 2019). The primary challenge with this technique is dividing the model into portions for distribution to the workforce (Mayer et al., 2017).

So, depending on model parallelization is ineffective at scaling to various devices (Mirhoseini et al., 2017) since it needs substantial relationships between workers. Parallelism in pipelines separates the Deep network's training into several processing steps. Each phase takes the output of the previous phase as input and immediately transfers the results downstream. On the other hand, parallel pipelining has the drawback of being bound by the slowest stages and exhibiting limited scalability. Recently, a hybrid parallelization strategy combining model and data parallelization has been investigated to maximize both methods' advantages while minimizing communication overhead during multi-device parallel training of neural network models. The present inquiry into ways to expedite machine learning training is motivated by both the successes and problems in the neural network area in terms of obtaining accurate and high-efficiency computer architectures in terms of enhanced floating-point abilities. The chapter's objective is to raise understanding of the possibilities of accelerated learning on massive datasets using HPC. Parallel machine learning tries to maximize the performance of complicated machine learning algorithms by executing them concurrently on contemporary hardware architectures. Significant effort is spent on integrating High-Performance Computing (HPC) technology into big data frameworks and commercially viable deep learning systems that are reliable and performant.

In light of these trends, there is a strong connection between machine learning and high-performance computing, even though machine learning algorithms have been used to perform auto-tuning on multicore-based paths for optimization and HPC technologies have been used to boost the effectiveness and throughput of numerous big data frameworks. Auto tuning may be capable of producing a high-quality result at a rate several times that of the simple implementation. To ensure higher and high-accuracy large-scale deep learning applications, the community has made significant progress toward decentralized heterogeneous deep learning systems. Distributed high-performance data analysis has developed into a fascinating but challenging endeavour. The study of CNN in detail in HPC platforms like GPU and TPU has been performed to analyze the impact on layers and networks (Ravikumar et al., 2022).

HIGH-PERFORMANCE COMPUTING

GPUs are programmed using the single-instruction, multiple threads (SIMT) approach, in which several processors execute lock-step warps of the same instruction. In comparison, CPUs programme in the various instructions, multiple data (MIMD) format, enabling multiprocessing and context switching. MIC architectures are composed of a group of CPU cores connected to a high-speed memory bus, each having SIMT capability. Memory accesses are also distinct, with CPUs focusing on data alignment with the memory hierarchy while GPUs transport data bulk-synchronously. The use of HPC to scale up machine learning training gives computational capacity and dynamic scheduling flexibility as more nodes become available. Synchronization, fault tolerance, and resilience are all performance considerations. A client launches a session by specifying the computation graph to be executed. The master accepts a session object from the client and arranges the task among one or more workers, coordinating the graph's execution.

Multiple systems, multiple cores and processors are the central HPC systems with different levels of parallel systems. A multiple-core processor is a single unit with many processing units or cores shown in Figure 1.

Figure 1. Multi-Core HPC Architecture

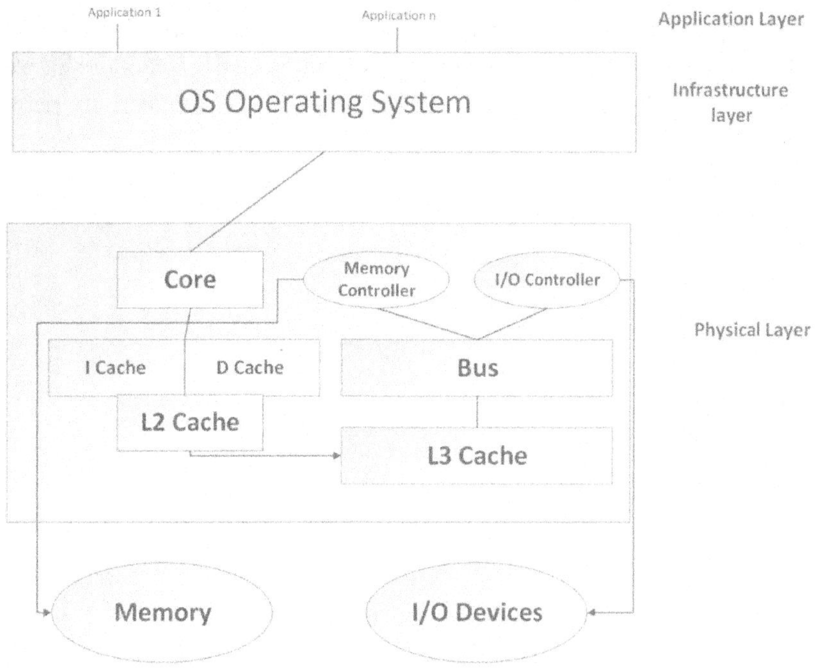

A multiple processor system is one in which more than one single core or multiple core processing units with the same memory access unit. The symmetric multiple processor system has the same access to the memory unit of the system shown in Figure 2.

Figure 2. Multi Processor HPC Architecture

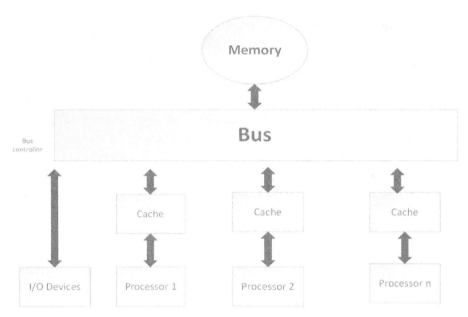

A multisystem is a collection of symmetric multiprocessor computers linked together via a high-speed data network. Due to infrastructure delay, one system's processors cannot share a memory with another. Such devices are mainly utilized for workloads that need less connectivity between processors shown in Figure 3.

Figure 3. Multi-System HPC Architecture

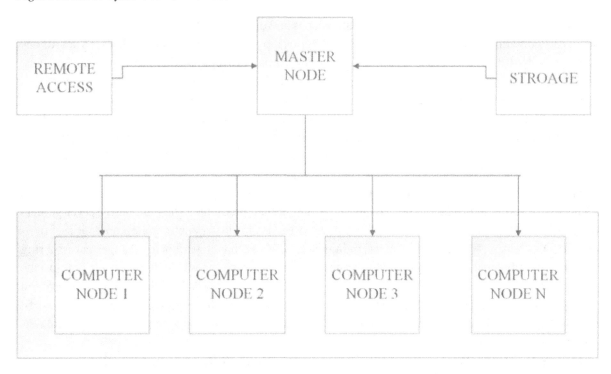

PARALLEL AND DISTRIBUTED DEEP LEANING

The progress of deep learning across numerous fields in recent years is enormous. Neural networks are proficient in extracting relevant data and modelling it for specific purposes. Whenever the data is high-dimensional or the amount of model parameters is large, the model must undertake intensive calculations. In such circumstances, parallel or distributed deep learning may aid in lowering the time and effort required by intensive computing. Occasionally, the volume of data is so great that a single computer cannot store it.

Consequently, using single compute strategies, we must use ways that may lessen the storage and computing issues. Parallel and distributed algorithms may dramatically reduce the training period and calculation time.

Current parallel and distributed DNN training models fall into four major categories: data parallelism, model parallelism, pipeline parallelism, and hybrid parallelism. The parameter server strategy, the dataflow approach, and dynamic run time systems are examples of distributed machine learning processes. During training, the parameter server approach delegates computation to workers, who push and pull changes to and from parameter servers. The dataflow technique functions from state transformations, simplifying model construction for more enormous datasets. Dynamic runtime systems provide changeable states, which allow for the modification of the dataflow graph for performance and flexibility reasons, as well as scheduling among available computing nodes.

Data Parallelism

Data parallelism divides a dataset into small batches and distributes them over numerous GPUs, with each GPU containing an exact replica of the prediction step and computing the gradient. Synchronous training involves all GPUs waiting for one another to finish computing the gradients for their local models, after which the calculated gradients are aggregated and utilized to update the model. In asynchronous training, on the other hand, the gradient from a single GPU is used to update the global model without waiting for additional GPUs to change. The asynchronous training approach has a better throughput than the synchronous training method because it avoids the waiting time associated with the synchronous training mode. Aggregated gradients may be shared across GPUs in both asynchronous pieces of training using one of two fundamental data-parallel training frameworks: parameter server architecture or AllReduce architecture. The parameter server architecture is a centralized design in which all GPUs connect with a single dedicated GPU to aggregate and update gradients. The parameter server gathers gradients and distributes the global model to all GPUs for use in subsequent iteration operations. Alternatively, AllReduce is a decentralized design in which GPUs exchange parameter changes across a ring network. The advantages are mainly it accelerates the pace at which the whole dataset contributes to the optimization, which is an important characteristic. Additionally, it needs less communication between nodes because of the large number of calculations per weight. On the other hand, the model must fit entirely on each node, and it is mainly used to accelerate the computation of convolutional neural networks with massive datasets.

Parameter Server: Weights are maintained on a collection of clusters by parameter servers, whereas workers are a set of nodes trained on such a local model replica and send weight changes to the parameter server, as shown in Figure 4. The parameter server stores weights in the form of a distributed table with parameters included inside the cells. There is no communication between worker nodes. Key-value pairs, range-based push-pull updates, and vector clocks were added to the parameter server technique to improve communication efficiency, scalability, and fault tolerance (Li, 2014). The parameter server design uses key-value vectors as data structures, which results in sparsity and allows the invocation of highly efficient linear algebra libraries. Push-and-pull operations transfer data between nodes, but range-based push-pull operations aggregate updates, improving network bandwidth efficiency. Servers save parameters as hashed key-value pairs. Entries are repeated and compressed on both data and range-based vector clocks to provide fault tolerance. Each key-value pair is assigned a vector clock that keeps track of the aggregation's state. Any changes made to the master node are replicated with their timestamp to the slave nodes, where they are pushed synchronously to slaves.

Ring all-reduce: In distributed data processing tools, such as TensorFlow, are deployed using All reduce, as shown in Figure 5. The high communication overhead of the central nodes is one bottleneck of the centralized algorithm. Baidu was the first to implement the ring-based all-reduce technique in DL. This is a significant advancement in the realm of dispersed training. Since then, Uber has expanded these concepts and included them in the outstanding Horovod library. When the number of nodes rises, the ring all-reduce technique significantly lowers the communication strain. The conventional ring all-reduce design has a few disadvantages with the increasing complexity of training systems. The delay of ring reduction is related to the number of compute nodes and is dominated by the network connection with the slowest throughput. The aggregation and updating of gradients amongst GPUs are often done simultaneously or asynchronously in data parallelism, as shown in Figure 6.

Figure 4. Parameter Server Architecture

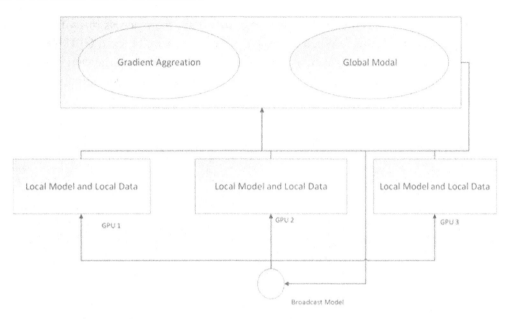

Figure 5. All Reduce Architecture

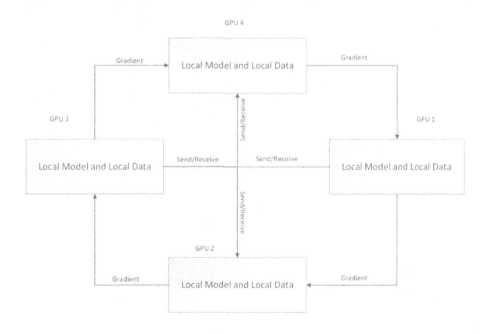

Model Parallelism

Model parallelization partitions the model layers and distributes them across many GPUs enabling concurrent training shown in Figure 7. When training the model in parallel, each GPU has its own set of parameters and calculations for each layer, as well as the flexibility to adjust the weights of allocated model layers. For forward and backward passes, intermediate data such as layer outputs and gradients are exchanged across GPUs.

Figure 6. Data Parallelism

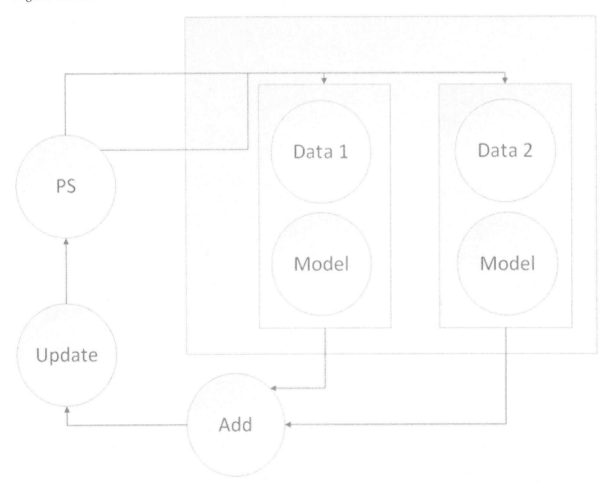

Figure 7. Model Parallelism

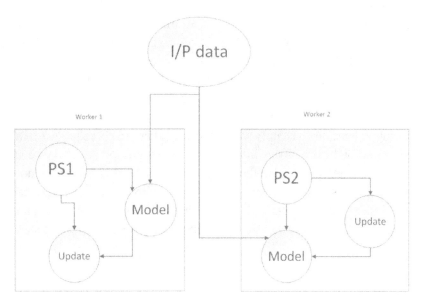

Pipelining Parallelism

Pipeline Parallelism decomposes the work into a series of processing phases. Each step accepts the previous level's output as input, with the outcomes being promptly transferred downstream. This approach has been used in a variety of works. Deep Stacking Networks (DSN) used overlapping neural network layer calculations to improve the training process's performance. DSN comprises three modules, each of which computes a distinct hidden layer of raw data. PipeDream (Narayanan et al., 2019) is another deep learning system that uses the pipeline approach.

Hybrid Parallelism

Onoufriou et al. (Onoufriou et al. 2019) introduced Nemesyst, a unique end-to-end hybrid parallelism-based framework for deep learning in which model partitions are trained concurrently with separate data sets. Oyama et al. (Oyama et al., 2020) suggested end-to-end hybrid-parallel training techniques for 3D convolutional neural networks on a wide scale. The strategies maximize performance and minimize I/O scaling bottlenecks by combining data and model parallelisms. The effectiveness of performance evaluations using CosmoFlow and 3D U-Net networks demonstrate the algorithms' efficacy. To increase the performance of DNN model training, the techniques mentioned above-used data, model, and pipeline parallelization singly or in combination. However, none of the prior approaches took into account the resource consumption and allocation issue in deep learning and gave solutions for efficient distributed learning performance.

Because most distributed deep learning methods are either synchronous or asynchronous, designers address distributed optimization techniques in terms of these two elements.

Synchronous algorithms: Parallel SGD calculates gradients for randomized samplings from the training set for each iteration and then sends the gradients to the parameter server (PS) shown in Figure 8. The PS collects the gradients and updates the global parameter. Parallel SGD is mathematically equal to SGD but with larger sample size. As a result, the convergence proof of P-SGD is straightforward. Because PS must receive data from all nodes throughout each iteration, PS's communication is extensive.

Asynchronous algorithms: The Asynchronous SGD (ASGD), PS conducts parameter updates while worker nodes parallelize the computation of stochastic gradients using local information. Due to asynchrony, ASGD delays will grow. Compared to synchronous algorithms, asynchronous parallel iterative algorithms allow agents to execute constantly without idling. They are not required to wait for the slowest agent to complete an iteration before proceeding to the next. And, despite its many benefits, asynchrony cannot escape certain disadvantages. Due to the delay introduced by the sharing memory, asynchronous algorithms have substantially smaller step sizes than synchronous algorithms. The main problems that occur due to the parallelism are stragglers and stale gradients (Ravikumar & Sriraman, 2021), and they have to be effectively mitigated for the better performance of the network (Ravikumar, 2021).

Figure 8. Synchronous Data Parallelism

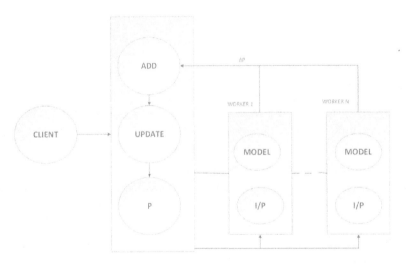

The effectiveness of data parallelism increases with the quantity of the training data since we can scan the data quicker with more nodes. Model parallelism is much more appropriate when the size of a model exceeds the memory capacity of a single node, as it allows the partitioning of models and the utilization of extra memory across many nodes. In distributed computing, it is ideal for getting as many speeds - up as the number of allotted machines. Allocate K nodes, and our systems can scan information K times quicker than on a node in unit time than our system has scalability K, also known as linear scalability. The ideal scalability for these systems is linearity. Due to the cost of synchronization operations, one cycle of learning on a distributed systems cluster often takes substantially longer to complete than with a single node. To guarantee convergence of the machine learning training process, we must spend additional time synchronizing (network connection) among several nodes after computation. In reality, synchronization might take as much time as or even longer than the calculation. Some worker nodes in the cluster operate more slowly than others. To synchronize with them, the quicker workers must wait until their calculation workloads are complete – the slower workers constantly limit system performance. In many instances, combining K machines would undoubtedly result in negative scalability, which would be a tremendous waste of time and resources.

TOOLS AND LIBRARIES

Python and other computer languages are rapidly being used to provide sensible interaction to libraries written in lower-level computer languages and to design utilizing several proposed elements. Along with the increased need for parallel processing, this change away from implementation toward orchestration necessitates rethinking how parallelism is represented in programs. Scientific portals are expanding in number to support this fast-evolving ecosystem, and to facilitate transparent, scaled implementation of various research. Science portals often rely on workflow systems to define and perform experiments fast and reliably. On the other side, incorporating process systems into scientific gateways may be challenging, especially when analyses become more engaging and dynamically, needing complicated coordination and administration of data and applications and adaptation for varied execution environments. The significant tools and libraries used for parallel and distributed deep learning are listed below.

PARSL

Parsl (Babuji et al., 2019) is a parallel scripting framework for Python that expands it with simple, scalable, and flexible parallelism encoding capabilities. Parsl uses these approaches to construct a dynamic dependency tree of components, which is then efficiently executed on one or more processors. Parsl abstracts away the complexities associated with interfacing with various resource fabrics and implementation models. Rather than that, it enables the creation of resource-independent Python programs. Additionally, it incorporates multiple sophisticated features, including automatic elasticity, multi-site execution support, fault tolerance, and automatic direct and wide-area information management. Parsl is intended to enable not just standard multi-task workflow models but also novel analytical models increasingly being supported by scientific gateways. (Chen et al., 2015b), a Python module for parallelizing the creation and execution of data-oriented processes. Developers may simply annotate Python scripts with Python functions or calls to other applications using Parsl directives. The Parsl library interfaces effortlessly with Python-based gateways, allowing for excellent process management and scaling.

The DataFlow Kernel decomposes Parsl scripts into a simple dependency tree. The DFK orchestrates the execution of single Parsl Apps across many locations. Unlike parallel programming languages such as Swift, which require users to label functions executed asynchronously based on data requirements, Parsl depends on users to document functions that will be run asynchronously derived from data dependencies. The DFK implements a minimal data management layer that facilitates the staging of Python objects and files to an execution location through a dedicated communication channel via Globus. Kernel for Dataflow: On top of several execution resources, the DFK offers a single lightweight abstraction. The DFK is responsible for controlling the execution of a script by making ordinary operations aware of futures, ensuring that these functions are only executed if all dependent futures have been resolved. This provides totally asynchronous administration of all launched processes, with the order of execution determined only by data dependencies. A Parsl script comprises regular Python code and several Apps—

annotated pieces of Python code or external programs that describe their input and output properties and are capable of running in parallel. An App may be created by using the @App decorator to surround an existing function or execute an external command-line program. When an App is invoked, there is no assurance about the timing of the return of the result. Rather than delivering an effect directly, Parsl produces an AppFuture: a structure that contains the actual development and the status and exceptions for the asynchronous function execution.

Additionally, Parsl provides ways for inspecting the future construct, such as monitoring its state, blocking on completion, and obtaining results. Parsl does this by using Python's concurrent.futures package. Parsl architecture is shown in Figure 9.

Figure 9. Parsl Architecture

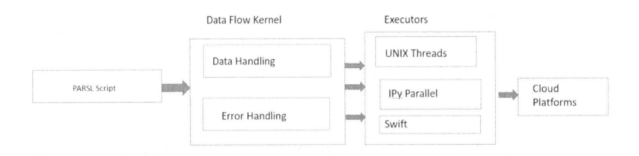

KERAS

Keras is an open neural network library written in Python. It facilitates experimentation and simplifies the process of developing code. Keras prioritizes maintaining minimum modifications to the current model and code while distributing training. The tf.distribute.Strategy API enables to distribute training over numerous processor units. It allows you to do distributed training with little modifications to current models and training. The tf.distribute.MirroredStrategy to execute in-graph replication with synchronized training on a single computer using many GPUs. Essentially, the method replicates all the model's variables across all processors. Then, it applies the combined value to all instances of the model using all-reduce to aggregate the gradients from all processors.

Multiple Device Synchronous Training

Each machine would execute a replicated version of the model (replica). At every stage of training, the current set of information (referred to as the global batch) is divided into distinct sub-batches (local batches). Each replicas processes a local batch independently: they do a forward pass and then a backward pass, returning the weight gradient relative to the model's loss on the locally batch. Local gradient-based weight modifications are efficiently integrated across the eight copies. As this is performed after each phase, the clones will always synchronize. Synchronously upgrading the model replicas' weights is done at the actual weight variable level. To do synchronous training with a Keras model on a single host and several devices, utilize the tf.distribute. API for MirroredStrategy. Implement a MirroredStrategy, with the ability to specify which individual devices to operate. Using the strategy object, create a scope and build all the Keras objects that include your required variables. This entails developing and constructing the model inside the scope of the distribution and training the model using fit ().

Multiple Workers Distributed Synchronous Training

Multiple computers (referred to as workers), all with one or more GPUs. Similarly, to single-host learning, each accessible GPU will execute 1 model replica, with the values of each replica's variables being maintained in synchronization after each batch.

1. Establish a cluster
2. Configure each worker with the proper TF CONFIG environment variable. This explains the worker's function and how to interact with their peers.
3. Similar to single-host training, execute your model creation and compilation code on each worker inside the scope of a MultiWorkerMirroredStrategy object.
4. Execute evaluation code on an evaluator machine that has been specified.

TENSOR FLOW

TensorFlow's primary distributed training technique is tf.distribute.Strategy. This technique lets users spread your training model over several PCs, Graphics processing units and TPUs. It is meant to be simple, deliver great performance, and facilitate strategy switching. Additionally, the distribution technique serves as the foundation for various other ways:

Mirrored Strategy

tf.distribute.MirroredStrategy is a technique for distributing training synchronously over many GPUs. This approach allows you to make mirrored copies of your model parameters across multiple GPUs. These mirrored variables are clustered together in a MirroredVariable during operation and maintained in sync using all-reduce techniques.

TPU Strategy

tf.distribute.experimental.TPUStrategy is a technique for allocating training across TPUs. This technique behaves the same as MirroredStrategy. The distinction is that it contains a customized implementation of all-reduce.

Multi Worker Mirrored Strategy

MultiWorkerMirroredStrategy is similar to MirroredStrategy yet allows for the distribution of training over several computers. This approach uses a collection of collectiveOps methods to maintain variable synchronization among your workers. This set consolidates your actions into a single unit in your TensorFlow graph, from which the suitable all-reduce method is selected. Additionally, TensorFlow offers a mechanism for doing synchronous data parallelism across several computers, each with a potentially large number of GPU devices. This approach is called MultiWorkerMirrorredStrategy, as shown in Figure 10. This distribution strategy operates like that of MirroredStrategy. The Ring All Reduce and Hierarchical All Reduce is shown in Figure 11 and Figure 12.

Figure 10. Multi Worker Mirrored Strategy

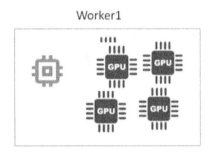

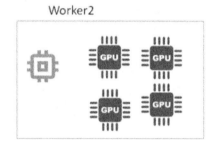

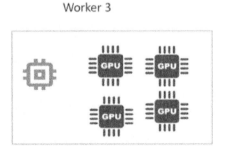

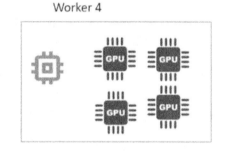

Figure 11. Ring All Reduce

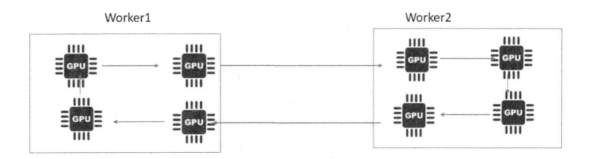

Figure 12. Hierarchal All Reduce

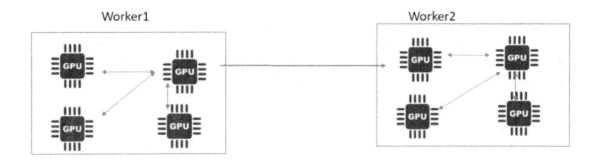

Central Storage Strategy

tf.distribute.experimental.CentralStorageStrategy is a technique for doing synchronous training from a single CPU. This solution centralizes variable management and replicates activities across multiple GPUs. This permits the execution of the same procedures on distinct data sets, as shown in Figure 13.

Figure 13 Central Storage

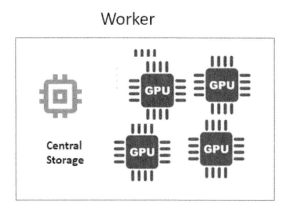

Worker

Parameter Server Strategy

tf.distribute.experimental.ParameterServerStrategy is a technique for simultaneously training various parameter servers over different machines, as shown in Figure 14. In this manner, you may divide your machines into parameter servers and workers. Your variables are distributed across multiple parameter servers, and your computations are replicated on numerous worker GPUs.

Figure 14. Parameter Server Strategy

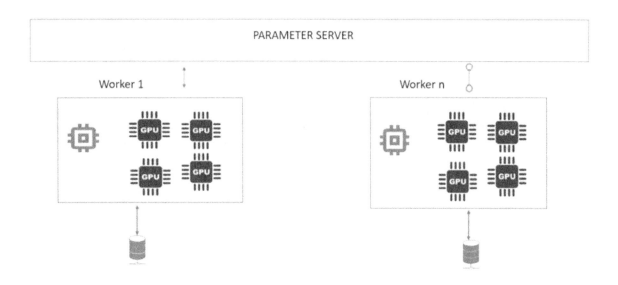

Distributed TensorFlow is mainly used for data parallelism, the stable paradigm of computing over the dynamic paradigm, a part of the Google Cloud environment and has a lot of data and requires a lot of processing power.

Mesh Tensor flow is another version of Tensor flow distributed learning; however, it is optimized for training massive deep learning models using Tensor Processing Units (TPUs), which are similar to GPUs but quicker. While Mesh TensorFlow supports data parallelism, its primary goal is to address distributed learning for huge models with parameters that can fit on a single device. Mesh TensorFlow is influenced by a synchronous data-parallel approach, in which each worker participates in all operations. Besides that, all employees use the same tool, which utilizes group communication in the same way Allreduce does. Mesh TensorFlow is used for model parallelism, creating massive models and experimenting with fast prototyping.

PyTorch

PyTorch has been one of Facebook's top advanced deep learning platforms. It is among the most adaptable and simple-to-learn frameworks available. PyTorch makes constructing and executing neural net modules simple, and its distributed training modules make it simple to perform parallel learning with only a few lines of code.PyTorch has a variety of methods for doing distributed training, and PyTorch distributed training is powerful on data parallelism. The packages were nn.DataParallel(This function enables parallel training on a single system equipped with many GPUs.), nn.DistributedDataParallel (This function allows for parallel training on many GPUs on various computers.) and torch.distributed. RPC (This function implements a model-parallelism technique. It is exceptionally effective if the model is enormous and cannot be represented by a single GPU.) is used for distributed training in PyTorch.

DeepSpeed, which is based on PyTorch, focuses on additional elements, such as model parallelism. Microsoft is developing DeepSpeed to provide distributed training for large systems. DeepSpeed can effectively address memory constraints associated with training networks with millions of parameters. It minimizes memory usage while optimizing computation and communication. Interestingly, DeepSpeed supports 3D parallelism, enabling data, models, and pipelines to be distributed. This implies that you can now train enormous models and use a vast amount of data.

Ray is yet another open-source distributed learning system based on Pytorch. Ray is a parallel distributed computing framework. Ray is a lightweight distributed execution platform that simplifies the process of scaling your apps and using cutting-edge machine learning libraries. With Ray, you can convert sequential Python code to a distributed application with few code modifications. It includes tools for deploying GPU clusters across many cloud providers. Unlike the other libraries covered so far, Ray is very adaptable and can be used in various environments, including Azure, GCD, AWS, Apache Spark, and Kubernetes. Ray's package includes the following libraries: hyperparameter tweaking, reinforcement learning, learning techniques, and scaling. Ray is utilized in the following situations to execute distributed reinforcement learning, distributed tweaking of hyperparameters, and divide data loading and computation over many computers. Ray inhabits a unique liminal space. Rather than offering new notions. Ray takes the existing ideas of functions and classes and converts them to tasks and actors for use in a distributed environment. This API option enables the parallelization of serial programs without requiring significant adjustments.

Dask is indeed one destination for all things big data. Whether you're a Python developer trying to accelerate current source code, or a data researcher seeking insight from complex data analyzing gigabytes of photos, Dask has you covered. Dask is unique in that it was built entirely in Python. Due to its collaboration with the Pandas, scikit-learn, and Jupyter teams, it includes several features that PySpark does not. Python programmers no longer need to decipher complex Java error messages, frequently switch between various syntaxes, or rewrite entirely their script to take advantage of distributed computing.

Additionally, Dask streamlines the big data process. Its outstanding single-machine performance accelerates prototyping and results in quicker model deployment. Parallelizing current workflows with Dask is straightforward and needs only minor adjustments for anybody familiar with Pandas, NumPy, or SciPy. Dask is the most straightforward approach to install not just statistical data analysis pipelines on clusters but also deep learning and image processing pipelines. Dask is a Python module for solving computational problems by exploiting task scheduling. Dask makes large-scale data processing possible by providing the most extensively used data structures inherited from Pandas and Numpy and fundamental massively parallel interfaces depending on its self-developed task scheduling mechanism. Whether you're running Dask on a laptop or a cluster of CPUs, the technique is the same, ensuring excellent accuracy and resilience. Lazy evaluation, a method for reducing the amount of work required to compute, is used to plan and optimize the program's operations before obtaining the final result. The full task graph may be shown with a single line of code, which assists you in determining where and how to improve your entire process.

DEAP is a Python-based platform for constructing bespoke evolutionary algorithms. The design ethos emphasizes precise algorithms and visible data structures, in contrast to most other evolutionary computing software, which often encapsulates standardized methods through a black-box approach. This attitude distinguishes it as a platform for rapidly developing new ideas in EA research. Its architecture enables simple distributed execution through numerous distribution libraries.

HOROVOD

Uber initially created Horovod to accelerate and simplify the usage of distributed machine learning, reducing model training from weeks to minutes and hours. Horovod enables you to scale a current training script to hundreds of GPUs with only a few words of Python code. Horovod may be installed on-premises or deployed as a service on cloud platforms such as AWS, Azure, and Databricks. Horovod can also operate on top of Apache Spark, allowing data analysis and model development to be combined into a single pipeline. Once set up, Horovod may be used to train models with any framework, making it simple to switch between TensorFlow, PyTorch, MXNet, and future frameworks as deep learning tech stacks expand. Horovod Runner is an API for executing distributed deep learning tasks on Databricks using the Horovod platform. Databricks can offer more excellent stability for long and deep learning training tasks on Spark by combining Horovod with the barrier mode. Horovod Runner accepts a Python function that provides Horovod-enabled deep learning training code. Horovod Runner encrypts and distributes the technique on the driver to Spark workers. A Horovod MPI work is integrated as a Spark job to use the barrier execution mode. The first executor uses Barrier Task Context to gather the IP addresses of all task processors and then uses mpi run to initiate a Horovod job. The Python MPI process loads, deserializes and executes the pickled user application.

DistBelief

DistBelief is a Google-developed solution for highly distributed deep learning. It enables parallel data and model training. Parallelism is supported in DistBelief for both data and model. It is one of the first that requires special skills of large-scale distributed machine learning, created by Google. Communication is necessary only when the output of a node is utilized as the input of another machine's trained node. Partitioning the model across clusters is transparent and does not need fundamental changes. However, the effectiveness of partitioning is highly dependent on the model's architecture, which needs careful planning.

MXNet

MXNet offers almost linear speedups while training Google Net on a small cluster of ten computers equipped with a GPU. The models, similar to TensorFlow, are expressed as dataflow graphs. MXNet (Chen et al., 2015) follows a similar method to TensorFlow in that models are written as dataflow graphs run on abstracted hardware and controlled through a parameter server. MXNet, on the other hand, offers the imperative specification of dataflow networks as actions on n-dimensional arrays, simplifying the design of certain types of networks. User-defined update logic is supported and is run whenever a new value is pushed.

SPARK

Apache Spark is a framework for distributing a dataflow graph over all compute nodes and caching frequently used data in memory, including checkpointing and fault tolerance support. RDDs are data structures composed of records distributed among compute nodes for replication, checkpointing, and fault tolerance.

A client driver takes requests for submitted tasks from the master and distributes them to available workers. RDDs use lazy evaluation, which involves performing a transform after the dataflow graph is generated. Spark's approach with a single driver becomes a bottleneck when the issue scales to millions of parameters and changes must be sent among workers.

SystemML is a Spark-based declarative machine learning (DML) framework that offers a MATLAB-like environment for linear algebra and numerical techniques and support for networked machine learning training. Spark-specific rewrites, memory budgets and limitations, operator selection, and an extended parallel for loop are all included in the optimizer integration. Caching and checkpoint injection are performed using Spark-specific rewrites, allowing RDDs to survive at multiple storage levels, while checkpoints are injected after persistent reads to avoid repeated lazy evaluation. Memory budgets and constraints provide an upper limit on memory needs based on driver memory, executor memory, the number of executors, the data fraction, and the shuffle fraction. Operator selection looks for patterns in linear algebra that may be solved by fusing physical operators. It was enhanced by adding three physical operators: a local executor for multithreading, a remote executor for a Spark task, and a remote disjoint executor for partitioning the matrices. The runtime integration consists of distributed matrix representation, which separates dense and sparse matrices according to their compressed storage format, and buffer pool integration, which handles all reads and writes of matrix objects and RDDs with lineage tracking.. The ratio of column cardinality to row cardinality assesses redundancy regardless of the actual values. Column co-coding divides columns into groups, with columns within each group being strongly connected and wrapped into a single unit.

TensorFlowOnSpark is a deep learning framework that enables distributed training for Apache Spark and Apache Hadoop clusters, developed by Yahoo. The framework allows for distributed training and interpretation with little modifications to the shared grid's current TensorFlow code.

BigDL: An open-source platform for Apache Spark distributed training. And Hadoop Intel created it to enable deep learning algorithms to operate on Apache Spark and Hadoop clusters. One significant feature of BigDL is that it allows the rapid development and processing of production data in an end-to-end pipeline for data analysis and machine learning applications. BigDL presents two alternatives:

1. Usage of BigDL in the same way you would any other library provided by Apache Spark for machine learning, data analytics, and so on.
2. Python libraries like PyTorch, TensorFlow, and Keras may be scaled up inside the Spark environment.

Main Advantages of BigDL

1. Pipeline: If big data is chaotic and complicated, as it often is with continuous streaming data, BigDL is a good fit since it merges data science with machine learning in a single pipeline.
2. Efficient development, deployment, and operations: Including an integrated approach across Spark BigDL's many elements, advancement, implementations, and processes are simple, smooth, and effective throughout all aspects.
3. Connectivity and Processing: Because all hardware and software are integrated, they operate seamlessly but without disruption, simplifying interaction with various processes and speeding up processing.

HADOOP AND MAP-REDUCE

Intensive applications are dispersed across clusters of computers using simple programming techniques. It is conceived and implemented in a way that allows it to grow from a single node to thousands of nodes, each of which provides local processing and storage. This framework offers a Hadoop MapReduce libraryfor processing massive data sets in parallel, as shown in Figure 15. Harp is a collective communication library that integrates with Hadoop to transfer MapReduce operations to Map-Collective jobs, hence improving the efficiency of in-memory interaction directly in map tasks.

Figure 15. Spark / Hadoop DL Architecture

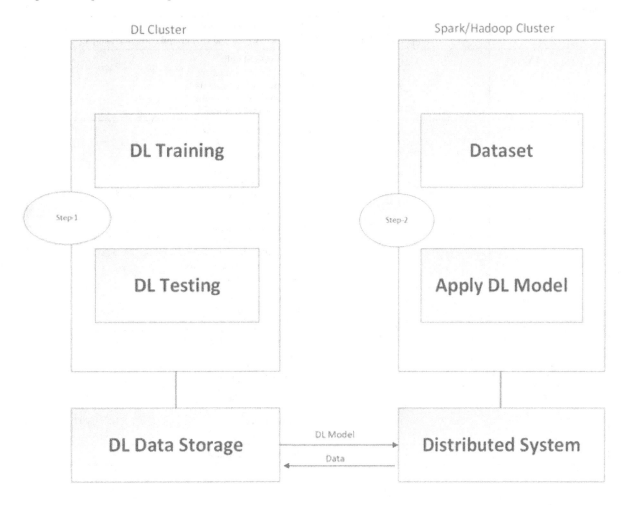

The significant tools and libraries are summarized in Table 1, along with the details of their use and technologies used.

Table 1. Tools for distributed deep learning

Sl No	Tools	Features
1	Parsl	Portable parallel programming Support cloud platforms AWS, Google Cloud and cluster and container setups
2	MXNet	Centralized only Data and Model Parallelism Synchronous, Asynchronous No Communication scheduling Provide Multi GPU support
3	PyTorch	Centralized and Decentralized Synchronous, Asynchronous Data and Model Parallelism No Model quantization No Communication scheduling No visualization Tools
4	TensorFlow	Centralized Synchronous and Asynchronous Model quantization Support multi-GPU and TPU Data Visualization on Tensor Board No Communication scheduling
5	Keras	Model quantization supported Multi GPU support
6	Horovod	data-parallel model Easy scaling to multi-GPU No fault Tolerance
7	DistBelief	data and model parallel
8	Deep Speed	Model parallelism Pipeline parallelism Single to multi-GPU Faster
9	Dask	Dynamic task Scheduling

CLOUD PLATFORMS

The emergence of cloud computing, as well as the growth of deep learning, were mutually reinforcing. Consequently, incorporating AI into the cloud may significantly increase the cloud's performance, effectiveness, and ability to change (Pusztai et al., 2021). Using deep learning in a cloud computing environment is critical for enterprises to become more efficient, purposeful, and have additional perspectives while also increasing their adaptability, flexibility, and cost benefits (Tuli et al., 2022). Cloud-hosted data and apps enable organizations to be more flexible and adaptive while saving money (Abdelaziz et al., 2018). The capability of sensing acquires knowledge, and consumers enjoy an enhanced level of service due to the inclusion of an extra layer of deep learning that assists in the development of insights from data. By combining machine learning and cloud computing, enterprises may have a better relationship with their customers while enhancing operating effectiveness. Cloud computing platforms and solutions enable enterprises to be more flexible, adaptive, and cost-efficient by drastically reducing infrastructure management costs (Younas et al., 2020). DL empowers businesses by allowing them to manage massive data warehouses, clarify data, optimize processes, and provide insightful information for day-to-day operations. Technology and data may be delegated to processes and people (Pop, 2016).

The software as a Service (SaaS) model is being utilized effectively to implement cloud-based artificial intelligence. SaaS firms are implementing AI into their systems, enhancing their abilities for customers and end-users. Another way for organizations to use AI is via AI as a service (Abad et al., n.d.) Using AI improves applications' flexibility and efficiency, minimizing errors and improving productivity. Cloud computing's cloud-native architecture has resulted in the demise of the old monolithic cloud platform in favour of lightweight, loosely linked, and fine-grained modules (Zhong et al., 2021). This approach enables apps to be changed far more efficiently. Microservices' effective administration, on the other hand, might be problematic owing to their increasing quantity and moment characteristics. AI/ML-based solutions may solve some of these issues; for example, a neural network-based method can be used to forecast microservices' workloads, and machine learning-based approaches can be used to examine microservices' dependencies.

Several benefits of employing DL on the cloud include the following:

- Improved data management: In today's information world, information is king, necessitating improved data management. A company's capacity to keep track of the data is a significant challenge. Cloud-based data analytics tools and applications recognize, update, catalogue, and give customers accurate data analytics.

- Automation: Intelligent automation could only be applied across an entire organization, owing to the marriage of AI and the clouds, eliminating the final outstanding impediments. DL improves predictiveness by using past data and other patterns in insights. DL automates the transition from semi-structured to unstructured documents while also testing the bounds of efficient deployments, which is likely to result in this little disruption and effect (Jha et al., 2021). Consequently, both the cost of business operations and the customer experience are improved.

- Cost Savings: Technology enables organizations to pay for the services they use. This results in considerable cost savings compared to the traditional infrastructure costs associated with the construction and maintenance of enormous data centres (Robertson et al., 2021). Savings can be leveraged to develop more strategic AI tools and accelerators, which can subsequently be used to boost revenue just to save extra income at the heart of the business(Horn et al., 2019). This should result in improved operational quality and cost savings.

AWS

Amazon Web Services (AWS) offers a diverse environment of platforms that help the development of machine learning algorithms. Amazon Web Services' different value model includes data storage, high-performance computing instances using Graphics processing units, and high-performance networking devices. A WS offers end-to-end solutions for machine learning, like SageMaker and Deep Learning Containers.

Amazon SageMaker simplifies the process of training neural network models throughout a cluster of computers. This is not a simple task, but SageMaker's designed methods and pre-built MXNet and TensorFlow containers abstract most of the complexity. Nonetheless, choices concerning data structure will affect how distributed training is performed. Amazon SageMaker is a highly scalable deep learning service that allows computer scientists and programmers to build and train neural network models, including deep learning architectures, and then deploy them in a cloud-based manufacturing environment. SageMaker incorporates a Jupyter notebook, enabling data scientists to access data sources without needing to maintain server infrastructure readily. It allows the execution of typical machine learning and deep learning algorithms that have been pre-optimized for use in a distributed setting. SageMaker also has an integrated Jupyter Notebook, which enables data scientists and deep learning programmers to rapidly prototype and refine pipeline algorithms and instantly deploy them in a hosted environment. You can configure hardware and settings from SageMaker Studio or the SageMaker interface. AWS SageMaker supports distributed training with both data parallelism and model parallelism. Indeed, SageMaker supports a hybrid training technique in which both model and data parallelism is used.

AWS Deep Learning AMI (DLAMI)

AWS DLAMI is a customized EC2 device image that works with various instance types, including primary CPU instances and high-performance GPU instances such as P4. It enables developers and system scientists to quickly provide a pre-configured deep learning environment on AWS, CUDA, cuDNN, and significant libraries such as PyTorch, TensorFlow, and Horovod.

AWS Containers for Deep Learning

A pre-configured Docker image for deep learning contains a complete development ecosystem for deep learning. It has TensorFlow and PyTorch pre-installed and can be installed on SageMaker or Amazon container services such as EKS and ECS. Deep Learning Containers are free to use; customers only pay for the Amazon resources required to operate the container.

Elastic Inference on Amazon

A technique for adding GPU acceleration to standard Amazon EC2 instances in the same way you would add a GPU to a standard CPU-based computer. It may result in considerable cost reductions by enabling you to operate SageMaker and learning techniques instances on standard compute instances that are much less expensive than GPU instances.

AWS ParallelCluster

ParallelCluster, based on the open-source CfnCluster project, allows you to deploy an HPC computing environment in AWS easily. It automatically configures the appropriate computational resources, Slurm Scheduler, and shared file system. AWS ParallelCluster enables rapid prototyping and operational implementations.

GOOGLE CLOUD PLATFORM

Google Cloud Computing is built within the same architecture as Google's other platforms. Google cloud computing has a system that will allow for frameworks like TensorFlow, Pytorch, and Scikit-Learn. In addition to installing GPUs in the pipeline, TPUs can be included to accelerate the training phase significantly. As previously stated, you may link your Google Colab to the Google Cloud Platform and take advantage of its advantages. Google Cloud also offers a hardware acceleration option in the form of the Tensorflow Processing Unit (TPU). While not a GPU in the strictest sense, TPUs are an excellent option for machine learning tasks, intense learning. A TPU is a Google-developed application-specific integrated circuit designed for machine learning acceleration. Google offers TPU on-demand with its Cloud TPU machine learning cloud storage service. Cloud TPU is strongly coupled with Google's open-source machine learning (ML) framework, TensorFlow, which includes TPU-specific APIs. Cloud TPU enables the creation of TensorFlow to compute unit clusters comprised of TPUs, GPUs, and conventional CPUs.

MICROSOFT AZURE

The Azure deep learning service is intended for both programmers and non-programmers. It only provides a drag-and-drop interface that may help you streamline your productivity. Additionally, it eliminates manual labour via automation learning, which might assist you in developing more intelligent functioning prototypes. Azure Python SDK enables interaction with any Python environment, including Jupyter Notebooks, Visual Studio Code, and several others. In terms of service offerings, it is pretty comparable to both AWS and GCP.

Additionally, Azure Machine Learning may be utilized to train massively parallel deep learning models. The following is a Microsoft-provided reference design demonstrating how to distribute deep learning workloads across VM clusters with GPU capability. Although the reference model is for an image classification model, it may be utilized for various deep learning applications. The main features of the three-cloud server are shown in Table 2.

Table 2. Cloud service providers

Features	Cloud Providers		
	GCP	**AWS**	**Microsoft Azure**
Storage	GCS Big Query	RedShift S3	Blob Data Lake
Dataset	AI Platform	Sage Maker	Data Factory
Data Visualization	Data Studio	Quick Signal	Power BI
Data Exploration	Auto ML AI Platform	Sage Maker Athena	Data Bricks ML Studio
Model Deployment	AI Platform	Sage Maker	Azure ML Notebooks
Distributed Training	Available	Available	Available
Error Handling	Auto ML with Big Query	Sage Maker	Azure ML Notebooks

continued on following page

Table 2. Continued

Features	Cloud Providers		
	GCP	**AWS**	**Microsoft Azure**
Batch Prediction	Available	Available	Available
Logical Data Storage	VPC	VPC	VNet
Virtual Servers	VM Instances	Instances	VMs
Serverless Computing	Cloud Functions	Lambda	Azure Function
Docker Management	Container Engine	ECS	Container Service
Kubernetes Management	Kubernetes engine	EKS	Kubernetes Service
Auto ML	Auto ML Table	Sage Maker	Auto ML

SERVERLESS COMPUTING

Serverless computing is a cloud computing paradigm which extracts away operations and management(Akkus et al., 2018). Since programmers are no longer eligible for infrastructure maintenance, serverless technology is projected to grow much faster (Slominski, n.d.). As a result, cloud providers can manage infrastructure and automated provisioning more simply using serverless computing. Additionally, (Al-Ali et al., 2018) reduce the time and resources necessary for network administration. The objective of serverless computing is to ensure that the best serverless technologies are chosen to minimize investments and maximize returns (Akkus et al., 2018).

The following concepts are used to describe serverless computing:

- Functions: Serverless computing implements serverless functions using event-driven models. Because the program is automated in response to events may accelerate the design process (Lee et al., 2018). As a consequence, the current application may be connected to a large number of services. Using these characteristics, you may successfully implement the pay-per-execution approach (Jangda et al., 2019). It is invoiced for the time and resources used by this model while running code.
- Kubernetes: Users may use Serverless Kubernetes to add their containers to Kubernetes (Lloyd et al., 2018). These containers can be automatically scaled up or down in a Kubernetes-managed cluster. This automated scaling capability can cope with high-volume traffic scenarios and varying workloads.
- Workflows: Serverless workflows use a low-code or no-code approach (Al-Ali et al., 2018). This strategy aims to minimize the planning overheads involved in many operations concurrently. Developers may use these procedures to link multiple cloud and on-premises services. Serverless computing can learn new APIs or standards, which eliminates the need for interactions to be programmed (Mohanty et al., 2018).

FUTURE RESEARCH DIRECTIONS

Several unresolved issues and suggestions for further studies need more exploration.

- New techniques to ensemble deep learning for container management technologies such as Docker Swarm and Kubernetes are required to manage the user-based quality of service-based container clusters.
- Reliability and quality of service (QoS) of cloud services must be maintained via sophisticated machine or deep learning approaches.
- Network virtualization must be supplied at a reasonable cost in an SDN-based cloud computing environment. This uses AI/ML models to reduce energy usage and increase reliability.
- Using AI/ML, cloud-based Big Data analysis tools can uncover patterns in customer behaviours, enabling businesses to make more informed choices. A complete understanding of their consumers. DL-based algorithms execute or process scaling decisions in a timely way.
- By incorporating new DL-inspired approaches, thermal-aware job and resource scheduling may be enhanced.
- As the Internet of Things and scientific applications expand, autonomic computing powered by DL will become more vital.
- The development of rapid and computationally efficient serial algorithms for deep learning network training
- Deep learning is currently being used to solve various complicated problems with the development of quick and computationally efficient serial methods for training deep learning networks. Training deep learning architectures is now a computationally intensive task well-suited to HPC settings. Using parallel and distributed approaches in conjunction with high-performance computing (HPC) technology significantly reduces the time required to train deep learning networks. The scalability of distributed and parallel algorithms enables deep learning to be applied to an increasing number of big datasets and contributes to the progress of deep understanding.

CONCLUSION

Modern digital technologies have addressed many real-world challenges that need low latency and reaction time. Deep Learning (DL) has grown in popularity in the latest years of the efficiency advancements developed in fields like object recognition, language processing, and other related applications. Researchers and professionals in computing should be familiar with AI/ML/DL methods and models. Contemporary computing may benefit from more effective management when combined with DL, and high-performance computing is a critical platform for running DL services due to its massive processing power. This signifies that both parties' benefit from the relationship. Numerous AI/ML/DL approaches need large-scale processing capacity and external data, which may be more readily accessed through computer systems. This is particularly critical now that techniques for training advanced AI, machine learning, and deep learning models can be applied in massive numbers and also in parallel. To that aim, it is anticipated that sustained interest in DL applications will stimulate the latest findings into the reasonable datacenter resources concerns such as VM provisioning, aggregation, and task scheduling, even while rendering scale-out obstacles simpler to overcome.

REFERENCES

Abad, C., Foster, I. T., Herbst, N., & Iosup, A. (n.d.). *Serverless Computing*. 60.

Abadi, M., Barham, P., Chen, J., Chen, Z., Davis, A., Dean, J., Devin, M., Ghemawat, S., Irving, G., Isard, M., Kudlur, M., Levenberg, J., Monga, R., Moore, S., Murray, D. G., Steiner, B., Tucker, P., Vasudevan, V., Warden, P., … Zheng, X. (n.d.). *TensorFlow: A system for large-scale machine learning*. 21.

Abdelaziz, A., Elhoseny, M., Salama, A. S., & Riad, A. M. (2018). A machine learning model for improving healthcare services in cloud computing environment. *Measurement*, 119, 117–128. DOI: 10.1016/j.measurement.2018.01.022

Adek, R. T., & Ula, M. (2020). A Survey on The Accuracy of Machine Learning Techniques for Intrusion and Anomaly Detection on Public Data Sets. *2020 International Conference on Data Science, Artificial Intelligence, and Business Analytics (DATABIA)*. DOI: 10.1109/DATABIA50434.2020.9190436

Akkus, I. E., Chen, R., Rimac, I., Stein, M., Satzke, K., Beck, A., Aditya, P., & Hilt, V. (2018). *{SAND}: Towards {High-Performance} Serverless Computing*. 923–935. https://www.usenix.org/conference/atc18/presentation/akkus

Al-Ali, Z., Goodarzy, S., Hunter, E., Ha, S., Han, R., Keller, E., & Rozner, E. (2018). Making Serverless Computing More Serverless. *2018 IEEE 11th International Conference on Cloud Computing (CLOUD)*, 456–459. DOI: 10.1109/CLOUD.2018.00064

Babuji, Y., Woodard, A., Li, Z., Katz, D. S., Clifford, B., Kumar, R., Lacinski, L., Chard, R., Wozniak, J. M., Foster, I., Wilde, M., & Chard, K. (2019). Parsl: Pervasive Parallel Programming in Python. *Proceedings of the 28th International Symposium on High-Performance Parallel and Distributed Computing*, 25–36. DOI: 10.1145/3307681.3325400

Chen, T., Li, M., Li, Y., Lin, M., Wang, N., Wang, M., Xiao, T., Xu, B., Zhang, C., & Zhang, Z. (2015). MXNet: A Flexible and Efficient Machine Learning Library for Heterogeneous Distributed Systems. *ArXiv:1512.01274[Cs]*. http://arxiv.org/abs/1512.01274

Deng, L., Yu, D., & Platt, J. (2012). Scalable stacking and learning for building deep architectures. *2012 IEEE International Conference on Acoustics, Speech and Signal Processing (ICASSP)*, 2133–2136. DOI: 10.1109/ICASSP.2012.6288333

Horn, G., Skrzypek, P., Materka, K., & Przeździk, T. (2019). Cost Benefits of Multi-cloud Deployment of Dynamic Computational Intelligence Applications. In Barolli, L., Takizawa, M., Xhafa, F., & Enokido, T. (Eds.), *Web, Artificial Intelligence and Network Applications* (pp. 1041–1054). Springer International Publishing., DOI: 10.1007/978-3-030-15035-8_102

Huo, Z., Gu, B., Yang, Q., & Huang, H. (2018). Decoupled Parallel Backpropagation with Convergence Guarantee. *ArXiv:1804.10574[Cs, Stat]*. http://arxiv.org/abs/1804.10574

Jangda, A., Pinckney, D., Brun, Y., & Guha, A. (2019). Formal Foundations of Serverless Computing. *Proceedings of the ACM on Programming Languages, 3*(OOPSLA), 1–26. DOI: 10.1145/3360575

Jha, N., Prashar, D., & Nagpal, A. (2021). Combining Artificial Intelligence with Robotic Process Automation—An Intelligent Automation Approach. In Ahmed, K. R., & Hassanien, A. E. (Eds.), *Deep Learning and Big Data for Intelligent Transportation: Enabling Technologies and Future Trends* (pp. 245–264). Springer International Publishing., DOI: 10.1007/978-3-030-65661-4_12

Kim, S., Yu, G.-I., Park, H., Cho, S., Jeong, E., Ha, H., Lee, S., Jeong, J. S., & Chun, B.-G. (2019). Parallax: Sparsity-aware Data Parallel Training of Deep Neural Networks. *ArXiv:1808.02621[Cs]*. http://arxiv.org/abs/1808.02621 DOI: 10.1145/3302424.3303957

Lee, H., Satyam, K., & Fox, G. (2018). Evaluation of Production Serverless Computing Environments. *2018 IEEE 11th International Conference on Cloud Computing (CLOUD)*, 442–450. DOI: 10.1109/CLOUD.2018.00062

Li, M. (2014). Scaling Distributed Machine Learning with the Parameter Server. *Proceedings of the 2014 International Conference on Big Data Science and Computing - BigDataScience '14*, 1–1. DOI: 10.1145/2640087.2644155

Lloyd, W., Ramesh, S., Chinthalapati, S., Ly, L., & Pallickara, S. (2018). Serverless Computing: An Investigation of Factors Influencing Microservice Performance. *2018 IEEE International Conference on Cloud Engineering (IC2E)*, 159–169. DOI: 10.1109/IC2E.2018.00039

Mayer, R., Mayer, C., & Laich, L. (2017). The TensorFlow Partitioning and Scheduling Problem: It's the Critical Path! *Proceedings of the 1st Workshop on Distributed Infrastructures for Deep Learning*, 1–6. DOI: 10.1145/3154842.3154843

Mirhoseini, A., Pham, H., Le, Q. V., Steiner, B., Larsen, R., Zhou, Y., Kumar, N., Norouzi, M., Bengio, S., & Dean, J. (2017). Device Placement Optimization with Reinforcement Learning. *ArXiv:1706.04972[Cs]*. http://arxiv.org/abs/1706.04972

Mohanty, S. K., Premsankar, G., & di Francesco, M. (2018). An Evaluation of Open Source Serverless Computing Frameworks. *2018 IEEE International Conference on Cloud Computing Technology and Science (CloudCom)*, 115–120. DOI: 10.1109/CloudCom2018.2018.00033

Narayanan, D., Harlap, A., Phanishayee, A., Seshadri, V., Devanur, N. R., Ganger, G. R., Gibbons, P. B., & Zaharia, M. (2019). PipeDream: Generalized pipeline parallelism for DNN training. *Proceedings of the 27th ACM Symposium on Operating Systems Principles*, 1–15. DOI: 10.1145/3341301.3359646

Ono, J., Utiyama, M., & Sumita, E. (2019). Hybrid Data-Model Parallel Training for Sequence-to-Sequence Recurrent Neural Network Machine Translation. *ArXiv:1909.00562[Cs]*. http://arxiv.org/abs/1909.00562

Onoufriou, G., Bickerton, R., Pearson, S., & Leontidis, G. (2019). Nemesyst: A hybrid parallelism deep learning-based framework applied for internet of things enabled food retailing refrigeration systems. *Computers in Industry*, 113, 103133. DOI: 10.1016/j.compind.2019.103133

Oyama, Y., Maruyama, N., Dryden, N., McCarthy, E., Harrington, P., Balewski, J., Matsuoka, S., Nugent, P., & Van Essen, B. (2020). The Case for Strong Scaling in Deep Learning: Training Large 3D CNNs with Hybrid Parallelism. *ArXiv:2007.12856[Cs]*. http://arxiv.org/abs/2007.12856

Pusztai, T., Morichetta, A., Pujol, V. C., Dustdar, S., Nastic, S., Ding, X., Vij, D., & Xiong, Y. (2021). SLO Script: A Novel Language for Implementing Complex Cloud-Native Elasticity-Driven SLOs. *2021 IEEE International Conference on Web Services (ICWS)*, 21–31. DOI: 10.1109/ICWS53863.2021.00017

Ravikumar, A. (2021). Non-relational multi-level caching for mitigation of staleness & stragglers in distributed deep learning. *Proceedings of the 22nd International Middleware Conference: Doctoral Symposium*, 15–16. DOI: 10.1145/3491087.3493678

Ravikumar, A., & Sriraman, H. (2021). Staleness and Stagglers in Distibuted Deep Image Analytics. *2021 International Conference on Artificial Intelligence and Smart Systems (ICAIS)*, 848–852. DOI: 10.1109/ICAIS50930.2021.9395782

Ravikumar, A., Sriraman, H., Saketh, P. M. S., Lokesh, S., & Karanam, A. (2022). Effect of neural network structure in accelerating performance and accuracy of a convolutional neural network with GPU/TPU for image analytics. *PeerJ. Computer Science*, 8, e909. DOI: 10.7717/peerj-cs.909 PMID: 35494877

Robertson, J., Fossaceca, J. M., & Bennett, K. W. (2021). A Cloud-Based Computing Framework for Artificial Intelligence Innovation in Support of Multidomain Operations. *IEEE Transactions on Engineering Management*, ●●●, 1–10. DOI: 10.1109/TEM.2021.3088382

Slominski, P. C. Vatche Ishakian, Vinod Muthusamy, Aleksander. (n.d.). *The Rise of Serverless Computing*. Retrieved April 19, 2022, from https://cacm.acm.org/magazines/2019/12/241054-the-rise-of-serverless-computing/fulltext

Tuli, S., Gill, S. S., Xu, M., Garraghan, P., Bahsoon, R., Dustdar, S., Sakellariou, R., Rana, O., Buyya, R., Casale, G., & Jennings, N. R. (2022). HUNTER: AI-based Holistic Resource Management for Sustainable Cloud Computing. *Journal of Systems and Software*, 184, 111124. DOI: 10.1016/j.jss.2021.111124

Younas, M., Jawawi, D. N. A., Shah, M. A., Mustafa, A., Awais, M., Ishfaq, M. K., & Wakil, K. (2020). Elicitation of Nonfunctional Requirements in Agile Development Using Cloud Computing Environment. *IEEE Access : Practical Innovations, Open Solutions*, 8, 209153–209162. DOI: 10.1109/ACCESS.2020.3014381

ADDITIONAL READING

Ben Youssef, B. (2015). A parallel cellular automata algorithm for the deterministic simulation of 3-D multicellular tissue growth. *Cluster Computing*, 18(4), 1561–1579. DOI: 10.1007/s10586-015-0455-7

Carneiro, T., Medeiros Da Nobrega, R. V., Nepomuceno, T., Bian, G.-B., De Albuquerque, V. H. C., & Filho, P. P. R. (2018). Performance Analysis of Google Colaboratory as a Tool for Accelerating Deep Learning Applications. *IEEE Access : Practical Innovations, Open Solutions*, 6, 61677–61685. DOI: 10.1109/ACCESS.2018.2874767

Chen, C.-C., Yang, C.-L., & Cheng, H.-Y. (2019). Efficient and Robust Parallel DNN Training through Model Parallelism on Multi-GPU Platform. *ArXiv:1809.02839[Cs]*. http://arxiv.org/abs/1809.02839

Hegde, V., & Usmani, S. (n.d.). *Parallel and Distributed Deep Learning*. 8.

Li, M. (2014). Scaling Distributed Machine Learning with the Parameter Server. *Proceedings of the 2014 International Conference on Big Data Science and Computing - BigDataScience '14*, 1–1. https://doi.org/DOI: 10.1145/2640087.2644155

Pop, D. (2016). Machine Learning and Cloud Computing: Survey of Distributed and SaaS Solutions. *ArXiv:1603.08767[Cs]*. http://arxiv.org/abs/1603.08767

Zhang, Z., Yin, L., Peng, Y., & Li, D. (2018). A Quick Survey on Large Scale Distributed Deep Learning Systems. *2018 IEEE 24th International Conference on Parallel and Distributed Systems (ICPADS)*, 1052–1056. https://doi.org/DOI: 10.1109/PADSW.2018.8644613

Zheng, L., Li, Z., Zhang, H., Zhuang, Y., Chen, Z., Huang, Y., Wang, Y., Xing, E. P., Xu, Y., Zhuo, D., Gonzalez, J. E., & Stoica, I. (2022). Alpa: Automating Inter- and Intra-Operator Parallelism for Distributed Deep Learning (arXiv:2201.12023). arXiv. http://arxiv.org/abs/2201.12023

KEY TERMS AND DEFINITIONS

Cloud Computing: Cloud computing is an on deployment of information systems assets, including data storage and processing power, without the user's direct administration. Large clouds usually divide their services over numerous sites, each of which is a data center. These services include storage, workstations, databases and software. Cloud infrastructure comprises the necessary hardware and software tools for implementing a cloud computing architecture.

Data parallelism: It focuses on spreading data over several nodes that act in parallel with the data. The data is split among worker nodes and the model remains the same in each of the nodes.

Deep Learning: Deep Learning is a branch of artificial intelligence dealing with artificial neural network learning algorithms and brain function. These neural networks seek to imitate the activity of the human brain, though imperfectly, allowing them to "learn" from massive amounts of data.

High-Performance Computing: HPC is the capacity to analyze data and execute complicated computations rapidly. High-performance computing is sometimes used interchangeably with supercomputing. A supercomputer is a system that operates at or close to the maximum operating rate for computers.

Serverless Computing: "Serverless" is a term since cloud service providers still employ servers to execute arbitrary code for developers. However, serverless application developers aren't worried about capacity management, configuration, administration, maintenance, high availability, or scalability of containers, virtual machines (VMs), or physical servers. Instead of storing resources in volatile memory, serverless computing computes the results stored in storage in brief bursts. When an application is not in use, no computer resources are assigned. An application's cost depends on the number of resources it consumes.

Task parallelism: Method of code parallelization over several processors in concurrent computing systems. Task parallelism focuses on spreading simultaneously executed tasks or threads across many processors. Pipelining is a popular sort of task parallelism that consists of transferring a single piece of data through a sequence of discrete jobs that may operate independently of one another.

Tensor Flow: A free, open-source artificial intelligence and machine learning software library. It may be used for various applications, but training and inference of deep neural networks are its primary emphasis.

Chapter 9
Accelerating Scientific Discovery With Machine Learning and HPC–Based Simulations

Sai Krishna Gunda
https://orcid.org/0009-0006-6033-9825
Department of Computer Software Engineering, University of Houston, USA

ABSTRACT

An integration of machine learning (ML) with high-performance computing (HPC) is radically transforming research in the scientific field. ML algorithms can span large-scale simulations and predict a great deal in materials science, climate modeling, and drug discovery by optimizing resource allocation and finding novel insights. HPC has accelerated complex data-sets processing, and ML models allow automation in pattern recognition and advanced analytics. The synergy of these technologies accelerates the experimentation rate, shortens time-to-discovery, and improves the scalability to tackle complex scientific challenges. It explores different key methodologies, case studies, and directions with future impacts that illustrate how advances in ML and HPC can revolutionize scientific innovation across disciplines. It demonstrates improved problem-solving capacity and accuracy in prediction as it addresses some of the most profound global challenges.

INTRODUCTION

Actually, by integrating machine learning with high-performance computing, one fundamentally changes the landscape for scientific discovery. Scientific breakthroughs in areas like materials science, climate modeling, molecular biology, or drug discovery have, traditionally, been achieved through this blend of theoretical modeling and experimental validation and simulation at large scales. Yet, since the complexity of problems had increased, there was a corresponding increase in the complexity of computation tools to deal with these big data sets and extract new insights or previously unknown facts. This chapter looks at the emergent trend in the convergence of ML and HPC as potentially powerful means

DOI: 10.4018/978-1-6684-3795-7.ch009

of improving such challenges so that phenomena can be simulated more efficiently, computations run faster, and breakthrough discoveries are made in many disciplines of science(Peterson et al., 2022).

Scientific simulations have always depended on high-performance computing. High performance computing systems allow scientists to model complex phenomena with high degrees of accuracy by using huge computational power for solving mathematical models that describe the processes for realistic study. Such simulations are important because they would be often too expensive, too dangerous, or too time-consuming to study directly. Without the computational power of modern HPC infrastructure, it would be almost impossible to simulate extreme conditions on materials or climate change over decades. Even using the most powerful tools, tradition simulation methods turn out to be quite slow and computationally expensive, especially with multiscale phenomena that demand higher resolution in time and space(Kurz et al., 2022).

That's where machine learning comes into play. In the methods of ML, but specifically in deep learning, researchers have really seen breakthroughs the last few years. These methods specialize in pattern recognition and prediction of large data sets-a task that has become increasingly important in scientific research. This means that by training models on historical data or simulation outputs, ML algorithms can now make real-time predictions and inferences with dramatic reductions in the time spent on experiments and analyses. In addition, ML can be used to optimize the simulations themselves: identifying redundant computations or accelerating the solution of complex mathematical equations leads to reduced computational costs and faster results. It is thus that the conjunction of ML and HPC shows a step forward, both in terms of speed and accuracy of scientific computations(Fox et al., 2019).

One of the most exciting applications of this convergence is in the field of materials science. Finding new materials with specific properties involves exploring vast spaces of potential compositions and structures-something that can be prohibitively expensive to do by using traditional experimental methods. By coupling HPC simulations with ML models trained on known material properties, the likely candidates for desired properties can now be rapidly predicted among the vast combinations of elements and structures. This approach not only accelerates the discovery process but opens up new possibilities for designing new materials with a degree of precision that has never been seen before. For example, materials can be found for energy storage, light aerospace components, or more efficient semiconductors, something that, in a timeframe and price point, would take one order of magnitude longer and cost much more with traditional methods(Paul et al., 2021).

Together, ML and HPC enable climate science to better model complex systems that span multiple scales and involve countless interacting variables. Climate models are computationally intensive because of the range of processes involved in capturing, such as atmospheric dynamics, ocean currents, land surface changes, and human activities. High-order simulations on the HPC are feasible; however, ML can provide further enhancements to the representation of sub-grid-scale processes, i.e., the processes that are too small to be resolved within the models but are relevant to capturing the fine details of the overall system(Ward et al., 2021). For example, trained ML models can predict the formation and behavior of clouds from history data, and then such data can be used in large climate simulations, thus improving the accuracy of climate predictions and getting them much faster, enabling scientists to better understand and predict the effects of global warming, impact of extreme weather, and other environmental changes.

The transformation of pharmaceutical and biotech drug discovery processes is being made possible by the union of ML in conjunction with HPC. New drug candidates used to be identified for years and millions of dollars by screening large libraries through laborious experimental methods. Currently, HPC allows for the simulation of molecular interaction on such a scale that scientists can forecast how drugs would react to specific targets while ML algorithms can filter through enormous biological and chemical data to predict which compounds stand more likely to be effective against certain targets(Ejarque et al., 2022). This also accelerates the identification of potential drug candidates, and researchers estimate their toxicity, solubility, and similar important attributes right at the initial steps of the research process. Hence, the time and cost associated with taking a new drug to the market are highly minimized(Mira et al., 2023).

The power of ML once again accelerates scientific discovery even in the field of fundamentals where researchers simulate phenomena that are at present beyond current experimental capabilities. For example, cosmology uses HPC simulations to model the growth of the universe from the very early epochs of Big Bang and up to the present. In those simulations, one needs to solve extremely complicated equations describing dark matter and energy and galactic formation over billions of years. This is where ML techniques find their use in optimizing simulations through knowledge acquired from previous iterations, which therefore reduces the time and computational resources taken to make various explorations. In particle physics, like experiments carried out in the Large Hadron Collider, huge volumes of data require adequate ML algorithms to recognize patterns and give meaning to underlying physical processes(Farrell et al., 2021).

The integration of ML and HPC is also taking new methodologies in scientific research itself. There is a new concept of "in silico" experiments, meaning that computers with ML augmentation can carry out impossible or impractical experiments in the real world. The advantage of this approach is that the researchers can consider hypotheses and test new theories without necessitating physical prototypes or lab experiments. For instance, ML can be developed to create synthetic data mimicking a real-world scenario so that scientists can ponder "what if" scenarios or fill gaps in data that may have been collected but could not be completed with available resources. This is not only designed to expedite the discovery process, but it also carries a level of precision and control that is very difficult to deliver in a traditional experiment setting(Kadupitiya et al., 2020).

Advancements in machine learning and high-performance computing are continuously improving and ensuring that the ability of such technologies in speeding up scientific discovery will continue to grow. Science research will hence become ever more data-driven, with ML emerging as a key to extracting insights from complex datasets and HPC providing the computational horsepower to run increasingly detailed simulations. Moreover, as even more disciplines start using these technologies, we might expect opportunities for cross-field interdisciplinary approaches to new discoveries and innovations. Whether the challenge is finding new materials, predicting climate change, or developing drugs likely to save thousands of lives, this synergistic union of ML and HPC has a high potential of being an indispensable tool in solving the scientific challenges of tomorrow(Kadupitiya et al., 2019; Sarma et al., 2024).

Hence, the combined synergy of machine learning and high-performance computing is revolutionizing the scientific process: much faster, more accurate simulations and predictive models. This now allows researchers to pose problems that are previously unsolvable or too resource-intensive to take into their full consideration. As these technologies continue to develop, so will their impact on scientific discovery, paving new frontiers of knowledge while fostering progress in a wide range of fields.

Objectives

The main aims of this chapter are to look at the integration of Machine Learning (ML) and High-Performance Computing (HPC) to effect synergy between accelerating discovery and enhancing simulation capabilities in scientific research. We elucidate elementary concepts and techniques behind ML, the architecture of and infrastructure for HPC systems, and illustrate applications in areas such as drug discovery, climate modeling, materials science, and fundamental physics. In this regard, this chapter also attempts to deal with the challenges and limitations that can be garnered by integrating these technologies while casting a foresight of future trends and innovations that may blur the lines and reshape scientific inquiry and discovery.

MACHINE LEARNING: FUNDAMENTALS AND TECHNIQUES

Machine learning is the kind of transformative technology which allows a computer to learn and make decisions without explicit programs, actually discovering patterns or distinguishing features from data. Two main categories in which machine learning falls under are supervised and unsupervised learning. In supervised learning, there exists labelled datasets where the input-output pairs are already known, so the model learns to predict outputs for new inputs by recognizing what pattern the data contains. Among its most common applications, classification tasks such as image recognition and regression tasks like predicting climate trends are highlighted. In contrast, unsupervised learning deals with unlabelled data in the process. The goal is finding hidden structures or patterns. Clustering and dimensionality reduction are examples of unsupervised learning, especially for data exploration and anomaly detection. These methods are highly utilized in scientific analysis to identify natural groups of data, such as genetic sequences or chemical compounds(Partee et al., 2022).

Deep learning represents a field of machine learning which has profoundly altered many domains due to the ability to learn hierarchical representations of data, using neural networks, which essentially contain numerous layers of neurons processed at increasingly abstract levels. Deep learning models, especially CNNs and RNNs, have proved to be significantly powerful in areas like image and speech recognition. They come with invaluable importance in medical imaging and natural language processing. Deep learning helps sift through large datasets, for example, satellite imagery for monitoring environmental conditions or particle physics data for finding new subatomic particles, providing a new way to make predictions for complex, high-dimensional data(Ihde et al., 2022).

The second key area of machine learning is reinforcement learning (RL). It focuses on how an agent learns to make choices by interacting with an environment in ways that maximise cumulative rewards. RL is fundamentally different from supervised learning since there is no reliance on labelled data. In RL, an agent learns through experiencing an association between actions and outcomes through trial and error. In scientific applications, for example, RL is optimizing experimental conditions, which may include control of plasma in nuclear fusion reactors or even the design of the chemical experiment used for drug discovery. Due to the dynamic and complex nature of the problems, it is highly suited to applying RL to automate scientific processes and under circumstances of uncertainty. Among the key algorithms used for scientific research are SVMs, decision trees and random forests-better algorithms for applications such as classification and regression tasks. In addition, the important use of genetic algorithms and

Bayesian networks in optimization and probabilistic reasoning is there. Together with these algorithms along with HPC infrastructure, scientists can achieve solutions to the most complex problems today.

HIGH-PERFORMANCE COMPUTING: CONCEPTS AND INFRASTRUCTURE

High-Performance Computing is the use of supercomputers and parallel processing in performing very complex calculations much faster than can be done within the regular system. HPC systems are specifically designed to perform huge data sets or carry out complex simulations, thus forming the basis of scientific research and engineering as well as data analyses. In general, they will have a network of connected nodes that have powerful processors, well-fitted with memory and fast storage solutions(Lee et al., 2019). Classification of HPC systems is based on architecture, ranging from tightly-coupled super-computers to rather loosely-coupled clusters. The fundamental argument about HPC is to achieve high throughput at low latency, enabling scientists to solve the problems that demand significant computational resources- like climate modeling, molecular dynamics simulations, and large-scale data analytics.

Parallel Computing and Distributed Systems

The core of HPC is the concept of parallel computing-that is, splitting up a computationally intensive task to smaller components that, in turn, are executable simultaneously across several nodes or processors. In this way, dramatic decreases in computation time occur especially with complex problems. Parallelism goes down to all levels of computing, from bit-level to instruction-level and finally to task-level(Dhanalakshmi et al., 2024). In HPC, task-level parallelism is typically applied. That is, a number of independent tasks are executed in parallel. Several independent computing entities work together in solving a problem to make up a distributed system. The systems are characterized by the sharing of various resources among network nodes, for example, data and power in computations. The combination of parallel and distributed computing made it possible for researchers to use several processors at the same time performing computations, which gave rise to unprecedented capabilities and scalability in computation.

GPU and TPU Acceleration in HPC

The integration of GPUs and TPUs into HPC architectures has been the revolution that changes the computational performance. GPUs are more intended for parallel processing; thus, they are used on very large-scale computing operations and machine learning. An HPC system can acquire several orders of magnitude more speedup than what is delivered by systems that only have a CPU due to the fact that certain computations can be offloaded onto GPUs. TPUs: Developed by Google, this is a special hardware accelerator particularly built for performing workloads for machine learning, set to optimize tensor operations to execute faster training and inference of deep learning models. With the embracing of the HPC environment with GPUs and TPUs, it is possible to tackle increasingly complex scientific problems like real-time simulations and predictive modeling. There, data sizes grow exponentially as does the complexity of the calculations.

Scalability and Optimization in HPC Environments

Scalability is one of those issues taken into consideration when it comes to HPC environments; basically, it demonstrates the ability of a system to sustain its performance even at increased numbers of processors or nodes. Horizontal scalability incorporates adding additional nodes to a cluster while vertical scalability boosts the existing nodes' capabilities. Scalability can only be achieved through careful planning of the architecture, possibly through efficient communication protocols and workload balancing. Optimization is also critical for full utilization and performance of HPC system resources(Boopathi & Kanike, 2023; Maheswari et al., 2023; Syamala et al., 2023). This can be achieved at the algorithmic level through fine-tuning the algorithm, optimizing the access patterns to data, and also through techniques like load balancing. Profiling and performance analysis tools help identify problems and inefficiencies so that these bottlenecks can be corrected by the adjustments made by the researchers. Concludingly, scalability and optimization fit very well together in order to make HPC systems more efficient on the whole and able to power scientific challenges that we have yet to face or even imagine.

THE INTERSECTION OF MACHINE LEARNING AND HPC

It is at the intersection of Machine Learning (ML) and High-Performance Computing (HPC) that the revolution in scientific research and engineering becomes catalyzed. On combining their strengths, a synergy can produce acceleration of discovery, optimization of simulations, and innovation in solutions to problems. This synergy realizes itself in four major aspects: speeding up simulation through acceleration by the use of ML, reduction of the computational complexity associated with high performance computing simulations, use of data-driven models within scientific applications using a hybrid approach, and the creation of real-time predictive models using both ML and HPC technologies(X. Chen et al., 2021). The figure 1 depicts the intersection of Machine Learning (ML) and High-Performance Computing (HPC).

Figure 1. Intersection of Machine Learning (ML) and High-Performance Computing (HPC)

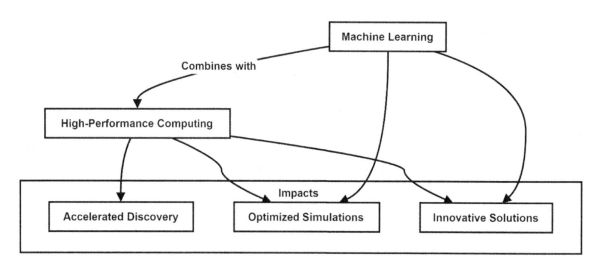

Boosting Simulation Speed Through the Use of ML

Use of ML within HPC leads to a number of benefits one of which is fast simulation. Traditional simulations that scientists use often are computationally intensive and time-consuming. Hence, those demand considerable resources on computers along with long periods of computation. Instead of re-running the expensive simulation codes, it is possible to train the ML algorithms on the available simulation data so that surrogate models could be developed, approximating the outcomes of complex simulations more efficiently. Those surrogate models may become much faster substitutes for traditional approaches to simulation, which can then allow researchers to investigate a larger parameter space in shorter time frames.

For instance, modelers relying on CFD simulations in fluid dynamics could run hours or days. Using ML models to predict fluid behaviors based on historical data from simulation could save tremendous amounts of computation time for analysis and optimization. The field, in particular, of aerospace engineering is especially requiring such improvements because it relies so much on rapid prototyping and design iteration. Such an approach can open the possibility for the analysis of multiple design scenarios within a relatively short time frame and speed up the decision-making process and reduce innovation cycles.

Computational Complexity Reduction in HPC Simulations

Another very important advantage ML bestows is to minimize the computational cost in HPC simulations. Many scientific problems are framed with high-dimensional data that portrays an interaction among the variables complicatedly, and this leads to exponentially high requirements of simulation for computational resources. Techniques using ML, especially methods of dimension reduction like PCA or t-SNE, may reduce complex datasets while retaining essential features. It reduces data dimensionality and, therefore, the complexity of data simulations. Perhaps in this respect, genomics is particularly promising-for example, because ML algorithms can actually process thousands of variables in genetic data to identify the key factors that influence the outcomes of disease. Such reduction in complexity gives scientists more focus on the most relevant data, which renders results more accurate and easier to interpret.

ML can also aid in resource optimization provision within HPC environments. This is achieved by analyzing performance for algorithms related to specific tasks by the ML models, leading to the identification of optimal configurations for these simulations. Dynamic resource allocation would thus provide researchers with optimal performance without unnecessary computational cost.

Data-Driven Scientific Models: A Hybrid Approach

A use of data-driven scientific models combines traditional approaches to modeling and those of ML techniques. Many established theories and equations applied in traditional models can greatly contribute to the understanding of a specific problem. However, these models are usually incapable of precisely describing complexities and nonlinear effects, which occur in real-world systems. The old models are further enriched with the power of ML so that researchers can predict by data-driven insights. For example, climate science can be represented by using the old models that predict temperature and precipitation patterns on the basis of history and physical equations. With ML integrated into the algorithm, the model further allows the researcher to fine-tune such predictions on the basis of real-time information, thereby increasing the responsiveness of the model to changing conditions(Tanash et al., 2021).

This hybrid approach works most effectively in conditions where existing models lack detail or where empirical data are abundant. In such conditions, machine learning algorithms learn from such data to identify patterns and relationships that might not be so evident when using traditional modeling alone. The result of this combination of both theoretical and empirical approaches is a more powerful scientific model capable of yielding deeper insight into the complex phenomena.

Real-Time Predictive Models Using ML and HPC

Another important application of the overlap between ML and HPC is in real-time predictive models. Applications in healthcare, finance, and environmental monitoring revolve around the idea of having accurate predictions made in real-time. This now allows researchers to develop systems that can process streaming data and make almost instantaneous predictions by taking the computational power from the HPC side and the predictive capabilities of ML(Khetawat et al., 2019).

For example, in healthcare, real-time predictive models can analyze data from patients to give potential risks and treatment recommendations. The ML algorithms have the capability of obtaining a pattern from patient histories, lab test results, and current real-time monitoring results, which may provide the healthcare professional with the capacity to make timely decisions. The real-time predictive model would thus be used in the financial markets to analyze patterns in trading as well as news sentiment, allowing the trader to change his strategy dynamically according to the current market conditions. The system combines the strength of ML and HPC, handling vast amounts of data in real time, so the predictions are based on the most recent information possible. This capacity enhances decision-making and leads to better results in all domains-to personal medicine and risk management in finance.

Machine learning and high-performance computing at the intersection create a new paradigm in the conduct of scientific research and engineering. This is achieved through increased simulation speed, reduced computational complexity, the use of hybrid data-driven models, and enabling real-time predictability. As these fields continue to evolve, their integration will surely accelerate breakthrough discoveries in the comprehension of complex systems as well as critical challenges across a wide range of scientific domains. Researchers and their institutions who can tap into the power of both ML and HPC will be at the forefront of this revolution wave, continuing the next generation of scientific inquiry and technology development.

Figure 2. Applications of Machine Learning (ML) and High-Performance Computing (HPC) in various scientific research domains

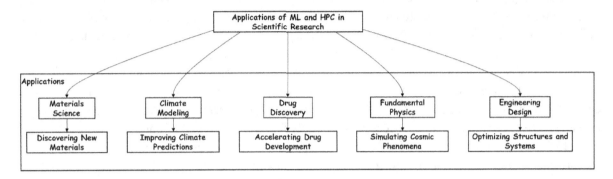

APPLICATIONS OF ML AND HPC IN SCIENTIFIC RESEARCH

With the advent of Machine Learning (ML) and High-Performance Computing (HPC), many areas of scientific study have changed with the enhancement of researchers' capabilities to solve complex problems. This combination is particularly potent in materials science, climate modeling, drug discovery, fundamental physics, and engineering design. Next, in depth, are discussions of how ML and HPC are applied in these diverse domains(Khetawat et al., 2019; Morales-Hernández et al., 2020). The figure 2 depicts the diverse applications of Machine Learning (ML) and High-Performance Computing (HPC) in various scientific research fields.

Materials Science: Discovering New Materials

These newly developed materials go to the heart of new technologies in the fields of energy storage, electronics, and nanotechnology. The process of discovery through experimentation is slow and resource-consuming, relying on trial and error. Machine Learning and HPC enabled this process by the prediction of material properties from chemical composition and structure.

Machine learning algorithms, such as regression models and neural networks, can find patterns and correlations between the compositions of materials and their properties using a large dataset of known materials. HPC systems enable these analyses by providing necessary computational capabilities dealing with large datasets quickly. For example, ML has been used to predict mechanical, thermal, and electronic properties of new alloys, polymers, and composites to quickly identify candidates for specific applications. In addition, ML-based methods such as generative design and optimization algorithms allow scientists to search much larger spaces of design and thereby identify materials with superior performance properties. The marriage of computational modeling with ML allows scientists to accelerate the materials discovery process that could likely unlock great breakthroughs in renewables, electronics, and structural materials.

Climate Modeling: Improving Predictions and Projections

Bringing together ML and HPC has immense implications for climate modeling. Since such climate models are instrumental in climate change understanding, weather pattern prediction, and much more policy-informed decisions, classical climate models rely predominantly on complex mathematical equations to simulate physical processes but often are limited by massive computational requirements and sheer complexity of systems involved. Through ML, the accuracy and efficiency of climate models may be enhanced. To give an example, ML algorithms could be trained on historical climate data to identify certain patterns for prediction on future climate scenarios. Deep learning techniques have been applied to enhance the precision of weather forecasts by analyzing satellite imagery and other meteorological data. The new models are enabled for simulations at scales they have never reached before using HPC resources with high resolutions to know the impacts on both global and local climate.

Aside from this, it can also be used for model calibration and uncertainty quantification; that way, scientists will be able to quantify the reliability of their predictions. Hybrid models can then be produced by integrating the ML techniques into the traditional climate models, thereby giving the researchers better predictive capabilities as well as an enhanced understanding of climate dynamics.

Drug Discovery: Accelerating Biomedical Research

The domain of drug discovery has revolutionized the methods with which investigators identify new therapeutics by the integration of machine learning and high-performance computing. The entire process of current drug discovery takes over a decade and billions of dollars to get a single drug in the market. In such a scenario, it is possible that the ML algorithms could greatly speed up this process by facilitating fast screening of potential candidates and determining their efficacy and safety profiles. With access to HPC resources, researchers can analyze large datasets produced from high-throughput screening assays, genomic studies, and clinical trials. It can facilitate the identification of promising compounds or biomarkers. Building these models allows machine learning to predict how different compounds interact with different biological targets; thus, scientists can fast-track the drug development phase. Deep learning techniques have been used to predict binding affinities of drug-like molecules for certain targets, which helps researchers develop lead candidates for further development(Rebecca et al., 2024).

Patient stratification and personalized medicine can also be furthered by ML through patient data analysis to find various subpopulations most likely to receive a treatment: The strategy not only accelerates the rate at which new drugs are discovered but also ensures that the right therapies are given to the right people, thereby leading to better outcomes.

Physics at the Basis: New Physical Phenomena Discovery

In fundamental physics, using an advanced computational technique, a new type of physical phenomenon may be explored to analyze the complex dataset produced by experimental data, such as produced at a particle accelerator or astronomical observatory. The ML and HPC integration will enable physicists to wring large volumes of data and find patterns in data that may not be interpreted by a method that would otherwise not reveal anything. For instance, in particle physics, ML algorithms can assist a researcher in sifting the tremendous data produced by experiments such as LHC. Such algorithms can potentially identify anomalies that are very rare events and could be results of the existence of new particles or new types of interactions, therefore speeding up the search for new physics beyond the Standard Model.

Astrophysicists rely on ML techniques to understand data emanating from the analysis of telescopes and satellite missions in the search for exoplanets, gravitational waves, and much more. Complex simulations regarding cosmic events such as supernovae and galaxy formation make it possible for researchers to gain information at the most fundamental working level within the universe with the help of HPC resources. The marriage of the analytical capabilities of ML with the computational abilities of HPC shall unlock frontiers of knowledge so that new physical phenomena can be unveiled, which would deepen our understanding of the cosmos.

Engineering and Design: Optimizing Structures and Systems

The integration of ML and HPC in engineering leads to significant advancement in optimizing structures and systems. Be it civil, mechanical, or aerospace engineering, the designing part demands simulation and analysis under several conditions that ensure safety and performance, as well as efficiency.

Machine learning algorithms may further analyze historical performance data and simulation results to identify design faults or suggest areas for optimization. For instance, in structural engineering, ML can be used to optimize the design of buildings and bridges using parameters such as material properties, load distribution, and environmental conditions. Thus, engineers would perform thousands of simulations evaluating different configurations of design, where they could identify effective solutions through HPC resources(Gopi et al., 2024; Pitchai et al., 2024).

The integration of ML and HPC into aerospace engineering allows optimizing aircraft design in both aerodynamic efficiency and fuel consumption benefits. Simulation of airflow over designs and resultant analysis by ML algorithms result in better refined designs for optimal performance. Moreover, the integration of ML and HPC monitors the constant structural integrity and performance to avoid sudden failure and permits proactive maintenance. This application is highly critical in critical infrastructure where both safety and reliability come into play.

Applications of Machine Learning and High-Performance Computing in Scientific Research

The applications of Machine Learning and High-Performance Computing are infinite and revolutionizing scientific research. From new materials discoveries to the improvement in climate models, accelerating drug discovery, revealing fundamental physical phenomena, and so much more, these technologies combined are already transforming how investigators address complex problems(Brayford et al., 2019; Khetawat et al., 2019; Morales-Hernández et al., 2020). Further evolution of ML and HPC will likely produce a synergistic effect of major innovation and breakthroughs in a very wide cross-section of scientific disciplines, enhancing our understanding of the world and improving quality of life for all.

Figure 3. Case studies showcasing the integration of Machine Learning (ML) and High-Performance Computing (HPC)

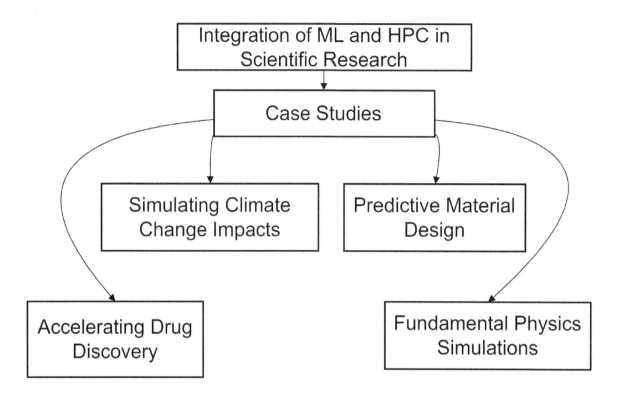

CASE STUDIES

The technological revolution described by ML and HPC above is applied in several strands of scientific research. Of course, this is only the tip of the iceberg; such potential can be harnessed through ML and HPC. In the next section, four case studies are presented to demonstrate successful integration of ML and HPC to speed up drug discovery, climate change impact simulation, predictive material design, and fundamental physics simulations(Brayford et al., 2019; Isakov et al., 2020; Morales-Hernández et al., 2020). Figure 3 showcases case studies demonstrating the integration of Machine Learning (ML) and High-Performance Computing (HPC).

Accelerating Drug Discovery with ML and HPC

ML and HPC have significantly cut the time that the pharmaceutical industry takes to develop drugs. In comparison, the outdated drug development process is so cumbersome and expensive that it often may take more than a decade and billions of dollars to put a novel drug on the market. Researchers can quickly analyze enormous datasets collected through high-throughput screening and genomic studies by using ML algorithms to identify potential drug candidates. For instance, one significant application was in the use of deep learning models to predict the bioactivity of compounds against particular biological targets. This has assisted scientists to filter several million compounds rapidly and identify promising candidates to further test. HPC has been key here in providing computational power that was critical for running extensive simulations in the optimization of molecular structures, thus accelerating the timescale for bringing in new drugs to clinical trials.

ML-Enhanced HPC Models for Simulating Climate Change Impacts

One of the greatest and most valuable usages of ML-enhanced HPC models have been within climate studies- specifically in simulating climate change impacts. Additionally, scientists will be able to predict more accurately future temperature changes, sea-level rise, and extreme weather events by including ML strategies into climate models. For instance, one case study was a hybrid model integrating traditional climate models and ML algorithms to make historical climate data amenable to pattern formulation. The model was then used to forecast the probable future climate scenarios based on different greenhouse gas emission pathways. The output provided critical information to the policymakers so they may have understanding of risks that may take place and strategies of mitigation and adaptation. The processing of large quantities of data from satellite observations and climate simulations using HPC enabled scientists to produce high-resolution models that improve the precision of climate predictions.

Predictive Material Design: Case of New Energy Storage Materials

Material science has benefited especially well from ML/HPC in designing new materials with predictive properties, especially energy storage ones. Next-generation batteries will maybe be discovered using ML-algorithm application when analyzing data coming from previous experiments and computational simulations to pick prospective candidates. They predicted the electrochemical properties of new materials before synthesizing them physiochemically in the lab using regression models and neural networks. HPC enabled quick computation of complex simulations, such that thousands of materials performances could be obtained simultaneously by these researchers. The researchers identified a few new compounds that have superior energy density and stability, and their discovery has significantly advanced efficient and sustainable energy storage solutions.

Physics Simulation

Dark Matter and the Cosmos Machine learning are helping open new avenues for better understanding of the universe-related topics, notably in studies on dark matter, and cosmic structures. Indeed, a hypothetical example of dark matter has been demonstrated through ML-based processing of large-scale numerical simulations describing the cosmic evolution process and which can be used to help recover some of the mysterious features surrounding the role of dark matter in cosmic structure formation. Here, deep learning algorithms classify and predict the behavior of simulated galaxies while revealing patterns that traditional analysis techniques can't. In this regard, HPC was significant because it provided the required computational resources to run extensive simulations which modeled complex interactions over billions of years. These simulations have helped not only to deepen our understanding of dark matter but to also strategize strategies for observational astronomy in up-coming astral surveys.

These case studies have formed the basis for transforming various scientific research domains through the accelerating impact of ML and HPC. Indeed, the fastening and deepening of the science discovery process through accelerating drug discovery, improving climate simulations, the possibility of predictive material design, and advancing frontiers physics are leading to a better understanding of complex systems and bring solutions to critical global challenges.

CHALLENGES AND LIMITATIONS

ML and HPC, when applied in science, would unlock tremendous advances in domains. Challenges and limitations exist within this integration. Understanding them is crucial for researchers and practitioners who seek to effectively apply such technologies. This section covers challenges with computations, data constraints, ethical issues, and reproducibility in ML and HPC(Anderson et al., 2020; Villa et al., 2021). The integration of Machine Learning (ML) and High-Performance Computing (HPC) in scientific research faces challenges and limitations as shown in Figure 4.

Figure 4. Challenges and limitations of integrating Machine Learning (ML) and High-Performance Computing (HPC) in scientific research

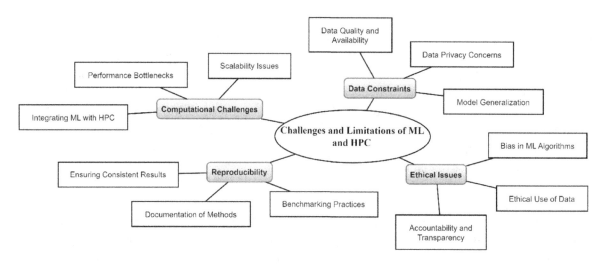

Computational Complexity in the Integration of ML with HPC

The specific problem in the integration of ML and HPC lies in the particular computational complexity in each of these technologies. While theoretically designed to handle massive computations, HPC systems are often burdened by ML algorithms and models of extreme complexity requiring high-computer computational resources. Thus, there appears to be a gap between what the HPC system can do and what modern ML models require. For instance, deep learning models have recently gained much popularity due to their great success in many applications. Generally, such models need large datasets to train. Training those models results in computational requirements greater than the available resources and therefore leads to training times increasing and increasing costs. Moreover, parallelization of the algorithms for ML is quite hard to take full advantage of HPC capabilities. Many ML algorithms, especially iterative processes of training, are hard to parallelize; therefore, only a relatively small advantage can be obtained by applying HPC.

It is also that integration of ML in the domain of HPC workflows often requires competent knowledge in the two domains. Researchers must be aware of the subtleties of parallel computing, algorithm optimization, as well as resource management to integrate ML in HPC environments effectively. This is a likely knowledge gap that can serve as an entry barrier to a whole number of researchers and organizations.

Data Limitations and Model Generalization

Data limitations are a significant challenge for effective adoption of ML in scientific research. Training good models with accurate ML requires fine, labeled datasets. It happens that the availability of such datasets is a big issue across many scientific fields. For example, experimental data can be very scarce in quantity or might not correspond to all possible scenarios to which the model is exposed. This leads to overfitting: a model that fits the training data well, yet performs poorly on unseen data. Besides these, generalization is typically impeded by the existence of biases in the training data of ML models. If the data used in training the model does not reflect the population at large or variations in the phenomena from which data are collected, the models obtained might give false conclusions. This is serious in a critical application like health care, where biased data can direct inequitable treatment recommendations or misdiagnosis(Palaniappan et al., 2023; Senthil et al., 2023). Besides, most real-world phenomena occur in complex form, which further complicates the development of ML models. Relationships between variables in most scientific domains cannot be linear but would be dependent upon multiple parameters. Such complicated relationships can be represented only by advanced modeling techniques which are difficult to design and validate. Therefore, ensuring that the models are robust, interpretable, and generalizable presents a difficult challenge to scientific research.

Ethical Concerns in ML-Based Scientific Research

Given the trends of ML in scientific research, the integration of ethics would be more important in the same process. One of the biggest concerns about ML is the possibility for bias in ML algorithms, which could translate into unfair and unethical outcomes. This would be most relevant in fields where ethics play a significant role, such as healthcare and criminal justice, since it would promote "unconscious" perpetuation or amplification of existing biases present in training data.

An added issue with the use of ML in scientific research is data privacy and consent. When using their data, researchers are held responsible for ensuring that they employ their data ethically and that they have been given sufficient permissions from the subjects whose data they are using. This is particularly important when fields such as genomics and personalized medicine are involved, as personal data can be very revealing in nature. Other ethical issues are transparency and explainability of ML models. Many ML algorithms, especially complex ones like deep neural networks, operate as "black boxes," meaning decisions made by a model cannot be easily understood. It could later constrain trust in the models and also raise questions of accountability, where consequences of ML-driven decisions have major implications for the individuals or for society.

Last but not the least, there is the environmental aspect of HPC and ML. Major power consumption for gigantic computations and storage can result in massive carbon footprint and destruction of the environment. The researchers in the field who seek to implement ML and HPC toward scientific excellence also have to be concerned with keeping their carbon footprints within a sustainable baseline in addition to environmentally friendly practices.

Ensuring Reproducibility in Big-Scale ML and HPC Projects

A third fundamental element of the scientific method is reproducibility: the ability to confirm and extend on previous research results. However, as discussed above, large-scale ML and HPC projects offer interesting reproducibility challenges; their complexity often involves issues such as choice of algorithms, parameter settings, and computational environments, which can make reproducing results challenging.

Another major contributor to the nonsustainability of research results is a lack of standardized practices to document and share ML models and HPC workflows. This happens because many researchers do not give details related to methodology, including data preprocessing steps, model architectures, and hyperparameter tuning processes, which makes the results nonuniform when trying to replicate them. Furthermore, the dynamic nature of ML and HPC technologies can contribute to making it harder to accomplish reproducibility. With new algorithms, frameworks, and hardware, models may become outdated or be incompatible with new systems. The pace at which they are being churned out makes it challenging for researchers to try reproducing studies conducted earlier or using a different tool. Such challenges are requiring the scientific community to increase their calls for best practices in reproducibility. Open-source code sharing, detailed documentation, and making use of containerization technologies can make an ML or HPC project reproduceable. Since such transparency promotes collaboration, it allows researchers to build the robustest foundation for scientific discovery, which future advancements can validate and extend.

Integration of Machine Learning and High-Performance Computing: This application holds out a world of tremendous opportunities in scientific research while consisting of numerous challenges and limitations in such domain and the subjects that are to be analyzed against these criteria. These include computational, data, ethical, and reproducibility issues. We would be able to identify and take up the challenges as a single scientific community to leverage ML and HPC towards innovative ways of sensing, analyzing, and understanding the complex phenomena better for advancing what will otherwise be revolutionary advances in all fields.

FUTURE TRENDS AND INNOVATIONS

Advances in Machine Learning (ML) and High-Performance Computing (HPC) are transforming the scientific research landscape. These emerging advances will transform how we discover new science, that is, efficient and effective research in an enormous variety of disciplines. This section includes ML inventions, HPC, quantum, and autonomous scientific discovery(Anderson et al., 2020; C. Chen et al., 2024; Doi et al., 2019). The figure 5 depicts the upcoming trends and innovations in machine learning and high-performance computing (HPC) in scientific research.

Figure 5. Future trends and innovations in ML and HPC in scientific research

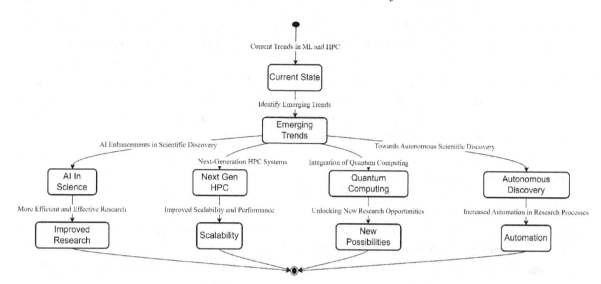

New ML Techniques for Scientific Discovery

Emerging ML techniques are going to change the way scientific discoveries are made about scientific discovery in terms of improvements in analysis capabilities, better performance of models, and new means for generating innovative insights. A new trend includes self-supervised learning where models learn a considerable amount of unlabeled data by making predictions of parts of inputs from other parts. This is especially useful when labeled datasets are scarce or expensive to obtain, as in genomics or particle physics fields. Another promising method is transfer learning which allows one ML model trained on one task or dataset to adapt to a quite different, though related, task requiring almost zero additional training. This is useful particularly in science, since data collection and training models are costly in terms of time. One application of transfer learning is that it can enable the development of models much more quickly than it might otherwise be possible where, in a field like drug discovery for instance, previous research findings will inform new inquiry.

There are also, of course, many exciting advancements in NAS. Such advancements automate the design of neural network architectures, thus opening avenues for researchers in general to find optimal configurations tailored for specific scientific problems. It might mean better performance of models and avoid the commonly used approach of trial and error in determining model architecture. Increasingly, XAI becomes important in scientific research. As ML models are getting increasingly complex, so it becomes essential to ensure that such ML models are interpretable, particularly when related to imperative fields such as healthcare and environmental science. Techniques of XAI help in understanding the reasoning behind predictions made by a model. This leads to better trust and facilitates better adoption of insights generated based on ML.

Next-Generation HPC Systems for Research

Following a long period of steadily increasing computing power, next-generation HPC systems promise unprecedented computational power, allowing scientists and researchers to tackle ever more complex and data-intensive scientific challenges. Next-generation systems will thus be characterized by a transition to exascale computing, where systems capable of performance above one exaFLOP, or 10^{18} calculations per second, are estimated to provide orders of magnitude increases in simulation capabilities and data processing speeds-for breakthroughs in everything from climate modeling to materials science to drug discovery. Other than exascale systems, heterogeneous computing architectures are taking center stage. The approach collects CPUs and GPUs along with specialized accelerators into one design-to-optimize performance for diverse workloads. Advanced accelerators, including FPGAs and TPUs, also come into play; this enables researchers to leverage tailored processing capabilities for specific tasks, which can further improve computational efficiency.

It democratizes high-performance computing resources with cloud-based HPC services. With scalable cloud infrastructure, researchers can run simulations and analyses without necessary significant capital investment in hardware. In terms of competing in this arena of scientific research, it favors smaller institutions and startups.

Future Role of Quantum Computing in Simulations

Quantum computers may represent the future transformation technology that changes science-based simulations fundamentally. Unlike a classical computer, where bits form the basic unit of information, a quantum computer uses qubits, thereby representing and processing information in fundamentally different ways. This means quantum computers can solve problems whose resolution is intractable for purely classical computers at present. Most importantly, answers to questions in material science will be provided by quantum computers, with unprecedented accuracy in the interactions of atoms and molecules. For example, the simulation of new behavior at the quantum level of certain materials can greatly accelerate the discovery of novel compounds with desirable properties, thus opening a huge possibility for breakthroughs in energy storage, catalysis, and pharmaceuticals(Bhattacharya et al., 2019; Louw & McIntosh-Smith, 2021; Villa et al., 2021).

Quantum algorithms are also being built with the dual intent of realizing the full potential of quantum computing and combining this with traditional ML techniques. Some hybrid approaches will further improve training and performance of ML models, while further areas of data analysis and discovery will be opened. Quantum computing, although highly promising, is still in its infancy in the general adoption of scientific research. This has to be overcome by reducing error rates and other unavoidable qubit coherence times, for example, while developing appropriate algorithms tailored toward quantum systems. Still, as these progressions unfold, quantum computing is firmly poised to assume a significant position in scientific simulations and discoveries into the future.

Towards Autonomous Scientific Discovery with AI and HPC

The ultimate vision of the integration of AI and HPC would be systems that can autonomously find scientific insight. These will be deploying ML capabilities combined with all aspects of HPC to posit hypotheses, design experiments, analyze data and draw insights to accelerate by orders of magnitude the research process. An area being researched is drug discovery whereby AI-based platforms can assess biological data, identify potential drug candidates, and predict their effectiveness. These processes, then, would be automated, enabling researchers to focus on validation and application, considerably reducing time and costs.

It, therefore, continued to improve more modern robotics and automation of experiments leading to the development of completely autonomous laboratories, which can experiment autonomously and independently without human interference. These systems are capable of continually being self-learned by their findings while refining their methods for eventual precision over time. The convergence of AI, HPC, and automation will no longer speed up scientific discovery only but will help researchers inquire about questions too complex or resource-intensive to be tried so far. From these perspectives, the scientific community stands at the doorstep of a new era defined by unprecedented discovery and innovation.

The future of scientific discovery is being defined by transformative trends and innovations in ML and HPC: accelerating scientific insights and breakthroughs are promised by emerging techniques, next-generation systems, quantum computing, and autonomous discovery. These possibilities are to be unlocked by locking in the current breakthroughs to facilitate a better understanding of the natural world and the march toward the greatest challenges to humanity.

CONCLUSION

This synergy represents a paradigm shift in scientific research: ML and HPC, together, enable unprecedented advancements across fields. Case studies from drug discovery, climate modeling, materials science, and even fundamental physics illustrate how synergy between ML and HPC accelerates the pace of discovery, improve simulation precision, and promotes a new approach to solving complex scientific challenges. That is, it enhances the analysis of large collections of data and provides researchers with possibilities to find patterns and insights that the classic approach might miss. HPC, on the other hand, delivers the computational power required to run extended simulations or process billions of data points within minutes. The synergy of these two allows for faster time-to-research while uncovering new frontiers in science-the next generation of materials and dark matter.

Into the future, the emergence of next-generation techniques for both ML and HPC will further enhance the research capabilities toward autonomous scientific discovery-the breakthroughs already unimaginable just a few years ago. These, however, come with the caveats: challenges that include missing data, ethical considerations, and demands for reproducibility. Overall, the synergy between ML and HPC will end up casting transformative impacts on scientific research; indeed, it will open the avenues for innovations that, even now, are being proposed to tackle some of the world's biggest challenges and ultimately enable a better understanding of the universe.

REFERENCES

Anderson, J. A., Glaser, J., & Glotzer, S. C. (2020). HOOMD-blue: A Python package for high-performance molecular dynamics and hard particle Monte Carlo simulations. *Computational Materials Science*, 173, 109363. DOI: 10.1016/j.commatsci.2019.109363

Bhattacharya, T., Brettin, T., Doroshow, J. H., Evrard, Y. A., Greenspan, E. J., Gryshuk, A. L., Hoang, T. T., Lauzon, C. B. V., Nissley, D., Penberthy, L., Stahlberg, E., Stevens, R., Streitz, F., Tourassi, G., Xia, F., & Zaki, G. (2019). AI meets exascale computing: Advancing cancer research with large-scale high performance computing. *Frontiers in Oncology*, 9, 984. DOI: 10.3389/fonc.2019.00984 PMID: 31632915

Boopathi, S., & Kanike, U. K. (2023). Applications of Artificial Intelligent and Machine Learning Techniques in Image Processing. In *Handbook of Research on Thrust Technologies' Effect on Image Processing* (pp. 151–173). IGI Global. DOI: 10.4018/978-1-6684-8618-4.ch010

Brayford, D., Vallecorsa, S., Atanasov, A., Baruffa, F., & Riviera, W. (2019). Deploying AI frameworks on secure HPC systems with containers. *2019 Ieee High Performance Extreme Computing Conference (Hpec)*, 1–6. DOI: 10.1109/HPEC.2019.8916576

Chen, C., Nguyen, D. T., Lee, S. J., Baker, N. A., Karakoti, A. S., Lauw, L., Owen, C., Mueller, K. T., Bilodeau, B. A., Murugesan, V., & Troyer, M. (2024). Accelerating Computational Materials Discovery with Machine Learning and Cloud High-Performance Computing: From Large-Scale Screening to Experimental Validation. *Journal of the American Chemical Society*, 146(29), 20009–20018. DOI: 10.1021/jacs.4c03849 PMID: 38980280

Chen, X., Proietti, R., Fariborz, M., Liu, C.-Y., & Yoo, S. B. (2021). Machine-learning-aided cognitive reconfiguration for flexible-bandwidth HPC and data center networks. *Journal of Optical Communications and Networking*, 13(6), C10–C20. DOI: 10.1364/JOCN.412360

Dhanalakshmi, M., Tamilarasi, K., Saravanan, S., Sujatha, G., Boopathi, S., & Associates. (2024). Fog Computing-Based Framework and Solutions for Intelligent Systems: Enabling Autonomy in Vehicles. In *Computational Intelligence for Green Cloud Computing and Digital Waste Management* (pp. 330–356). IGI Global.

Doi, J., Takahashi, H., Raymond, R., Imamichi, T., & Horii, H. (2019). Quantum computing simulator on a heterogenous hpc system. *Proceedings of the 16th ACM International Conference on Computing Frontiers*, 85–93. DOI: 10.1145/3310273.3323053

Ejarque, J., Badia, R. M., Albertin, L., Aloisio, G., Baglione, E., Becerra, Y., Boschert, S., Berlin, J. R., D'Anca, A., Elia, D., Exertier, F., Fiore, S., Flich, J., Folch, A., Gibbons, S. J., Koldunov, N., Lordan, F., Lorito, S., Løvholt, F., & Volpe, M. (2022). Enabling dynamic and intelligent workflows for HPC, data analytics, and AI convergence. *Future Generation Computer Systems*, 134, 414–429. DOI: 10.1016/j.future.2022.04.014

Farrell, S., Emani, M., Balma, J., Drescher, L., Drozd, A., Fink, A., Fox, G., Kanter, D., Kurth, T., & Mattson, P. (2021). MLPerf™ HPC: A holistic benchmark suite for scientific machine learning on HPC systems. *2021 IEEE/ACM Workshop on Machine Learning in High Performance Computing Environments (MLHPC)*, 33–45. DOI: 10.1109/MLHPC54614.2021.00009

Fox, G., Glazier, J. A., Kadupitiya, J., Jadhao, V., Kim, M., Qiu, J., Sluka, J. P., Somogyi, E., Marathe, M., & Adiga, A. (2019). Learning everywhere: Pervasive machine learning for effective high-performance computation. *2019 IEEE International Parallel and Distributed Processing Symposium Workshops (IPDPSW)*, 422–429. DOI: 10.1109/IPDPSW.2019.00081

Gopi, B., Sworna Kokila, M. L., Bibin, C. V., Sasikala, D., Howard, E., & Boopathi, S. (2024). Distributed Technologies Using AI/ML Techniques for Healthcare Applications. In *Advances in Human and Social Aspects of Technology* (pp. 375–396). IGI Global. DOI: 10.4018/979-8-3693-2569-8.ch019

Ihde, N., Marten, P., Eleliemy, A., Poerwawinata, G., Silva, P., Tolovski, I., Ciorba, F. M., & Rabl, T. (2022). A survey of big data, high performance computing, and machine learning benchmarks. *Performance Evaluation and Benchmarking: 13th TPC Technology Conference, TPCTC 2021, Copenhagen, Denmark, August 20, 2021, Revised Selected Papers 13*, 98–118.

Isakov, M., Del Rosario, E., Madireddy, S., Balaprakash, P., Carns, P., Ross, R. B., & Kinsy, M. A. (2020). HPC I/O throughput bottleneck analysis with explainable local models. *SC20. International Conference for High Performance Computing, Networking, Storage and Analysis : [proceedings]. SC (Conference : Supercomputing)*, ●●●, 1–13.

Kadupitiya, J., Fox, G. C., & Jadhao, V. (2019). Machine learning for performance enhancement of molecular dynamics simulations. *International Conference on Computational Science*, 116–130. DOI: 10.1007/978-3-030-22741-8_9

Kadupitiya, J., Sun, F., Fox, G., & Jadhao, V. (2020). Machine learning surrogates for molecular dynamics simulations of soft materials. *Journal of Computational Science*, 42, 101107. DOI: 10.1016/j.jocs.2020.101107

Khetawat, H., Zimmer, C., Mueller, F., Atchley, S., Vazhkudai, S. S., & Mubarak, M. (2019). Evaluating burst buffer placement in hpc systems. *2019 IEEE International Conference on Cluster Computing (CLUSTER)*, 1–11. DOI: 10.1109/CLUSTER.2019.8891051

Kurz, M., Offenhäuser, P., Viola, D., Shcherbakov, O., Resch, M., & Beck, A. (2022). Deep reinforcement learning for computational fluid dynamics on HPC systems. *Journal of Computational Science*, 65, 101884. DOI: 10.1016/j.jocs.2022.101884

Lee, H., Turilli, M., Jha, S., Bhowmik, D., Ma, H., & Ramanathan, A. (2019). Deepdrivemd: Deep-learning driven adaptive molecular simulations for protein folding. *2019 IEEE/ACM Third Workshop on Deep Learning on Supercomputers (DLS)*, 12–19. DOI: 10.1109/DLS49591.2019.00007

Louw, T., & McIntosh-Smith, S. (2021). Using the Graphcore IPU for traditional HPC applications. *3rd Workshop on Accelerated Machine Learning (AccML)*.

Maheswari, B. U., Imambi, S. S., Hasan, D., Meenakshi, S., Pratheep, V., & Boopathi, S. (2023). Internet of things and machine learning-integrated smart robotics. In *Global Perspectives on Robotics and Autonomous Systems: Development and Applications* (pp. 240–258). IGI Global. DOI: 10.4018/978-1-6684-7791-5.ch010

Mira, D., Pérez-Sánchez, E. J., Borrell, R., & Houzeaux, G. (2023). HPC-enabling technologies for high-fidelity combustion simulations. *Proceedings of the Combustion Institute*, 39(4), 5091–5125. DOI: 10.1016/j.proci.2022.07.222

Morales-Hernández, M., Sharif, M. B., Gangrade, S., Dullo, T. T., Kao, S.-C., Kalyanapu, A., Ghafoor, S., Evans, K., Madadi-Kandjani, E., & Hodges, B. R. (2020). High-performance computing in water resources hydrodynamics. *Journal of Hydroinformatics*, 22(5), 1217–1235. DOI: 10.2166/hydro.2020.163

Palaniappan, M., Tirlangi, S., Mohamed, M. J. S., Moorthy, R. S., Valeti, S. V., & Boopathi, S. (2023). Fused Deposition Modelling of Polylactic Acid (PLA)-Based Polymer Composites: A Case Study. In *Development, Properties, and Industrial Applications of 3D Printed Polymer Composites* (pp. 66–85). IGI Global.

Partee, S., Ellis, M., Rigazzi, A., Shao, A. E., Bachman, S., Marques, G., & Robbins, B. (2022). Using machine learning at scale in numerical simulations with SmartSim: An application to ocean climate modeling. *Journal of Computational Science*, 62, 101707. DOI: 10.1016/j.jocs.2022.101707

Paul, A. K., Karimi, A. M., & Wang, F. (2021). Characterizing machine learning i/o workloads on leadership scale hpc systems. *2021 29th International Symposium on Modeling, Analysis, and Simulation of Computer and Telecommunication Systems (MASCOTS)*, 1–8.

Peterson, J. L., Bay, B., Koning, J., Robinson, P., Semler, J., White, J., Anirudh, R., Athey, K., Bremer, P.-T., Di Natale, F., Fox, D., Gaffney, J. A., Jacobs, S. A., Kailkhura, B., Kustowski, B., Langer, S., Spears, B., Thiagarajan, J., Van Essen, B., & Yeom, J.-S. (2022). Enabling machine learning-ready HPC ensembles with Merlin. *Future Generation Computer Systems*, 131, 255–268. DOI: 10.1016/j.future.2022.01.024

Pitchai, R., Guru, K. V., Gandhi, J. N., Komala, C. R., Kumar, J. R. D., & Boopathi, S. (2024). Fog Computing-Integrated ML-Based Framework and Solutions for Intelligent Systems: Digital Healthcare Applications. In *Technological Advancements in Data Processing for Next Generation Intelligent Systems* (pp. 196–224). IGI Global. DOI: 10.4018/979-8-3693-0968-1.ch008

Rebecca, B., Kumar, K. P. M., Padmini, S., Srivastava, B. K., Halder, S., & Boopathi, S. (2024). Convergence of Data Science-AI-Green Chemistry-Affordable Medicine: Transforming Drug Discovery. In *Handbook of Research on AI and ML for Intelligent Machines and Systems* (pp. 348–373). IGI Global.

Sarma, R., Inanc, E., Aach, M., & Lintermann, A. (2024). Parallel and scalable AI in HPC systems for CFD applications and beyond. *Frontiers in High Performance Computing*, 2, 1444337. DOI: 10.3389/fhpcp.2024.1444337

Senthil, T., Puviyarasan, M., Babu, S. R., Surakasi, R., Sampath, B., & Associates. (2023). Industrial Robot-Integrated Fused Deposition Modelling for the 3D Printing Process. In *Development, Properties, and Industrial Applications of 3D Printed Polymer Composites* (pp. 188–210). IGI Global.

Syamala, M., Komala, C., Pramila, P., Dash, S., Meenakshi, S., & Boopathi, S. (2023). Machine Learning-Integrated IoT-Based Smart Home Energy Management System. In *Handbook of Research on Deep Learning Techniques for Cloud-Based Industrial IoT* (pp. 219–235). IGI Global. DOI: 10.4018/978-1-6684-8098-4.ch013

Tanash, M., Yang, H., Andresen, D., & Hsu, W. (2021). Ensemble prediction of job resources to improve system performance for slurm-based hpc systems. In *Practice and experience in advanced research computing* (pp. 1–8). DOI: 10.1145/3437359.3465574

Villa, O., Lustig, D., Yan, Z., Bolotin, E., Fu, Y., Chatterjee, N., Jiang, N., & Nellans, D. (2021). Need for speed: Experiences building a trustworthy system-level gpu simulator. *2021 IEEE International Symposium on High-Performance Computer Architecture (HPCA)*, 868–880. DOI: 10.1109/HPCA51647.2021.00077

Ward, L., Sivaraman, G., Pauloski, J. G., Babuji, Y., Chard, R., Dandu, N., Redfern, P. C., Assary, R. S., Chard, K., & Curtiss, L. A. (2021). Colmena: Scalable machine-learning-based steering of ensemble simulations for high performance computing. *2021 IEEE/ACM Workshop on Machine Learning in High Performance Computing Environments (MLHPC)*, 9–20. DOI: 10.1109/MLHPC54614.2021.00007

KEY TERMS

HPC: High-Performance Computing
ML: Machine Learning
CNN: Convolutional Neural Network
RNN: Recurrent Neural Network
RL: Reinforcement Learning
SVM: Support Vector Machine
GPU: Graphics Processing Unit
TPU: Tensor Processing Unit
CPU: Central Processing Unit
CFD: Computational Fluid Dynamics
PCA: Principal Component Analysis
SNE: Stochastic Neighbor Embedding
LHC: Large Hadron Collider
NAS: Neural Architecture Search
XAI: Explainable Artificial Intelligence
FLOP: Floating Point Operations Per Second
FPGA: Field-Programmable Gate Array
AI: Artificial Intelligence

Chapter 10
Harnessing High–Performance Computing for AI–Driven Energy Harvesting and Environmental Monitoring

Immanuel D. Godwin

Department of Electrical and Electronics Engineering, Sathyabama Institute of Science and Technology, Chennai, India

Dhivakar Poospadi

https://orcid.org/0009-0009-5492-1458

Quest Global North America, Windsor, USA

Chevuri Pavan Kumar

Department of Civil Engineering, St. Ann's College of Engineering and Technology, Chirala, India

S. Senthil Kumar

Department of Electrical and Electronics Engineering, K.S.R. College of Engineering, Tiruchengode, India

R. Manikandan

https://orcid.org/0009-0002-4269-5480

Department of Electronics and Communication Engineering, Panimalar Engineering College, Chennai, India

ABSTRACT

This chapter explores how high-performance computing (HPC) can be a transformative force towards further acceleration of AI-driven energy harvesting and environmental monitoring systems. With increasing demand for sustainable energy solutions and effective environmental management, this affords a golden opportunity through the integration of HPC and AI, which can largely optimize the processing of large datasets with respect to energy collection and increase monitoring precision. The methods used in harvesting renewable energy, such as solar and wind-based methods using AI algorithms, that analyze the energy output to optimize system efficiencies, are discussed. The chapter also discusses how HPC allows

DOI: 10.4018/978-1-6684-3795-7.ch010

real-time analysis of environmental data that can be used in decision-making and in being proactive when there are changes in ecosystems. Case studies that focus on successful implementations show the synergistic benefits of this integration, which may directly contribute to the global sustainability agenda.

INTRODUCTION

An electric vehicle (EV), for sure, will be the defining trend of the automotive industry in response to the pressing need for the reduction of carbon emissions, an enhancement in energy efficiency, and the shift towards solutions in sustainable transportation. The changes of the last ten years have created a new atmosphere through modifications in the face of the auto industry, drawing further ongoing pursuits in innovations such as better vehicle performance, improved energy storage, and power management. The increasing importance of High-Performance Computing (HPC) in the analysis and simulation of EV performance also brings about further transformation. HPC ensures the real-time simulation of complex systems due to the provision of computational power, enabling researchers and engineers to make very precise evaluation and optimization of a vehicle's performance. In this chapter, I indicate where it becomes possible to find an intersection between EV technology and HPC, wherein performance analysis and simulation play a pivotal role in driving innovations (Aghabali et al., 2020a).

The primary distinction between EVs and conventional internal combustion engine (ICE) vehicles is the utilization of electric powertrains and battery systems. As such, some questions arise in vehicle design, performance analysis, and testing because of the absence of fuel-burning engines and the presence of advanced electronic components. Therefore, the capabilities of EVs can only be maximized if designers simulate all conceivable factors-affecting factors including battery dynamics, thermal management, energy consumption, and powertrain efficiency. Each one of these encompasses complex, multi-physics problems that require advanced computational models and simulation to understand. That is where HPC steps in as the ability to run complicated simulations that would otherwise be computationally infeasible using traditional computing systems is possible (Alawneh et al., 2023).

HPC is using the techniques of supercomputers and parallel processing to solve problems computationally at high speeds that appear too difficult for traditional computers. In EV technology, HPC enables the simulation of hundreds of thousands of variables and scenarios whose optimization is critical to a well-performance vehicle. This means that an EV's battery system, consisting of thousands of individual cells, requires monitoring and management for optimal operational characteristics to last for a long time. This will demand vast computational resources in simulating the thermal and electrical behavior of these cells and their interaction with other cells within the battery pack. Such detail in HPC models will bring factors like temperature, charge cycles, and energy demand under different operating conditions (Pozzato et al., 2023).

Aerodynamics is another thing related to EVs and tremendously affects overall efficiency. Unlike in the ICE vehicles, wherein the primary goal is to focus on efficiency at the engine level, for EVs, it shall be focused on drag and airflow optimization toward attaining full range. Simulation of aerodynamics performance of an EV usually involves complex fluid dynamics which require significant computational effort to represent with adequate precision. The HPC will allow detailed simulation for interactions between body design and power-consuming energy of airflow to further the aerodynamics efficiency of the vehicle, thus increasing its driving range and lowering its energy consumption (Sharma et al., 2019).

The development of EVs is also influenced by HPC in an important area: powertrain optimization. Optimization begins with ensuring that there is a fluid interaction between the electric motor, inverter, and battery. The simulation of these systems under various load conditions, drive patterns, and environmental factors is computationally intensive. HPC allows engineers to build models of these systems to a level of intricacy that is exact; therefore, the systems can be optimized for maximal efficiency and performance. For example, HPC can be used to simulate the interaction of motor with its battery pack during acceleration, regenerative braking, and charging to optimize its reduction in energy loss and longevity enhancement (Du et al., 2019).

Aside from that, HPC plays a very vital role in the optimization of battery management systems (BMS). The BMS monitors and controls health, charge, and safety of the EV pack. This is achieved by advanced BMS algorithms relying on real-time data processing and predictive modeling to enable safe usage with maximum energy efficiency. HPC ensures that this kind of large data processing can be done speedily and accurately, thus allowing the battery conditions to be monitored in real time, and predictive maintenance is conducted for keeping the battery in optimal condition. Overcharging, overheating, or deep discharging can significantly affect battery lifespan (Bucaioni, 2019).

Apart from battery management and powertrain optimization, HPC revolutionizes prototyping and testing in EVs. The traditional processes of prototyping are building a physical model followed by real-world testing, expensive and time-consuming. Digital prototypes or "digital twins" will be replicas of the physical characteristics and behavior of the vehicle or components created through HPC-driven simulations. Digital twins give engineers the means to test many iterations of design, or optimized vehicle parts, and simulate different driving scenarios without physical prototypes. This can shorten the cycle time, reduce costs, and expand the amount of testing for a wide range of conditions (Ahmed & Liu, 2019).

HPC is beneficial in simulating real-time scenarios, which is probably one of the most significant advantages in EV development. EVs have to be tested under a variety of real-world conditions-persistently changing temperatures, road surfaces, and driving patterns-to work efficiently and safely. Simulations powered by HPC can do this natively in a virtual world, yielding useful insight into how the vehicle will serve under a range of situations. Manufacturers will use this to recognize problems ahead of time and thus make products more reliable and safer (Taghavipour et al., 2019).

HPC also has a role in the solutions geared toward the challenges of the infrastructure for EV charging. With more electric cars on the road, there is an increased requirement for effective and accessible charging stations. HPC can be applied toward modeling and optimization of the placement and operation of charging stations such that they are sited in a strategic manner to meet the required demand and reduce strain on the grid. HPCs simulate EV charging patterns and impacts on the electrical grid, allowing utility companies and policymakers to design and build charging networks much more efficiently to promote widespread EV use (Lyu et al., 2021).

This is a paradigm shift in the automobile industry. Such influence of EVs could go a long way to affect energy consumption, environmental sustainability and, for sure, transport infrastructure. HPC is an enabling factor for this new transition, providing the computational power required to analyze, optimize, and innovate all points related to EV performance. HPC is transforming the design, testing, and deployment of EVs via optimization of battery management, power train efficiency, aerodynamics, and real-time simulation (Yi et al., 2021). HPC will play an increasingly critical role for these vehicles to meet the relevant performance, safety, and efficiency standards for their acceptance as transportation that could be widely used because of the high demand in EVs. This chapter explores how HPC is changing the face of the future of EVs, insights into cutting-edge simulations and analyses driving next-generation sustainable transportation solutions.

HIGH-PERFORMANCE COMPUTING IN ELECTRIC VEHICLE DEVELOPMENT

High Performance Computing has emerged as a vital tool in EV development. It does provide the computational power required to simulate and analyze and optimize a complex structure of systems involved in designing and achieving the performance of EVs. They range from optimized battery management to efficient power trains, aerodynamics, to thermal dynamics - the workhorse behind automobile design engineers' ability to model and test innumerable aspects of EVs in a virtual environment. The above accelerates innovation to offer manufacturers more efficient, reliable, and sustainable vehicles by minimizing physical prototyping time and the cost of real-world testing (McIntosh-Smith et al., 2019). Figure 1 depicts the use of HPC in the development of EVs.

Figure 1. High-performance computing in EV development

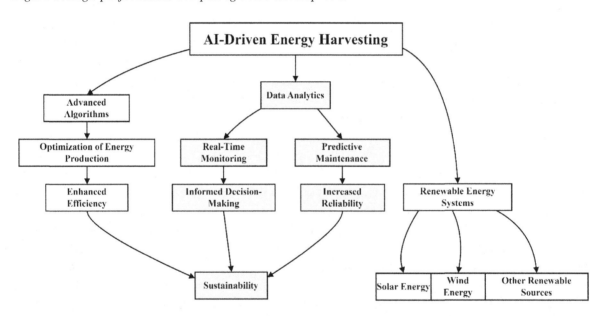

Definition and Importance of HPC

This article is making use of supercomputers or computing clusters working simultaneously to process large datasets or carry out computationally intensive computations at high-speed performance. The primary reason for embracing HPC in the design of an EV is in the processing of huge data quantities and detailed running simulations. In the study of EV, possibly with regards to battery packs and power-trains systems, along with its diverse interlocking interactions between the mechanical, electrical, and even thermal parts, computation indeed goes by a very large scale. HPC enables automobile engineers to simulate these systems without wasting precious time, with a basis to analyze perfectly for optimal vehicle designs.

HPC Architecture

HPC architecture of HPC systems involves a network of processors which work in parallel. Sums up to millions of calculations per unit of time by having processors distributed across several servers or nodes and high-speed interconnects. These computational tools include central processing units, graphics processing units, and memory subsystems. This architecture will enable engineers to run very complex simulations of multi-physics problems-for example, thermal management system interactions with battery performance-in the design of EVs. It is the potential for access beyond pure computing power, however, which makes this architecture really interesting: it also provides access to high-end data processing and storage abilities, which are essential when dealing with the large datasets generated by sensors in EVs, simulations, and real-world testing.

Applications of HPC in Automotive Engineering

One of the largest applications in HPC is related to the automotive industry, where it has particularly been most valuable in EV development. Some of the most important areas include: simulation and optimization of the battery system and, within the EV, HPC users can model the electrochemical processes occurring in each cell, predict the behaviour of those cells under thermal conditions, thereby optimizing overall BMS and leading to improved energy efficiency, lifespan, and safety in batteries. Another key application is in the aerodynamics for EVs: with HPC, engineers can actually optimize vehicle body shape design to reduce drag through computational fluid dynamics (CFD) simulations. In powertrain optimization, HPC is also applied. In this case, powertrain engineers simulate a multitude of interactions between the motor, inverter, and battery by simulating conditions in order to find the optimum performance and efficiency (Saldaña et al., 2019).

Application of Parallel Processing in EV Simulations

Parallel processing forms the core of HPC and is critical to the execution of simulations in the EV systems, as these comprise numerous subsystems. These comprise the powertrain, the battery, and cooling systems, all of which require a detailed simulation and analysis. All the work related to these subsystems can be executed in parallel using parallel processing, thus decreasing the time requirements for running complex models. Thus, for example, simulating the whole thermal management system of an EV, which, among other things, includes a battery cooling system, motor cooling system, and inverter heat dissipation system, can take a lot of time. Engineers may use parallel processing to divide a simulation into smaller tasks being executed concurrently; that is, the whole process is speeded up significantly, and one can test more iteratively, optimize faster, and execute more scenarios in a shorter time scale. With parallel processing, it would also be possible to simulate in real time. For instance, testing an EV system with all possible operating conditions-such as varying driving environments, temperature, and load-can be monitored (Babu et al., 2022).

Hence, HPC has that transformative ability in the development of EVs-by giving the unparallel capability to simulate and optimize complex systems in a manner not possible at any previous time. Through its architecture and parallel processing capabilities, HPC enables rapid testing and refinement of EV designs, ultimately leading to the optimization of vehicles in efficiency, reliability, and sustainability.

METRICS OF PERFORMANCE

Metrics of Performance: Instead of traditional internal combustion engine vehicles, EVs carry quite different performance metrics. Such critical parameters for understanding and optimizing these allow an even greater scope to enhance overall efficiency, reliability, and longevity. Chief among those are energy efficiency, battery life and management, powertrain and motor performance, and thermal dynamics-the essence of each such aspect playing a pivotal role in defining performance, cost, or sustainability of these electrical vehicles. We discuss each of these metrics in depth below and outline their roles in the performance of EVs (Miri et al., 2021; Yao et al., 2021). The performance and optimization cycle of EVs are influenced by various performance parameters, as shown in Figure 2.

Figure 2. Different performance parameters: performance and optimization cycle of electric vehicles

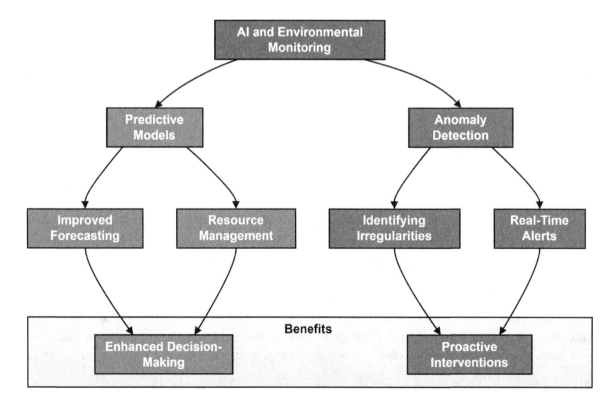

Energy Efficiency and Consumption

Energy efficiency is a critical determinant of the performance of EVs, as it directly correlates to range and, therefore, environmental impact. Energy consumption in electric vehicles often is quantified by kilowatt-hours per mile (kWh/mi) or kilowatt-hours per kilometer (kWh/km). This metric helps in comparing the efficiency with which this mechanical motion is obtained from the energy stored in a battery. While for ICE vehicles, the fuel efficiency is measured in miles per gallon, or mpg, the EV has much higher conversion efficiency, typically 85-90%, compared to the 20-30% for ICE (Chandrika et al., 2023; Devi et al., 2024).

Several factors affect energy efficiency, which include the weight of the vehicle, aerodynamics, and conditions of driving. Obviously, the more massive a vehicle, the more energy it will consume. Similarly, a hilly terrain or a high speed is not very suitable for energy efficiency. However, in cases where deceleration is involved, regenerative braking helps recover some of the energy lost, thereby managing the efficiency of the vehicle to increase overall value.

Management Systems for the Battery

The leading indicator of long-term performance and overall cost of ownership of an EV is battery life. The capacity of an EV battery determines its life span, and this changes with every shift in charging patterns, operating temperatures, and depth of discharge. It is a tough goal for manufacturers to make EVs such that they last anywhere from 8 to 15 years under normal usage conditions. Additionally, the capacity of an EV battery degrades with time, and losses approach about 2-3% per year under normal use.

This BMS is intended to play a very important role in ensuring optimum functioning of the battery pack. For this reason, it controls cell voltage, temperature, and current to ensure proper balance among cells and prevents overcharging, thus ensuring safe operation. Another way in which the BMS assists is in estimating State of Charge (SoC) and State of Health (SoH), primarily used for precise range prediction and evaluation of the life of the batteries.

Powertrain and Motor Performance

The powertrain of an EV consists of the motor, inverter, and transmission that combine to transform electrical energy from the battery into mechanical motion. Motor performance is a determining factor in the calculation of acceleration, torque, and speed for such a vehicle. Generally, electric motors are more efficient as they produce peak torque from zero revolution, hence enabling the customer to get instantaneous power delivery.

This motor efficiency depends on the type used. The common types of motors for use in EVs are the permanent magnet synchronous motors (PMSM) and induction motors. The high-performance applications prefer PMSMs due to their efficiency as well as reduced weight. Induction motors are, however heavier and often preferred due to strength and mainly commercial vehicle use. Also, another efficiency enhancing feature of the powertrain is its regenerative braking; this system reclaims energy which would otherwise not be recovered.

Inverters are integral to controlling the flow of electricity between the battery and the motor. The simple change in them adjusts the direct current from the battery to alternating current, which the motor can now run. High-design inverters improve conversion efficiency by minimizing losses and enhancing the overall powertrain performance.

Thermal Dynamics and Cooling Systems

The performance of EVs is generally influenced by thermal management, however, especially on the battery and motor. It is necessary to maintain proper temperatures for efficient working, prevention of degradation, and risk-free scenarios. Overheating can potentially lead to loss in the performance of a battery and cause thermal runaway, reducing the efficiency of the motor (Giri et al., 2024; Godwin Immanuel et al., 2024).

There are a few cooling systems in place in EVs that cool down some of the generated heat by the vehicle when in operation. One such system is liquid cooling that involves circulating coolant to cool battery cells, motors, and inverters. Air cooling is another system that is used but is mostly less efficient, particularly in applications for high performance. The above systems play a key role in battery thermal management, where, in a pack of batteries, they must be maintained within a given range, preferably 15°C-35°C because extreme temperatures degrade rapidly.

Thermal simulation models are utilized widely to predict the heat generation and optimization of design on cooling systems. Real-time monitoring of thermal dynamics using HPC tools is realized. The dynamics in thermal domains are extremely critical for ensuring safe and efficient operation of a system, especially when it undergoes high-stress driving conditions such as rapid acceleration or high ambient temperatures.

For an electric vehicle to be optimal, it has to be optimized in terms of four significant performance metrics-battery life, powertrain efficiency, energy efficiency, and thermal management. All these pose unique challenges, but advances in simulation and real-time monitoring open up significant avenues for enhancement. The better use of HPC and sophisticated management systems is making EVs more efficient and reliable while able to meet the requirements of modern transportation. Proper management of these performance metrics will be very key in advancing the next generation of electric vehicles and ensuring greater sustainability in the automotive industry.

SIMULATION OF EV BATTERY SYSTEMS

The electric vehicle's battery systems are the heart of a vehicle. A battery system involves multiple factors in determining the range, performances, and overall efficiency of a vehicle. Simulation of these systems will play a key role in optimization for their design, management, and longevity. Advanced simulation techniques allow automotive engineers to explore how these batteries would behave with varied conditions (Loeb & Kockelman, 2019; Tran et al., 2020). This helps bring about better heat management, the energy efficiency of the system, and long-term durability of that system. Discussion of the main areas of EV battery system simulation, namely, battery dynamics and chemistry models, thermal management in battery packs, HPC for real-time monitoring and optimization, and predictive maintenance for improving lifetime. Figure 3 illustrates the integral steps involved in simulating and optimizing EV battery systems.

Figure 3. Integral steps in simulating and optimizing EV battery systems

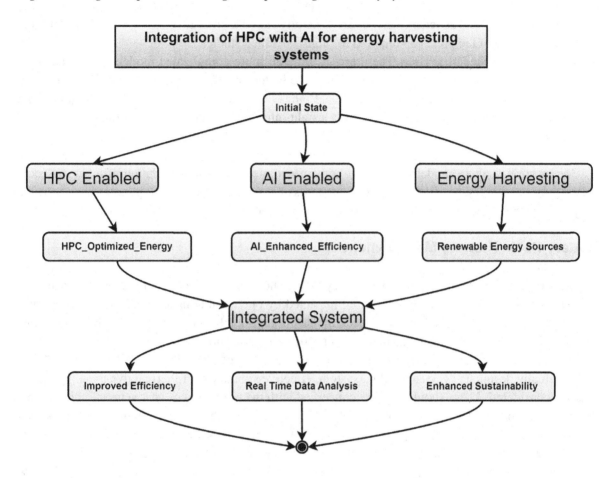

Battery Dynamics and Chemistry Models

The simulation of EV battery systems starts from the inside dynamics of the batteries, from electrochemical processes. This can involve charge/discharge cycles, energy storage efficiency, or voltage under different loads. Such processes depend on the type of chemistry being used for the battery, such as from lithium to solid-state, or nickel-metal hydride (NiMH) (Naresh et al., 2024; Rajan et al., 2024).

The most common type used in the latest generation of EVs is the lithium-ion battery. They are assembled with their electrochemistry based on the intercalation of lithium ions between the anode and cathode during both charging and discharging. Therefore, good simulation models should take into account several parameters such as cell voltage, current, capacity fade, and rate of ion diffusion through the electrolyte. The two commonly used models for simulating these electrochemical processes are equivalent circuit models and physics-based models (Aghabali et al., 2020b).

a) Equivalent Circuit Models (ECM): The battery is represented here as an assembly of electrical components: resistors, capacitors. A model can be used as a means to simulate charge/discharge behavior quickly and efficiently. ECMs are generally suited for real-time applications but will often sacrifice some of the precision required for highly detailed studies.

b) Physics-Based Models (PBM): These are, in general, more complicated models that actually attempt to model the chemistry occurring within the battery itself. Parameters include ion transport, electrochemical kinetics, and heat generation. Being computationally intensive, PBMs require more computational resources but provide better insight into long-term battery performance and degradation behavior.

Combination of these models will enable a more complete dynamic simulation of a battery pack, helping engineers optimize cell design, predict patterns of degradation, and develop strategies to enhance the performance of the battery and further extend its lifespan.

Battery Pack Thermal Management

Thermal management, therefore, plays a very important role in an electric vehicle battery system as the performance of, and its safety are visibly impacted by operation temperatures. The batteries, naturally, generate heat during operation, especially during high load conditions like acceleration or fast charging operations. Excess generated heat can result in thermal runaway, a condition that can lead to uncontrollable temperature rise with risks of fire or explosion (Muhammed et al., 2020; Yi et al., 2022).

To actually design an efficient cooling system, effective simulation of thermal dynamics in battery packs is considered. These simulations are concerned with the prediction of heat generation in various driving scenarios and the evaluation of the effectiveness of the used thermal management strategies such as liquid cooling or air cooling systems. Thermal management systems must ensure that battery cells are kept within an optimal temperature range between 15°C and 35°C not to degrade and to safe operation. There are liquid cooling systems, which may work better on high-performance EVs by letting coolant flow through channels surrounding the battery cells to dissipate heat. Then there are air cooling systems, which are simpler, less expensive, but less effective for high temperature or performance-oriented applications.

Simulations also optimize the layouts and flow dynamics of such cooling systems to obtain balanced temperature distribution in the battery pack. Moreover, it can also predict the effects of environment-based conditions, such as ambient temperatures and humidity, on the thermal performance. This information helps in the development of sophisticated thermal management algorithms that can give adaptive real-time control for cooling based on the current batteries' performance.

HPC for Real-Time Battery Monitoring and Optimization

HPC is instrumental in real-time monitoring and optimization of the systems being used in electric vehicles' batteries. Using HPC, engineers are able to process large amounts of data coming from sensors installed inside the battery pack that monitor temperature, voltage, and current for distribution. With this amount of real-time data, adjustments can be made in precise points for optimization, enhancing safety and preventing possible failures. Besides such high-level simulations of electrochemical behavior, HPC simulations enable multi-physics simulations where thermal, electrochemical, and mechanical behaviors are modeled concurrently. In fact, this is necessary for predicting how different components of a system within the battery would interact under any given condition, such as fast charging or high-speed driving. Such HPC can simulate thousands of operating scenarios in a short period and thus helps engineers more effectively refine battery designs and control strategies (Giri et al., 2024; Godwin Immanuel et al., 2024; Muthukumar et al., 2024).

In addition to real-time optimization, HPC enables machine learning models to predict what will happen in the battery sometime later with dependence on historical data. It makes possible developing smart BMSs that could be adapted to change in driving patterns or environmental conditions to ensure longer battery life as well as better performance from the vehicle.

Predictive Maintenance and Battery Longevity

An important area of investigation in pursuit of increasing the lifetime of a battery and enhancing the general reliability of vehicles lies in the long-term simulation of EV battery systems. Predictive maintenance strategies, supported by HPC simulations, coupled with real-time data analysis, can identify early warnings of the degradation conditions likely to end up in significant performance loss or system failure. Important indications include capacity fade, increased internal resistance, and imbalanced cell voltages. Predictive models would use data from sensors, past driving patterns, and environmental conditions to make predictions for when maintenance or replacements are going to be required. This is when the automobile owner or fleet manager can schedule a process of maintenance prior to an essential failure happening, thus reducing downtime as well as expenditure. SoH and SoC estimations are also constantly improved by such simulations; as such, the battery will perform at its optimal best during the entire cycle of its life.

Operating conditions, such as the depth of charge (DoD), and also the charging habits affect the usable life of a battery. Simulations may reveal desirable charge strategies in terms of optimal charge cycles, adaptive rates of charging and others which lessen the stress on the battery and expand its usability life. Such strategies, for instance, may include reducing high-current fast charging and deep discharges altogether. All these can greatly reduce degradation, thus elongating the life of the battery.

Simulations of electric vehicle battery systems are something that is highly needed and complex in developing better-performing, safe, and prolonged batteries. Advanced models of both battery dynamics and chemistry; optimum thermal management systems; using HPC for on-real-time monitoring; and predictive maintenance models can all work together towards an electricity vehicle that would be highly efficient and reliable. The above-mentioned simulations will energize future innovations into better battery technology, leading to more effective and sustainable electric transportation options.

PERFORMANCE OF SIMULATION OF EV AERODYNAMICS

Aerodynamics is possibly the most critical area of an electric vehicle's design that, on one hand, determines great efficiency and performance along with a range. In light of an ever-growing demand for energy efficiency and sustainable mobility, this is definitely one parameter in which automakers will need to tread very carefully if they want to stretch the range of EVs without sacrificing top performance (Meintz et al., 2023; Tan & Yuan, 2022). It encompasses the importance of aerodynamics in the design of EVs, the use of CFD and HPC for simulations, methodologies for drag reduction and range improvement, and case studies of aerodynamics optimization in EVs. The process of aerodynamics performance simulation for electric vehicles is depicted in Figure 4.

Figure 4. Process of aerodynamics performance simulation for electric vehicles

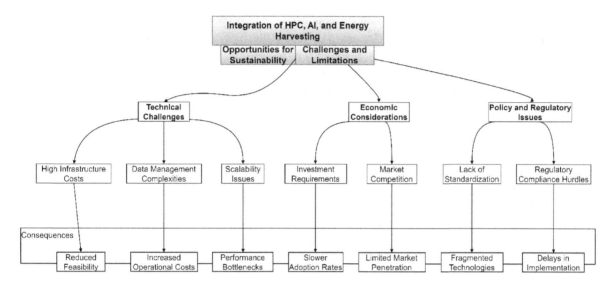

Importance of Aerodynamics in EV Design

This basically explains how aerodynamics performance can make the difference in the movement of a vehicle through air. For EVs, which run mainly on battery power, the most significant way to take it a long distance is through reduced air resistance. Poor aerodynamics use up more energy on the vehicle, which means that the battery has to work overtime, thus using lots of energy and reducing mileage. Aerodynamics has impacts on several aspects of how a vehicle performs. These include:

a) Drag: Air resistance when the vehicle is moving forward.
b) Lift: The force vertically upward which may reduce the stabilities.
c) Noise: Aerodynamics design also affects noise from wind at high velocities.

One of the most important influences of aerodynamics is that on drag, where an increased drag coefficient (Cd) means more energy used to push a vehicle. Reduction in the drag coefficient for an electric vehicle can provide a longer range and less energy usage. Since EVs do not possess traditional engines and mechanical noise, aerodynamics design can also minimize wind noise in the cabin which will mean an inherently quieter cabin environment. So, in terms of efficiency as well as of comfort, aerodynamics optimization is of absolute importance.

Computational Fluid Dynamics and High-Performance Computing

Aerodynamics testing was done using a great number of wind tunnels in the conventional approach. Today, more requirements are placed on CFD, which utilizes numerical methods to simulate an air flow around a vehicle, where pressure distribution, drag, and other aerodynamics parameters are numerically visualized. From this simulation, designers could point out the areas of high drag so that they could alter the design to minimize drag.

The complexity of such simulation demands huge computational power, where HPC plays its part: With HPC, huge simulations of complex fluid flows with high resolutions can be modeled very realistically, simulating realistic real-world conditions for the vehicles to be designed for. Thousands of such simulations run quickly, documenting as many design iterations and configurations as possible. HPC-powered CFD Simulation has advantages as follows:

a) Accuracy: High resolution in the simulation can provide very accurate predictions for airflow behavior.
b) Speed: Simulations that would take days or weeks on a conventional system can be completed in hours.
c) Optimization: Many design variables such as vehicle shape, size and placements of individual components can be tested in parallel, which accelerates the optimization process.

Such capabilities make HPC-driven CFD simulations the go-to tool for modern EV aerodynamics design, giving insight into how different design features affect performance in a much more nuanced way than has been possible to date.

Simulation of Drag Reduction and Range Improvement

Drag reduction, therefore, is the key objective of aerodynamics optimization for an electric vehicle. Given that the drag force accelerates exponentially with the speed, even a slight reduction in the drag coefficient is good enough to save quite a lot of energy at faster velocities. In electric vehicles, it directly translates into extended driving ranges, improved efficiency, and better performance.

CFD can predict how different vehicle shapes, surface textures, and components contribute to drag. Areas to be tackled at the front grille, side mirrors, underbody create drag and need to be reduced. Aerodynamics features to optimize or even eliminate drag:

a) Active Grille Shutters: These automatically open or close depending on cooling requirements to optimize airflow.
b) Low-Drag Side Mirrors: Compact mirrors or camera-based systems can reduce the turbulence caused by traditional mirrors.
c) Smooth Underbody Panels: A flat underbody is a traditional aerodynamic modification that helps minimize airflow disruptions beneath the vehicle, and it is commonly linked to reductions in drag.

In fact, scientists are now trying to cut their Cd below 0.25, which is a pretty much smaller number than what is attained in current production designs. These cuts have indeed meant a 5 to 10% gain in electric vehicle range, and that's well worth it.

The aerodynamics drag also is created by the vehicle's tires and wheels; hence, it adds to a great deal of the aerodynamics drag. Aero wheel covers can benefit more from the aerodynamics efficiency when combined with low-rolling-resistance tires.

POWERTRAIN OPTIMIZATION USING HPC

In maximizing the efficiency as well as performance and overall driving experience of an EV, powertrain optimization would prove to be important. With the capability of simulating complicated models and performing data analysis that earlier would be impossible on conventional computing resources, HPC has come to play a critical role in powertrain optimization. This section discusses the modeling of electric powertrains and the key roles of components like inverters, motors, and control algorithms played in such simulations.In addition to the simulations of energy flow, we also elaborate on how HPC may optimize powertrain efficiency (Naresh et al., 2024; Rajan et al., 2024). The powertrain optimization process in EVs can be undertaken by using HPC, as depicted in Figure 5.

Figure 5. Powertrain optimization process in electric vehicles using HPC

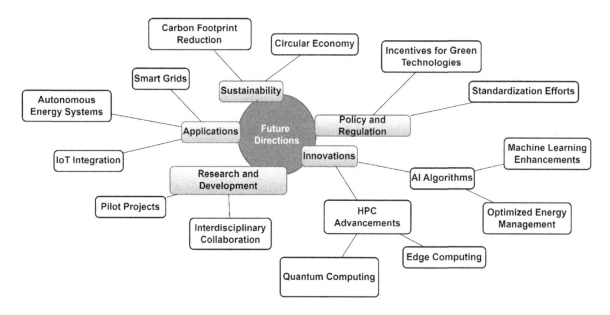

Electric Powertrain Modelling: Challenges and Opportunities

Electric powertrain modeling involves simulation behavior of different components, such as batteries, motors, inverters, and drivetrain, considering driving dynamics and environment-related effects. High modeling complexity is one of the major challenges in modeling the different components because of their nonlinear behavior and interdependencies. Opportunities are present in the potential to do predictive models that could provide valuable information on how energy consumption and performance might be best optimized under any set of driving conditions. Traditional methods generally fail to pick the nuances of modern EV powertrains and result in inefficient designs and lost opportunities to save energy. HPC enables much more detailed simulations as engineers can create highly accurate models accounting for hundreds of parameters (Giri et al., 2024; Muthukumar et al., 2024; Naresh et al., 2024). Additionally, parallel execution reduces time drastically for design iterations.

Inverters, Motors, and Control Algorithms

The key components are inverters and motors, along with the algorithms to control their interaction, and the performance of the electric powertrain depends on these. The inverters convert the direct current of the battery to alternating current to feed into the electric motor. Efficiency in inverter design through simulation is an important factor that can significantly minimize energy losses in vehicles.

The motor is the heart of the EV powertrain and transforms electrical energy into mechanical energy. Problem: without a significant variation in speed and load, this has to be achieved. Several motor designs-from PMSMs to induction motors-can be simulated using HPC to find the best configuration for specific vehicle types. The control algorithms controlling the coordination between the motor, inverter and the battery ensure that energy is consumed in an optimal manner and the vehicle goes on to operate just as it was expected. Testing of several scenarios by simulation of the control algorithms through HPC helps engineers find an optimal trade-off between performance, energy consumption and thermal management.

Simulation of Energy Flow and Regenerative Braking

Energy flow in an electric vehicle is nothing but complex and needs to be accurately regulated to optimize performance. It's also very important in simulating the flow of energy through the vehicle from the battery, through to the motor and back again through regenerative braking, to improve efficiency. Regenerative braking recovers kinetic energy, which would otherwise be lost as heat when braking, and transfers it back to the battery. HPC enables such energy flows under different conditions to be simulated in great detail, allowing the engineers to use all the energy recovered through regenerative braking to the maximum extent. Simulations also provide insight into thermal behavior in the powertrain, where energy loss by heat can be the most substantial efficiency degradation. Energy flow through drivetrain and, in some cases, regenerative systems will be optimized to push the vehicle range further and make it more efficient overall.

HPC-Enabled Powertrain Efficiency and Performance Improvements

HPC usage provides unprecedented improvements in powertrain efficiency and performance. Engineers can run a series of complex scenarios in parallel to test hundreds, if not thousands, of different powertrain configurations in a fraction of the time that would be possible with conventional methods, thus making it possible to identify optimal solutions for energy efficiency, component reliability, and overall vehicle performance (Devi et al., 2024; Godwin Immanuel et al., 2024).

For instance, HPC simulations can be used to optimize the motor-inverter-battery interface for the minimum energy loss with better power supply to the automakers. Real-time optimization becomes feasible with HPC in which the powertrain dynamically adapts to driving conditions to ensure peak performance at all times. Acceleration will be better, with extended range and comfort while driving.

Moreover, HPC-based simulations enable the virtual testing of new architectures and control strategies for the powertrain before they are brought into actual physical configuration. It decreases the high costs and time involved in the prototyping process, which is considered pretty crucial in a fast-paced industry like EV, where innovation cycles are getting tighter by the day and the demand for higher performance, efficiency, and sustainability is growing very rapidly.

In summary, HPC-driven optimization of the powertrain has enormous potential to revolutionize the design of electric vehicles. It enables quite advanced simulations that support the overcoming of key problems such as complex component interactions and dynamic energy flows for more efficient, high-performance powertrains with a greater range, driving experience, and sustainability.

REAL-TIME SIMULATION FOR ELECTRIC VEHICLES

Electric vehicles are increasing in popularity and require real-time simulation in the design, development, and testing processes. It is very critical for dynamic modeling and performance evaluation of EVs under different real-world driving conditions. Engineers can simulate systems that entail advanced computer computation to know system behavior in real time by using real-time computing. This resulted in large improvement in the prototyping process and in the final vehicle performance achieved. In this section, we look at the requirement for real-time performance testing, the role of digital twins in EV development, cost and time savings through simulation, and how real-time simulations can bridge the varying driving conditions and load scenarios (Babu et al., 2022; Boopathi et al., 2018; Rajan et al., 2024).

The Need for Real-Time Performance Testing

Electric vehicles operate in dynamic environments that are complex and subject to incessant fluctuations caused by road conditions, weather, and driver inputs. Real-time performance testing is therefore very critical because it will simulate such dynamic conditions and allow engineers to know exactly how the vehicle performs in real time. Real-time tests provide instant feedback whereas traditional tests' returns are mostly delayed and therefore lead to slower design iteration and refinement in vehicle systems. For example, real-time testing can determine variations in how battery charge, motor efficiency, or regenerative braking may affect overall performance so that control algorithms may be tuned to ensure optimal performance for most scenarios, a requirement for the diverse demands of modern drivers.

Digital Twins in EV Design and Development

A big step in real-time simulation is the advent of the concept of digital twins. A digital twin is essentially the virtual replica of any physical EV system and can be used to simulate performance in real time. The digital twin behaves just like a mimetic representation of any real vehicle by getting its data synchronized through continuously updating the sensors and other input sources. In this manner, engineers work in real time on analysis, testing, and optimization of a vehicle's systems without having to run the physical vehicle. Digital twins are most beneficially applied to test complicated subsystems such as battery management, powertrain dynamics, and thermal performance. Testing in a controlled environment can help manufacturers find early potential faults in their designs, which may save them from generating more prototypes. Digital twins could improve parts of EVs much faster by making sure the smooth functioning of components under all sorts of operating conditions.

Rapid Prototyping with Simulations Ends Up Being Less Time-Consuming and Cheaper

The development and testing of electric vehicles through traditional methods take a long time and are very costly since multiple physical prototypes have to be created along with extensive tests in varied conditions. Finally, with the support of HPC, real-time simulations may decrease the cost and time for such processes. Simulations permit the virtual test of different configurations and scenarios without needing many physical prototyping. This approach also reduces the likelihood of costly mistakes or failures since problems can be identified during the preliminary stages of design. Through real-time simulations, manufacturers refine designs, fine-tune systems, and verify compliance with regulations without using an excessive amount of physical resources, thus saving much cost and allowing the possibility of getting to market quickly with new EV models.

Simulation of Drive Conditions and Load Scenarios

These would then be run dependably over a wide range of driving conditions-that is to say, including all load variations, terrain, and external environmental conditions. Real-time simulations of the above conditions allow one to see how a vehicle can behave in response, for example, while climbing steeply, accelerating sharply, or in stop-and-go traffic, where its demands for energy vary considerably. Load cases may include passenger weight, cargo, or trailer towing variations to simulate these conditions on energy consumption, powertrain stress, and range. Extreme temperature regimes can also be evaluated in real-time simulations of importance in the effects on the battery and its thermal management. All done in optimizing operation of EVs over a broad spectrum of real-world conditions toward both performance and reliability improvement.

In a nutshell, real-time simulation is a tool for electric vehicles and their development, testing, giving immediate responses on the performance of the system, and always optimizing the fast process. Digital twins can really make modeling of many driving conditions, therefore decrease the cost of prototyping, help in improving the efficiency of the vehicle, and ensure the performance at the level of modern consumers' expectations for EVs. Hence, real-time simulation even accelerates innovation. In addition, it helps make the electric vehicle strong and adaptable to the competitive changing market.

HPC AND ELECTRIC VEHICLE CHARGING INFRASTRUCTURE

Growing popularity of electric cars becomes the reason why proper and effective charging infrastructure, for example, sturdy charging stations, is necessary. HPC thereby plays a transformative role in optimizing the efficiency of EV charging networks, solving the problems with the grid, and working to improve the effectiveness of charging stations in general. This section focuses on the challenges in EV charging infrastructure, a role HPC plays in optimization of charging networks, simulating charging patterns and their impacts on the electrical grid, and the strategic placement of charging stations to optimize their efficiency (Boopathi et al., 2024; Chandrika et al., 2023; Devi et al., 2024).

Challenges in EV Charging Infrastructure

There are several challenges EV charging infrastructure development is facing. Charging imbalances would form a salient issue when it comes to range anxiety, especially in sparsely populated regions. The integration of an ultra-high level of EVs into the power grid also raises some complex issues relating to load management, including the potential overloading of the power grid and fluctuations in power demand. Those charging times vary with types of charger, size of the car's battery and the availability of the grid. Coordination for such a system must be effectively handled to avoid disrupting charging. There is a dire need for detailed models and analysis in the design of a resilient yet efficient network to support growing adoption of EVs with minimal disruption in the grid.

HPC for Charging Network Optimization

HPC enables optimal charging infrastructure for electric vehicles overall through the handling of large volumes of data which will simulate and analyze charging patterns, energy flows, and network performance. Engineers can therefore model scenarios for various types of vehicles, different charging rates, and different power demands at different times of day and regions. With HPC, real-time data can be aggregated and analyzed from a thousand charging stations to determine the optimal configurations of network expansions that will minimize congestion and reduce energy distribution. HPC also makes demand forecasting much more precise, predicting where the likelihood of demand at which hour of the day and at what locations, therefore far ahead on future-proofing the structure of infrastructure development and preparation for a burst in EV adoption.

Simulation of Charging Patterns and Impact on Grid

Simulating charging patterns and their effects on the power grid is the most critical application of HPC in EV charging infrastructure. Charging a fully electric vehicle imposes extremely high demands on the grid at times when most are charging, especially peak hours. Such simulation by HPC helps to model those patterns of interaction with the existing grid infrastructure to enable utilities to balance loads more effectively. This is vital from the point of view of grid stability and will especially become quite critical with the increasing inclusions of renewable sources in the overall energy mix. Grid operators can apply simulation of diverse charging patterns across different geographic areas to optimize flow of energy as well as avoid any potential or possible strain on the grid and prevent outages, thereby making the growing EV load manageable by the grid without performance drop.

Strategic Siting for Maximum Efficiency

HPC helps in strategic location of charging stations, simulating traffic patterns and population density as well as projected EV adoption rates. This analysis would help in finding the best location for new stations, ensuring that demand is at its highest level in those areas and grid impact is at a minimum. Optimized placement of charging stations in cities and regions can support access to EV charging services and reduce the risk of congestion in certain areas where the grid's transmission capacity may be limited. For example, HPC-computer simulations can choose which placement of fast-charging stations on highways or in urban centers would deliver better vehicle driving ranges and lower time charges for filling, greatly improving the EV ownership experience. Station placement overall can also reduce the costs of infrastructure as investments will be targeted to where they will deliver the most impact.

Thus, HPC is an extremely important tool in dealing with the issues of charging infrastructure for electric vehicles. Therefore, it would further enable the effective optimization of the charging network, better integration of charging stations with the grid, and strategical station placement, ensuring a scalable and sustainable future for electric mobility.

FUTURE TRENDS IN HPC-DRIVEN ELECTRIC VEHICLE INNOVATIONS

HPC is at the forefront of innovation in electric vehicle designs, performance, and possibilities when technology is developed further. With the tremendous progress in artificial intelligence (AI), and especially machine learning (ML), as well as the emergence of quantum computing, it is now an exciting future area to explore. The subsequent section will focus on the key future trends in HPC-driven EV innovation, AI/ML, quantum integration, sustainability, challenges, and opportunities ahead (Dall-Orsoletta et al., 2022; Prud'homme & Koning, 2012; Rapson & Muehlegger, 2023).

AI and Machine Learning Integration with HPC in EV Design

Perhaps one of the most promising applications of AI and machine learning is the integration into the HPC for designing electric vehicles: AI algorithms can analyze the data coming from sensors, simulation results, and real-world operations of vehicles to ensure that everything, right from battery management to motor control, is optimized. It also enables quick simulation of vehicle performance under different conditions by trained machine learning models in an HPC environment, with a higher-degree prediction to make the design process more efficient.

AI can also be applied for more complex decisions, such as optimization of energy flow or fault detection in EV systems. Combined with HPC, AI-powered simulation would provide real-time feedback, thus accelerating the production cycle by aiding automakers to develop more intelligent and efficient EVs.

Next-Generation Simulations of EV

The more it evolves, the more insights reveal regarding its potential to revolutionize EV simulation. So far in its infancy, AI promises to solve problems hitherto intractable for classical computers. Multivariable optimizations, such as materials science, battery chemistry, and aerodynamics, can now be solved by quantum computers. Quantum computers will be able to simulate at the molecular level interactions within battery materials. This is a major breakthrough with regard to augmenting battery life, charging speeds, and energy density. Quantum computers might be capable of doing calculations exponentially faster than traditional HPCs, so potentially model much more complex systems in real-time, which would radically improve EV design and performance optimization.

Sustainable EV Innovations through HPC

With sustainability emerging as a very important focus area in EV development, HPC shall play a decisive role in making eco-friendly innovations possible. Simulations based on HPC can help determine the optimal selection of materials and energy efficiency during EV manufacturing to reduce the carbon footprint of the production process. Moreover, efficiency and aerodynamics of the vehicle are further improved by HPC, saving energy.

In relation to battery technology, HPC allows modeling of advanced chemistries and recycling methods and facilitates sustainable energy storage solutions while fostering innovations in battery life cycle management and environmental impacts.

Future Challenges and Opportunities in HPC for EVs

Although the future of HPC in EV innovation appears very bright, there are still many challenges for which HPC will be necessary. Rising complexity in simulations will ever increasingly require more computing power, and the cost of scaling up could prove too costly for smaller auto manufacturers. Balancing AI, quantum computing, and initiatives toward sustainability will require multidisciplinary collaboration. But these challenges also represent opportunities. Cloud-based HPC services will democratize greater access to powerful computing resources. What develops from current research in AI algorithms might provide altogether different avenues for optimizing both vehicle design and performance. It is with such proper investments and technological advances that HPC will lead electric vehicles in shaping their future, including driving both performance and sustainability in the industry.

Thus, it might be stated that in integrating AI, quantum computing, and sustainable practices into HPC-driven EV innovation, the automotive world is bound to transform and open new avenues, but pose great challenges and difficulties for further considerations.

CONCLUSION

This chapter highlights the significant importance of HPC for electric vehicle development: the automotive industry today leverages HPC as an essential tool for maximizing powertrain performance, simulating battery systems and aerodynamics, and transforming innovation, efficiency, and sustainable advancement. Manufacturers will be able to run complex simulations using HPC, which can decrease prototyping time, improve design, lead to better overall performance, and cost and time-to-market savings. Future: Increasingly data- and high-performance computer-driven, the revolution and transformation in design and testing processes, especially with AI and possibly quantum computers, would be critically important. HPC simulation of real-world scenarios, prediction of system failures, and optimization of energy consumption are some of the critical steps to overcome the challenges identified, including degradation of batteries, infrastructure for charging, and aerodynamics.

While the areas that relate to scalability, infrastructure cost, and the development of innovative emerging technologies remain, HPC certainly finds its way into the future electric vehicle generation. Progress in HPC capabilities is continuously evolving; it will unlock further sustainable innovations that set electric vehicles ahead in transportation of the future.

REFERENCES

Aghabali, I., Bauman, J., Kollmeyer, P. J., Wang, Y., Bilgin, B., & Emadi, A. (2020a). 800-V electric vehicle powertrains: Review and analysis of benefits, challenges, and future trends. *IEEE Transactions on Transportation Electrification*, 7(3), 927–948. DOI: 10.1109/TTE.2020.3044938

Aghabali, I., Bauman, J., Kollmeyer, P. J., Wang, Y., Bilgin, B., & Emadi, A. (2020b). 800-V electric vehicle powertrains: Review and analysis of benefits, challenges, and future trends. *IEEE Transactions on Transportation Electrification*, 7(3), 927–948. DOI: 10.1109/TTE.2020.3044938

Ahmed, K., & Liu, J. (2019). Simulation of energy-efficient demand response for high performance computing systems. *2019 Winter Simulation Conference (WSC)*, 2560–2571. DOI: 10.1109/WSC40007.2019.9004781

Alawneh, S. G., Zeng, L., & Arefifar, S. A. (2023). A Review of High-Performance Computing Methods for Power Flow Analysis. *Mathematics*, 11(11), 2461. DOI: 10.3390/math11112461

Babu, B. S., Kamalakannan, J., Meenatchi, N., Karthik, S., & Boopathi, S. (2022). Economic impacts and reliability evaluation of battery by adopting Electric Vehicle. *IEEE Explore*, 1–6.

Boopathi, S., Ananth, J., Raghuram, K. S., Kistan, A., Velumani, M., & Gopinathan, R. (2024, January). *6342734- Machine for Analysis of the resistance of welded parts by the electrical resistance process.*

Boopathi, S., Saranya, A., Raghuraman, S., & Revanth, R. (2018). Design and Fabrication of Low Cost Electric Bicycle. *International Research Journal of Engineering and Technology*, 5(3), 146–147.

Bucaioni, A. (2019). Boosting the development of high-performance automotive systems. *Junior Researcher Community Event at Software Technologies: Applications and Foundations 2019 STAF-JRC19.*

Chandrika, V., Sivakumar, A., Krishnan, T. S., Pradeep, J., Manikandan, S., & Boopathi, S. (2023). Theoretical Study on Power Distribution Systems for Electric Vehicles. In *Intelligent Engineering Applications and Applied Sciences for Sustainability* (pp. 1–19). IGI Global. DOI: 10.4018/979-8-3693-0044-2.ch001

Dall-Orsoletta, A., Ferreira, P., & Dranka, G. G. (2022). Low-carbon technologies and just energy transition: Prospects for electric vehicles. *Energy Conversion and Management: X, 16*, 100271.

Devi, J. V., Argiddi, R. V., Renuka, P., Janagi, K., Hari, B. S., & Boopathi, S. (2024). Study on Integrated Neural Networks and Fuzzy Logic Control for Autonomous Electric Vehicles. In *Advances in Web Technologies and Engineering* (pp. 104–127). IGI Global. DOI: 10.4018/979-8-3693-1487-6.ch006

Du, J., Mo, X., Li, Y., Zhang, Q., Li, J., Wu, X., Lu, L., & Ouyang, M. (2019). Boundaries of high-power charging for long-range battery electric car from the heat generation perspective. *Energy*, 182, 211–223. DOI: 10.1016/j.energy.2019.05.222

Giri, R. B., N., Alhamad, A. M., Mamidi, P. L., R., S., & Boopathi, S. (2024). Human-Centered Design Approach to Autonomous Electric Vehicles: Revolutionizing Mobility. In *Advances in Logistics, Operations, and Management Science* (pp. 91–109). IGI Global. DOI: 10.4018/979-8-3693-1862-1.ch006

Godwin Immanuel, D., Solaimalai, G., Chandrakala, B. M., Bharath, V. G., Singh, M. K., & Boopathi, S. (2024). Advancements in Electric Vehicle Management System: Integrating Machine Learning and Artificial Intelligence. In *Advances in Web Technologies and Engineering* (pp. 371–391). IGI Global. DOI: 10.4018/979-8-3693-1487-6.ch018

Loeb, B., & Kockelman, K. M. (2019). Fleet performance and cost evaluation of a shared autonomous electric vehicle (SAEV) fleet: A case study for Austin, Texas. *Transportation Research Part A, Policy and Practice*, 121, 374–385. DOI: 10.1016/j.tra.2019.01.025

Lyu, C., Lin, N., & Dinavahi, V. (2021). Device-level parallel-in-time simulation of mmc-based energy system for electric vehicles. *IEEE Transactions on Vehicular Technology*, 70(6), 5669–5678. DOI: 10.1109/TVT.2021.3081534

McIntosh-Smith, S., Price, J., Deakin, T., & Poenaru, A. (2019). A performance analysis of the first generation of HPC-optimized Arm processors. *Concurrency and Computation*, 31(16), e5110. DOI: 10.1002/cpe.5110

Meintz, A., Slezak, L., Thurston, S., Carlson, B., Thurlbeck, A., Kisacikoglu, J., Kandula, P., Rowden, B., Chinthavali, M., Wojda, R., & Associates. (2023). *Electric vehicles at scale (EVs@ Scale) laboratory consortium deep-dive technical meetings: High power charging (HPC) summary report*. National Renewable Energy Laboratory (NREL), Golden, CO (United States).

Miri, I., Fotouhi, A., & Ewin, N. (2021). Electric vehicle energy consumption modelling and estimation—A case study. *International Journal of Energy Research*, 45(1), 501–520. DOI: 10.1002/er.5700

Muhammed, T., Mehmood, R., Albeshri, A., & Alsolami, F. (2020). HPC-smart infrastructures: A review and outlook on performance analysis methods and tools. *Smart Infrastructure and Applications: Foundations for Smarter Cities and Societies*, 427–451.

Muthukumar, R., & Pratheep, G. V. G., S. J., S., Kunduru, K. R., Kumar, P., & Boopathi, S. (2024). Leveraging Fuel Cell Technology With AI and ML Integration for Next-Generation Vehicles: Empowering Electric Mobility. In *Advances in Mechatronics and Mechanical Engineering* (pp. 312–337). IGI Global. DOI: 10.4018/979-8-3693-5247-2.ch016

Naresh, M., Subhahan, D. A., Narula, V. N., Roslin, D. K., Narula, S., & Boopathi, S. (2024). Edge Computing and Machine Learning Integration for Autonomous Electrical Vehicles. In *Solving Fundamental Challenges of Electric Vehicles* (pp. 99–127). IGI Global., DOI: 10.4018/979-8-3693-4314-2.ch005

Pozzato, G., Allam, A., Pulvirenti, L., Negoita, G. A., Paxton, W. A., & Onori, S. (2023). Analysis and key findings from real-world electric vehicle field data. *Joule*, 7(9), 2035–2053. DOI: 10.1016/j.joule.2023.07.018

Prud'homme, R., & Koning, M. (2012). Electric vehicles: A tentative economic and environmental evaluation. *Transport Policy*, 23, 60–69. DOI: 10.1016/j.tranpol.2012.06.001

Rajan, T. S., Rex, C. R. E. S., Shastri, D. S., Naidu, G., Senthil Kumar, C., & Boopathi, S. (2024). Study on Environmental and Social Impacts Through Electric Vehicles. In *Solving Fundamental Challenges of Electric Vehicles* (pp. 352–383). IGI Global., DOI: 10.4018/979-8-3693-4314-2.ch013

Rapson, D. S., & Muehlegger, E. (2023). The economics of electric vehicles. *Review of Environmental Economics and Policy*, 17(2), 274–294. DOI: 10.1086/725484

Saldaña, G., San Martín, J. I., Zamora, I., Asensio, F. J., & Oñederra, O. (2019). Analysis of the current electric battery models for electric vehicle simulation. *Energies*, 12(14), 2750. DOI: 10.3390/en12142750

Sharma, T., Glynn, J., Panos, E., Deane, P., Gargiulo, M., Rogan, F., & Gallachóir, B. Ó. (2019). High performance computing for energy system optimization models: Enhancing the energy policy tool kit. *Energy Policy*, 128, 66–74. DOI: 10.1016/j.enpol.2018.12.055

Taghavipour, A., Vajedi, M., & Azad, N. L. (2019). *Intelligent control of connected plug-in hybrid electric vehicles*. Springer. DOI: 10.1007/978-3-030-00314-2

Tan, L., & Yuan, Y. (2022). Computational fluid dynamics simulation and performance optimization of an electrical vehicle Air-conditioning system. *Alexandria Engineering Journal*, 61(1), 315–328. DOI: 10.1016/j.aej.2021.05.001

Tran, D.-D., Vafaeipour, M., El Baghdadi, M., Barrero, R., Van Mierlo, J., & Hegazy, O. (2020). Thorough state-of-the-art analysis of electric and hybrid vehicle powertrains: Topologies and integrated energy management strategies. *Renewable & Sustainable Energy Reviews*, 119, 109596. DOI: 10.1016/j.rser.2019.109596

Yao, M., Gan, Y., Liang, J., Dong, D., Ma, L., Liu, J., Luo, Q., & Li, Y. (2021). Performance simulation of a heat pipe and refrigerant-based lithium-ion battery thermal management system coupled with electric vehicle air-conditioning. *Applied Thermal Engineering*, 191, 116878. DOI: 10.1016/j.applthermaleng.2021.116878

Yi, H., Deng, C., Gong, X., Deng, X., & Blatnik, M. (2021). 1D-3D Online Coupled Transient Analysis for Powertrain-Control Integrated Thermal Management in an Electric Vehicle. *SAE International Journal of Advances and Current Practices in Mobility*, 3(2021-01–0237), 2410–2420.

Yi, H., Li, A., Sun, R., Hu, Y., Zhou, A., Zan, J., & Peng, Q. (2022). *1D-3D Coupled Analysis for Motor Thermal Management in an Electric Vehicle*. SAE Technical Paper.

ADDITIONAL READING

Chougule, S. B., Chaudhari, B. S., Ghorpade, S. N., & Zennaro, M. (2024). Exploring Computing Paradigms for Electric Vehicles: From Cloud to Edge Intelligence, Challenges and Future Directions. *World Electric Vehicle Journal*, 15(2), 39. DOI: 10.3390/wevj15020039

Donald, A., & Brian, A. (2023). AI-Driven horizons: Electric vehicles, cloud computing, and the future of automation. *International Journal of Advanced Engineering Technologies and Innovations*, 1(02), 100–115.

Farooqi, A. M., Alam, M. A., Hassan, S. I., & Idrees, S. M. (2022). A fog computing model for VANET to reduce latency and delay using 5G network in smart city transportation. *Applied Sciences (Basel, Switzerland)*, 12(4), 2083. DOI: 10.3390/app12042083

George, D., & Ronald, R. (2023). Connected Futures: Antenna Breakthroughs in the Era of Cloud Computing, AI Automation, and Electric Vehicles. *International Journal of Advanced Engineering Technologies and Innovations*, 1(02), 131–144.

Jeslin, J. G., Sujatha, M., Aghalya, S., Jehan, C., Ishwarya, M., & Vinayagam, P. V. (2024). 5G-Enabled V2X Communication with Cloud-Powered XGBoost Algorithm for Electric Transportation. 2024 10th International Conference on Communication and Signal Processing (ICCSP), 1388–1393.

Raviprolu, L., Molakatala, N., Argiddi, R. V., Dilavar, S. N., & Srinivasan, P. (2024). Performance Improvements of Electric Vehicles Using Edge Computing and Machine Learning Technologies. In Solving Fundamental Challenges of Electric Vehicles (pp. 248–281). IGI Global. DOI: 10.4018/979-8-3693-4314-2.ch010

Rimal, B. P., Kong, C., Poudel, B., Wang, Y., & Shahi, P. (2022). Smart electric vehicle charging in the era of internet of vehicles, emerging trends, and open issues. *Energies*, 15(5), 1908. DOI: 10.3390/en15051908

Salek, M. S., Khan, S. M., Rahman, M., Deng, H.-W., Islam, M., Khan, Z., Chowdhury, M., & Shue, M. (2022). A review on cybersecurity of cloud computing for supporting connected vehicle applications. *IEEE Internet of Things Journal*, 9(11), 8250–8268. DOI: 10.1109/JIOT.2022.3152477

Tappeta, V. S. R., Appasani, B., Patnaik, S., & Ustun, T. S. (2022). A review on emerging communication and computational technologies for increased use of plug-in electric vehicles. *Energies*, 15(18), 6580. DOI: 10.3390/en15186580

KEY TERMS AND DEFINITIONS

AI: Artificial Intelligence, enables machines to simulate human intelligence.
BMS: Battery Management System, regulates battery performance and health.
CFD: Computational Fluid Dynamics, simulates fluid flow around objects.
ECM: Electric Control Module, controls electric vehicle functions.
EV: Electric Vehicle, powered entirely by electricity.
HPC: High-Performance Computing, powerful computing systems for complex simulations.
ICE: Internal Combustion Engine, traditional engine using fuel.
MH: Motor Horsepower, measure of motor power output.
ML: Machine Learning, AI subset that learns from data patterns.
PBM: Powertrain Battery Management, oversees battery usage in powertrains.
PMSM: Permanent Magnet Synchronous Motor, efficient electric motor type.

Chapter 11
AI–Driven Energy Optimization in High–Performance Computing:
Smart Solutions for Sustainable Efficiency

S. Subashree
https://orcid.org/0000-0003-2034-847X

Department of Computer Science and Engineering, E G.S. Pillay Engineering College, Nagapattinam, India

T. Akila

Department of Information Technology, Mahendra College of Engineering, Salem, India

Pravin A Dwaramwar
https://orcid.org/0000-0002-8479-9053

Department of Electronic and Computer Science, Ramdeobaba University, Nagpur, India

Saurabh Chandra
https://orcid.org/0000-0003-4172-9968

School of Law, Bennett University, Greater Noida, India

Ketki P. Kshirsagar

Department of Electronics and Telecommunication, Vishwakarma Institute of Technology, Pune, India

ABSTRACT

The rapid digital transformation in this era has led to the rise of high-performance computing (HPC) systems as a hub for addressing computationally intensive requirements, but their energy consumption is also a growing concern due to sustainability efforts. This chapter surveys the potential transformative impact of Artificial Intelligence (AI) in optimizing energy management in the context of HPC systems. With machine learning algorithms and predictive analytics, an AI system can dynamically adapt to power use levels, optimize workload distributions, and reduce energy consumption without compromising computational performance. The techniques discussed in this chapter include AI-driven techniques founded on computational methods such as reinforcement learning and neural network models that change HPC

DOI: 10.4018/978-1-6684-3795-7.ch011

workloads appropriately to support real-time decision-making and energy-efficient operations. This chapter presents successful AI-based system implementations while highlighting high performance and energy savings.

INTRODUCTION

High-performance computing (HPC) is a leader in modern technological advances, as it enables the opportunity for incredibly complicated computational tasks in such dissimilar fields as scientific research and weather forecasting, data analysis, and artificial intelligence (AI). However, with extensive growth in HPC capabilities, its associated challenge is high energy consumption. As the demand for processing power accelerates, so does the need for more efficient energy solutions. As such, traditional ways of managing energy have been proven to be insufficient in efficiently managing increasing power demands within HPC, which inevitably leads to associated operation costs along with environmental implications. In this context, AI-driven energy optimization appears to be the next big hope for HPC systems in terms of how energy is consumed and managed and conserved (Long, 2023).

The integration of AI in energy management is more than a technology effort; it's really a paradigm shift in the approach to achieving energy efficiency in HPC environments. The AI technologies related to machine learning and reinforcement learning enable intelligent monitoring and real-time prediction of energy usage. The approach makes use of data-driven insights to be informative to make energy management more responsive, adaptive, and efficient. In fact, with AI algorithms, one can progressively adjust energy consumption by analyzing humongous amounts of data from high-performance computing systems based on real-time workload patterns, system performance, and environmental factors, such as cooling requirements. It offers a dynamic and more sustainable energy management strategy that fits into the increasing drive towards green computing and carbon footprint reduction (G. Wang et al., 2024).

Economic pressure and environmental sustainability are two chief factors that make the importance of energy efficiency increasing in HPC systems. Their computational tasks are becoming increasingly resource-intensive, and the data centers carrying HPC systems are facing entirely new operational costs, mainly because of the quantity of electricity these systems require to run and keep cool (Kaushik et al., 2024). In addition to that, on the issue of environment, these power-guzzling systems are a massive strain in that data centers take the most significant share of energy globally. Therefore, it is anticipated that the regulatory bodies and other industry players will begin to lobby for energy-efficient solutions that could reduce carbon footprint from the data centers while still boasting massive computational performance. AI-based energy optimization is a very attractive solution that offers the ability to make significant savings in terms of cost and environmental impact without an offset in performance. AI-based optimization of energy consumption of HPC systems is, for the most part, based on the actual prediction and adaptation of dynamic workloads (S. Wang et al., 2024).

Static models that underlie most traditional energy management do not account for the dynamic nature of workloads in an HPC system, with the results being waste of energy usage. In contrast, AI algorithms can learn from historical data and adjust energy consumption automatically with the real-time demand. For example, machine learning models may analyze the patterns of system performance and workload distribution in order to bring an optimal perspective to save energy. It may adjust the power level of a dormant or underutilized component, for instance. Reinforcement learning techniques could also be used to enable systems to make autonomous decisions relating to power management, continually refining their efficiency through trial and error (Kwaku, 2023).

One area of promise with AI applying to HPC energy management is predictive analytics: Predicting future workloads and system performance allows AI algorithms to make changes to energy usage in advance to ensure resources are allocated appropriately. For example, predictive models can predict peaks in processing times and adjust the cooling system or power supply levels accordingly, reducing reactive strategies to energy management, which are inherently less efficient. It is not just the saving in the energy consumption, as it extends the lifetime of HPC components by reducing the effects of fluctuating power levels and temperatures (Sathupadi & others, 2023).

One more major area of energy optimization with AI is smart energy systems. Here, smart energy refers to the integration of AI technologies with advanced hardware solutions like energy-efficient processors and cooling mechanisms into an all-rounded energy management framework. For instance, AI can enable temperature and airflow management in data centers so that cooling systems operate at optimal levels. With AI-powered energy management systems whose cooling level changes dynamically according to real-time system performance and environmental conditions, the energy required to sustain ideal operating conditions for HPC systems will be significantly reduced (Sathupadi & others, 2023).

AI-driven optimization benefits extend far beyond cost savings and environmental sustainability. More efficient HPC systems directly map to higher levels of computational performance, so these organizations can solve problems that are much more complex and process larger datasets. Moreover, scalability increases because the amount of energy consumed by HPC systems is not proportionally scalable. On the other hand, as the AI-based technologies move forward with time, more advanced energy optimization strategies are bound to come up, offering better possibilities for increased sustainability and efficiency in HPC systems in the long run (Huang et al., 2019).

Quite promising as the AI-based energy optimization may be, there is still a downside to it. Of course, implementing AI-driven energy management systems would entail a good deal of investment in hardware and software and the people who are involved in AI as well as HPC. Questioning further, the infusion of AI in this regard raises data security and privacy issues, particularly where sensitive information is processed. These challenges require this holistic approach to AI-driven energy management as best practices in data security are embraced and presented with an AI system that is transparent, explainable, and aligned with broader organizational goals (Gregory et al., 2019).

AI-Powered Energy Optimization stands for a change in principles of managing energy at HPCs. Leveraging AI technologies in the form of machine learning, reinforcement learning, and predictive analytics is going to present unprecedented efficiency, cost savings, and sustainability levels. With more and more demands rising in the high-performance computing sector, energy management based on AI will soon be one of the main players in the near future of HPC-with a scalable, sustainable solution for challenges with energy consumption and environmental impacts (Ligozat et al., 2022).

Scope

This chapter focuses on the intersection of AI and energy optimization in high-performance computing. Techniques for AI encompass machine learning, reinforcement learning, and predictive analytics, and their applications in improving the energy efficiency of a heterogeneous set of systems in HPC. Additionally, this chapter examines the integration of AI with energy-efficient hardware, data center cooling, and smart grid systems. This chapter therefore depicts in a comprehensive way the ability of AI to drive sustainable, energy-efficient HPC operations; insights are also drawn about emerging technologies and best practices in energy management through case studies and discussion of current challenges and future trends.

Objectives

This chapter presents a clear understanding of the role of AI in optimizing energy consumption in high performance computing (HPC) systems. The key objectives are to

i.   Explore machine learning, reinforcement learning, and predictive analytics-related AI technologies in pursuit of more energy-efficient systems.
ii. Examine how AI was integrated with hardware-based energy-efficient hardware, smart grids, and cooling systems in the context of an HPC.
iii. Explore real-world application case studies that leverage AI-driven energy management practices.
iv. Identify the challenges and opportunities presented by AI in the optimization of energy in an HPC environment
v.   Draw out future trends and directions of AI as well as sustainable computing to create a roadmap leading toward a green HPC.

HIGH-PERFORMANCE COMPUTING AND ENERGY CONSUMPTION

High-performance computing has become the workhorse of many cutting-edge technologies and scientific initiatives-from climate modelling to pharmaceutical research, to future artificial intelligence. Along with escalating demand for computational capacity comes increasing energy consumption; therefore, yet another great challenge in the pursuit of sustainability and operational efficiency lies in the energy demands of HPC infrastructures that come with power processors, memory, and storage. As such, energy usage management in HPC becomes an increasingly important research focus area for researchers, policymakers, and organizations around the globe (Ligozat et al., 2022; Wu et al., 2022).

HPC Energy Requirements and Environmental Impact

Some high-performance computing systems have incredible energy demands. HPC systems, especially at the top tier of performance, such as exascale machines, require great amounts of electric power to support their enormous computation loads. These mainly run as "24/7," processing huge amounts of data, running simulations, and executing tasks requiring highly intensive computation. The more computational power consumed, the more energy consumed with some of the world's largest supercomputers consuming megawatts of electricity.

The environmental impact of such energy demands is enormous. HPC systems are typically deployed in massive data centers whose carbon footprint contributes to the expanding carbon footprint of global computing infrastructure. Data centers account for about 1% of the world's total energy consumption-a figure that only promises to grow as the digital economy expands. Increased usage of HPC in both research and industry serves only to further exacerbate this problem. Another layer of components contributes to energy usage: cooling systems are required to ensure the optimal operation temperatures of HPC hardware. Environmental concerns multiply, as the carbon footprint of computing systems, which have become more important in recent times with an emphasis on sustainability, automatically puts pressure on the HPC community to handle energy usage minimally without being inferior in performance.

The environmental effect of the carbon footprint isn't the only one. These are highly energy-intensive HPC systems that exert significant pressure on the power grid, making their operating costs still more expensive and more unsustainable. Many organizations reliant upon HPC are finding alternative sources of renewable energy, such as solar and wind power. These measures alone however are inadequate to combat the level of energy consumed in that way by an HPC system. Hence, there is an emergent need for more efficient modes of energy optimization that can be incorporated into both levels: hardware and software level.

Conventional Methods of Energy Management

Usually, the conventional way of managing energy in HPCs focuses on several methods; however, most of these approaches are reactive or static, in which optimization was mainly made on individual components rather than approaching the holistic energy consumption. Traditional techniques depend largely on hardware solutions, such as power-aware processors, power capping, and dynamic voltage and frequency scaling (DVFS). Such methods decrease the power footprint through control of required powers according to computation needs. While useful for energy-constrained computing systems, DVFS and other techniques do not perform as well for more complex systems that require a high level of computationally intensive activity (Troisi et al., 2020).

Another classic approach is to use the cooling systems of data centers that house HPC machines to manage energy. Energy-related efficiency at the cooling level through liquid cooling or airflow management can be great in terms of lowering the amount of energy needed to maintain optimum temperatures for HPC operations. However, cooling optimizations address only one end, leaving primarily the overall energy demand of the computational processes essentially the same.

Other job scheduling and load balancing are also mechanisms as part of software-level solutions that adapt to savings in terms of reducing energy consumption by optimizing the way workloads are distributed across computing resources. Distribution of workloads without running such unnecessary processes or during low demand periods and excessive power usage will avoid running needlessly or using more power than needed at specific instances. Most rely on static models that do not change over time based on the changing nature of the workloads, which locks into perpetuating inefficiencies. Traditional techniques for managing energy are helpful but cannot capture the requirements of modern HPC workloads as they change dynamically thus requiring a more intelligent and flexible approach in trying to optimize energy expenditure.

Economic and Environmental Drivers for Energy Optimization

The motivation behind energy optimization for HPC systems is driven both economically and environmentally. This leads to extremely high costs for electricity to power and cool HPC systems, and is arguably one of the significant operational expenses incurred by organizations that rely more on computing power. As global energy prices continue to escalate, organizations are increasingly driven by such cost-saving strategies to reduce energy consumption. The savings potential of proper energy management is enormous cost savings for large data centers running energy-hungry HPC systems all day, every day (Hanelt et al., 2021).

Beyond cost is the environmental footprint high-energy-consuming computing systems are leaving. Global awareness about climate change and sustainability is on the rise, and industries are being held accountable for their carbon footprints. Data centers and their brethren who host HPC workloads are among the larger contributors to CO_2 emissions globally. More strict energy efficiency standards are being set by governments, environmental agencies, and industry regulators that require organizations to adopt greener practices. Failure to comply might attract fines or higher regulation, further stimulating the demands for energy optimization.

A shift towards renewable energy sources is the first essential step, but it does not satisfy all the needs of HPC in terms of energy. Renewable energy is often variable and does not often coincide with the steady power demanded by data centers. Efficiency is still a major objective. Companies and organizations are increasingly seeking ways to establish their bona fides on issues of environmental responsibility. Energy-efficient HPC operation can become a key differentiator. Savvy consumers, investors, and stakeholders are increasingly attaching importance to sustainability, and hence energy-efficient HPC is a strategic business imperative.

To this end, one important driving factor will be cloud computing and HPC as a service. It is in this context that the cloud service providers, which offer most of the industries HPC capabilities, are being forced to optimize energy consumption in order to maintain competitive pricing models. In a very competitive market place, energy efficiency simply translates into lower cost and higher margins. As more organizations send their HPC workloads to the cloud, energy efficiency becomes one service provider's competitive advantage and an environmental requirement.

In addition to the carbon cuts mentioned above, energy optimization in HPC has wider environmental benefits. Electricity management will reduce the pressure on electrical grids, thus obviating the investment needed to construct new energy infrastructure to feed power-hungry computing systems. This will benefit not only specific organizations but also the efforts toward global energy sustainability in the long run. The more we are going to rely on digital and computational power, the more important it will be to sustain these technologies for both the future environment and the economy.

The consumption of energy in HPC systems is a challenge that interlinks three major ideas: technology, economics, and sustainability. Although they have met with some success on aspects of energy management, traditional techniques face inherent limitations from their static and hardware-centric views. It is only when energy costs escalate and environmental regulations become more stringent that organizations will need to consider more dynamic and intelligent approaches to optimize their energy usage in HPC operations. It comes with its underlying drivers: economic savings, environmental responsibility, and healthy competitive positioning through efficient energy management. Ultimately, AI and machine learning, together with the most advanced technologies, will feature as fundamental components in forming the full power and sustainability of optimized energy in HPC systems.

ARTIFICIAL INTELLIGENCE FOR ENERGY MANAGEMENT

The integration of artificial intelligence in the energy management system, particularly high-performance computing, changes the paradigms of energy consumption, optimization, and sustenance. With increasingly high demands for energy and traditional methods way below the standards set by such demand, AI-powered solutions open the possibilities for a dynamic, intelligent, real-time approach to energy efficiency. AI can sieve through very large sets of data, make decisions in real time, and adapts to changing conditions, making AI an essential tool of modern energy management (Ejarque et al., 2022; Hanelt et al., 2021). Figure 1 depicts the integration of artificial intelligence into energy management systems for high-performance computing.

Figure 1. Artificial intelligence for energy management

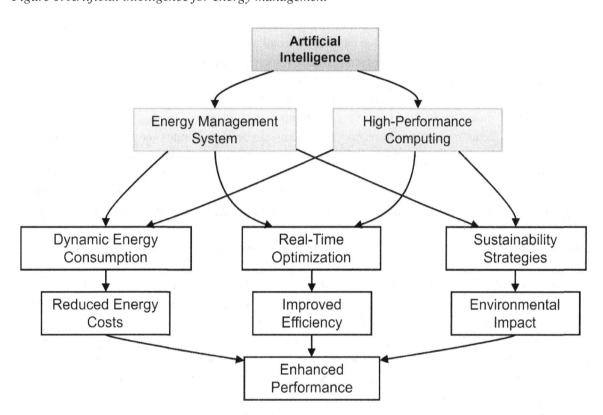

AI and Machine Learning in Energy Systems

Artificial intelligence, and more specifically the machine learning part, is a critical component of energy management. This is because it will permit predictive and adaptive systems, which could potentially achieve optimization in terms of energy consumption. AI-driven energy management systems in the context of HPC, where energy usage is significant and often fluctuating according to workload, offer granular control of power consumption, making resource utilization much more efficient. AI can track and manage system parameters according to current computational load, varying energy costs, and environmental factors to prevent waste, providing optimality in performance (Ciabattoni et al., 2020; Czarnul et al., 2019; Tovazzi et al., 2020).

Energy usage patterns and trends are very well discovered with the help of machine learning algorithms. For example, supervised learning can well be used for the achievement of predictable statements regarding the possible level of energy usage by using historical data, which unsupervised learning would pinpoint anomalies or inefficiencies in the use of energy likely to be ignored. Such an ability is invaluable in environments such as data centers or HPC systems where small inefficiencies lead to large energy expenditures over time.

In addition, deep learning models are increasingly deployed to support more sophisticated energy management strategies. These models are capable of simulating complex energy scenarios, optimizing the distribution of energy across the components, and even predicting future energy needs. The predictive capabilities of AI and ML result in proactive controls over energy usage with a reduced wastage of such an important resource and ensuring that the best is extracted out of it.

The use of AI is well beyond the step of merely monitoring and energy management. With the incorporation of AI in the entire infrastructure, energy systems can be made "smart" enough to autonomously respond in accordance with changing conditions. For example, if the system recognizes that certain hardware components are unused, it can dynamically reduce their usage of power-or vice versa, increase energy delivery when those particular components are highly in use. Such flexibility and adaptability are the main advantages of AI in energy management, making it an asset in sustainable computing.

Dynamic Optimization Using Reinforcement Learning

One of the most promising AI techniques that has been developing in energy management is reinforcement learning (RL). Unlike supervised learning, it works with pre-labeled data; reinforcement learning learns from interaction with a particular environment. Reinforcement learning is, therefore, well-suited for dynamic and complex systems like HPC infrastructures. In the context of energy management, reinforcement learning allows systems to learn autonomously how to optimize energy consumption in real time on the basis of feedback and adjust to new situations without human intervention (Bouhamed, 2022a; Kelechi et al., 2020).

Reinforcement learning algorithms maximize a cumulative reward function, which for the case of energy management may be energy consumption while maintaining performance. Processing various workloads, the RL agent continually refines its energy optimization strategy and hence improves with every interaction. For instance, in HPC systems, RL can dynamically scale the power consumption across processors and other hardware components according to the system's current performance and its current energy requirement.

One key benefit of RL is that it can solve challenging, multi-objective optimization tasks. Generally, for energy management, the potential for a trade-off between energy efficiency and performance exists more often. The reinforcement learning algorithm can master navigating this trade-off by learning how to balance objectives. For instance, an RL system could learn when to bring down the clock speed of processors in order to save energy without inducing significant penalties to total system performance.

Additional benefits of RL are that it optimizes energy usage in HPC across all layers including processor-level optimization to entire data center infrastructures. It can learn with the real-time assessment of workload predictions or even optimize the scheduling of tasks so that peak energy demand periods might be minimized. Since an RL-based energy management system learns from its environment constantly, it gets more efficient with time, cuts down energy consumption, and improves sustainability.

Another application of RL in energy management is dynamic voltage and frequency scaling, whereby the system automatically tunes the processor power consumption to meet the requirements of the workload. The most relevant aspect of this process can be learned by RL agents through reinforcement learning to determine when it would be optimal to scale up or down the voltage and frequency and therefore balance the need for energy efficiency with computational demand.

Predictive Analytics for Energy Efficiency

Another critical AI-driven technique employed in the management of energy is predictive analytics, especially for the improvement of efficiency from HPC systems. By applying vast datasets from sensors, logs, and historical consumption of energy, AI algorithms will give predictions of future energy consumption and aid in their adjustment ahead of time. This kind of predictability of future energy demand is important in an environment as presented by HPC systems, whose workloads and energy demands change dramatically within a short period (Mohammad & Mahjabeen, 2023; Salama & Abdellatif, 2022).

Predictive analytics therefore engages the application of machine learning models analyzing historical data to identify patterns for energy usage prediction. The applied models will predict when peak energy periods are most likely to occur and give guidelines on how to avoid energy excesses during such times. For example, when HPC workloads are running on a data center, predictive models can predict which systems are likely to consume more energy based on the past performance; therefore, the energy management system will prepare for this by optimizing resource allocation.

Perhaps the most important application of predictive analytics in energy efficiency is load forecasting. It ensures that a data center or an HPC system will neither over-provision nor under-provision energy, thus wasting more energy. AI-based models for predicting the energy demands with variables like time of day, workload intensity, and environmental conditions help the systems plan better in terms of energy usage.

Preventive maintenance is another major energy management factor, in which predictive analytics is applied. AI models analyze data coming from sensors embedded within HPC hardware and predict when various components are likely to fail or need to be maintained. Preventive maintenance helps minimize energy wastage due to an inefficient performance of the hardware. For example, if one cooling fan fails, then the system would overload and increase in temperature, consuming an excess amount of energy to keep temperatures in check. That's what predictive maintenance addresses: identifying potential malfunctions before they degrade into energy inefficiencies.

Optimization of cooling systems is among the major constituents in the energy consumption in HPC environments with predictive analytics powered by AI. While patterns in temperature fluctuations and system workload are analyzed, the predictive models can adjust cooling strategies so that there is a maintained minimal energy usage of optimization of temperatures. For example, peak periods of workload can be predicted using AI as to when it will probably show up and aligned the cooling systems for optimal energy use when such instances rarely show up.

Integration of artificial intelligence and machine learning into the energy management system can change the way energy is consumed and optimized, especially in high-demand environments like HPC systems. With its ability to allow predictive and adaptive energy management strategies, machine learning offers up-front, in situ optimization based on actual system performance; reinforcement learning could offer dynamic, real-time optimization based on real system performance. Predictive analytics enables such optimizations by developing insights and forecasts to predict future energy requirements and enhancing energy efficiency through proactive energy resource management. Together, these AI-driven technologies open the path for smarter and more sustainable energy management systems that don't just result in reduced operational costs but also support the global need to reduce the environmental impact of computing systems. The more evolving the landscape of AI technologies becomes, the more important the role will play toward achieving sustainability and efficiency in high-performance computing systems.

AI-DRIVEN TECHNIQUES FOR OPTIMIZING ENERGY IN HPC

The growing energy demand for HPC systems raises the challenge on both the operating efficiency and environmental sustainability. Since AI as an intelligent computation tool can analyze huge data sets in real time and make decisions right away, it has emerged as the backbone for optimizing energy usage in HPC systems. AI strategies for energy management focus on areas that decrease energy consumption while optimizing system performance to a required level because this is very critical in balancing efficiency with computational power. This section details three AI-driven techniques in optimizing energy in HPC: workloads predicting and adapting to power management, real-time decision making in energy systems, and AI algorithms for performance-energy trade-offs (Bouhamed, 2022b; Mahmoud & Slama, 2023). Figure 2 depicts AI-driven techniques for optimizing energy in HPC systems.

Figure 2. AI-driven techniques for optimizing energy in high-performance computing systems

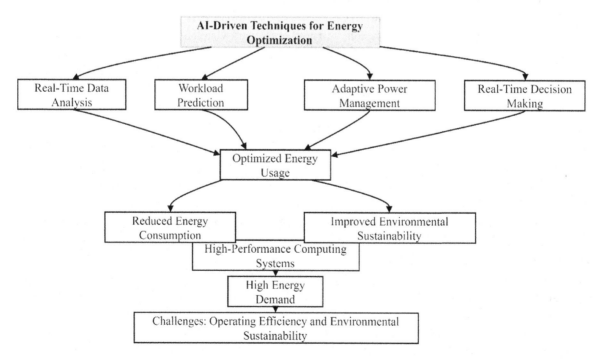

Workload Prediction and Adaptive Power Management

Workloads in high-performance computing are dynamic. This is due to fluctuations which depend on computational tasks and their size. Such fluctuation makes it challenging to maintain energy efficiency without affecting the performance. AI through predictive analytics and machine learning enables more effective prediction of workloads and adaptive power management (Esnaola-Gonzalez et al., 2021; Tovazzi et al., 2020).

Workload forecasting is an analysis of historical data and current performance of other existing systems to ascertain or predict future demands in computing. Machine learning models have the capacity to deal with enormous amounts of data, identify patterns in workload behavior, and predict when peak usage periods occur. For example, it could surge incredibly during peak periods of the day or when certain actions are initiated. The AI can learn to predict these patterns and assist with optimization in energy allocation so that resources are best utilized during peak periods but scaled back during off-peak periods.

Adaptive power management extends this principle by dynamically adapting energy usage based on the predicted workload. These AI-driven adaptive power management systems can dynamically adjust power levels in real time by analyzing the predicted needs of the HPC system. In this way, during peak predictive computation, such as highly resource-demanding tasks, the system can surge preemption of power delivery to the task. During times of low resource usage, such as during largely light or idle tasks, AI can cut energy use, thus avoiding waste. It maintains the power efficiency up but does not compromise on performance.

Some of the adaptive power management techniques used are dynamic voltage and frequency scaling. DVFS control the time-varying voltage and clock frequency of processors based on their workload. AI can optimize this by predicting the perfect time for power down or up and so keeping the system at peak efficiency. It also manages the cooling systems of buildings more effectively by predicting the alterations in temperature and adjusting power usage so that the system temperatures are stable without using too much energy.

Real-time Decision-Making Systems in Energy Systems

High-performance computing requires real-time decisions for optimization of energy usage. Compared to the traditional energy management techniques based on static models, AI-driven energy systems can process data and perform analysis in real time; hence, such adjustments in power consumption made based on the current operational conditions are directly applicable (Ciabattoni et al., 2020; Esnaola-Gonzalez et al., 2021; Tovazzi et al., 2020).

In terms of real-time decision-making in complex environments such as HPCs, AI algorithms, but more importantly RL algorithms, are robust. This way, the RL systems learn through an interaction with their environment and get feedback and continually try to optimize their strategies for making decisions. Such an RL agent used in energy management will automatically keep track of the performance of the system, the workload demands, and the energy consumption of the system and adjust the parameters on the fly dynamically, according to the needs of the system in terms of energy. The real-time nature of the RL lets it adjust its energy usage based on how it is going and adjusts to variations in workload and any effect caused by environmental factors like temperature or cooling requirement.

For example, if the system determines that a particular device, such as a processor or memory module, is at its maximum utilization, the agent can optimize the allocation of energy to that device so that the performance would not degrade. Conversely, if the system's resources are in surplus, the agent can reduce the energy utilization in that department thus saving power. The real-time decision-making capability is very valuable in large scale HPC environments because the state of operations of the system changes fast.

Real-time energy management also enjoys benefits of real-time processing of large datasets by AI. In this regard, AI systems can identify inefficiencies which might not be visible using traditional methods by analyzing data on consumption in real time. For example, in live monitoring, those parts that need to draw power over the rated values or those areas in which the cooling systems overcompensate in temperature fluctuations can be identified. Such inefficiencies can be addressed by AI algorithms that immediately make corrections. In this way, the lost energy is minimized, and the overall performance of the system optimized.

AI Algorithms to Maintain Performance-Energy Trade-Offs

This leads to the central problem of performance-energy efficiency. High-performance computing systems are designed to handle computations that are really complex at maximum speeds. However, this comes at a considerable energy cost; thus, AI algorithms navigate the performance-energy tradeoff so that the HPC systems operate optimally without excessive consumption of energy (Domakonda et al., 2022; Kumara et al., 2023; Samikannu et al., 2022; Venkateswaran et al., 2023).

For managing performance-energy trade-offs, AI techniques in multi-objective optimization are best-suited algorithms. Such algorithms might be able to optimize the system towards two or more conflicting objectives simultaneously, say, maximizing the computational performance of a computer while minimizing energy consumption. AI algorithms can calculate the performance and current energy usage level of a system and adjust several parameters such as processor speed, voltage, and cooling to achieve the optimal balance between the two objectives.

For instance, if a task demands high levels of computation, then the AI algorithm may estimate minimum energy consumption without degrading the performance of that task. Conversely, if the task computationally demands less, then the system could be adapted so that it consumes less energy while still offering proper performance. This adaptive approach can help HPC systems reduce consumption of energy without affecting the ability to process demanding workloads.

Reinforcement learning also comes into the management of performance-energy trade-offs. Based on historical and online feedback, RL agents can be trained on simultaneous optimization of performance with energy usage. Decisions based on such learning, where an intelligent RL agent understands the other components' interplay within the HPC system, may be made regarding efficient resources. For example, an RL agent learns to optimize the power allocation to some hardware resources during low-demand periods only, so as not to compromise the overall system performance while reducing energy usage significantly.

AI-powered algorithms also make energy usage management at any of the layers in HPC systems more granular. Deep learning models, for instance, can fine-tune efficiency at the layer of components by making sure processors, memory, and storage devices are all optimized in using energy. This would lead to drastic reduction in the overall energy footprint associated with HPC environments by optimizing energy usage at each layer in a system.

AI-driven techniques transform energy management in high-performance computing systems through more intelligent, adaptive, and efficient usage of resources. The developed methods of workload prediction and adaptive power management enabled AI to predict the energy requirements and consumption dynamically, thereby ensuring real-time decision making about optimal energy usage based upon varying operational conditions. AI algorithms in performance-energy trade-offs can help balance the needs of HPC systems in terms of performance with the imperative mandate to reduce energy consumption, thereby providing a new frontier of sustainable computing along the way toward more energy-efficient high-performance systems that meet the increasingly demanding needs of computing tasks.

INTEGRATION OF SMART ENERGY SYSTEMS IN HPC

The integration of smart energy systems into high-performance computing environments can be seen as a precursor to reducing energy usage and increasing efficiency. As the demand for computing power is on the increase, so are energy requirements; therefore, advanced energy management solutions need to be adopted in HPC environments. Organizations will be able to minimize the operation expenses of their HPC systems with much retained power by combining AI with energy-efficient hardware, enhancing data center cooling systems using AI, and optimizing energy distribution through AI-driven smart grids (Hema et al., 2023; Kavitha et al., 2023; Saravanan et al., 2024). Figure 3 depicts the integration of smart energy systems into high-performance computing.

Figure 3. Integration of smart energy systems in high-performance computing

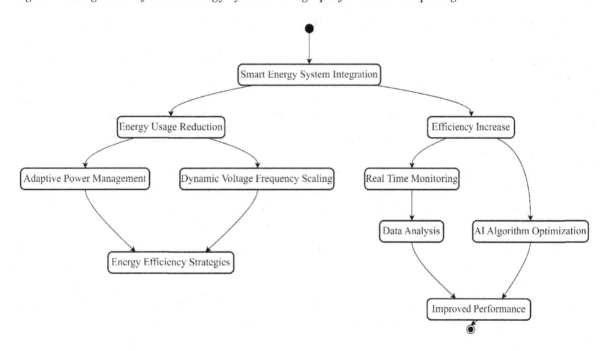

Combining AI with Energy-Efficient Hardware

The energy consumption of an HPC system is mostly dependent on the energy efficiency of the hardware used. Typically, the HPC processors, memory units, and storage devices are designed to be as fast as possible while sacrificing energy efficiency. Analogous to other hardware technologies, recent improvements in processor and storage systems toward energy efficiency opened up new possibilities to further reduce the power footprint of HPC infrastructures.

The potential for AI-driven energy management integrated with energy-efficient hardware would optimize performance while saving energy. As a typical example, many of the modern processors support power-saving modes; among the more notable examples is dynamic voltage and frequency scaling (DVFS). AI can analyze the real-time data associated with demand and change the voltage and frequency of processors at appropriate instances without hindering performance when the demand comes back to the level needed.

Apart from this, AI models are likely to predict when memory or storage components in the system might go idle and consume powers based on those predictions. For example, AI-based memory management algorithms can reduce unnecessary power consumption by selectively putting unused modules of memory into a low-power state without affecting the computational performance.

Integration of AI with energy-efficient hardware extends to the development of neuromorphic chips that emulate the energy-frugal processes that occur in human brains. These chips require orders of magnitude less power than traditional processors, and AI algorithms ensure optimal use, thereby further reducing energy consumption. This kind of smart technology represents an important integration of HPC systems in order to reduce the energy footprint of computationally intensive tasks.

Role of Artificial Intelligence in Data Center Cooling and Infrastructure

Cooling systems are among the biggest energy consumers in HPC data centers-the share reached 40-50% recently. One of the most effective ways to maintain the performance and extend the lifetime of HPC hardware is through effective cooling, but conventional cooling strategies are mainly inefficient because they often lead to important wastes of energy. More and more, AI-based cooling technologies come into play with the goal of maximizing those processes while minimizing both the costs and environmental implications.

AI-powered cooling systems have the ability to continuously monitor and sense data center environments and track temperature, humidity, and airflow amongst other things to find the best way to cool. Machine learning algorithms can predict very early when any areas of the data centre are likely to go into high temperatures, which would enable it to proactively adjust the cooling strategy for those zones. For instance, with AI, overheating in a particular zone of server racks might be detected, and then cooling resources can be targeted to those areas to prevent overheating but only provide minimal cooling at less active zones when not necessary.

Another aspect is how AI models can actually balance the conflicting requirements of air conditioning, liquid cooling, and other parts of the infrastructure to minimize energy usage. Based on real-time loads of the systems, ambient temperatures, and energy prices, AI algorithms can dynamically change the strategy of cooling to switch off or downsize particular cooling units when no one is using them.

In large data centers, AI can even manage the cooling in tandem with all the hardware power management strategies. For instance, AI systems will temporarily minimize the power consumption of specific components during cooling-intensive operations, thus further reducing the total energy load. In this manner, hardware and cooling will synergistically combine their efficiency so that the infrastructure runs absolutely at maximum efficiency without incurring as much waste in terms of energy.

Smart Grids and AI-Driven Energy Distribution

Energy usage optimization by AI does not stop there in HPC systems and data centers, but further engagement with smart grids embodies an innovative approach to energy management in a high-performance computing environment that integrates AI even more into energy distribution networks (Boopathi, 2024; Saravanan et al., 2024).

Energy from providers and data centers, along with any other energy consumers, will be communicated in real time using a smart grid. The AI algorithms would process that real-time demand and supply of energy data to predict the peak usage periods and optimize energy distribution in time. HPC systems can, therefore, have power allocated more efficiently according to the needs of the data center and avoid unnecessary energy consumption.

For example, in peak periods of computation, artificial intelligence systems can cut off the amount of energy supply to secondary users so that HPC operations continue uninterrupted. However, AI systems can scale down energy during low-demand times so as not to consume too much. This is a mechanism by which the data centre will strike a real-time balance in power usage without compromising performance.

Renewable energy sources can also be systematically integrated into energy management in HPC systems through smart grids. AI can determine when such sources are most productive by analyzing data from solar panels, wind turbines, and other renewable sources, then tweaking energy use within the data center to tap into those cleaner energy options. Such HPC systems can thus increase their computations when renewable energy is abundant, but scale down their energy usage when renewable energy generation is low.

Moreover, AI controls energy storage solutions in smart grids, which comprises batteries, holding excess energy generated when the usage of energy is low. AI-based algorithms determine patterns in the consumption of energy and figure out the right time to store the excess energy or release the energy for consumption in the data center when most required, therefore ensuring full deployment of energy efficiency and sustainability.

The integration of smart energy systems into high-performance computing leads to dramatic drifts towards more environmentally friendly operation and efficiency. AI integration with energy-efficient hardware for data centers can severely minimize power intake without impacting performance. Data centers equipped with cooling systems powered by AI adjust their infrastructure in real time with certain environmental factors to reduce energy usage. Simultaneously, smart grids and AI-based energy distribution systems ensure power delivery through means that are efficient and renewable whenever possible. This itself is not just an enhancement to bring the environmental impact of HPC systems further down but also a way in which data centers manage to get operational costs down, making them more competitive and sustainable in the long run.

CASE STUDIES: AI-POWERED ENERGY OPTIMIZATION IN HPC

Case studies regarding the future use of AI in optimizing energy usage in HPC environments have also been taken into account, which greatly reduced power consumption while maintaining an exceptionally high degree of computational performance (Glady et al., 2024; Prasad et al., 2024; Vijaya Lakshmi et al., 2024).

Case Study 1: AI-Optimized Power Efficiency in Scientific Computing

AI was deployed to enhance the power efficiency in high-performance, computationally intensive systems at a huge research institution involved in climate modeling and molecular simulations. The institution employed machine learning algorithms to monitor and predict power consumption of systems. In this way, due to automatic power setting adjustments according to the intensity of the workload, waste energy was reduced around low computation values periods and overall power consumption was reduced by 20%. The AI system not only kept the energy consumption at efficient levels but also preserved all the performance levels demanded by complex scientific simulations without interruption.

Case Study 2: Predictive AI in Data Center Energy Management

A large cloud service provider applied predictive analytics influenced by AI to manage energy consumption at its global data centers. The AI model analyzed historical data about energy usage patterns and the performance of cooling systems to make predictions about future energy demands and dynamically allocate coolings and powers through multiple data centers. This predictive approach helped the provider cut its cooling energy consumption by 30% and run at a lower cost, reducing its carbon footprint. The system always learned from changing environmental conditions and workload variation to deliver the best possible energy management.

Case Study 3: AI for Workload Scheduling to Save Energy

In one of the centers focused on AI and machine learning, AI-based workload scheduling was used to reduce energy consumption. The incoming workloads were checked through AI-based schedulers that scheduled the work in off-peak hours when energy usage was low as the energy cost as well as its demand was low. In addition to this, the AI algorithm also used dynamic resource allocation subject to energy efficiency parameters for an overall 15% decrease in energy intake from the system. Apart from these advantages, this wise scheduling scheme ensured a smooth completion of high priority jobs and reduced the energy cost.

CHALLENGES AND OPPORTUNITIES IN AI-DRIVEN ENERGY MANAGEMENT

On the one hand, there are a lot of opportunities to increase efficiency as well as sustainability in energy management systems by embedding AI into these, but on the other hand, these come with huge hurdles. The understanding of these barriers is important to effectively tapping into AI-driven energy management (Domakonda et al., 2022; Kumara et al., 2023; Samikannu et al., 2022). Figure 4 presents both challenges and opportunities in AI-driven energy management.

Figure 4. Challenges and opportunities in AI-driven energy management.

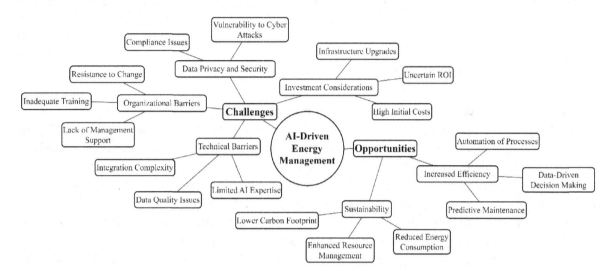

Technical and Organizational Barrier to Adoption

The main technical challenge associated with adopting AI-driven energy management is integrating disparate systems. Many organizations face legacy infrastructure that by no means is compatible with advanced AI technologies. This generally means that even the normal data collection and analysis tasks prove inefficient and deprive the AI applications of their due effectiveness. Additionally, usually, there is a gap in skills within any organization because the workforce might lack expertise on AI and machine learning, which further hampers the effective implementation and maintenance of such a system.

Organizational barriers to change are very serious. Some of the essential reasons for stakeholders not wanting to adopt AI solutions include the fear of disruption and uncertainty on the possible return that would be made. Organizational culture also speaks; if leadership does not add emphasis or understand the core value that AI can add in terms of energy management, then the project initiatives will lack enough support and are doomed to death.

Investment and Infrastructure Considerations

It is high costs that can be one of the demotivational factors for most organizations, particularly SMEs, since investing in AI-driven energy management is a very costly affair. High initial costs are incurred in technology acquisition, upgradation of existing infrastructure, and training personnel. Moreover, the long-term nature of ROI for AI investments might dissuade decision-makers who operate under the lens of short-term financial performance.

In addition, the infrastructure for AI-driven systems usually needs to be developed to face more demanding requirements. For instance, modernized data gathering and storage with high-speed connectivity for real-time analytics must be provided. Thus, organizations have to assess the existing infrastructure already in place to establish whether it can support AI technologies or whether significant upgrades will be required.

Data Privacy and Security in AI-Based Systems

Collection and processing concerns of data include privacy and security issues on account of the incredible amounts of data that AI systems need to rely on to operate. Huge amounts of energy consumption data raise information security concerns about seeing and using information that should not be seen or used without explicit consent. Data governance policies should, therefore, be very strict within organizations and aligned to various regulations, such as GDPR or CCPA, that demand explicit transparency about the usage of data and explicit consent from the users.

Most AI systems are vulnerable to cyber-attacks, which may breach not only the integrity of the energy management system but also the privacy of user data. Organizations have, therefore, to invest significantly in cybersecurity for protection. The process involves continuous monitoring of security measures, updating security protocols, and educating employees on potential threats.

All that complexity and obstruction to the adoption of AI-driven energy management notwithstanding, the scope for innovation and efficiency are limitless. Key technical and organizational barriers must be addressed, including strategic investment in infrastructure of data privacy and security. And if organizations embrace them, they will be able to unlock all that AI technology can be - further sound the drum for sustainability and operational efficiency, and establish organizations competitively in a fast-changing landscape: energy-related.

FUTURE DIRECTIONS IN AI AND HPC ENERGY OPTIMIZATION

As HPC usage expands, the urgent requirements for efficiency are not lost sight of with respect to energy usage. Here, one sees AI playing the most important role, in which the whole set of emerging technologies and trends promises to make HPC infrastructures at once more sustainable and scalable (Domakonda et al., 2022; Kumara et al., 2023; Vennila et al., 2022). Figure 5 outlines the future directions in AI and energy optimization for high-performance computing.

Figure 5. Future directions in AI and energy optimization for high-performance computing

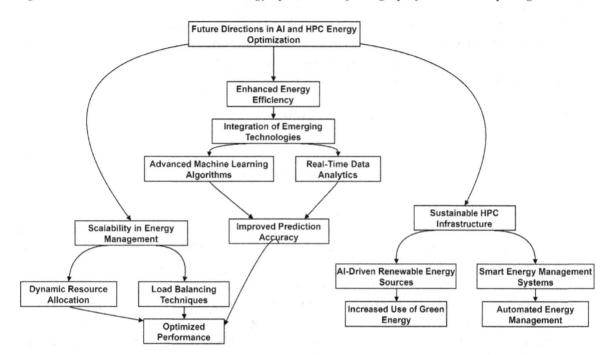

Emerging AI Technologies for Energy Efficiency

There are several emerging cutting-edge AI technologies that promise to change the landscape of energy optimization in HPC systems. Deep Reinforcement Learning (DRL) could empower systems to learn from complex environments and optimally use energy on the fly within a given scenario. DRL can dynamically manage power settings, cooling systems, and hardware utilization to downsize energy consumption while maintaining computational performance.

Another trend of interest that's emerging is Federated Learning, where AI models can be trained in the presence of multiple decentralized data sources without transferring sensitive data. This approach allows energy consumption to be optimized within geographically distributed HPC environments and may support local energy optimization strategies while maintaining an overview of system performance worldwide.

The other rapidly advancing trend is AI-oriented edge computing, which pushes data processing closer to its origin, thereby reducing the energy and bandwidth tied up in data transfers to central HPC systems. AI thus done at the edge may lead to more energy-efficient HPC operations while enhancing efficiency.

Scalability and Future Outlook of Green HPC

Scalability becomes an important factor for future HPC platforms, with the amount of data and computation showing no signs of decline. Resource allocation using AI is poised to become quite central in the management of scaling of the HPC environment. The workload demands can be predicted using machine learning algorithms and accordingly energy resources can be allocated. The high and large-scale HPC environments thus are able to work with varied loads efficiently.

In addition, green HPC will be furthered by growth in the use of renewable energy supplies, especially solar and wind. Such renewable energy sources are incorporated more effectively into HPC systems through the power of AI. The smart energy grids with AI-driven load balancing can make greater utilization of renewable energy by the HPC data centers, allowing for a greener future.

The Evolution of Sustainable Computing in AI

There will be more involvement of AI in sustainable computing because the objective of mitigating the associated operational impact is still intensely imbided in the management of organizations. Predictive analytics will make it possible to determine energy consumption and increase resource utilization efficiency by multiple rounds of forecasting and optimal resource allocation. This will consequently result in waste reduction, improved uptime, and energy-efficient computation. Looking forward, quantum computing can also find use in energy optimization for HPC systems. Although it is still at the embryonic stage of realization, the fact that quantum computing promises to perform complex computations with largely reduced energy compared to traditional HPC means a lot for the future of sustainable computing.

With their maturing vision, the next leap for future AI-driven energy optimization in HPC will arrive via technologies now emerging: DRL, federated learning, and edge computing. As they advance, these innovations will make scalable, green, and sustainable HPC systems a reality. By managing and incorporating renewable energy through AI, organizations can drastically reduce their carbon footprint toward the evolutionary foray into sustainable computing.

CONCLUSION

High-Performance Computing AI-driven energy optimization can be a significant step toward a sustainable transformation and maximizing efficiency. Techniques such as machine learning, reinforcement learning, and predictive analytics could significantly optimize several aspects of energy usage in HPC operations-ranging from scheduling workloads to cooling-at the organizational level-with reductions in operating costs while minimizing or reducing all environmental impacts, hence serving the growing concerns of modern computing related to energy consumption.

As AI technologies continue to grow, their adoption with HPC systems will keep advancing developments within energy management toward the greener, more effective infrastructure. Because AI is an adaption to dynamic workloads that predicts the energy demand, it also promises several future breakthroughs in these areas, considering how more organizations today are gravitating towards sustainability.

However, integrating AI for energy management comes with its technical, organizational, and infrastructural challenges that will definitely need to be addressed in order to harvest the complete potential of AI. Scalability of HPC towards sustainability is critically dependent on achieving its full promise and is well supported by all the ongoing efforts in making AI an enabler in this vision-a move toward a much more energy-efficient and environmentally responsible computing landscape.

REFERENCES

Boopathi, S. (2024). Advancements in Optimizing Smart Energy Systems Through Smart Grid Integration, Machine Learning, and IoT. In *Advances in Environmental Engineering and Green Technologies* (pp. 33–61). IGI Global. DOI: 10.4018/979-8-3693-0492-1.ch002

Bouhamed, O. (2022a). *AI-Powered Time Series Forecasting Frameworks For Building Energy Management Systems* [PhD Thesis]. Concordia University.

Bouhamed, O. (2022b). *AI-Powered Time Series Forecasting Frameworks For Building Energy Management Systems* [PhD Thesis]. Concordia University.

Ciabattoni, L., Comodi, G., Ferracuti, F., & Foresi, G. (2020). Ai-powered home electrical appliances as enabler of demand-side flexibility. *IEEE Consumer Electronics Magazine*, 9(3), 72–78. DOI: 10.1109/MCE.2019.2956197

Czarnul, P., Proficz, J., & Krzywaniak, A. (2019). Energy-aware high-performance computing: Survey of state-of-the-art tools, techniques, and environments. *Scientific Programming*, 2019, 2019. DOI: 10.1155/2019/8348791

Domakonda, V. K., Farooq, S., Chinthamreddy, S., Puviarasi, R., Sudhakar, M., & Boopathi, S. (2022). Sustainable Developments of Hybrid Floating Solar Power Plants: Photovoltaic System. In *Human Agro-Energy Optimization for Business and Industry* (pp. 148–167). IGI Global.

Ejarque, J., Badia, R. M., Albertin, L., Aloisio, G., Baglione, E., Becerra, Y., Boschert, S., Berlin, J. R., D'Anca, A., Elia, D., Exertier, F., Fiore, S., Flich, J., Folch, A., Gibbons, S. J., Koldunov, N., Lordan, F., Lorito, S., Løvholt, F., & Volpe, M. (2022). Enabling dynamic and intelligent workflows for HPC, data analytics, and AI convergence. *Future Generation Computer Systems*, 134, 414–429. DOI: 10.1016/j.future.2022.04.014

Esnaola-Gonzalez, I., Jelić, M., Pujić, D., Diez, F. J., & Tomašević, N. (2021). An AI-powered system for residential demand response. *Electronics (Basel)*, 10(6), 693. DOI: 10.3390/electronics10060693

Glady, J. B. P., D'Souza, S. M., Priya, A. P., Amuthachenthiru, K., Vikram, G., & Boopathi, S. (2024). A Study on AI-ML-Driven Optimizing Energy Distribution and Sustainable Agriculture for Environmental Conservation. In *Harnessing High-Performance Computing and AI for Environmental Sustainability* (pp. 1–27). IGI Global., DOI: 10.4018/979-8-3693-1794-5.ch001

Gregory, G. D., Ngo, L. V., & Karavdic, M. (2019). Developing e-commerce marketing capabilities and efficiencies for enhanced performance in business-to-business export ventures. *Industrial Marketing Management*, 78, 146–157. DOI: 10.1016/j.indmarman.2017.03.002

Hanelt, A., Bohnsack, R., Marz, D., & Antunes Marante, C. (2021). A systematic review of the literature on digital transformation: Insights and implications for strategy and organizational change. *Journal of Management Studies*, 58(5), 1159–1197. DOI: 10.1111/joms.12639

Hema, N., Krishnamoorthy, N., Chavan, S. M., Kumar, N., Sabarimuthu, M., & Boopathi, S. (2023). A Study on an Internet of Things (IoT)-Enabled Smart Solar Grid System. In *Handbook of Research on Deep Learning Techniques for Cloud-Based Industrial IoT* (pp. 290–308). IGI Global. DOI: 10.4018/978-1-6684-8098-4.ch017

Huang, Y., Fan, X., Chen, S.-C., & Zhao, N. (2019). Emerging technologies of flexible pressure sensors: Materials, modeling, devices, and manufacturing. *Advanced Functional Materials*, 29(12), 1808509. DOI: 10.1002/adfm.201808509

Kaushik, N., Gill, A., & Raghavendra, R. (2024). Frontiers of Artificial Intelligence Through Accelerated Model Training and Optimization Techniques. *2024 IEEE 13th International Conference on Communication Systems and Network Technologies (CSNT)*, 995–1002.

Kavitha, C., Varalatchoumy, M., Mithuna, H., Bharathi, K., Geethalakshmi, N., & Boopathi, S. (2023). Energy Monitoring and Control in the Smart Grid: Integrated Intelligent IoT and ANFIS. In *Applications of Synthetic Biology in Health, Energy, and Environment* (pp. 290–316). IGI Global.

Kelechi, A. H., Alsharif, M. H., Bameyi, O. J., Ezra, P. J., Joseph, I. K., Atayero, A.-A., Geem, Z. W., & Hong, J. (2020). Artificial intelligence: An energy efficiency tool for enhanced high performance computing. *Symmetry*, 12(6), 1029. DOI: 10.3390/sym12061029

Kumara, V., Mohanaprakash, T., Fairooz, S., Jamal, K., Babu, T., & Sampath, B. (2023). Experimental Study on a Reliable Smart Hydroponics System. In *Human Agro-Energy Optimization for Business and Industry* (pp. 27–45). IGI Global. DOI: 10.4018/978-1-6684-4118-3.ch002

Kwaku, W. K. (2023). Sustainable Cloud Computing with AI-Driven Resource Optimization. *Advances in Computer Sciences, 6*(1).

Ligozat, A.-L., Lefevre, J., Bugeau, A., & Combaz, J. (2022). Unraveling the hidden environmental impacts of AI solutions for environment life cycle assessment of AI solutions. *Sustainability (Basel)*, 14(9), 5172. DOI: 10.3390/su14095172

Long, L. D. (2023). An AI-driven model for predicting and optimizing energy-efficient building envelopes. *Alexandria Engineering Journal*, 79, 480–501. DOI: 10.1016/j.aej.2023.08.041

Mahmoud, M., & Slama, S. B. (2023). Peer-to-Peer Energy Trading Case Study Using an AI-Powered Community Energy Management System. *Applied Sciences (Basel, Switzerland)*, 13(13), 7838. DOI: 10.3390/app13137838

Mohammad, A., & Mahjabeen, F. (2023). Revolutionizing Solar Energy with AI-Driven Enhancements in Photovoltaic Technology. *BULLET: Jurnal Multidisiplin Ilmu*, 2(4), 1174–1187.

Prasad, M. S. C., Dhanalakshmi, M., Mohan, M., Somasundaram, B., Valarmathi, R., & Boopathi, S. (2024). Machine Learning-Integrated Sustainable Engineering and Energy Systems: Innovations at the Nexus. In *Harnessing High-Performance Computing and AI for Environmental Sustainability* (pp. 74–98). IGI Global. DOI: 10.4018/979-8-3693-1794-5.ch004

Salama, A. K., & Abdellatif, M. M. (2022). AIoT-based Smart Home Energy Management System. *2022 IEEE Global Conference on Artificial Intelligence and Internet of Things (GCAIoT)*, 177–181.

Samikannu, R., Koshariya, A. K., Poornima, E., Ramesh, S., Kumar, A., & Boopathi, S. (2022). Sustainable Development in Modern Aquaponics Cultivation Systems Using IoT Technologies. In *Human Agro-Energy Optimization for Business and Industry* (pp. 105–127). IGI Global.

Saravanan, S., Khare, R., Umamaheswari, K., Khare, S., Krishne Gowda, B. S., & Boopathi, S. (2024). AI and ML Adaptive Smart-Grid Energy Management Systems: Exploring Advanced Innovations. In *Principles and Applications in Speed Sensing and Energy Harvesting for Smart Roads* (pp. 166–196). IGI Global. DOI: 10.4018/978-1-6684-9214-7.ch006

Sathupadi, K. (2023). Ai-driven energy optimization in sdn-based cloud computing for balancing cost, energy efficiency, and network performance. *International Journal of Applied Machine Learning and Computational Intelligence*, 13(7), 11–37.

Tovazzi, D., Faticanti, F., Siracusa, D., Peroni, C., Cretti, S., & Gazzini, T. (2020). GEM-Analytics: Cloud-to-Edge AI-Powered Energy Management. *Economics of Grids, Clouds, Systems, and Services:17th International Conference, GECON 2020,Izola, Slovenia,September 15–17, 2020, Revised Selected Papers 17*, 57–66.

Troisi, O., Maione, G., Grimaldi, M., & Loia, F. (2020). Growth hacking: Insights on data-driven decision-making from three firms. *Industrial Marketing Management*, 90, 538–557. DOI: 10.1016/j.indmarman.2019.08.005

Venkateswaran, N., Vidhya, K., Ayyannan, M., Chavan, S. M., Sekar, K., & Boopathi, S. (2023). A Study on Smart Energy Management Framework Using Cloud Computing. In *5G, Artificial Intelligence, and Next Generation Internet of Things: Digital Innovation for Green and Sustainable Economies* (pp. 189–212). IGI Global. DOI: 10.4018/978-1-6684-8634-4.ch009

Vennila, T., Karuna, M., Srivastava, B. K., Venugopal, J., Surakasi, R., & Sampath, B. (2022). New Strategies in Treatment and Enzymatic Processes: Ethanol Production From Sugarcane Bagasse. In *Human Agro-Energy Optimization for Business and Industry* (pp. 219–240). IGI Global.

Vijaya Lakshmi, V., Mishra, M., Kushwah, J. S., Shajahan, U. S., Mohanasundari, M., & Boopathi, S. (2024). Circular Economy Digital Practices for Ethical Dimensions and Policies for Digital Waste Management. In *Harnessing High-Performance Computing and AI for Environmental Sustainability* (pp. 166–193). IGI Global., DOI: 10.4018/979-8-3693-1794-5.ch008

Wang, G., Luo, Z., Desta, H. G., Chen, M., Dong, Y., & Lin, B. (2024). AI-driven development of high-performance solid-state hydrogen storage. *Energy Reviews*, 100106.

Wang, S., Zheng, H., Wen, X., & Fu, S. (2024). Distributed high-performance computing methods for accelerating deep learning training. *Journal of Knowledge Learning and Science Technology ISSN: 2959-6386 (Online), 3*(3), 108–126.

Wu, C.-J., Raghavendra, R., Gupta, U., Acun, B., Ardalani, N., Maeng, K., Chang, G., Aga, F., Huang, J., & Bai, C. (2022). Sustainable ai: Environmental implications, challenges and opportunities. *Proceedings of Machine Learning and Systems*, 4, 795–813.

ADDITIONAL READING

Boopathi, S. (2024). Energy Cascade Conversion System and Energy-Efficient Infrastructure. In *Sustainable Development in AI, Blockchain, and E-Governance Applications* (pp. 47–71). IGI Global. DOI: 10.4018/979-8-3693-1722-8.ch004

Domakonda, V. K., Farooq, S., Chinthamreddy, S., Puviarasi, R., Sudhakar, M., & Boopathi, S. (2022). Sustainable Developments of Hybrid Floating Solar Power Plants: Photovoltaic System. In *Human Agro-Energy Optimization for Business and Industry* (pp. 148–167). IGI Global.

Glady, J. B. P., D'Souza, S. M., Priya, A. P., Amuthachenthiru, K., Vikram, G., & Boopathi, S. (2024). A Study on AI-ML-Driven Optimizing Energy Distribution and Sustainable Agriculture for Environmental Conservation. In *Harnessing High-Performance Computing and AI for Environmental Sustainability* (pp. 1–27). IGI Global., DOI: 10.4018/979-8-3693-1794-5.ch001

Khare, R., Chinnasamy, A., Shashibhushan, G., Suresh Kumar, P., Hemalatha, R., & Boopathi, S. (2024). Energy Cascade Conversion System and Energy-Efficient Infrastructure: Experimentation, Results, Discussion, and Case Studies. In *Advances in Environmental Engineering and Green Technologies* (pp. 115–139). IGI Global. DOI: 10.4018/979-8-3693-0492-1.ch006

Nishanth, J., Deshmukh, M. A., Kushwah, R., Kushwaha, K. K., Balaji, S., & Sampath, B. (2023). Particle Swarm Optimization of Hybrid Renewable Energy Systems. In *Intelligent Engineering Applications and Applied Sciences for Sustainability* (pp. 291–308). IGI Global. DOI: 10.4018/979-8-3693-0044-2.ch016

S., B. (2024). Advancements in Optimizing Smart Energy Systems Through Smart Grid Integration, Machine Learning, and IoT. In *Advances in Environmental Engineering and Green Technologies* (pp. 33–61). IGI Global. DOI: 10.4018/979-8-3693-0492-1.ch002

Tirlangi, S., Teotia, S., Padmapriya, G., Senthil Kumar, S., Dhotre, S., & Boopathi, S. (2024). Cloud Computing and Machine Learning in the Green Power Sector: Data Management and Analysis for Sustainable Energy. In *Developments Towards Next Generation Intelligent Systems for Sustainable Development* (pp. 148–179). IGI Global. DOI: 10.4018/979-8-3693-5643-2.ch006

Venkateswaran, N., Kumar, S. S., Diwakar, G., Gnanasangeetha, D., & Boopathi, S. (2023). Synthetic Biology for Waste Water to Energy Conversion: IoT and AI Approaches. *Applications of Synthetic Biology in Health. Energy & Environment*, ●●●, 360–384.

KEY TERMS AND DEFINITIONS

AI: Artificial Intelligence. Simulation of human intelligence in machines for solving problems.

CCPA: California Consumer Privacy Act. It is the data privacy regulation introduced by the state of California.

CO: Carbon Monoxide. Emission associated with energy consumption.

DRL: Deep Reinforcement Learning. This is an advanced technique of Reinforcement Learning coupled with deep learning techniques.

DVFS: Dynamic Voltage and Frequency Scaling. A technique to decrease the power consumption of systems.

GDPR: General Data Protection Regulation. A legal regulation of the European Union regarding data privacy.

HPC: High-Performance Computing. A computer system that performs complex computations with high efficiency.

ML: Machine Learning. Subset of AI to analyze data.

RL: Reinforcement Learning. Method of ML for effective decision making.

ROI: Return on Investment. A measure of the profitability of investment.

SME: Small and Medium Enterprises. Business organizations with limited resources.

Chapter 12
Application of Federated Learning and Gestural Technology in Healthcare

C. Indhumathi

Department of Computer and Business Systems, Sri Sairam Engineering College, Chennai, India

Shaik Abdul Hameed

Department of Computer Science and Engineering, VNR VJIET, Hyderabad, India

R. Jothilakshmi

Department of Information Technology, R.M.D. Engineering College, Chennai, India

Syed Musthafa A.

Department of Information Technology, M. Kumarasamy College of Engineering, Karur, India

M. Ramesh Babu

Department of Electrical and Electronics Engineering, St. Joseph's College of Engineering, Chennai, India

S. Muthuvel

https://orcid.org/0009-0000-1194-2907

Kalasalingam Academy of Research and Education, Srivilliputhur, India

ABSTRACT

This chapter explores the integration of federated learning and gestural technology in the healthcare sector, aiming to enhance patient care, diagnostics, and treatment. Federated learning allows decentralized machine learning models to train on patient data from multiple healthcare institutions while maintaining privacy, making it ideal for protecting sensitive medical data. Gestural technology is mainly utilized in human-computer interaction to assist healthcare professionals in the management of accessibility and usability of healthcare systems, especially during remote diagnostics and rehabilitation. The integration of these two technologies ensures that individualized care can be achieved, workflow operations streamlined, and outcomes improved without compromising data security. It also explores use cases of telemedicine, rehabilitation, and clinical decision support, addressing challenges like data privacy, model accuracy, and technical integration.

DOI: 10.4018/978-1-6684-3795-7.ch012

INTRODUCTION

Healthcare technology has evolved at a very rapid pace, especially regarding the diagnosis of patients and their respective treatments and care. Among the new innovations that herald a new way of healthcare delivery and management are federated learning and gestural technology. Federated learning is decentralized and focuses on data privacy, while gestural technology is involved in intuitive human-computer interaction, wherein numerous benefit flows from one another. Together they provide an avenue through which accessibility, efficiency, and personalization of health care can be optimized (Navaz et al., 2021).

Federated learning (FL) is particularly suitable for healthcare because it responds to one of the industry's most pressing concerns: privacy in patient data. Traditional machine learning requires data to be centralized and even moves sensitive medical information to third-party servers for analysis. This centralized approach works well in other sectors, but it is a huge challenge in healthcare due to the privacy laws governing health care in jurisdictions such as the Health Insurance Portability and Accountability Act (HIPAA) in the United States and the the General Data Protection Regulation (GDPR) in Europe. This is where federated learning has come in as a valuable solution. Machine learning models are now able to be trained locally on the devices or servers of different healthcare institutions, without having to transfer the data from patients. Instead, model updates are exchanged between the institutions (Nguyen et al., 2022). Thus, patient data remains confidential. The fully decentralized scheme of the system ensures the fact that health care providers can avail themselves of robust data-driven insights while staying compliant with data protection laws.

In addition to preserving privacy, federated learning enables healthcare institutions to aggregate their pool of data without allowing the access of security to be compromised. Medical data is fragmented by nature since each hospital, clinic, and specialized institution holds patient records. Federated learning allows these parties to collaborate through training of machine-learning models on different datasets and thus improves the model generalization and accuracy. This method could significantly improve the development of predictive models for the detection of diseases, planning treatments, and monitoring patients through federated learning. Furthermore, since sensitive information resides in the local environment, federated learning minimizes the attack surface for any potential cyber threats and thereby reduces data breaches (Sun & Wu, 2022).

In contrast, gestural technology is a new field for interaction between healthcare providers and digital systems. With the advent of digitization in the health care sector, the increasing trend of electronic health records and telemedicine platforms, combined with the initiation of robotic-assisted surgeries, making interfaces intelligent and efficient has become an issue of burgeoning importance. This is supported by gestural technology because body control of digital systems can be rich with hand gestures or even facial expressions. This interface is especially useful in aseptic environments, such as operating rooms, where keyboards and touch screens are either impractical or even dangerous to use. A surgeon can use gestures to manipulate medical imaging, access patient data, or control robotic instruments without touching anything, thus avoiding the risk of contamination (Sun & Wu, 2022).

Patient input and participation in their cure processes can also be enhanced through gestural technology, helping patients rehabilitate more effectively after treatment. Gesture-based systems are utilized for patients recovering from accidents or through physical therapy. Such a system can make a patient perform exercises by keeping an eye on his improvements, providing the user with instantaneous feedback. Usually, such systems use motion sensors or camera-based technology, so they can be applied even in the clinical environment or at home for continuous monitoring and personalized care. The simplicity of access and usage, offered by gestural interfaces, has great appeal for people with mobility impairments or lack the expertise to work with sophisticated devices; this aspect of gestural interfaces promotes accessibility in the health fields (Singh et al., 2022).

The federated learning and gestural technology combined hold transformative possibilities that may simplify the health systems involved. Alone, but within a singular application, the two technologies may offer much more responsive, personalized care while strictly maintaining the tightest data security standards. This, for example may be the federated learning models that adapt to the progress of each patient in real-time and improve continuously the exercise and recovery plans based on anonymized data from several patients located in various places. It basically represents a feedback loop which creates an effective dynamic system: in use, with each iteration it becomes better suited to patient-specific problems (Bashir et al., 2023).

In telemedicine, an area where there has been exponential growth, especially during and after the COVID-19 pandemic, federated learning combined with the combination of gestural technologies is promising. Telemedicine platforms with gesture-based control can facilitate user experience both to healthcare providers and patients. Telehealth professionals can easily touch navigators for patient information or change the settings of teleconferences with easy hand gestures, while federated learning can be used to carry out real-time analysis on telemedicine data to offer predictors to clinicians on the outcome of patients through big decentralized datasets of all the previous telehealth consultations. This not only improves the accuracy of diagnosis but also provides proactive, patient-centric care delivery even in remote locations (Chaddad et al., 2023).

The gestural technology with federated learning has significant ramifications in clinical decision support systems (CDSS). CDSS is a critical support system in contemporary health care because it delivers real-time, evidence-based suggestions to the clinicians at the time of diagnosis or treatment planning. Such systems can utilize interoperability to develop gestural interfaces that allow clinicians to intuitively interact with complex data visualizations or treatment pathways liberated from the constraints of traditional methods of input. Federated learning advances these systems by making optimal use of insights derived from a wide array of institutions in providing recommendations based upon more comprehensive and current information (Gahlan & Sethia, 2024). This can, therefore lead to more informed decision-making and better patient outcomes especially in fast-paced environments like emergency rooms or intensive care units

Federated learning as well as the gestural technology in health care is not without challenges. Data security is the major concern. Federated learning still has a potential cyber threat in the process of transferring model updates between institutions despite offering higher privacy compared to traditional approaches to machine learning. A cyber-attack to model updates may damage model integrity or steal personal information held in data if not encrypted appropriately. Also, gestural technology applies sensors and cameras to capture user movements. This can raise patient privacy concerns, especially when practiced in sensitive environments like hospitals. Increasing usage by many health care systems also will depend in large part on assurance of adequate security and compliance with key health care regulations (Bashir et al., 2023).

There also are technical barriers. Federated learning models are computationally intensive and require significant infrastructure, which may be a limiting factor for smaller health care providers or those in developing regions. Ensuring model accuracy in the presence of disparate datasets with variable quality also remains one of the biggest challenges. Even though gestural technology is intuitive, it would have to be extremely refined to capture a lot of user movement with good accuracy and consistency. Lighting differences, user positioning, or background noise are among the factors that influence the performance of the systems; therefore, software developers should create strong and flexible systems (Ali et al., 2022).

Besides that, ethical and regulatory considerations have to be faced in these technologies. In order not to perpetuate disparities in patient care through the biased models, federated learning models must be free of bias. Similarly, in the deployment of gestural technology, the patient's consent with regard to considerations of ethical use of motion data must be accommodated. Regulated frameworks in such innovative and emerging arenas of AI and healthcare technology must keep pace with the technology itself, so these uses are responsibly applied for the good of all patients (Chen et al., 2021).

Federated learning combined with gestural technology is not only a great combination that has the potential to reshape health care but also can become a vessel for realizing a more efficient, accessible, and personalized healthcare system satisfying both innovation and patient well-being.

FEDERATED LEARNING IN HEALTHCARE

Federated learning, in this case, is a rather revolutionary approach to machine learning that precisely responds to issues related to privacy and security inherent in industries such as the healthcare sector. Traditional, classic machine learning models demand centralization, and therefore, large datasets need to be brought together in a single location for purposes of training. Such an approach introduces grave privacy risks, which are also critical in healthcare, considering the strict regulations under which sensitive patient data is protected, such as the HIPAA for the U.S. and GDPR in Europe. The alternative is to provide a way to create machine learning models without allowing raw data transfer. Instead, training happens locally at each site using local private datasets, but the model updates, that is the learned patterns and parameters-are shared back to a central server in return. This decentralized approach retains patient data privacy while facilitating collaboration on machine learning across institutions. Figure 1 illustrates the iterative and decentralized nature of federated learning, highlighting its suitability for sensitive applications like healthcare (Jiang et al., 2024).

Figure 1. Process of federated learning in healthcare

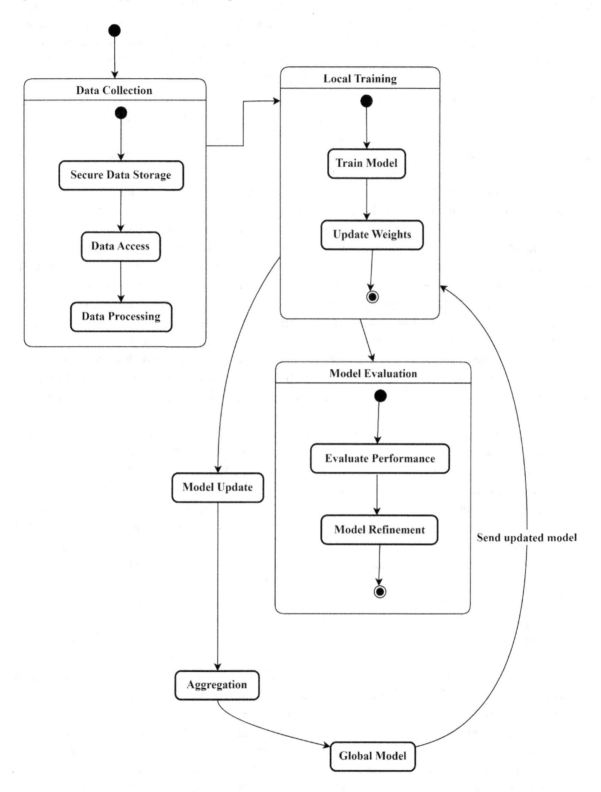

Federated learning is founded on the concepts of decentralization, collaboration, and privacy. Federated learning differs from the traditional machine learning, which relies on transferring raw data for centralized processing. In the federated learning system, raw data is meant to be kept locally in hospitals or clinics. An individual entity trains its local version of the machine learning model on its local dataset, sometimes transmitting the updates of the model itself, namely, the parameters or gradients of the model, to a central server for aggregation at periods. This server aggregates updates coming from all participating entities and proceeds to produce a global model that benefits from the insights gleaned across the network. No raw data is allowed to leave the local environment and sensitive information is never exposed beyond its origin. Since patient data would be stored within the federation boundaries, federated learning tends to support a privacy-preserving structure and thereby decrease the likelihood of data breaches as well as respect data protection regulations.

One of the important features of privacy-preserving machine learning models is collaboration without possibly compromising the confidentiality of the data. For example, in healthcare applications, where the data are dispersed across multiple systems and organizations, federated learning facilitates an organization-centric way of developing more accurate and resilient models within organizations. For instance, hospitals from diverse regions or countries can train the same model on local datasets, integrating insights from various populations with different characteristics and medical histories. Differential privacy and homomorphic encryption are some of the applicable techniques for additional augmentation to the security of the dataset. Differential privacy ensures that the results of statistical analysis on the data are such that the re-identification of individuals is minimized, regardless of the extent to which many datasets are combined. Homomorphic encryption is an encryption method which effectively permits computations to be conducted on encrypted data so that information remains safeguarded during the entire process. These advanced privacy measures make federated learning an ideal solution for data-driven industries like healthcare.

The applications in patient data and diagnostics are immense, as federated learning allows institutes to use machine learning without breaching the confidentiality of patient data. Predictive analytics in disease detection is one of the first successful applications of federated learning. Through federated learning, models can be trained from multiple hospital data sets for increasing the precision in diagnosis-related predictive outputs about conditions like cancer, diabetes, or heart disease. These models are more likely to generalize and make precise predictions on different populations of patients as they enjoy a higher diversity of patient data. Federated learning also aids in enhancing the precision of the treatment plans. In precision medicine where treatments are administered according to an individual's genetic makeup and clinical history, federated learning enables institutions to train a larger dataset from different sources, resulting in better treatment recommendations and outcomes. Another application of federated learning is in the usage of real-time patient monitoring, particularly in intensive care units, where analytics-based machine learning models might analyze data streams from hundreds of patients to alert healthcare providers to potential complications or adverse events.

Despite the advantages discussed above, federated learning also presents a variety of challenges in healthcare environments. The first challenge is that each participating institution requires robust computational infrastructure. Training federated machine learning models is extremely computationally intensive, and small health-care facilities may not have the necessary computational infrastructure to participate in federated learning networks. Additionally, the data used by different institutions would vary in quality and format, making it challenging to harmonize model updates. For instance, while hospital A in one region uses sensors for data collection in a manner that is far from that of a hospital in another region, it is then very difficult to confirm whether model updates will actually be compatible and relevant. This is why, on one hand, uniform model updates as well as the fact that data is still representative of the general population is what plays an important role in determining whether federated learning shall prove successful in healthcare.

While federated learning improves privacy because it keeps the data localized, the mechanism of aggregating model updates is vulnerable to certain attacks, for example, model inversion or poisoning attacks. A model inversion attack could allow an adversary to reconstruct sensitive patient data from the model updates that were shared with the central server. Another form of attack is known as poisoning. Here, an attacker corrupted the training data for local models, thus invalidating the validity of the global model. Countermeasures to such security threats include sophisticated cryptography and robust authentication with regards to guaranteeing the integrity of every update of the model.

Taking all these considerations into account, it appears that federated learning for healthcare can solve some of the most major challenges in medical data analysis- that is, privacy and security issues but on a cooperation basis. That decentralized approach enables institutions to build genuinely powerful models of machine learning without exposing sensitive information about patients, thus being attractive for use in diagnostics, personalized medicine, and patient monitoring. While it opens many avenues for achieving the benefits of federated learning, there is also a corresponding technical and security approach on the part of the healthcare providers to ensure that it is private and useful.

GESTURAL TECHNOLOGY IN HEALTHCARE

With gestural technology, interaction with digital systems will be changed in a more natural and intuitive manner in the control of devices and data interaction. It leads this revolution concerning patient care, medical training, rehabilitation, and surgical procedures in healthcare. Gestural interfaces help health care practitioners and patients share information with technology using gestures and facial expressions or by body gestures, thus reducing face-to-face contact with surfaces and devices and, consequently, hygiene, precision, and access are improved (Ali et al., 2022; Chen et al., 2021; Gahlan & Sethia, 2024). Figure 2 explores the utilization of gestural interfaces in patient care, medical training, rehabilitation, and surgical procedures.

Figure 2. Structure of gestural technology in healthcare

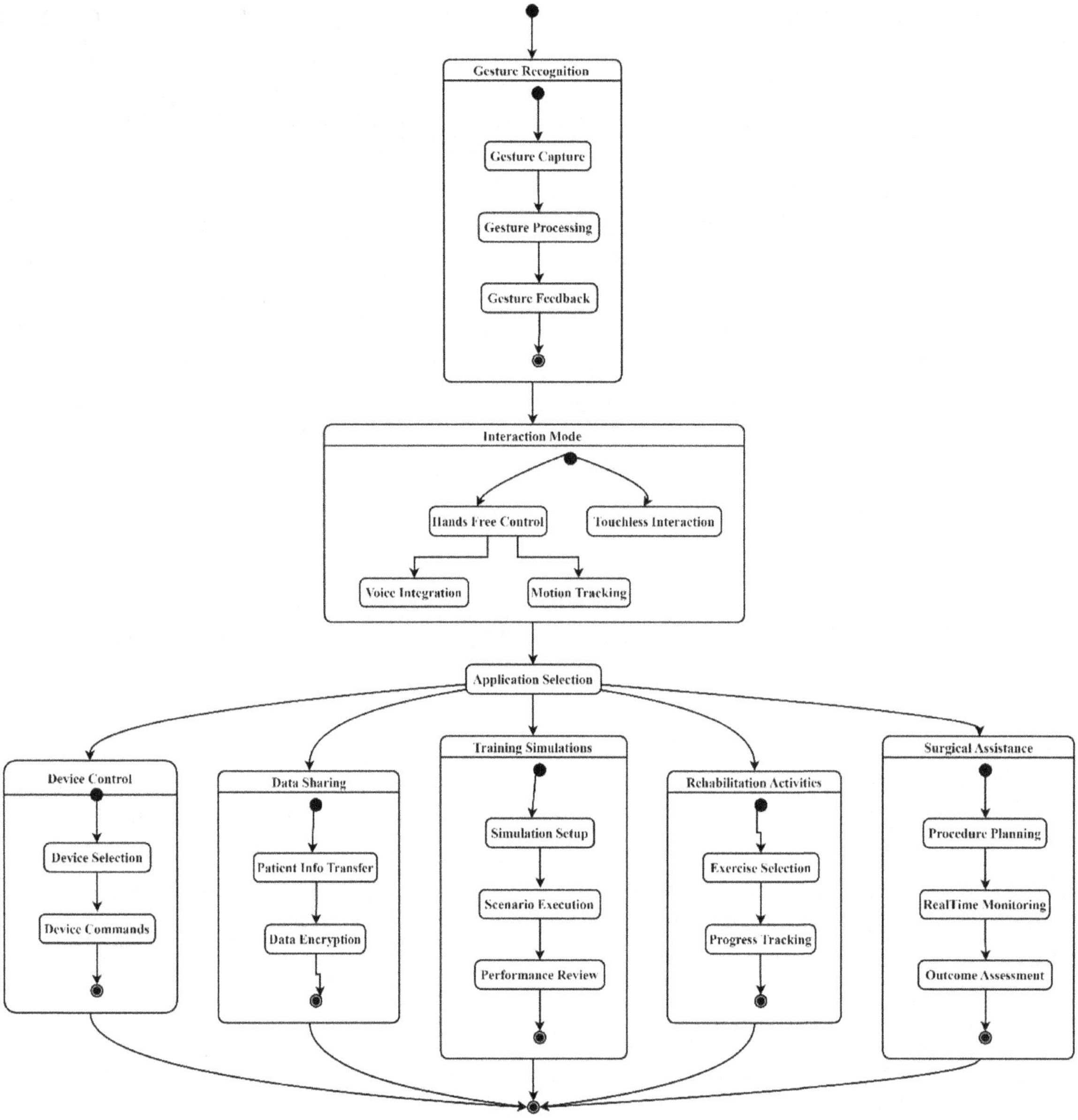

Basics of Gestural Interfaces

Gesture interaction allows for the remote access of digital systems through direct use of physical gestures instead of keyboards or touch screens. Computer vision, motion sensors, depth-sensing cameras, and algorithms of machine learning are used to record real-time human movement through gesture recognition. In gestures, movements which identify by hand or arm, or even the full body, in order to issue commands or control virtual objects (Jiang et al., 2024).

Another general categorization of the overarching gestural interfaces is into two categories: touchless and touch-based. Touchless gestural systems rely upon sensors that can catch movements from distances, much like Microsoft Kinect or Leap Motion devices. These are highly appreciated in a sterile environment such as the operating room, where the prevention of superficial invasion of microbes is one of the bases of infection control. Touch-based systems rely on contact, where the gestures applied can include swiping or pinching on touch screens to give a command. However, in healthcare, the touchless version proves most useful, particularly in clinical settings where hygiene and contact minimization may be key concerns.

Gestural interfaces have great benefits such as easing workflow and mental burden from people, and it also ensures that technology is accessed by everyone despite physical disabilities. For instance, it can assist health workers to control diagnostic equipment, gain access to patient records, or explore three-dimensional models of medical scans without having to touch a screen or click on the mouse and free both hands for anything else.

Rehabilitation, Surgery, and Telemedicine

Gestural technology offers significant application in rehabilitation. It tracks and analyzes the execution of movements by patients undergoing therapy by the services of physical therapists and doctors. In turn, systems identifying and evaluating motor skill can be of great help to provide real-time feedback, to patients recovering from strokes and injuries, that encourages movement in the right way and thus may lead to better output. Gesture-controlled exoskeletons and robotic systems allow for the guidance of patients through rehabilitation exercises according to the needs and progress of each. They have proven to be very effective in enhancing muscle strength, coordination, and range of movement because of the engaging and interactive nature of therapy.

In surgery, gestural interfaces enable surgeons to interact with medical imaging and patient data during surgical procedures without leaving the sterile field. Surgeons could zoom in on, or grasp parts of a scan, or adjust the settings of a robotic surgical instrument using an equivalent of a gesture, executed through a smartphone. This is free from the constraints of performing controls elsewhere in the operating room-those external keyboards and touchpads, for example. This is because in critical surgeries, where minute changes may be urgently required, the risk of infection through mere insertion of a gadget would be avoided. The gestural technology can be integrated into robotic-assisted surgery systems like the *da-Vinci* robot to further aid surgeons in high-precision minimally invasive procedures.

The development of gestural technology has also made inroads into telemedicine. It has been followed by new trends in remote patient monitoring, and telehealth consultations have become especially relevant during the COVID-19 pandemic. The use of gestural systems would make the telemedicine sessions much more natural and interactive. For example, with the help of gesture-controlled cameras or wearables, patients can present symptoms or movements to the doctor, and the clinicians can assess the condition without actually being in the same space as the patient. Besides, gesture recognition in wearable device, such as smartwatches, will help patients monitor the vital signs or alert the medical staff if an emergency occurs due to fall or arrhythmia, thereby improving the quality of remote care.

Advancements in Patient Interaction Using Gestural Systems

Probably, the most hopeful feature of gestural technology is to increase the patient's contact with medical devices and surroundings. Of course, user interfaces that can be used most easily by immobile patients would be either keyboards or touchscreens (Kumar et al., 2021). However, in these gesture-based systems, there exists much more intuitive means to get in touch with medical technologies and in this way have more control over their health care. For instance, a hospital patient who is in a bed could manage the illumination of the room, or change their position by adjusting the bed, or even request assistance by simply performing a gesture that the computer will interpret.

The gesture-controlled interface may be integrated in patient rooms or homes within smart environments to let patients access and use devices in an essentially contact-free way. This is a huge help to the elderly or the disabled because it keeps them independent. These systems can also monitor compliance with medication usage. Gesture recognition can monitor whether a patient is, indeed taking his/her prescription medicines correctly, providing reminders and instructions where necessary.

Gestural technology also enables people to make interactions with a medical information system more interesting and accessible. Electronic health record (HER)-based technologies enable physicians to manipulate 3D EHRs so that they can see complex data in three-dimensional space, such as with magnetic resonance imaging (MRI) scans or genomic information. Hands-free access to data allows clinicians to make quicker and better-informed decisions at critical times. In educational setups, this tool allows the medical students to practice handling procedures by interactive participation in a virtual setup guided through gesture. With this, the practice becomes more immersive.

Technical and Clinical Challenges

Despite all these potential benefits, gestural technology faces several technical as well as clinical challenges that need to be addressed before its benefits can be enjoyed in healthcare. Great accuracy in gesture recognition remains as one of the main technical challenges faced. Gestural systems have to interpret numerous movements by humans, often in a lit, noisy, or background-interfered environment. Errors in gesture recognition may pose risks for medical procedures or miscommunication during sessions of rehabilitation or telemedicine, thereby jeopardizing patient safety. So, continuous enhancement of algorithms from computer vision and machine learning is supposed to be warranted to ensure very high accuracy and reliability (Hu et al., 2023; Kumar et al., 2021).

Another challenge is hardware-related. Advanced cameras and sensors are widely used in gesture-based systems and are very expensive, adding problems to integrate in already saturated healthcare infrastructures. The device needs also to be integrated with existing hospital systems-most notably, EHRs or robotic surgery tools, to provide true ease of adoption. Further, the hardware must last and be suitable for use in a sterile environment where cleaning and maintenance may be even harder.

Adopting these systems clinically is one of the biggest challenges. Acceptance by users and the training process are significant problems in this regard. In this regard, clinician discomfort will depend on the perceptions of these clinicians unfamiliar with technology. This is seen in that they may be unwilling to use gestural systems if they perceive these systems as difficult to master or clumsy. High-powered training and intuitive user interfaces are critical points in their ability to seamlessly adopt these systems into their workflows. Moreover, any such technology has to be clinically tested in clinical trials before its actual benefit and safety on humans can be confirmed (Ramudu et al., 2023; Sreedhar et al., 2024; Ugandar et al., 2023).

Privacy is another concern especially with gestural technology in telemedicine and remote monitoring applications. They might involve the monitoring and recording of patient movements and interactions, where sensitive data may be involved, hence systems would need to ensure these aspects are covered in their safety, and assured regulatory compliance as applicable in HIPAA and GDPR. The integration of gestural technology into medical systems has to meet the stancher regulation; hence patient safety and privacy won't be compromised.

Gestural technology holds great promise for changing healthcare through offering novel ways to interact with medical devices, enhancing patient care, and ultimately better clinical outcomes. The technical as well as the clinical challenges that its introduction into health systems presents may be overcome in ways to make more efficient, interactive, and patient-centered environments.

INTEGRATING FEDERATED LEARNING AND GESTURAL TECHNOLOGY

Federated learning and gestural technology (GT) could be conjoined to form one of the most important developments in healthcare, bringing together a decentralized AI capability with an intuitive, touchless human-machine interface. It would be surprising if this integration between FL and GT did not start a fundamental shift in how patient data is gathered, analyzed, and used to improve health care for better outcomes in a more personalized medicine. The privacy-preserving capabilities of machine learning with FL suggest potential complementary relationships with gesture-based systems, allowing health care professionals an accessible and non-intrusive user experience without compromising patient privacy with critical data (Ali et al., 2022; Bashir et al., 2023; Gahlan & Sethia, 2024). Figure 3 illustrates the interconnected states and processes of these two technologies, highlighting their collaboration to improve patient care and data management.

Figure 3. Integration of federated learning and gestural technology in healthcare

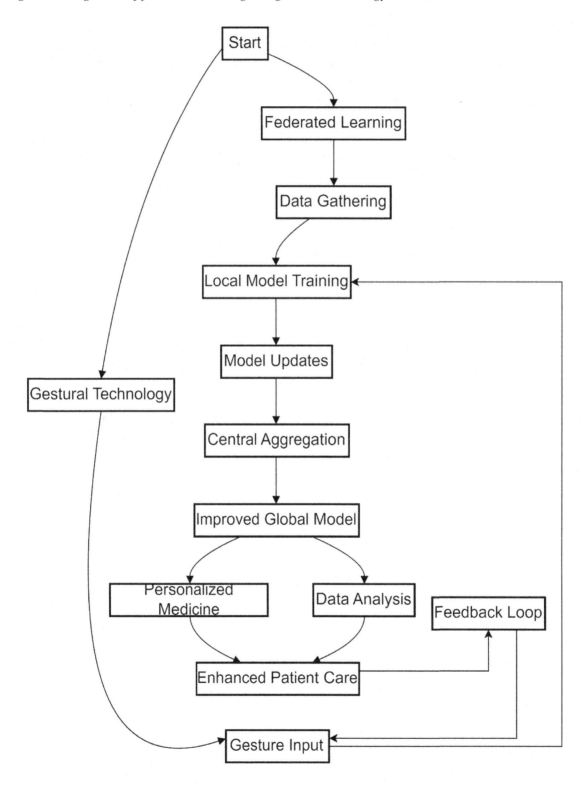

Synergism Between Federated Learning and Gestural Interaction

Synergism between federated learning and gestural interaction forms the core of this integration. In federated learning, it enables training machine learning models on multiple decentralized devices without raw patient data being shared; therefore, sensitive health information remains locked down on local devices such as hospital servers or patient-owned wearable devices. This decentralized approach, in the light of the health care industry, where in the context of HIPAA and GDPR, data protection can come across as being of utmost importance, is all the more relevant.

Gestural technology, by its very nature, offers a natural contactless interface with digital systems. Healthcare professionals and patients will interact more intuitively with data and medical equipment. Integration of these technologies will enable the creation of more efficient, privacy-preserving systems with correct secure processing of patient data and seamless interactions with technology. For instance, in an operating room, a doctor might use hand gestures to manipulate the 3D model of a patient's anatomy itself, whereas the model itself has been powered by federated learning algorithms trained on data from multiple hospitals. In this manner, the system will constantly learn without ever compromising on the privacy of its patients.

The above collaborative framework addresses two of the greatest challenges for healthcare technology: the ability to maintain patient confidentiality while allowing for the benefits of AI-driven diagnostics to be seized upon, and the design of intuitive systems with no overload of cognition on the healthcare professional. Gesture interfaces allow doctors, nurses, and surgeons to operate directly on patient data, medical images, or robot surgical instruments without having to touch screens or buttons, thus minimizing risks of contamination in sterile environments and maintaining high precision levels.

Data-Driven Patient Care and Personalized Medicine

The federated learning-concept, coupled with gestural technology, comes across as being particularly effective in the field of personalized medicine. Personalized medicine relies considerably on the analysis of vast patient-specific data, such as genomic sequences, medical histories, lifestyle factors, and much more to develop individualized treatment plans for patients. Federated learning enables such an analysis across multiple healthcare institutions without centralizing data to protect confidentiality about patients and allows the models to learn from a far larger and more diverse dataset that leads to more accurate predictions and recommendations about patient care (Naresh et al., 2024; Vaithianathan et al., 2024).

Alongside gestural technology, delivering personalized care also becomes dynamic and interactive. Healthcare providers can make some decisions in real-time and tailored to the individual needs of the patient as they cut through genomic patterns or disease progression models through gestures. This integration can really be crucial in oncology, especially since the treatment plan is continuously based on continuous monitoring and analytics of response to therapies. The use of gesture-controlled interfaces allows for the visualization of continuous changes in tumor growth or treatment efficacy over time through models of federated learning, which continuously update based on new data, thus making the evolving treatment plan dependent on the condition of the patient.

Similarly, gesture-controlled interfaces enhance data-driven patient care in any telemedicine setting. Federated learning-based remote monitoring systems can then analyze data from wearables and smart devices for patients as patients will interact with them via gestures to report symptoms or monitor vital signs and receive guidance on treatment adherence. Such as patient who undergoes surgery and is operated at home might utilize gestural commands which interact with a continuously learning telemedicine platform infused with data collected across multiple similar cases so that the system's ability to provide the patient with improved, personally tailored recovery advice increases.

Case Studies: Successful Integration of Federated Learning in Healthcare

There are many case studies that have proven that healthcare can be achieved in more aspects by integrating federated learning with gestural technology. For instance, the field of robotic surgery is among the prominent uses of robotics. There, in a renowned medical facility, surgeons can control the robotic-assisted surgery tools by gestural interfaces and achieve greater accuracy with reduced risks of exposure to contamination in the operating room. Based on this system, federated learning algorithms had learned continuously from data collected from previous surgeries at many institutions. This meant the robotic system was continually improving, provided real-time feedback to surgeons based on the latest data, all this done without compromising patient privacy. The system improved surgical outcomes and reduced recovery times for patients (Ramudu et al., 2023; Sreedhar et al., 2024; Ugandar et al., 2023).

Stroke rehabilitation is another application to have been successful. A network of rehabilitation centers used federated learning models to enhance the accuracy of patient recovery predictions across centers. These models were trained on data coming from multiple centers and hence could learn to generalize to a broad spectrum of cases while keeping the data secure. Patients undergoing rehabilitation could interact with virtual exercises in recovery through gesture-based systems, thereby making the process more interesting and dependent less on patients physically interacting with devices. The federated learning models adjusted the intensity and challenge of exercise considering the rate of improvement of different patients and, therefore, provided every patient with a tailored dynamic plan of rehabilitation. This led to quicker recovery times and increased patient satisfaction.

Further, federated learning and gestural technology have also been applied in telemedicine. A network of hospitals introduced a system whereby patients can remotely monitor chronic conditions such as diabetes or heart disease using wearable devices. Federated learning algorithms trained on data from such devices would determine potential health risks, while patients interact with the system via gestural commands. For example, patients may wave their hand to show that they indeed took their medication. Another easy gesture could be performed to call for help while their wearable device identified the abnormality in patient vital signs. This made it possible to incorporate technology, assess, and manage the patients remotely in high personalization and security.

Thus, this integration of federated learning and gestural technology is nothing less than revolutionary in its steps toward much more efficient, safe, and personalized patient care. The two pieces combined will allow healthcare providers to build systems that respect the privacy of their patients while providing cutting-edge, AI-driven insights. There will be even more improvements in clinical outcomes, patient engagement, and the delivery of care as even more healthcare institutions come to accept these technologies.

APPLICATIONS

The integration of federated learning and gestural technology has begun to change the landscape in healthcare, bringing in innovative solutions that improve the care for patients and the efficiency of their operations (Karthik et al., 2023; Malathi et al., 2024). The integration of Federated learning and gestural technology is being extensively utilized in healthcare, as illustrated in Figure 4.

Figure 4. Various applications of the integration of federated learning and gestural technology in healthcare

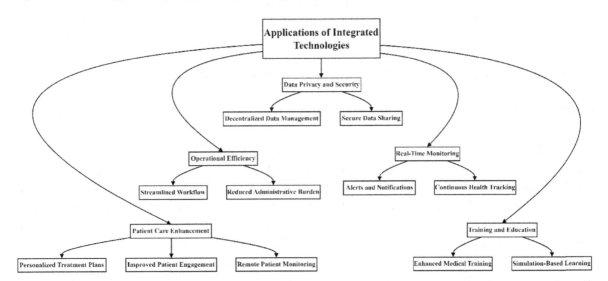

Remote Diagnostics and Monitoring

This new health scenario makes remote diagnostics and monitoring absolutely essential to the care of chronic conditions as well as the provision of continuity of care. In the federated learning context, advanced machine learning models developed for healthcare providers look at the information about the patients without exposing sensitive details to fraudulent third parties. Then, devices such as wearables and remote monitoring systems take in, analyze data like vital signs and activity levels, and do not send back raw data to the central servers.

This application is therefore enhanced by gestural technology through patients' seamless interaction with monitoring systems. For instance, patients may use hand gestures to advance their dashboards, report symptoms, or confirm having taken medication. In most cases, such interactions reduce physical contact with devices in efforts to prevent infections. Moreover, federated learning algorithms can fine-tune their predictions based on data gathered from similar patients who are across different healthcare settings, thus leading to improvements in precision without compromising either privacy or personalizes care.

Smart Rehabilitation Systems

Federated learning and gestural technology are beneficial to smart rehabilitation systems. Gesture-based interfaces in rehabilitation allow therapists in real time to monitor the patients' progress and guide them accordingly. The same stroke or post-orthopedic surgery patient will be able to do prescribed exercises while being engaged with a system that incorporates federated learning in exercising by adjusting exercises based on patient performance and recovery pace.

As these systems gather the details regarding patients' activities and rehabilitation progress, federated learning enables them to improve exercise recommendations without storing centrally any sensitive information concerning the patients. This privacy-preserving approach encourages more patients to take part in rehabilitation courses; patients become safe knowing their health data is protected. Simultaneously, therapists could benefit from insights generated from a vast pool of anonymized data at different rehabilitation centers, which will lead to even more efficient and individual-specific rehabilitation plans.

Telemedicine and Virtual Care Solutions

Telemedicine became a household name, particularly during the COVID-19 pandemic, as it enables health care professionals to deliver care from afar. Federated learning with gestural technology can be used together to enhance the interactivity as well as the effectiveness of the telemedicine platforms. In systems associated with telehealth, federated learning facilitates the analysis of patient data arising from thousands of virtual consultations conducted with enhanced diagnostic accuracy along with treatment prescriptions with the privacy of the patients ensured (Sreedhar et al., 2024).

Gestural technology can make a consultation between a patient and their provider more intuitive when done virtually. For example, using gestures, a patient can be indicating symptoms, interacting with their virtual interface or asking a question to make the consultation experience look interactive and engaging. Also, a patient might use a gesture to zoom in on some aspect of an imaging report that they wish to discuss with their physician. Such functionalities serve to enhance communication, thereby guaranteeing clear and effective conveyance of important information.

In addition, the federated learning's results can be applied to inform the practitioner of population health trends and the treatment effectiveness of a specific diagnosis, which can then allow evidence-based care with respect to individual patient's privacy.

Clinical Decision Support Tools

Clinical decision support tools have been very important in helping clinicians make diagnostic and treatment decisions. Adding federated learning into the clinical decision support tools boosts their capabilities since they can learn various cases without exposing sensitive data to the institution. It assists the models in aggregation of various insights from multiple health care institutions, improving their predictive abilities for a different kind of patient population.

In conjunction with gestural technology, clinicians can better interact with such decision support systems. For example, a physician may use gestures to navigate through patient records, visualize treatment options, or simulate the outcomes of differences in clinical decisions. This can be particularly useful for high-stakes environments like emergency room or surgery settings, where quicker access to relevant data and rapid decision-making are paramount.

Besides, these tools can give live recommendations within a consultation session, helping the clinicians to make well-informed decisions very swiftly. For that matter, the felicitous integration of federated learning with gestural interfaces not only enhances the usability of clinical decision support tools but also boosts the quality of care given to the patients in general.

A vast range of applications that have a positive impact on healthcare can result from combining federated learning with gestural technology. These range from remote diagnostics and smart rehabilitation systems, and telemedicine, to clinical decision support tools, thereby assisting patients in recording better outcomes, making healthcare delivery more efficient, and protecting the privacy of individual patients. Continued advancement in the healthcare sector is bound to produce even more innovative solutions as it grows. In addition, combining federated learning with gestural technology would undoubtedly lead to enhanced patient care.

CHALLENGES AND CONSIDERATIONS

Although the integration of federated learning and gestural technology in healthcare is bristling with immense potential, many challenges and considerations must be addressed in order to achieve successful implementation and optimal outcomes. These technical, regulatory, and practical challenges are serious and warrant great consideration and strategic planning (Navaz et al., 2021; Nguyen et al., 2022). The integration of federated learning and gestural technology in healthcare presents various challenges and considerations, as illustrated in Figure 5.

Figure 5. Challenges and considerations related to the integration of federated learning and gestural technology in healthcare

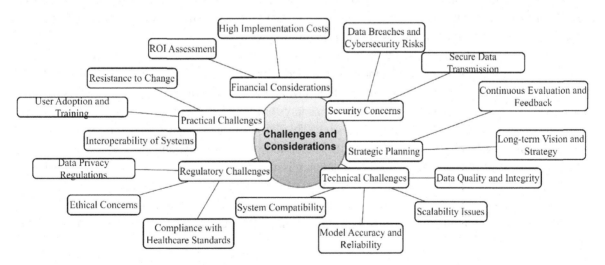

Technical Challenges

Federated learning provides one of the promises of privacy-preserving AI in healthcare, but there are many technical challenges to overcome before it can be fully realized. The major ones among those relate to heterogeneity in data, quality of data, complexity of integrating systems, and necessity for low latency and real-time processing.

Data Heterogeneity and Quality: Data heterogeneity presents one of the significant challenges in federated learning, more so in the healthcare sector. The data from different medical institutions may vary greatly because the collection methodologies, patient demographics, and clinical practices differ. For example, imaging data coming from one hospital may be collected based on different protocols or pieces of equipment than another. Furthermore, patient demographics, such as age, ethnicity, and location, introduce variability that can limit model generalizability. Federated learning models should be strong enough to generalize across different types of datasets, yet provide highly accurate results in diagnostics and treatment recommendations. Data quality from wearables, gesture-based systems, and other Internet of Things (IoT) devices may not be uniform. Sensor inaccuracy, environmental conditions, and user behavior can reduce the reliability of data collected. It may lead to degradation of the model, demanding advanced preprocessing and robust algorithms to counteract it.

Complexity of Integration: Integration of FL within healthcare systems is yet another important challenge. Many healthcare institutions are depending on legacy systems not designed with decentralized architecture in mind. They usually don't have the interoperability needed with modern technologies, thus making the integration with FL models somewhat technically complex. Wide modifications to pre-existing infrastructure and development of middleware between disparate systems would be required for its effective implementation. Another pertinent issue related to data integrity and security during integration. Federated learning transfers model updates and not raw data; however, ensuring that the integrity of these model updates is preserved across heterogeneous systems is not a trivial task. Moreover, organizations in the healthcare sector are obligated to adhere to more stringent regulations like HIPAA and GDPR, which add to the complexities of integration processes.

Latency and Real-Time Processing: Healthcare applications, for instance, require real-time processing capabilities; for example, in remote diagnostics, telemedicine, or robotic surgical interventions. FL-based models need to make predictions within time that have a low latency. However, low latency is difficult to achieve, especially because FL is a decentralized system, where data cannot be processed centrally but must be performed at a large number of sites. This leads to many delays caused by computational and communication overheads. Local compute loads, network reliability, and the need to synchronize updates across multiple nodes can exacerbate latency issues. Balancing the trade-off between real-time performance and model accuracy is a critical aspect of designing FL systems for healthcare.

Addressing these challenges will require advancements in robust algorithms, system interoperability, and efficient communication protocols to unlock the potential of federated learning in healthcare applications.

Privacy and Security Concerns

Data security: Federated learning helps in enhancement of privacy because the sensitive data is persisted locally at local devices. Nonetheless, still related to data security, wearables or tablets with healthcare applications are susceptible to hacking or data breaches. Therefore, robust security measures must be implemented in the form of encryption and secure communication protocols to protect sensitive patient data against unauthorized access.

Adherence to Laws: Health care institutions are now navigating extremely complex regulatory landscapes, including HIPAA and GDPR on data protection as well as individual rights. The challenge lies in ensuring adherence when working with federated learning and gestural technology; for example, as in aggregating data from multiple sources. Further, there is responsibility on the part of the institution to put in place processes that ensure conformity to such regulations while optimizing the benefits of integrated technologies.

Clinical and Operational Considerations

Resistance to Adoption of New Technologies: Health care providers may resist the adoption of new technologies, such as reliance on AI-driven systems. These technologies may be deemed unreliable or inaccurate by providers. They also may resist change by established workflows that have provided them with adequate support so far. Training, demonstrations of effectiveness of the technologies, and showing promise for improvement over disorganization in clinical practice should all be implemented towards facilitating their adoption.

User Experience and Usability: This aspect is mostly based on user experience and usability in gestural technology. The gestural interfaces, which the healthcare providers and patients interact with should give an impression of intuitive and easy usage. If the interfaces are not well designed, it leads to frustration and disengagement. Thorough rigorous testing with users and the availability of a feedback loop during the development phases of such technology, user experience can be enhanced.

Interdisciplinary Collaboration: The integration of federated learning and gestural technology requires collaboration across multiple stakeholders: data scientists, healthcare providers, computer engineers, and technology developers. Building effective communication channels and collaborative frameworks is a challenging process but, basically, it ensures that the goals are aligned with what insights are shared, and then technologies are developed according to clinical needs.

Ethical Considerations

Bias and Fairness: Machine learning-based systems, including federated learning models, intrinsically inherit biases from the training data. The risk of gathering data through federated learning that is not representative of the majority population can lead to an uneven character of the model's outcomes and can drive unintended care differentials. Continuous bias reviews of these models and ensuring an equitable access of technology to diverse patient populations have become important interventions.

Informed Consent: Federated learning and gestural technologies add complexities to obtaining informed consent. There is a requirement to inform patients of the use of their data, that what it means by the use of AI-driven systems, and that what technology is in interaction with them. Clear communication and transparency about the usage of data and protection of their data are crucial for building trust between patients and providers of health care.

Therefore, it is quite challenging to implement the application of federated learning and gestural technology in healthcare. In this regard, health care organizations must resolve the technical complexity, concerns over privacy and security, operational hurdles, and ethical considerations for successful integration and implementation of such technologies to maximally enhance patient care and outcomes through strategic navigation across challenges and fostering collaborations among various stakeholders. With this ever-changing healthcare landscape, the necessity to proactively anticipate challenges for innovation and to ensure quality care becomes increasingly important.

FUTURE DIRECTIONS

The federated learning and gestural technology that brings these technologies together will change the healthcare delivery paradigm. With such developments, various future directions are brought about including improving patients' outcomes, enhancing data security, and developing innovation in clinical practices (Khalid et al., 2023; Navaz et al., 2021; Nguyen et al., 2022; Thilagam et al., 2022). Below, we discuss some of the key future directions worthy of note.

Enhanced Personalization of Patient Care

The future for healthcare is one of personalized medicine. This means that both treatment and intervention are tailored to individual patient needs, while federated learning unlocks the potential of those systems by analyzing vast amounts of patient data from diverse populations in a privacy-preserving manner. Its capacity will enable the development of more accurate predictive models of patient outcomes and possibly customized treatment plans based on the unique characteristics of the patient.

Gestural technology will further personalize patient care because of increased intuitive patient interactions with health management systems. Emerging applications in the future will allow patients to access the system according to preference, thus making healthcare delivery more user-friendly and engaging. For instance, a patient could use gestures to change the care protocol-in real time, offering instant feedback and revision to the treatment plan.

Interoperability and Integration with Other Technologies

The advancement of healthcare technology will increasingly depend on the interoperability with other computing technologies. Future directions should integrate federated learning and gestural technology with other new and advanced technologies such as IoT and EHRs. The seamless data integration across systems would make the decision-making tools function better in making the right determinations as it would ensure that the healthcare providers are informed on the comprehensive states of their patients.

For example, using federated learning with IoT devices is feasible in order to enable real-time monitoring and analysis of patients' data for more proactive care. Similarly, the effective conjunction of gestural interfaces and AI-driven analytics could make health applications considerably more responsive and interactive, opening a way for patients to have highly accessible systems for their health journeys.

Advanced Research and Development

A combination of federated learning and gestural technology may help open up opportunities for research and development in healthcare. Such technologies may be studied based on their effectiveness in different domains of medicine, such as oncology, cardiology, or mental health. Further studies may be undertaken to verify the usability of gestural technology in clinical environments and to assess whether such technology could enhance patient engagement, satisfaction, or outcomes.

Besides, there is a great need to develop more powerful federated learning algorithms. Algorithms may be improved further with increased focus on optimization that may enhance its handling of data heterogeneity and eventually decrease the computational requirements. Stronger models would lead to stronger predictive functions across different healthcare systems.

Ethical Regulatory Frameworks

With more federated learning and gestural technology deployment, the establishment of ethical and regulatory frameworks will become necessary. They should include developing comprehensive guidelines to recognize data privacy, consent, and security concerns. Such frameworks would evolve and need to be developed within the unique challenges of federated learning, addressing questions about data provenance and accountability.

However, there is a need for ethical concerns about algorithmic bias and fairness to be at the center of future development of these models. It is upon both researchers and policymakers to collaborate in setting the standards in which the AI systems are fair and do not widen the differences currently faced in health care. The continuous evaluation and observation of algorithms is paramount in keeping ahead of the public trust and making sure that such technologies are all applied rightly towards all patients.

CONCLUSION

Federated learning and gestural technology could be integrated together to introduce a completely new way in which care for patients might be improved, the security of data ensured, and proper clinical decisions made. Thus, decentralized analysis of data is one of the means through which federated learning helps healthcare institutions unleash the full capacity that extensive diverse datasets have while retaining patient privacy. Such collaboration promotes not only improved predictive models but also enables the utilization of individualized treatment plans that are customized to each patient's specific needs.

Gestural technology enhances patient experience because it provides intuitive and interactive interfaces in which to share information between health care providers and patients. Since the patients in this context are more engaged in managing their health, there will be an extremely high potential for improved adherence to treatment and better health outcomes.

Many challenges still lie ahead in integrating these technologies into daily practices. The sustainability of the implementations will be largely based on technical complexity, the data security requirements, and considering ethics and laws in practice. Continuing education and training of health professionals on developing their knowledge of these technologies will bridge this gap between technology and clinical applications so that all stakeholders can apply them to their fullest potential.

More synergy will be created in the future through the further development of federated learning and gestural technologies. The myriad of demands on interoperability, interdisciplinary collaboration, and caution against ethical considerations is simply part of the road to unlocking the next levels of patient care and operational efficiency in healthcare systems. Next-generation progress in these technologies promises to shake up the very foundations of health care delivery, changing patient experience at the levels of individual, organizational, and systemic ones. This will lay a path toward a truly connected, responsive, and patient-centric health ecosystem.

REFERENCES

Ali, M., Naeem, F., Tariq, M., & Kaddoum, G. (2022). Federated learning for privacy preservation in smart healthcare systems: A comprehensive survey. *IEEE Journal of Biomedical and Health Informatics*, 27(2), 778–789. DOI: 10.1109/JBHI.2022.3181823 PMID: 35696470

Bashir, A. K., Victor, N., Bhattacharya, S., Huynh-The, T., Chengoden, R., Yenduri, G., Maddikunta, P. K. R., Pham, Q.-V., Gadekallu, T. R., & Liyanage, M. (2023). Federated learning for the healthcare metaverse: Concepts, applications, challenges, and future directions. *IEEE Internet of Things Journal*, 10(24), 21873–21891. DOI: 10.1109/JIOT.2023.3304790

Chaddad, A., Lu, Q., Li, J., Katib, Y., Kateb, R., Tanougast, C., Bouridane, A., & Abdulkadir, A. (2023). Explainable, domain-adaptive, and federated artificial intelligence in medicine. *IEEE/CAA Journal of Automatica Sinica, 10*(4), 859–876.

Chen, M., Shlezinger, N., Poor, H. V., Eldar, Y. C., & Cui, S. (2021). Communication-efficient federated learning. *Proceedings of the National Academy of Sciences of the United States of America*, 118(17), e2024789118. DOI: 10.1073/pnas.2024789118 PMID: 33888586

Gahlan, N., & Sethia, D. (2024). Federated learning inspired privacy sensitive emotion recognition based on multi-modal physiological sensors. *Cluster Computing*, 27(3), 3179–3201. DOI: 10.1007/s10586-023-04133-4

Hu, C.-Y., Hu, L.-S., Yuan, L., Lu, D.-J., Lyu, L., & Chen, Y.-Q. (2023). FedIERF: Federated Incremental Extremely Random Forest for Wearable Health Monitoring. *Journal of Computer Science and Technology*, 38(5), 970–984. DOI: 10.1007/s11390-023-3009-0

Jiang, S., Shuai, X., & Xing, G. (2024). ArtFL: Exploiting data resolution in federated learning for dynamic runtime inference via multi-scale training. *2024 23rd ACM/IEEE International Conference on Information Processing in Sensor Networks (IPSN)*, 27–38.

Karthik, S., Hemalatha, R., Aruna, R., Deivakani, M., Reddy, R. V. K., & Boopathi, S. (2023). Study on Healthcare Security System-Integrated Internet of Things (IoT). In *Perspectives and Considerations on the Evolution of Smart Systems* (pp. 342–362). IGI Global.

Khalid, N., Qayyum, A., Bilal, M., Al-Fuqaha, A., & Qadir, J. (2023). Privacy-preserving artificial intelligence in healthcare: Techniques and applications. *Computers in Biology and Medicine*, 158, 106848. DOI: 10.1016/j.compbiomed.2023.106848 PMID: 37044052

Kumar, K. S., Nair, S. A. H., Roy, D. G., Rajalingam, B., & Kumar, R. S. (2021). Security and privacy-aware artificial intrusion detection system using federated machine learning. *Computers & Electrical Engineering*, 96, 107440. DOI: 10.1016/j.compeleceng.2021.107440

Malathi, J., Kusha, K., Isaac, S., Ramesh, A., Rajendiran, M., & Boopathi, S. (2024). IoT-Enabled Remote Patient Monitoring for Chronic Disease Management and Cost Savings: Transforming Healthcare. In *Advances in Explainable AI Applications for Smart Cities* (pp. 371–388). IGI Global.

Naresh, M., Subhahan, D. A., Narula, V. N., Roslin, D. K., Narula, S., & Boopathi, S. (2024). Edge Computing and Machine Learning Integration for Autonomous Electrical Vehicles. In *Solving Fundamental Challenges of Electric Vehicles* (pp. 99–127). IGI Global., DOI: 10.4018/979-8-3693-4314-2.ch005

Navaz, A. N., Serhani, M. A., El Kassabi, H. T., Al-Qirim, N., & Ismail, H. (2021). Trends, technologies, and key challenges in smart and connected healthcare. *IEEE Access : Practical Innovations, Open Solutions*, 9, 74044–74067. DOI: 10.1109/ACCESS.2021.3079217 PMID: 34812394

Nguyen, D. C., Pham, Q.-V., Pathirana, P. N., Ding, M., Seneviratne, A., Lin, Z., Dobre, O., & Hwang, W.-J. (2022). Federated learning for smart healthcare: A survey. *ACM Computing Surveys*, 55(3), 1–37. DOI: 10.1145/3501296

Ramudu, K., Mohan, V. M., Jyothirmai, D., Prasad, D., Agrawal, R., & Boopathi, S. (2023). Machine Learning and Artificial Intelligence in Disease Prediction: Applications, Challenges, Limitations, Case Studies, and Future Directions. In *Contemporary Applications of Data Fusion for Advanced Healthcare Informatics* (pp. 297–318). IGI Global.

Singh, S., Rathore, S., Alfarraj, O., Tolba, A., & Yoon, B. (2022). A framework for privacy-preservation of IoT healthcare data using Federated Learning and blockchain technology. *Future Generation Computer Systems*, 129, 380–388. DOI: 10.1016/j.future.2021.11.028

Sreedhar, P. S. S., Sujay, V., Rani, M. R., Melita, L., Reshma, S., & Boopathi, S. (2024). Impacts of 5G Machine Learning Techniques on Telemedicine and Social Media Professional Connection in Healthcare. In *Advances in Medical Technologies and Clinical Practice* (pp. 209–234). IGI Global. DOI: 10.4018/979-8-3693-1934-5.ch012

Sun, L., & Wu, J. (2022). A scalable and transferable federated learning system for classifying healthcare sensor data. *IEEE Journal of Biomedical and Health Informatics*, 27(2), 866–877. DOI: 10.1109/JBHI.2022.3171402 PMID: 35486556

Thilagam, K., Beno, A., Lakshmi, M. V., Wilfred, C. B., George, S. M., Karthikeyan, M., Peroumal, V., Ramesh, C., & Karunakaran, P. (2022). Secure IoT Healthcare Architecture with Deep Learning-Based Access Control System. *Journal of Nanomaterials*, 2022(1), 2638613. DOI: 10.1155/2022/2638613

Ugandar, R., Rahamathunnisa, U., Sajithra, S., Christiana, M. B. V., Palai, B. K., & Boopathi, S. (2023). Hospital Waste Management Using Internet of Things and Deep Learning: Enhanced Efficiency and Sustainability. In *Applications of Synthetic Biology in Health, Energy, and Environment* (pp. 317–343). IGI Global.

Vaithianathan, V., Subbulakshmi, N., Boopathi, S., & Mohanraj, M. (2024). Integrating Project-Based and Skills-Based Learning for Enhanced Student Engagement and Success: Transforming Higher Education. In *Adaptive Learning Technologies for Higher Education* (pp. 345–372). IGI Global. DOI: 10.4018/979-8-3693-3641-0.ch015

ADDITIONAL READING

Ben Youssef, B., Alhmidi, L., Bazi, Y., & Zuair, M. (2024). Federated Learning Approach for Remote Sensing Scene Classification. *Remote Sensing (Basel)*, 16(12), 2194. DOI: 10.3390/rs16122194

Gopi, B., Sworna Kokila, M. L., Bibin, C. V., Sasikala, D., Howard, E., & Boopathi, S. (2024). Distributed Technologies Using AI/ML Techniques for Healthcare Applications. In Advances in Human and Social Aspects of Technology (pp. 375–396). IGI Global. DOI: 10.4018/979-8-3693-2569-8.ch019

Kushwah, J. S., Gupta, M., Shrivastava, S., Saxena, N., Saini, R., & Boopathi, S. (2024). Psychological Impacts, Prevention Strategies, and Intervention Approaches Across Age Groups: Unmasking Cyberbullying. In Change Dynamics in Healthcare, Technological Innovations, and Complex Scenarios (pp. 89–109). IGI Global.

Malathi, J., Kusha, K., Isaac, S., Ramesh, A., Rajendiran, M., & Boopathi, S. (2024). IoT-Enabled Remote Patient Monitoring for Chronic Disease Management and Cost Savings: Transforming Healthcare. In Advances in Explainable AI Applications for Smart Cities (pp. 371–388). IGI Global.

Pitchai, R., Guru, K. V., Gandhi, J. N., Komala, C. R., Kumar, J. R. D., & Boopathi, S. (2024). Fog Computing-Integrated ML-Based Framework and Solutions for Intelligent Systems: Digital Healthcare Applications. In Technological Advancements in Data Processing for Next Generation Intelligent Systems (pp. 196–224). IGI Global. DOI: 10.4018/979-8-3693-0968-1.ch008

Ramudu, K., Mohan, V. M., Jyothirmai, D., Prasad, D., Agrawal, R., & Boopathi, S. (2023). Machine Learning and Artificial Intelligence in Disease Prediction: Applications, Challenges, Limitations, Case Studies, and Future Directions. In Contemporary Applications of Data Fusion for Advanced Healthcare Informatics (pp. 297–318). IGI Global.

Satav, S. D., Hasan, D. S., Pitchai, R., Mohanaprakash, T., Sultanuddin, S., & Boopathi, S. (2023). Next generation of internet of things (ngiot) in healthcare systems. In *Sustainable Science and Intelligent Technologies for Societal Development* (pp. 307–330). IGI Global.

Sreedhar, P. S. S., Sujay, V., Rani, M. R., Melita, L., Reshma, S., & Boopathi, S. (2024). Impacts of 5G Machine Learning Techniques on Telemedicine and Social Media Professional Connection in Healthcare. In Advances in Medical Technologies and Clinical Practice (pp. 209–234). IGI Global. DOI: 10.4018/979-8-3693-1934-5.ch012

Subha, S., Inbamalar, T., Komala, C., Suresh, L. R., Boopathi, S., & Alaskar, K. (2023). A Remote Health Care Monitoring system using internet of medical things (IoMT). IEEE Explore, 1–6.

Ugandar, R., Rahamathunnisa, U., Sajithra, S., Christiana, M. B. V., Palai, B. K., & Boopathi, S. (2023). Hospital Waste Management Using Internet of Things and Deep Learning: Enhanced Efficiency and Sustainability. In Applications of Synthetic Biology in Health, Energy, and Environment (pp. 317–343). IGI Global.

KEY TERMS AND DEFINITIONS

Artificial Intelligence (AI): AI refers to the simulation of human intelligence and cognitive processes in machines that can learn, reason, and problem-solve. It enables systems to perform tasks such as understanding language, recognizing patterns, and making decisions.

Clinical Decision Support System (CDSS): CDSS is a health information technology system designed to assist healthcare providers in making clinical decisions. It analyzes patient data and provides evidence-based recommendations to improve diagnosis, treatment, and patient outcomes. CDSS enhances decision-making by offering timely, relevant information at the point of care.

COVID-19: An infectious disease caused by the novel coronavirus SARS-CoV-2, first identified in December 2019 in Wuhan, China. It primarily spreads through respiratory droplets and can cause symptoms ranging from mild to severe, including fever, cough, and difficulty breathing. The pandemic led to widespread global health, social, and economic challenges, prompting significant public health measures and vaccination efforts.

Electronic Health Record (HER): HER is a digital version of a patient's medical history, stored and managed electronically. It allows healthcare providers to easily access, update, and share patient information for better care coordination and decision-making.

Federated Learning (FL): FL is a machine learning approach that enables multiple decentralized devices or servers to collaboratively train a model without sharing raw data. Instead of sending data to a central server, each participant trains the model locally and only shares updates or model parameters. This method enhances privacy, security, and efficiency, as sensitive data remains on the local device.

General Data Protection Regulation (GDPR): This is a regulation in the European Union (EU) that governs the collection, storage, and processing of personal data. It aims to protect individuals' privacy and give them greater control over their personal information. GDPR imposes strict rules on organizations, with penalties for non-compliance.

Gestural Technology: This technology refers to systems that enable users to interact with digital devices through body movements, such as hand gestures, facial expressions, or body positioning. It utilizes sensors, cameras, or motion detectors to interpret and respond to these physical actions. This technology offers a more intuitive and hands-free way of controlling devices, enhancing user experience in fields like gaming, healthcare, and virtual reality.

Health Insurance Portability and Accountability Act (HIPAA): This is a U.S. law designed to protect the privacy and security of individuals' health information. It sets standards for the electronic exchange, confidentiality, and safeguarding of medical data. HIPAA also ensures that individuals can maintain health insurance coverage when changing jobs.

Machine Learning (ML): ML is a subset of artificial intelligence allowing computers to learn from data and improve performance over time without being explicitly programmed. It involves algorithms that identify patterns and make predictions or decisions based on input data.

Magnetic Resonance Imaging (MRI): MRI is one of the various systems of medical imaging techniques that uses strong magnetic fields and radio waves to create detailed images of the inside of the body. It is commonly used to examine the brain, spinal cord, muscles, and joints. MRI provides high-resolution images without using ionizing radiation, thus making it a safe diagnostic tool.

Chapter 13
Advances in Computational Visual Information Processing for Neuroscience and Healthcare Applications

E. Afreen Banu

https://orcid.org/0000-0001-8654-9851

Department of Computer Engineering, Shah and Anchor Kutchhi Engineering College, Mumbai, India

Chalumuru Suresh

Department of Computer Science and Engineering, VNRVJIET, Hyderabad, India

V. Nyemeesha

Department of Computer Science and Engineering, VNRVJIET, Hyderabad, India

Mannepalli Venkata Krishna Rao

Department of Computer Science and Engineering, VNRVJIET, Hyderabad, India

B. Muthuraj

Department of Electrical and Electronics Engineering, Panimalar Engineering College, Chennai, India

S. Muthuvel

https://orcid.org/0009-0000-1194-2907

Kalasalingam Academy of Research and Education, Srivilliputhur, India

ABSTRACT

Advances in visual information processing have revolutionized computational neuroscience and healthcare by enhancing our understanding of neural mechanisms and developing new medical solutions. Techniques like deep learning algorithms, convolutional neural networks, and computer vision applications have provided unprecedented insights into brain activity and visual organ function. These technologies also enhance our ability to model and simulate cognitive processes, making them crucial in understanding and improving medical outcomes. Visual information processing enhances healthcare diagnostics, medical imaging, and treatment personalization, ranging from radiology to pathology. It integrates advanced technology with neural interfaces and AI, revolutionizing patient care and neurological research. Further, ethical considerations, data privacy, and the challenge of transforming complex visual data into actionable insights for healthcare professionals and neuroscientists are discussed in this chapter.

DOI: 10.4018/978-1-6684-3795-7.ch013

INTRODUCTION

Visual information processing has significantly advanced in recent years, transforming computational neuroscience and healthcare disciplines. Visual data, including medical images, neural activity maps, and brain simulations, has become a crucial part of research and practical applications. Methods like machine learning and deep learning, particularly CNNs, have significantly improved the interpretation of visual data. Visual information analysis has become a powerful tool for diagnosing diseases, monitoring health conditions, and understanding the human brain. This chapter explores the potential and challenges of these advances in computational neuroscience and healthcare (Sarishma et al., 2022).

Visual information processing involves the extraction and analysis of visual data such as images, videos, and multi-dimensional datasets for interpretation.It has been important in the development of computational neuroscience in modeling neural circuits and in understanding diseases such as Alzheimer's, Parkinson's, and epilepsy. The process of visual information plays a very crucial role in medical imaging technologies like MRI, CT scans, and X-rays, which ease health workers in noticing abnormalities more efficiently and accurately. The integration of AI and machine learning in these domains enhanced the capacity to process large volumes of complex visual data, which eventually leads to better and improved insights as well as decision-making. In particular, CNNs, with their ability to automatically extract hierarchical features from images, have played an important role in moving forward research and practice in both computational neuroscience and healthcare (Yu et al., 2020).

The most interesting challenge in computational neuroscience is the study of how the brain represents the world of visual information. Human vision is inherently more complex than other senses because it involves many regions of the brain that process color, motion, shape, and depth, among other features. Scientists have focused on understanding for decades how those processes occur, how they integrate, and how the brain creates meaningful visual experiences from raw sensory input (Ienca & Ignatiadis, 2020). While traditional methods in neuroscience, like electrophysiological recordings and behavioral experiments, are undoubtedly very valuable, they are particularly limited by the sheer volume of data they can work with, and the level of detail they can offer. This is where advances in the handling of visual information, particularly in AI and computational models, have really begun to make a big impact. Models in machine learning, especially deep learning, are able to process large neural data and find patterns and relations that are generally hard to determine with manual analysis. This not only improved our understanding of simple neural processes but also contributed to the development of brain-machine interfaces wherein the neural signals were translated into commands to computers or prosthetic limbs, thus opening new channels of augmenting disabled individuals (Behera et al., 2019).

Healthcare has revolutionized in the visual information processing of medical images in central health care treatment diagnosis and monitoring many conditions. Traditional interpretation of medical images relied on highly trained specialists to visually scan the images for signs of disease or abnormality. The time that it took was just too long and very susceptible to human error. However, the integration of AI and machine learning has greatly improved the accuracy and speed with which image analysis is accomplished. For example, CNNs can prove highly efficient in the automatic analysis of medical images intended to help in identifying features like tumors, fractures, and lesions that could go unnoticed by the human eye. This has resulted in more accurate diagnoses, early detection of diseases, and the ability to prepare more personalized treatment plans for patients. For example, in oncology, deep learning algorithms could look into mammograms or CT scans and detect where cancer might be present, possibly even before it is visible to the human eye (Ahad et al., 2019). Similarly, in cardiology, AI could look at echocardiograms to start noticing early signs of heart disease so that the intervention can take place in due time.

Visual information processing has a lot to do with diagnostics, but it does not stop there; it also is very much involved in surgical planning and real-time surgery. Robotics of surgeries have the advantage of processing visual information to offer much higher precision than is possible with the human hand when manipulating the surgical instrument. Surgeons can now use AR as well as VR technologies that have recourse to real-time visual information processing in order to visualize a patient's anatomy in 3D for planning complex surgeries with more accuracy with fewer complications and better outcomes. Furthermore, post-operative examination of visual information helps medical practitioners assess the outcome of treatments and modify treatment plans accordingly (Tripathi et al., 2021).

One of the most concrete technologies that spearhead the field of visual information processing technology is the convolutional neural network (CNN). This is a class of deep learning models that is peculiar to the processing of visual information. It can automatically learn features from images based on its feature-learning abilities. Unlike machine learning models, which have to rely on feature extraction to perform their tasks, CNNs learn hierarchical representations starting from simple edges up to shapes and textures. The approach of hierarchical representation makes the CNNs extremely effective in doing tasks like image classification, object detection, and segmentation. CNNs have been used in vast applications in healthcare; it has been applied to every imaging modality from retinal scans to MRI images such as enhancing the accuracy of diagnoses to allow more detailed analysis of medical conditions. In computational neuroscience, CNNs are used to model the brain's visual processing pathways, providing insights into how different regions of the brain work together to interpret visual stimuli (Wood et al., 2019).

Despite significant advancements in visual information processing, plenty of challenges remain. The first one is about large annotated datasets needed for training deep models. Data obtained and required in a health environment for deep learning is very difficult as it needs to be labeled by medical experts. Labels can then only be added to images correctly if the labeling is done by knowledgeable professionals. Besides, data, especially sensitive and personal patient information, is also confidential to some extent. Interpretability of AI models also adds to the challenges, especially in the fields of healthcare, where mistakes in this case cannot be risked. If AI algorithms make wrong decisions, it could prove fatal. Deep learning models, particularly CNNs, have been proven to be highly accurate but their "black box" nature makes it hard to understand how the output is arrived at. Such limitations raise ethical concerns in both healthcare and neuroscience (Kording et al., 2020).

Advances in processing the information coming through the visual pathways paved the way for breakthrough development in research and application, be it in computational neuroscience or healthcare. Processing big volumes of complex data about the image by AI and ML has opened new doors toward leaps in understanding the brain and how to diagnose and treat various medical conditions. However, all these technologies are yet to be fully exploited and some challenges include the availability of data, privacy in some cases, and in most cases, model interpretability. As these fields grow, interdisciplinary collaboration will be very vital to ensure that the advantages of these advancements are completely realized and applied in proper ways by whoever owns them or utilizes them that are advantageous for society and the social good (Maturi et al., 2022).

BACKGROUND: VISUAL INFORMATION PROCESSING

The human visual system is a complex system that processes external stimuli into meaningful perceptions, starting with the eye's retina, which captures light through photoreceptor cells, rods, and cones. These cells convert light into electrical signals, which are transmitted through the optic nerve to other parts of the brain, such as the lateral geniculate nucleus (LGN) and the primary visual cortex (V1). The visual information is then processed further in higher-order regions within the brain for an interpretation of such matters as shape, color, depth, and motion. This is what gives humans an understanding of the outside world and the way to act (Stevens et al., 2019).

Some of the major concepts in visual perception outline how the brain interprets the countless facets of visual stimulation: object identification, depth, motion, and color discrimination. The use of parallel processing by the brain allows the brain to perform these tasks by looking at various facets of a visual scene simultaneously by specific areas of the brain. For example, visual recognition is thought to use "what" and "where" pathways, known as ventral and dorsal streams, to describe object identification from spatial awareness. These are crucial for how human subjects interact with their environment in terms of decision-making driving the motor responses.

Computational models are also broadly useful in furthering our understanding of visual information processing in neuroscience. These mimic how the brain processes visual stimuli through neural mechanisms, thus simulating perception. For example, these computational models like the CNN are inspired by the visual cortex. They are designed to recognize patterns as well as features in visual data. Developing these models informs neuroscientists how the model processes images, driving new discoveries into the function of the human brain and possibly opening the door to fixes for neurological disorders characterized by deficits in visual processing.

UNSUPERVISED LEARNING IN MACHINE LEARNING

Unsupervised learning, a branch of machine learning, focuses on analyzing and organizing unstructured data without predefined labels. Unlike supervised learning, which relies on labeled datasets, unsupervised learning explores hidden patterns, structures, or clusters in data. Key techniques include clustering, dimensionality reduction, and association analysis. These methodologies are pivotal in fields like computational neuroscience and healthcare, where interpreting complex and voluminous datasets is essential (Alsenan et al., 2022; Ramudu et al., 2023; Sreedhar et al., 2024).

Indeed, unsupervised learning performs its magic in analysis of brain functions and neurological procedures. Neuroscientists rely on clustering algorithms like k-means or hierarchical clustering in order to categorize neural activity patterns. This then allows insight into cognitive states or interaction between brain regions. For instance, spike train data from neurons can be used to identify activity patterns that may be linked to behaviors or disorders. Such dimensionality reduction methods as PCA and t-SNE simplify huge neural datasets of high dimensionality. They help in the visualization and interpretation of complex neural connections and temporal dynamics, thus supporting the detection of biomarkers for neurological disorders such as Alzheimer's or epilepsy. In addition, unsupervised learning is helpful in the development of BMI, which decodes neural signals controlling prosthetic devices to enable mobility for patients who suffer from paralysis.

In healthcare, unsupervised learning drives advancements in patient care, diagnosis, and personalized medicine. Clustering techniques are employed to group patients with similar medical profiles, enabling targeted interventions. For instance, cancer subtyping using gene expression data allows oncologists to customize treatments. Unsupervised learning algorithms find unknown patterns embedded in electronic health records and identify possible comorbidities or predict the course of disease. Association rule mining describes relationships between symptoms, medications, and outcomes and their interactions to improve clinical decision-making.

Moreover, dimensionality reduction helps analyze large-scale genomic data. Finding variance in gene expression profiles can identify some genetic predispositions to the diseases, thus supporting precision medicine. In radiology, unsupervised learning algorithms help detect anomalies in medical imaging, such as tumors in MRI or CT scans, cut down the possibilities of diagnostic errors, and improves efficiency. When data collection in neuroscience and healthcare is increasing, unsupervised learning of novel insights is highly probable. These methods can be integrated with deep learning, such as autoencoders, to provide deeper insight into neural dynamics and sharpen tools for diagnostics. The synergy between computational neuroscience and healthcare applications promises breakthrough innovations fostered to lead better lives and improve quality of life.

DEEP LEARNING AND CONVOLUTIONAL NEURAL NETWORKS (CNNS)

CNNs, or Convolutional Neural Networks, form a specific class of deep models aimed to process and interpret visual information. The network exhibits superiority in the area of image recognition, classification, and object detection since it learns spatial hierarchies automatically from input images. A CNN consists of several layers designed to extract progressively increasingly complex features in the input data. There are mainly convolution layers, pooling layers, and fully connected layers that combine to form the architecture of a CNN (Wood et al., 2019). The workflow of Convolutional Neural Networks (CNNs) is illustrated in Figure 1.

Figure 1. Workflow of Convolutional Neural Networks (CNNs) in processing visual information

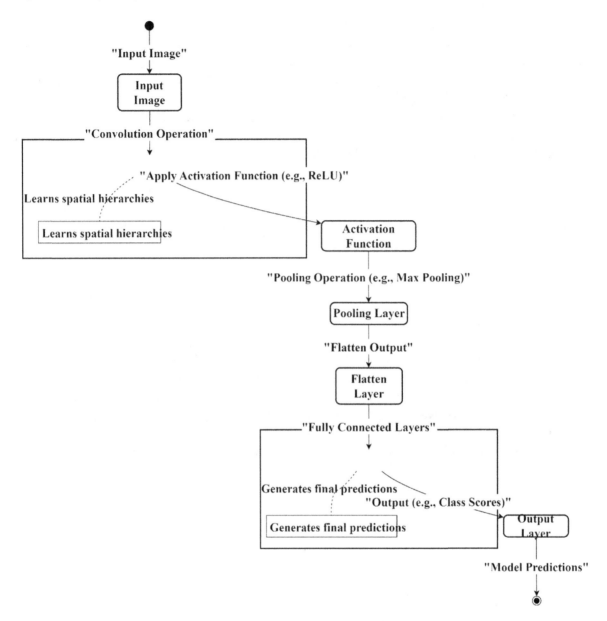

This layer is the core component of a CNN. It contains a group of filters or kernels that slide over the input image to generate feature maps. With each filter capturing specific patterns, it can highlight edges, textures, or color gradients. The pooling layer usually comes right after that, as it reduces the dimensionality of these feature maps while retaining the most important features. It makes the network more efficient. Max pooling is very popular because it selects the maximum value from each patch in the feature map. Fully connected layers finally interpret these high-level features derived by previous layers and output the prediction or classification.

CNNs are trained with very large labeled image datasets. In training, the network adjusts the weights of its filters by backpropagation, minimizing the difference between the predicted output and the actual label. It is because of this iterative process that CNNs can learn to recognize images at high accuracy in terms of objects and patterns. CNNs have become the core of many applications related to the state-of-the-art visual data analysis through their unmatched performance compared with other traditional models in machine learning.

Applications of CNNs in Visual Data Analysis

CNNs revolutionized the application of visual data analysis. From health and neuroscience applications to driverless cars and security systems, applications of CNNs spread across all industries. Their automatic property of identifying features from complex image data makes them the choice methodology for applications such as image classification, object detection, and semantic segmentation (Fellous et al., 2019; Sodhro et al., 2022).

In the medical field, CNNs have broad applications in medical imaging and are used to detect diseases and abnormalities in patients. For example, in radiology, CNNs may analyze MRI, CT scan, and X-rays in order to get more information about tumors, fractures, or other pathological signs in the images. In oncology, CNNs are used to analyze mammograms to check for early detection of breast cancer; they can pick subtle characteristics that are sometimes unable to be determined by human radiologists. Another area where CNNs have proven to be quite promising is histopathology slides, through which they enabled classification of cancerous versus non-cancerous tissue samples, thus allowing for even more accurate and precise diagnoses than their analytical counterparts.

Other applications of CNNs in healthcare include significant use in ophthalmology, whereby CNNs analyze images of retinal conditions such as diabetic retinopathy, macular degeneration, and glaucoma. As a result, use of CNNs in these areas not only aids in early diagnosis but also monitors the progression of disease over time, thereby enabling more personalized interventions.

In computational neuroscience, they apply the CNN to model the processing pathways of vision within the brain. Researchers will use the CNN to simulate how the brain will process visual stimuli in order to understand the neural mechanisms that underlie vision, such as object recognition and motion perception. Therefore, advances in BMIs and prosthetics are possible because of CNNs through decoding of neural signals into visual or motor responses, providing new possibilities for those with impairments in either the visual or motor system.

Outside the field of health care, CNNs have transformed many other spheres, for example, self-driving cars, which rely on input from cameras mounted on cars to detect, in real-time, obstacles, lanes, pedestrians, and traffic signs. In surveillance and security systems, CNNs could be utilized to enhance the ability of those systems toward distinguishing between individuals and identifying suspicious behaviors. The fact that one can use them in agriculture by, for instance, analyzing the images taken by drones above farmlands for the diseases or growth irregularities of a crop, makes it clear that CNN's flexibility in domains transcends visual data analysis.

Benefits and Limitations of CNNs in Neuroscience and Healthcare

CNNs offer numerous advantages in neuroscience and healthcare, but they also have certain limitations (Leo et al., 2020; Srivani et al., 2023; Zhang et al., 2024).

Benefits

Another major advantage associated with the use of CNNs is that it features automatic extraction of features. While models of traditional machine learning perform feature extraction through laboriously step-wise processes that are mostly required in this process and which demand some domain knowledge, learning these features can directly come from an n-dimensional data space within the CNNs, thus making them more flexible and scalable.

High Accuracy: CNNs performed outstandingly well at tasks such as image classification or object detection by outperforming human comparison. These are great abilities for medical diagnostics, where getting a disease right can be a matter of life and death.

Efficient Visual Data Processing: CNNs are primarily useful in handling vast amounts of visual data, such as scans of medical images or neural scans. Their hierarchical structure allows the processing of data at different levels of abstraction-from simple edges to complex shapes-which facilitates more efficient processing of visual data.

Adaptability to Different Domains: Initially, CNNs were designed for image recognition tasks. However, such adaptability allows them to be the most widely applied in the most versatile areas, from healthcare and neuroscience to robotics and further. By that aspect, it is an excellent instrument for interdisciplinary applications and research.

Limitations

Data Requirements: CNNs require very large amounts of labeled data to be trained effectively. Normally, it is quite challenging in healthcare and neuroscience to obtain large annotated datasets because it involves the requirement of expert labeling, which would take a lot of time and money. For instance, for the application of medical imaging, one requires annotated datasets, which may require radiologists to label each image meticulously resulting in slow development of CNN models.

Interpretability: The biggest criticism, currently, of CNNs is that they are "black boxes." It is really very difficult to understand how a CNN arrives at some given decision, especially if that field is healthcare, in which transparency in those results is paramount. Lack of interpretability can raise many significant ethical concerns based on the applications of CNNs in medical diagnostics or treatment recommendations.

APPLICATIONS IN COMPUTATIONAL NEUROSCIENCE

Therefore, one of the most significant applications of computational neuroscience is through closing the gap between neuroscience and advanced computational technologies by using mathematical models, algorithms, and data-driven techniques for understanding and simulating the functions of the brain. One such application is in the processing of visual information by the brain. Important areas for developing computational models that will advance our understanding of brain functions: visual perception, neural circuitry, and BCIs. Following are some of the major applications of computational techniques in neuroscience: modeling of visual perception, analysis of neural circuits, and integration of visual information into BCIs (Leo et al., 2020; Srivani et al., 2023). Figure 2 depicts the various applications of computational neuroscience, specifically focusing on visual information processing.

Figure 2. Applications of computational neuroscience focused on visual information processing

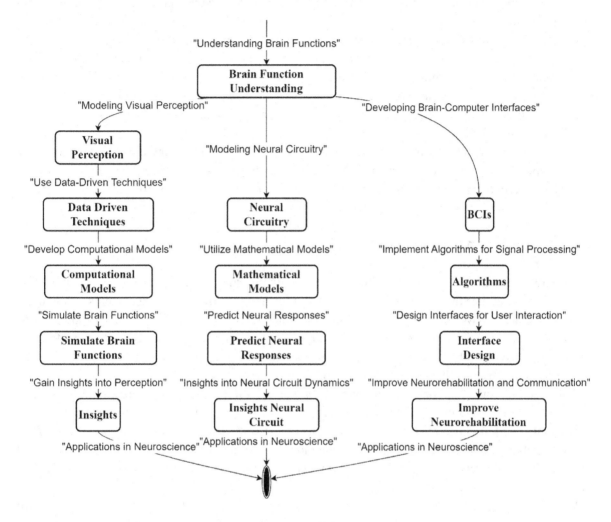

Modeling Visual Perception and Cognitive Processes

Visual perception is such an elementary cognitive process through which people often perceive the world around them. From the computational standpoint, there has been a significant move forward in modeling the neuronal processes underlying the processes involved in visual information processing within the brain and thus provides the inside into the mechanisms that result in object recognition, depth perception, motion detection, among other perceptual functions.

An important modeling approach of visual perception is neural network models, which significantly include CNNs inspired by the visual cortex in the brain. The CNNs are structured to simulate a hierarchical nature of the visual processing system of the brain, where each layer produces progressively more complex features of the visual stimuli. Basic features like edges and corners are drawn out at the initial layers of CNNs, whereas complicated patterns like objects or faces appear at deeper layers. The current models give researchers toolsets with which they can understand how visual information is processed in the human brain as well as offer frameworks for investigation into the perceptual deficit of neurological disorder conditions.

Additionally, computational models show in detail how the visual perception is integrated with other cognitive processes in the brain. For instance, attention mechanisms allow the brain to selectively focus on relevant visual stimuli while ignoring distractors, and those are modelled at the computation level using attention-driven neural networks. Such models explain how different parts of the brain cooperate when visual tasks are performed and help identify impairments in attention-related disorders such as ADHD and schizophrenia.

In addition, computational models help understand visual illusions in how the brain misinterprets sensory input. Researchers can understand mechanisms leading to misperception by simulating neural responses to deceptive visual stimuli, which leads to better understanding of disorders like visual agnosia or synesthesia, where perception is atypical.

Neural Circuits and Brain Mapping

Actually, the complexity of neural circuits in the brain provides a great challenge in understanding how regions coordinate their effort to process visual information. However, advancements in computational neuroscience have allowed mapping of these neural circuits and deciphering the intricate patterns of how different brain regions communicate. Brain mapping includes determination of the patterns of neuron connectivity and how these networks contribute to specific cognitive functions such as visual processing (Glomb et al., 2022; Srivani et al., 2023).

With neural circuit mapping and data-driven approaches of machine learning, researchers can now study large-scale brain networks with unprecedented resolutions, including the visual cortex. Researchers use tools like functional magnetic resonance imaging (fMRI) and electrophysiological recording to gather data about brain activity and computational models help analyze this data to determine functional networks. These models may represent how components of the brain function together to perform, for example, object recognition or motion analysis or depth perception.

In terms of vision research, the visual pathway in the brain is usually subdivided into large two streams: one dorsal stream, which processes spatial information and motion (the "where" pathway), and the other ventral stream, which is responsible for object recognition and form processing (the "what" pathway). Computational models have played an important part in studying these pathways and how specific regions within those streams might contribute to visual processing.

Furthermore, computational models allow for grasping neural plasticity: the brain's ability to change itself and compensate by generating new neural connections through injury or experience. For instance, if a person's visual cortex is damaged, sometimes the human brain compensates by re-routing visual information to other areas of the brain. Such a compensation process can be modeled using a computational simulation, and it indicates rehabilitation strategies that could be devised for people suffering from stroke-induced visual loss, traumatic visual loss, or neurodegenerative disease-related visual loss.

Finally, construction of high-resolution neural circuit models greatly advances the current effort to characterize the complete human brain, a so-called "connectome". Understanding neurocircuitry that supports vision is fundamentally part of that effort and discovery in this area has many applications which can result in breakthroughs in treatment conditions such as cortical blindness or amblyopia, commonly known as lazy eye.

Visual Information in Brain-Computer Interfaces (BCIs)

BCIs are speedy-emerging systems that directly link the brain with devices outside it, such as computers or robotic limbs. BCIs rely on significant decoding of visual information from the brain in order to enable users to interact, in real-time, with digital or physical environments. Computational models have a prominent part to play in interpreting the visual signals produced by the brain and converting them into actionable commands for BCIs (Stevens et al., 2019; Zhang et al., 2024).

Among the main neuroscience applications of BCIs lies the access of the device and computer systems for those suffering from motor disability, to control their prosthetic devices. Many BCI applications require visual feedback since a user needs to see the results of the brain commands to adjust and improve their control over the device. Computational neuroscience comes into play here because it develops algorithms that enable the translation of visual information and neural signals into control of the device.

For example, in a typical BCI system, a user may wear an EEG headset that is recording his brain activity while looking at the computer screen. In this way, the visual stimuli presented on the screen are processed by the brain of the user, yielding such neural signals that can be decoded with the aid of machine learning algorithms with the purpose of understanding the intentions of the user. Such decoded signals can then be used in the control of a cursor or robotic limb, for example, or even to initiate communication with people who suffer from locked-in syndrome.

Advances in computational modeling also influence the accuracy and precision in BCIs. Several algorithms have been refined to boost signal-to-noise ratios of the brain signal to simplify the interpretation of complex visual information. In addition, deep learning techniques improved the decoding of neural signals related to visual stimuli to more sophisticated applications of BCI, such as partial vision restoration in blind or visually impaired persons.

Integration of visual information into BCIs is considered for use in neurorehabilitation. In this particular case, BCIs can be applied in order to rehabilitate brain circuits in patients with a condition such as stroke or traumatic brain injury by the stimulation of visual stimuli and registering feedbacks by the brain. For example, BCIs of VR type, which expose patients to controlled visual settings, are applied for brain plasticity enhancement and motor rehabilitation in rehabilitating practice.

The field of computational neuroscience opens a new avenue to the understanding and simulation of how the brain works with regard to visual information. From modeling visual perception and cognitive processes through the mapping of neural circuits to the development of brain-computer interfaces, computational approaches have completely revolutionized our capability to manipulate and study the brain's visual systems. These have immediate implications in the treatment of neurological conditions, improved brain mapping techniques, and new technologies for brain-computer interaction, which feeds into the overarching scope of making basic neuroscience research and healthcare applications better. The future prospects of visual information processing in neuroscience hold promises of new discoveries in brain function and innovative treatments for visual and cognitive impairments.Case Studies: Neurological Disorders and Neural Simulations.

APPLICATIONS IN HEALTHCARE

The integration of visual data with advanced computational techniques has significantly transformed healthcare practice, especially in fields such as medical imaging, diagnosis, and customized treatment. Advances in computational models and AI-driven technologies have increased the accuracy and precision of medical evaluation, thereby influencing the outcome of the patient while permitting early disease detection. In the health sector, dealing with visual information involves anything from conducting complex medical images to creating predictive healthcare models that apply individual patients' data to make personalized treatment plans (Al Mamun et al., 2021; Stevens et al., 2019; Zhang et al., 2024). Figure 3 illustrates the various applications of visual data integration in healthcare.

Figure 3. Applications of visual data integration in healthcare

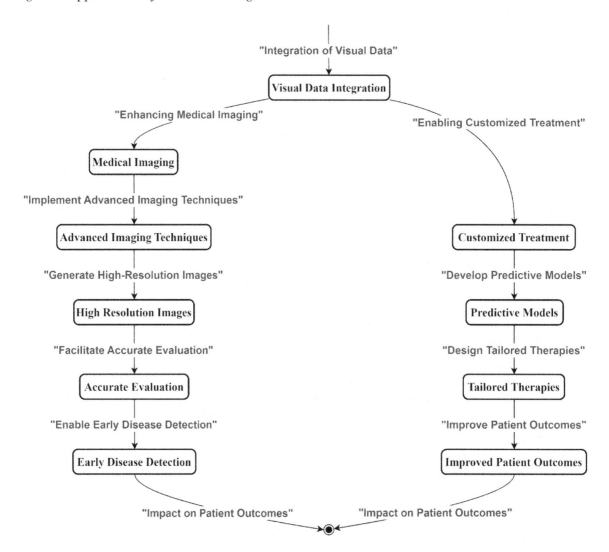

Visual Data in Medical Imaging: MRI, CT, X-rays

Medical imaging represents perhaps one of the most vital areas where visual information plays a critically important role in diagnostics as well as the planning of treatment. The use of such technologies as Magnetic Resonance Imaging, Computed Tomography, and X-rays creates high-resolution images of inner organs, tissues, and bones such that physicians are able to detect ailments that may not be visible to the naked eye. These images have important data, which are highly complicated to be interpreted manually. Thus, at such junctures computation models and processing of visual information are very significant.

This MRI uses powerful magnetic fields along with radio waves to develop detailed images of the brain and muscles as well as other soft tissues in the body. High multidimensionality rich data from the scans of MRI have significant and important information regarding the organization functionally and structurally of the body. On the other side, CT represents a combination of X-rays taken from various angles to create cross sections of the body, especially useful in lung and abdominal conditions. X-rays, being one of the oldest imaging tools, continue to be considered for fractures, infections, and chest or abdominal-related diseases.

Recently, deep learning models such as CNNs have supplemented the ability to enhance and interpret such images. With AI and computer systems, they can auto-detect several patterns in medical images believed to be relevant in cases where an individual may have a tumor or lesion that were otherwise not seen during hand analysis. Coupled with these computational tools, medical professionals are better placed to reduce the time spent analyzing diseases significantly with augmented accuracy and speed.

Other medical image datasets have been used to create predictive models. Feeding thousands of labeled images into machine learning algorithms, predictions are made about the development of diseases like cancer, cardiovascular disorders, and neurodegenerative diseases. This becomes an important application for early detection: faster and more accurate identification means it can be treated effectively and survival rates improved.

Improved Diagnostics Using AI and Early Detection

Artificial intelligence or AI has indeed revolutionized healthcare, especially in diagnostics and the detection of diseases at early stages. Traditional methods of diagnosis depend so much on the professional interpretation of symptoms and data. In most cases, it would be erring humanly. With AI-integrated systems, huge amounts of medical data - even visual ones from scans and clinical reports - can be analyzed promptly and accurately, thus making more accurate diagnosis (Al Mamun et al., 2021; Stevens et al., 2019).

AI has brought to diagnosis is that it can detect even the most elusive patterns and anomalies in medical data beyond naked human vision. As an example, in visual diagnostics, AI models have been trained to be able to inspect medical images for evidence of diseases such as cancer, diabetic retinopathy, and pneumonia. But deep learning algorithms, especially CNNs proved to be a vital tool in this area because they work very well in the area of pattern recognition and anomalies of visual data. For example, AI algorithms prove useful in a mammography analysis system due to its ability to identify early signs of breast cancer, even sometimes before the symptoms will begin to develop or even before the radiologist may note it.

AI is enhancing diagnostic skills in radiology, dermatology and pathology by processing a vast quantity of visual data. In the field of dermatology, AI-based models can classify skin lesions and can quite accurately estimate their malignancy rates as well as seasoned dermatologists. In radiology, AI boosts detection rates of small nodules in the lungs through CT scans-a harbinger of lung cancer.

Early detection is important for effective improvement in survival outcomes, especially in diseases such as cancer or cardiovascular disease, where prompt intervention often results in complete recovery. Automated systems of AI are being incorporated into routine screenings that determine a possibility of the risk factors based on medical imaging, genetic markers, or other related information. This process can automate the decision-making, enabling the health care providers to prioritize further evaluations and treatments for patients with high-risk profiles.

Another usage of AI is in predictive models applied to predict the progression of diseases. Using visual data, patient history, or other clinical information, AI models are able to predict how a disease will evolve and tailor a treatment scheme. For instance, in the treatment of tumor growth, AI can predict patterns of tumor growth; therefore, oncologists can proactively change their treatment strategies.

Personalized Treatment and Predictive Healthcare

AI and machine learning have also ushered in significant strides in personalized medicine, where treatment is specifically tailored to the characteristics of each individual patient. With superior data analytics and visual information processing, health providers can now plan individualized treatments based on the medical history, genetic makeup of a patient, lifestyle issues, and diagnostic images. This move from one-size-fits-all to more individualised methodology will offer better treatment and greater patient satisfaction (Karthik et al., 2023; Pramila et al., 2023; Subha et al., 2023).

While there are a number of applications for personalised treatment, one area of importance impacts on the main area: oncology. There have always been treatments mainly through surgery, chemotherapy, and radiation for any type of cancer, applied alike to all patients. Now, it is possible for oncologists to take into account many other factors with AI-driven predictive models, like the molecular profile of a tumor and how a treatment may work based on past case scenarios. Even with the inclusion of genetic information in MRI and PET scans and all other imaging techniques, visual data is what forms the basis of what the oncologists design to be an individualized plan of treatment to enhance the prognosis.

Similarly, AI also accelerates precision medicine in cardiology through predictive models that give a patient an estimate of his or her risk of heart disease or stroke based on visual data such as coronaries or echocardiograms. By comparing these images with patient-specific data, AI algorithms can help cardiologists develop individualized plans for treatment and prevention, such as lifestyle adjustments, medication, or surgical interventions.

Predictive healthcare models in neurology can be used to diagnose and manage neurodegenerative diseases such as Alzheimer's or Parkinson's. The data regarding brain atrophy or plaque build-up can be detected early by visualizing brain scans with AI analysis, so such cases may give a reasonably early intervention, and the treatments for slowing down the progress of the disease and enhancing the quality of life for patients are further decided with the help of predictive algorithms.

Beyond diagnosis and prediction, personalized therapy includes rehabilitation. AI-based systems can monitor the progress of patients and adjust the rehabilitation programs in real time, thereby providing, effectively, continuous feedback and modifying exercises' intensity or focus to the patient's response.

Visual data, like the tracking of movements made by a patient in physical therapy, can be analyzed to better service the development of treatment programs as to ensure maximum recovery.

Visual information processing combined with AI and machine learning is changing healthcare positively through better imaging, higher accuracy in diagnosis, and customized treatment planning. From MRI to CT and X-ray imaging and from imaging to AI-enhanced diagnostics, the heavy guns for early detection of disease and customized care are now at the disposal of healthcare professionals. The updated computational models make healthcare more predictive and should go a long way in early intervention, good prognosis, and more personalized care to the patients. These developments stand out as an example of the prospects that may be realized through AI and visualization in information processing to a great extent in changing the methodology of diagnosing, treating, and managing health conditions across the medical spectrum.

TECHNOLOGICAL INTEGRATION: AI, ML, AND NEURAL INTERFACES

The conjugation of AI, ML, and neural interfaces is a giant leap in neuroscience research and applications in healthcare. These technologies helped advance what is known about the brain but now are also revolutionizing clinical practices that lead to better health outcomes and greater precision during surgery. Integration of AI and ML with neural interfaces makes it possible to have an approach at both aspects - understanding complex neural processes and applying what is known in real-life medical scenarios (Gopi et al., 2024; Pitchai et al., 2024). The integration of AI, machine learning, and neural interfaces is gaining prominence in neuroscience research and healthcare applications, as depicted in Figure 4.

Figure 4. Technological integration of AI, machine learning (ML), and neural interfaces in neuroscience research and healthcare applications

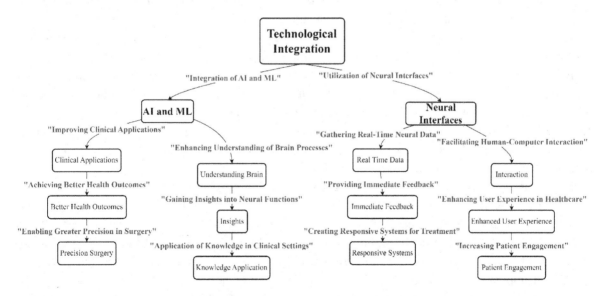

AI-Driven Neuroscience Research

The neuroscience research landscape has changed with the help of AI-driven approaches that permit the analysis of volumes of data of unprecedented rapidity and accuracy. Conventional neuroscience approaches require lengthy, although subjective, steps to analyze manually, but machine learning algorithms now permit such complex datasets, for instance neuroimaging studies, electrophysiological recordings, and genetic profiling to be processed automatically. Therefore, the adoption of machine learning has sparked revolutions in neuroscience.

For instance, AI models could recognize the patterns associated with brain activities related to certain kinds of cognitive processes, such as memory formation, decision-making, or emotional responses. Applying deep learning techniques can begin dissecting complex neural circuits and understanding how parts of the brain communicate with each other. Such insights are crucial to unravel mysteries behind neurodegenerative diseases, mental health disorders and more.

Moreover, the analytics made possible by AI can be used to predict individual responses to treatment. Enabling large data sources from patient histories and neuroimaging as well as genomic information, researchers can develop predictive models for disease course and treatment efficacy. This will not only elucidate the mechanisms underlying neurological disorders but also inform targeted therapies that are more specific and improve care for patients.

Another significant advantage that AI provides in experimental neuroscience is processing and analyzing huge amounts of data online. For example, AI facilitates adaptive learning during brain-machine interface experiments. The system adjusts to the neural signals of the subject in real time. This real-time feedback loop is necessary in developing neuroprosthetic devices that will effectively improve functionality.

Neural Interfaces for Enhanced Visual Processing

Neural interfaces-both BCIs and retinal implants-situate the place where neuroscience intersects with technology to render human vision more efficient and allow the brain to access such devices outside the human body. The state of being visually impaired can be restored by these interfaces, hence presenting new avenues for research and therapeutic studies (Boopathi, 2024; Gopal et al., 2024; Teja et al., 2024).

BCI systems have been developed in order to interpret neural signals coming out from the brain and translate them into actionable commands for external devices. Whereas the technology has immense implications for patients who are suffering from motor disorders, it has succeeded in helping them exercise some degree of control over prosthetic limbs, wheelchairs, or even computer cursors through thoughts alone. New applications focus on visual processing and use BCIs in order to improve the vision of the patient or help them recover some visual functions.

For instance, efforts are underway to create cortical visual prostheses, with a direct activation of the visual cortices designed to bypass damaged retinal cells. Such implants have been applied in clinically applied conditions to offer patients certain forms of artificial vision, such as shape, motion, or patterns. This development not only extends and improves the quality of life for some of those who are visually impaired but also helps contribute to our understanding of how such information enters our brains.

Retinal implants, such as the Argus II, are another type of neural interface envisioned for visual restoration. These capture images from a camera mounted on the body as a pair of glasses and then transmit that image to an implant that activates existing cells in the retina. AI integration can improve the functionality of such devices by enhancing the processing of images in an improved intuitive visual experience.

Neural interfaces can be integrated with augmented reality technologies to create an immersive visual experience. In this connection, augmented reality technologies find applications in creating real-time visual data integration with neural inputs to probe into the way a brain interacts with an augmented environment. Synergizing neural interfaces with AR technologies opens such new frontiers in neurology and enables rehabilitation and cognitive training opportunities.

AI Assisted Surgery: Precision, Robotics, and Visualization

AI-assisted surgery is another groundbreaking application of the integration of AI, ML, and neural interfaces within health care. The use of systems that incorporate AI algorithms has enhanced the use of robotics in surgery, consequently changing the nature of surgical procedures to achieve sharp accuracies, shorter periods of recovery, and decreased complications and risk factors. Such advanced systems have helped surgeons carry out intricate operations with a precision degree unattainable through traditional techniques (Ahamed et al., 2024; Puranik et al., 2024; Revathi et al., 2024; Srinivas et al., 2023).

AI algorithms can review a patient's preoperative imaging data and collaborate in the design of surgical approaches tailor-made for that particular patient. For example, an AI could assist surgeons in determining the optimal entry sites to reach brain tumors to ensure as little destruction to adjacent healthy brain tissue as possible. It can integrate real-time imaging data with insights provided by machine learning algorithms, making it possible for surgeons to make informed decisions about their surgeries.

Robotic surgical systems, such as the da Vinci Surgical System, can improve dexterity and control in minimally invasive procedures, for example with high-definition three-dimensional visualization. These systems do not just provide surgeons with leading edge visualization tools but also use AI algorithms to improve those with the potential for predictive analytics over the course of surgery, thus alerting a surgeon to potential complications or suggesting alternative approaches based on real-time data.

Another much-desired integration would be that of neural interfaces with surgical systems. For example, neurosurgeons can monitor neural activity during surgeries using BCIs to better navigate delicate procedures involving areas critical for the brain. In such instances, real-time feedback could guide surgical maneuvers and increase the safety of deep brain stimulations or tumor resections.

In addition, advances in AI-algorithm-driven visualization methods like AR/VR will likely provide the surgeon with vivid experiences of immersive training and enhanced situational awareness of the scene during surgery. Technologies of this nature can realistically mimic diverse complex surgical conditions and allow surgeons to learn and practice skills in safe conditions. Real-time AR over a surgery can also draw attention to critical structures and assist surgical instruments to ensure higher accuracy.

This technological integration of AI, ML, and neural interfaces is actually changing the landscape of neuroscience and healthcare. Research into brain function, due to the enablement of AI-driven research, is going faster now, and there is also easier access to personal medicine through these interfaces. Neural interfaces improve visual processing by enabling innovative treatments for impairments. The AI-assisted techniques have evolved surgical practices in improving intricate procedures' precision and safety to transform how surgeries are conducted. These technologies are going to open new avenues in the care of a patient and bring a revolution about in our understanding of the human brain.

CHALLENGES IN VISUAL INFORMATION PROCESSING

As visual information processing is developed further, especially in the areas of computational neuroscience and healthcare, several issues surface that need to be considered in order for the effect to be meaningful and safe (Gopi et al., 2024; Mohanraj et al., 2024; Upadhyaya et al., 2024).

Data Availability and Annotation

One of the major challenges facing visual information processing is the availability and quality of the data. High-quality labeled datasets are the most fundamental requirement for training machine learning models, particularly CNNs, which need large amounts of annotated visual data in order to become operational. However, this also proves expensive and time-consuming to generate. Most datasets that appear in the literature are too small or do not provide sufficient diversity in choices to lead to developed models that perform well in real-world applications.

nnotation of the visual data especially on medical imaging requires specific knowledge. Labeling images must be done carefully by radiologists or experts. The process, however is lengthy. Poor or incoherent annotations can impact the performance of AI models, and the answers might become completely wrong even dangerous in real clinical settings. Thus, making availability more extensive and improving procedures associated with annotation are significant to advance the utilization of processing visible information in health care and neuroscience.

Privacy and Security in Health Care Data

The introduction of AI and visual information processing in health care has raised critical questions regarding privacy and security. The client data is very sensitive, and misuse or unauthorized access can create major ethical as well as legal implications. In this regard, issues relate to the anonymization and safe storage of data used for training and analysis, yet accessible for legit research and clinical purposes. The country of the United States does have strict requirements in the use of medical data, as stipulated in legislation in its handling, most notably under HIPAA, but complexity has also been cited as a barrier to the advancement of innovative applications of AI. Access to such information will always play against the patient's right to privacy, and balancing the two remains one of the vital challenges faced today.

Interpretable AI Models in Critical Applications

An issue with AI models, specifically critical applications such as healthcare and neuroscience, lies with their interpretability. Most advanced AI models, specifically deep learning algorithms, are regarded as "black boxes," allowing little insight into how they came to a decision. Such a lack of transparency can be problematic in the clinical setting in which the rationale for a model's prediction is key to garnering the trust of healthcare professionals and patients. How such decisions are arrived at, for instance, becomes critical knowledge for physicians and clinicians during the planning of surgery or even the diagnosis of serious medical conditions. Improved interpretability of AI systems is a requirement for their responsible application to health care.

Ethical Issues in Neuroscience and Medicine

Finally, ethical issues in neuroscience and medicine continue to haunt them. The use of AI technologies in both fields raises issues of consent, accountability, and potential biases and unfair practices in algorithms. For instance, the phenomenon of differential disadvantages in access and their related healthcare treatment can be inadvertently perpetuated with nonrepresentative training datasets for AI models. Moreover, the use of neural interfaces and other invasive technologies raises questions about autonomy and the potential for misuse. Collaborative involvement among technologists, ethicists, healthcare providers, and regulatory bodies will be needed to develop guidelines for the development and use of AI applications while truly prioritizing the welfare of patients and equitable access to innovation.

These challenges need to be addressed to ensure that visual information processing technologies are properly integrated into the domain of neuroscience and health care. Available data, along with related processes such as annotation, will be promoted by protecting privacy and security, model interpretability, and the necessary taking of ethical aspects into account for the benefits realized through the development of such technologies while limiting risks and promoting responsible use. Figure 5 highlights the challenges and future work in visual information processing for computational neuroscience and healthcare.

Figure 5. Challenges and future work: Advances in visual information processing for computational neuroscience and healthcare

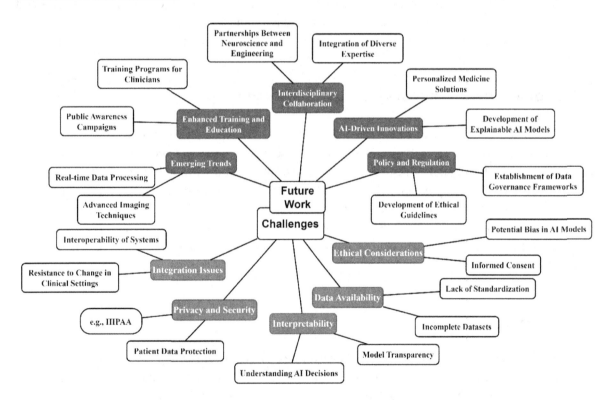

FUTURE DIRECTIONS AND INNOVATIONS

Emerging Trends in Visual Data Processing

The next phase of visual data processing promises to be quite revolutionary, while some of the trends which are driving this are better algorithms, more powerful computing, and improved integration techniques. In terms of trendy applications, generative models such as GANs might be leveraged for the synthesis of realistic visual data for training and testing AI systems. This can give the possibility to handle problems of scarcity of data, especially in specific domains such as medical imaging. Simultaneously, multimodal data which integrates visual with textual, auditory, and sensor information can potentially add more depth and richness of visual inputs within their context for more holistic models to tackle complex tasks both in neuroscience and healthcare (Gopi et al., 2024; Pitchai et al., 2024).

Interdisciplinary Collaboration and Research

Interdisciplinary research will be crucial to drive innovation in visual information processing. The integration of neuroscience with computer science, engineering, and ethics will be beneficial in cross-disciplinary solutions to the various problems encountered in the fields. Advances in neural interfaces might be achieved through such interdisciplinary research initiatives. Such programs can further develop AI-driven diagnostics and enhanced therapeutic strategies to pursue more effective treatments and interventions. Coordinated efforts, such as joint academic-industry collaborations, will speed up the translation of theoretical scientific discoveries into practice. This would make research and implementation walk hand in hand.

Future of AI-Driven Neuroscience and Healthcare

Neuroscience and healthcare with AI - A view: The long-term perspective for precision and personalization. Powerhouse AI algorithms with the strong visual data processing techniques would facilitate aspiration towards the design of personalized treatment plans tailored to unique patient profiles. The same vision will be used in predictive analytics AI models to forecast disease progression and treatment responses to employ proactive health care strategies. Improvements to Brain Computer Interfaces, and other neural technologies, can empower disabled persons to regain lost functions, improving quality of life. Finally, the infusion of AI into neuroscience and healthcare brings a revolution in patient care that is now going to be efficient, accurate, and accessible.

CONCLUSION

There lies a massive intersection between the world of visual information processing, computational neuroscience, and health. As we have thus far found out, the foundations of visual perception along with the use of deep learning techniques, such as convolutional neural networks, provided a sense of hope for increased applications in these fields. Everything, from medical imaging and diagnostics to advanced brain-computer interfaces, could eventually be driven by powerful AI solutions that turn these ideas into reality.

It has to be acknowledged that the journey is not without problems. There are several concerns related to issues of data availability, privacy, interpretability, and ethics, among others, that need to be ironed out so that these technologies are designed responsibly and deployed effectively. Towards this end, the future direction of visual data processing would lie in the encouragement of interdisciplinary collaborations and bridging gaps between neurosciences, technologies, and health care, which would ultimately promote research with real-world applications and therefore better patient benefits. Looking ahead, neuroscience and healthcare thus might be envisaged in an AI-enhanced landscape: "precision and personalization," finally enabling patients and healthcare providers alike. Embracing these innova-tions even as we keep vigilant attention on their implications might perhaps unlock the full human potential for processing visual information to better human health and well-being.

REFERENCES

Ahad, M. A. R., Antar, A. D., & Shahid, O. (2019). Vision-based Action Understanding for Assistive Healthcare: A Short Review. *CVPR Workshops*, 1–11.

Ahamed, B. S., Chakravarthy, K. S., Arputhabalan, J., Sasirekha, K., Prince, R. M. R., Boopathi, S., & Muthuvel, S. (2024). Revolutionizing Friction Stir Welding With AI-Integrated Humanoid Robots. In *Advances in Computational Intelligence and Robotics* (pp. 120–144). IGI Global. DOI: 10.4018/979-8-3693-2399-1.ch005

Al Mamun, S., Kaiser, M. S., & Mahmud, M. (2021). An artificial intelligence based approach towards inclusive healthcare provisioning in society 5.0: A perspective on brain disorder. *International Conference on Brain Informatics*, 157–169. DOI: 10.1007/978-3-030-86993-9_15

Alsenan, A., Ben Youssef, B., & Alhichri, H. (2022). Mobileunetv3—A combined unet and mobilenetv3 architecture for spinal cord gray matter segmentation. *Electronics (Basel)*, 11(15), 2388. DOI: 10.3390/electronics11152388

Behera, R. K., Bala, P. K., & Dhir, A. (2019). The emerging role of cognitive computing in healthcare: A systematic literature review. *International Journal of Medical Informatics*, 129, 154–166. DOI: 10.1016/j.ijmedinf.2019.04.024 PMID: 31445250

Boopathi, S. (2024). Influences of nano-green lubricants on the performance of grinding machining process. In *Lecture Notes in Mechanical Engineering* (pp. 45–53). Springer Nature Singapore.

Fellous, J.-M., Sapiro, G., Rossi, A., Mayberg, H., & Ferrante, M. (2019). Explainable artificial intelligence for neuroscience: Behavioral neurostimulation. *Frontiers in Neuroscience*, 13, 1346. DOI: 10.3389/fnins.2019.01346 PMID: 31920509

Glomb, K., Cabral, J., Cattani, A., Mazzoni, A., Raj, A., & Franceschiello, B. (2022). Computational models in electroencephalography. *Brain Topography*, 35(1), 142–161. DOI: 10.1007/s10548-021-00828-2 PMID: 33779888

Gopal, M., Lurdhumary, J., Bathrinath, S., Priya, A. P., Sarojwal, A., & Boopathi, S. (2024). Energy Harvesting and Smart Highways for Sustainable Transportation Infrastructure: Revolutionizing Roads Using Nanotechnology. In *Principles and Applications in Speed Sensing and Energy Harvesting for Smart Roads* (pp. 136–165). IGI Global. DOI: 10.4018/978-1-6684-9214-7.ch005

Gopi, B., Sworna Kokila, M. L., Bibin, C. V., Sasikala, D., Howard, E., & Boopathi, S. (2024). Distributed Technologies Using AI/ML Techniques for Healthcare Applications. In *Advances in Human and Social Aspects of Technology* (pp. 375–396). IGI Global. DOI: 10.4018/979-8-3693-2569-8.ch019

Ienca, M., & Ignatiadis, K. (2020). Artificial intelligence in clinical neuroscience: Methodological and ethical challenges. *AJOB Neuroscience*, 11(2), 77–87. DOI: 10.1080/21507740.2020.1740352 PMID: 32228387

Karthik, S., Hemalatha, R., Aruna, R., Deivakani, M., Reddy, R. V. K., & Boopathi, S. (2023). Study on Healthcare Security System-Integrated Internet of Things (IoT). In *Perspectives and Considerations on the Evolution of Smart Systems* (pp. 342–362). IGI Global.

Kording, K. P., Blohm, G., Schrater, P., & Kay, K. (2020). Appreciating the variety of goals in computational neuroscience. *arXiv Preprint arXiv:2002.03211.*

Leo, M., Carcagnì, P., Mazzeo, P. L., Spagnolo, P., Cazzato, D., & Distante, C. (2020). Analysis of facial information for healthcare applications: A survey on computer vision-based approaches. *Information (Basel)*, 11(3), 128. DOI: 10.3390/info11030128

Maturi, M. H., Satish, S., Gonaygunta, H., & Meduri, K. (2022). The Intersection of Artificial Intelligence and Neuroscience: Unlocking the Mysteries of the Brain. *International Journal of Creative Research In Computer Technology and Design*, 4(4), 1–21.

Mohanraj, G., Krishna, K. S., Lakshmi, B. S., Vijayalakshmi, A., Pramila, P. V., & Boopathi, S. (2024). Optimizing Trust and Security in Healthcare 4.0: Human Factors in Lightweight Secured IoMT Ecosystems. In *Lightweight Digital Trust Architectures in the Internet of Medical Things (IoMT)* (pp. 52–72). IGI Global. DOI: 10.4018/979-8-3693-2109-6.ch004

Pitchai, R., Guru, K. V., Gandhi, J. N., Komala, C. R., Kumar, J. R. D., & Boopathi, S. (2024). Fog Computing-Integrated ML-Based Framework and Solutions for Intelligent Systems: Digital Healthcare Applications. In *Technological Advancements in Data Processing for Next Generation Intelligent Systems* (pp. 196–224). IGI Global. DOI: 10.4018/979-8-3693-0968-1.ch008

Pramila, P., Amudha, S., Saravanan, T., Sankar, S. R., Poongothai, E., & Boopathi, S. (2023). Design and Development of Robots for Medical Assistance: An Architectural Approach. In *Contemporary Applications of Data Fusion for Advanced Healthcare Informatics* (pp. 260–282). IGI Global.

Puranik, T. A., Shaik, N., Vankudoth, R., Kolhe, M. R., Yadav, N., & Boopathi, S. (2024). Study on Harmonizing Human-Robot (Drone) Collaboration: Navigating Seamless Interactions in Collaborative Environments. In *Cybersecurity Issues and Challenges in the Drone Industry* (pp. 1–26). IGI Global.

Ramudu, K., Mohan, V. M., Jyothirmai, D., Prasad, D., Agrawal, R., & Boopathi, S. (2023). Machine Learning and Artificial Intelligence in Disease Prediction: Applications, Challenges, Limitations, Case Studies, and Future Directions. In *Contemporary Applications of Data Fusion for Advanced Healthcare Informatics* (pp. 297–318). IGI Global.

Revathi, S., Babu, M., Rajkumar, N., Meti, V. K. V., Kandavalli, S. R., & Boopathi, S. (2024). Unleashing the Future Potential of 4D Printing: Exploring Applications in Wearable Technology, Robotics, Energy, Transportation, and Fashion. In *Human-Centered Approaches in Industry 5.0: Human-Machine Interaction, Virtual Reality Training, and Customer Sentiment Analysis* (pp. 131–153). IGI Global.

Sarishma, D., Sangwan, S., Tomar, R., & Srivastava, R. (2022). A review on cognitive computational neuroscience: Overview, models, and applications. *Innovative Trends in Computational Intelligence*, 217–234.

Sodhro, A. H., Sennersten, C., & Ahmad, A. (2022). Towards cognitive authentication for smart healthcare applications. *Sensors (Basel)*, 22(6), 2101. DOI: 10.3390/s22062101 PMID: 35336276

Sreedhar, P. S. S., Sujay, V., Rani, M. R., Melita, L., Reshma, S., & Boopathi, S. (2024). Impacts of 5G Machine Learning Techniques on Telemedicine and Social Media Professional Connection in Healthcare. In *Advances in Medical Technologies and Clinical Practice* (pp. 209–234). IGI Global. DOI: 10.4018/979-8-3693-1934-5.ch012

Srinivas, B., Maguluri, L. P., Naidu, K. V., Reddy, L. C. S., Deivakani, M., & Boopathi, S. (2023). Architecture and Framework for Interfacing Cloud-Enabled Robots. In *Handbook of Research on Data Science and Cybersecurity Innovations in Industry 4.0 Technologies* (pp. 542–560). IGI Global. DOI: 10.4018/978-1-6684-8145-5.ch027

Srivani, M., Murugappan, A., & Mala, T. (2023). Cognitive computing technological trends and future research directions in healthcare—A systematic literature review. *Artificial Intelligence in Medicine*, 138, 102513. DOI: 10.1016/j.artmed.2023.102513 PMID: 36990590

Stevens, R., Galloway, T., & Willemsen-Dunlap, A. (2019). Advancing our understandings of healthcare team dynamics from the simulation room to the operating room: A neurodynamic perspective. *Frontiers in Psychology*, 10, 1660. DOI: 10.3389/fpsyg.2019.01660 PMID: 31456706

Subha, S., Inbamalar, T., Komala, C., Suresh, L. R., Boopathi, S., & Alaskar, K. (2023). A Remote Health Care Monitoring system using internet of medical things (IoMT). *IEEE Explore*, 1–6.

Teja, N. B., Kannagi, V., Chandrashekhar, A., Senthilnathan, T., Pal, T. K., & Boopathi, S. (2024). Impacts of Nano-Materials and Nano Fluids on the Robot Industry and Environments. In *Advances in Computational Intelligence and Robotics* (pp. 171–194). IGI Global. DOI: 10.4018/979-8-3693-5767-5.ch012

Tripathi, U., Chamola, V., Jolfaei, A., & Chintanpalli, A. (2021). Advancing remote healthcare using humanoid and affective systems. *IEEE Sensors Journal*, 22(18), 17606–17614. DOI: 10.1109/JSEN.2021.3049247

Upadhyaya, A. N., Saqib, A., Devi, J. V., Rallapalli, S., Sudha, S., & Boopathi, S. (2024). Implementation of the Internet of Things (IoT) in Remote Healthcare. In *Advances in Medical Technologies and Clinical Practice* (pp. 104–124). IGI Global. DOI: 10.4018/979-8-3693-1934-5.ch006

Wood, D., Cole, J., & Booth, T. (2019). NEURO-DRAM: a 3D recurrent visual attention model for interpretable neuroimaging classification. *arXiv Preprint arXiv:1910.04721*.

Yu, Z., Liu, J. K., Jia, S., Zhang, Y., Zheng, Y., Tian, Y., & Huang, T. (2020). Toward the next generation of retinal neuroprosthesis: Visual computation with spikes. *Engineering (Beijing)*, 6(4), 449–461. DOI: 10.1016/j.eng.2020.02.004

Zhang, Y., Gao, J., Tan, Z., Zhou, L., Ding, K., Zhou, M., Zhang, S., & Wang, D. (2024). Data-centric foundation models in computational healthcare: A survey. *arXiv Preprint arXiv:2401.02458*.

ADDITIONAL READING

Karthik, S., Hemalatha, R., Aruna, R., Deivakani, M., Reddy, R. V. K., & Boopathi, S. (2023). Study on Healthcare Security System-Integrated Internet of Things (IoT). In Perspectives and Considerations on the Evolution of Smart Systems (pp. 342–362). IGI Global.

Kushwah, J. S., Gupta, M., Shrivastava, S., Saxena, N., Saini, R., & Boopathi, S. (2024). Psychological Impacts, Prevention Strategies, and Intervention Approaches Across Age Groups: Unmasking Cyberbullying. In Change Dynamics in Healthcare, Technological Innovations, and Complex Scenarios (pp. 89–109). IGI Global.

Malathi, J., Kusha, K., Isaac, S., Ramesh, A., Rajendiran, M., & Boopathi, S. (2024). IoT-Enabled Remote Patient Monitoring for Chronic Disease Management and Cost Savings: Transforming Healthcare. In Advances in Explainable AI Applications for Smart Cities (pp. 371–388). IGI Global.

Mohanraj, G., Krishna, K. S., Lakshmi, B. S., Vijayalakshmi, A., Pramila, P. V., & Boopathi, S. (2024). Optimizing Trust and Security in Healthcare 4.0: Human Factors in Lightweight Secured IoMT Ecosystems. In Lightweight Digital Trust Architectures in the Internet of Medical Things (IoMT) (pp. 52–72). IGI Global. DOI: 10.4018/979-8-3693-2109-6.ch004

Pitchai, R., Guru, K. V., Gandhi, J. N., Komala, C. R., Kumar, J. R. D., & Boopathi, S. (2024). Fog Computing-Integrated ML-Based Framework and Solutions for Intelligent Systems: Digital Healthcare Applications. In Technological Advancements in Data Processing for Next Generation Intelligent Systems (pp. 196–224). IGI Global. DOI: 10.4018/979-8-3693-0968-1.ch008

Satav, S. D., Hasan, D. S., Pitchai, R., Mohanaprakash, T., Sultanuddin, S., & Boopathi, S. (2023). Next generation of internet of things (ngiot) in healthcare systems. In *Sustainable Science and Intelligent Technologies for Societal Development* (pp. 307–330). IGI Global.

Sreedhar, P. S. S., Sujay, V., Rani, M. R., Melita, L., Reshma, S., & Boopathi, S. (2024). Impacts of 5G Machine Learning Techniques on Telemedicine and Social Media Professional Connection in Healthcare. In Advances in Medical Technologies and Clinical Practice (pp. 209–234). IGI Global. DOI: 10.4018/979-8-3693-1934-5.ch012

Upadhyaya, A. N., Saqib, A., Devi, J. V., Rallapalli, S., Sudha, S., & Boopathi, S. (2024). Implementation of the Internet of Things (IoT) in Remote Healthcare. In *Advances in Medical Technologies and Clinical Practice* (pp. 104–124). IGI Global., DOI: 10.4018/979-8-3693-1934-5.ch006

KEY TERMS AND DEFINITIONS

Artificial Intelligence (AI): simulation of processes involved in human intelligence by machines, allowing them to learn, reason, and make decisions.

Attention Deficit Hyperactivity Disorder (ADHD): This is one of those neurodevelopmental disorders of the kind that affects focus and behavior.

Augmented Reality (AR): Supplementing reality with the aid of computer-generated elements.

Brain-Computer Interface (BCI): Similar to BMI, an interface of the computer with human brains and facilitating devices to be controlled through the neural signals.

Brain-Machine Interface (BMI): A direct pathway of communication from the brain to devices and vice versa.

Computed Tomography (CT): A technique of combining measurements with X-rays to provide cross-sectional images.

Convolutional Neural Network (CNN): A a deep learning model designed for processing grid-like data, such as images, using convolutional layers to automatically learn spatial hierarchies of features.

Deep Learning (DL): This is a subfield of ML. It utilizes neural networks with multiple internal layers modeling complex patterns in large datasets.

Generative Adversarial Network (GAN): This is a class of deep learning models consisting of two neural networks, a generator and a discriminator, that compete to create and evaluate realistic data.

Health Insurance Portability and Accountability Act (HIPAA): This is a U.S. legislation designed to protect patients' health information.

Lateral Geniculate Nucleus (LGN): A relay centre of the thalamus with regard to visual information.

Machine Learning (ML): This is a subset of AI concentrating on algorithms that learn from data in a given sample without the use of explicit programming.

Magnetic Resonance Imaging (MRI): It is a technique for visualizing internal images of the body for medical purposes.

Positron Emission Tomography (PET): This is an imaging test which makes possible the acquisition of a picture of how tissues and organs function.

Virtual Reality (VR): A hypothetical world synthesized by computer.

Chapter 14
High–Performance Computer–Integrated Microcontrollers for Enhancing Food Quality Monitoring:
Innovations and Applications

Prachi Rajendra Salve

Department of Computer Engineering, MKSSS's Cummins College of Engineering for Women, Pune, India

M. R. Mano Jemila

Department of Biomedical Engineering, Dr. NGP Institute of Technology, Coimbatore, India

S. Sridharan

Department of Electrical and Electronics Engineering, St. Joseph's College of Engineering, Chennai, India

Vinod Kumar V. Meti

https://orcid.org/0000-0001-5692-9693

Department of Automation and Robotics, KLE Technological University, Hubballi, India

Bhaskar Roy

https://orcid.org/0009-0000-3045-3834

Department of Computer Science and Engineering, Asansol Engineering College, India

ABSTRACT

Application of high-performance computer systems and microcontrollers in food quality monitoring pays extra attention to their improvements in accuracy, efficiency, and real-time analysis. Advanced microcontrollers allow the accomplishment of more precise monitoring of critical parameters such as temperature, humidity, and gas composition in order to ensure food safety and quality from supply chain outlets. Innovations in sensor technology, data processing, and wireless communication gave birth to smart systems for detecting contamination, spoilage, or adulteration. These systems feed real-time data

DOI: 10.4018/978-1-6684-3795-7.ch014

that enables instantaneous decisions and reduces food waste. Microcontroller-based solutions allow for IoT connectivity and machine learning algorithms with a better possibility of predictive analytics and automation in the management of food quality. The chapter is focused on the key technologies, applications, and challenges, giving insight into the future regarding food quality monitoring in this very connected world, particularly about food industries.

INTRODUCTION

This is an essential ingredient in ensuring food safety and, above all, keeping the consumers' trust as globalization interlinks myriad complexity in the food supply chain. As more awareness is gained pertaining to food quality issues, regulatory bodies set up strict safety standards that call for more resilient monitoring systems. In this end, the integration of computer high-performance systems with microcontrollers offers a transformative approach toward improving food quality monitoring. This chapter discusses recent innovations and applications involving these advanced technologies, including their impact on food safety, quality assurance, and sustainability (Rebecca et al., 2024).

A microcontroller is a small integrated circuit that has been designed with the aim of controlling specific operations in an embedded system, which is at the heart of systems that monitor food quality. The microcontrollers provide the much needed computational capability for processing sensor data, carrying out control algorithms, and communicating with other devices. The most impressive in-built functionality included in microcontrollers is the integration of high-performance computing, which can be used for sophisticated data analysis and decision-making. Thus, this integration gives food producers, processors, and retailers real-time monitoring solutions that could drastically mitigate risks related to food safety and quality degradation (Ahmad et al., 2017).

The development of smart food quality monitoring systems has been further accelerated with the integration of IoT technology. IoT-equipped sensors now make it possible to capture, record, and compare data from various supply chain locations; this provides stakeholders with the ability to follow close records of events impacting the quality of food-temperature, humidity, and even atmospheric gas concentrations. For instance, in cold chain logistics for perishables, a real-time temperature monitoring check ensures that products are stored and transported within optimal conditions and thus minimize the risk of spoilage. The collected data are then processed and analyzed through machine learning algorithms for underlying patterns that might predict a possible malfunction, such as equipment breakdown or unsuitable storage conditions (Malouche et al., 2015).

Sensor technology advancements have also played an important role in the improvement of food quality monitoring. Modern sensors can measure a wide range of parameters, from physical attributes to chemical indicators like pH and volatile organic compounds. The connection of microcontrollers to these sensors enables the creation of the most sophisticated monitoring systems that may eventually offer useful insight into food quality and safety. For example, the sensing of ethylene gas, which fruits emit during ripening, with the help of gas sensors, allows producers to achieve optimal storage conditions and extend shelf life (Ibrahim, 2006).

The capacity to process and analyze huge quantities of data in real-time is also fundamental to the effective food quality monitoring system. These new high-performance microcontrollers can process complex algorithms and workloads related to data analytics that have been for a long time relegated to larger computing systems. This means that food manufacturers could deploy advanced quality control in quality assessment and management of their equipment in real-time with predictive maintenance of equipment during production. The early notification of deviations from established quality parameters allows companies to take corrective action before defects reach the consumer, with minimum waste and, consequently, the overall inefficiency (Yadav, 2004).

The use of wireless communications technologies in food quality monitoring systems also supports the stated efficiency of quality control. Since wireless networks can deliver real-time information transmission by remote sensors directly to the center of the database, full supply chain monitoring in real-time is possible. This function is highly useful for companies having multi-location business or large distribution channels. A decentralized cloud-based data storage and analytical approach give access to stakeholders to the information needed so that in alignment with the supply chain, decisions can be made and coordinated by them (Sadraey, 2017).

Despite tremendous developments in technology, food quality monitoring is apparently still facing several problems in adopting high-performance computer-integrated microcontrollers. Most fundamentally, it is in sensor technology and data formats that should be standardized; sensor interoperability has been one of the concerns because of the many different kinds that manufacturers have in their production lines plus their communication protocols. Consolidated standards can help integrate various systems and promote better effectiveness in food quality monitoring solutions (Al-Dhaher, 2004).

In addition, upfront investment in the advanced monitoring system may keep some of the small and medium-sized enterprises from using such technologies. Long-term advantages of prevention of food wastes due to fresh food and improved food safety are obvious, but the upfront cost towards implementing high-performance microcontrollers and sensor technologies can be discouraging to business decision-makers. This calls for policymakers and industry stakeholders to come together in designing incentives and support systems that would encourage the use of advanced monitoring systems up and down the food supply chain (Al-Dhaher, 2004).

In addition to economic barriers, there are also the technical problems, especially related to data security and privacy. With increased dependency on connected devices for food quality monitoring, the threat of potentially exposing sensitive data to cyber hacking is a potential concern. Only through robust cybersecurity measures can proprietary information be safely guarded while maintaining consumer trust. The process of making food quality monitoring systems increasingly interconnected requires establishing secured forms of communication protocol and data encryption methods to mitigate risk (Swathi et al., 2018).

The future of high-performance computer-integrated microcontrollers in food quality monitoring seems boundless. The emergent future technologies, such as AI and blockchain, open new ways to escalate the previously mentioned dimensions toward increasing food safety and traceability. AI can be exploited to analyze a vast source of data and may inform predictive analytics systems that can predict possible problems before they occur. The blockchain technology will provide an immutable record of all transactions in the food chain to help ensure transparency and accountability throughout the food supply chain. And collectively, these technologies will help build a better food system-a quality-and safety-focused one (Castiglia et al., 2018).

High performance computer systems married with microcontrollers represents outstanding progress with respect to food quality monitoring. The capacity of food supply chain stakeholders to view and control food quality will improve with the use of IoT technology, new sensor innovations, and real-time data processing capabilities. Notwithstanding the stated barriers against standardization, investment costs, and cybersecurity, there are prosiderable benefits. As the food industry continues to evolve, embracing high-performance computer-integrated microcontrollers will be crucial in ensuring the safety, quality, and sustainability of our food supply. This chapter goes into more detail about specific case studies, emerging trends, and future directions regarding food quality monitoring, offering a robust overview of the developments and opportunities in this critical area (Crepaldi et al., 2021).

Objectives

This chapter focuses on the applications of high-performance computer systems and microcontrollers towards food quality monitoring with respect to their applications for high accuracy, high efficiency and real time analysis. It considers how complex advances in microcontrollers allied with innovations in sensor technologies, data processing, and wireless communication are changing the food safety and quality dimensions at the supply chain level. This will bring the limelight on the integration of IoT connectivity and machine learning in predictive analytics as well as automation within food management. Finally, the chapter addresses the essential problems of key technologies, applications, and challenges and draws a vision about future perspectives for industries concerning agriculture, manufacture, and logistics relating to food quality monitoring.

HIGH-PERFORMANCE MICROCONTROLLERS

Definition and Functionality

High-performance microcontrollers are specialized application-specific processors that may be used to control particular functions within any embedded system. It may, or it may not have improved processing power, greater memory capacity, and more complex functions than those of the common microcontrollers. MCUs engineered for such sophisticated computing tasks are best for applications that require real-time processing and multitasking capabilities. Unlike ordinary MCUs that, in the majority of cases, deal with basic control functions, high-performance microcontrollers are provided with strong architectures in order to include advanced instruction sets, a high clock, and integrated peripherals and hence can be more efficient and be used in a wider range of applications (Xu et al., 2024).

High performance microcontrollers are not only restricted to simple processing. They usually consist of onboard elements, such as ADCs, DACs, UART, SPI, I2C, etc., and timers. Onboard elements facilitate circuit designs through fewer external components in a system, making it easier; these factors cut down expenses and reliability as well. Most high-performance MCUs provide sophisticated programming environments and development tools that facilitate rapid prototyping and deployment of applications embedded in them. The main benefit of these microcontrollers is the ability to fit them to a broad spectrum of applications, such as automotive, consumer electronics, medical devices, as well as food quality monitoring.

Comparison with the Standard Microcontrollers

Comparing high-performance microcontrollers and standard microcontrollers reveals several principal differences, particularly regarding processing capabilities, architecture, and their intended applications. Standard microcontrollers are typically designed for straightforward control tasks, like a turn-on/off operation or reading data from a sensor. Typically, they usually offer less processing power, less memory capacity, and fewer integrated peripherals compared to others. For instance, 8-bit traditional microcontroller can be expected to work at a clock of around 16 MHz and hold about 1-2 KB of memory; it is, therefore, suitable for very simple applications, such as household appliances or simple electronic devices (S. Wang et al., 2024a).

High-performance microcontrollers, on the other hand, run at a much higher clock speed-often above 100 MHz and support 32-bit or even 64-bit architectures where such chips are well-equipped to execute more complex algorithms and handle larger data sets efficiently. In addition, they can run with hundreds of kilobytes up to several megabytes of flash memory and SRAM to facilitate a much more extensive kind of software application. With the advent of improved computation capabilities, high-performance MCUs can run multiple operations at faster speeds. Therefore, one area where they may be preferable is in real-time processing applications such as autonomous vehicles, advanced robotics, and sophisticated food monitoring systems.

Another critical difference lies in the integrated features. While highly advanced microcontrollers have several differences from their traditional counterparts, ones of the most important aspects is how these devices will integrate advanced peripherals - things such as high resolution ADCs for sensor reading, highspeed communication interfaces such as Ethernet and USB for data transfer, and robust security capabilities for protecting data. These extra features make them much more versatile for complex applications, whereas sometimes traditional microcontrollers may need to make use of external components to do the same jobs, thereby increasing design complexity and perhaps introducing reliability problems.

Processing Capabilities and Benefits

The processing capabilities of high-performance microcontrollers make them even more useful in so many applications. For example, real-time data processing can be the biggest advantage; this is very crucial in applications that require timely responses. In food quality monitoring systems, for instance, high-performance MCUs can process information from several sensors with the real-time adjustment of storage conditions or alerts when the range is out of the quality parameters. This way, it improves protection regarding food safety, while operation efficiency is also improved since delays in response times are minimized (Ramesh, 2024).

Advanced algorithms, such as AI and ML-based, often involve high-performance microcontrollers: This means that predictive analytics can be built into systems to predict and prevent possible issues of quality before they even start to happen. For instance, an MCU will determine when there is a likelihood to cause spoilage based on its analysis of historical data on temperature and humidity conditions. With this prediction, the stakeholders will proactively take their measures to prevent the occurrence. This is a very important characteristic in supply chain management where the integrity of the products depends on optimal conditions.

Energy efficiency is also one of the merits that high-performance MCUs can offer. Some of these devices include the use of low-power modes and sophisticated power management capabilities, making it possible to operate efficiently in energy-scarce environments. For example, remote monitoring applications demand only low power input-this is where the efficiency of high-performance MCUs can prove useful. Therefore, optimizing power consumption can help reduce the cost of operations and increase sustainability in food quality monitoring systems.

Furthermore, with a high-performance microcontroller-based food quality monitoring system, design is simplified and reliability is enhanced. Combining many functionalities into one device means that fewer individual components take up less space than if they were standalone devices, so designs are less bulky. Decreasing the number of parts to manufacture reduces manufacturing costs while minimizing possible points of failure, thus enhancing system reliability. Integration of in-built high-security features such as encryption and secure boot mechanisms protects sensitive data from unauthorized access which is strongly needed in this age where a data breach can prove disastrous to both consumers and business alike.

Another salient advantage of high-performance microcontrollers is their versatility. In fact, these devices are designed keeping in mind scalability because technological advancements occur at a very rapid pace. Such devices allow for up-gradation and modification as newer technologies come into existence. The benefits ensure that food quality monitoring systems can be developed incorporating newer sensors, communication protocols, or more analytical tools without necessarily designing from scratch. Such adaptability assumes important contours in a competitive environment where the onus lies on business houses to continually innovate to meet the changing demands of consumers and to remain up-to-date with the changing scenarios of regulatory requirements.

Hence, high-performance microcontrollers are an important step forward in embedded system technology that features enhanced processing capabilities, integrated functionalities, and real-time data processing required for applications such as food quality monitoring. Their capability to process complex tasks, coupled with features to ensure energy efficiency and system reliability, positions them as integral components in the present food supply chain. The need for such high-performance microcontrollers will only increase as the industry continues to evolve, particularly to ensure food safety and quality and to sustain such food longer, thereby increasing production, commercializing, and consuming value for both producers and consumers.

INNOVATIONS IN SENSOR TECHNOLOGY

High technological advancement is emerging in sensor technology, and the landscape of food quality monitoring is changing fast. Enhanced requirements for better food safety, quality assurance, and traceability continue to grow, while high-tech sensors ensure that food products are safe to consume and meet regulatory standards. There are now various types of sensors being used in food monitoring systems, with each different in application and requirement. Sensors can be generally classified as follows: there are temperature sensors, humidity sensors, gas sensors, and optical sensors, among others (Isik et al., 2023; Ramachandran et al., 2024). Figure 1 illustrates advancements in sensor technology for monitoring food quality.

Figure 1. Innovations in Sensor Technology

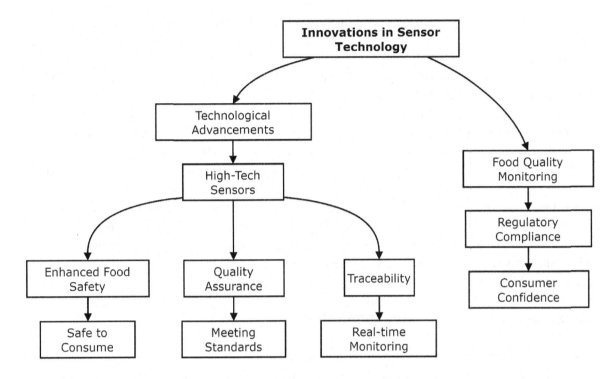

Types of Sensors Used in Food Monitoring

Maybe the most widely used temperature sensors in food quality monitoring are those related to temperature, as this is one of the most relevant variables that will determine the shelf life and food safety. Thermocouples and thermistors are the most common types of temperature sensors used in monitoring systems, providing real-time data on temperature fluctuations during storage and transportation. The other critical sensors within the food sensing system are humidity sensors, which consist of capacitive and resistive humidity sensors. Moisture levels can significantly affect the quality of food, particularly for perishable products. Humidity sensors ensure the maintenance of appropriate humidity levels that are critical for preventing the spoilage of food items, thereby elongating shelf life (Wu & Xie, 2022).

Gas sensors play an increasingly crucial role in food monitoring systems since they detect specific gases produced due to food deterioration. For example, volatile organic compounds (VOCs) are used as an index for the ripeness or spoilage of fruits and vegetables. Advanced sensors in gases utilize metal oxide semiconductors (MOS), electrochemical methods, and optical sensing techniques to detect these gases with high accuracy. The types of sensors employed include NIR and fluorescence sensors. Sensors have the ability to carry out non-destructive analysis of food products, meaning that quality attributes such as sugar content, ripeness, and nutrient levels may be assessed without damaging the items.

Advanced Sensor Resolution and Sensitivity Improvement

In the past couple of years, sensor technology has been improving significantly the resolution and sensitivity of food monitoring sensors. Advances in nanotechnology, material science, and microfabrication provide for the ability to explore fabrication of smaller sensors, yet highly sensitive, to detect minute changes in environmental conditions or chemical compositions. As an illustration, nano-scale materials integrated into sensor designs have led to the realization of sensors that are much more sensitive for the detection of analytes of interest. Other materials under thorough consideration for the design of new sensors are graphene-based materials with high surface area and electrical conductivity, and carbon nanotubes, to detect high accuracy spoilage indicators of food products (Usman et al., 2022).

Other sensor calibration and signal processing strategies further improve the reliability and performance of the food monitoring sensors. In analyzing sensor data, machine learning algorithms are increasingly used for making real-time adjustments in accordance with environmental changes or trends in food quality. These algorithms will learn from data history and provide better predictions to support food decision-making processes in storage and handling applications. Hence, food monitoring systems will be able to determine potential problems in quality before they become critical, so that preventive actions can be made on time.

Microcontrollers and Sensors Integration

This integration with high-performance microcontrollers represents an important innovation in food quality monitoring systems. It can connect, thus ensuring good data acquisition, handling, and transmission capabilities toward enhancing the efficiency and effectiveness of monitoring processes. High-performance microcontrollers, possessing more powerful processing capacity and more extensive communication interfaces, can handle more data from several sensors at one time and support real-time comprehensive monitoring of food quality parameters (Wu & Xie, 2022).

For instance, a food monitoring system may incorporate temperature sensors, humidity sensors, and gas sensors with a microcontroller. In this design, the system will monitor temperature and humidity levels but also be able to feel the presence of spoilage gases for an even larger, more complete view of the quality of food. The data obtained from these sensors are then analyzed at the microcontroller's end, which makes decisions based on predefined thresholds and algorithms. If any parameter exceeds acceptable limits, then it can send a signal to the system to start an alarm, trigger the cooling mechanism, and notify stakeholders to take necessary measures.

The integration of sensors and microcontrollers is enabled to allow IoT applications, hence the creation of food monitoring systems. These are able to send data to cloud-based platforms; this allows remote monitoring and analysis. This allows stakeholders access to real-time information related to food quality, from anywhere in the world. They instill transparency up and down the supply chain, where producers, distributors, and retailers can ensure compliance with safety regulations on food while delivering superior-quality products.

This also paves the way for sensor integration with the microcontrollers, resulting in advancements in predictive analytics and machine learning. Such types of data collection and analysis result in the identification of trends or patterns, which will thus allow development of systems for predictive maintenance or proactive management of food quality. For example, if it is discovered that a particular storage environment contributes significantly to spoilage because humidity levels are too high, then control over the environment can be altered before such losses will occur again.

Moreover, some of the wireless communication technologies, such as the LoRaWAN, Zigbee, and Wi-Fi capabilities, have made it possible for sensors and microcontrollers to be connected to wider networks, hence making food monitoring systems scale up highly. Besides, this wireless technology allows deployment of sensor networks easily almost everywhere-from farms and processing facilities to retail locations-in order to offer wide coverage and to monitor areas comprehensively.

Thus, innovations in sensor technology revolutionally transform food quality monitoring through advanced sensing devices, intensifying the chance and sensitivity of choosing the device, as well as streamlining integration with high-performance microcontrollers. It is in this evolution of the industry that all of these technological progressions are going to play the important part of ensuring food safety, quality, and sustainability to one day claim this benefit to consumers and the food supply chain as a whole. Research and development ongoing in this area promise further high-end solutions to enhance our monitoring and maintenance capabilities in food safety.

INTERNET OF THINGS (IOT) IN FOOD QUALITY MONITORING

IoT is the most powerful transforming technology that enables devices, systems, and services to connect over the internet in order to be able to communicate with each other and exchange data. In the context of food quality monitoring, IoT has become a powerful force developing the efficiency of the working process with regard to food safety and ensuring regulatory compliance. Integrated IoT technologies into food quality monitoring systems aid in real-time data collection, analysis, and management, thereby enabling the stakeholders to effectively monitor and control food quality throughout the supply chain (Upadhyaya et al., 2024; Venkateswaran et al., 2024). The Internet of Things (IoT) is being utilized in food quality monitoring to improve safety, efficiency, and regulatory compliance through the integration of various devices and systems as shown in Figure 2.

Figure 2. Internet of Things (IoT) in food quality monitoring

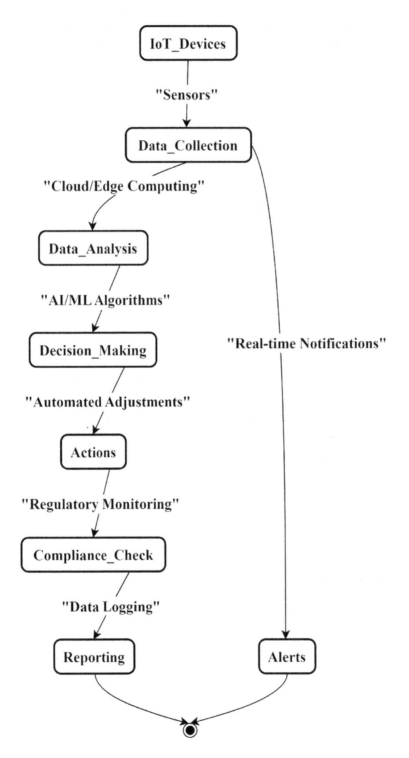

IoT Applications in Food Safety

IoT applications of food safety range from the production and processing stage to the transportation and retailing stages. One of the primary applications is also at the environmental conditions levels for food storage and transportation. The sensors can be buried in the storage facilities and transport vehicles and will be able to continuously monitor critical parameters like temperature, humidity, and the concentrations of gases. Thus, food products will be stored and transported under optimal conditions that minimize the risk of spoilage and contamination (Molakatala et al., 2024; Pachiappan et al., 2024).

In cold chain logistics, for instance, temperature and humidity sensors can be mounted on refrigerated trucks or storage units and can monitor and report real-time environmental conditions. In case there occurs a deviation in temperature outside the tolerance limit, alerts may be sent to the managers and operators to take appropriate corrective action to avoid the risk of spoilage. This protects the integrity of food products and saves businesses from costly losses and keeps customers satisfied. IoT technologies can be implemented in food processing units for monitoring quality parameters that are pH-based, microbial counts, and chemical residues among other things. Manufacturers can gather real-time product quality and safety insights by deploying IoT-enabled sensors along the entire production process. Thus, smart sensors would detect contamination or pathogen presence in raw materials in real time to take remediation measures before the same food reaches consumers. The proactive approach to food safety reduces the risks of foodborne illnesses and increases consumer confidence in food products.

Data Collection and Analysis in Real-Time

Real-time data collection and analysis is one of the major benefits of employing IoT on food quality monitoring. Traditional tactics for monitoring foods mostly delay in pointing out potential issues in regards to its quality, as it usually follows the periodical checking of food quality and manual entry of data. IoT systems, however, continuously gather data from sensors and other devices that help have a more accurate view of food quality at any time. This ability allows stakeholders to make informed decisions, which will enable them to be as efficient as possible.

Advanced analytics tools and machine learning algorithms can then analyze data collected by IoT devices. Such analysis of voluminous data indicates trends, patterns, and anomalies that can indicate a quality problem in the system. For example, IoT can predict potential spoilage through predictive analytics techniques using trends learnt from historical data along with prevailing environmental conditions. Predictability empowers businesses to take preventive actions before the problem gets out of hand, thus reducing waste and improved resource use.

In addition, the method of IoT with cloud computing enables data to be stored in large volumes across different sources. Such a cloud-based approach benefits stakeholders along the supply chain, and they will have access to data anywhere in the world to monitor food quality. For instance, producers, distributors, and retailers can track the quality of their products in real-time on dashboards or see how well they are complying with safety standards and respond aggressively to emerging matters.

The collected data also supports compliance with food safety regulations and standards by means of systems enabled by IoT. Regulatory agencies require food businesses to maintain detailed records of their products, including the source of the produce, processing, storage conditions, etc. The ability to automatically collect this data from IoT systems ensures that accurate and comprehensive records are maintained without the burden of manual input. Therefore, with this automation, besides the fact that it makes the management of the production process more efficient, it also reduces the chances of human error, which could influence food safety.

Real-time data analysis would therefore also mean continued improvement in best practices monitoring food quality. From the analyzed data trends, areas in which the processes can be thus improved could be identified to optimize resource utilization and improve product quality. For example, once temperature fluctuations while storage are understood, improved insulation strategies can be implemented or better designed refrigeration systems hence improving the overall quality of food products. Hence, the use of IoT technologies in the implementation of monitoring systems of food quality revolutionizes management of food safety from the point of collection at the field towards the supply chain. From data collection to real-time analysis and applications regarding traceability and environmental monitoring, IoT proves an all-rounded solution for ensuring safe and quality food products. With this industry adopting these new innovations, the stakeholders will even more effectively meet the challenges and contribute to increasing consumer trust in improving a safer and more efficient food supply chain. All of what has been presented has tremendous potential in the context of monitoring food quality through IoT, and future models are predicted to be even further advanced and complex.

DATA PROCESSING AND ANALYTICS

In the food quality monitoring sector, data processing and analytics play a significant role as raw data must be transformed into actionable insight. Technology is continuously getting advanced, which has led to gathering big data from various sources - including sensors, IoT devices, as well as other monitoring devices. To appropriately utilize these data for food quality and safety enhancement, three fundamental essentials must be considered on the part of organizations: real-time data processing, machine learning algorithms in predictive analytics, and data visualization techniques (Pramila et al., 2023; Srinivas et al., 2023). All of the pieces will be able to provide an overall perspective on food quality and safety and will therefore eventually lead to good decision-making and operational efficiency. The figure 3 depicts data processing and analytics in the food quality monitoring sector.

Figure 3. Data Processing and Analytics in the food quality monitoring sector

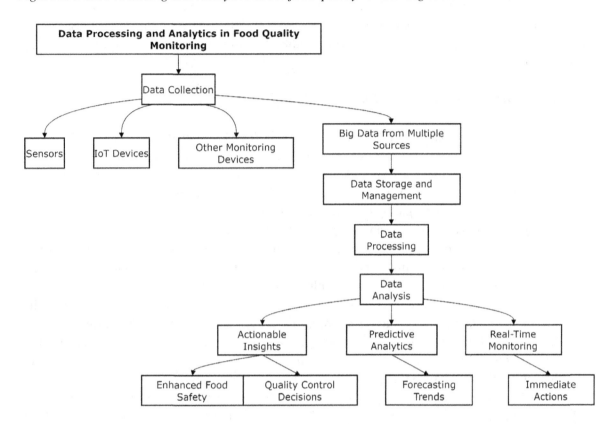

Importance of Real-Time Data Processing

Real-time data processing is important to food quality monitoring systems because they can analyze information as soon as it is available. This characteristic is very important in places where food safety is strictly observed - processing facilities, storage units, and transportation networks - because in these industries, time plays a crucial role in solving any possible quality issues. It reduces risks and increases conformity to safety standards due to its prompt detection of potential quality problems. Another key benefit of real-time data processing is anomaly and deviation detection from the set parameters. For example, if the sensors monitoring temperature in a cold storage facility begin recording an increase in temperature, then real-time processing just has it that alerts are sent to the managers or operators. Early warning allows for quick intervention, where they can take appropriate measures, such as adjusting the refrigeration systems or relocating sensitive products, thus preventing spoilage and ensuring food safety.

Continuous processing of real-time data further assists with proactive decision-making. In fact, constant observations of key quality indicators help an organization spot trends and patterns that may serve as a warning of possible outbreaks of problems before they reach critical conditions; for example, if humidity levels in some storage area are always near critical limits, predictive measures can be taken toward adjusting environmental controls- thus decreasing the possibility of mold and spoilage. Apart from enhanced transparency, real-time data processing enhances traceability in the supply chain. Stakeholders can tap into the current data related to food quality conditions and, therefore, build cooperation and trust among producers, distributors, and retailers. With such transparency, this food industry is one of the key issues today. Consumers demand accountability and assurance regarding the safety and quality of products for consumption.

Machine Learning Algorithms for Predictive Analytics

Indirectly, predictive capabilities are enhanced when machine learning algorithms are used for food quality monitoring. Predictive analytics is a process whereby historical and real-time data are used to predict future outcomes, while allowing stakeholders to make choices based on data-driven insights. Machine learning models can analyze complicated data sets, identify trends, and produce predictions that can inform operational strategies (Rebecca et al., 2024).

Some of the deployed machine learning algorithms that are rather effective in food quality monitoring occur in successful practices of predictive analytics. For instance, regression algorithms can be used to model the relationship between environmental factors and food quality metrics, thus enabling organizations to predict shelf life in varied conditions. Fitted with historical data by feeding these models, businesses can now develop accurate forecasts informing the inventory management and distribution strategy. Other key applications for classification algorithms are decision trees and support vector machines (SVM), which can be used to classify food products based on quality indicators. For example, these algorithms can analyze sensor data classifying products as "fresh," "at risk," or "spoiled" and hence provide operators with actionable information that could be used for early interventions.

Additionally, unsupervised learning techniques, such as clustering, allow for the identification of product groups that are homogeneous in their similarity regarding quality characteristics. This allows companies to tailor the quality assurance processes based on the different categories of products, taking into account how resources might better be allocated in order to maximize quality management overall. It also continually adjusts in time to make it more accurate and effective because new information continues to accumulate over time. This will enable the algorithm to adapt better to a dynamic environment where variables affecting the quality of food may change with time, such as variability in temperature and humidity levels or a disruption in the supply chain.

The analysis and forecasting of patterns, trends, and outcome based on historical data constitute the very core elements of machine learning algorithms in predictive analytics. Algorithms such as decision trees, neural networks, and support vector machines are just some of the important algorithms that can recognize patterns and dig out meaningful correlations to make predictive modeling feasible. Machine learning also plays a critical role within high-performance computer integrated microcontrollers by making the system more efficient through process optimization and adaptive control. Complex applications that involve real-time data analysis, anomaly detection, and predictive maintenance are feasible with microcontrollers in conjunction with machine learning models. Such operations are of utmost relevance in industrial automation, healthcare, and IoT-based applications.

Data Visualization Techniques

Data visualization is the process of representing data or information in an easier to understand way. The proper tools for visualization would allow easy interpretation of the data by the stakeholders; this would determine trends, hence making better decisions afterward. Data visualization forms within food quality monitoring occur as dashboards, graphs, and heat maps (Pitchai et al., 2024).

Dashboards are powerful tools aggregating data from all sources in a view, giving a total view of the key indicators and aspects about the quality indicators in real time. Stakeholders can also monitor at glance some key metrics relating to temperature, humidity, and spoilage rate for quick decision-making. Interactive dashboards enable users to click down into specific data points to deepen analysis and check and explore trends. Graphs and charts are some of the typical representations, but a line graph, bar charts, pie charts or whatever type, reflect over time the trends in graphs. For instance, if one plots over time temperature variations in a storage area, such a graph would possibly reflect patterns regarding effectiveness of temperature controls or problems with refrigeration systems. Yet again, visualization would help stakeholders identify, at a glance, what is being done right or not. Another is heat maps, which are particularly useful for monitoring environmental conditions across large areas. For example, temperature variation in a storage facility could be represented by a heat map to point out certain areas of hotspots or areas most at risk from spoilage. Such visualization increases situational awareness and allows pinpoint interventions to maintain the optimal conditions. Advanced tools are also coming along to provide visualization in innovative ways, such as AR and VR. Through which possibilities are opened up whereby stakeholders may experience data visualized through such immersion realities so that one can see, understand, and retains the information in that way; thus becomes essential, effectively done.

To conclude, in effective food quality monitoring, should constituents like data processing and analytics. The processing of data in real-time becomes an important constituent, without which anomalies in performance are hardly discovered immediately, or drastic decisions cannot be made proactively.

WIRELESS COMMUNICATION TECHNOLOGIES

Wireless communication has improved the use of food quality monitoring by enhancing its application in various industries where data exchange no longer waits for the limitations of physical wiring. In food monitoring, wireless networks offer real-time data transmission from sensors, IoT devices, as well as other monitoring equipment and equipment in monitoring food safety and quality levels along the supply chain. This section discusses primary communication protocols used in wireless networks and some advantages that these technologies offer when using them in food monitoring applications (Agrawal et al., 2023; Koshariya et al., 2023). The flow of real-time data transmission from sensors and IoT devices through wireless networks across the food supply chain is depicted in Figure 4.

Figure 4. Flow of real-time data transmission from sensors and IoT devices through wireless networks across the food supply chain

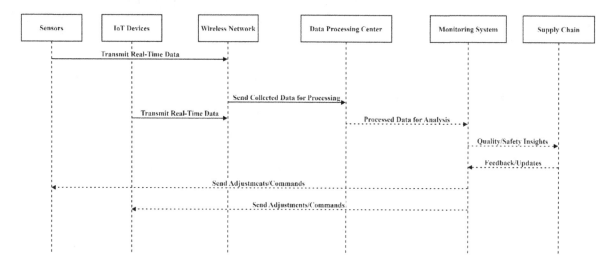

Communication Protocols

Communication protocols are important mechanisms that define the standards and rules used in data exchange between devices in a wireless network. In food quality monitoring systems, several communication protocols are in use, all with different characteristics and advantages.

i.   Wi-Fi (Wireless Fidelity) is another widely known wireless communication protocol. It is utilized in the most commercial applications for the sake of sharing these applications for mass-scale internet connectivity with higher speeds. For the purpose of food monitoring, Wi-Fi is also useful, as it allows IoT devices to be integrated with existing networks and infrastructures there through which data can be communicated effectively. Wi-Fi is very helpful within a processing facility and retail environments, where high throughputs of data are needed for the sake of real-time monitoring and analysis. However, its limited range and susceptibility to interference can be drawbacks for large-scale agricultural settings.

ii. Bluetooth and Bluetooth Low Energy: Bluetooth technology, while BLE is meant for point-to-point communication; BLE has special advantages in the monitoring of food where low power consumption is crucial. For example, BLE sensors with Bluetooth can be able to do continuous rounds of temperature and humidity in storage without frequent changes of the battery for it. Bluetooth is adopted for use when there are applications that require direct device-to-device communications and handhelds on usage by inspectors or workers in food processing plants.

iii. Zigbee: This is a low-power, low data rate wireless communication protocol specifically designed for short-range applications. In the Zigbee mesh network topology, devices can converse with other devices and provide extended coverage of the network. The suitability of this protocol for the food monitoring of environments with many sensors to be deployed makes it ideal. Zigbee's energy-efficient design makes it fit for battery-powered sensors that may operate long-term without regular maintenance or replacement.

iv. LoRa (Long Range):LoRa is one of LPWAN technologies that enable low power and wide area networks. This technology enables a long range with minimum energy consumption. It is very effective for agricultural applications wherein sensors are spread over vast areas to monitor environmental conditions. Due to this, LoRa can allow data transmission over several kilometers in remote monitoring in the fields so that the required data can be collected without setting up extensive infrastructure.

v. NFC (Near Field Communication) It is short-range communication where data can be exchanged from one device to another at close proximity. NFC is normally not used in continuous monitoring but can be applied in food traceability applications. Smart labels with NFC tags are embedded in a given packaging, whereby information relating to origin, storage conditions, and expiration dates is known by the consumers when scanned using a smartphone.

vi. Cellular Networks (2G, 3G, 4G, 5G): Cellular networks enable communication among devices across wide geographic areas through wireless and mobile communication. It can be useful to employ such networks in food monitoring systems that are installed in distant locations and not directly connected to the Internet. Cellular communication is enhanced by speed and reliability in 5G, which allows real-time data transmission and the greater deployment of IoT devices in food monitoring applications.

Benefits of Wireless Networks in Food Monitoring

The integration of wireless communication technologies into food quality monitoring systems brings along a multitude of benefits that are meant to increase efficiency in operations and enhance safety in foods:

i. Real-Time Data Transmission: With wireless networks, sensors and monitoring devices can transmit data in real-time to central systems. This makes it easier for stakeholders to track quality throughout, allowing a decision to be made at once where deviation from set safety standards occurs.

ii. Scalability and Flexibility. Wireless networks are flexible to expand the food monitoring system. New sensors and new devices may be simply included in the network without extensive wiring and changes in infrastructure. Scalability is mostly useful in applications where the needs of monitoring should change over time, such as seasonal fluctuations of agricultural production.

iii. Cost-Effectiveness: Wireless communication technologies reduce installation and then maintenance costs as opposed to traditional wired systems. Wireless networks do not require lots of cabling, making them much more cost-effective and easier to deploy in various settings, from farms to processing plants.

This facilitates remote monitoring and control of food quality systems via wireless networks. The stakeholders can access data and monitor equipment using smartphones or computers. This is very useful for businesses with multiple locations or farmers monitoring crops in more remote areas. More mobility in food monitoring applications: Wireless communication makes more mobility possible in food monitoring applications. Inspectors, workers, and managers can now access real-time data through mobile devices, be alerted, and make on-the-job decisions. This mobility enhances operational efficiency, enabling a quicker response time toward major quality issues. Data Integration: Wireless networks integrate data coming from sensors and databases as well as cloud-based applications. Data integration allows the food quality conditions to be perceived holistically so that the business operations can be analyzed at all angles to act on the extracted insights toward improving operations.

Wireless communication technologies basically play a crucial role in enhancing food quality monitoring systems. With these communication protocols, these technologies enable real-time data transmission, scalability, cost-effectiveness, and traceability. Emerging innovative solutions for food safety and quality requirements will be integrated with the inclusion of wireless networks to shape the future of food monitoring and management. A significant indirect benefit of using these technologies is improving efficiency in operations, better decision making, and, hence, ensuring that safe, quality food is provided to consumers.

APPLICATIONS IN THE FOOD SUPPLY CHAIN

It involves a complex sequence of processes, from agricultural production through to delivery to consumers, with all such processes being important to ensure safety and quality of food. High-performance computer-integrated microcontrollers with improvements in sensor technology and wireless communications have been instrumental in the optimization of these processes. We now describe three of these major applications: monitoring in agriculture, quality control in food processing, and logistics and distribution (Mohanty et al., 2023; Vangeri et al., 2024; Verma et al., 2024).

Monitoring in Agriculture

Hence, environmental monitoring in crop-growing conditions is very vital within the agriculture sector, relating to high yields and quality. High-performance microcontrollers that come with advanced sensors allow real-time monitoring of soil moisture, temperature, humidity, and light levels. Data gathered by these sensors can be used for gauging the optimal requirements in growth conditions for any plant. For instance, through IoT-enabling sensors, farmers are able to adopt precision agriculture by now being informed about the need for irrigation, application of fertilizers, or pest management, thereby conserving resources and improving the output. In addition, wireless communication technologies enable the farmer to access information remotely that might inform a timely intervention. For instance, based on low soil moisture that has been detected by a sensor, an alarm can be issued instantly to the farmer and through mobile apps, the irrigation system is activated. This real-time feedback loop is one major factor that leads to sustainable farming because it minimizes the usage of water while maximizing crop health.

Quality Control during Food Processing

High-performance sensing microcontrollers are being used to monitor critical parameters like temperature, pH, and humidity in food processing, such as meat processing. This enhances food safety and compliance with regulatory standards. Machine learning algorithms are also being used to detect potential quality issues in real-time, preventing waste and enhancing efficiency. Data visualization methods are also integrated.

Logistics and Distribution

Cold chain logistics ensures food products are transported at appropriate conditions, maintaining their quality. High-performance microcontrollers monitor environmental conditions, while IoT technologies track shipment location and condition. Real-time tracking improves traceability and response time. Data analytics optimizes routing and delivery schedules, minimizing delays and improving supply chain efficiency.

That is to say, highly effective implementations of microcontrollers and sensor technologies along the chain have significantly improved how agriculture is monitored, quality control executed in food processing, and logistics and distribution occur. Such improved technologies enhance food safety and quality but also result in greater sustainability in food production and consumption practices and contribute to efficiency for the good of both the consumer and the producer.

CASE STUDY: APPLICATIONS IN THE FOOD SUPPLY CHAIN

Applications of high-performance computer systems and microcontrollers have become very essential in the supply chain of food, ensuring safety of food, quality of food, and minimum resultant waste. For instance, IoT-enabled microcontrollers can be embedded in cold chain logistics, especially for perishable products such as dairy, meat, and seafood. In that regard, advanced microcontrollers have internal memory to store temperature, humidity, and gas sensors, which continuously monitor the environmental condition during transportation and storage. The sensors now provide logistics managers with real-time information on critical parameters for decisions in maintaining optimal storage conditions and prevention of spoilage (Mohanty et al., 2023; Vangeri et al., 2024; Verma et al., 2024).

An example of dairy transportation is at a high risk of spoilage because of temperature variations. Microcontroller-based systems can now monitor temperatures in real time and send alerts instantly if the situations go outside the safe range. The microcontroller alerts the handlers or dispatch teams to attend to the problem immediately when a refrigeration unit breaks down or the doors are left open. Real-time data are also recorded and used to refine operations and cut energy costs by just adjusting what is necessary in the refrigeration. Improved crop storage facilities monitoring: Applications of microcontrollers in agriculture. For instance, grain storage is highly prone to moisture and temperature because poor conditions lead to mold and infestation by pests, which consequently affects quality and safety of the crop. IoT sensor networks integrated with microcontrollers track the environment variables so grains are stored in stable environmental conditions. If the moisture content surpasses the predetermined level, the system will activate ventilation or alert the personnel to rectify the situation to avoid damaging the crop quality.

Predictive models based on microcontrollers have also proven highly beneficial for the meat industry. Through analysis of historical data stored under certain conditions, food companies can predict through trends possible risks of spoilage. For example, if data analysis indicates a probable tendency towards bacterial growth due to temperature trends, logistics managers act early and minimize food waste while saving consumer health.

The case studies portray how IoT and machine learning of high-performance microcontrollers bring automation, predictive maintenance, as well as real-time decision-making to food supply chains. These technologies not only help improve quality and safety of food, with energy consumption and operational costs being reduced but also continuously monitor, alert, and take preventive actions. With the increased complexity and openness, applications of these types are likely to gain penetration throughout the food supply chain, which in turn will contribute to increasing control, sustainability, and reliability for producers and end-users alike.

CHALLENGES AND BARRIERS TO ADOPTION

Despite promising trends in high-performance microcontrollers and sensor technologies for improving food quality monitoring, several issues act as barriers to their widespread application in the food supply chain (G. Wang et al., 2024; S. Wang et al., 2024b).

Issues of Standardization in Sensor Technology

One of the major issues is the lack of standardization in sensor technology. Most manufacturers produce different sensors, and so differences in specifications and protocols often lead to compatibility problems.

Cost Implications for Small and Medium Enterprises (SMEs)

The other key challenge is cost, particularly to the small and medium enterprise as they do not have the capacity to invest in high-end monitoring devices. The start-up costs of high-performance microcontrollers and sensors and, ancillary infrastructure are expensive. Maintenance costs and possible upgradations quickly become very straining on the resources of SMEs, allowing huge companies to innovate and evolve at the blurring of competition at a higher setting. This financial gap could lead to a technological gap as SME's would not be able to enhance their practices of food safety effectively.

Cyber Security Threats

Lastly, cyber security threats are one of the critical challenges for the adaptation of the connected monitoring system. By using IoT devices and cloud-based data storage for quality monitoring of food, the threat of a cyber attack is enhanced. It can facilitate unauthorized entry into monitoring systems, breach data confidentiality, manipulation of food safety data records, and operations disruption. The provision of strong cybersecurity measures calls for supplementary investment in protective technologies and continuous employee training, which can deter organizations already limited in terms of resources.

Hence, high-performance microcontrollers and sensor technologies show great promise in the further improvement of monitoring the quality of food, but issues with standardization, added cost to SMEs, and concerns about cybersecurity must be considered to make them more acceptable in the food supply chain.

Despite such exciting potential from high performance microcontrollers and sensor technologies in monitoring the quality of food, there are several challenges that have remained as barriers in the general uptake and integration into the food supply chain. Among these, the one-time large cost of installation and integration of advanced IoT systems, microcontrollers, and sensors into the production lines is quite a challenge. Most firms in the food sector are SMEs, and such costs are too unbearable for most of them, since some specialized equipment must be serviced regularly and upgraded after a given period.

More Challenges

a) Another challenge is posed by the lack of standardization across sensor technologies and data communication protocols. Various systems are provided by different manufacturers, adding complexity and cost to an effort to integrate diverse devices into one coherent platform. Lack of standardization leads to compatibility issues and raises the bar for companies to scale or integrate newer technologies with the old without heavy restructuring investments.

b) Barriers also exist in the form of data security and privacy because food companies fear to adopt IoT-based monitoring systems generating and transmitting massive volumes of data. Food quality data is perceived sensitive if compromised could damage the company's reputation or lead to financial losses with growing cybersecurity threats, setting up robust measures for cybersecurity often calls for added resources and skill sets, creating further reluctance on the part of potential adopters.

c) For instance, environmental and operational conditions such as harsh storage conditions will pose challenges regarding the environments and operations that limit the effectiveness and life of sensors and microcontrollers. Sensors used in extreme temperature or high humidity conditions, for example, refrigerated trucks, may incur frequent recalibration or replacement issues leading to an escalation of maintenance costs and interruptions in continuous monitoring.

d) Another problem could be a lack of digital literacy within particular parts of the food industry, in general and especially by those businesses that still operate with traditional principles. The proper use and maintenance of such highly sophisticated monitoring solutions require expertise and education that may not be available or even impossible in those resource-poor companies.

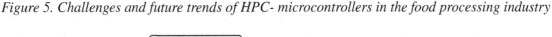

Figure 5. Challenges and future trends of HPC- microcontrollers in the food processing industry

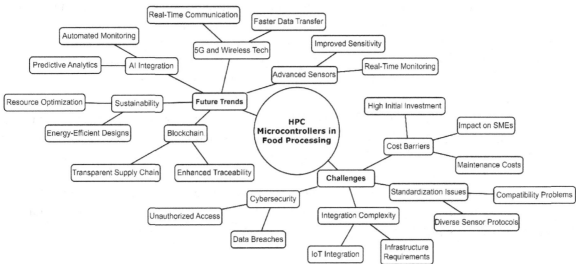

FUTURE TRENDS AND INNOVATIONS

Several main trends and innovations will characterize the future of food quality monitoring as the practice of food quality monitoring continues to evolve (Kaushik et al., 2024; S. Wang et al., 2024b).

Integration of Artificial Intelligence (AI)

Artificial intelligence will revolutionize food monitoring systems by processing vast data, enabling predictive analytics to anticipate quality issues, enhancing food safety and optimizing resource usage, thereby increasing efficiency.

Blockchain for Traceability and Transparency

Blockchain technology is enhancing traceability and transparency in food supply chains by providing a decentralized record of transactions. It can trace food products from farm to table, enhancing accountability and reducing food-borne contamination risks. Emerging technologies like IoT, advanced robotics, and 5G communication are also impacting food monitoring quality. The integration of AI, blockchain, and other technologies will drive improvements in safety, efficiency, and transparency in food supply chains.

CONCLUSION

The application of high-performance computer microcontrollers and advanced sensor technologies to food quality monitoring is a step into ensuring safety, quality, and sustainability in food products. These technologies could transform industry practice through application along the food supply chain-from agricultural production to processing and distribution to consumers-as considered in this chapter. The road is not, however, without difficulties as issues related to standardization; cost implications, particularly to small and medium-sized enterprises; and cybersecurity concerns have to be sorted out carefully to create the right conditions for innovation. Efficiency in standards and frameworks can be achieved through the collaboration of manufacturers, policymakers, and industry associations.

Looking forward, new technologies such as artificial intelligence, blockchain for traceability, etc., will be added to elevate the quality of food monitoring systems. It will ensure proper proactive and responsive measures on food safety so that its benefits also touch consumers, producers, and the rest of the food supply chain. Quality monitoring of food embraces a welcoming attitude toward the evolution of technologies with the complications coming along with them. In this regard, encouraging collaboration and innovation between industry sectors will allow the food industry to craft a more adaptable and effective system that not only will respond but also lead in adjusting to the speeding changes global in nature. Indeed, in the future, we should stay responsive and adaptable to such changes to maintain the integrity of our food supply.

REFERENCES

Agrawal, A. V., Magulur, L. P., Priya, S. G., Kaur, A., Singh, G., & Boopathi, S. (2023). Smart Precision Agriculture Using IoT and WSN. In *Handbook of Research on Data Science and Cybersecurity Innovations in Industry 4.0 Technologies* (pp. 524–541). IGI Global. DOI: 10.4018/978-1-6684-8145-5.ch026

Ahmad, A., Roslan, M. F., & Amira, A. (2017). Throughput, latency and cost comparisons of microcontroller-based implementations of wireless sensor network (WSN) in high jump sports. *AIP Conference Proceedings*, 1883(1), 020010. DOI: 10.1063/1.5002028

Al-Dhaher, A. (2004). Development of Microcontroller/FPGA-based systems. *International Journal of Engineering Education*, 20(1), 52–60.

Castiglia, V., Ciotta, P., Di Tommaso, A., Miceli, R., & Nevoloso, C. (2018). High performance foc for induction motors with low cost atsam3x8e microcontroller. *2018 7th International Conference on Renewable Energy Research and Applications (ICRERA)*, 1495–1500.

Crepaldi, M., Merello, A., & Di Salvo, M. (2021). A multi-one instruction set computer for microcontroller applications. *IEEE Access : Practical Innovations, Open Solutions*, 9, 113454–113474. DOI: 10.1109/ACCESS.2021.3104150

Ibrahim, D. (2006). *Microcontroller based applied digital control*. John Wiley. DOI: 10.1002/0470863374

Isik, M., Inadagbo, K., & Aktas, H. (2023). Design optimization for high-performance computing using FPGA. *Annual International Conference on Information Management and Big Data*, 142–156. DOI: 10.21203/rs.3.rs-2679691/v1

Kaushik, N., Gill, A., & Raghavendra, R. (2024). Frontiers of Artificial Intelligence Through Accelerated Model Training and Optimization Techniques. *2024 IEEE 13th International Conference on Communication Systems and Network Technologies (CSNT)*, 995–1002.

Koshariya, A. K., Kalaiyarasi, D., Jovith, A. A., Sivakami, T., Hasan, D. S., & Boopathi, S. (2023). AI-Enabled IoT and WSN-Integrated Smart Agriculture System. In *Artificial Intelligence Tools and Technologies for Smart Farming and Agriculture Practices* (pp. 200–218). IGI Global. DOI: 10.4018/978-1-6684-8516-3.ch011

Malouche, I., Abbes, A. K., & Bouani, F. (2015). Automatic model predictive control implementation in a high-performance microcontroller. *2015 IEEE 12th International Multi-Conference on Systems, Signals & Devices (SSD15)*, 1–6.

Mohanty, A., Venkateswaran, N., Ranjit, P., Tripathi, M. A., & Boopathi, S. (2023). Innovative Strategy for Profitable Automobile Industries: Working Capital Management. In *Handbook of Research on Designing Sustainable Supply Chains to Achieve a Circular Economy* (pp. 412–428). IGI Global.

Molakatala, N., Kumar, D. A., Patil, U., Mhatre, P. J., Sambathkumar, M., & Boopathi, S. (2024). Integrating 5G and IoT Technologies in Developing Smart City Communication Networks. In *Blockchain-Based Solutions for Accessibility in Smart Cities* (pp. 147–170). IGI Global. DOI: 10.4018/979-8-3693-3402-7.ch006

Pachiappan, K., Anitha, K., Pitchai, R., Sangeetha, S., Satyanarayana, T., & Boopathi, S. (2024). Intelligent Machines, IoT, and AI in Revolutionizing Agriculture for Water Processing. In *Handbook of Research on AI and ML for Intelligent Machines and Systems* (pp. 374–399). IGI Global.

Pitchai, R., Guru, K. V., Gandhi, J. N., Komala, C. R., Kumar, J. R. D., & Boopathi, S. (2024). Fog Computing-Integrated ML-Based Framework and Solutions for Intelligent Systems: Digital Healthcare Applications. In *Technological Advancements in Data Processing for Next Generation Intelligent Systems* (pp. 196–224). IGI Global. DOI: 10.4018/979-8-3693-0968-1.ch008

Pramila, P., Amudha, S., Saravanan, T., Sankar, S. R., Poongothai, E., & Boopathi, S. (2023). Design and Development of Robots for Medical Assistance: An Architectural Approach. In *Contemporary Applications of Data Fusion for Advanced Healthcare Informatics* (pp. 260–282). IGI Global.

Ramachandran, S., Jayalal, M., Vasudevan, M., Das, S., & Jehadeesan, R. (2024). Combining machine learning techniques and genetic algorithm for predicting run times of high performance computing jobs. *Applied Soft Computing*, 165, 112053. DOI: 10.1016/j.asoc.2024.112053

Ramesh, R. S. (2024). Scalable Systems and Software Architectures for High-Performance Computing on cloud platforms. *arXiv Preprint arXiv:2408.10281*.

Rebecca, B., Kumar, K. P. M., Padmini, S., Srivastava, B. K., Halder, S., & Boopathi, S. (2024). Convergence of Data Science-AI-Green Chemistry-Affordable Medicine: Transforming Drug Discovery. In *Handbook of Research on AI and ML for Intelligent Machines and Systems* (pp. 348–373). IGI Global.

Sadraey, M. H. (2017). Microcontroller. In *Unmanned Aircraft Design: A Review of Fundamentals* (pp. 123–137). Springer. DOI: 10.1007/978-3-031-79582-4_7

Srinivas, B., Maguluri, L. P., Naidu, K. V., Reddy, L. C. S., Deivakani, M., & Boopathi, S. (2023). Architecture and Framework for Interfacing Cloud-Enabled Robots. In *Handbook of Research on Data Science and Cybersecurity Innovations in Industry 4.0 Technologies* (pp. 542–560). IGI Global. DOI: 10.4018/978-1-6684-8145-5.ch027

Swathi, K., Sandeep, T. U., & Ramani, A. R. (2018). Performance Analysis of Microcontrollers Used In IoT Technology. *International Journal of Scientific Research in Science, Engineering and Technology*, 4(4), 1268–1273.

Upadhyaya, A. N., Saqib, A., Devi, J. V., Rallapalli, S., Sudha, S., & Boopathi, S. (2024). Implementation of the Internet of Things (IoT) in Remote Healthcare. In *Advances in Medical Technologies and Clinical Practice* (pp. 104–124). IGI Global. DOI: 10.4018/979-8-3693-1934-5.ch006

Usman, S., Mehmood, R., Katib, I., & Albeshri, A. (2022). Data locality in high performance computing, big data, and converged systems: An analysis of the cutting edge and a future system architecture. *Electronics (Basel)*, 12(1), 53. DOI: 10.3390/electronics12010053

Vangeri, A. K., Bathrinath, S., Anand, M. C. J., Shanmugathai, M., Meenatchi, N., & Boopathi, S. (2024). Green Supply Chain Management in Eco-Friendly Sustainable Manufacturing Industries. In *Environmental Applications of Carbon-Based Materials* (pp. 253–287). IGI Global., DOI: 10.4018/979-8-3693-3625-0.ch010

Venkateswaran, N., Kiran Kumar, K., Maheswari, K., Kumar Reddy, R. V., & Boopathi, S. (2024). Optimizing IoT Data Aggregation: Hybrid Firefly-Artificial Bee Colony Algorithm for Enhanced Efficiency in Agriculture. *AGRIS On-Line Papers in Economics and Informatics*, 16(1), 117–130. DOI: 10.7160/aol.2024.160110

Verma, R., Christiana, M. B. V., Maheswari, M., Srinivasan, V., Patro, P., Dari, S. S., & Boopathi, S. (2024). Intelligent Physarum Solver for Profit Maximization in Oligopolistic Supply Chain Networks. In *AI and Machine Learning Impacts in Intelligent Supply Chain* (pp. 156–179). IGI Global. DOI: 10.4018/979-8-3693-1347-3.ch011

Wang, G., Luo, Z., Desta, H. G., Chen, M., Dong, Y., & Lin, B. (2024). AI-driven development of high-performance solid-state hydrogen storage. *Energy Reviews*, 100106.

Wang, S., Zheng, H., Wen, X., & Fu, S. (2024a). Distributed high-performance computing methods for accelerating deep learning training. *Journal of Knowledge Learning and Science Technology ISSN: 2959-6386 (Online), 3*(3), 108–126.

Wang, S., Zheng, H., Wen, X., & Fu, S. (2024b). Distributed high-performance computing methods for accelerating deep learning training. *Journal of Knowledge Learning and Science Technology ISSN: 2959-6386 (Online), 3*(3), 108–126.

Wu, N., & Xie, Y. (2022). A survey of machine learning for computer architecture and systems. *ACM Computing Surveys*, 55(3), 1–39. DOI: 10.1145/3494523

Xu, H., Song, S., & Mao, Z. (2024). Characterizing the performance of emerging deep learning, graph, and high performance computing workloads under interference. *2024 IEEE International Parallel and Distributed Processing Symposium Workshops (IPDPSW)*, 468–477. DOI: 10.1109/IPDPSW63119.2024.00098

Yadav, D. (2004). *Microcontroller: Features and applications*. New Age International.

ADDITIONAL READING

Gopi, B., Sworna Kokila, M. L., Bibin, C. V., Sasikala, D., Howard, E., & Boopathi, S. (2024). Distributed Technologies Using AI/ML Techniques for Healthcare Applications. In Advances in Human and Social Aspects of Technology (pp. 375–396). IGI Global. DOI: 10.4018/979-8-3693-2569-8.ch019

K. S. K. K., Isaac, J. S., Pratheep, V. G., Jasmin, M., Kistan, A., & Boopathi, S. (2024). Smart Food Quality Monitoring by Integrating IoT and Deep Learning for Enhanced Safety and Freshness. In Edible Electronics for Smart Technology Solutions (pp. 79–110). IGI Global. DOI: 10.4018/979-8-3693-5573-2.ch004

Kumar, M., Kumar, K., Sasikala, P., Sampath, B., Gopi, B., & Sundaram, S. (2023). Sustainable Green Energy Generation From Waste Water: IoT and ML Integration. In Sustainable Science and Intelligent Technologies for Societal Development (pp. 440–463). IGI Global.

Pachiappan, K., Anitha, K., Pitchai, R., Sangeetha, S., Satyanarayana, T., & Boopathi, S. (2024). Intelligent Machines, IoT, and AI in Revolutionizing Agriculture for Water Processing. In Handbook of Research on AI and ML for Intelligent Machines and Systems (pp. 374–399). IGI Global.

Pitchai, R., Guru, K. V., Gandhi, J. N., Komala, C. R., Kumar, J. R. D., & Boopathi, S. (2024). Fog Computing-Integrated ML-Based Framework and Solutions for Intelligent Systems: Digital Healthcare Applications. In Technological Advancements in Data Processing for Next Generation Intelligent Systems (pp. 196–224). IGI Global. DOI: 10.4018/979-8-3693-0968-1.ch008

Saravanan, S., Khare, R., Umamaheswari, K., Khare, S., Krishne Gowda, B. S., & Boopathi, S. (2024). AI and ML Adaptive Smart-Grid Energy Management Systems: Exploring Advanced Innovations. In Principles and Applications in Speed Sensing and Energy Harvesting for Smart Roads (pp. 166–196). IGI Global. DOI: 10.4018/978-1-6684-9214-7.ch006

Venkateswaran, N., Kiran Kumar, K., Maheswari, K., Kumar Reddy, R. V., & Boopathi, S. (2024). Optimizing IoT Data Aggregation: Hybrid Firefly-Artificial Bee Colony Algorithm for Enhanced Efficiency in Agriculture. *AGRIS On-Line Papers in Economics and Informatics*, 16(1), 117–130. DOI: 10.7160/aol.2024.160110

KEY TERMS AND DEFINITIONS

Chemical and biological sensors: They detect freshness markers, allergens, pathogens, adulterants, and toxicants in food. They are crucial for maintaining food safety and quality. On the other hand, intelligent packaging involves packaging that can monitor the quality of food in real-time. It helps in extending shelf life and ensuring the highest quality and safety during storage and transportation.

Food quality monitoring: It involves the use of various techniques and technologies to ensure that food products meet safety and quality standards throughout their lifecycle.

High-performance microcontrollers (MCUs): They are advanced computing devices designed to handle complex tasks with high efficiency and speed. MCUs often feature powerful cores, such as the Arm Cortex-M series, which provide high computational performance for demanding applications. Despite their high performance, MCUs are designed to be energy-efficient, making them suitable for applications that require low power consumption.

IoT systems: Smart IoT systems use sensors to monitor environmental factors like temperature, humidity, and gas composition. This data is transmitted wirelessly for real-time analysis, helping to prevent food spoilage and waste.

Machine Learning (ML): It is a subfield of artificial intelligence that focuses on developing algorithms and statistical models that enable computers to perform tasks without explicit instructions. ML algorithms build models based on sample data, known as training data, to make predictions or decisions without being explicitly programmed to perform the task.

Real-time analysis: It refers to the immediate processing and evaluation of data as it is generated. This capability is crucial in various fields, including food quality monitoring, where it allows for the continuous assessment of food safety and quality parameters. Real-time analysis helps in making instantaneous decisions, reducing waste, and ensuring that food products remain safe and of high quality throughout the supply chain.

Sensor technology: It plays a crucial role in various fields by enabling the detection and measurement of physical, chemical, and biological parameters. Sensor technology is widely used in industries.

Spoilage detection: It involves identifying when food products have deteriorated to the point where they are no longer safe or desirable to consume.

Types of sensors: Sensors can be classified into different types based on what they measure, such as temperature sensors, pressure sensors, chemical sensors, and biological sensors. Each type has specific applications and advantages.

Chapter 15
Integrating IoT and Machine Learning for Advanced Nuclear Structure Analysis

R. Muthukumar

https://orcid.org/0009-0008-1383-5396

Department of Electrical and Electronics Engineering, Erode Sengunthar Engineering College, India

Divakar Harekal

Department of Information Science and Engineering, Jyothy Institute of Technology, Bengaluru, India

Sk. Mastan Sharif

https://orcid.org/0000-0003-2399-5795

Department of Advanced Computer Science Engineering, Vignan's Foundation for Science, Technology, and Research, Vadlamudi, India

Dhivakar Poosapadi

https://orcid.org/0009-0009-5492-1458

Quest Global North America, Windsor, USA

P. Suresh Kumar

Department of Mechanical Engineering, R.V.R. & J.C. College of Engineering, Guntur, India

M. Sudhakar

Mechanical Engineering, Sri Sai Ram Engineering College, Chennai, India

ABSTRACT

The integration of Internet of Things (IoT) and Machine Learning (ML) technologies presents groundbreaking advancements in nuclear structure analysis. This chapter explores how IoT devices and sensors, combined with ML algorithms, can enhance the precision and efficiency of nuclear research. IoT enables real-time data collection from various sensors distributed across nuclear facilities, providing a comprehensive view of nuclear reactions and structural parameters. ML algorithms then process and analyze this vast amount of data, identifying patterns and anomalies that traditional methods might miss. The chapter discusses the implementation of advanced ML techniques such as neural networks and ensemble methods for predictive modeling and anomaly detection in nuclear systems. It also highlights the challenges and potential solutions related to data integration, security, and computational demands. The convergence of IoT and ML in nuclear structure analysis promises significant improvements in safety, operational efficiency, and research capabilities.

DOI: 10.4018/978-1-6684-3795-7.ch015

INTRODUCTION

Nuclear structure analysis is a crucial component of nuclear science and engineering, aimed at understanding the intricate dynamics and safety parameters of nuclear reactors and facilities. Traditionally, this field relied on manual inspection methods and static analytical techniques, which, despite their importance, often fell short in addressing the complex, real-time challenges inherent in nuclear operations. As the demands for enhanced safety, efficiency, and operational insight have grown, there has been a significant shift towards leveraging advanced technologies. Among these, the integration of Internet of Things (IoT) and Machine Learning (ML) has emerged as a transformative approach, promising to revolutionize the field of nuclear structure analysis(Knöll et al., 2023).

The Internet of Things (IoT) refers to the network of interconnected devices that communicate and share data through the internet. In the context of nuclear facilities, IoT involves deploying an array of sensors and devices that monitor various parameters such as temperature, pressure, radiation levels, and structural integrity. These sensors continuously collect real-time data, providing a comprehensive view of the operational conditions within a nuclear reactor or related infrastructure. This real-time data collection capability of IoT systems is pivotal in capturing the dynamic nature of nuclear processes, which traditional methods might miss(Gao et al., 2021).

Machine Learning (ML), a subset of artificial intelligence, encompasses a range of algorithms and techniques designed to analyze large volumes of data, identify patterns, and make predictions. ML algorithms can process data far beyond the capacity of human analysis, learning from historical data to forecast future conditions and detect anomalies. When applied to the data collected from IoT sensors, ML models can uncover complex relationships and trends that might not be immediately apparent through manual analysis. The integration of IoT and ML offers a synergistic approach to nuclear structure analysis. IoT provides the necessary data infrastructure, while ML delivers the analytical prowess to interpret and act upon that data. This convergence enables a more nuanced understanding of nuclear systems, leading to improved predictive maintenance, enhanced safety measures, and more efficient operational management(Wilson, 2019).

One of the primary advantages of integrating IoT with ML in nuclear structure analysis is the enhancement of real-time monitoring capabilities. Traditional monitoring methods, often based on periodic checks and manual inspections, can be limited in their ability to detect and respond to dynamic changes within a nuclear facility. IoT systems, by providing continuous data streams, allow for a more immediate and comprehensive assessment of operational conditions. ML algorithms then analyze this data to identify patterns, forecast potential issues, and provide actionable insights. For instance, predictive maintenance models can forecast equipment failures before they occur, allowing for timely interventions that prevent costly downtimes or safety incidents(Pang, 2021).

Another significant benefit is the improvement in anomaly detection. Nuclear facilities operate under stringent safety regulations, and even minor deviations from normal parameters can have serious consequences. ML algorithms can be trained to recognize normal operational patterns and identify deviations that may indicate potential problems. By integrating these advanced analytical techniques with IoT data, nuclear facilities can enhance their ability to detect anomalies early, reducing the risk of accidents and improving overall safety. Despite these promising advancements, the integration of IoT and ML in nuclear structure analysis also presents several challenges. One of the key issues is the quality and integration of data. IoT systems generate vast amounts of data, which can vary in quality and relevance(Steinheimer et al., 2019).

Ensuring that this data is accurate, consistent, and integrated effectively with ML models is crucial for reliable analysis and predictions. Moreover, the security and privacy of data are paramount in nuclear facilities, where breaches can have severe implications. Implementing robust security measures to protect data integrity and prevent unauthorized access is essential. Computational resources also pose a challenge. ML algorithms, particularly those involving deep learning and complex models, require significant computational power. Managing these resources efficiently while ensuring timely processing of real-time data is a critical consideration. Advances in cloud computing and edge computing are helping to address these challenges by providing scalable and flexible computational solutions(Gong et al., 2022).

The implementation of IoT and ML in nuclear structure analysis represents a significant shift towards more intelligent and adaptive systems. By harnessing the power of these technologies, nuclear facilities can achieve unprecedented levels of safety, efficiency, and operational insight. The continuous evolution of IoT and ML technologies, along with ongoing research and development, will further enhance their capabilities and applications in nuclear science. As this integration becomes more refined, it is expected to drive innovations in nuclear safety protocols, operational management, and overall research advancements(Nakagawa et al., 2022).

In conclusion, the integration of IoT and Machine Learning offers a transformative approach to nuclear structure analysis, promising to address the limitations of traditional methods and unlock new possibilities for safety and efficiency. The synergy between real-time data collection and advanced analytical techniques holds the potential to revolutionize how nuclear facilities operate, manage risks, and conduct research. As these technologies continue to evolve, their application in nuclear structure analysis will likely expand, leading to even more significant advancements and improvements in the field(Xu et al., 2021).

Background of Research:

Nuclear structure analysis involves studying the intricate details of nuclear reactors and facilities to ensure their safe and efficient operation. Traditionally, this analysis relied on manual inspections and static data assessments, which could be limited in scope and prone to human error. The advent of Internet of Things (IoT) and Machine Learning (ML) technologies offers transformative potential in this field. IoT provides a framework for deploying a network of sensors that collect real-time data on various parameters such as temperature, pressure, and radiation levels within nuclear systems. This continuous data stream enables a more comprehensive understanding of operational conditions and potential anomalies.

Machine Learning, on the other hand, excels at processing large volumes of data, identifying patterns, and making predictions. By applying ML algorithms to the data gathered by IoT devices, researchers can gain deeper insights into nuclear structure behavior, improve predictive maintenance, and enhance anomaly detection. The integration of IoT and ML represents a significant leap forward from traditional methods, promising increased accuracy, efficiency, and safety in nuclear structure analysis. This research aims to explore and harness the synergy between these technologies to advance nuclear science and engineering.

Scope: This chapter explores the integration of Internet of Things (IoT) and Machine Learning (ML) in nuclear structure analysis. It discusses the deployment of IoT devices for real-time data collection and the application of ML techniques for advanced data analysis. The chapter also explores ML methods used for predictive analytics, anomaly detection, and pattern recognition in nuclear data, including neural networks, deep learning models, and statistical methods. It also addresses challenges such as data integration, security, and computational resources, proposing strategies for effective integration and management. The chapter concludes with practical applications and tangible benefits of these integrated technologies for enhanced safety, efficiency, and research capabilities in nuclear facilities.

Objectives: This chapter explores the integration of Internet of Things (IoT) and Machine Learning (ML) in nuclear structure analysis. It demonstrates the role of IoT in real-time data collection and monitoring of structural parameters, highlighting sensor types, data acquisition methods, and benefits of continuous monitoring. It also showcases ML applications, such as neural networks and ensemble methods, for processing and analyzing large datasets generated by IoT systems. The chapter addresses integration challenges, such as data quality, security concerns, and computational resource requirements, and highlights the potential for improved safety protocols, operational efficiency, and research advancements in nuclear structure analysis.

TECHNOLOGICAL FOUNDATIONS

Introduction to Internet of Things (IoT)

The Internet of Things (IoT) represents a transformative technological paradigm characterized by the interconnection of physical devices via the internet. In essence, IoT extends the internet beyond traditional computing devices like computers and smartphones to encompass a vast array of physical objects embedded with sensors, software, and other technologies. These "smart" devices collect, exchange, and act upon data, creating a network of interconnected systems that can communicate and interact autonomously(Upadhyaya et al., 2024; Venkateswaran et al., 2024).

In the context of nuclear structure analysis, IoT involves deploying a network of sensors throughout nuclear facilities to monitor critical parameters such as temperature, pressure, radiation levels, and structural integrity. These sensors provide real-time data, which is crucial for maintaining operational safety and efficiency. IoT's capability to offer continuous, real-time monitoring makes it an invaluable tool in environments where timely and accurate data is essential for preventing accidents and ensuring optimal performance.

Types of Sensors and Devices

The effectiveness of an IoT system in nuclear facilities largely depends on the types of sensors and devices deployed(BOOPATHI et al., 2024; Jha et al., 2024; Malathi et al., 2024). Various sensors serve specific functions and provide critical data:

Temperature Sensors: These sensors monitor thermal conditions within the reactor and surrounding infrastructure. Maintaining the correct temperature is crucial for safe and efficient reactor operation.

Pressure Sensors: These devices measure the pressure within reactor vessels and pipelines, ensuring that operational pressures remain within safe limits.

Radiation Sensors: Radiation detectors monitor radiation levels, which is essential for safety and compliance with regulatory standards.

Vibration Sensors: These sensors detect vibrations within structural components, helping to identify potential issues such as mechanical failures or structural weaknesses.

Flow Meters: Flow sensors measure the flow rate of fluids through pipes and systems, providing data critical for maintaining proper reactor cooling and system performance.

These sensors transmit data to centralized systems, where it can be aggregated, analyzed, and utilized for decision-making and operational control.

Data Acquisition and Communication Protocols

Data acquisition refers to the process of collecting and digitizing data from various sensors and devices. In IoT systems, data acquisition involves interfacing sensors with data collection systems, which then transmit this data to central repositories for analysis. This process typically involves several key steps:

Data Collection: Sensors capture environmental or operational parameters and convert them into digital signals.

Data Transmission: The digital data is transmitted from the sensors to a central processing unit or cloud-based system. Common communication protocols for this transmission include MQTT (Message Queuing Telemetry Transport), HTTP/HTTPS (Hypertext Transfer Protocol), and CoAP (Constrained Application Protocol).

Data Storage: The collected data is stored in databases or cloud storage systems. Effective data management ensures that data is organized, secure, and accessible for analysis.

Data Processing: Data processing involves cleaning, aggregating, and preparing the data for analysis. This step ensures that the data is accurate and ready for subsequent analytical tasks.

Communication protocols are crucial in ensuring efficient and reliable data transmission. Protocols like MQTT are lightweight and designed for low-bandwidth, high-latency networks, making them ideal for IoT applications. HTTPS provides secure data transmission over the internet, which is essential for protecting sensitive information.

Introduction to Machine Learning (ML)

Machine Learning (ML) is a subset of artificial intelligence (AI) focused on developing algorithms that enable computers to learn from and make predictions based on data. Unlike traditional programming, where explicit instructions are provided, ML algorithms learn patterns and insights from historical data, improving their performance over time without being explicitly programmed for specific tasks(S., 2024; Syamala et al., 2023).

In the context of nuclear structure analysis, ML can process and analyze large volumes of data collected by IoT sensors. ML algorithms can identify trends, predict future conditions, and detect anomalies, offering valuable insights that enhance operational safety and efficiency.

Key ML Algorithms and Techniques

Several ML algorithms and techniques are particularly relevant for analyzing data in nuclear structure contexts:

Supervised Learning: This approach involves training models on labeled data, where the input data is paired with known outcomes. Algorithms such as Linear Regression, Support Vector Machines (SVM), and Decision Trees fall under this category.

Unsupervised Learning: Involves analyzing data without predefined labels to identify patterns or groupings. Techniques such as Clustering (e.g., K-Means) and Principal Component Analysis (PCA) are commonly used.

Deep Learning: A subset of supervised learning that uses neural networks with multiple layers (deep neural networks) to model complex patterns. Convolutional Neural Networks (CNNs) and Recurrent Neural Networks (RNNs) are prominent examples.

Anomaly Detection: Specialized algorithms designed to identify unusual or outlier data points. Techniques such as Isolation Forest and One-Class SVM are used for detecting anomalies in operational data.

Role of ML in Data Analysis

In nuclear structure analysis, ML plays a critical role by providing advanced analytical capabilities. ML algorithms can process the vast amounts of data generated by IoT sensors to uncover insights that are not immediately obvious(Sreedhar et al., 2024; Tirlangi et al., 2024; Verma et al., 2024). Key roles include:

Predictive Maintenance: ML models can forecast equipment failures or maintenance needs based on historical data, reducing unplanned downtimes and enhancing operational reliability.

Anomaly Detection: ML algorithms detect deviations from normal operational patterns, enabling early identification of potential issues or safety hazards.

Trend Analysis: ML helps in understanding long-term trends and patterns in the data, which can inform strategic decision-making and operational improvements.

Optimization: By analyzing data, ML algorithms can optimize processes, such as reactor performance or resource allocation, leading to increased efficiency and cost savings.

The integration of IoT and ML represents a powerful synergy that enhances the capabilities of nuclear structure analysis, offering unprecedented levels of safety, efficiency, and operational insight.

MACHINE LEARNING: FUNDAMENTALS AND TECHNIQUES

Machine learning (ML) is the new vital tool in advanced nuclear structure analysis, processing large datasets, modeling the phenomena of nuclei, and predicting properties that traditional approaches could not really capture. In nuclear physics, advanced ML techniques enable in-depth understanding of nuclear reactions, decay modes, and even the structure of atomic nuclei, particularly for complex, less well-studied isotopes. These ML models have helped unravel the otherwise very dense and knotty data patterns produced by nuclear experiments, often yielding insights not easily accessible otherwise through physics-based models(Chandra et al., 2024; Naresh et al., 2024; S., 2024).

Machine learning, at its very core, relies on algorithms that enable such systems to learn from data patterns without explicit programming. One of the widely adopted ML approaches is supervised learning, which teaches a model, using labeled data, in the form of input-output pairs depicting known relationships. In the analysis of nuclear structure, supervised learning can predict a variety of nuclear properties, like binding energies, neutron-proton ratios, deformation parameters. A model trained on known nuclear properties can generalize and, hence, predict properties of less-explored isotopes. This amounts to a huge contribution to research in nuclear physics and practical applications in nuclear energy and medicine.

Important additional techniques from ML have come from unsupervised learning, which finds hidden structures in an unlabeled dataset. Unsupervised learning applications of dimensionality reduction and clustering techniques are exceedingly useful in the context of nuclear data analysis, which often contains millions of variables from raw data coming from particle detectors or simulations. PCA and t-SNE are two examples of dimensionality reduction techniques that keep the essential relationships while bringing down the data's dimension. These techniques can help find hidden nuclear states or even correlations between isotopic characteristics. More importantly, clustering algorithms can identify isotopes that share similar structural or energetic properties, which can have implications for the theoretical models by exhibiting systematic features in the nuclear landscape.

Another breakthrough area of ML is reinforcement learning (RL). As one of the newer ML techniques, this has the potential to be applied in many areas of nuclear physics where sequential decision-making and adaptive strategies are needed, such as dynamically optimizing conditions in nuclear reactions in simulations. For instance, in accelerator experiments whose aim is to produce specific isotopes or study particular nuclear states, the experimental parameters could be adjusted iteratively so that the probability of their success is maximized. RL algorithms would offer, in this case, a new level of efficiency and precision particularity when dealing with short-lived isotopes or complex reaction chains.

DL is also that type of ML subset which has neural networks, and it has been transformative in nuclear physics. The capacity of DL to process high-dimensional data can take it up to very useful applications for analyzing data from nuclear detectors, which often catch some very intricate spatial and temporal signals. Convolutional Neural Networks (CNNs) applied over the spatial data coming from the nuclear experiments, allow pattern detection to be made about specific nuclear interactions or events. Recurrent Neural Networks (RNNs) also fit well over sequential data analysis and therefore time-series data from the detectors are interpreted. They shine in cases where the data dependencies span several time steps, such as in many applications of nuclear decay studies and reactor simulations.

The integration of ML techniques within nuclear structure analysis is leading innovations across the board. Hybrid models combining the use of ML with traditional physics approaches increasingly consist of known physical laws augmented by insights provided by the power of data. Hybrid models are also very useful in various areas where the traditional model does not perform effectively. For example, in predicting structures of exotics nuclei far from stability. As nuclear research shifts to high-throughput experiments with gigantic datasets generation, scalability also becomes a really important criterion for ML algorithms. The ability of ML in processing and analyzing the data in an efficient manner is assisting researchers in managing the complexity of nuclear datasets; new isotopes are discovered faster, and uncharted regions of the nuclear chart are explored much more easily(Pachiappan et al., 2024; S., 2024).

Machine learning impacts on nuclear physics are going to rise with improved algorithms and increasing computational resources. The future will bring explainable ML models with interpretable insights into nuclear structure, thereby building trust and insight into the predictions of ML amongst the physics community. Furthermore, ML is relevant beyond research applications as it identifies potential applications in domains such as the production of nuclear energy and nuclear medicine, where detailed knowledge of the properties of isotopes and their radioactive decay pathways is crucial. The adoption of ML techniques is expected to take nuclear physics into revolutionary strides, both theoretically and in applications, in the revelation of atomic nuclei and their complex behavior.

INTEGRATION OF IOT AND MACHINE LEARNING

Figure 1. Integration of IoT and Machine Learning (ML)

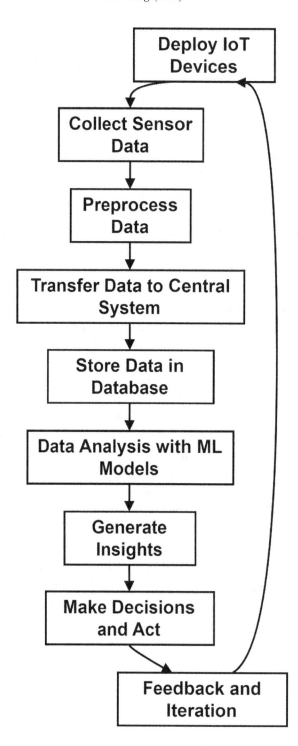

The integration of IoT and Machine Learning (ML) involves data collection, illustrated using a flow-chart to illustrate the sequential steps involved as showun in Figure 1.

Framework for Combining IoT with ML

The integration of Internet of Things (IoT) with Machine Learning (ML) involves creating a framework that seamlessly connects data collection with advanced analytical capabilities(Trindade et al., 2019). This framework consists of several key components:

IoT Device Network: At the core of the framework is a network of IoT devices, including sensors and actuators, deployed throughout the nuclear facility. These devices continuously collect data on various parameters such as temperature, pressure, radiation, and vibrations. The data collected by these sensors forms the foundation for further analysis.

Data Aggregation Layer: Data from multiple IoT devices is aggregated in this layer. Data aggregation involves collecting, consolidating, and organizing data from different sensors into a coherent format. This layer often includes edge computing nodes that preprocess data locally, reducing the volume of data transmitted to centralized systems and enabling real-time processing.

Data Transmission and Storage: Aggregated data is transmitted to centralized storage systems or cloud-based platforms. Communication protocols such as MQTT, HTTP/HTTPS, and CoAP are used to ensure reliable and secure data transfer. The data is then stored in databases or data lakes, where it can be accessed for analysis.

Data Processing and Preparation: Before applying ML algorithms, the data must be cleaned, normalized, and prepared. This step involves handling missing values, outliers, and ensuring that data is in a suitable format for ML models. Techniques such as data transformation and feature extraction are used to enhance the quality and relevance of the data.

Machine Learning Models: Once the data is prepared, it is fed into ML models. These models can range from simple linear regression to complex deep learning networks, depending on the specific analytical needs. The ML models are trained on historical data to learn patterns, correlations, and anomalies.

Model Deployment and Integration: After training, ML models are deployed and integrated into the IoT system. They can operate in real-time, analyzing incoming data from IoT devices to generate predictions, detect anomalies, or provide actionable insights. This integration allows for continuous, automated analysis of the data as it is collected.

Visualization and Reporting: The results of the ML analysis are often visualized through dashboards and reporting tools. These tools present the insights derived from the data in a user-friendly format, enabling operators and decision-makers to make informed decisions based on real-time information.

Data Flow from IoT Devices to ML Models

The data flow from IoT devices to ML models involves several key stages(Wang et al., 2022):

a) **Data Collection:** IoT devices continuously collect data from their environment. For instance, sensors might record temperature fluctuations or radiation levels at frequent intervals. This raw data is transmitted from the devices to a central repository.

b) **Data Transmission:** The collected data is sent to the data aggregation layer using communication protocols. Protocols like MQTT are often employed due to their lightweight nature and efficiency in handling intermittent data transmission. The data is transmitted securely to ensure integrity and confidentiality.

c) **Data Aggregation and Preprocessing:** Upon reaching the central system, data is aggregated from multiple sources and preprocessed. This step involves cleaning the data to remove noise and inconsistencies, normalizing values to ensure consistency, and transforming the data into a format suitable for ML analysis.

d) **Data Storage:** Processed data is stored in databases or cloud storage solutions. Data lakes or data warehouses may be used to handle large volumes of data, providing a centralized location for access and further analysis.

e) **Feature Engineering:** During preprocessing, relevant features are extracted from the data. Feature engineering involves selecting or creating variables that will be most informative for the ML models. This might include aggregating data over time or deriving new metrics from raw data.

f) **Model Training and Testing:** ML models are trained using historical data to learn patterns and relationships. During training, the model adjusts its parameters to minimize prediction errors. Once trained, the model is tested on new data to evaluate its performance and accuracy.

g) **Real-Time Analysis:** Deployed ML models analyze incoming data from IoT devices in real-time. The models use learned patterns to make predictions, detect anomalies, or generate insights based on the live data stream.

h) **Decision Making and Action:** The insights and predictions generated by ML models are used to make informed decisions. For instance, an anomaly detection model might alert operators to potential safety issues, allowing them to take corrective action before a problem escalates.

By integrating IoT with ML, nuclear facilities can achieve a sophisticated analytical framework that enhances their ability to monitor, predict, and optimize operations. This integration facilitates real-time insights and automated responses, improving safety, efficiency, and operational effectiveness.

APPLICATIONS IN NUCLEAR STRUCTURE ANALYSIS

Figure 2. Applications of IoT and Machine Learning (ML) in nuclear structure analysis

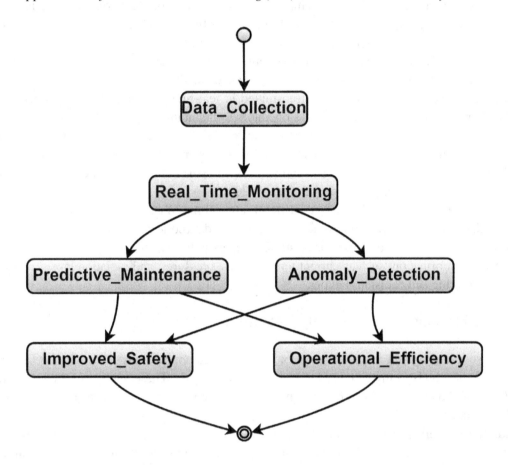

The use of IoT and Machine Learning (ML) in nuclear structure analysis is depicted in Figure 2. IoT devices collect data from sensors in nuclear facilities, enabling real-time monitoring to track system parameters and performance. This data is then used for predictive maintenance, predicting and preventing equipment failures. Anomaly detection helps identify deviations or unusual patterns, enhancing safety and operational efficiency. This results in improved safety and reduced downtime, while optimizing maintenance schedules through IoT and ML applications. Overall, these advancements contribute to safer operations(Murarka et al., 2022).

Real-Time Monitoring and Data Collection

Real-time monitoring and data collection represent the foundational applications of integrating IoT and Machine Learning (ML) in nuclear structure analysis. In a nuclear facility, continuous monitoring is crucial for ensuring operational safety and efficiency. The deployment of IoT devices throughout the facility allows for comprehensive, real-time data collection on various critical parameters such as temperature, pressure, radiation levels, and structural integrity(Trindade et al., 2019).

IoT sensors are strategically placed at key locations within the reactor, cooling systems, and structural components to gather data. For instance, temperature sensors monitor the thermal conditions of reactor components, ensuring they remain within safe operational limits. Radiation sensors provide constant updates on radiation levels, crucial for both safety and regulatory compliance. Pressure sensors track the pressure within reactor vessels and piping systems to prevent overpressure scenarios that could lead to catastrophic failures(Pachiappan et al., 2024; Syamala et al., 2023).

The data collected by these sensors is transmitted in real-time to centralized data processing systems. This continuous stream of data allows operators to maintain an up-to-date view of the facility's operational state. Real-time monitoring enables the immediate detection of deviations from normal operating conditions, allowing for prompt intervention. For example, if a temperature sensor detects an anomaly, operators can quickly investigate and address the issue before it escalates into a more serious problem(Agrawal et al., 2023; Venkateswaran et al., 2024).

Moreover, the integration of IoT devices with ML algorithms enhances the ability to manage and interpret this data. ML models can process the vast amounts of data collected, providing actionable insights and visualizations that help operators understand complex patterns and trends. Real-time dashboards display critical information, such as current temperatures, pressures, and radiation levels, allowing for efficient monitoring and decision-making.

Predictive Modeling and Anomaly Detection

Predictive modeling and anomaly detection are advanced applications of combining IoT and ML technologies that significantly enhance nuclear structure analysis. These applications leverage historical and real-time data to anticipate future conditions and identify potential issues before they become critical(Murarka et al., 2022).

Predictive Modeling: Predictive modeling involves using historical data to forecast future conditions and performance. In nuclear facilities, predictive models are employed to anticipate equipment failures, maintenance needs, and other operational issues. For example, ML algorithms can analyze historical data from temperature and pressure sensors to predict when a piece of equipment might fail. This predictive capability allows for scheduled maintenance before a failure occurs, reducing the risk of unplanned outages and improving overall operational efficiency.

One common approach in predictive modeling is the use of regression algorithms, which identify relationships between different variables and use these relationships to make predictions. For instance, a regression model might be trained to predict reactor temperatures based on historical temperature data and other influencing factors. Advanced techniques such as time series forecasting and ensemble methods further refine these predictions, providing more accurate and reliable forecasts.

Anomaly Detection: Anomaly detection focuses on identifying deviations from normal operational patterns that may indicate potential problems. ML algorithms are trained to recognize what constitutes normal behavior based on historical data, and they continuously monitor real-time data to detect deviations. For example, if a sensor detects a sudden spike in temperature or an unusual pattern in pressure readings, the anomaly detection system flags this as a potential issue(Sonia et al., 2024; Sreedhar et al., 2024; Sundar et al., 2024).

Several techniques are used for anomaly detection, including statistical methods, clustering algorithms, and advanced deep learning models. Statistical methods may involve setting thresholds for acceptable ranges of sensor readings, while clustering algorithms group similar data points to identify outliers. Deep learning models, such as autoencoders and recurrent neural networks (RNNs), can learn complex patterns and detect subtle anomalies that might be missed by simpler methods.

Anomaly detection not only helps in identifying immediate issues but also provides valuable insights into underlying problems. For instance, a recurring anomaly in vibration data might indicate a developing fault in mechanical components, prompting further investigation and preventive maintenance.

The integration of predictive modeling and anomaly detection with IoT and ML technologies transforms nuclear structure analysis by enabling proactive management and enhanced safety measures. Predictive models offer foresight into potential issues, allowing for timely interventions and maintenance, while anomaly detection ensures that unexpected deviations are promptly identified and addressed. Together, these applications contribute to a more reliable and efficient operation of nuclear facilities, reducing risks and improving overall performance.

In summary, the integration of IoT and ML in nuclear structure analysis offers significant advancements in real-time monitoring and data collection, predictive modeling, and anomaly detection. By leveraging these technologies, nuclear facilities can achieve enhanced operational safety, efficiency, and reliability, ultimately leading to more effective management and optimization of their systems.

Enhancing Safety: The integration of IoT and Machine Learning (ML) significantly enhances safety in nuclear facilities. IoT sensors continuously monitor critical parameters such as radiation levels, temperature, and pressure. By analyzing this real-time data with ML algorithms, facilities can detect anomalies and potential safety hazards more effectively. For example, ML models can identify unusual patterns or deviations from normal operational conditions, which may indicate impending equipment failures or hazardous situations. Early detection allows for timely interventions, preventing accidents and ensuring compliance with safety regulations. Additionally, predictive maintenance enabled by ML can forecast potential equipment failures before they occur, reducing the likelihood of unexpected breakdowns and enhancing overall safety(K. S. et al., 2024).

Operational Efficiency: Operational efficiency in nuclear facilities is greatly improved through the use of IoT and ML. IoT devices provide continuous, granular data on various operational metrics, such as energy consumption, flow rates, and system performance. ML algorithms analyze this data to identify inefficiencies and optimize processes. For instance, ML can be used to fine-tune reactor operations, improve cooling system performance, and optimize resource utilization. This leads to more efficient energy production, reduced operational costs, and extended equipment lifespans. Furthermore, ML-driven insights can support decision-making by providing actionable recommendations for process improvements and operational adjustments.

Overall, the application of IoT and ML in nuclear structure analysis offers a dual advantage: enhancing safety through proactive hazard detection and improving operational efficiency through data-driven optimization. This integration ensures that nuclear facilities operate safely, efficiently, and in accordance with regulatory standards, ultimately contributing to more reliable and sustainable energy production.

CHALLENGES AND SOLUTIONS

Figure 3. Challenges and solutions associated with integrating IoT and Machine Learning (ML) in a nuclear structure analysis

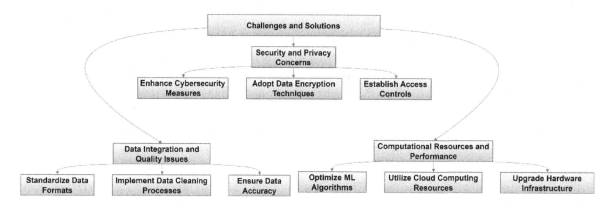

Figure 3 illustrates the challenges and solutions to improve data integration and quality in IoT systems. It emphasizes the importance of standardizing data formats, implementing data cleaning processes, and regularly validating data to maintain accuracy. It also highlights the need for enhanced cybersecurity measures, data encryption techniques, and strict access controls. The text also suggests optimizing machine learning algorithms, leveraging cloud computing resources for large-scale data processing, and upgrading hardware infrastructure to enhance processing capabilities and performance. These measures aim to ensure the smooth functioning of IoT systems(Lee & Chien, 2020; Saleem et al., 2020).

Data Integration and Quality Issues

Challenges: One of the primary challenges in integrating IoT with Machine Learning (ML) for nuclear structure analysis is managing data integration and ensuring data quality. IoT systems generate vast amounts of data from diverse sensors, each with different formats, frequencies, and scales. This data must be aggregated and synchronized for effective analysis, but discrepancies in data formats and quality can hinder this process. Issues such as missing data, sensor malfunctions, and variations in data collection methods can impact the accuracy and reliability of the ML models(Ramaprasad et al., 2022; Yi et al., 2020).

Solutions: To address data integration and quality issues, it is essential to implement robust data preprocessing and management strategies. Standardizing data formats and protocols ensures consistency across different sensors and sources. Data cleansing techniques, such as interpolation for missing values and outlier detection, improve data quality. Implementing comprehensive data validation procedures helps identify and rectify errors early in the data collection process. Furthermore, integrating edge computing capabilities can preprocess data locally, reducing the volume of data that needs to be transmitted and improving data quality before it reaches the central system. Leveraging data integration platforms and middleware can also facilitate seamless aggregation and synchronization of data from disparate sources.

Security and Privacy Concerns

Challenges: The integration of IoT and ML systems raises significant security and privacy concerns. IoT devices and data communication channels are vulnerable to cyber-attacks, which could compromise sensitive information and disrupt operations. In nuclear facilities, where data confidentiality and operational integrity are paramount, ensuring secure data transmission and storage is crucial. Additionally, privacy concerns arise with the collection and handling of potentially sensitive data, including operational metrics and system performance information(Do Koo et al., 2020; Galib et al., 2021).

Solutions: To mitigate security and privacy risks, implementing robust cybersecurity measures is essential. This includes encrypting data both in transit and at rest to protect against unauthorized access and data breaches. Regular security updates and patches should be applied to IoT devices and software to address vulnerabilities. Implementing strong authentication and authorization mechanisms ensures that only authorized personnel can access critical systems and data. Additionally, adopting a defense-in-depth strategy, which includes multiple layers of security controls, can provide comprehensive protection against potential threats. Privacy-preserving techniques, such as data anonymization and aggregation, can further enhance data security while complying with regulatory requirements.

Computational Resources and Performance

Challenges: The deployment of ML models in real-time IoT environments requires substantial computational resources. ML algorithms, especially those involving deep learning, can be computationally intensive, necessitating significant processing power and memory. In nuclear facilities, where timely and accurate analysis is critical, managing computational resources efficiently is a challenge. The need for real-time processing can strain existing infrastructure and impact system performance, leading to potential delays in data analysis and decision-making.

Solutions: To address computational resource challenges, leveraging edge computing and cloud-based solutions can provide scalable and flexible processing power. Edge computing allows for the local processing of data, reducing latency and bandwidth usage while improving real-time performance. Cloud computing offers on-demand resources that can be scaled up or down based on workload requirements, ensuring efficient management of computational resources. Additionally, optimizing ML algorithms and employing techniques such as model pruning and quantization can reduce computational demands while maintaining performance. Implementing efficient data management and processing workflows helps streamline operations and ensures timely analysis. Regularly evaluating and upgrading hardware infrastructure to meet evolving computational needs is also crucial.

The integration of IoT and ML in nuclear structure analysis presents several challenges, including data integration and quality issues, security and privacy concerns, and computational resource management. Addressing these challenges requires a multi-faceted approach, incorporating robust data management practices, comprehensive cybersecurity measures, and efficient computational strategies. By implementing these solutions, nuclear facilities can enhance the effectiveness and reliability of their IoT and ML systems, ultimately improving safety, operational efficiency, and overall performance. As technology continues to advance, ongoing research and development will further refine these solutions, paving the way for more sophisticated and resilient systems in nuclear structure analysis.

IMPLEMENTATION STRATEGIES

Figure 4. Implementation strategies for integrating IoT and Machine Learning in nuclear structure analysis

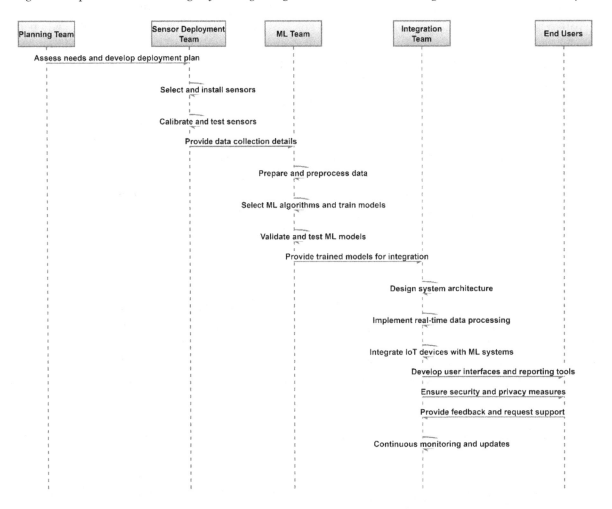

Guidelines for Deploying IoT Devices

Needs Assessment and Planning: Before deploying IoT devices, conduct a comprehensive assessment to identify specific monitoring needs and objectives. This includes determining which parameters need to be measured (e.g., temperature, pressure, radiation) and selecting appropriate sensor types and quantities. Develop a detailed deployment plan that outlines sensor locations, data transmission methods, and integration with existing systems(Clerbaux et al., 2021; Keeble & Rios, 2020; Yüksel et al., 2021).

Figure 4 depicts the implementation strategies for integrating IoT and Machine Learning in nuclear structure analysis.

Selection of Reliable Sensors: Choose high-quality, reliable sensors that meet the requirements of the nuclear facility. Consider factors such as accuracy, durability, and resistance to environmental conditions. Ensure that sensors are capable of operating under the extreme conditions often found in nuclear environments.

Installation and Calibration: Proper installation and calibration of IoT devices are crucial for accurate data collection. Follow manufacturer guidelines for installation and perform initial calibration to ensure that sensors provide accurate readings. Regular maintenance and recalibration should be scheduled to maintain sensor performance over time.

Connectivity and Communication: Establish robust connectivity and communication channels for data transmission. This involves selecting appropriate communication protocols (e.g., MQTT, CoAP) and ensuring that network infrastructure can handle the data volume and frequency. Implement redundancy and failover mechanisms to ensure continuous data flow in case of network disruptions.

Data Management and Storage: Set up a data management system to handle the large volumes of data generated by IoT devices. Implement data storage solutions that provide scalability and reliability, such as cloud storage or on-premises databases. Ensure that data is stored securely and is accessible for analysis and reporting.

ML Model Training and Validation

Data Preparation: Before training ML models, prepare the data collected from IoT devices by cleaning, normalizing, and transforming it into a format suitable for analysis. This involves handling missing values, removing outliers, and performing feature extraction to enhance the quality and relevance of the data(Clerbaux et al., 2021; Yüksel et al., 2021).

Model Selection: Choose appropriate ML algorithms based on the objectives of the analysis. For supervised learning tasks, algorithms such as Linear Regression, Support Vector Machines (SVM), and Decision Trees can be used. For anomaly detection, consider algorithms like Isolation Forest or One-Class SVM. For complex patterns, deep learning models like Convolutional Neural Networks (CNNs) or Recurrent Neural Networks (RNNs) may be appropriate.

Training and Hyperparameter Tuning: Train ML models using historical data and optimize them through hyperparameter tuning. Split the data into training, validation, and test sets to evaluate model performance and prevent overfitting. Use techniques such as cross-validation to assess model generalization and robustness.

Model Validation and Testing: Validate and test ML models to ensure their accuracy and reliability. Perform rigorous testing using unseen data to evaluate how well the models perform in real-world scenarios. Metrics such as accuracy, precision, recall, and F1 score should be used to assess model performance.

Continuous Monitoring and Updating: Once deployed, continuously monitor the performance of ML models and update them as needed. Retrain models with new data to adapt to changing conditions and improve accuracy. Implement a feedback loop to refine models based on real-time performance and user feedback.

Integrating IoT and ML Systems Effectively

System Architecture Design: Design a robust architecture that integrates IoT devices with ML systems. The architecture should include data collection, preprocessing, ML model deployment, and visualization components. Ensure that the architecture supports scalability and can handle the volume and variety of data generated by IoT devices(Garcia-Cardona et al., 2019; Murarka et al., 2022; Trindade et al., 2019).

Real-Time Data Processing: Implement real-time data processing capabilities to enable timely analysis and decision-making. Use edge computing to preprocess data locally before sending it to centralized systems. This reduces latency and bandwidth usage, ensuring that ML models receive high-quality data for analysis.

Interoperability and Integration: Ensure that IoT devices and ML systems can communicate and interact seamlessly. Use standardized communication protocols and data formats to facilitate interoperability. Implement APIs and integration platforms to connect disparate systems and enable smooth data flow between IoT devices and ML models.

User Interface and Reporting: Develop user-friendly interfaces for monitoring and interacting with IoT and ML systems. Dashboards and reporting tools should present insights in a clear and actionable format, allowing operators to make informed decisions based on real-time data and ML predictions.

Security and Privacy Measures: Incorporate robust security and privacy measures to protect data and systems. Implement encryption for data transmission and storage, and enforce strong authentication and authorization controls. Regularly update security protocols and conduct vulnerability assessments to address potential threats.

Training and Support: Provide training and support for personnel involved in managing and operating IoT and ML systems. Ensure that staff are familiar with system components, data interpretation, and troubleshooting procedures. Ongoing support and education help maintain system effectiveness and address any issues that arise.

Implementing IoT and ML systems in nuclear structure analysis involves careful planning, selection of reliable technologies, and effective integration strategies. By following these guidelines for deploying IoT devices, training and validating ML models, and integrating systems, nuclear facilities can enhance safety, operational efficiency, and overall performance. Addressing challenges and leveraging advanced technologies will ensure that IoT and ML systems deliver valuable insights and support informed decision-making in complex and critical environments.

FUTURE DIRECTIONS

Figure 5. Emerging Technologies and Innovations

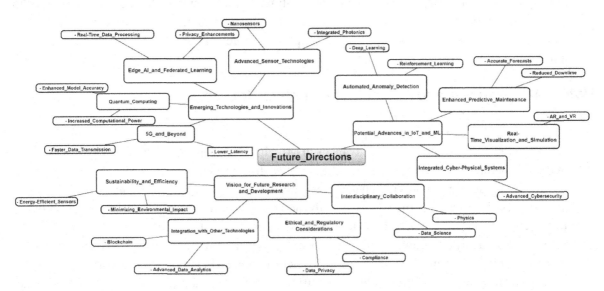

Emerging Technologies and Innovations

As technology continues to advance, the integration of IoT and Machine Learning (ML) in nuclear structure analysis is poised for significant evolution. Emerging technologies are shaping the future of this integration, offering new possibilities for enhancing safety, efficiency, and research capabilities(Garcia-Cardona et al., 2019; Murarka et al., 2022; Trindade et al., 2019). The figure 5 depicts the development and advancements in emerging technologies and innovations.

a) Quantum Computing: Quantum computing holds the potential to revolutionize ML by significantly increasing computational power. This advancement could enable more complex and accurate models, enhancing the ability to predict and analyze nuclear phenomena with unprecedented precision. Quantum algorithms could handle vast amounts of data from IoT devices more efficiently, leading to faster insights and improved decision-making.

b) Advanced Sensor Technologies: The development of more sophisticated sensors with higher accuracy, sensitivity, and resilience is crucial for monitoring nuclear facilities. Innovations such as nanosensors and integrated photonics could provide more detailed and reliable data. These sensors would be capable of detecting minute changes in environmental parameters and nuclear processes, thereby improving the quality of data for ML analysis.

c) Edge AI and Federated Learning: Edge AI involves deploying ML models directly on IoT devices, enabling real-time data processing and decision-making at the source. Federated learning allows ML models to be trained collaboratively across multiple devices without centralized data aggregation.

These approaches can enhance the efficiency and scalability of ML applications in nuclear research by reducing data transmission latency and improving privacy.

d) 5G and Beyond: The rollout of 5G networks promises faster data transmission speeds, lower latency, and improved connectivity. This will facilitate real-time data transfer from IoT devices to centralized systems and enable more responsive ML applications. Future advancements beyond 5G, such as 6G, could further enhance network capabilities, supporting more extensive and complex IoT networks in nuclear facilities.

Potential Advances in IoT and ML for Nuclear Research

a) Enhanced Predictive Maintenance: Advances in ML algorithms and sensor technologies will refine predictive maintenance strategies for nuclear facilities. Improved models will provide more accurate forecasts of equipment failures and maintenance needs, leading to reduced downtime and enhanced operational efficiency. Real-time data from advanced sensors will feed into these models, improving their accuracy and reliability(Knöll et al., 2023; Ramaprasad et al., 2022; Wang et al., 2022).

b) Automated Anomaly Detection: Future ML models will leverage more sophisticated techniques, such as deep learning and reinforcement learning, to detect anomalies in nuclear processes with greater precision. These models will be able to identify subtle patterns and deviations that may indicate potential safety hazards or operational issues, providing early warnings and enabling proactive measures.

c) Integrated Cyber-Physical Systems: The integration of IoT and ML with advanced cybersecurity measures will lead to more secure cyber-physical systems. Innovations in encryption, intrusion detection, and secure communication protocols will enhance the resilience of IoT and ML systems against cyber threats. This will ensure the integrity and confidentiality of data in nuclear research environments.

d) Real-Time Visualization and Simulation: Advances in visualization technologies, such as augmented reality (AR) and virtual reality (VR), will provide immersive and interactive ways to analyze and interpret data from IoT devices and ML models. Real-time simulations and visualizations will enable researchers and operators to explore complex scenarios and make informed decisions based on dynamic data.

Vision for Future Research and Development

a) Interdisciplinary Collaboration: Future research in IoT and ML for nuclear structure analysis will benefit from interdisciplinary collaboration. Bringing together experts in fields such as physics, data science, engineering, and cybersecurity will foster innovation and drive the development of new technologies and methodologies. Collaborative research efforts will address complex challenges and create integrated solutions for nuclear facilities.

b) Ethical and Regulatory Considerations: As IoT and ML technologies advance, addressing ethical and regulatory considerations will be essential. Developing frameworks for the responsible use of data, ensuring privacy and security, and adhering to regulatory standards will guide the implementation of these technologies in nuclear research. Ongoing dialogue with regulatory bodies and stakeholders will ensure that advancements align with safety and ethical guidelines.

c) Sustainability and Efficiency: Future research will focus on enhancing the sustainability and efficiency of IoT and ML systems. This includes developing energy-efficient sensors and computing solutions, optimizing data management practices, and minimizing the environmental impact of technological deployments. Sustainable practices will ensure that advancements contribute to long-term benefits for nuclear research and energy production.

d) Integration with Other Technologies: The integration of IoT and ML with other emerging technologies, such as blockchain and advanced data analytics, will open new possibilities for nuclear research. Blockchain can provide secure and transparent data management, while advanced analytics can offer deeper insights into complex data sets. Exploring these synergies will drive innovation and expand the capabilities of IoT and ML systems.

The future of integrating IoT and ML in nuclear structure analysis is bright with the potential for transformative advancements. Emerging technologies, such as quantum computing, advanced sensors, and edge AI, will drive the evolution of these systems, enhancing their capabilities and impact(Kumar et al., 2023; Pachiappan et al., 2024). As research and development continue to progress, interdisciplinary collaboration, ethical considerations, and sustainability will guide the implementation of these technologies, ensuring their benefits are realized in a responsible and effective manner. The vision for the future encompasses a holistic approach that integrates technological innovations, research advancements, and collaborative efforts to advance nuclear structure analysis and improve safety, efficiency, and operational effectiveness.

CONCLUSION

The integration of Internet of Things (IoT) and Machine Learning (ML) in nuclear structure analysis represents a significant leap forward in enhancing safety, efficiency, and operational capabilities within nuclear facilities. By leveraging IoT devices to collect real-time data on critical parameters and applying ML algorithms for advanced data analysis, we can achieve unprecedented levels of precision in monitoring and managing nuclear systems.

This chapter has explored the technological foundations of IoT and ML, detailing how advancements in sensor technologies and computational techniques contribute to more effective nuclear structure analysis. The framework for integrating IoT with ML highlights the importance of seamless data flow, robust system architecture, and real-time processing capabilities. These integrations not only improve operational efficiency and safety but also offer innovative solutions for predictive maintenance and anomaly detection. However, the journey towards fully realizing these benefits is not without its challenges. Issues related to data integration and quality, security and privacy concerns, and computational resource demands must be addressed to ensure the effective implementation of IoT and ML systems. Solutions such as standardizing data formats, implementing strong cybersecurity measures, and optimizing computational resources are crucial for overcoming these challenges.

Emerging technologies like quantum computing, advanced sensors, and edge AI are set to revolutionize the integration of IoT and ML in nuclear structure analysis, enhancing accuracy, safety measures, and operational efficiencies. However, interdisciplinary collaboration, ethical considerations, and sustainability will be crucial in developing and deploying these technologies.

In conclusion, the ongoing advancements in IoT and ML offer transformative potential for nuclear research and facility management. Embracing these technologies with a forward-thinking approach will drive continuous improvements, ensuring that nuclear facilities operate at the highest standards of safety and efficiency.

REFERENCES

Agrawal, A. V., Magulur, L. P., Priya, S. G., Kaur, A., Singh, G., & Boopathi, S. (2023). Smart Precision Agriculture Using IoT and WSN. In *Handbook of Research on Data Science and Cybersecurity Innovations in Industry 4.0 Technologies* (pp. 524–541). IGI Global. DOI: 10.4018/978-1-6684-8145-5.ch026

BOOPATHI, S., KARTHIKEYAN, K. R., JAISWAL, C., DABI, R., SUNAGAR, P., & MALIK, S. (2024). *IoT based Automatic Cooling Tower.*

Chandra, S., Ghule, G., Bilfaqih, S. M., Thiyagarajan, A., Sharmila, J., & Boopathi, S. (2024). Adaptive Strategies in Online Marketing Using Machine Learning Techniques. In *Digital Transformation Initiatives for Agile Marketing* (pp. 67–100). IGI Global., DOI: 10.4018/979-8-3693-4466-8.ch004

Clerbaux, B., Molla, M. C., Petitjean, P.-A., Xu, Y., & Yang, Y. (2021). Study of using machine learning for level 1 trigger decision in JUNO experiment. *IEEE Transactions on Nuclear Science*, 68(8), 2187–2193. DOI: 10.1109/TNS.2021.3085428

Do Koo, Y., Jo, H. S., Yoo, K. H., & Na, M. G. (2020). *Identification of Initial Events in Nuclear Power Plants Using Machine Learning Methods.*

Galib, S., Bhowmik, P., Avachat, A., & Lee, H. (2021). A comparative study of machine learning methods for automated identification of radioisotopes using NaI gamma-ray spectra. *Nuclear Engineering and Technology*, 53(12), 4072–4079. DOI: 10.1016/j.net.2021.06.020

Gao, Z.-P., Wang, Y.-J., Lü, H.-L., Li, Q.-F., Shen, C.-W., & Liu, L. (2021). Machine learning the nuclear mass. *Nuclear Science and Techniques*, 32(10), 109. DOI: 10.1007/s41365-021-00956-1

Garcia-Cardona, C., Kannan, R., Johnston, T., Proffen, T., Page, K., & Seal, S. K. (2019). Learning to predict material structure from neutron scattering data. *2019 IEEE International Conference on Big Data (Big Data)*, 4490–4497. DOI: 10.1109/BigData47090.2019.9005968

Gong, H., Cheng, S., Chen, Z., & Li, Q. (2022). Data-enabled physics-informed machine learning for reduced-order modeling digital twin: Application to nuclear reactor physics. *Nuclear Science and Engineering*, 196(6), 668–693. DOI: 10.1080/00295639.2021.2014752

Jha, S. K., & Beevi, S. J. P., H., Babitha, M. N., Chinnusamy, S., & Boopathi, S. (2024). Artificial Intelligence-Infused Urban Connectivity for Smart Cities and the Evolution of IoT Communication Networks. In *Blockchain-Based Solutions for Accessibility in Smart Cities* (pp. 113–146). IGI Global. DOI: 10.4018/979-8-3693-3402-7.ch005

K. S. K. K., Isaac, J. S., Pratheep, V. G., Jasmin, M., Kistan, A., & Boopathi, S. (2024). Smart Food Quality Monitoring by Integrating IoT and Deep Learning for Enhanced Safety and Freshness. In *Edible Electronics for Smart Technology Solutions* (pp. 79–110). IGI Global. DOI: 10.4018/979-8-3693-5573-2.ch004

Keeble, J., & Rios, A. (2020). Machine learning the deuteron. *Physics Letters. [Part B]*, 809, 135743. DOI: 10.1016/j.physletb.2020.135743

Knöll, M., Wolfgruber, T., Agel, M. L., Wenz, C., & Roth, R. (2023). Machine learning for the prediction of converged energies from ab initio nuclear structure calculations. *Physics Letters. [Part B]*, 839, 137781. DOI: 10.1016/j.physletb.2023.137781

Kumar, M., Kumar, K., Sasikala, P., Sampath, B., Gopi, B., & Sundaram, S. (2023). Sustainable Green Energy Generation From Waste Water: IoT and ML Integration. In *Sustainable Science and Intelligent Technologies for Societal Development* (pp. 440–463). IGI Global.

Lee, M.-F. R., & Chien, T.-W. (2020). Artificial intelligence and Internet of Things for robotic disaster response. *2020 International Conference on Advanced Robotics and Intelligent Systems (ARIS)*, 1–6. DOI: 10.1109/ARIS50834.2020.9205794

Malathi, J., Kusha, K., Isaac, S., Ramesh, A., Rajendiran, M., & Boopathi, S. (2024). IoT-Enabled Remote Patient Monitoring for Chronic Disease Management and Cost Savings: Transforming Healthcare. In *Advances in Explainable AI Applications for Smart Cities* (pp. 371–388). IGI Global.

Murarka, U., Banerjee, K., Malik, T., & Providência, C. (2022). The neutron star outer crust equation of state: A machine learning approach. *Journal of Cosmology and Astroparticle Physics*, 045(01), 045. DOI: 10.1088/1475-7516/2022/01/045

Nakagawa, M., Kasagi, A., Liu, E., Ekawa, H., Yoshida, J., Dou, W., He, Y., Muneem, A., Nakazawa, K., Rappold, C., Saito, N., Saito, T. R., Sugimoto, S., Taki, M., Tanaka, Y. K., Wang, H., Gao, Y., Yanai, A., & Yoshimoto, M. (2022). Unique approach for precise determination of binding energies of hypernuclei with nuclear emulsion and machine learning. *EPJ Web of Conferences*, 271, 11006. DOI: 10.1051/epjconf/202227111006

Naresh, M., Subhahan, D. A., Narula, V. N., Roslin, D. K., Narula, S., & Boopathi, S. (2024). Edge Computing and Machine Learning Integration for Autonomous Electrical Vehicles. In *Solving Fundamental Challenges of Electric Vehicles* (pp. 99–127). IGI Global., DOI: 10.4018/979-8-3693-4314-2.ch005

Pachiappan, K., Anitha, K., Pitchai, R., Sangeetha, S., Satyanarayana, T., & Boopathi, S. (2024). Intelligent Machines, IoT, and AI in Revolutionizing Agriculture for Water Processing. In *Handbook of Research on AI and ML for Intelligent Machines and Systems* (pp. 374–399). IGI Global.

Pang, L.-G. (2021). Machine learning for high energy heavy ion collisions. *Nuclear Physics. A.*, 1005, 121972. DOI: 10.1016/j.nuclphysa.2020.121972

Ramaprasad, A. S. E., Smith, M. T., McCoy, D., Hubbard, A. E., La Merrill, M. A., & Durkin, K. A. (2022). Predicting the binding of small molecules to nuclear receptors using machine learning. *Briefings in Bioinformatics*, 23(3), bbac114. DOI: 10.1093/bib/bbac114 PMID: 35383362

S., B. (2024). Advancements in Optimizing Smart Energy Systems Through Smart Grid Integration, Machine Learning, and IoT. In *Advances in Environmental Engineering and Green Technologies* (pp. 33–61). IGI Global. DOI: 10.4018/979-8-3693-0492-1.ch002

Saleem, R. A., Radaideh, M. I., & Kozlowski, T. (2020). Application of deep neural networks for high-dimensional large BWR core neutronics. *Nuclear Engineering and Technology*, 52(12), 2709–2716. DOI: 10.1016/j.net.2020.05.010

Sonia, R., Gupta, N., Manikandan, K., Hemalatha, R., Kumar, M. J., & Boopathi, S. (2024). Strengthening Security, Privacy, and Trust in Artificial Intelligence Drones for Smart Cities. In *Analyzing and Mitigating Security Risks in Cloud Computing* (pp. 214–242). IGI Global. DOI: 10.4018/979-8-3693-3249-8.ch011

Sreedhar, P. S. S., Sujay, V., Rani, M. R., Melita, L., Reshma, S., & Boopathi, S. (2024). Impacts of 5G Machine Learning Techniques on Telemedicine and Social Media Professional Connection in Healthcare. In *Advances in Medical Technologies and Clinical Practice* (pp. 209–234). IGI Global. DOI: 10.4018/979-8-3693-1934-5.ch012

Steinheimer, J., Pang, L.-G., Zhou, K., Koch, V., Randrup, J., & Stoecker, H. (2019). A machine learning study to identify spinodal clumping in high energy nuclear collisions. *The Journal of High Energy Physics*, 2019(12), 1–26. DOI: 10.1007/JHEP12(2019)122

Sundar, R., Srikaanth, P. B., Naik, D. A., Murugan, V. P., Karumudi, M., & Boopathi, S. (2024). Achieving Balance Between Innovation and Security in the Cloud With Artificial Intelligence of Things: Semantic Web Control Models. In *Advances in Web Technologies and Engineering* (pp. 1–26). IGI Global. DOI: 10.4018/979-8-3693-1487-6.ch001

Syamala, M., Komala, C., Pramila, P., Dash, S., Meenakshi, S., & Boopathi, S. (2023). Machine Learning-Integrated IoT-Based Smart Home Energy Management System. In *Handbook of Research on Deep Learning Techniques for Cloud-Based Industrial IoT* (pp. 219–235). IGI Global. DOI: 10.4018/978-1-6684-8098-4.ch013

Tirlangi, S., Teotia, S., Padmapriya, G., Senthil Kumar, S., Dhotre, S., & Boopathi, S. (2024). Cloud Computing and Machine Learning in the Green Power Sector: Data Management and Analysis for Sustainable Energy. In *Developments Towards Next Generation Intelligent Systems for Sustainable Development* (pp. 148–179). IGI Global. DOI: 10.4018/979-8-3693-5643-2.ch006

Trindade, M. G., Coelho, A., Valadares, C., Viera, R. A., Rey, S., Cheymol, B., Baylac, M., Velazco, R., & Bastos, R. P. (2019). Assessment of a hardware-implemented machine learning technique under neutron irradiation. *IEEE Transactions on Nuclear Science*, 66(7), 1441–1448. DOI: 10.1109/TNS.2019.2920747

Upadhyaya, A. N., Saqib, A., Devi, J. V., Rallapalli, S., Sudha, S., & Boopathi, S. (2024). Implementation of the Internet of Things (IoT) in Remote Healthcare. In *Advances in Medical Technologies and Clinical Practice* (pp. 104–124). IGI Global. DOI: 10.4018/979-8-3693-1934-5.ch006

Venkateswaran, N., Kiran Kumar, K., Maheswari, K., Kumar Reddy, R. V., & Boopathi, S. (2024). Optimizing IoT Data Aggregation: Hybrid Firefly-Artificial Bee Colony Algorithm for Enhanced Efficiency in Agriculture. *AGRIS On-Line Papers in Economics and Informatics*, 16(1), 117–130. DOI: 10.7160/aol.2024.160110

Verma, R., Christiana, M. B. V., Maheswari, M., Srinivasan, V., Patro, P., Dari, S. S., & Boopathi, S. (2024). Intelligent Physarum Solver for Profit Maximization in Oligopolistic Supply Chain Networks. In *AI and Machine Learning Impacts in Intelligent Supply Chain* (pp. 156–179). IGI Global. DOI: 10.4018/979-8-3693-1347-3.ch011

Wang, Y., Gao, Z., Lü, H., & Li, Q. (2022). Decoding the nuclear symmetry energy event-by-event in heavy-ion collisions with machine learning. *Physics Letters. [Part B]*, 835, 137508. DOI: 10.1016/j. physletb.2022.137508

Wilson, J. (2019). *Machine learning for nuclear fission systems: Preliminary investigation of an autonomous control system for the MGEP* [PhD Thesis]. Massachusetts Institute of Technology.

Xu, X., Han, T., Huang, J., Kruger, A. A., Kumar, A., & Goel, A. (2021). Machine learning enabled models to predict sulfur solubility in nuclear waste glasses. *ACS Applied Materials & Interfaces*, 13(45), 53375–53387. DOI: 10.1021/acsami.1c10359 PMID: 34516090

Yi, L., Deng, X., Yang, L. T., Wu, H., Wang, M., & Situ, Y. (2020). Reinforcement-learning-enabled partial confident information coverage for IoT-based bridge structural health monitoring. *IEEE Internet of Things Journal*, 8(5), 3108–3119. DOI: 10.1109/JIOT.2020.3028325

Yüksel, E., Soydaner, D., & Bahtiyar, H. (2021). Nuclear binding energy predictions using neural networks: Application of the multilayer perceptron. *International Journal of Modern Physics E*, 30(03), 2150017. DOI: 10.1142/S0218301321500178

KEY TERMS

AI: Artificial Intelligence
AP: Access Point (or Application Processor, depending on context)
API: Application Programming Interface
AR: Augmented Reality
CNN: Convolutional Neural Network
HTTP: Hypertext Transfer Protocol
HTTPS: Hypertext Transfer Protocol Secure
ML: Machine Learning
MQTT: Message Queuing Telemetry Transport
PCA: Principal Component Analysis
RNN: Recurrent Neural Network
SVM: Support Vector Machine
VR: Virtual Reality

Chapter 16
High–Performance Computing for Electric Vehicle Performance Analysis and Simulation

D. Venkata Srihari Babu

Department of Electronics and Communication Engineering, G. Pulla Reddy Engineering College, India

Ramaprasad Maharana
https://orcid.org/0000-0001-8411-7334

Department of Electronics and Communication Engineering, Sri Sai Ram Institute of Technology, Chennai, India

M. Ponrekha
https://orcid.org/0009-0005-6316-1754

Department of Electrical and Electronics Engineering, Karpagam Academy of Higher Education, Coimbatore, India

S. Ramesh

Department of Electrical and Electronics Engineering, K.S.R. College of Engineering, Tiruchengode, India

D. Kirubakaran

Department of Electrical and Electronics Engineering, St. Joseph's Institute of Technology, Chennai, India

ABSTRACT

High Performance Computing (HPC) has established an important place in the performance analysis and simulation of electric vehicles. An enhanced study built on HPC answers to the high computational requirements of performance evaluation of electric vehicles, namely battery management, energy efficiency, and thermal dynamics. HPC, with parallel processing and improved algorithms, can intensively simulate powertrain systems, aerodynamics, and vehicle dynamics, keeping a stream of avenues to improve the design and functionality of electric vehicles. Further, it optimizes battery life and energy consumption as well as charging systems. This is useful for manufacturers and researchers to work toward enhancing

DOI: 10.4018/978-1-6684-3795-7.ch016

Copyright ©2025, IGI Global Scientific Publishing. Copying or distributing in print or electronic forms without written permission of IGI Global Scientific Publishing is prohibited.

the efficiency of EVs. The current chapter also deals with real-time simulations of HPC that allow pro-
totyping, reduce development costs, and enable sustaining innovations in the electric vehicle business.

INTRODUCTION

An electric vehicle (EV), for sure, will be the defining trend of the automotive industry in response to the pressing need for the reduction of carbon emissions, an enhancement in energy efficiency, and the shift towards solutions in sustainable transportation. The changes of the last ten years have created a new atmosphere through modifications in the face of the auto industry, drawing further ongoing pursuits in innovations such as better vehicle performance, improved energy storage, and power management. The increasing importance of High-Performance Computing (HPC) in the analysis and simulation of EV performance also brings about further transformation. HPC ensures the real-time simulation of complex systems due to the provision of computational power, enabling researchers and engineers to make very precise evaluation and optimization of a vehicle's performance. In this chapter, I indicate where it becomes possible to find an intersection between EV technology and HPC, wherein performance analysis and simulation play a pivotal role in driving innovations (Aghabali et al., 2020a).

The primary distinction between EVs and conventional internal combustion engine (ICE) vehicles is the utilization of electric powertrains and battery systems. As such, some questions arise in vehicle design, performance analysis, and testing because of the absence of fuel-burning engines and the presence of advanced electronic components. Therefore, the capabilities of EVs can only be maximized if designers simulate all conceivable factors-affecting factors including battery dynamics, thermal management, energy consumption, and powertrain efficiency. Each one of these encompasses complex, multi-physics problems that require advanced computational models and simulation to understand. That is where HPC steps in as the ability to run complicated simulations that would otherwise be computationally infeasible using traditional computing systems is possible (Alawneh et al., 2023).

HPC is using the techniques of supercomputers and parallel processing to solve problems computationally at high speeds that appear too difficult for traditional computers. In EV technology, HPC enables the simulation of hundreds of thousands of variables and scenarios whose optimization is critical to a well-performance vehicle. This means that an EV's battery system, consisting of thousands of individual cells, requires monitoring and management for optimal operational characteristics to last for a long time. This will demand vast computational resources in simulating the thermal and electrical behavior of these cells and their interaction with other cells within the battery pack. Such detail in HPC models will bring factors like temperature, charge cycles, and energy demand under different operating conditions (Pozzato et al., 2023).

Aerodynamics is another thing related to EVs and tremendously affects overall efficiency. Unlike in the ICE vehicles, wherein the primary goal is to focus on efficiency at the engine level, for EVs, it shall be focused on drag and airflow optimization toward attaining full range. Simulation of aerodynamics performance of an EV usually involves complex fluid dynamics which require significant computational effort to represent with adequate precision. The HPC will allow detailed simulation for interactions between body design and power-consuming energy of airflow to further the aerodynamics efficiency of the vehicle, thus increasing its driving range and lowering its energy consumption (Sharma et al., 2019).

The development of EVs is also influenced by HPC in an important area: powertrain optimization. Optimization begins with ensuring that there is a fluid interaction between the electric motor, inverter, and battery. The simulation of these systems under various load conditions, drive patterns, and environmental factors is computationally intensive. HPC allows engineers to build models of these systems to a level of intricacy that is exact; therefore, the systems can be optimized for maximal efficiency and performance. For example, HPC can be used to simulate the interaction of motor with its battery pack during acceleration, regenerative braking, and charging to optimize its reduction in energy loss and longevity enhancement (Du et al., 2019).

Aside from that, HPC plays a very vital role in the optimization of battery management systems (BMS). The BMS monitors and controls health, charge, and safety of the EV pack. This is achieved by advanced BMS algorithms relying on real-time data processing and predictive modeling to enable safe usage with maximum energy efficiency. HPC ensures that this kind of large data processing can be done speedily and accurately, thus allowing the battery conditions to be monitored in real time, and predictive maintenance is conducted for keeping the battery in optimal condition. Overcharging, overheating, or deep discharging can significantly affect battery lifespan (Bucaioni, 2019).

Apart from battery management and powertrain optimization, HPC revolutionizes prototyping and testing in EVs. The traditional processes of prototyping are building a physical model followed by real-world testing, expensive and time-consuming. Digital prototypes or "digital twins" will be replicas of the physical characteristics and behavior of the vehicle or components created through HPC-driven simulations. Digital twins give engineers the means to test many iterations of design, or optimized vehicle parts, and simulate different driving scenarios without physical prototypes. This can shorten the cycle time, reduce costs, and expand the amount of testing for a wide range of conditions (Ahmed & Liu, 2019).

HPC is beneficial in simulating real-time scenarios, which is probably one of the most significant advantages in EV development. EVs have to be tested under a variety of real-world conditions-persistently changing temperatures, road surfaces, and driving patterns-to work efficiently and safely. Simulations powered by HPC can do this natively in a virtual world, yielding useful insight into how the vehicle will serve under a range of situations. Manufacturers will use this to recognize problems ahead of time and thus make products more reliable and safer (Taghavipour et al., 2019).

HPC also has a role in the solutions geared toward the challenges of the infrastructure for EV charging. With more electric cars on the road, there is an increased requirement for effective and accessible charging stations. HPC can be applied toward modeling and optimization of the placement and operation of charging stations such that they are sited in a strategic manner to meet the required demand and reduce strain on the grid. HPCs simulate EV charging patterns and impacts on the electrical grid, allowing utility companies and policymakers to design and build charging networks much more efficiently to promote widespread EV use (Lyu et al., 2021).

This is a paradigm shift in the automobile industry. Such influence of EVs could go a long way to affect energy consumption, environmental sustainability and, for sure, transport infrastructure. HPC is an enabling factor for this new transition, providing the computational power required to analyze, optimize, and innovate all points related to EV performance. HPC is transforming the design, testing, and deployment of EVs via optimization of battery management, power train efficiency, aerodynamics, and real-time simulation (Yi et al., 2021). HPC will play an increasingly critical role for these vehicles to meet the relevant performance, safety, and efficiency standards for their acceptance as transportation that could be widely used because of the high demand in EVs. This chapter explores how HPC is changing the face of the future of EVs, insights into cutting-edge simulations and analyses driving next-generation sustainable transportation solutions.

HIGH-PERFORMANCE COMPUTING IN ELECTRIC VEHICLE DEVELOPMENT

High Performance Computing has emerged as a vital tool in EV development. It does provide the computational power required to simulate and analyze and optimize a complex structure of systems involved in designing and achieving the performance of EVs. They range from optimized battery management to efficient power trains, aerodynamics, to thermal dynamics - the workhorse behind automobile design engineers' ability to model and test innumerable aspects of EVs in a virtual environment. The above accelerates innovation to offer manufacturers more efficient, reliable, and sustainable vehicles by minimizing physical prototyping time and the cost of real-world testing (McIntosh-Smith et al., 2019). Figure 1 depicts the use of HPC in the development of EVs.

Figure 1. High-performance computing in EV development

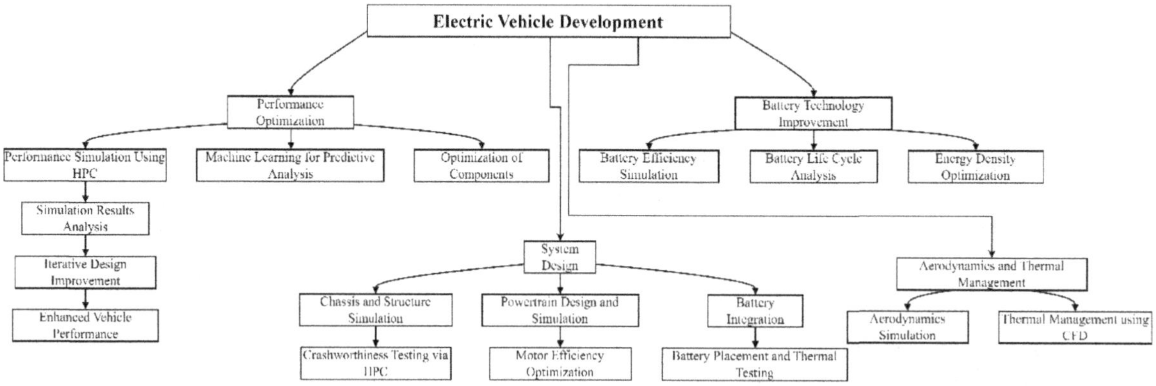

Definition and Importance of HPC

This article is making use of supercomputers or computing clusters working simultaneously to process large datasets or carry out computationally intensive computations at high-speed performance. The primary reason for embracing HPC in the design of an EV is in the processing of huge data quantities and detailed running simulations. In the study of EV, possibly with regards to battery packs and powertrains systems, along with its diverse interlocking interactions between the mechanical, electrical, and even thermal parts, computation indeed goes by a very large scale. HPC enables automobile engineers to simulate these systems without wasting precious time, with a basis to analyze perfectly for optimal vehicle designs.

HPC Architecture

HPC architecture of HPC systems involves a network of processors which work in parallel. Sums up to millions of calculations per unit of time by having processors distributed across several servers or nodes and high-speed interconnects. These computational tools include central processing units, graphics processing units, and memory subsystems. This architecture will enable engineers to run very complex simulations of multi-physics problems-for example, thermal management system interactions with battery performance-in the design of EVs. It is the potential for access beyond pure computing power, however, which makes this architecture really interesting: it also provides access to high-end data processing and storage abilities, which are essential when dealing with the large datasets generated by sensors in EVs, simulations, and real-world testing.

Applications of HPC in Automotive Engineering

One of the largest applications in HPC is related to the automotive industry, where it has particularly been most valuable in EV development. Some of the most important areas include: simulation and optimization of the battery system and, within the EV, HPC users can model the electrochemical processes occurring in each cell, predict the behaviour of those cells under thermal conditions, thereby optimizing overall BMS and leading to improved energy efficiency, lifespan, and safety in batteries. Another key application is in the aerodynamics for EVs: with HPC, engineers can actually optimize vehicle body shape design to reduce drag through computational fluid dynamics (CFD) simulations. In powertrain optimization, HPC is also applied. In this case, powertrain engineers simulate a multitude of interactions between the motor, inverter, and battery by simulating conditions in order to find the optimum performance and efficiency (Saldaña et al., 2019).

Application of Parallel Processing in EV Simulations

Parallel processing forms the core of HPC and is critical to the execution of simulations in the EV systems, as these comprise numerous subsystems. These comprise the powertrain, the battery, and cooling systems, all of which require a detailed simulation and analysis. All the work related to these subsystems can be executed in parallel using parallel processing, thus decreasing the time requirements for running complex models. Thus, for example, simulating the whole thermal management system of an EV, which, among other things, includes a battery cooling system, motor cooling system, and inverter heat dissipation system, can take a lot of time. Engineers may use parallel processing to divide a simulation into smaller tasks being executed concurrently; that is, the whole process is speeded up significantly, and one can test more iteratively, optimize faster, and execute more scenarios in a shorter time scale. With parallel processing, it would also be possible to simulate in real time. For instance, testing an EV system with all possible operating conditions-such as varying driving environments, temperature, and load-can be monitored (Babu et al., 2022).

Hence, HPC has that transformative ability in the development of EVs-by giving the unparallel capability to simulate and optimize complex systems in a manner not possible at any previous time. Through its architecture and parallel processing capabilities, HPC enables rapid testing and refinement of EV designs, ultimately leading to the optimization of vehicles in efficiency, reliability, and sustainability.

METRICS OF PERFORMANCE

Metrics of Performance: Instead of traditional internal combustion engine vehicles, EVs carry quite different performance metrics. Such critical parameters for understanding and optimizing these allow an even greater scope to enhance overall efficiency, reliability, and longevity. Chief among those are energy efficiency, battery life and management, powertrain and motor performance, and thermal dynamics-the essence of each such aspect playing a pivotal role in defining performance, cost, or sustainability of these electrical vehicles. We discuss each of these metrics in depth below and outline their roles in the performance of EVs (Miri et al., 2021; Yao et al., 2021). The performance and optimization cycle of EVs are influenced by various performance parameters, as shown in Figure 2.

Figure 2. Different performance parameters: performance and optimization cycle of electric vehicles

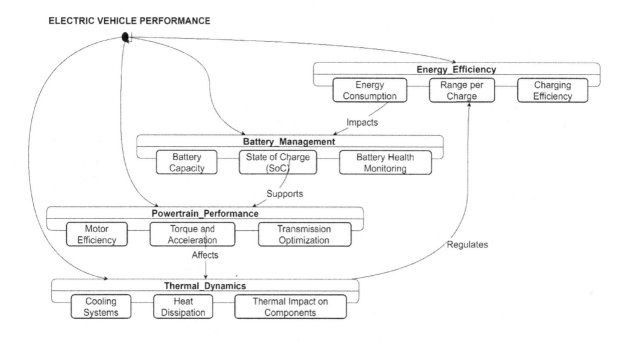

Energy Efficiency and Consumption

Energy efficiency is a critical determinant of the performance of EVs, as it directly correlates to range and, therefore, environmental impact. Energy consumption in electric vehicles often is quantified by kilowatt-hours per mile (kWh/mi) or kilowatt-hours per kilometer (kWh/km). This metric helps in comparing the efficiency with which this mechanical motion is obtained from the energy stored in a battery. While for ICE vehicles, the fuel efficiency is measured in miles per gallon, or mpg, the EV has much higher conversion efficiency, typically 85-90%, compared to the 20-30% for ICE (Chandrika et al., 2023; Devi et al., 2024).

Several factors affect energy efficiency, which include the weight of the vehicle, aerodynamics, and conditions of driving. Obviously, the more massive a vehicle, the more energy it will consume. Similarly, a hilly terrain or a high speed is not very suitable for energy efficiency. However, in cases where deceleration is involved, regenerative braking helps recover some of the energy lost, thereby managing the efficiency of the vehicle to increase overall value.

Management Systems for the Battery

The leading indicator of long-term performance and overall cost of ownership of an EV is battery life. The capacity of an EV battery determines its life span, and this changes with every shift in charging patterns, operating temperatures, and depth of discharge. It is a tough goal for manufacturers to make EVs such that they last anywhere from 8 to 15 years under normal usage conditions. Additionally, the capacity of an EV battery degrades with time, and losses approach about 2-3% per year under normal use.

This BMS is intended to play a very important role in ensuring optimum functioning of the battery pack. For this reason, it controls cell voltage, temperature, and current to ensure proper balance among cells and prevents overcharging, thus ensuring safe operation. Another way in which the BMS assists is in estimating State of Charge (SoC) and State of Health (SoH), primarily used for precise range prediction and evaluation of the life of the batteries.

Powertrain and Motor Performance

The powertrain of an EV consists of the motor, inverter, and transmission that combine to transform electrical energy from the battery into mechanical motion. Motor performance is a determining factor in the calculation of acceleration, torque, and speed for such a vehicle. Generally, electric motors are more efficient as they produce peak torque from zero revolution, hence enabling the customer to get instantaneous power delivery.

This motor efficiency depends on the type used. The common types of motors for use in EVs are the permanent magnet synchronous motors (PMSM) and induction motors. The high-performance applications prefer PMSMs due to their efficiency as well as reduced weight. Induction motors are, however heavier and often preferred due to strength and mainly commercial vehicle use. Also, another efficiency enhancing feature of the powertrain is its regenerative braking; this system reclaims energy which would otherwise not be recovered.

Inverters are integral to controlling the flow of electricity between the battery and the motor. The simple change in them adjusts the direct current from the battery to alternating current, which the motor can now run. High-design inverters improve conversion efficiency by minimizing losses and enhancing the overall powertrain performance.

Thermal Dynamics and Cooling Systems

The performance of EVs is generally influenced by thermal management, however, especially on the battery and motor. It is necessary to maintain proper temperatures for efficient working, prevention of degradation, and risk-free scenarios. Overheating can potentially lead to loss in the performance of a battery and cause thermal runaway, reducing the efficiency of the motor (Giri et al., 2024; Godwin Immanuel et al., 2024).

There are a few cooling systems in place in EVs that cool down some of the generated heat by the vehicle when in operation. One such system is liquid cooling that involves circulating coolant to cool battery cells, motors, and inverters. Air cooling is another system that is used but is mostly less efficient, particularly in applications for high performance. The above systems play a key role in battery thermal management, where, in a pack of batteries, they must be maintained within a given range, preferably 15°C-35°C because extreme temperatures degrade rapidly.

Thermal simulation models are utilized widely to predict the heat generation and optimization of design on cooling systems. Real-time monitoring of thermal dynamics using HPC tools is realized. The dynamics in thermal domains are extremely critical for ensuring safe and efficient operation of a system, especially when it undergoes high-stress driving conditions such as rapid acceleration or high ambient temperatures.

For an electric vehicle to be optimal, it has to be optimized in terms of four significant performance metrics-battery life, powertrain efficiency, energy efficiency, and thermal management. All these pose unique challenges, but advances in simulation and real-time monitoring open up significant avenues for enhancement. The better use of HPC and sophisticated management systems is making EVs more efficient and reliable while able to meet the requirements of modern transportation. Proper management of these performance metrics will be very key in advancing the next generation of electric vehicles and ensuring greater sustainability in the automotive industry.

SIMULATION OF EV BATTERY SYSTEMS

The electric vehicle's battery systems are the heart of a vehicle. A battery system involves multiple factors in determining the range, performances, and overall efficiency of a vehicle. Simulation of these systems will play a key role in optimization for their design, management, and longevity. Advanced simulation techniques allow automotive engineers to explore how these batteries would behave with varied conditions (Loeb & Kockelman, 2019; Tran et al., 2020). This helps bring about better heat management, the energy efficiency of the system, and long-term durability of that system. Discussion of the main areas of EV battery system simulation, namely, battery dynamics and chemistry models, thermal management in battery packs, HPC for real-time monitoring and optimization, and predictive maintenance for improving lifetime. Figure 3 illustrates the integral steps involved in simulating and optimizing EV battery systems.

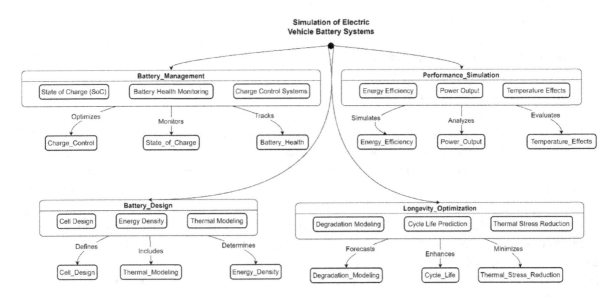

Battery Dynamics and Chemistry Models

The simulation of EV battery systems starts from the inside dynamics of the batteries, from electrochemical processes. This can involve charge/discharge cycles, energy storage efficiency, or voltage under different loads. Such processes depend on the type of chemistry being used for the battery, such as from lithium to solid-state, or nickel-metal hydride (NiMH) (Naresh et al., 2024; Rajan et al., 2024).

The most common type used in the latest generation of EVs is the lithium-ion battery. They are assembled with their electrochemistry based on the intercalation of lithium ions between the anode and cathode during both charging and discharging. Therefore, good simulation models should take into account several parameters such as cell voltage, current, capacity fade, and rate of ion diffusion through the electrolyte. The two commonly used models for simulating these electrochemical processes are equivalent circuit models and physics-based models (Aghabali et al., 2020b).

a) Equivalent Circuit Models (ECM): The battery is represented here as an assembly of electrical components: resistors, capacitors. A model can be used as a means to simulate charge/discharge behavior quickly and efficiently. ECMs are generally suited for real-time applications but will often sacrifice some of the precision required for highly detailed studies.

b) Physics-Based Models (PBM): These are, in general, more complicated models that actually attempt to model the chemistry occurring within the battery itself. Parameters include ion transport, electrochemical kinetics, and heat generation. Being computationally intensive, PBMs require more computational resources but provide better insight into long-term battery performance and degradation behavior.

Combination of these models will enable a more complete dynamic simulation of a battery pack, helping engineers optimize cell design, predict patterns of degradation, and develop strategies to enhance the performance of the battery and further extend its lifespan.

Battery Pack Thermal Management

Thermal management, therefore, plays a very important role in an electric vehicle battery system as the performance of, and its safety are visibly impacted by operation temperatures. The batteries, naturally, generate heat during operation, especially during high load conditions like acceleration or fast charging operations. Excess generated heat can result in thermal runaway, a condition that can lead to uncontrollable temperature rise with risks of fire or explosion (Muhammed et al., 2020; Yi et al., 2022).

To actually design an efficient cooling system, effective simulation of thermal dynamics in battery packs is considered. These simulations are concerned with the prediction of heat generation in various driving scenarios and the evaluation of the effectiveness of the used thermal management strategies such as liquid cooling or air cooling systems. Thermal management systems must ensure that battery cells are kept within an optimal temperature range between 15°C and 35°C not to degrade and to safe operation. There are liquid cooling systems, which may work better on high-performance EVs by letting coolant flow through channels surrounding the battery cells to dissipate heat. Then there are air cooling systems, which are simpler, less expensive, but less effective for high temperature or performance-oriented applications.

Simulations also optimize the layouts and flow dynamics of such cooling systems to obtain balanced temperature distribution in the battery pack. Moreover, it can also predict the effects of environment-based conditions, such as ambient temperatures and humidity, on the thermal performance. This information helps in the development of sophisticated thermal management algorithms that can give adaptive real-time control for cooling based on the current batteries' performance.

HPC for Real-Time Battery Monitoring and Optimization

HPC is instrumental in real-time monitoring and optimization of the systems being used in electric vehicles' batteries. Using HPC, engineers are able to process large amounts of data coming from sensors installed inside the battery pack that monitor temperature, voltage, and current for distribution. With this amount of real-time data, adjustments can be made in precise points for optimization, enhancing safety and preventing possible failures. Besides such high-level simulations of electrochemical behavior, HPC simulations enable multi-physics simulations where thermal, electrochemical, and mechanical behaviors are modeled concurrently. In fact, this is necessary for predicting how different components of a system within the battery would interact under any given condition, such as fast charging or high-speed driving. Such HPC can simulate thousands of operating scenarios in a short period and thus helps engineers more effectively refine battery designs and control strategies (Giri et al., 2024; Godwin Immanuel et al., 2024; Muthukumar et al., 2024).

In addition to real-time optimization, HPC enables machine learning models to predict what will happen in the battery sometime later with dependence on historical data. It makes possible developing smart BMSs that could be adapted to change in driving patterns or environmental conditions to ensure longer battery life as well as better performance from the vehicle.

Predictive Maintenance and Battery Longevity

An important area of investigation in pursuit of increasing the lifetime of a battery and enhancing the general reliability of vehicles lies in the long-term simulation of EV battery systems. Predictive maintenance strategies, supported by HPC simulations, coupled with real-time data analysis, can identify early warnings of the degradation conditions likely to end up in significant performance loss or system failure. Important indications include capacity fade, increased internal resistance, and imbalanced cell voltages. Predictive models would use data from sensors, past driving patterns, and environmental conditions to make predictions for when maintenance or replacements are going to be required. This is when the automobile owner or fleet manager can schedule a process of maintenance prior to an essential failure happening, thus reducing downtime as well as expenditure. SoH and SoC estimations are also constantly improved by such simulations; as such, the battery will perform at its optimal best during the entire cycle of its life.

Operating conditions, such as the depth of charge (DoD), and also the charging habits affect the usable life of a battery. Simulations may reveal desirable charge strategies in terms of optimal charge cycles, adaptive rates of charging and others which lessen the stress on the battery and expand its usability life. Such strategies, for instance, may include reducing high-current fast charging and deep discharges altogether. All these can greatly reduce degradation, thus elongating the life of the battery.

Simulations of electric vehicle battery systems are something that is highly needed and complex in developing better-performing, safe, and prolonged batteries. Advanced models of both battery dynamics and chemistry; optimum thermal management systems; using HPC for on-real-time monitoring; and predictive maintenance models can all work together towards an electricity vehicle that would be highly efficient and reliable. The above-mentioned simulations will energize future innovations into better battery technology, leading to more effective and sustainable electric transportation options.

PERFORMANCE OF SIMULATION OF EV AERODYNAMICS

Aerodynamics is possibly the most critical area of an electric vehicle's design that, on one hand, determines great efficiency and performance along with a range. In light of an ever-growing demand for energy efficiency and sustainable mobility, this is definitely one parameter in which automakers will need to tread very carefully if they want to stretch the range of EVs without sacrificing top performance (Meintz et al., 2023; Tan & Yuan, 2022). It encompasses the importance of aerodynamics in the design of EVs, the use of CFD and HPC for simulations, methodologies for drag reduction and range improvement, and case studies of aerodynamics optimization in EVs. The process of aerodynamics performance simulation for electric vehicles is depicted in Figure 4.

Figure 4. Process of aerodynamics performance simulation for electric vehicles

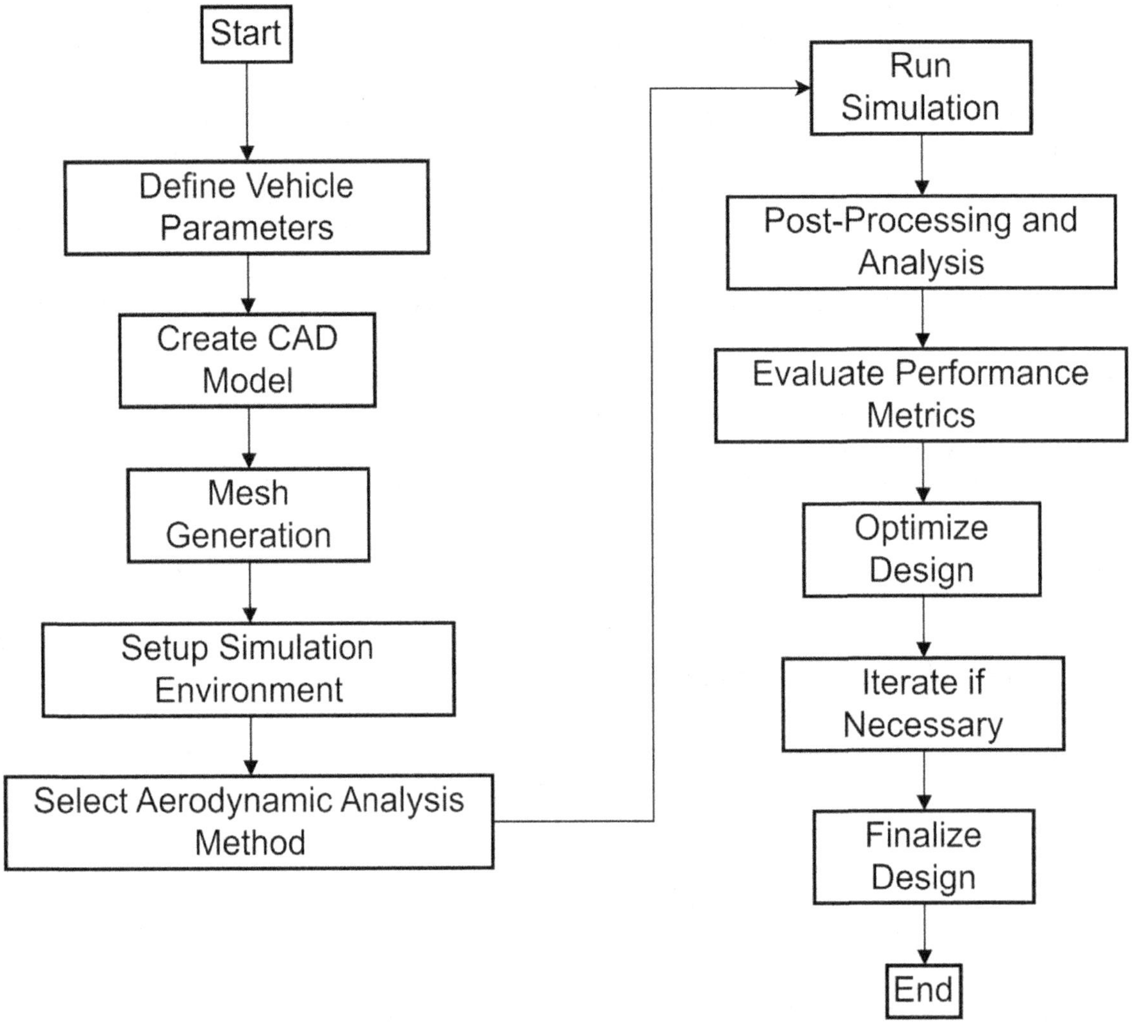

Importance of Aerodynamics in EV Design

This basically explains how aerodynamics performance can make the difference in the movement of a vehicle through air. For EVs, which run mainly on battery power, the most significant way to take it a long distance is through reduced air resistance. Poor aerodynamics use up more energy on the vehicle, which means that the battery has to work overtime, thus using lots of energy and reducing mileage. Aerodynamics has impacts on several aspects of how a vehicle performs. These include:

a) Drag: Air resistance when the vehicle is moving forward.
b) Lift: The force vertically upward which may reduce the stabilities.

c) Noise: Aerodynamics design also affects noise from wind at high velocities.

One of the most important influences of aerodynamics is that on drag, where an increased drag coefficient (Cd) means more energy used to push a vehicle. Reduction in the drag coefficient for an electric vehicle can provide a longer range and less energy usage. Since EVs do not possess traditional engines and mechanical noise, aerodynamics design can also minimize wind noise in the cabin which will mean an inherently quieter cabin environment. So, in terms of efficiency as well as of comfort, aerodynamics optimization is of absolute importance.

Computational Fluid Dynamics and High-Performance Computing

Aerodynamics testing was done using a great number of wind tunnels in the conventional approach. Today, more requirements are placed on CFD, which utilizes numerical methods to simulate an air flow around a vehicle, where pressure distribution, drag, and other aerodynamics parameters are numerically visualized. From this simulation, designers could point out the areas of high drag so that they could alter the design to minimize drag.

The complexity of such simulation demands huge computational power, where HPC plays its part: With HPC, huge simulations of complex fluid flows with high resolutions can be modeled very realistically, simulating realistic real-world conditions for the vehicles to be designed for. Thousands of such simulations run quickly, documenting as many design iterations and configurations as possible. HPC-powered CFD Simulation has advantages as follows:

a) Accuracy: High resolution in the simulation can provide very accurate predictions for airflow behavior.
b) Speed: Simulations that would take days or weeks on a conventional system can be completed in hours.
c) Optimization: Many design variables such as vehicle shape, size and placements of individual components can be tested in parallel, which accelerates the optimization process.

Such capabilities make HPC-driven CFD simulations the go-to tool for modern EV aerodynamics design, giving insight into how different design features affect performance in a much more nuanced way than has been possible to date.

Simulation of Drag Reduction and Range Improvement

Drag reduction, therefore, is the key objective of aerodynamics optimization for an electric vehicle. Given that the drag force accelerates exponentially with the speed, even a slight reduction in the drag coefficient is good enough to save quite a lot of energy at faster velocities. In electric vehicles, it directly translates into extended driving ranges, improved efficiency, and better performance.

CFD can predict how different vehicle shapes, surface textures, and components contribute to drag. Areas to be tackled at the front grille, side mirrors, underbody create drag and need to be reduced. Aerodynamics features to optimize or even eliminate drag:

a) Active Grille Shutters: These automatically open or close depending on cooling requirements to optimize airflow.

b) Low-Drag Side Mirrors: Compact mirrors or camera-based systems can reduce the turbulence caused by traditional mirrors.

c) Smooth Underbody Panels: A flat underbody is a traditional aerodynamic modification that helps minimize airflow disruptions beneath the vehicle, and it is commonly linked to reductions in drag.

In fact, scientists are now trying to cut their Cd below 0.25, which is a pretty much smaller number than what is attained in current production designs. These cuts have indeed meant a 5 to 10% gain in electric vehicle range, and that's well worth it.

The aerodynamics drag also is created by the vehicle's tires and wheels; hence, it adds to a great deal of the aerodynamics drag. Aero wheel covers can benefit more from the aerodynamics efficiency when combined with low-rolling-resistance tires.

POWERTRAIN OPTIMIZATION USING HPC

In maximizing the efficiency as well as performance and overall driving experience of an EV, powertrain optimization would prove to be important. With the capability of simulating complicated models and performing data analysis that earlier would be impossible on conventional computing resources, HPC has come to play a critical role in powertrain optimization. This section discusses the modeling of electric powertrains and the key roles of components like inverters, motors, and control algorithms played in such simulations. In addition to the simulations of energy flow, we also elaborate on how HPC may optimize powertrain efficiency (Naresh et al., 2024; Rajan et al., 2024). The powertrain optimization process in EVs can be undertaken by using HPC, as depicted in Figure 5.

Figure 5. Powertrain optimization process in electric vehicles using HPC

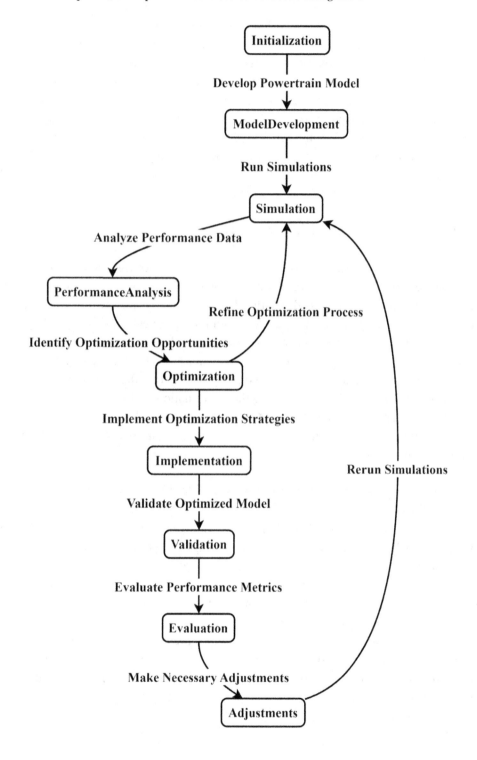

Electric Powertrain Modelling: Challenges and Opportunities

Electric powertrain modeling involves simulation behavior of different components, such as batteries, motors, inverters, and drivetrain, considering driving dynamics and environment-related effects. High modeling complexity is one of the major challenges in modeling the different components because of their nonlinear behavior and interdependencies. Opportunities are present in the potential to do predictive models that could provide valuable information on how energy consumption and performance might be best optimized under any set of driving conditions. Traditional methods generally fail to pick the nuances of modern EV powertrains and result in inefficient designs and lost opportunities to save energy. HPC enables much more detailed simulations as engineers can create highly accurate models accounting for hundreds of parameters (Giri et al., 2024; Muthukumar et al., 2024; Naresh et al., 2024). Additionally, parallel execution reduces time drastically for design iterations.

Inverters, Motors, and Control Algorithms

The key components are inverters and motors, along with the algorithms to control their interaction, and the performance of the electric powertrain depends on these. The inverters convert the direct current of the battery to alternating current to feed into the electric motor. Efficiency in inverter design through simulation is an important factor that can significantly minimize energy losses in vehicles.

The motor is the heart of the EV powertrain and transforms electrical energy into mechanical energy. Problem: without a significant variation in speed and load, this has to be achieved. Several motor designs-from PMSMs to induction motors-can be simulated using HPC to find the best configuration for specific vehicle types. The control algorithms controlling the coordination between the motor, inverter and the battery ensure that energy is consumed in an optimal manner and the vehicle goes on to operate just as it was expected. Testing of several scenarios by simulation of the control algorithms through HPC helps engineers find an optimal trade-off between performance, energy consumption and thermal management.

Simulation of Energy Flow and Regenerative Braking

Energy flow in an electric vehicle is nothing but complex and needs to be accurately regulated to optimize performance. It's also very important in simulating the flow of energy through the vehicle from the battery, through to the motor and back again through regenerative braking, to improve efficiency. Regenerative braking recovers kinetic energy, which would otherwise be lost as heat when braking, and transfers it back to the battery. HPC enables such energy flows under different conditions to be simulated in great detail, allowing the engineers to use all the energy recovered through regenerative braking to the maximum extent. Simulations also provide insight into thermal behavior in the powertrain, where energy loss by heat can be the most substantial efficiency degradation. Energy flow through drivetrain and, in some cases, regenerative systems will be optimized to push the vehicle range further and make it more efficient overall.

HPC-Enabled Powertrain Efficiency and Performance Improvements

HPC usage provides unprecedented improvements in powertrain efficiency and performance. Engineers can run a series of complex scenarios in parallel to test hundreds, if not thousands, of different powertrain configurations in a fraction of the time that would be possible with conventional methods, thus making it possible to identify optimal solutions for energy efficiency, component reliability, and overall vehicle performance (Devi et al., 2024; Godwin Immanuel et al., 2024).

For instance, HPC simulations can be used to optimize the motor-inverter-battery interface for the minimum energy loss with better power supply to the automakers. Real-time optimization becomes feasible with HPC in which the powertrain dynamically adapts to driving conditions to ensure peak performance at all times. Acceleration will be better, with extended range and comfort while driving. Moreover, HPC-based simulations enable the virtual testing of new architectures and control strategies for the powertrain before they are brought into actual physical configuration. It decreases the high costs and time involved in the prototyping process, which is considered pretty crucial in a fast-paced industry like EV, where innovation cycles are getting tighter by the day and the demand for higher performance, efficiency, and sustainability is growing very rapidly.

In summary, HPC-driven optimization of the powertrain has enormous potential to revolutionize the design of electric vehicles. It enables quite advanced simulations that support the overcoming of key problems such as complex component interactions and dynamic energy flows for more efficient, high-performance powertrains with a greater range, driving experience, and sustainability.

REAL-TIME SIMULATION FOR ELECTRIC VEHICLES

Electric vehicles are increasing in popularity and require real-time simulation in the design, development, and testing processes. It is very critical for dynamic modeling and performance evaluation of EVs under different real-world driving conditions. Engineers can simulate systems that entail advanced computer computation to know system behavior in real time by using real-time computing. This resulted in large improvement in the prototyping process and in the final vehicle performance achieved. In this section, we look at the requirement for real-time performance testing, the role of digital twins in EV development, cost and time savings through simulation, and how real-time simulations can bridge the varying driving conditions and load scenarios (Babu et al., 2022; Boopathi et al., 2018; Rajan et al., 2024).

The Need for Real-Time Performance Testing

Electric vehicles operate in dynamic environments that are complex and subject to incessant fluctuations caused by road conditions, weather, and driver inputs. Real-time performance testing is therefore very critical because it will simulate such dynamic conditions and allow engineers to know exactly how the vehicle performs in real time. Real-time tests provide instant feedback whereas traditional tests' returns are mostly delayed and therefore lead to slower design iteration and refinement in vehicle systems. For example, real-time testing can determine variations in how battery charge, motor efficiency, or regenerative braking may affect overall performance so that control algorithms may be tuned to ensure optimal performance for most scenarios, a requirement for the diverse demands of modern drivers.

Digital Twins in EV Design and Development

A big step in real-time simulation is the advent of the concept of digital twins. A digital twin is essentially the virtual replica of any physical EV system and can be used to simulate performance in real time. The digital twin behaves just like a mimetic representation of any real vehicle by getting its data synchronized through continuously updating the sensors and other input sources. In this manner, engineers work in real time on analysis, testing, and optimization of a vehicle's systems without having to run the physical vehicle. Digital twins are most beneficially applied to test complicated subsystems such as battery management, powertrain dynamics, and thermal performance. Testing in a controlled environment can help manufacturers find early potential faults in their designs, which may save them from generating more prototypes. Digital twins could improve parts of EVs much faster by making sure the smooth functioning of components under all sorts of operating conditions.

Rapid Prototyping with Simulations Ends Up Being Less Time-Consuming and Cheaper

The development and testing of electric vehicles through traditional methods take a long time and are very costly since multiple physical prototypes have to be created along with extensive tests in varied conditions. Finally, with the support of HPC, real-time simulations may decrease the cost and time for such processes. Simulations permit the virtual test of different configurations and scenarios without needing many physical prototyping. This approach also reduces the likelihood of costly mistakes or failures since problems can be identified during the preliminary stages of design. Through real-time simulations, manufacturers refine designs, fine-tune systems, and verify compliance with regulations without using an excessive amount of physical resources, thus saving much cost and allowing the possibility of getting to market quickly with new EV models.

Simulation of Drive Conditions and Load Scenarios

These would then be run dependably over a wide range of driving conditions-that is to say, including all load variations, terrain, and external environmental conditions. Real-time simulations of the above conditions allow one to see how a vehicle can behave in response, for example, while climbing steeply, accelerating sharply, or in stop-and-go traffic, where its demands for energy vary considerably. Load cases may include passenger weight, cargo, or trailer towing variations to simulate these conditions on energy consumption, powertrain stress, and range. Extreme temperature regimes can also be evaluated in real-time simulations of importance in the effects on the battery and its thermal management. All done in optimizing operation of EVs over a broad spectrum of real-world conditions toward both performance and reliability improvement.

In a nutshell, real-time simulation is a tool for electric vehicles and their development, testing, giving immediate responses on the performance of the system, and always optimizing the fast process. Digital twins can really make modeling of many driving conditions, therefore decrease the cost of prototyping, help in improving the efficiency of the vehicle, and ensure the performance at the level of modern consumers' expectations for EVs. Hence, real-time simulation even accelerates innovation. In addition, it helps make the electric vehicle strong and adaptable to the competitive changing market.

HPC AND ELECTRIC VEHICLE CHARGING INFRASTRUCTURE

Growing popularity of electric cars becomes the reason why proper and effective charging infrastructure, for example, sturdy charging stations, is necessary. HPC thereby plays a transformative role in optimizing the efficiency of EV charging networks, solving the problems with the grid, and working to improve the effectiveness of charging stations in general. This section focuses on the challenges in EV charging infrastructure, a role HPC plays in optimization of charging networks, simulating charging patterns and their impacts on the electrical grid, and the strategic placement of charging stations to optimize their efficiency (Boopathi et al., 2024; Chandrika et al., 2023; Devi et al., 2024).

Challenges in EV Charging Infrastructure

There are several challenges EV charging infrastructure development is facing. Charging imbalances would form a salient issue when it comes to range anxiety, especially in sparsely populated regions. The integration of an ultra-high level of EVs into the power grid also raises some complex issues relating to load management, including the potential overloading of the power grid and fluctuations in power demand. Those charging times vary with types of charger, size of the car's battery and the availability of the grid. Coordination for such a system must be effectively handled to avoid disrupting charging. There is a dire need for detailed models and analysis in the design of a resilient yet efficient network to support growing adoption of EVs with minimal disruption in the grid.

HPC for Charging Network Optimization

HPC enables optimal charging infrastructure for electric vehicles overall through the handling of large volumes of data which will simulate and analyze charging patterns, energy flows, and network performance. Engineers can therefore model scenarios for various types of vehicles, different charging rates, and different power demands at different times of day and regions. With HPC, real-time data can be aggregated and analyzed from a thousand charging stations to determine the optimal configurations of network expansions that will minimize congestion and reduce energy distribution. HPC also makes demand forecasting much more precise, predicting where the likelihood of demand at which hour of the day and at what locations, therefore far ahead on future-proofing the structure of infrastructure development and preparation for a burst in EV adoption.

Simulation of Charging Patterns and Impact on Grid

Simulating charging patterns and their effects on the power grid is the most critical application of HPC in EV charging infrastructure. Charging a fully electric vehicle imposes extremely high demands on the grid at times when most are charging, especially peak hours. Such simulation by HPC helps to model those patterns of interaction with the existing grid infrastructure to enable utilities to balance loads more effectively. This is vital from the point of view of grid stability and will especially become quite critical with the increasing inclusions of renewable sources in the overall energy mix. Grid operators can apply simulation of diverse charging patterns across different geographic areas to optimize flow of energy as well as avoid any potential or possible strain on the grid and prevent outages, thereby making the growing EV load manageable by the grid without performance drop.

Strategic Siting for Maximum Efficiency

HPC helps in strategic location of charging stations, simulating traffic patterns and population density as well as projected EV adoption rates. This analysis would help in finding the best location for new stations, ensuring that demand is at its highest level in those areas and grid impact is at a minimum. Optimized placement of charging stations in cities and regions can support access to EV charging services and reduce the risk of congestion in certain areas where the grid's transmission capacity may be limited. For example, HPC-computer simulations can choose which placement of fast-charging stations on highways or in urban centers would deliver better vehicle driving ranges and lower time charges for filling, greatly improving the EV ownership experience. Station placement overall can also reduce the costs of infrastructure as investments will be targeted to where they will deliver the most impact.

Thus, HPC is an extremely important tool in dealing with the issues of charging infrastructure for electric vehicles. Therefore, it would further enable the effective optimization of the charging network, better integration of charging stations with the grid, and strategical station placement, ensuring a scalable and sustainable future for electric mobility.

FUTURE TRENDS IN HPC-DRIVEN ELECTRIC VEHICLE INNOVATIONS

HPC is at the forefront of innovation in electric vehicle designs, performance, and possibilities when technology is developed further. With the tremendous progress in artificial intelligence (AI), and especially machine learning (ML), as well as the emergence of quantum computing, it is now an exciting future area to explore. The subsequent section will focus on the key future trends in HPC-driven EV innovation, AI/ML, quantum integration, sustainability, challenges, and opportunities ahead (Dall-Orsoletta et al., 2022; Prud'homme & Koning, 2012; Rapson & Muehlegger, 2023). The future trends in HPC-driven innovations for electric vehicles are illustrated in Figure 6.

Figure 6. Future trends in HPC-driven innovations for electric vehicles

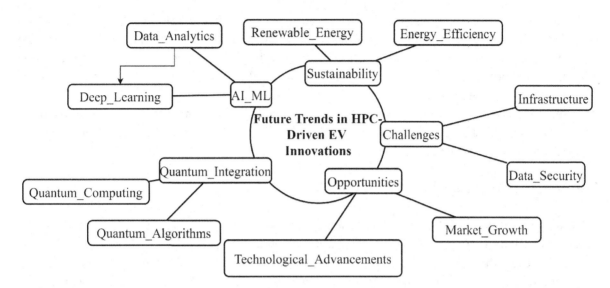

AI and Machine Learning Integration with HPC in EV Design

Perhaps one of the most promising applications of AI and machine learning is the integration into the HPC for designing electric vehicles: AI algorithms can analyze the data coming from sensors, simulation results, and real-world operations of vehicles to ensure that everything, right from battery management to motor control, is optimized. It also enables quick simulation of vehicle performance under different conditions by trained machine learning models in an HPC environment, with a higher-degree prediction to make the design process more efficient.

AI can also be applied for more complex decisions, such as optimization of energy flow or fault detection in EV systems. Combined with HPC, AI-powered simulation would provide real-time feedback, thus accelerating the production cycle by aiding automakers to develop more intelligent and efficient EVs.

Next-Generation Simulations of EV

The more it evolves, the more insights reveal regarding its potential to revolutionize EV simulation. So far in its infancy, AI promises to solve problems hitherto intractable for classical computers. Multivariable optimizations, such as materials science, battery chemistry, and aerodynamics, can now be solved by quantum computers. Quantum computers will be able to simulate at the molecular level interactions within battery materials. This is a major breakthrough with regard to augmenting battery life, charging speeds, and energy density. Quantum computers might be capable of doing calculations exponentially faster than traditional HPCs, so potentially model much more complex systems in real-time, which would radically improve EV design and performance optimization.

Sustainable EV Innovations through HPC

With sustainability emerging as a very important focus area in EV development, HPC shall play a decisive role in making eco-friendly innovations possible. Simulations based on HPC can help determine the optimal selection of materials and energy efficiency during EV manufacturing to reduce the carbon footprint of the production process. Moreover, efficiency and aerodynamics of the vehicle are further improved by HPC, saving energy.

In relation to battery technology, HPC allows modeling of advanced chemistries and recycling methods and facilitates sustainable energy storage solutions while fostering innovations in battery life cycle management and environmental impacts.

Future Challenges and Opportunities in HPC for EVs

Although the future of HPC in EV innovation appears very bright, there are still many challenges for which HPC will be necessary. Rising complexity in simulations will ever increasingly require more computing power, and the cost of scaling up could prove too costly for smaller auto manufacturers. Balancing AI, quantum computing, and initiatives toward sustainability will require multidisciplinary collaboration. But these challenges also represent opportunities. Cloud-based HPC services will democratize greater access to powerful computing resources. What develops from current research in AI algorithms might provide altogether different avenues for optimizing both vehicle design and performance. It is with such proper investments and technological advances that HPC will lead electric vehicles in shaping their future, including driving both performance and sustainability in the industry.

Thus, it might be stated that in integrating AI, quantum computing, and sustainable practices into HPC-driven EV innovation, the automotive world is bound to transform and open new avenues, but pose great challenges and difficulties for further considerations.

CONCLUSION

This chapter highlights the significant importance of HPC for electric vehicle development: the automotive industry today leverages HPC as an essential tool for maximizing powertrain performance, simulating battery systems and aerodynamics, and transforming innovation, efficiency, and sustainable advancement. Manufacturers will be able to run complex simulations using HPC, which can decrease prototyping time, improve design, lead to better overall performance, and cost and time-to-market savings. Future: Increasingly data- and high-performance computer-driven, the revolution and transformation in design and testing processes, especially with AI and possibly quantum computers, would be critically important. HPC simulation of real-world scenarios, prediction of system failures, and optimization of energy consumption are some of the critical steps to overcome the challenges identified, including degradation of batteries, infrastructure for charging, and aerodynamics.

While the areas that relate to scalability, infrastructure cost, and the development of innovative emerging technologies remain, HPC certainly finds its way into the future electric vehicle generation. Progress in HPC capabilities is continuously evolving; it will unlock further sustainable innovations that set electric vehicles ahead in transportation of the future.

REFERENCES

Aghabali, I., Bauman, J., Kollmeyer, P. J., Wang, Y., Bilgin, B., & Emadi, A. (2020a). 800-V electric vehicle powertrains: Review and analysis of benefits, challenges, and future trends. *IEEE Transactions on Transportation Electrification*, 7(3), 927–948. DOI: 10.1109/TTE.2020.3044938

Aghabali, I., Bauman, J., Kollmeyer, P. J., Wang, Y., Bilgin, B., & Emadi, A. (2020b). 800-V electric vehicle powertrains: Review and analysis of benefits, challenges, and future trends. *IEEE Transactions on Transportation Electrification*, 7(3), 927–948. DOI: 10.1109/TTE.2020.3044938

Ahmed, K., & Liu, J. (2019). Simulation of energy-efficient demand response for high performance computing systems. *2019 Winter Simulation Conference (WSC)*, 2560–2571. DOI: 10.1109/WSC40007.2019.9004781

Alawneh, S. G., Zeng, L., & Arefifar, S. A. (2023). A Review of High-Performance Computing Methods for Power Flow Analysis. *Mathematics*, 11(11), 2461. DOI: 10.3390/math11112461

Babu, B. S., Kamalakannan, J., Meenatchi, N., Karthik, S., & Boopathi, S. (2022). Economic impacts and reliability evaluation of battery by adopting Electric Vehicle. *IEEE Explore*, 1–6.

Boopathi, S., Ananth, J., Raghuram, K. S., Kistan, A., Velumani, M., & Gopinathan, R. (2024, January). *6342734- Machine for Analysis of the resistance of welded parts by the electrical resistance process.*

Boopathi, S., Saranya, A., Raghuraman, S., & Revanth, R. (2018). Design and Fabrication of Low Cost Electric Bicycle. *International Research Journal of Engineering and Technology*, 5(3), 146–147.

Bucaioni, A. (2019). Boosting the development of high-performance automotive systems. *Junior Researcher Community Event at Software Technologies: Applications and Foundations 2019 STAF-JRC19.*

Chandrika, V., Sivakumar, A., Krishnan, T. S., Pradeep, J., Manikandan, S., & Boopathi, S. (2023). Theoretical Study on Power Distribution Systems for Electric Vehicles. In *Intelligent Engineering Applications and Applied Sciences for Sustainability* (pp. 1–19). IGI Global. DOI: 10.4018/979-8-3693-0044-2.ch001

Dall-Orsoletta, A., Ferreira, P., & Dranka, G. G. (2022). Low-carbon technologies and just energy transition: Prospects for electric vehicles. *Energy Conversion and Management: X, 16*, 100271.

Devi, J. V., Argiddi, R. V., Renuka, P., Janagi, K., Hari, B. S., & Boopathi, S. (2024). Study on Integrated Neural Networks and Fuzzy Logic Control for Autonomous Electric Vehicles. In *Advances in Web Technologies and Engineering* (pp. 104–127). IGI Global. DOI: 10.4018/979-8-3693-1487-6.ch006

Du, J., Mo, X., Li, Y., Zhang, Q., Li, J., Wu, X., Lu, L., & Ouyang, M. (2019). Boundaries of high-power charging for long-range battery electric car from the heat generation perspective. *Energy*, 182, 211–223. DOI: 10.1016/j.energy.2019.05.222

Giri, R. B., N., Alhamad, A. M., Mamidi, P. L., R., S., & Boopathi, S. (2024). Human-Centered Design Approach to Autonomous Electric Vehicles: Revolutionizing Mobility. In *Advances in Logistics, Operations, and Management Science* (pp. 91–109). IGI Global. DOI: 10.4018/979-8-3693-1862-1.ch006

Godwin Immanuel, D., Solaimalai, G., Chandrakala, B. M., Bharath, V. G., Singh, M. K., & Boopathi, S. (2024). Advancements in Electric Vehicle Management System: Integrating Machine Learning and Artificial Intelligence. In *Advances in Web Technologies and Engineering* (pp. 371–391). IGI Global. DOI: 10.4018/979-8-3693-1487-6.ch018

Loeb, B., & Kockelman, K. M. (2019). Fleet performance and cost evaluation of a shared autonomous electric vehicle (SAEV) fleet: A case study for Austin, Texas. *Transportation Research Part A, Policy and Practice*, 121, 374–385. DOI: 10.1016/j.tra.2019.01.025

Lyu, C., Lin, N., & Dinavahi, V. (2021). Device-level parallel-in-time simulation of mmc-based energy system for electric vehicles. *IEEE Transactions on Vehicular Technology*, 70(6), 5669–5678. DOI: 10.1109/TVT.2021.3081534

McIntosh-Smith, S., Price, J., Deakin, T., & Poenaru, A. (2019). A performance analysis of the first generation of HPC-optimized Arm processors. *Concurrency and Computation*, 31(16), e5110. DOI: 10.1002/cpe.5110

Meintz, A., Slezak, L., Thurston, S., Carlson, B., Thurlbeck, A., Kisacikoglu, J., Kandula, P., Rowden, B., Chinthavali, M., Wojda, R., & Associates. (2023). *Electric vehicles at scale (EVs@ Scale) laboratory consortium deep-dive technical meetings: High power charging (HPC) summary report*. National Renewable Energy Laboratory (NREL), Golden, CO (United States).

Miri, I., Fotouhi, A., & Ewin, N. (2021). Electric vehicle energy consumption modelling and estimation—A case study. *International Journal of Energy Research*, 45(1), 501–520. DOI: 10.1002/er.5700

Muhammed, T., Mehmood, R., Albeshri, A., & Alsolami, F. (2020). HPC-smart infrastructures: A review and outlook on performance analysis methods and tools. *Smart Infrastructure and Applications: Foundations for Smarter Cities and Societies*, 427–451.

Muthukumar, R., & Pratheep, G. V. G., S. J., S., Kunduru, K. R., Kumar, P., & Boopathi, S. (2024). Leveraging Fuel Cell Technology With AI and ML Integration for Next-Generation Vehicles: Empowering Electric Mobility. In *Advances in Mechatronics and Mechanical Engineering* (pp. 312–337). IGI Global. DOI: 10.4018/979-8-3693-5247-2.ch016

Naresh, M., Subhahan, D. A., Narula, V. N., Roslin, D. K., Narula, S., & Boopathi, S. (2024). Edge Computing and Machine Learning Integration for Autonomous Electrical Vehicles. In *Solving Fundamental Challenges of Electric Vehicles* (pp. 99–127). IGI Global., DOI: 10.4018/979-8-3693-4314-2.ch005

Pozzato, G., Allam, A., Pulvirenti, L., Negoita, G. A., Paxton, W. A., & Onori, S. (2023). Analysis and key findings from real-world electric vehicle field data. *Joule*, 7(9), 2035–2053. DOI: 10.1016/j.joule.2023.07.018

Prud'homme, R., & Koning, M. (2012). Electric vehicles: A tentative economic and environmental evaluation. *Transport Policy*, 23, 60–69. DOI: 10.1016/j.tranpol.2012.06.001

Rajan, T. S., Rex, C. R. E. S., Shastri, D. S., Naidu, G., Senthil Kumar, C., & Boopathi, S. (2024). Study on Environmental and Social Impacts Through Electric Vehicles. In *Solving Fundamental Challenges of Electric Vehicles* (pp. 352–383). IGI Global., DOI: 10.4018/979-8-3693-4314-2.ch013

Rapson, D. S., & Muehlegger, E. (2023). The economics of electric vehicles. *Review of Environmental Economics and Policy*, 17(2), 274–294. DOI: 10.1086/725484

Saldaña, G., San Martín, J. I., Zamora, I., Asensio, F. J., & Oñederra, O. (2019). Analysis of the current electric battery models for electric vehicle simulation. *Energies*, 12(14), 2750. DOI: 10.3390/en12142750

Sharma, T., Glynn, J., Panos, E., Deane, P., Gargiulo, M., Rogan, F., & Gallachóir, B. Ó. (2019). High performance computing for energy system optimization models: Enhancing the energy policy tool kit. *Energy Policy*, 128, 66–74. DOI: 10.1016/j.enpol.2018.12.055

Taghavipour, A., Vajedi, M., & Azad, N. L. (2019). *Intelligent control of connected plug-in hybrid electric vehicles*. Springer. DOI: 10.1007/978-3-030-00314-2

Tan, L., & Yuan, Y. (2022). Computational fluid dynamics simulation and performance optimization of an electrical vehicle Air-conditioning system. *Alexandria Engineering Journal*, 61(1), 315–328. DOI: 10.1016/j.aej.2021.05.001

Tran, D.-D., Vafaeipour, M., El Baghdadi, M., Barrero, R., Van Mierlo, J., & Hegazy, O. (2020). Thorough state-of-the-art analysis of electric and hybrid vehicle powertrains: Topologies and integrated energy management strategies. *Renewable & Sustainable Energy Reviews*, 119, 109596. DOI: 10.1016/j.rser.2019.109596

Yao, M., Gan, Y., Liang, J., Dong, D., Ma, L., Liu, J., Luo, Q., & Li, Y. (2021). Performance simulation of a heat pipe and refrigerant-based lithium-ion battery thermal management system coupled with electric vehicle air-conditioning. *Applied Thermal Engineering*, 191, 116878. DOI: 10.1016/j.applthermaleng.2021.116878

Yi, H., Deng, C., Gong, X., Deng, X., & Blatnik, M. (2021). 1D-3D Online Coupled Transient Analysis for Powertrain-Control Integrated Thermal Management in an Electric Vehicle. *SAE International Journal of Advances and Current Practices in Mobility, 3*(2021-01–0237), 2410–2420.

Yi, H., Li, A., Sun, R., Hu, Y., Zhou, A., Zan, J., & Peng, Q. (2022). *1D-3D Coupled Analysis for Motor Thermal Management in an Electric Vehicle*. SAE Technical Paper.

ADDITIONAL READING

Chougule, S. B., Chaudhari, B. S., Ghorpade, S. N., & Zennaro, M. (2024). Exploring Computing Paradigms for Electric Vehicles: From Cloud to Edge Intelligence, Challenges and Future Directions. *World Electric Vehicle Journal*, 15(2), 39. DOI: 10.3390/wevj15020039

Donald, A., & Brian, A. (2023). AI-Driven horizons: Electric vehicles, cloud computing, and the future of automation. *International Journal of Advanced Engineering Technologies and Innovations*, 1(02), 100–115.

Farooqi, A. M., Alam, M. A., Hassan, S. I., & Idrees, S. M. (2022). A fog computing model for VANET to reduce latency and delay using 5G network in smart city transportation. *Applied Sciences (Basel, Switzerland)*, 12(4), 2083. DOI: 10.3390/app12042083

George, D., & Ronald, R. (2023). Connected Futures: Antenna Breakthroughs in the Era of Cloud Computing, AI Automation, and Electric Vehicles. *International Journal of Advanced Engineering Technologies and Innovations*, 1(02), 131–144.

Jeslin, J. G., Sujatha, M., Aghalya, S., Jehan, C., Ishwarya, M., & Vinayagam, P. V. (2024). 5G-Enabled V2X Communication with Cloud-Powered XGBoost Algorithm for Electric Transportation. 2024 10th International Conference on Communication and Signal Processing (ICCSP), 1388–1393.

Raviprolu, L., Molakatala, N., Argiddi, R. V., Dilavar, S. N., & Srinivasan, P. (2024). Performance Improvements of Electric Vehicles Using Edge Computing and Machine Learning Technologies. In Solving Fundamental Challenges of Electric Vehicles (pp. 248–281). IGI Global. DOI: 10.4018/979-8-3693-4314-2.ch010

Rimal, B. P., Kong, C., Poudel, B., Wang, Y., & Shahi, P. (2022). Smart electric vehicle charging in the era of internet of vehicles, emerging trends, and open issues. *Energies*, 15(5), 1908. DOI: 10.3390/en15051908

Salek, M. S., Khan, S. M., Rahman, M., Deng, H.-W., Islam, M., Khan, Z., Chowdhury, M., & Shue, M. (2022). A review on cybersecurity of cloud computing for supporting connected vehicle applications. *IEEE Internet of Things Journal*, 9(11), 8250–8268. DOI: 10.1109/JIOT.2022.3152477

Tappeta, V. S. R., Appasani, B., Patnaik, S., & Ustun, T. S. (2022). A review on emerging communication and computational technologies for increased use of plug-in electric vehicles. *Energies*, 15(18), 6580. DOI: 10.3390/en15186580

KEY TERMS AND DEFINITIONS

AI: Artificial Intelligence, enables machines to simulate human intelligence.
BMS: Battery Management System, regulates battery performance and health.
CFD: Computational Fluid Dynamics, simulates fluid flow around objects.
ECM: Electric Control Module, controls electric vehicle functions.
EV: Electric Vehicle, powered entirely by electricity.
HPC: High-Performance Computing, powerful computing systems for complex simulations.
ICE: Internal Combustion Engine, traditional engine using fuel.
MH: Motor Horsepower, measure of motor power output.
ML: Machine Learning, AI subset that learns from data patterns.
PBM: Powertrain Battery Management, oversees battery usage in powertrains.
PMSM: Permanent Magnet Synchronous Motor, efficient electric motor type.

Chapter 17
Architectures of High-Performance Computing Systems for Machine Learning Workloads

M. Raju
https://orcid.org/0009-0009-0909-3403

Department of Software Systems, Sri Krishna Arts and Science College, Kuniamuthur, India

Saurabh Chandra
https://orcid.org/0000-0003-4172-9968

School of Law, Bennett University, Greater Noida, India

Kimsy Gulhane
https://orcid.org/0009-0006-6791-8651

School of Management, Ramdeobaba University, Nagpur, India

Pravin A. Dwaramwar
https://orcid.org/0000-0002-8479-9053

Department of Electronics and Computer Science, Ramdeobaba University, Nagpur, India

Gulshan Banu A.

Department of Artificial Intelligence and Data Science, SNS College of Engineering, Coimbatore, India

Sampath Boopathi
https://orcid.org/0000-0002-2065-6539

Department of Mechanical Engineering, Muthayammal Engineering College, Namakkal, India

ABSTRACT

This chapter explores the architectures of high-performance computing (HPC) systems designed for machine learning (ML) workloads with special attention paid to advanced hardware and software optimizations intended to accelerate computational efficiency. It discusses the state-of-the-art use of GPUs, TPUs, and FPGAs in parallelizing operations, optimizing deep learning models during training and inference periods. The final section covers distributed computing frameworks, such as Apache Spark and Hadoop, that also provide support for big data processing in clusters. It also examines the challenges arising from the handling of data, distribution of resources, and scalability aspects as well as emerging solutions, such as memory-centric architectures and quantum computing, respectively. This chapter provides a comprehensive understanding of the evolution of HPC systems to meet the requirements of modern ML workloads, faster model development, reduced energy consumption, and better scalability, along with some of the trends and future research directions in HPC for ML.

DOI: 10.4018/978-1-6684-3795-7.ch017

INTRODUCTION

The current revolution in computing has been attributed, largely, to machine learning (ML) and artificial intelligence (AI) advancements in many industries. It has accounted for excellent growth in health care and finance and has impacted various sectors like transport and entertainment highly, among many others. As ML models continue to increase in complexity and data size, it gets harder and harder for regular computing systems to fulfill the computational requirements that would be needed for effectively training and deploying such models (Wang et al., 2024). This challenge has brought to the forefront high-performance computing (HPC) systems, where specialized hardware and scalable architectures provide the necessary infrastructure for running ML workloads. HPC systems have a long history of application in various domains, including scientific simulations, large-scale data processing, and complex problem-solving tasks, ranging from the field of physics to climate modeling and genomics (Ande & Khair, 2019). Today, such architectures are adapted and optimized in a way for machine learning workloads so that they can support training times, efficient data processing, and excellent scalability.

Many machine learning applications-in particular, deep learning models-require great computational loads in the processing of large amounts of dataset and repeatedly adjusting the parameters in a given model for its training. In all such models, be it neural networks, support vector machines, or even reinforcement learning algorithms, the biggest challenge, indeed a requirement, lies in processing huge volumes of data with high precision as well as high velocity. The perfect answer to their needs has been HPC architectures designed precisely for handling the massive parallel processing and high-speed data transfer (Correa-Baena et al., 2018). The architectures for high-performance computing systems generally contain many constituent components and configurations, such as distributed systems, cloud-based infrastructure, and hardware accelerators including graphics processing units (GPUs), tensor processing units (TPUs), and field-programmable gate arrays (FPGAs). These are crucial elements in the optimization of workloads resulting from machine learning, reducing time to solution, and enabling real-time inference in applications like autonomous vehicles, natural language processing, and recommendation systems (Sterling et al., 2017).

Another fantastic advancement of HPC for using machine learning workloads is the repurposing to GPUs and TPUs. Central processing units (CPUs) are typically too general purpose and thus incapable of handling the scale of parallelism calculated in ML tasks. In fact, deep learning particularly draws much more resources than the other aspects of the work. In reality, GPUs were originally designed to aid with graphics rendering but are very suitable for parallel processing, such that they are rapidly gaining popularity as the hardware of choice for training deep models. Designed with thousands of cores, GPUs speed up training greatly because they focus on rather heavy matrix multiplications and convolutions so typical for neural network training (Li et al., 2022). TPUs stand for Tensor Processing Units and are developed by Google, Inc. These are specialized processors designed to accelerate deep learning tasks-that specifically focus on tensor operations across neural networks. The accelerators drive further optimization in the performance of machine learning models especially upon dealing with large-scale data and complicated architectures.

FPGAs are also an important application for high performance computing for machine learning. Unlike GPUs and TPUs, which have fixed architectures, FPGAs are reconfigurable. One can tweak them to optimum performance of specific ML algorithms or workloads. This way they present tailored, optimized performance improvement in targeted applications. Because of these traits, FPGAs can come in very handy for edge computing scenarios, where power efficiency and low-latency processing play crucial roles. As many machine learning applications are moving toward the edge, in other words, to Internet of Things (IoT) devices, or even entirely autonomous systems, FPGAs can offer a great balance between computational performance and energy efficiency (Wu & Xie, 2022).

Hardware accelerators aside, the other very important constituent of high-performance computing architectures for machine learning is distributed computing frameworks. These frameworks, including Apache Spark and Hadoop, enable massive, distributed datasets to be processed in parallel across multiple machines. Distributed systems allow for the horizontal scaling of machine learning workloads-whereas data volumes increase, ever more nodes can be added to distribute the load without performance penalties. The real strength, especially in deep learning training, where datasets grow to petabyte scales, is that the training times of those systems easily stretch over days or even weeks on traditional systems (Robey & Zamora, 2021). The HPC system reduces the training time and allows faster iteration of the model development process by distributing the computational load on multiple nodes.

Despite these enormous benefits for machine learning workloads from high-performance computing systems, several challenges have to be addressed. One of these challenges is data management. Such models require large volumes of high-quality, labeled training data. The storage solutions that must be brought to support the requirements for such large datasets, efficient data pipelines, and fast access times pose a very real challenge. HPC architectures have to be designed with the rapid ingestion and processing of data to make sure that data bottlenecks do not hinder the overall performance of the system (Ahn et al., 2018).

Resource allocation is the next major challenge in HPC for machine learning. With growing demand in both computational resources and shared environments like the cloud computing platform, it becomes imperative to ensure that resources are efficiently allocated to various ML tasks. Dynamic resource allocation is one such possible solution: it allows provisioning of computing resources based on the workload demands so that provisioning may be de-provisioned in response to demand drops. However, it comes with an orchestration and scheduling requirement and ensures that resources are utilized so that nothing is over-provisioned or underutilized (Mutlu, 2021).

Another concern in high-performance computing systems architecture when dealing with machine learning workloads is scalability. With the size and complexity of the machine learning model, distributing those models across multiple nodes or clusters presents a whole different set of challenges. Efficient parallelization of computations as well as communication among nodes are essential to realize efficiency for distributed systems. Network latency, communication overhead, and synchronization problems may become major issues for ML workloads on HPC systems. More advanced techniques, such as model parallelism and data parallelism, where different parts of the model or dataset are computed across different nodes, can help alleviate these issues but rely on careful implementation and optimization (Mutlu, 2021; Usman et al., 2022).

Emerging technologies that also promise improvement in the performance of high-performance computing systems for machine learning are memory-centric architectures and quantum computing. Memory-centric architectures focus on optimizing data movement and memory accesses. One of the biggest challenges on traditional HPC systems arises from the separation of processing and memory. By bringing memory closer to the processor, with smaller distances and without mediaries and inter-domain errors, those are reduced and the efficiency of the workloads dramatically increases, especially for the data-intensive ones in ML (Isik et al., 2023; Kalamkar et al., 2020). Despite its infancy, quantum computing holds the promise of revolutionizing machine learning in a true sense by allowing exponential speedups for certain kinds of computation. While practical quantum computing is still many years away, there is rapid acceleration in research on quantum algorithms in machine learning, and HPCs will eventually be married to quantum processors to solve the most complex computationally intensive ML tasks (Dongarra et al., 2005; Isik et al., 2023).

The role of high-performance computing systems will become critical with the advance of machine learning, its expansion into new domains, and the shift toward big machine learning that awaits the future. HPC architectures will have to power both training, deployment, and scaling of ML models in all aspects of applications. High-performance computing systems are particularly well-suited to assume the ever-growing computational demands of modern machine learning workloads by leveraging advances in hardware accelerators, distributed computing frameworks, and emerging technologies (Kalamkar et al., 2020; Lupión et al., 2023).

HPC system architecture is critical for this new generation of applications based on machine learning. Each one of these acceleration means for ML tasks--GPUs, TPUs, FPGAs, distributed computing frameworks--is accompanied by memory-centric architectures and quantum computers, opening up extremely promising avenues for future development. However, critical data management, resource allocation, and scalability issues have to be overcome to fully capitalize on the power of HPC systems for applications in machine learning. As those issues continue to be overcome, the supercomputer, high-performance computing systems will be a grand tool in advancing the field of machine learning (Bernholdt et al., 2006; Lupión et al., 2023).

BACKGROUND: HIGH-PERFORMANCE COMPUTING FOR MACHINE LEARNING

Therefore, machine learning -which, nowadays, is very much placed at the forefront of modern industries -requires supercomputing systems to undertake huge machine learning workloads. High-performance computing systems, which were initially proposed for scientific simulations and complex computations, have increasingly been applied to manage the higher computational demands of ML tasks. The core fundamentals of HPC systems are the ability to process large volumes of data quickly and efficiently, which makes them absolutely requisite for modern machine learning applications. In this section, we discuss the evolution of HPC systems, major components of HPC architectures, and the critical role that parallel processing plays in optimizing machine learning workloads (Penney & Chen, 2019; Ramachandran et al., 2024). Figure 1 depicts the connection between high-performance computing and machine learning.

Figure 1. Relationship between high-performance computing and machine learning

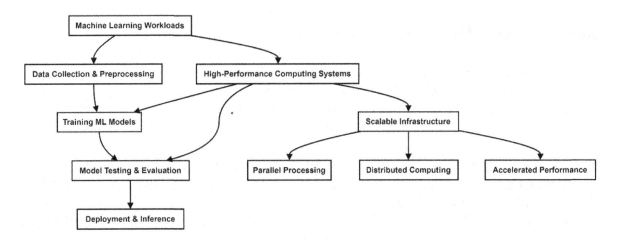

Evolution of HPC Systems

The history of HPC is said to date back to the mid-20th century, during which early developments of supercomputers aimed at solving some of the complicated problems in physics and cryptography. These early machines were already big and expensive, with strongly specialized hardware. In fact, through the integration of semiconductor technology and the development of computing theory over the decades, HPC systems have provided high performance, scalability, and accessibility in their architectures. By the late 20th century, HPC systems had pervaded fields from climate modeling to genomics and even financial modeling that required a huge amount of computational capability (Mališa et al., 2020; Vasilache et al., 2018).

Parallel computing emerged during the 1990s, and it really marked the new wave changeover in the development of HPC systems. In parallel computing, instead of a single powerful processor, multiple processors can be created to work together to solve a given problem more quickly and effectively. This enabled full-scale horizontal scaling of HPC systems, spreading the workload across many processing units. As the pursuit for faster computing continued, using clusters came to be one of the primary means of scaling up an HPC system: groups of interconnected computers. In today's scenario, HPC systems have become easier and widespread, as cloud-based HPC platforms also opened avenues for enterprises and researchers to exploit the latent power of computations without pinning on the physical existence of infrastructure.

Advancement in machine learning models has resulted in increasing complexity in HPC systems, particularly in deep learning. Deep learning is a subset of machine learning which requires a highly computational power for processing tasks like recognizing images, processing natural languages, and autonomous systems. To address these needs, present-day HPC systems have incorporated various types of specialized hardware, such as GPUs, TPUs, and FPGAs, which can process enormous numerical workloads in parallel more effectively than the traditional, single-core central processing units. This trend also indicates the increased marriage of HPC and ML technologies toward more efficient, scalable, and powerful systems.

Building Blocks of HPC Architectures

An HPC system is built upon the amalgamation of a set of hardware and software elements, designed to maximize performance, specifically computational performance. Critical elements of the structures include processors, memory, storage, interconnects, and software frameworks, each contributing crucially to delivering high performance for ML workloads (Muralidhar et al., 2022; Xu et al., 2024).

a) Processors: The CPU will still be the core of HPCs but in recent years has specialized toward becoming more on the GPUs, TPUs, etc. Again, one specialty of the GPUs will be parallelism, which is the workhorse for these machine learning types of applications, such as matrix multiplications in deep learning models. TPU is developed by Google, designed to accelerate tensor operations and is especially suited for machine learning. It enhances the computing powers of the HPC system in running large-scale models of machine learning with better speed and accuracy of operation.

b) Memory and Storage: Most HPC systems process large amounts of data and therefore require high-speed memory for data storage. Larger volumes of data are stored and maintained through long-term data storage solutions, such as solid-state drives or hard disk drives. For providing fast access to periodically needed data, the processors use the RAM. Distributed HPC systems distribute the data across multiple nodes which necessitates advanced storage management techniques to provide both low-latency performance and fast data access.

c) Interconnects: The interconnects of HPC architectures provide for communication across different components of the system, particularly distributed environments. High-speed networks such as InfiniBand or Ethernet are typically used to allow fast transfers of data between processors, memory, and storage across nodes. Therefore, the interconnect in HPC architectures has to be efficient with low latency in terms of process communication so that ML workloads can run as smoothly as possible in a parallelized environment.

d) Software Frameworks: The HPC system critically relies upon a set of software frameworks that manage and optimize computational workloads. It is mainly helped by the MPI and OpenMP frameworks in the way of task distribution among multiple processors or nodes for parallel computing. Similarly, adaptation is done of some of the famous machine learning software frameworks like TensorFlow, PyTorch, and Apache Spark that allows easy integration with machine learning algorithms along with the architecture of HPC.

Parallel Processing and its Significance in Machine Learning

High-performance computing is basically the principle of performing multiple jobs within parallel processing units of a computer, hence several operations can be performed simultaneously. Parallel processing in machine learning is absolutely inevitable in terms of reaching the optimization goal, especially in the case of big datasets and complex algorithms (Ramesh, 2024; Tuncer et al., 2017).

This is achieved through the highly significant number of matrix multiplications and other linear algebra operations, which in conventional CPUs are extremely time-consuming. By exploiting parallel processing, HPC systems will allow the operator to split these operations between more than one processor and thus to reduce the time taken to train a model as well as to make inferences from the model. For instance, with thousands of cores, GPUs are engineered to support many operations at the same time-this is an attribute particularly valuable for training deep neural networks. Another good feature of parallel processing is its feasibility in handling large datasets, a trait that is usually common with tasks performed in machine learning. The sequential processing of data is not required since HPC can ensure that the data is distributed to the nodes; processes are, therefore fast, and memory usage also becomes efficient. Another area of relevance is parallel processing in distributed HPC systems, where workloads are distributed over several nodes or clusters. Such computing is indispensable to machine learning models requiring huge amounts of computation power for large applications such as natural language processing, image recognition, or even autonomous systems. By parallelizing data and computation, HPC systems make possible the faster and higher-accuracy training of machine learning models, enabling more complex and powerful AI applications to be accomplished.

Thus, with their evolution, they, along with the high-performance computing systems' key architectural components and parallel processing capabilities, represent HPC as an important tool that propels advancements in machine learning models. With complexity and scale gaining machine learning model dimensions, integration of HPC systems will, increasingly, be important due to the fact that further innovation and development in AI technologies call for it.

HARDWARE ACCELERATORS FOR MACHINE LEARNING IN HPC

HPC is one of the main things needed to handle big machine learning workloads, while hardware accelerators make the difference in terms of performance optimization. These accelerators are specifically designed to handle the heavy computational loads of modern ML tasks, such as deep learning, neural networks, and real-time data processing. Each of these hardware components has its unique architecture and use cases and, henceforth, makes ML workloads faster and more efficient within HPC environments (Clevenger et al., 2015; Ramachandran et al., 2024). Figure 2 depicts the significant role of hardware accelerators in machine learning within high-performance computing systems.

Figure 2. Role of hardware accelerators in machine learning within high-performance computing systems

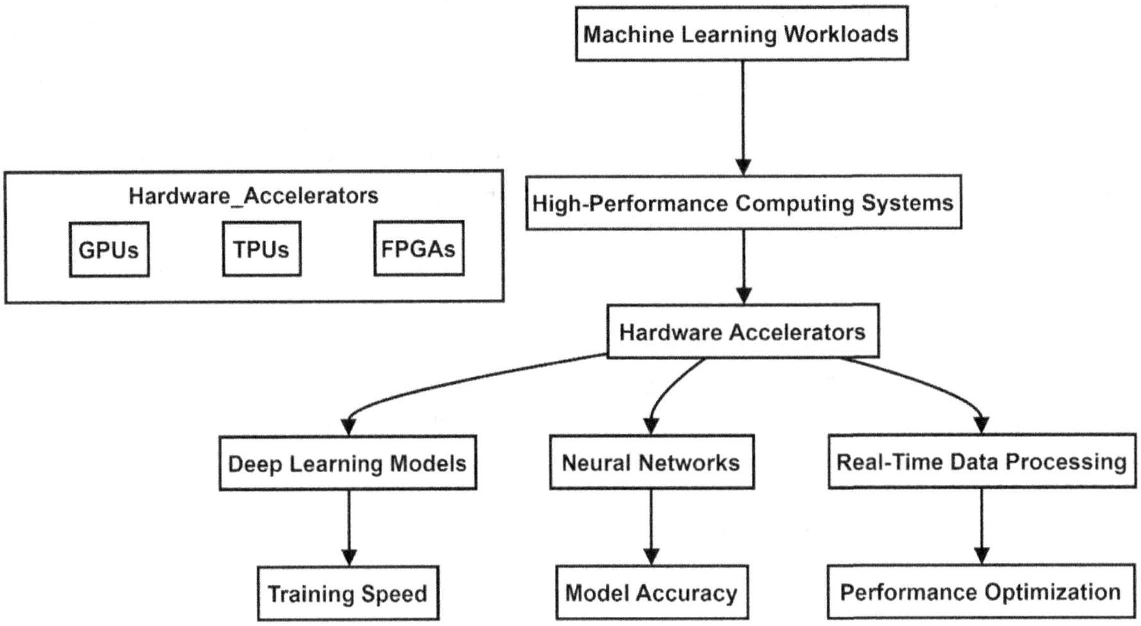

GPUs and Their Role in Machine Learning

Because of these capabilities, GPUs have become an essential component in the HPC systems for machine learning. In fact, the primary design objective of developing such units was specifically to render images and video in graphics-intensive applications. But these units have since evolved in general-purpose computing, especially with matrix operations-the mainstay of all machine learning algorithms. The reason why GPUs are efficient for ML workloads is because they are parallel, with thousands of cores that execute lots of operations at the same time. This runs completely opposite to the design of the standard CPU, which is optimized for tasks given sequentially and with fewer numbers of cores. Deep tasks like the training of neural networks rely on the execution of a large number of mathematical operations in parallel. Because of this, GPUs are utilized to speed the training phase of machine learning models. This is especially for deep learning algorithms like convolutional neural networks (CNNs) and recurrent neural networks (RNNs) (Balaprakash et al., 2018; Georganas et al., 2018).

From amongst these popular frameworks that harness the use of the GPUs for machine learning is NVIDIA's CUDA (Compute Unified Device Architecture). CUDA lets the developer write code that is natively run on an NVIDIA GPU to unlock the full potential of parallel computing inside these accelerators. Deep learning libraries like TensorFlow and PyTorch also optimize their usage on a GPU, offering APIs that integrate really well with a HPC environment. In general, GPU acceleration greatly decreases the training times for complex models, further speeding up the pace of research and development of AI.

In addition, GPUs play a critical role in inference workloads, where pre-trained models are required to make predictions on new data. Inference workloads can be done on the CPU, but the advantage in terms of speed is much more pronounced for applications like autonomous vehicles, image recognition, and natural language processing using GPUs. A combination of flexibility and powerful parallel computing capabilities has made GPUs indispensable for HPC systems designed for modern machine learning workloads.

Deep Learning Tensor Processing Units

Tensor Processing Units are specially designed hardware accelerators developed by Google for the application of machine learning and deep learning. In contrast to GPUs, which provide a wide range of general-purpose computing, TPUs are optimized for the specific requirements of deep learning algorithms, especially those based on tensor operations - building blocks of neural networks (Georganas et al., 2018; Shams et al., 2017).

TPUs were specifically optimised to accelerate the execution of deep learning models for TensorFlow, Google's deep learning framework. Their architecture was optimised for throughput tensor computations, including matrix multiplication and convolution, that are crux deep learning operations. This focus on tensor processing allows the TPU to perform significantly better than even high-performance GPUs when it comes to energy efficiency and deep learning operations speed. The most significant advantage of the TPUs is that they can support large-scale deep learning workloads with significantly reduced energy usage. This makes them suitable for large-scale data centers and cloud-based HPC environments, which mostly require focus on energy efficiency. For instance, Google offers TPU-based instances in its cloud infrastructure, wherein researchers and developers can avail high-performance deep learning capabilities without specific hardware requirements.

This has proved to be extremely useful in applications such as image classification, natural language processing, and machine translation. Because TPUs reduce the time required for model training and the computational resources required to produce models, experimentation and iteration in AI research is faster than before. Second, because TPUs are cloud-based, they are highly accessible to a larger audience.

Field-Programmable Gate Arrays and Edge Computing

The approach here is completely different with FPGAs, providing the mix of flexibility and the ability for high-performance computing, while GPUs and TPUs are fixed architectures with specialization either in parallel processing or deep learning. Because FPGAs allow for reprogramming, specific tasks can be run efficiently. This reconfigurable architecture makes FPGAs easily customizable for various machine learning applications, holding high versatility in HPC environments (Kalamkar et al., 2020; Lupión et al., 2023).

One of the major advantages of FPGAs is the ability to deliver low-latency computation, exactly what is demanded by real-time learning machine tasks in edge computing. In edge computing, because data is processed closer to where it emanates-for example, from sensors or other IoT devices-rather than in some central data center, huge amounts of data do not need to be transferred across networks and processed in distant locations and thus remove latency. The edge cases of FPGAs have an advantage in this because they can customize the design based on specific machine learning models and workloads, leading to a high performance with low power usage compared to GPUs or TPUs. In most applications related to autonomous systems, industrial automation, and healthcare devices requiring real-time processing and decision-making, it puts FPGAs at the top of the list. For example, one can program an FPGA to speed inference in a compact edge device that can then process data and make predictions without resorting to the use of cloud-based HPC systems.

This flexibility is complemented with the energy efficiency required by battery-powered or low-power edge devices. Optimizing hardware to perform only the specific computations required for a particular task minimizes overall power consumption, thus maintaining high computational throughput. Therefore, the ability of FPGAs to sustain flexibility, low-latency performance, and energy efficiency makes them key players in future edge computing and distributed machine learning systems. Truly, hardware accelerators, such as GPUs, TPUs, and FPGAs, have become indispensable in the fast-evolving field of machine learning for HPCs. While GPUs with massively parallel computing have great momentum in building up and deployment of complex models, TPUs are specialized deep learning accelerators well suited to large-scale cloud environments. Edge computing will provide a valid opportunity for FPGAs with reprogrammable architecture and low-latency performance, unfolding for many real-time applications in the ML domain. As the demands of ML continue to grow, these hardware accelerators will remain at the forefront in innovation when facing faster, more efficient, and more scalable solutions for ML workloads across industries.

DISTRIBUTED COMPUTING FRAMEWORKS FOR ML WORKLOADS

Distributed computing frameworks include the deployment as well as the runtime of ML workloads especially during data that is large in volume and complex algorithms. Such as Apache Spark and Hadoop, technologies enable scalable computation of large datasets across many machines for efficient analysis of data, training models, as well as inference. Such frameworks enable parallel processing with tools for resource allocation and load balancing to provide the best performance and efficiency in ML applications (Dongarra et al., 2005; Isik et al., 2023). The process of utilizing distributed computing frameworks for machine learning workloads is illustrated in Figure 3.

Figure 3. Process of using distributed computing frameworks for machine learning workloads

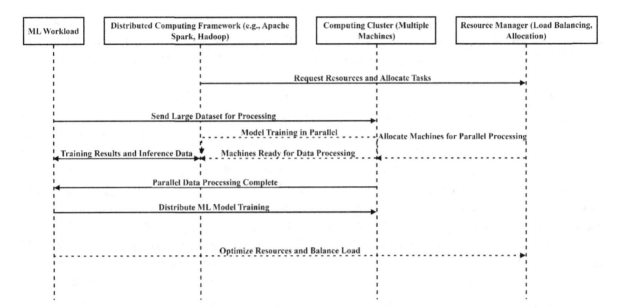

Apache Spark and Hadoop are two of the most popular distributed computing frameworks; widely adopted across large vistas in the realm of machine learning. Hadoop is an open-source framework, allowing for distributed storage and processing of big data across a cluster of commodity hardware. It is based on the idea of the Hadoop Distributed File System, or HDFS, for storing data and uses the MapReduce programming model for parallel data processing across the cluster. Hadoop's architecture is very efficient for batch processing. When data is divided into segments, then it's processed in bits and pieces, thus applied suitably for different operations when tasks are done on data for ML. Apache Spark, on the other hand, allows better improvements over Hadoop by providing an in-memory computing model that highly enhances processing speed. The data can also be operated on HDFS and other storage systems so that Spark can fetch and process it much more efficiently. Its Resilient Distributed Datasets (RDDs) makes the data processing fault tolerant and parallel, which is a necessity for training machine learning models on large data sets. Further, Spark includes libraries like MLlib, which offer a vast reservoir of machine learning algorithms and tools for scalable ML tasks further simplify the implementation of ML workflows.

These frameworks help deal with huge volumes of data that may have to be processed in most domains, including finance, healthcare, and e-commerce. By distributing data and computation across multiple nodes, organizations can then use the combined processing power of the resources for faster analytical and training computation on machine learning models. With horizontal scaling capabilities-implementing more nodes within the cluster-the flexibility is improved, and the infrastructure will always be able to respond accordingly to growing loads in terms of data or processing.

Scaling Machine Learning Workloads Across Clusters

Scaling machine learning workloads across clusters is a dimension that improves the performance and efficiency of ML tasks. One node can only carry so much information, and certainly not large enough to hold complex models, which are too big to fit inside the memory of one node, so how is the workload going to be distributed across multiple nodes? This has led to the development of popular computing frameworks, such as Spark and Hadoop, that support effective distributed computation.

In a distributed environment, the ML workloads may be broken down into smaller tasks that are executed concurrently on different nodes within the cluster, yielding enormous parallel processing capability and, hence significantly reduced time to train models and analyze data. For instance, during the training of large deep learning models, the dataset may be subdivided into smaller batches; such batches could then be processed by the different nodes in parallel, with the results aggregated to update the model parameters efficiently. Scaling the ML workloads also presents the same problems of locality, bandwidth, and intra-node communication. In fact, these factors play a critical role in order to keep latency at a minimum and increase through put. For instance, Spark relies on the concept of "data locality," which tries to process data on the same node on which it resides and which in turn reduces the overhead involved in transferring the data over the network. Another alternative to increase efficiency in scaling up is by the use of techniques like distributed training, which includes both data parallelism and model parallelism. In data parallelism, the dataset is split and processed in parallel across several nodes, while in model parallelism, the model is split across the nodes into different parts and trained on it in combination.

Another relevant aspect of scaling ML workloads relates to the usage of orchestration tools and cluster management systems. Any of the orchestration tools, like Kubernetes, can be readily integrated with frameworks such as Spark and Hadoop to manage distributed application deployment, scaling, and management. By automating resource management and workload distribution, orchestration tools enable an ML workload to dynamically scale according to demand.

Resource Allocation and Load Balancing

Distributed ML workloads can have real utilization and effective load balancing if they effectively allocate resources. In a distributed environment, when many jobs are running at the same time, there is a heavy requirement for the allocation of several types of computational resources like CPU, memory, and storage to avoid bottlenecks and ensure high efficiency.

In a distributed computing framework, the resource allocation strategy depends on the nature of workload and available resources in a cluster. Very few frameworks incorporate dynamic resource allocation, and in them, the resources are supplied based on real-time demand. For instance, Apache Spark dynamically adjusts the amount of resources allocated to various tasks so that high-priority jobs are given the required power of computation while at the same time maintaining the overall system in balance. Another central consideration in the distributed systems is load balancing, which is generally characterized by uneven distribution of workload across nodes, thus degrading the overall performance and resource underutilization. Techniques such as scheduling tasks and prioritizing jobs are used to ensure workload distribution across nodes is balanced and uniform. For instance, round-robin scheduling can further divide the tasks between different nodes fairly. Algorithms can be much more detailed, taking into consideration how much load each node is carrying and how much processing power it maintains to allocate tasks as ideally as possible.

Monitoring and performance metrics are also crucial for proper resource allocation as well as load balancing. The system administrator has to continually monitor both resource utilization and performance to make optimal decisions about the usage of resources. Some monitoring tools come built into the frameworks to identify bottlenecks, track job progress, and make adjustments in proper resource allocation.

Those distributed computing frameworks, such as Apache Spark and Hadoop, given their functionalities on scaling on clusters and how to optimize resource allocation and load balancing, are able to support organizations in making full use of their volumes of data toward adding value and insights into the organization. The future of the use of machine learning will heighten the importance of frameworks like these in the support of large-scale, distributed ML applications, particularly in enabling and simplifying organizations' ability to extract insight and value from data.

CHALLENGES IN HPC FOR MACHINE LEARNING

HPCs are critical for advancing machine learning applications: large high-performance computing systems can provide plenty of computational power to process huge amounts of data and complex models. Despite all these potential benefits, however, several challenges arise during the implementation and operational stages of HPC systems for machine learning workloads. In this section, three critical challenges are addressed: data management and storage solutions, resource allocation and optimization, and scalability and performance bottlenecks (Ahn et al., 2018; Mutlu, 2021). Figure 4 depicts the challenges encountered by high-performance computing in machine learning models.

Figure 4. Challenges faced by high-performance computing (HPC) in machine learning (ML)

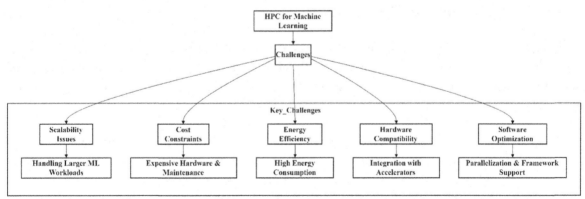

Data Management and Storage Solutions

Data management and storage solutions come handy in HPC environments, especially in a field such as machine learning, which mainly relies on big volumes of data. The main tasks involved with data management include data acquisition, preprocessing, storage, and retrieval.

a) Data Acquisition and Preprocessing: Most machine learning workflows involve the inclusion of data of all types coming from diverse sources like structured and unstructured data, real-time streams of data, and historical datasets. Enough measures must be taken for quality and integrity during acquisition. Data cleaning, normalization, and transformation are computationally intensive processes and may require very effective techniques of management in order to avoid model training delays.

b) Storage: In ML, the traditional storage mechanism might not suffice. High-throughput storage solutions that might include parallel file systems (e.g., Lustre, GPFS) and object storage (e.g., Amazon S3, OpenStack Swift) are usually required for all HPC applications with large data volumes. The system must also support access speeds and concurrent read and writes. For example, ML workloads often have multiple nodes accessing the same dataset at the same time.

c) Data Retrieval and Locality: Achieving efficient data retrieval will ensure that the requirements to maintain high performance in the ML workflows are preserved. The concept of data locality, that is, process data close to its storage location, significantly reduces transfer times of data and thereby enhances the total efficiency of the system. Data locality in distributed environments, however, poses highly complex challenges particularly with large distributed datasets across multiple nodes.

d) Data Security and Compliance: For most applications in healthcare and finance, for instance, data is required to adhere to higher security and compliance standards. Therefore, the strong data management solutions that can suit these regulations without compromising the access and performance add another level of complexity.

Resource Allocation and Optimization

Resource allocation and optimization, just like any other HPC system, is pertinent to ascertain that such systems perform in an efficient and effective way when the ML workloads are executed (Li et al., 2022; Wu & Xie, 2022). Several challenges will arise for the ML tasks, which inherently are dynamic and heterogeneous in their nature:

a) Dynamic Workloads: Machine learning applications are usually characterized by dynamic computational loads that depend on the size of the dataset to which the model is applied, the complexity of the model, and algorithmic needs. Traditional resource allocation strategies are static and may lead to underutilization or overloading of resources. Such issues can be mitigated, however, with dynamic resource allocation approaches that take into consideration the time-variant characteristics of the workload; such sophisticated monitoring and decision-making algorithms are needed to implement such systems.

b) Contention for Resources: The contention in multi-tenant HPC environments likely results in lower performance because of the competing shared resources from various users and applications. Efficient management of this kind of contention through scheduling and prioritization is key to preserving performance levels, particularly when running resource-intensive ML workloads.

c) Load Balancing: Load balancing efficiently distributes the workload across accessible resources. Uneven distribution of loads can cause some nodes to become highly loaded while other nodes are unused or idle, which takes longer to complete jobs and wastes computational resources. In place is the complex challenge of providing certain effective load balancing algorithms to satisfy the unique characteristics of the ML workloads through monitoring and adaptation.

d) Resource Provisioning: Determining the number of resources required for specific ML tasks can be quite challenging in a situation where workload varies. To make resource usage optimal and cost-effective, therefore, a sharp estimation of the resource requirement considering history and a workload trend is necessary.

Scalability and Performance Bottlenecks

Scalability is one of the key features of HPC systems within machine learning, and scalability represents the ability to economically handle growing workloads as well as bigger data sets (Muthukumar et al., 2024). However, there are also several problems that may relate to scalability and performance bottlenecks:.

a) Performance Bottlenecks: Performance bottlenecks can occur anywhere in the ML workflow, including data loading, preprocessing, model training, and inference. Thus, proper identification of bottlenecks and rectification of them are very important for optimizing the total performance of HPC systems. For instance, if data loading is taking too high time, then the entire process of training gets unnecessarily delayed, along with resource utilization becoming inefficient.

b) Network Latency and Bandwidth: Networks can easily turn into bottlenecks in distributed HPC systems because their latency and bandwidth often cause a lot of performance problems. The communications between nodes incur heavy overhead, causing delays in data transfer and synchronization; hence this quality damages when training large-scale ML models. The mitigation of the problem is done by optimizing communication patterns through the use of high-speed networking technologies such as InfiniBand.

c) Algorithmic Scalability: Not all ML algorithms scale well with large data sizes or model complexity. Some algorithms degrade in the speed of performance when scaled up. Algorithms, therefore, have to be chosen judiciously along with their optimization in such a way that scalability is ensured. This can be enhanced with some techniques such as mini-batch training, distributed training frameworks, and efficient optimization algorithms.

d) Infrastructure Limitations: Most of the time, scale is constrained by what the underlying infrastructure, that is the hardware, is able to do. If there is not enough memory, CPU, or even GPU, for example, then the size of a dataset and a model could not be processed efficiently. Upgrades in hardware as well as adopting specialized computing resources can be of help in these regards.

It also becomes very challenging when various software components and tools are included in HPC environments. Indeed, very critical is making sure that those tools and frameworks-talked data storage solutions, distributed computing frameworks, and ML libraries-are compatible with each other and can communicate with each other in an efficient manner for achieving the best performance in such environments.

Although the HPC system holds a lot of promise in leading the advancements to capability in machine learning, it is also plagued by some critical challenges. Challenges in terms of data management and storage, resource allocation and optimization, scalability and performance bottlenecks have to be addressed so that one can actually realize the benefits of HPCs with machine learning workloads. The need for continuous innovation in hardware, software, and algorithms will be of utmost importance for the eventual challenge-coming resolutions in leading to even more efficient and effective applications of ML.

EMERGING TRENDS IN HPC ARCHITECTURES FOR Machine Learning

An ever-changing landscape for HPC architectures is needed to cope with the burgeoning demands of workloads in machine learning. With ever-increasing sizes and complexity of ML models, traditional HPC architectures are being reimagined to offer better performance, scalability, and efficiency. Memory-centric architectures, quantum computing, and considerations around energy efficiency and green computing will change the future landscape of HPC for ML applications (Robey & Zamora, 2021; Wu & Xie, 2022). Figure 5 depicts the latest trends in high -performance computing architectures for machine learning models.

Figure 5. Emerging trends in HPC architectures for machine learning models

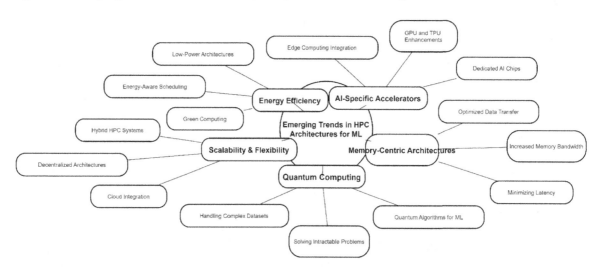

Memory-Centric Architectures

One of the main challenges involved in supporting ML workloads in existing HPC architectures is memory management. Large ML models, in particular the deep learning network, require a lot of memory for storing, processing, and maintaining parameters and intermediate results as well as for data sets. In most traditional architectures, memory was treated as a relatively secondary resource over computing capabilities, and this will make quite a challenge in the efficient management of data flow between processing units and memory stores (Correa-Baena et al., 2018).

Memory-Centric Design Memory-centric architecture is designed with considerations of achieving a faster, higher-capacity memory interface and greater bandwidth-all those things come together to make minima latency among computation and storage. Here, unlike the separation between a processor and its memory, such architectures place as much memory as close as possible to computational resources. This includes some integration of High Bandwidth Memory and NVMe. -centric designs exploit the benefits of improved locality to bring data closer to the processing unit, reducing transfer time between different hierarchies of memory. This is important in deep learning models as iterative matrix operations require high speed access to large data blocks. New architectures have been moving towards unified memory systems that, at the same time, allow GPUs, CPUs, and other accelerators to access the same pool of memory. Deprecates data copying and synchronization. NVIDIA's Unified Memory is a similar example which enables direct access of GPU to CPU memory. It simplifies the programming and minimizes memory overhead.

Emerging memory technologies, including 3D XPoint, a non-volatile memory that combines DRAM speed with NAND flash persistence, are opening the doors to even faster and larger memory storage systems, potentially supporting huge ML workloads.

Quantum Computing and Its Potential for Machine Learning

The quantum computing, though still in very early stages, is growing rapidly and witnesses huge interest as a game-changer both for HPC as well as ML workloads. Quantum computers use principles of quantum mechanics to perform computations infeasible or impossible with classical computers, with the hope of solving for things that would take years on traditional systems in a matter of minutes. An exponential speed-up is one of the promises of quantum computing, in certain classes of problems, including optimization tasks, which are indeed at the core of many machine learning algorithms. A quantum computer uses qubits, which can represent and process much more complex states than can classical bits, so that many calculations are performed in parallel.

Quantum machine learning (QML) is a very recent area of research which discovers how quantum algorithms can be applied to improve the ML technique. A QML model could speed up tasks, such as training deep neural networks or performing dimensionality reduction or large-scale optimization problems. In the near term HPC systems will be hybrid quantum-classical, meaning that they will combine the best strengths of classical HPC systems with quantum processors for ML workloads. Here specific parts of the computation are done on the quantum processors, such as linear algebra operations or optimization problems, while the remaining workload is done on traditional HPC systems. Despite the promise of quantum computing to ML, challenges abound including those related to error correction, qubit coherence, and designing of quantum algorithms specific to the problems of ML. However, companies such as IBM, Google, and Microsoft are actively developing their quantum systems and making them available through cloud platforms to be experimented by researchers interested in quantum computing for ML.

Energy Efficiency and Green Computing

With further scaling and increased complexity of the ML workloads, energy consumption in HPC systems becomes a challenge of high priority. Very large-scale ML models would directly consume enormous amounts of power while training on a traditional HPC system, also raising environmental concerns and increasing their operational costs. Energy-efficient and environmentally friendly computing practices are new and emerging key priorities in the design of future HPC architectures.

a) Energy-Efficient Hardware: Another important trend is the development of specialized hardware - GPUs, TPUs and FPGAs- optimized to minimize energy usage while still providing large computational power. Accelerators are much less power-hungry compared to traditional CPUs in executing ML workloads and thus are a favored choice in the state-of-the-art HPC systems. Low-power processors and AI chips (such as Apple's Neural Engine) are another trend toward energy efficiency.

b) Dynamic Power Management: Dynamic power management techniques can be increasingly deployed inside modern HPC systems in order to regulate their power usage as per the workload demand. These techniques include voltage scaling, power gating, and dynamic frequency adjustments of the system to make it more capable of running in reduced power activity for activities where full computational capability is not required. This reduces the overall energy footprint of the system without loss of any performance capability.

c) Cooling Solutions: Some of the classical designs for cooling systems used in data centers rely heavily on prevention of overheating. These constitute a large share of energy utilization. Emergent architectures for HPC aim to enable innovative cooling solutions including liquid cooling and immersion cooling. Such cooling solutions can significantly reduce HPC operational costs by reducing reliance on energy-intensive air cooling.

d) Renewable Energy Integration: Another such important green computing element is the integration of renewable energy. Companies have begun using renewable energy sources, such as solar power, wind power, or other renewable energies, to power HPC systems. As well as minimizing carbon footprint related to running big ML workloads, it also aligns with the objectives at the global scale in terms of sustainability.

e) Hardware Inventions: These can be complemented by energy-aware algorithms for ML. These algorithms have to maintain a minimum performance loss while minimizing the energy consumption. Algorithms like sparsity, low-rank approximations, and quantization drastically reduce the computational complexity and energy demands without compromising accuracy in ML models.

f) Carbon Footprint Accountability: Companies and researchers argue that such large training ML models should be tracked and reported. This trend may increase the responsibility of organizations toward adoption of more sustainable practices and investment in energy-efficient infrastructure while containing the adverse environmental impacts of large-scale training.

With an increased requirement of ML, HPC architecture must evolve for the computational and energy-intensive requirements of workloads that would be involved with such workloads. One big trend in shaping the future of HPC for ML is the directions and advancements along memory-centric architectures, quantum computing, and energy-efficient design practices. Not only will they help to foster improvements in performance and scalability provided by HPC systems, but they also advance towards environmental impact reduction for longer-term sustainability and efficiency of HPC.

FUTURE DIRECTIONS IN HPC FOR MACHINE LEARNING

As advances in HPC are integrated with ML, new innovations soon to be heralded are expected to transform this field. Breakthroughs in the realm of distributed systems and hardware accelerators and research opportunities emerging in the context of distributed and heterogeneous computing mark new directions for the future of HPC toward ML. All these breakthroughs are proposed to provide enhancements in performance, scalability, and efficiency as related to the ever-increasing complexity of ML workloads (Ramachandran et al., 2024).

Next-Generation Hardware Accelerators

The increasing demand for faster and more efficient processing of ML workloads has inspired the conception of next-generation hardware accelerators. These accelerators are designed with the potential requirements of deep learning, neural networks, and other ML algorithms in mind (Ramudu et al., 2023).

a) Advanced GPUs: This is because GPUs have been the original accelerators for ML, primarily because they support multithreading. Future GPUs are again devised to support even higher computing and higher bandwidth memory, but in a more energy-efficient way. Technologies such as Multi-Instance GPUs (MIG) allow for the division of a single GPU into multiple instances, thereby enabling the flexible and efficient use of resources in multi-tenanted environments.

b) Next-Generation Tensor Processing Units: TPUs represent specialized accelerators focused on deep learning workloads, Google says. The AI models continue to become bigger, more and more complex, while the new version of TPUs will come with increased speeds and optimized performance for tensor-based computations, which constitutes the very basis of these popular deep learning workloads. Scalability, energy efficiency, and integration into much wider distributed systems are likely to be the focus points of the next generation of TPUs.

c) AI-Specific Chips: Many companies are working on bespoke AI chips that are optimized specifically for ML workloads. Cerebras, Graphcore, and the Intel Nervana, among others, are designed to understand the enormous data and computational needs of deep learning models. AI-specific accelerators may rule the future HPC environment with extreme parallelism and highly optimized ML algorithm performance.

d) Neuromorphic Computing: Inspired by the structure and function of the human brain, neuromorphic chips represent one of the emerging directions in AI hardware. Such chips rely on spiking neural networks (SNNs) to emulate biological neural processes, thus allowing more energy-efficient and parallel computation. The future implementation of neuromorphic computing technology could therefore provide a highly efficient alternative for handling ML tasks in low-power, high-throughput contexts.

Advances in Distributed Computing

Distributed computing will, therefore, be a necessity to scale ML workloads across HPC clusters. Future research in this area will continue to engineer improvements toward better processing efficiency, resource utilization, and load distribution across very large networks(Gopi et al., 2024).

a) Federated Learning: Federated learning, a decentralized method for training ML models where multiple devices or servers contribute for model training without exposing the raw data, improves privacy and saves data transfer cost while distributed resources can be used for training large ML models. Future of federated learning will see more developments toward achievement of efficiency in communication, security, and scalability in distributed environments.

b) Edge Computing: Scaling ML to edge devices including smartphones, sensors, and IoT devices will necessitate further integration of edge computing with central HPC systems. This can be accomplished in distributed computing frameworks where a computation can be performed closer to its data source, thus avoiding more latency and the associated bandwidth cost. Future work will include developing new distributed algorithms to balance optimizations between edge devices and central HPC systems.

c) Enhanced Distributed Frameworks: The existing distributed computing frameworks include Apache Spark, Hadoop, and so on, which are made better from time to time to support workloads in ML. Future versions of distributed computing frameworks will focus more on large-scale data processing better with minimal latencies and overheads. Innovations in the area of distributed frameworks would be focused on the optimization for better utilization of resources and reduced communication bottlenecks in order to increase fault tolerance towards efficient scaling of ML models across multi-node clusters.

d) Autonomous Resource Management: Resources will be allocated completely in real time based on workload demands and managed through even more pervasive automated systems. These will change computing resources based on ML model complexity in real time to optimize performance and energy consumption. AI will play a significantly bigger role in managing distributed systems more intelligently and efficiently with better orchestration tools.

Research Opportunities and Technological Advancements

The intersection of HPC and ML has brought about many new areas for research, bringing exciting technological advancements for future development (Maliṭa et al., 2020; Vasilache et al., 2018).

a) Energy-Efficient Computing: Advances in the amount of required computation in ML models correlate with the exponentially growing energy consumption of HPC systems. Key opportunities include the design of power-efficient algorithms and hardware, as well as data center infrastructure that can harness renewable sources of energy optimally. Innovations include low-power computing, liquid cooling technologies, and developing more sustainable data centers with renewable energy sources.

b) Quantum Computing for ML: Such a quantum computer can lead to revolutionary steps in ML through exponentiating speed-ups in many computations. Research in quantum algorithms for ML has been initiated and is very much in its infancy; exciting prospects include quantum optimization, quantum neural networks. Hybrid quantum-classical systems, such as a quantum processor combined with a traditional HPC system, will unlock new research and possibly practical applications.

c) Interdisciplinary Research: There has been a growing trend of integrating HPC, ML, and other scientific domains. New avenues for breakthroughs are opened up, such as that in genomics, drug discovery, climate modeling, and physics simulations. The interdisciplinary research combines the power of ML applied to the analysis of large datasets and complex simulations; new avenues of solutions for scientific challenges will come across that have been beyond one's reach.

d) Algorithmic Development: Another significant research field is developing more efficient algorithms for ML with fewer computational resources. Methods such as model pruning, quantization, and knowledge distillation can reduce the size and complexity of ML models without any compromise in their accuracy ratings while making them appropriate enough for deployment in some HPC environments, where less resources could be available.

e) Secure and Private ML: Distributed ML systems and federated learning pose increasing research challenges on the security and privacy of data. Techniques like differential privacy, homomorphic encryption, and secure multi-party computation are being explored for protecting sensitive information while efficiently enabling large-scale ML collaboration. Future work here will be about developing robust, scalable mechanisms of privacy preservation for HPC systems.

This means that future HPC systems for machine learning are going to be transformed by next-generation hardware accelerators, innovation in distributed computing, and significantly more advanced research. As ML models keep incresing in scale and complexity, there would be only growing demands for greater efficiency, scalability, and energy considerations in HPC systems. Harnessing developments in hardware, distributed systems, and interdisciplinary research, the future wave of innovations in HPC promises to be an enabler of innovation on what is possible with machine learning, thus revolutionizing breakthroughs in many scientific disciplines and diverse industries.

CONCLUSION

HPC has emerged as a necessary backbone to speed up machine learning workloads, all set to grow exponentially with respect to data complexity and model size. Convergence of HPC and ML will drive breakthroughs in applications such as artificial intelligence, scientific research, and industry-specific applications. Advances in hardware accelerators, including GPUs, TPUs, and other AI-specific chips, coupled with distributed computing frameworks, are pushing the boundaries of scalability and efficiency for HPC-based ML applications.

Nonetheless, there are still many challenges including those about data management, optimum resource utilization, and performance bottlenecks. Sustained innovation, especially in memory-centric architectures and energy-efficient designs, and possibly disruptive technologies like quantum computing, would be needed to deal with these issues. Next-generation hardware accelerators, complex distributed systems, and continued growth in interdisciplinary research will drive the integration of ML with HPC. The increasing complexity within ML models will create new opportunities for handling these models as these fields advance, leading to higher performance, scalability, and energy efficiency in general. It is this integrated direction between HPC and ML that will play a leadership role in shaping the future of various computing-based fields.

REFERENCES

Ahn, S., Kim, J., & Kang, S. (2018). A novel shared memory framework for distributed deep learning in high-performance computing architecture. *Proceedings of the 40th International Conference on Software Engineering: Companion Proceeedings*, 191–192. DOI: 10.1145/3183440.3195091

Ande, J. R. P. K. R., & Khair, M. A. (2019). High-Performance VLSI Architectures for Artificial Intelligence and Machine Learning Applications. *International Journal of Reciprocal Symmetry and Theoretical Physics*, 6(1), 20–30.

Balaprakash, P., Dongarra, J., Gamblin, T., Hall, M., Hollingsworth, J. K., Norris, B., & Vuduc, R. (2018). Autotuning in high-performance computing applications. *Proceedings of the IEEE*, 106(11), 2068–2083. DOI: 10.1109/JPROC.2018.2841200

Bernholdt, D. E., Allan, B. A., Armstrong, R., Bertrand, F., Chiu, K., Dahlgren, T. L., Damevski, K., Elwasif, W. R., Epperly, T. G., Govindaraju, M., Katz, D. S., Kohl, J. A., Krishnan, M., Kumfert, G., Larson, J. W., Lefantzi, S., Lewis, M. J., Malony, A. D., Mclnnes, L. C., & Zhou, S. (2006). A component architecture for high-performance scientific computing. *International Journal of High Performance Computing Applications*, 20(2), 163–202. DOI: 10.1177/1094342006064488

Clevenger, L. A., Eng, H., Khan, K., Maghsoudi, J., & Reid, M. (2015). *Parallel computing hardware and software architectures for high performance computing. Proceedings of Student-Faculty Research Day*. Seidenberg School of CSIS, Pace University.

Correa-Baena, J.-P., Hippalgaonkar, K., van Duren, J., Jaffer, S., Chandrasekhar, V. R., Stevanovic, V., Wadia, C., Guha, S., & Buonassisi, T. (2018). Accelerating materials development via automation, machine learning, and high-performance computing. *Joule*, 2(8), 1410–1420. DOI: 10.1016/j.joule.2018.05.009

Dongarra, J., Sterling, T., Simon, H., & Strohmaier, E. (2005). High-performance computing: Clusters, constellations, MPPs, and future directions. *Computing in Science & Engineering*, 7(2), 51–59. DOI: 10.1109/MCSE.2005.34

Georganas, E., Avancha, S., Banerjee, K., Kalamkar, D., Henry, G., Pabst, H., & Heinecke, A. (2018). Anatomy of high-performance deep learning convolutions on simd architectures. *SC18. International Conference for High Performance Computing, Networking, Storage and Analysis : [proceedings]. SC (Conference : Supercomputing)*, •••, 830–841.

Gopi, B., Sworna Kokila, M. L., Bibin, C. V., Sasikala, D., Howard, E., & Boopathi, S. (2024). Distributed Technologies Using AI/ML Techniques for Healthcare Applications. In *Advances in Human and Social Aspects of Technology* (pp. 375–396). IGI Global. DOI: 10.4018/979-8-3693-2569-8.ch019

Isik, M., Inadagbo, K., & Aktas, H. (2023). Design optimization for high-performance computing using FPGA. *Annual International Conference on Information Management and Big Data*, 142–156. DOI: 10.21203/rs.3.rs-2679691/v1

Kalamkar, D., Georganas, E., Srinivasan, S., Chen, J., Shiryaev, M., & Heinecke, A. (2020). Optimizing deep learning recommender systems training on cpu cluster architectures. *SC20. International Conference for High Performance Computing, Networking, Storage and Analysis : [proceedings]. SC (Conference : Supercomputing)*, ●●●, 1–15.

Li, L., Pandey, S., Flynn, T., Liu, H., Wheeler, N., & Hoisie, A. (2022). Simnet: Accurate and high-performance computer architecture simulation using deep learning. *Proceedings of the ACM on Measurement and Analysis of Computing Systems*, 6(2), 1–24.

Lupión, M., Cruz, N. C., Sanjuan, J. F., Paechter, B., & Ortigosa, P. M. (2023). Accelerating neural network architecture search using multi-GPU high-performance computing. *The Journal of Supercomputing*, 79(7), 7609–7625. DOI: 10.1007/s11227-022-04960-z

Malița, M., Popescu, G. V., & Ştefan, G. M. (2020). Heterogeneous computing system for deep learning. *Deep Learning: Concepts and Architectures*, 287–319.

Muralidhar, R., Borovica-Gajic, R., & Buyya, R. (2022). Energy efficient computing systems: Architectures, abstractions and modeling to techniques and standards. *ACM Computing Surveys*, 54(11s), 1–37. DOI: 10.1145/3511094

Muthukumar, R., & Pratheep, G. V. G., S. J., S., Kunduru, K. R., Kumar, P., & Boopathi, S. (2024). Leveraging Fuel Cell Technology With AI and ML Integration for Next-Generation Vehicles: Empowering Electric Mobility. In *Advances in Mechatronics and Mechanical Engineering* (pp. 312–337). IGI Global. DOI: 10.4018/979-8-3693-5247-2.ch016

Mutlu, O. (2021). Intelligent architectures for intelligent computing systems. *2021 Design, Automation & Test in Europe Conference & Exhibition (DATE)*, 318–323.

Penney, D. D., & Chen, L. (2019). A survey of machine learning applied to computer architecture design. *arXiv Preprint arXiv:1909.12373*.

Ramachandran, S., Jayalal, M., Vasudevan, M., Das, S., & Jehadeesan, R. (2024). Combining machine learning techniques and genetic algorithm for predicting run times of high performance computing jobs. *Applied Soft Computing*, 165, 112053. DOI: 10.1016/j.asoc.2024.112053

Ramesh, R. S. (2024). Scalable Systems and Software Architectures for High-Performance Computing on cloud platforms. *arXiv Preprint arXiv:2408.10281*.

Ramudu, K., Mohan, V. M., Jyothirmai, D., Prasad, D., Agrawal, R., & Boopathi, S. (2023). Machine Learning and Artificial Intelligence in Disease Prediction: Applications, Challenges, Limitations, Case Studies, and Future Directions. In *Contemporary Applications of Data Fusion for Advanced Healthcare Informatics* (pp. 297–318). IGI Global.

Robey, R., & Zamora, Y. (2021). *Parallel and high performance computing*. Simon and Schuster.

Shams, S., Platania, R., Lee, K., & Park, S.-J. (2017). Evaluation of deep learning frameworks over different HPC architectures. *2017 IEEE 37th International Conference on Distributed Computing Systems (ICDCS)*, 1389–1396.

Sterling, T., Brodowicz, M., & Anderson, M. (2017). *High performance computing: Modern systems and practices*. Morgan Kaufmann.

Tuncer, O., Ates, E., Zhang, Y., Turk, A., Brandt, J. M., Leung, V. J., Egele, M., & Coskun, A. K. (2017). Diagnosing Performance Variations in HPC Architectures Using Machine Learning. Sandia National Lab.(SNL-NM), Albuquerque, NM (United States).

Usman, S., Mehmood, R., Katib, I., & Albeshri, A. (2022). Data locality in high performance computing, big data, and converged systems: An analysis of the cutting edge and a future system architecture. *Electronics (Basel)*, 12(1), 53. DOI: 10.3390/electronics12010053

Vasilache, N., Zinenko, O., Theodoridis, T., Goyal, P., DeVito, Z., Moses, W. S., Verdoolaege, S., Adams, A., & Cohen, A. (2018). Tensor comprehensions: Framework-agnostic high-performance machine learning abstractions. *arXiv Preprint arXiv:1802.04730*.

Wang, S., Zheng, H., Wen, X., & Fu, S. (2024). Distributed high-performance computing methods for accelerating deep learning training. *Journal of Knowledge Learning and Science Technology ISSN: 2959-6386 (Online), 3*(3), 108–126.

Wu, N., & Xie, Y. (2022). A survey of machine learning for computer architecture and systems. *ACM Computing Surveys*, 55(3), 1–39. DOI: 10.1145/3494523

Xu, H., Song, S., & Mao, Z. (2024). Characterizing the performance of emerging deep learning, graph, and high performance computing workloads under interference. *2024 IEEE International Parallel and Distributed Processing Symposium Workshops (IPDPSW)*, 468–477. DOI: 10.1109/IPDPSW63119.2024.00098

ADDITIONAL READINGS

Chandra, S., Ghule, G., Bilfaqih, S. M., Thiyagarajan, A., Sharmila, J., & Boopathi, S. (2024). Adaptive Strategies in Online Marketing Using Machine Learning Techniques. In Digital Transformation Initiatives for Agile Marketing (pp. 67–100). IGI Global. DOI: 10.4018/979-8-3693-4466-8.ch004

Ingle, R. B., Swathi, S., Mahendran, G., Senthil, T., Muralidharan, N., & Boopathi, S. (2023). Sustainability and Optimization of Green and Lean Manufacturing Processes Using Machine Learning Techniques. In Circular Economy Implementation for Sustainability in the Built Environment (pp. 261–285). IGI Global. DOI: 10.4018/978-1-6684-8238-4.ch012

Maheswari, B. U., Imambi, S. S., Hasan, D., Meenakshi, S., Pratheep, V., & Boopathi, S. (2023). Internet of things and machine learning-integrated smart robotics. In Global Perspectives on Robotics and Autonomous Systems: Development and Applications (pp. 240–258). IGI Global. DOI: 10.4018/978-1-6684-7791-5.ch010

Prasad, M. S. C., Dhanalakshmi, M., Mohan, M., Somasundaram, B., Valarmathi, R., & Boopathi, S. (2024). Machine Learning-Integrated Sustainable Engineering and Energy Systems: Innovations at the Nexus. In Harnessing High-Performance Computing and AI for Environmental Sustainability (pp. 74–98). IGI Global. DOI: 10.4018/979-8-3693-1794-5.ch004

Ramudu, K., Mohan, V. M., Jyothirmai, D., Prasad, D., Agrawal, R., & Boopathi, S. (2023). Machine Learning and Artificial Intelligence in Disease Prediction: Applications, Challenges, Limitations, Case Studies, and Future Directions. In Contemporary Applications of Data Fusion for Advanced Healthcare Informatics (pp. 297–318). IGI Global.

Tirlangi, S., Teotia, S., Padmapriya, G., Senthil Kumar, S., Dhotre, S., & Boopathi, S. (2024). Cloud Computing and Machine Learning in the Green Power Sector: Data Management and Analysis for Sustainable Energy. In Developments Towards Next Generation Intelligent Systems for Sustainable Development (pp. 148–179). IGI Global. DOI: 10.4018/979-8-3693-5643-2.ch006

Veeranjaneyulu, R., Boopathi, S., Narasimharao, J., Gupta, K. K., Reddy, R. V. K., & Ambika, R. (2023). Identification of Heart Diseases using Novel Machine Learning Method. IEEE- Explore, 1–6.

Verma, R., Christiana, M. B. V., Maheswari, M., Srinivasan, V., Patro, P., Dari, S. S., & Boopathi, S. (2024). Intelligent Physarum Solver for Profit Maximization in Oligopolistic Supply Chain Networks. In AI and Machine Learning Impacts in Intelligent Supply Chain (pp. 156–179). IGI Global. DOI: 10.4018/979-8-3693-1347-3.ch011

KEY TERMS AND DEFINITIONS

CNN: Convolutional Neural Network. A CNN is a deep learning model designed for processing structured grid data, such as images. It uses convolutional layers to automatically detect patterns like edges, textures, and shapes, which are then used for tasks like classification and recognition. CNNs are widely used in computer vision, natural language processing, and other tasks requiring pattern recognition.

CUDA: Compute Unified Device Architecture. CUDA is a parallel computing platform and programming model developed by NVIDIA for utilizing GPUs for general-purpose computing. It allows developers to write programs that run on NVIDIA GPUs, accelerating computationally intensive tasks. CUDA is widely used in fields like machine learning, scientific computing, and graphics rendering to leverage the massive parallel processing power of GPUs.

FPGA: Field-Programmable Gate Array. FPGA is an integrated circuit that can be configured after manufacturing to perform specific tasks or algorithms. Unlike fixed-function hardware, FPGAs allow users to reprogram the hardware to meet changing requirements or optimize performance. They are widely used in applications requiring high-speed processing, such as telecommunications, cryptography, and embedded systems.

GPFS: General Parallel File System. GPFSis a high-performance, shared-disk file system designed for handling large-scale data across multiple nodes in a cluster. It provides parallel access to files, ensuring high throughput and low-latency performance. GPFS is used in environments that require fast data processing, such as scientific research, data analytics, and high-performance computing.

GPU: Graphics Processing Unit. A GPU is a specialized processor designed to handle complex graphical computations and rendering tasks. It excels at parallel processing, making it ideal for applications like gaming, 3D rendering, and scientific simulations. GPUs are also increasingly used in AI and machine learning for their ability to accelerate large-scale data processing tasks.

HDFS: Hadoop Distributed File System. HDFS is a distributed storage system designed to store large volumes of data across multiple machines. It splits data into blocks and replicates them across different nodes to ensure fault tolerance and high availability. HDFS is optimized for high-throughput access to large datasets, making it ideal for big data processing frameworks like Hadoop.

MIG: Multi-Instance GPU. This is is a technology that allows a single GPU to be partitioned into multiple smaller, isolated instances. Each instance can run independently, with its own dedicated resources like memory and compute cores.

MPI: Message Passing Interface. MPI is a standardized communication protocol that enables processes to exchange data in parallel computing environments. It allows processes running on different nodes or machines to send and receive messages, facilitating coordination and synchronization in distributed systems. MPI is widely used in high-performance computing (HPC) applications to achieve scalable and efficient parallelism.

QML: Quantum Machine Learning. QML combines quantum computing and classical machine learning to enhance computational power and efficiency. It leverages quantum algorithms to potentially accelerate tasks like optimization, pattern recognition, and data analysis.

RDD: Resilient Distributed Dataset. This is a fault-tolerant, distributed collection of data in Apache Spark. It allows for parallel processing across multiple nodes while maintaining data integrity through lineage information, which helps recover lost data.

SNN: Spiking Neural Network. SNN is a type of artificial neural network that mimics the behavior of biological neurons, using discrete spikes or pulses to encode and transmit information. Unlike traditional neural networks, SNNs process information through time-based events, capturing the temporal dynamics of signals. They are often used in neuromorphic computing and applications requiring energy-efficient processing or real-time sensory data analysis.

TPU: Tensor Processing Unit. A TPU is a specialized accelerator designed by Google for efficient machine learning and deep learning tasks. It is optimized for high-throughput tensor computations, particularly those used in neural network training and inference. TPUs provide significant performance gains over general-purpose CPUs and GPUs for AI workloads, particularly in Google's cloud infrastructure

Compilation of References

Abad, C., Foster, I. T., Herbst, N., & Iosup, A. (n.d.). *Serverless Computing*. 60.

Abadi, M., Barham, P., Chen, J., Chen, Z., Davis, A., Dean, J., Devin, M., Ghemawat, S., Irving, G., Isard, M., Kudlur, M., Levenberg, J., Monga, R., Moore, S., Murray, D. G., Steiner, B., Tucker, P., Vasudevan, V., Warden, P., … Zheng, X. (n.d.). *TensorFlow: A system for large-scale machine learning*. 21.

Abdelaziz, A., Elhoseny, M., Salama, A. S., & Riad, A. M. (2018). A machine learning model for improving healthcare services in cloud computing environment. *Measurement*, 119, 117–128. DOI: 10.1016/j.measurement.2018.01.022

Adayel, R., Bazi, Y., Alhichri, H., & Alajlan, N. (2020). Deep Open-Set Domain Adaptation for Cross-Scene Classification based on Adversarial Learning and Pareto Ranking. *Remote Sensing (Basel)*, 12(11), 11. Advance online publication. DOI: 10.3390/rs12111716

Adek, R. T., & Ula, M. (2020). A Survey on The Accuracy of Machine Learning Techniques for Intrusion and Anomaly Detection on Public Data Sets. *2020 International Conference on Data Science, Artificial Intelligence, and Business Analytics (DATABIA)*. DOI: 10.1109/DATABIA50434.2020.9190436

Aggarwal, C. C. (2018). *Neural networks and deep learning* (Vol. 10, No. 978, p. 3). Cham: springer.

Aghabali, I., Bauman, J., Kollmeyer, P. J., Wang, Y., Bilgin, B., & Emadi, A. (2020a). 800-V electric vehicle powertrains: Review and analysis of benefits, challenges, and future trends. *IEEE Transactions on Transportation Electrification*, 7(3), 927–948. DOI: 10.1109/TTE.2020.3044938

Ahad, M. A. R., Antar, A. D., & Shahid, O. (2019). Vision-based Action Understanding for Assistive Healthcare: A Short Review. *CVPR Workshops*, 1–11.

Ahamed, B. S., Chakravarthy, K. S., Arputhabalan, J., Sasirekha, K., Prince, R. M. R., Boopathi, S., & Muthuvel, S. (2024). Revolutionizing Friction Stir Welding With AI-Integrated Humanoid Robots. In *Advances in Computational Intelligence and Robotics* (pp. 120–144). IGI Global. DOI: 10.4018/979-8-3693-2399-1.ch005

Ahmad, A., Roslan, M. F., & Amira, A. (2017). Throughput, latency and cost comparisons of micro-controller-based implementations of wireless sensor network (WSN) in high jump sports. *AIP Conference Proceedings*, 1883(1), 020010. DOI: 10.1063/1.5002028

Ahmed, K., & Liu, J. (2019). Simulation of energy-efficient demand response for high performance computing systems. *2019 Winter Simulation Conference (WSC)*, 2560–2571. DOI: 10.1109/WSC40007.2019.9004781

Ahn, S., Kim, J., & Kang, S. (2018). A novel shared memory framework for distributed deep learning in high-performance computing architecture. *Proceedings of the 40th International Conference on Software Engineering: Companion Proceeedings*, 191–192. DOI: 10.1145/3183440.3195091

Akkus, I. E., Chen, R., Rimac, I., Stein, M., Satzke, K., Beck, A., Aditya, P., & Hilt, V. (2018). *{SAND}: Towards {High-Performance} Serverless Computing*. 923–935. https://www.usenix.org/conference/atc18/presentation/akkus

Aksonov, Y., Kombarov, V., Tsegelnyk, Y., Plankovskyy, S., Fojtů, O., & Piddubna, L. (2021). Visualization and analysis of technological systems experimental operating results. In *2021 IEEE 16th International Conference on Computer Sciences and Information Technologies (CSIT)* (Vol. 2, pp. 141–146). IEEE. DOI: 10.1109/CSIT52700.2021.9648592

Aksonov, Y., Kombarov, V., Fojtů, O., Sorokin, V., & Kryzhyvets, Y. (2019). Investigation of processes in high-speed equipment using CNC capabilities. *MM Science Journal*, 2019(04), 3271–3276. DOI: 10.17973/MMSJ.2019_11_2019081

Al Mamun, S., Kaiser, M. S., & Mahmud, M. (2021). An artificial intelligence based approach towards inclusive healthcare provisioning in society 5.0: A perspective on brain disorder. *International Conference on Brain Informatics*, 157–169. DOI: 10.1007/978-3-030-86993-9_15

Aladag, C. H., Egrioglu, E., & Yolcu, U. (2014). Robust multilayer neural network based on median neuron model. *Neural Computing & Applications*, 24(3-4), 945–956. DOI: 10.1007/s00521-012-1315-5

Alajaji, D., Alhichri, H. S., Ammour, N., & Alajlan, N. (2020). Few-Shot Learning For Remote Sensing Scene Classification. *2020 Mediterranean and Middle-East Geoscience and Remote Sensing Symposium (M2GARSS)*, 81–84. DOI: 10.1109/M2GARSS47143.2020.9105154

Al-Ali, Z., Goodarzy, S., Hunter, E., Ha, S., Han, R., Keller, E., & Rozner, E. (2018). Making Serverless Computing More Serverless. *2018 IEEE 11th International Conference on Cloud Computing (CLOUD)*, 456–459. DOI: 10.1109/CLOUD.2018.00064

Alawneh, S. G., Zeng, L., & Arefifar, S. A. (2023). A Review of High-Performance Computing Methods for Power Flow Analysis. *Mathematics*, 11(11), 2461. DOI: 10.3390/math11112461

Al-Dhaher, A. (2004). Development of Microcontroller/FPGA-based systems. *International Journal of Engineering Education*, 20(1), 52–60.

Alem, A., & Kumar, S. (2022). End-to-End Convolutional Neural Network Feature Extraction for Remote Sensed Images Classification. *Applied Artificial Intelligence*, 36(1), 2137650. DOI: 10.1080/08839514.2022.2137650

Alfons, A., Croux, C., & Gelper, S. (2013). Sparse least trimmed squares regression for analyzing high-dimensional large data sets. *The Annals of Applied Statistics*, 7(1), 226–248. DOI: 10.1214/12-AOAS575

Ali, M., Naeem, F., Tariq, M., & Kaddoum, G. (2022). Federated learning for privacy preservation in smart healthcare systems: A comprehensive survey. *IEEE Journal of Biomedical and Health Informatics*, 27(2), 778–789. DOI: 10.1109/JBHI.2022.3181823 PMID: 35696470

Alsalemi, A., Amira, A., Malekmohamadi, H., Diao, K., & Bensaali, F. (2021). *Elevating Energy Data Analysis with M2GAF: Micro-Moment Driven Gramian Angular Field Visualizations*. International Conference on Applied Energy. https://dora.dmu.ac.uk/handle/2086/21303

Alsalemi, A., Himeur, Y., Bensaali, F., Amira, A., Sardianos, C., Chronis, C., Varlamis, I., & Dimitrakopoulos, G. (2020). A Micro-Moment System for Domestic Energy Efficiency Analysis. *IEEE Systems Journal*, •••, 1–8. DOI: 10.1109/JSYST.2020.2997773

Alsalemi, A., Ramadan, M., Bensaali, F., Amira, A., Sardianos, C., Varlamis, I., & Dimitrakopoulos, G. (2019). Endorsing domestic energy saving behavior using micro-moment classification. *Applied Energy*, 250, 1302–1311. DOI: 10.1016/j.apenergy.2019.05.089

Alsenan, A., Ben Youssef, B., & Alhichri, H. (2022). Mobileunetv3—A combined unet and mobilenetv3 architecture for spinal cord gray matter segmentation. *Electronics (Basel)*, 11(15), 2388. DOI: 10.3390/electronics11152388

Aluru, S. S., Mathew, B., Saha, P., & Mukherjee, A. (2020). Deep learning models for multilingual hate speech detection. *arXiv preprint arXiv:2004.06465*.

Al-Zahrani, A. M. (2015). Cyberbullying among Saudi's Higher-Education Students: Implications for Educators and Policymakers. *World Journal of Education*, 5(3), 15–26. DOI: 10.5430/wje.v5n3p15

Ammour, N., Bashmal, L., Bazi, Y., Al Rahhal, M. M., & Zuair, M. (2018). Asymmetric Adaptation of Deep Features for Cross-Domain Classification in Remote Sensing Imagery. *IEEE Geoscience and Remote Sensing Letters*, 15(4), 597–601. DOI: 10.1109/LGRS.2018.2800642

Ande, J. R. P. K. R., & Khair, M. A. (2019). High-Performance VLSI Architectures for Artificial Intelligence and Machine Learning Applications. *International Journal of Reciprocal Symmetry and Theoretical Physics*, 6(1), 20–30.

Anderson, J. A., Glaser, J., & Glotzer, S. C. (2020). HOOMD-blue: A Python package for high-performance molecular dynamics and hard particle Monte Carlo simulations. *Computational Materials Science*, 173, 109363. DOI: 10.1016/j.commatsci.2019.109363

Anderson, M. (2018). *A majority of teens have experienced some form of cyberbullying*. Pew Research Center.

Ansys. (2011). *User's Guide – Maxwell 2D*. Ansys Inc.

Aravind, C. V., Grace, I., Rozita, T., Rajparthiban, R., Rajprasad, R., & Wong, Y. V. (2012). Universal computer aided design for electrical machines. In *2012 IEEE 8th International Colloquium on Signal Processing and its Applications* (pp. 99–104). IEEE. DOI: 10.1109/CSPA.2012.6194699

Arnoux, P. H., Caillard, P., & Gillon, F. (2015). Modeling finite-element constraint to run an electrical machine design optimization using machine learning. *IEEE Transactions on Magnetics*, 51(3), 7402504. DOI: 10.1109/TMAG.2014.2364031

Awwad, A. E., Al-Quteimat, A., Al-Suod, M., Ushkarenko, O. O., & AlHawamleh, A. (2021). Improving the accuracy of the active power load sharing in paralleled generators in the presence of drive motors shaft speed instability. *International Journal of Electronics and Telecommunications*, 67(3), 371–377. DOI: 10.24425/ijet.2021.137822

Ayesha, S., Hanif, M. K., & Talib, R. (2020). Overview and comparative study of dimensionality reduction techniques for high dimensional data. *Information Fusion*, 59, 44–58. DOI: 10.1016/j.inffus.2020.01.005

Babu, B. S., Kamalakannan, J., Meenatchi, N., Karthik, S., & Boopathi, S. (2022). Economic impacts and reliability evaluation of battery by adopting Electric Vehicle. *IEEE Explore*, 1–6.

Babuji, Y., Woodard, A., Li, Z., Katz, D. S., Clifford, B., Kumar, R., Lacinski, L., Chard, R., Wozniak, J. M., Foster, I., Wilde, M., & Chard, K. (2019). Parsl: Pervasive Parallel Programming in Python. *Proceedings of the 28th International Symposium on High-Performance Parallel and Distributed Computing*, 25–36. DOI: 10.1145/3307681.3325400

Back, T. (1996). *Evolutionary Algorithms in Theory and Practice: Evolution Strategies, Evolutionary Programming, Genetic Algorithms*. Oxford University Press. DOI: 10.1093/oso/9780195099713.001.0001

Ba, L. J., & Caruana, R. (2014). Do deep nets really need to be deep? *Advances in Neural Information Processing Systems*.

Balachandran, P. V. (2020). Adaptive machine learning for efficient materials design. *MRS Bulletin*, 45(7), 579–586. DOI: 10.1557/mrs.2020.163

Balaprakash, P., Dongarra, J., Gamblin, T., Hall, M., Hollingsworth, J. K., Norris, B., & Vuduc, R. (2018). Autotuning in high-performance computing applications. *Proceedings of the IEEE*, 106(11), 2068–2083. DOI: 10.1109/JPROC.2018.2841200

Bashir, A. K., Victor, N., Bhattacharya, S., Huynh-The, T., Chengoden, R., Yenduri, G., Maddikunta, P. K. R., Pham, Q.-V., Gadekallu, T. R., & Liyanage, M. (2023). Federated learning for the healthcare metaverse: Concepts, applications, challenges, and future directions. *IEEE Internet of Things Journal*, 10(24), 21873–21891. DOI: 10.1109/JIOT.2023.3304790

Bashmal, L., Bazi, Y., AlHichri, H., AlRahhal, M. M., Ammour, N., & Alajlan, N. (2018). Siamese-GAN: Learning Invariant Representations for Aerial Vehicle Image Categorization. *Remote Sensing (Basel)*, 10(2), 2. Advance online publication. DOI: 10.3390/rs10020351

Behera, R. K., Bala, P. K., & Dhir, A. (2019). The emerging role of cognitive computing in healthcare: A systematic literature review. *International Journal of Medical Informatics*, 129, 154–166. DOI: 10.1016/j.ijmedinf.2019.04.024 PMID: 31445250

Ben Ismail, M. M. (2020). Insult detection using a partitional CNN-LSTM model. *Computer Science and Information Technology*, 1(2), 84–92.

Ben Youssef, B., Alhmidi, L., Bazi, Y., & Zuair, M. (2024). Federated Learning Approach for Remote Sensing Scene Classification. *Remote Sensing (Basel)*, 16(12), 2194. DOI: 10.3390/rs16122194

Benamimour, T., Bentounsi, A., & Djeghloud, H. (2013). CAD of electrical machines using coupled FEMM-MATLAB softwares. In *2013 3rd International Conference on Electric Power and Energy Conversion Systems* (pp. 1–6). IEEE. DOI: 10.1109/EPECS.2013.6712995

Bengfort, B., Bilbro, R., & Ojeda, T. (2018). *Applied text analysis with Python: Enabling language-aware data products with machine learning*. O'Reilly Media, Inc.

Benjamini, Y., & Hochberg, Y. (1995). Controlling the false discovery rate: A practical and powerful approach to multiple testing. *Journal of the Royal Statistical Society. Series B, Statistical Methodology*, 57(1), 289–300. DOI: 10.1111/j.2517-6161.1995.tb02031.x

Benjamini, Y., & Yekutieli, D. (2001). The control of the false discovery rate in multiple testing under dependency. *Annals of Statistics*, 29(4), 1165–1188. DOI: 10.1214/aos/1013699998

Bernholdt, D. E., Allan, B. A., Armstrong, R., Bertrand, F., Chiu, K., Dahlgren, T. L., Damevski, K., Elwasif, W. R., Epperly, T. G., Govindaraju, M., Katz, D. S., Kohl, J. A., Krishnan, M., Kumfert, G., Larson, J. W., Lefantzi, S., Lewis, M. J., Malony, A. D., Mclnnes, L. C., & Zhou, S. (2006). A component architecture for high-performance scientific computing. *International Journal of High Performance Computing Applications*, 20(2), 163–202. DOI: 10.1177/1094342006064488

Bhattacharya, T., Brettin, T., Doroshow, J. H., Evrard, Y. A., Greenspan, E. J., Gryshuk, A. L., Hoang, T. T., Lauzon, C. B. V., Nissley, D., Penberthy, L., Stahlberg, E., Stevens, R., Streitz, F., Tourassi, G., Xia, F., & Zaki, G. (2019). AI meets exascale computing: Advancing cancer research with large-scale high performance computing. *Frontiers in Oncology*, 9, 984. DOI: 10.3389/fonc.2019.00984 PMID: 31632915

Blazques, D., & Domenech, J. (2018). Big Data sources and methods for social and economic analyses. *Technological Forecasting and Social Change*, 130, 99–113. DOI: 10.1016/j.techfore.2017.07.027

Bonneel, P., Le Besnerais, J., Pile, R., & Devillers, E. (2018). Pyleecan: an open-source Python object-oriented software for the multiphysic design optimization of electrical machines. In *2018 XIII International Conference on Electrical Machines (ICEM)* (pp. 948–954). IEEE. DOI: 10.1109/ICEL-MACH.2018.8506884

Boopathi, S. (2024). Advancements in Optimizing Smart Energy Systems Through Smart Grid Integration, Machine Learning, and IoT. In *Advances in Environmental Engineering and Green Technologies* (pp. 33–61). IGI Global. DOI: 10.4018/979-8-3693-0492-1.ch002

Boopathi, S., Ananth, J., Raghuram, K. S., Kistan, A., Velumani, M., & Gopinathan, R. (2024, January). *6342734- Machine for Analysis of the resistance of welded parts by the electrical resistance process.*

BOOPATHI, S., KARTHIKEYAN, K. R., JAISWAL, C., DABI, R., SUNAGAR, P., & MALIK, S. (2024). *IoT based Automatic Cooling Tower.*

Boopathi, S. (2024). Influences of nano-green lubricants on the performance of grinding machining process. In *Lecture Notes in Mechanical Engineering* (pp. 45–53). Springer Nature Singapore.

Boopathi, S., & Kanike, U. K. (2023). Applications of Artificial Intelligent and Machine Learning Techniques in Image Processing. In *Handbook of Research on Thrust Technologies' Effect on Image Processing* (pp. 151–173). IGI Global. DOI: 10.4018/978-1-6684-8618-4.ch010

Boopathi, S., Saranya, A., Raghuraman, S., & Revanth, R. (2018). Design and Fabrication of Low Cost Electric Bicycle. *International Research Journal of Engineering and Technology*, 5(3), 146–147.

Bouhamed, O. (2022a). *AI-Powered Time Series Forecasting Frameworks For Building Energy Management Systems* [PhD Thesis]. Concordia University.

Bouhamed, O. (2022b). *AI-Powered Time Series Forecasting Frameworks For Building Energy Management Systems* [PhD Thesis]. Concordia University.

Boyd, S., Parikh, N., Chu, E., Peleato, B., & Eckstein, J. (2010). Distributed optimization and statistical learning via the alternating direction method of multipliers. In *Foundations and Trends in Machine Learning* (Vol. 3, Issue 1, pp. 1–122). DOI: 10.1561/9781601984616

Bradlow, E. T., Gangwar, M., Kopalle, P., & Voleti, S. (2017). The role of Big Data and predictive analytics in retailing. *Journal of Retailing*, 93(1), 79–95. DOI: 10.1016/j.jretai.2016.12.004

Bramerdorfer, G., Tapia, J. A., Pyrhönen, J. J., & Cavagnino, A. (2018). Modern electrical machine design optimization: Techniques, trends, and best practices. *IEEE Transactions on Industrial Electronics*, 65(10), 7672–7684. DOI: 10.1109/TIE.2018.2801805

Brayford, D., Vallecorsa, S., Atanasov, A., Baruffa, F., & Riviera, W. (2019). Deploying AI frameworks on secure HPC systems with containers. *2019 Ieee High Performance Extreme Computing Conference (Hpec)*, 1–6. DOI: 10.1109/HPEC.2019.8916576

Bridge, J. & Dodds, J.C. (2019). Managerial decision making. Routledge, Abingdon-on-Thames.

Bucaioni, A. (2019). Boosting the development of high-performance automotive systems. *Junior Researcher Community Event at Software Technologies: Applications and Foundations 2019 STAF-JRC19.*

Bučková, B., Brunovský, M., Bareš, M., & Hlinka, J. (2020). Predicting sex from EEG: Validity and generalizability of deep-learning-based interpretable classifier. *Frontiers in Neuroscience*, 14, 589303. DOI: 10.3389/fnins.2020.589303 PMID: 33192274

Buhr, K., Fajtl, R., Lettl, J., & Plyugin, V. (2014). Electromobile drive diagnostics and property prediction. In *XX International Symposium on Electric Machinery* (pp. 38–44).

Bui, N., Truong, H., Nguyen, A., Ashok, A., Nguyen, P., Dinh, T., Deterding, R., & Vu, T. (2017). PhO2: Smartphone based Blood Oxygen Level Measurement Systems using Near-IR and RED Wave-guided Light. *SenSys 2017 - Proceedings of the 15th ACM Conference on Embedded Networked Sensor Systems*. DOI: 10.1145/3131672.3131696

Burkov, A. (2019). *The hundred-page machine learning book* (Vol. 1). Andriy Burkov.

Cai, H., Zhu, L., & Han, S. (2019). Proxylessnas: Direct neural architecture search on target task and hardware. *7th International Conference on Learning Representations, ICLR 2019*, 1–13.

Canziani, A., Culurciello, E., & Paszke, A. (n.d.). *AN ANALYSIS OF DEEP NEURAL NETWORK MODELS FOR PRACTICAL APPLICATIONS.*

Castiglia, V., Ciotta, P., Di Tommaso, A., Miceli, R., & Nevoloso, C. (2018). High performance foc for induction motors with low cost atsam3x8e microcontroller. *2018 7th International Conference on Renewable Energy Research and Applications (ICRERA)*, 1495–1500.

Cathey, J. J. (2001). *Electric Machines: Analysis and Design Applying Mathlab*. McGraw-Hil.

CDCP. (2021), "Adult Obesity Causes & Consequenc-es," Centers for Disease control and prevention, Mar. 22, 2021. https://www.cdc.gov/obesity/adult/causes.html

Chaddad, A., Lu, Q., Li, J., Katib, Y., Kateb, R., Tanougast, C., Bouridane, A., & Abdulkadir, A. (2023). Explainable, domain-adaptive, and federated artificial intelligence in medicine. *IEEE/CAA Journal of Automatica Sinica, 10*(4), 859–876.

Chandra, S., Ghule, G., Bilfaqih, S. M., Thiyagarajan, A., Sharmila, J., & Boopathi, S. (2024). Adaptive Strategies in Online Marketing Using Machine Learning Techniques. In *Digital Transformation Initiatives for Agile Marketing* (pp. 67–100). IGI Global., DOI: 10.4018/979-8-3693-4466-8.ch004

Chandrika, V., Sivakumar, A., Krishnan, T. S., Pradeep, J., Manikandan, S., & Boopathi, S. (2023). Theoretical Study on Power Distribution Systems for Electric Vehicles. In *Intelligent Engineering Applications and Applied Sciences for Sustainability* (pp. 1–19). IGI Global. DOI: 10.4018/979-8-3693-0044-2.ch001

Chappel, D. (2015). *Introduction Azure Machine Learning: a Guide for Technical Professionals*. Chappel & Associates.

Chaudhari, S., Mithal, V., Polatkan, G., & Ramanath, R. (2021). An attentive survey of attention models. [TIST]. *ACM Transactions on Intelligent Systems and Technology*, 12(5), 1–32. DOI: 10.1145/3465055

Chawla J and M. Wagner, (2016), "Using Machine Learning Techniques for User Specific Ac-tivity Recognition," Frankfurt University of Applied Science, May 2016, Accessed: Mar. 28, 2022. [Online].

CHEN, J., & WANG, X. (2022). Non-intrusive Load Monitoring Using Gramian Angular Field Color Encoding in Edge Computing. *Chinese Journal of Electronics*, 31(4), 1–9.

Chen, C., Nguyen, D. T., Lee, S. J., Baker, N. A., Karakoti, A. S., Lauw, L., Owen, C., Mueller, K. T., Bilodeau, B. A., Murugesan, V., & Troyer, M. (2024). Accelerating Computational Materials Discovery with Machine Learning and Cloud High-Performance Computing: From Large-Scale Screening to Experimental Validation. *Journal of the American Chemical Society*, 146(29), 20009–20018. DOI: 10.1021/jacs.4c03849 PMID: 38980280

Cheng, Y., Wang, D., Zhou, P., & Zhang, T. (2017). *A Survey of Model Compression and Acceleration for Deep Neural Networks*. 1–10.

Cheng, G., Han, J., & Lu, X. (2017). Remote sensing image scene classification: Benchmark and state of the art. *Proceedings of the IEEE*, 105(10), 1865–1883. DOI: 10.1109/JPROC.2017.2675998

Cheng, G., Xie, X., Han, J., Guo, L., & Xia, G.-S. (2020). Remote Sensing Image Scene Classification Meets Deep Learning: Challenges, Methods, Benchmarks, and Opportunities. *IEEE Journal of Selected Topics in Applied Earth Observations and Remote Sensing*, 13, 3735–3756. DOI: 10.1109/JSTARS.2020.3005403

Cheng, M., Han, P., & Hua, W. (2017). General airgap field modulation theory for electrical machines. *IEEE Transactions on Industrial Electronics*, 64(8), 6063–6074. DOI: 10.1109/TIE.2017.2682792

Chen, M., Shlezinger, N., Poor, H. V., Eldar, Y. C., & Cui, S. (2021). Communication-efficient federated learning. *Proceedings of the National Academy of Sciences of the United States of America*, 118(17), e2024789118. DOI: 10.1073/pnas.2024789118 PMID: 33888586

Chen, S., Wang, J., & He, K. (2024). Chinese Cyberbullying Detection Using XLNet and Deep Bi-LSTM Hybrid Model. *Information (Basel)*, 15(2), 93. DOI: 10.3390/info15020093

Chen, T., Li, M., Li, Y., Lin, M., Wang, N., Wang, M., Xiao, T., Xu, B., Zhang, C., & Zhang, Z. (2015). MXNet: A Flexible and Efficient Machine Learning Library for Heterogeneous Distributed Systems. *ArXiv:1512.01274[Cs]*. http://arxiv.org/abs/1512.01274

Chen, W., Ouyang, S., Tong, W., Li, X., Zheng, X., & Wang, L. (2022). GCSANet: A global context spatial attention deep learning network for remote sensing scene classification. *IEEE Journal of Selected Topics in Applied Earth Observations and Remote Sensing*, 15, 1150–1162. DOI: 10.1109/JSTARS.2022.3141826

Chen, W., Wilson, J. T., Tyree, S., Weinberger, K. Q., & Chen, Y. (2015). Compressing neural networks with the hashing trick. *32nd International Conference on Machine Learning, ICML 2015, 3*, 2275–2284.

Chen, X., Proietti, R., Fariborz, M., Liu, C.-Y., & Yoo, S. B. (2021). Machine-learning-aided cognitive reconfiguration for flexible-bandwidth HPC and data center networks. *Journal of Optical Communications and Networking*, 13(6), C10–C20. DOI: 10.1364/JOCN.412360

Chen, Y. H., Krishna, T., Emer, J. S., & Sze, V. (2017). Eyeriss: An Energy-Efficient Reconfigurable Accelerator for Deep Convolutional Neural Networks. *IEEE Journal of Solid-State Circuits*, 52(1), 127–138. Advance online publication. DOI: 10.1109/JSSC.2016.2616357

Chen, Y. H., Yang, T. J., Emer, J. S., & Sze, V. (2019). Eyeriss v2: A Flexible Accelerator for Emerging Deep Neural Networks on Mobile Devices. *IEEE Journal on Emerging and Selected Topics in Circuits and Systems*, 9(2), 292–308. Advance online publication. DOI: 10.1109/JETCAS.2019.2910232

Chi, M., Plaza, A., Benediktsson, J. A., Sun, Z., Shen, J., & Zhu, Y. (2016). Big Data for Remote Sensing: Challenges and Opportunities. *Proceedings of the IEEE*, 104(11), 2207–2219. DOI: 10.1109/JPROC.2016.2598228

Choi, B., & Kim, Y. S. (2021). New structure design of ferrite cores for wireless EV charging by machine learning. *IEEE Transactions on Industrial Electronics*, 68(12), 12162–12172. DOI: 10.1109/TIE.2020.3047041

Chollet, F. (2015). Keras. Github repository. [https://github.com/fchollet/keras]

Chollet, F. (2017). Xception: Deep learning with depthwise separable convolutions. *Proceedings - 30th IEEE Conference on Computer Vision and Pattern Recognition, CVPR 2017, 2017-Janua*, 1800–1807. DOI: 10.1109/CVPR.2017.195

Chollet, F. (2018). *Deep learning with Python*. Manning Publications Co.

Ciabattoni, L., Comodi, G., Ferracuti, F., & Foresi, G. (2020). Ai-powered home electrical appliances as enabler of demand-side flexibility. *IEEE Consumer Electronics Magazine*, 9(3), 72–78. DOI: 10.1109/ MCE.2019.2956197

Cioffi, R., Travaglioni, M., Piscitelli, G., Petrillo, A., & De Felice, F. (2020). Artificial intelligence and machine learning applications in smart production: Progress, trends, and directions. *Sustainability (Basel)*, 12(2), 492. DOI: 10.3390/su12020492

Clerbaux, B., Molla, M. C., Petitjean, P.-A., Xu, Y., & Yang, Y. (2021). Study of using machine learning for level 1 trigger decision in JUNO experiment. *IEEE Transactions on Nuclear Science*, 68(8), 2187–2193. DOI: 10.1109/TNS.2021.3085428

Cleveland clinic. (2019), "Aerobic Exercise Health Information | Cleveland Clinic," Cleveland Clinic, Jul. 16, 2019. https://my.clevelandclinic.org/health/articles/7050-aerobic-exercise

Clevenger, L. A., Eng, H., Khan, K., Maghsoudi, J., & Reid, M. (2015). *Parallel computing hardware and software architectures for high performance computing. Proceedings of Student-Faculty Research Day*. Seidenberg School of CSIS, Pace University.

Collier, M., & Shahan, R. (2015). *Microsoft Azure Essentials – Fundamentals of Azure*. Microsoft Press.

Corcoran, L., & McGuckin, C. (2014). Addressing bullying problems in Irish schools and in cyberspace: A challenge for school management. *Educational Research*, 56(1), 48–64. DOI: 10.1080/00131881.2013.874150

Correa-Baena, J.-P., Hippalgaonkar, K., van Duren, J., Jaffer, S., Chandrasekhar, V. R., Stevanovic, V., Wadia, C., Guha, S., & Buonassisi, T. (2018). Accelerating materials development via automation, machine learning, and high-performance computing. *Joule*, 2(8), 1410–1420. DOI: 10.1016/j.joule.2018.05.009

Crepaldi, M., Merello, A., & Di Salvo, M. (2021). A multi-one instruction set computer for microcontroller applications. *IEEE Access : Practical Innovations, Open Solutions*, 9, 113454–113474. DOI: 10.1109/ACCESS.2021.3104150

Crotti, R., & Misrahi, T. (2015). The Travel & Tourism Competitiveness Report 2015. Growth Through Shocks. World Economic Forum, Geneva. [http://www3.weforum.org/docs/TT15/WEF_ Global_Travel&Tourism_Report_2015.pdf]

Czarnul, P., Proficz, J., & Krzywaniak, A. (2019). Energy-aware high-performance computing: Survey of state-of-the-art tools, techniques, and environments. *Scientific Programming*, 2019, 2019. DOI: 10.1155/2019/8348791

Dall-Orsoletta, A., Ferreira, P., & Dranka, G. G. (2022). Low-carbon technologies and just energy transition: Prospects for electric vehicles. *Energy Conversion and Management: X, 16*, 100271.

Das, K. A., Baruah, A., Barbhuiya, F. A., & Dey, K. (2020, December). Checkpoint ensemble of transformers for hate speech classification. In *Proceedings of the fourteenth workshop on semantic evaluation* (pp. 2023-2029). DOI: 10.18653/v1/2020.semeval-1.267

Daukaev, K., Rassõlkin, A., Kallaste, A., Vaimann, T., & Belahcen, A. (2017). A review of electrical machine design processes from the standpoint of software selection. In *2017 IEEE 58th International Scientific Conference on Power and Electrical Engineering of Riga Technical University (RTUCON)* (pp. 1–6). IEEE. DOI: 10.1109/RTUCON.2017.8124818

Delaigle, A., & Hall, P. (2012). Achieving near perfect classification for functional data. *Journal of the Royal Statistical Society. Series A, (Statistics in Society)*, 74, 267–286.

Deng, J., Dong, W., Socher, R., Li, L.-J., Li, K., & Fei-Fei, L. (2009). Imagenet: A large-scale hierarchical image database. *2009 IEEE Conference on Computer Vision and Pattern Recognition*, 248–255. DOI: 10.1109/CVPR.2009.5206848

Deng, L., Yu, D., & Platt, J. (2012). Scalable stacking and learning for building deep architectures. *2012 IEEE International Conference on Acoustics, Speech and Signal Processing (ICASSP)*, 2133–2136. DOI: 10.1109/ICASSP.2012.6288333

Deshpande, M. V. (2011). *Electrical Machines*. PHI Learning Private Limited.

Devi, J. V., Argiddi, R. V., Renuka, P., Janagi, K., Hari, B. S., & Boopathi, S. (2024). Study on Integrated Neural Networks and Fuzzy Logic Control for Autonomous Electric Vehicles. In *Advances in Web Technologies and Engineering* (pp. 104–127). IGI Global. DOI: 10.4018/979-8-3693-1487-6.ch006

Dey, P., Gopal, M., Pradhan, P., & Pal, T. (2019). On robustness of radial basis function network with input perturbation. *Neural Computing & Applications*, 31(2), 523–537. DOI: 10.1007/s00521-017-3086-5

Dhanalakshmi, M., Tamilarasi, K., Saravanan, S., Sujatha, G., Boopathi, S., & Associates. (2024). Fog Computing-Based Framework and Solutions for Intelligent Systems: Enabling Autonomy in Vehicles. In *Computational Intelligence for Green Cloud Computing and Digital Waste Management* (pp. 330–356). IGI Global.

Digă, S. M., Năvrăpescu, V., Digă, N., & Dina, C. (2021). Considerations on the optimal computer-aided design of induction motors from the turbomachines drive systems in power plants. In *2021 12th International Symposium on Advanced Topics in Electrical Engineering (ATEE)* (pp. 1–6). IEEE. DOI: 10.1109/ATEE52255.2021.9425259

Dimiduk, D. M., Holm, E. A., & Niezgoda, S. R. (2018). Perspectives on the impact of machine learning, deep learning, and artificial intelligence on materials, processes, and structures engineering. *Integrating Materials and Manufacturing Innovation*, 7(3), 157–172. DOI: 10.1007/s40192-018-0117-8

Do Koo, Y., Jo, H. S., Yoo, K. H., & Na, M. G. (2020). *Identification of Initial Events in Nuclear Power Plants Using Machine Learning Methods*.

Doi, J., Takahashi, H., Raymond, R., Imamichi, T., & Horii, H. (2019). Quantum computing simulator on a heterogenous hpc system. *Proceedings of the 16th ACM International Conference on Computing Frontiers*, 85–93. DOI: 10.1145/3310273.3323053

Domakonda, V. K., Farooq, S., Chinthamreddy, S., Puviarasi, R., Sudhakar, M., & Boopathi, S. (2022). Sustainable Developments of Hybrid Floating Solar Power Plants: Photovoltaic System. In *Human Agro-Energy Optimization for Business and Industry* (pp. 148–167). IGI Global.

Dongarra, J., Sterling, T., Simon, H., & Strohmaier, E. (2005). High-performance computing: Clusters, constellations, MPPs, and future directions. *Computing in Science & Engineering*, 7(2), 51–59. DOI: 10.1109/MCSE.2005.34

Duan, Y., & Ionel, D. M. (2013). A review of recent developments in electrical machine design optimization methods with a permanent-magnet synchronous motor benchmark study. *IEEE Transactions on Industry Applications*, 49(3), 1268–1275. DOI: 10.1109/TIA.2013.2252597

Du, J., Mo, X., Li, Y., Zhang, Q., Li, J., Wu, X., Lu, L., & Ouyang, M. (2019). Boundaries of high-power charging for long-range battery electric car from the heat generation perspective. *Energy*, 182, 211–223. DOI: 10.1016/j.energy.2019.05.222

Eichelberger, M., Tanner, S., Luchsinger, K., & Wattenhofer, R. (2017). Indoor localization with aircraft signals. *SenSys 2017 - Proceedings of the 15th ACM Conference on Embedded Networked Sensor Systems*. DOI: 10.1145/3131672.3131698

Eisner, B., Rocktäschel, T., Augenstein, I., Bošnjak, M., & Riedel, S. (2016). emoji2vec: Learning emoji representations from their description. *arXiv preprint arXiv:1609.08359*. DOI: 10.18653/v1/W16-6208

Ejarque, J., Badia, R. M., Albertin, L., Aloisio, G., Baglione, E., Becerra, Y., Boschert, S., Berlin, J. R., D'Anca, A., Elia, D., Exertier, F., Fiore, S., Flich, J., Folch, A., Gibbons, S. J., Koldunov, N., Lordan, F., Lorito, S., Løvholt, F., & Volpe, M. (2022). Enabling dynamic and intelligent workflows for HPC, data analytics, and AI convergence. *Future Generation Computer Systems*, 134, 414–429. DOI: 10.1016/j.future.2022.04.014

Elbasani, E., & Kim, J. D. (2022). AMR-CNN: Abstract meaning representation with convolution neural network for toxic content detection. *Journal of Web Engineering*, 21(3), 677–692. DOI: 10.13052/jwe1540-9589.2135

Elshamli, A., Taylor, G. W., & Areibi, S. (2019). Multisource domain adaptation for remote sensing using deep neural networks. *IEEE Transactions on Geoscience and Remote Sensing*, 58(5), 3328–3340. DOI: 10.1109/TGRS.2019.2953328

Erricolo, D., Chen, P. Y., Rozhkova, A., Torabi, E., Bagci, H., Shamim, A., & Zhang, X. (2019). Machine learning in electromagnetics: A review and some perspectives for future research. In *2019 International Conference on Electromagnetics in Advanced Applications (ICEAA)* (pp. 1377–1380). IEEE. DOI: 10.1109/ICEAA.2019.8879110

Esnaola-Gonzalez, I., Jelić, M., Pujić, D., Diez, F. J., & Tomašević, N. (2021). An AI-powered system for residential demand response. *Electronics (Basel)*, 10(6), 693. DOI: 10.3390/electronics10060693

Evo, J. (2002). *EvoJ – Evolutionary Computations Framework*. http://evoj-frmw.appspot.com

Fan, J., Ke, Y., & Wang, K. (2020). Factor-adjusted regularized model selection. *Journal of Econometrics*, 216(1), 71–85. DOI: 10.1016/j.jeconom.2020.01.006 PMID: 32269406

Farahani, A., Voghoei, S., Rasheed, K., & Arabnia, H. R. (2021). A brief review of domain adaptation. *Advances in Data Science and Information Engineering: Proceedings from ICDATA 2020 and IKE 2020*, 877–894.

Farrell, S., Emani, M., Balma, J., Drescher, L., Drozd, A., Fink, A., Fox, G., Kanter, D., Kurth, T., & Mattson, P. (2021). MLPerf™ HPC: A holistic benchmark suite for scientific machine learning on HPC systems. *2021 IEEE/ACM Workshop on Machine Learning in High Performance Computing Environments (MLHPC)*, 33–45. DOI: 10.1109/MLHPC54614.2021.00009

Favi, C., Germani, M., Marconi, M., & Mengoni, M. (2012). Innovative software platform for eco-design of efficient electric motors. *Journal of Cleaner Production*, 37, 125–134. DOI: 10.1016/j.jclepro.2012.06.019

Fellous, J.-M., Sapiro, G., Rossi, A., Mayberg, H., & Ferrante, M. (2019). Explainable artificial intelligence for neuroscience: Behavioral neurostimulation. *Frontiers in Neuroscience*, 13, 1346. DOI: 10.3389/fnins.2019.01346 PMID: 31920509

Fernandes, S. L., & Bala, G. J. (2016). ODROID XU4 based implementation of decision level fusion approach for matching computer generated sketches. *Journal of Computational Science*, 16, 217–224. DOI: 10.1016/j.jocs.2016.07.013

Filzmoser, P., & Todorov, V. (2011). Review of robust multivariate statistical methods in high dimension. *Analytica Chimica Acta*, 705(1-2), 2–14. DOI: 10.1016/j.aca.2011.03.055 PMID: 21962341

Finkelshtein, V., Iegorov, O., Petrenko, O., & Koliada, O. (2020). The analytic-field method for calculating the squirrel-cage induction motor parameters. *Naukovyi Visnyk Natsionalnoho Hirnychoho Universytetu*, 2020(3), 67–72. DOI: 10.33271/nvngu/2020-3/067

Fordellone, M. (2019). *Statistical analysis of complex data. Dimensionality reduction and classification methods*. LAP LAMBERT Academic Publishing.

Founta, A. M., Chatzakou, D., Kourtellis, N., Blackburn, J., Vakali, A., & Leontiadis, I. (2019, June). A unified deep learning architecture for abuse detection. In *Proceedings of the 10th ACM conference on web science* (pp. 105-114). DOI: 10.1145/3292522.3326028

Fox, G., Glazier, J. A., Kadupitiya, J., Jadhao, V., Kim, M., Qiu, J., Sluka, J. P., Somogyi, E., Marathe, M., & Adiga, A. (2019). Learning everywhere: Pervasive machine learning for effective high-performance computation. *2019 IEEE International Parallel and Distributed Processing Symposium Workshops (IPDPSW)*, 422–429. DOI: 10.1109/IPDPSW.2019.00081

Frank, A., & Asuncion, A. (2010). *UCI Machine Learning Repository*. University of California. [http://archive.ics.uci.edu/ml]

Fraunhofer, I. F. F. (2015). *Expediting and Validating Development*. https://www.iff.fraunhofer.de/content/ dam/iff/en/documents/publications/expediting-and-validating-development-fraunhofer-iff.pdf

Gahlan, N., & Sethia, D. (2024). Federated learning inspired privacy sensitive emotion recognition based on multi-modal physiological sensors. *Cluster Computing*, 27(3), 3179–3201. DOI: 10.1007/s10586-023-04133-4

Galib, S., Bhowmik, P., Avachat, A., & Lee, H. (2021). A comparative study of machine learning methods for automated identification of radioisotopes using NaI gamma-ray spectra. *Nuclear Engineering and Technology*, 53(12), 4072–4079. DOI: 10.1016/j.net.2021.06.020

Ganin, Y., & Lempitsky, V. (2015). Unsupervised domain adaptation by backpropagation. *Proceedings of the 32nd International Conference on International Conference on Machine Learning-* Volume 37, 1180–1189.

Gao, Z.-P., Wang, Y.-J., Lü, H.-L., Li, Q.-F., Shen, C.-W., & Liu, L. (2021). Machine learning the nuclear mass. *Nuclear Science and Techniques*, 32(10), 109. DOI: 10.1007/s41365-021-00956-1

Garcia-Cardona, C., Kannan, R., Johnston, T., Proffen, T., Page, K., & Seal, S. K. (2019). Learning to predict material structure from neutron scattering data. *2019 IEEE International Conference on Big Data (Big Data)*, 4490–4497. DOI: 10.1109/BigData47090.2019.9005968

Gaudio, J. E., Gibson, T. E., Annaswamy, A. M., Bolender, M. A., & Lavretsky, E. (2019). Connections between adaptive control and optimization in machine learning. In *2019 IEEE 58th Conference on Decision and Control (CDC)* (pp. 4563–4568). IEEE. DOI: 10.1109/CDC40024.2019.9029197

Georgakopoulos, S. V., Tasoulis, S. K., Vrahatis, A. G., & Plagianakos, V. P. (2018, July). Convolutional neural networks for toxic comment classification. In *Proceedings of the 10th hellenic conference on artificial intelligence* (pp. 1-6). DOI: 10.1145/3200947.3208069

Georganas, E., Avancha, S., Banerjee, K., Kalamkar, D., Henry, G., Pabst, H., & Heinecke, A. (2018). Anatomy of high-performance deep learning convolutions on simd architectures. *SC18. International Conference for High Performance Computing, Networking, Storage and Analysis : [proceedings]. SC (Conference : Supercomputing)*, ●●●, 830–841.

Gholamalinezhad, H., & Khosravi, H. (2020). *Pooling Methods in Deep Neural Networks, a Review* (arXiv:2009.07485). arXiv. https://doi.org//arXiv.2009.07485DOI: 10.48550

Ghorbanian, V. (2018). *An HPC-based data-driven approach to system-level design process for integrated motor-drive systems* [Doctoral dissertation, McGill University]. McGill University's institutional digital repository. https://escholarship.mcgill.ca/concern/theses/t722hc204

Ghorbanian, V., Mohammadi, M.H., & Lowther, D. (2019). Design concepts of low-frequency electromagnetic devices based on a data-driven approach. *COMPEL – The International Journal for Computation and Mathematics in Electrical and Electronic Engineering, 38*(5), 1374–1385. DOI: 10.1108/COMPEL-12-2018-0524

Giri, R. B., N., Alhamad, A. M., Mamidi, P. L., R., S., & Boopathi, S. (2024). Human-Centered Design Approach to Autonomous Electric Vehicles: Revolutionizing Mobility. In *Advances in Logistics, Operations, and Management Science* (pp. 91–109). IGI Global. DOI: 10.4018/979-8-3693-1862-1.ch006

Gjoreski, H., Bizjak, J., Gjoreski, M., & Gams, M. (2016), "Comparing Deep and Classical Ma-chine Learning Methods for Human Activity Recognition using Wrist Accelerometer," Jozef Stefan International Postgraduate School, Jan. 2016.

Glady, J. B. P., D'Souza, S. M., Priya, A. P., Amuthachenthiru, K., Vikram, G., & Boopathi, S. (2024). A Study on AI-ML-Driven Optimizing Energy Distribution and Sustainable Agriculture for Environmental Conservation. In *Harnessing High-Performance Computing and AI for Environmental Sustainability* (pp. 1–27). IGI Global., DOI: 10.4018/979-8-3693-1794-5.ch001

Glomb, K., Cabral, J., Cattani, A., Mazzoni, A., Raj, A., & Franceschiello, B. (2022). Computational models in electroencephalography. *Brain Topography*, 35(1), 142–161. DOI: 10.1007/s10548-021-00828-2 PMID: 33779888

Glorot, X., Bordes, A., & Bengio, Y. (2011). Deep sparse rectifier neural networks. *Journal of Machine Learning Research*.

Godwin Immanuel, D., Solaimalai, G., Chandrakala, B. M., Bharath, V. G., Singh, M. K., & Boopathi, S. (2024). Advancements in Electric Vehicle Management System: Integrating Machine Learning and Artificial Intelligence. In *Advances in Web Technologies and Engineering* (pp. 371–391). IGI Global. DOI: 10.4018/979-8-3693-1487-6.ch018

Goldberg, D. E. (1989). *Genetic Algorithms in Search, Optimization and Machine Learning*. Addison-Wesley Longman Publishing., DOI: 10.5555/534133

Gong, Y., Liu, L., Yang, M., & Bourdev, L. (2014). *Compressing Deep Convolutional Networks using Vector Quantization*. 1–10.

Gong, H., Cheng, S., Chen, Z., & Li, Q. (2022). Data-enabled physics-informed machine learning for reduced-order modeling digital twin: Application to nuclear reactor physics. *Nuclear Science and Engineering*, 196(6), 668–693. DOI: 10.1080/00295639.2021.2014752

Gong, X., Xie, Z., Liu, Y., Shi, X., & Zheng, Z. (2018). Deep salient feature based anti-noise transfer network for scene classification of remote sensing imagery. *Remote Sensing (Basel)*, 10(3), 410. DOI: 10.3390/rs10030410

Goodfellow, I., Bengio, Y., & Courville, A. (2016). *Deep learning*. MIT Press.

Google. (2019). *TensorFlow Lite | TensorFlow*. Tensorflow.Org. https://www.tensorflow.org/lite

Gopal, M., Lurdhumary, J., Bathrinath, S., Priya, A. P., Sarojwal, A., & Boopathi, S. (2024). Energy Harvesting and Smart Highways for Sustainable Transportation Infrastructure: Revolutionizing Roads Using Nanotechnology. In *Principles and Applications in Speed Sensing and Energy Harvesting for Smart Roads* (pp. 136–165). IGI Global. DOI: 10.4018/978-1-6684-9214-7.ch005

Gopi, B., Sworna Kokila, M. L., Bibin, C. V., Sasikala, D., Howard, E., & Boopathi, S. (2024). Distributed Technologies Using AI/ML Techniques for Healthcare Applications. In *Advances in Human and Social Aspects of Technology* (pp. 375–396). IGI Global. DOI: 10.4018/979-8-3693-2569-8.ch019

Greco, L., Percannella, G., Ritrovato, P., Tortorella, F., & Vento, M. (2020). Trends in IoT based solutions for health care: Moving AI to the edge. *Pattern Recognition Letters*, 135, 346–353. DOI: 10.1016/j.patrec.2020.05.016 PMID: 32406416

Greene, W. H. (2017). *Econometric analysis* (8th ed.). Pearson.

Gregory, G. D., Ngo, L. V., & Karavdic, M. (2019). Developing e-commerce marketing capabilities and efficiencies for enhanced performance in business-to-business export ventures. *Industrial Marketing Management*, 78, 146–157. DOI: 10.1016/j.indmarman.2017.03.002

Guo, K., Zeng, S., Yu, J., Wang, Y., & Yang, H. (2019). [DL] A survey of FPGA-based neural network inference accelerators. In *ACM Transactions on Reconfigurable Technology and Systems*. DOI: 10.1145/3289185

Guo, W., Li, S., Yang, J., Zhou, Z., Liu, Y., Lu, J., Kou, L., & Zhao, M. (2022). Remote Sensing Image Scene Classification by Multiple Granularity Semantic Learning. *IEEE Journal of Selected Topics in Applied Earth Observations and Remote Sensing*, 15, 2546–2562. DOI: 10.1109/JSTARS.2022.3158703

Hall, P., & Pham, T. (2010). Optimal properties of centroid-based classifiers for very high-dimensional data. *Annals of Statistics*, 38(2), 1071–1093. DOI: 10.1214/09-AOS736

Han, S., Liu, X., Mao, H., Pu, J., Pedram, A., Horowitz, M. A., & Dally, W. J. (2016). EIE: Efficient Inference Engine on Compressed Deep Neural Network. *Proceedings - 2016 43rd International Symposium on Computer Architecture, ISCA 2016*. DOI: 10.1109/ISCA.2016.30

Han, S., Pool, J., Tran, J., & Dally, W. J. (2015). Learning both weights and connections for efficient neural networks. *Advances in Neural Information Processing Systems, 2015-Janua*, 1135–1143.

Hanelt, A., Bohnsack, R., Marz, D., & Antunes Marante, C. (2021). A systematic review of the literature on digital transformation: Insights and implications for strategy and organizational change. *Journal of Management Studies*, 58(5), 1159–1197. DOI: 10.1111/joms.12639

Han, S., Mao, H., & Dally, W. J. (2016a). Deep compression: Compressing deep neural networks with pruning, trained quantization and Huffman coding. *4th International Conference on Learning Representations, ICLR 2016 - Conference Track Proceedings*, 1–14.

Hastie, T., Tibshirani, R., & Wainwright, M. (2015). *Statistical learning with sparsity: The lasso and generalizations*. CRC Press. DOI: 10.1201/b18401

Hayakawa, S., & Hayashi, H. (2017). Using Azure machine learning for estimating indoor locations. In *2017 International Conference on Platform Technology and Service (PlatCon)* (pp. 1–4). IEEE. DOI: 10.1109/PlatCon.2017.7883736

Haykin, S. O. (2009). *Neural networks and learning machines: A comprehensive foundation* (2nd ed.). Prentice Hall.

He, Y., Lin, J., Liu, Z., Wang, H., Li, L. J., & Han, S. (2018). AMC: AutoML for model compression and acceleration on mobile devices. *Lecture Notes in Computer Science (Including Subseries Lecture Notes in Artificial Intelligence and Lecture Notes in Bioinformatics), 11211 LNCS*, 815–832. DOI: 10.1007/978-3-030-01234-2_48

Heidenreich, H. (2021, Dec. 21). *Stemming? Lemmatization? What?* [Available online] https://towardsdatascience.com/stemming-lemmatization-what-ba782b7c0bd8

Heinze, G., Wallisch, C., & Dunkler, D. (2017). Variable selection–A review and recommendations for the practicing statistician. *Biometrical Journal. Biometrische Zeitschrift*, 60(3), 431–449. DOI: 10.1002/bimj.201700067 PMID: 29292533

He, K., Zhang, X., Ren, S., & Sun, J. (2016). Deep residual learning for image recognition. *Proceedings of the IEEE Computer Society Conference on Computer Vision and Pattern Recognition.* DOI: 10.1109/CVPR.2016.90

Henaff, M., Bruna, J., & LeCun, Y. (2015). Deep convolutional networks on graph-structured data. *arXiv preprint arXiv:1506.05163.*

Hinton, G., Vinyals, O., & Dean, J. (2015). Distilling the Knowledge in a Neural Network. *CiteArxiv:1503.02531Comment: NIPS 2014 Deep Learning Workshop.* https://arxiv.org/abs/1503.02531

Hinton, G., Deng, L., Yu, D., Dahl, G. E., Mohamed, A., Jaitly, N., Senior, A., Vanhoucke, V., Nguyen, P., Sainath, T. N., & Kingsbury, B. (2012). Deep neural networks for acoustic modeling in speech recognition: The shared views of four research groups. *IEEE Signal Processing Magazine*, 29(6), 82–97. DOI: 10.1109/MSP.2012.2205597

Hoang, V.-T., & Jo, K. (2018). *PydMobileNet: Improved Version of MobileNets with Pyramid Depthwise Separable Convolution.*

Holder, A., & Eichholz, J. (2019). *An introduction to computational science.* Springer. DOI: 10.1007/978-3-030-15679-4

Horn, G., Skrzypek, P., Materka, K., & Prześdzi k, T. (2019). Cost Benefits of Multi-cloud Deployment of Dynamic Computational Intelligence Applications. In Barolli, L., Takizawa, M., Xhafa, F., & Enokido, T. (Eds.), *Web, Artificial Intelligence and Network Applications* (pp. 1041–1054). Springer International Publishing., DOI: 10.1007/978-3-030-15035-8_102

Howard, A. G., Zhu, M., Chen, B., Kalenichenko, D., Wang, W., Weyand, T., Andreetto, M., & Adam, H. (2017). *MobileNets: Efficient Convolutional Neural Networks for Mobile Vision Applications.*

Huang, H., & Xu, K. (2019). Combing triple-part features of convolutional neural networks for scene classification in remote sensing. *Remote Sensing (Basel)*, 11(14), 1687. DOI: 10.3390/rs11141687

Huang, Y., Fan, X., Chen, S.-C., & Zhao, N. (2019). Emerging technologies of flexible pressure sensors: Materials, modeling, devices, and manufacturing. *Advanced Functional Materials*, 29(12), 1808509. DOI: 10.1002/adfm.201808509

Huber, P. J. (2009). *Robust statistics* (2nd ed.). Wiley. DOI: 10.1002/9780470434697

Hu, C.-Y., Hu, L.-S., Yuan, L., Lu, D.-J., Lyu, L., & Chen, Y.-Q. (2023). FedIERF: Federated Incremental Extremely Random Forest for Wearable Health Monitoring. *Journal of Computer Science and Technology*, 38(5), 970–984. DOI: 10.1007/s11390-023-3009-0

Huo, Z., Gu, B., Yang, Q., & Huang, H. (2018). Decoupled Parallel Backpropagation with Convergence Guarantee. *ArXiv:1804.10574[Cs, Stat].* http://arxiv.org/abs/1804.10574

Iandola, F. N., Moskewicz, M. W., Ashraf, K., Han, S., Dally, W. J., & Keutzer, K. (2016). *Squeezenet: alexnet-level accuracy with 50x fewer parameters and < 0.5mb model size.* ArXiv.

IBM Cloud Education. (2020), "What is artificial intelligence (AI)?" IBM, Jun. 03, 2020. https://www.ibm.com/cloud/learn/what-is-artificial-intelligence

IBM. (2021, Dec. 15). *Text mining*. [Available online] https://www.ibm.com/cloud/learn/text-mining

Ibrahim, D. (2006). *Microcontroller based applied digital control*. John Wiley. DOI: 10.1002/0470863374

Iegorov, O., Iegorova, O., Kundenko, M., & Potryvaieva, N. (2020). Ripple torque synchronous reluctance motor with different rotor designs. In *2020 IEEE Problems of Automated Electrodrive. Theory and Practice (PAEP)* (pp. 1–4). IEEE. DOI: 10.1109/PAEP49887.2020.9240820

Ienca, M., & Ignatiadis, K. (2020). Artificial intelligence in clinical neuroscience: Methodological and ethical challenges. *AJOB Neuroscience*, 11(2), 77–87. DOI: 10.1080/21507740.2020.1740352 PMID: 32228387

Ihde, N., Marten, P., Eleliemy, A., Poerwawinata, G., Silva, P., Tolovski, I., Ciorba, F. M., & Rabl, T. (2022). A survey of big data, high performance computing, and machine learning benchmarks. *Performance Evaluation and Benchmarking: 13th TPC Technology Conference, TPCTC 2021, Copenhagen, Denmark, August 20, 2021, Revised Selected Papers 13*, 98–118.

Ioffe, S., & Szegedy, C. (2015). Batch normalization: Accelerating deep network training by reducing internal covariate shift. *32nd International Conference on Machine Learning, ICML 2015, 1*, 448–456.

Isakov, M., Del Rosario, E., Madireddy, S., Balaprakash, P., Carns, P., Ross, R. B., & Kinsy, M. A. (2020). HPC I/O throughput bottleneck analysis with explainable local models. *SC20. International Conference for High Performance Computing, Networking, Storage and Analysis : [proceedings]. SC (Conference : Supercomputing)*, ●●●, 1–13.

Isik, M., Inadagbo, K., & Aktas, H. (2023). Design optimization for high-performance computing using FPGA. *Annual International Conference on Information Management and Big Data*, 142–156. DOI: 10.21203/rs.3.rs-2679691/v1

Iwendi, C., Srivastava, G., Khan, S., & Maddikunta, P. K. R. (2023). Cyberbullying detection solutions based on deep learning architectures. *Multimedia Systems*, 29(3), 1839–1852. DOI: 10.1007/s00530-020-00701-5

Jackson, D., Belakaria, S., Cao, Y., Doppa, J. R., & Lu, X. (2021). Machine learning enabled design automation and multi-objective optimization for electric transportation power systems. *IEEE Transactions on Transportation Electrification*, 8(1), 1467–1481. DOI: 10.1109/TTE.2021.3113958

Jacob, B., Kligys, S., Chen, B., Zhu, M., Tang, M., Howard, A., Adam, H., & Kalenichenko, D. (2018). Quantization and Training of Neural Networks for Efficient Integer-Arithmetic-Only Inference. *Proceedings of the IEEE Computer Society Conference on Computer Vision and Pattern Recognition*, 2704–2713. DOI: 10.1109/CVPR.2018.00286

Jacobson, N. J., Bentley, K. H., Walton, A., Wang, S. B., Fortgang, R. G., Millner, A. J., Coombs, G.III, Rodman, A. M., & Coppersmith, D. D. L. (2020). Ethical dilemmas posed by mobile health and machine learning in psychiatry research. *Bulletin of the World Health Organization*, 98(4), 270–276. DOI: 10.2471/BLT.19.237107 PMID: 32284651

Jaderberg, M., Vedaldi, A., & Zisserman, A. (2014). Speeding up convolutional neural networks with low rank expansions. *BMVC 2014 - Proceedings of the British Machine Vision Conference 2014*. DOI: 10.5244/C.28.88

Jangda, A., Pinckney, D., Brun, Y., & Guha, A. (2019). Formal Foundations of Serverless Computing. *Proceedings of the ACM on Programming Languages, 3*(OOPSLA), 1–26. DOI: 10.1145/3360575

Jastrzebski, R. P., Jaatinen, P., Pyrhönen, O., & Chiba, A. (2018). Design optimization of permanent magnet bearingless motor using differential evolution. In *2018 IEEE Energy Conversion Congress and Exposition (ECCE)* (pp. 2327–2334). IEEE. DOI: 10.1109/ECCE.2018.8557878

Jha, S. K., & Beevi, S. J. P., H., Babitha, M. N., Chinnusamy, S., & Boopathi, S. (2024). Artificial Intelligence-Infused Urban Connectivity for Smart Cities and the Evolution of IoT Communication Networks. In *Blockchain-Based Solutions for Accessibility in Smart Cities* (pp. 113–146). IGI Global. DOI: 10.4018/979-8-3693-3402-7.ch005

Jha, N., Prashar, D., & Nagpal, A. (2021). Combining Artificial Intelligence with Robotic Process Automation—An Intelligent Automation Approach. In Ahmed, K. R., & Hassanien, A. E. (Eds.), *Deep Learning and Big Data for Intelligent Transportation: Enabling Technologies and Future Trends* (pp. 245–264). Springer International Publishing., DOI: 10.1007/978-3-030-65661-4_12

Jia, Y., Shelhamer, E., Donahue, J., Karayev, S., Long, J., Girshick, R., Guadarrama, S., & Darrell, T. (2014). Caffe: Convolutional architecture for fast feature embedding. *MM 2014 - Proceedings of the 2014 ACM Conference on Multimedia*, 675–678. DOI: 10.1145/2647868.2654889

Jiang, S., Shuai, X., & Xing, G. (2024). ArtFL: Exploiting data resolution in federated learning for dynamic runtime inference via multi-scale training. *2024 23rd ACM/IEEE International Conference on Information Processing in Sensor Networks (IPSN)*, 27–38.

Jia, X., Wei, X., Cao, X., & Foroosh, H. (2019). Comdefend: An efficient image compression model to defend adversarial examples. *Proceedings of the IEEE Computer Society Conference on Computer Vision and Pattern Recognition, 2019-June*, 6077–6085. DOI: 10.1109/CVPR.2019.00624

Jurečková, J., Picek, J., & Schindler, M. (2019). *Robust statistical methods with R* (2nd ed.). CRC Press. DOI: 10.1201/b21993

K. S. K. K., Isaac, J. S., Pratheep, V. G., Jasmin, M., Kistan, A., & Boopathi, S. (2024). Smart Food Quality Monitoring by Integrating IoT and Deep Learning for Enhanced Safety and Freshness. In *Edible Electronics for Smart Technology Solutions* (pp. 79–110). IGI Global. DOI: 10.4018/979-8-3693-5573-2.ch004

Kadupitiya, J., Fox, G. C., & Jadhao, V. (2019). Machine learning for performance enhancement of molecular dynamics simulations. *International Conference on Computational Science*, 116–130. DOI: 10.1007/978-3-030-22741-8_9

Kadupitiya, J., Sun, F., Fox, G., & Jadhao, V. (2020). Machine learning surrogates for molecular dynamics simulations of soft materials. *Journal of Computational Science*, 42, 101107. DOI: 10.1016/j.jocs.2020.101107

Kaggle (2022), "Inertia Sensors for Human Activity Recognition", www.kaggle.com. https://www.kaggle .com/datasets/owenagius/inertia-sensors-for-human-activity-recognition (accessed May 08, 2022).

Kahneman, D. (2013). *Thinking, fast and slow*. Farrar, Straus and Giroux.

Kalamkar, D., Georganas, E., Srinivasan, S., Chen, J., Shiryaev, M., & Heinecke, A. (2020). Optimizing deep learning recommender systems training on cpu cluster architectures. *SC20. International Conference for High Performance Computing, Networking, Storage and Analysis : [proceedings]. SC (Conference : Supercomputing)*, ●●●, 1–15.

Kalina, J., & Duintjer Tebbens, J. (2015). Algorithms for regularized linear discriminant analysis. Proceedings of the 6th International Conference on Bioinformatics Models Methods, and Algorithms (BIOINFORMATICS '15), Scitepress, Lisbon, 128-133. DOI: 10.5220/0005234901280133

Kalina, J. (2015). Three contributions to robust regression diagnostics. Journal of Applied Mathematics. *Statistics and Informatics*, 11(2), 69–78.

Kalina, J. (2018). A robust pre-processing of BeadChip microarray images. *Biocybernetics and Biomedical Engineering*, 38(3), 556–563. DOI: 10.1016/j.bbe.2018.04.005

Kalina, J., & Matonoha, C. (2020). A sparse pair-preserving centroid-based supervised learning method for high-dimensional biomedical data or images. *Biocybernetics and Biomedical Engineering*, 40(2), 774–786. DOI: 10.1016/j.bbe.2020.03.008

Kalina, J., & Rensová, D. (2015). How to reduce dimensionality of data: Robustness point of view. *Serbian Journal of Management*, 10(1), 131–140. DOI: 10.5937/sjm10-6531

Kalina, J., & Schlenker, A. (2015). A robust supervised variable selection for noisy high-dimensional data. *BioMed Research International*, 2015, 320385. DOI: 10.1155/2015/320385 PMID: 26137474

Kalina, J., Seidl, L., Zvára, K., Grünfeldová, H., Slovák, D., & Zvárová, J. (2013). System for selecting relevant information for decision support. *Studies in Health Technology and Informatics*, 186, 83–87. PMID: 23542973

Kalina, J., & Tichavský, J. (2020). On robust estimation of error variance in (highly) robust regression. *Measurement Science Review*, 20(1), 6–14. DOI: 10.2478/msr-2020-0002

Kalina, J., & Vidnerová, P. (2020). On robust training of regression neural networks. In Aneiros, G., Horová, I., Hušková, M., & Vieu, P. (Eds.), *Functional and high-dimensional statistics and related fields. IWFOS 2020. Contributions to Statistics* (pp. 145–152). Springer. DOI: 10.1007/978-3-030-47756-1_20

Kallaste, A., Vaimann, T., & Rassãlkin, A. (2018). Additive design possibilities of electrical machines. In *2018 IEEE 59th International Scientific Conference on Power and Electrical Engineering of Riga Technical University (RTUCON)* (pp. 1–5). IEEE. DOI: 10.1109/RTUCON.2018.8659828

Karthik, S., Hemalatha, R., Aruna, R., Deivakani, M., Reddy, R. V. K., & Boopathi, S. (2023). Study on Healthcare Security System-Integrated Internet of Things (IoT). In *Perspectives and Considerations on the Evolution of Smart Systems* (pp. 342–362). IGI Global.

Kaushik, N., Gill, A., & Raghavendra, R. (2024). Frontiers of Artificial Intelligence Through Accelerated Model Training and Optimization Techniques. *2024 IEEE 13th International Conference on Communication Systems and Network Technologies (CSNT)*, 995–1002.

Kavitha, C., Varalatchoumy, M., Mithuna, H., Bharathi, K., Geethalakshmi, N., & Boopathi, S. (2023). Energy Monitoring and Control in the Smart Grid: Integrated Intelligent IoT and ANFIS. In *Applications of Synthetic Biology in Health, Energy, and Environment* (pp. 290–316). IGI Global.

Keeble, J., & Rios, A. (2020). Machine learning the deuteron. *Physics Letters. [Part B]*, 809, 135743. DOI: 10.1016/j.physletb.2020.135743

Kelechi, A. H., Alsharif, M. H., Bameyi, O. J., Ezra, P. J., Joseph, I. K., Atayero, A.-A., Geem, Z. W., & Hong, J. (2020). Artificial intelligence: An energy efficiency tool for enhanced high performance computing. *Symmetry*, 12(6), 1029. DOI: 10.3390/sym12061029

Kelly, J., & Knottenbelt, W. (2015). The UK-DALE dataset, domestic appliance-level electricity demand and whole-house demand from five UK homes. *Scientific Data*, 2(1), 150007. DOI: 10.1038/sdata.2015.7 PMID: 25984347

Kemp, S. (2022, Feb. 26). *Digital 21: Global overview report*. [Available online] https://datareportal.com/reports/digital-2021-global-overview-report

Khalid, N., Qayyum, A., Bilal, M., Al-Fuqaha, A., & Qadir, J. (2023). Privacy-preserving artificial intelligence in healthcare: Techniques and applications. *Computers in Biology and Medicine*, 158, 106848. DOI: 10.1016/j.compbiomed.2023.106848 PMID: 37044052

Khan, A., & Lowther, D. A. (2020). Machine learning applied to the design and analysis of low frequency electromagnetic devices. In *2020 21st International Symposium on Electrical Apparatus & Technologies (SIELA)* (pp. 1–4). IEEE. DOI: 10.1109/SIELA49118.2020.9167158

Khatri, A. (2018, June). *Detecting offensive messages using deep learning: A micro-service based approach*. Pycon APAC Conference Presentation. [Available online] https://www.youtube.com/watch?v=6ciGTSrL-l4

Khelifi, L., & Mignotte, M. (2020). Deep learning for change detection in remote sensing images: Comprehensive review and meta-analysis. *IEEE Access : Practical Innovations, Open Solutions*, 8, 126385–126400. DOI: 10.1109/ACCESS.2020.3008036

Khetawat, H., Zimmer, C., Mueller, F., Atchley, S., Vazhkudai, S. S., & Mubarak, M. (2019). Evaluating burst buffer placement in hpc systems. *2019 IEEE International Conference on Cluster Computing (CLUSTER)*, 1–11. DOI: 10.1109/CLUSTER.2019.8891051

Kim, S., Yu, G.-I., Park, H., Cho, S., Jeong, E., Ha, H., Lee, S., Jeong, J. S., & Chun, B.-G. (2019). Parallax: Sparsity-aware Data Parallel Training of Deep Neural Networks. *ArXiv:1808.02621[Cs]*. http://arxiv.org/abs/1808.02621 DOI: 10.1145/3302424.3303957

Kim, Y. D., Park, E., Yoo, S., Choi, T., Yang, L., & Shin, D. (2016). Compression of deep convolutional neural networks for fast and low power mobile applications. *4th International Conference on Learning Representations, ICLR 2016 - Conference Track Proceedings*, 1–16.

Kitaev, N., Kaiser, Ł., & Levskaya, A. (2020). Reformer: The efficient transformer. *arXiv preprint arXiv:2001.04451*.

Kitagawa, W., Inaba, A., & Takeshita, T. (2019). Objective function optimization for electrical machine by using multi-objective genetic programming and display method of its results. *IEEJ Transactions on Electronics. Information Systems*, 139(7), 796–801. DOI: 10.1541/ieejeiss.139.796

Knöll, M., Wolfgruber, T., Agel, M. L., Wenz, C., & Roth, R. (2023). Machine learning for the prediction of converged energies from ab initio nuclear structure calculations. *Physics Letters. [Part B]*, 839, 137781. DOI: 10.1016/j.physletb.2023.137781

Ko, V., Oehmcke, S., & Gieseke, F. (2019). Magnitude and Uncertainty Pruning Criterion for Neural Networks. *Proceedings - 2019 IEEE International Conference on Big Data, Big Data 2019*. DOI: 10.1109/BigData47090.2019.9005692

Kombarov, V., Sorokin, V., Tsegelnyk, Y., Plankovskyy, S., Aksonov, Y., & Fojtů, O. (2021). Numerical control of machining parts from aluminum alloys with sticking minimization. *International Journal of Mechatronics and Applied Mechanics*, I(9), 209–216. DOI: 10.17683/ijomam/issue9.30

Kording, K. P., Blohm, G., Schrater, P., & Kay, K. (2020). Appreciating the variety of goals in computational neuroscience. *arXiv Preprint arXiv:2002.03211*.

Koshariya, A. K., Kalaiyarasi, D., Jovith, A. A., Sivakami, T., Hasan, D. S., & Boopathi, S. (2023). AI-Enabled IoT and WSN-Integrated Smart Agriculture System. In *Artificial Intelligence Tools and Technologies for Smart Farming and Agriculture Practices* (pp. 200–218). IGI Global. DOI: 10.4018/978-1-6684-8516-3.ch011

Krizhevsky, A., Sutskever, I., & Hinton, G. E. (2017). Imagenet classification with deep convolutional neural networks. *Communications of the ACM*, 60(6), 84–90. DOI: 10.1145/3065386

Kumar, M., Kumar, K., Sasikala, P., Sampath, B., Gopi, B., & Sundaram, S. (2023). Sustainable Green Energy Generation From Waste Water: IoT and ML Integration. In *Sustainable Science and Intelligent Technologies for Societal Development* (pp. 440–463). IGI Global.

Kumara, V., Mohanaprakash, T., Fairooz, S., Jamal, K., Babu, T., & Sampath, B. (2023). Experimental Study on a Reliable Smart Hydroponics System. In *Human Agro-Energy Optimization for Business and Industry* (pp. 27–45). IGI Global. DOI: 10.4018/978-1-6684-4118-3.ch002

Kumari, K., & Singh, J. P. (2019). Deep learning approach for identification of abusive content. In *Proceedings of forum for information retrieval evaluation* (FIRE) (pp. 328-335), vol. 2517.

Kumar, K. S., Nair, S. A. H., Roy, D. G., Rajalingam, B., & Kumar, R. S. (2021). Security and privacy-aware artificial intrusion detection system using federated machine learning. *Computers & Electrical Engineering*, 96, 107440. DOI: 10.1016/j.compeleceng.2021.107440

Kumbale, S., Singh, S., Poornalatha, G., & Singh, S. (2023). BREE-HD: A Transformer-Based Model to Identify Threats on Twitter. *IEEE Access : Practical Innovations, Open Solutions*, 11, 67180–67190. DOI: 10.1109/ACCESS.2023.3291072

Kurakin, A., Goodfellow, I. J., & Bengio, S. (2017). Adversarial machine learning at scale. *5th International Conference on Learning Representations, ICLR 2017 - Conference Track Proceedings*.

Kurz, M., Offenhäuser, P., Viola, D., Shcherbakov, O., Resch, M., & Beck, A. (2022). Deep reinforcement learning for computational fluid dynamics on HPC systems. *Journal of Computational Science*, 65, 101884. DOI: 10.1016/j.jocs.2022.101884

Kwaku, W. K. (2023). Sustainable Cloud Computing with AI-Driven Resource Optimization. *Advances in Computer Sciences, 6*(1).

Kwapisz, J. R., Weiss, G. M., & Moore, S. A. (2021, March). Activity recognition using cell phone accelerometers. *SIGKDD Explorations*, 12(2), 74–82. DOI: 10.1145/1964897.1964918

Lakshmanaprabu, S. K., Mohanty, S. N., Krishnamoorthy, S., Uthayakumar, J., & Shankar, K. (2019). Online clinical decision support system using optimal deep neural networks. *Applied Soft Computing*, 81, 105487. DOI: 10.1016/j.asoc.2019.105487

Lalmuanawma, S., Hussain, J., & Chhaakchhuak, L. (2020). Applications of machine learning and artificial intelligence for Covid-19 (SARS-CoV-2) pandemic: A review. *Chaos, Solitons, and Fractals*, 139, 110059. DOI: 10.1016/j.chaos.2020.110059 PMID: 32834612

Lasloum, T., Alhichri, H., Bazi, Y., & Alajlan, N. (2021). SSDAN: Multi-source semi-supervised domain adaptation network for remote sensing scene classification. *Remote Sensing (Basel)*, 13(19), 3861. DOI: 10.3390/rs13193861

LeCun, Y. (2015). *MNIST Demos on Yann LeCun's website*. https://yann.lecun.com/exdb/lenet/

LeCun, Y., Boser, B., Denker, J. S., Henderson, D., Howard, R. E., Hubbard, W., & Jackel, L. D. (1989). Backpropagation applied to handwritten zip code recognition. *Neural Computation*, 1(4), 541–551. DOI: 10.1162/neco.1989.1.4.541

Lee, H., Satyam, K., & Fox, G. (2018). Evaluation of Production Serverless Computing Environments. *2018 IEEE 11th International Conference on Cloud Computing (CLOUD)*, 442–450. DOI: 10.1109/CLOUD.2018.00062

Lee, H., Turilli, M., Jha, S., Bhowmik, D., Ma, H., & Ramanathan, A. (2019). Deepdrivemd: Deep-learning driven adaptive molecular simulations for protein folding. *2019 IEEE/ACM Third Workshop on Deep Learning on Supercomputers (DLS)*, 12–19. DOI: 10.1109/DLS49591.2019.00007

Lee, M.-F. R., & Chien, T.-W. (2020). Artificial intelligence and Internet of Things for robotic disaster response. *2020 International Conference on Advanced Robotics and Intelligent Systems (ARIS)*, 1–6. DOI: 10.1109/ARIS50834.2020.9205794

Lei, G., Zhu, J., Guo, Y., Liu, C., & Ma, B. (2017). A review of design optimization methods for electrical machines. *Energies*, 10(12), 1962. DOI: 10.3390/en10121962

Leo, M., Carcagnì, P., Mazzeo, P. L., Spagnolo, P., Cazzato, D., & Distante, C. (2020). Analysis of facial information for healthcare applications: A survey on computer vision-based approaches. *Information (Basel)*, 11(3), 128. DOI: 10.3390/info11030128

Li, Y., Orgerie, A.C., Rodero, I., Amersho, B.L., Parashar, M. et al. (2018). End-to-end models for edge cloud-based IoT platforms: Application to data stream analysis in IoT. [https://hal.archives-ouvertes.fr/hal-01673501]

Li, Z., Gong, Y., Ma, X., Liu, S., Sun, M., Zhan, Z., Kong, Z., Yuan, G., & Wang, Y. (2020). *SS-Auto: A Single-Shot, Automatic Structured Weight Pruning Framework of DNNs with Ultra-High Efficiency.*

Liang, Z., Liang, Z., Zheng, Y., Liang, B., & Zheng, L. (2021). Data analysis and visualization platform design for batteries using flask-based Python web service. *World Electric Vehicle Journal*, 12(4), 187. DOI: 10.3390/wevj12040187

Li, D., Wang, X., & Kong, D. (2018). DeePrebirth: Accelerating deep neural network execution on mobile devices. *32nd AAAI Conference on Artificial Intelligence, AAAI 2018*, 2322–2330. DOI: 10.1609/aaai.v32i1.11876

Ligozat, A.-L., Lefevre, J., Bugeau, A., & Combaz, J. (2022). Unraveling the hidden environmental impacts of AI solutions for environment life cycle assessment of AI solutions. *Sustainability (Basel)*, 14(9), 5172. DOI: 10.3390/su14095172

Li, J., Li, G., Shi, Y., & Yu, Y. (2021). Cross-domain adaptive clustering for semi-supervised domain adaptation. *Proceedings of the IEEE/CVF Conference on Computer Vision and Pattern Recognition*, 2505–2514. DOI: 10.1109/CVPR46437.2021.00253

Li, L., Pandey, S., Flynn, T., Liu, H., Wheeler, N., & Hoisie, A. (2022). Simnet: Accurate and high-performance computer architecture simulation using deep learning. *Proceedings of the ACM on Measurement and Analysis of Computing Systems*, 6(2), 1–24.

Li, M. (2014). Scaling Distributed Machine Learning with the Parameter Server. *Proceedings of the 2014 International Conference on Big Data Science and Computing - BigDataScience '14*, 1–1. DOI: 10.1145/2640087.2644155

Liu, D., Wang, M., & Catlin, A. G. (2024). Detecting Anti-Semitic Hate Speech using Transformer-based Large Language Models. *arXiv preprint arXiv:2405.03794.*

Liu, J., Zhuang, B., Zhuang, Z., Guo, Y., Huang, J., Zhu, J., & Tan, M. (2020). *Discrimination-aware Network Pruning for Deep Model Compression.* 1–14.

Liu, N., Xu, Z., Wang, Y., Tang, J., & Ye, J. (2018). *Ultra-High Compression Rates.*

Liu, Y., Ott, M., Goyal, N., Du, J., Joshi, M., Chen, D., Levy, O., Lewis, M., Zettlemoyer, L., & Stoyanov, V. (2019). RoBERTa: A robustly optimized BERT pretraining approach. *arXiv preprint arXiv:1907.11692.*

Liubarskyi, B., Petrenko, O., Iakunin, D., & Dubinina, O. (2017). Optimization of thermal modes and cooling systems of the induction traction motors of trams. *Eastern-European Journal of Enterprise Technologies, 3*(9-87), 59–67. DOI: 10.15587/1729-4061.2017.102236

Liu, P., Li, W., & Zou, L. (2019, June). NULI at SemEval-2019 task 6: Transfer learning for offensive language detection using bidirectional transformers. In *Proceedings of the 13th international workshop on semantic evaluation* (pp. 87-91). DOI: 10.18653/v1/S19-2011

Li, W., & Liewig, M. (2020). A Survey of AI Accelerators for Edge Environment. In Rocha, Á., Adeli, H., Reis, L. P., Costanzo, S., Orovic, I., & Moreira, F. (Eds.), *Trends and Innovations in Information Systems and Technologies* (pp. 35–44). Springer International Publishing., DOI: 10.1007/978-3-030-45691-7_4

Li, Y., Lei, G., Bramerdorfer, G., Peng, S., Sun, X., & Zhu, J. (2021). Machine learning for design optimization of electromagnetic devices: Recent developments and future directions. *Applied Sciences (Basel, Switzerland)*, 11(4), 1627. DOI: 10.3390/app11041627 PMID: 34671486

Lloyd, W., Ramesh, S., Chinthalapati, S., Ly, L., & Pallickara, S. (2018). Serverless Computing: An Investigation of Factors Influencing Microservice Performance. *2018 IEEE International Conference on Cloud Engineering (IC2E)*, 159–169. DOI: 10.1109/IC2E.2018.00039

Loeb, B., & Kockelman, K. M. (2019). Fleet performance and cost evaluation of a shared autonomous electric vehicle (SAEV) fleet: A case study for Austin, Texas. *Transportation Research Part A, Policy and Practice*, 121, 374–385. DOI: 10.1016/j.tra.2019.01.025

Long, L. D. (2023). An AI-driven model for predicting and optimizing energy-efficient building envelopes. *Alexandria Engineering Journal*, 79, 480–501. DOI: 10.1016/j.aej.2023.08.041

López-Robles, J. R., Rodríguez-Salvador, M., Gamboa-Rosales, N. K., Ramirez-Rosales, S., & Cobo, M. J. (2019). The last five years of Big Data Research in economics, econometrics and finance: Identification and conceptual analysis. *Procedia Computer Science*, 162, 729–736. DOI: 10.1016/j.procs.2019.12.044

Louw, T., & McIntosh-Smith, S. (2021). Using the Graphcore IPU for traditional HPC applications. *3rd Workshop on Accelerated Machine Learning (AccML)*.

Luo, X., Li, Y., Wang, W., Ban, X., Wang, J. H., & Zhao, W. (2020). A robust multilayer extreme learning machine using kernel risk-sensitive loss criterion. *International Journal of Machine Learning and Cybernetics*, 11(1), 197–216. DOI: 10.1007/s13042-019-00967-w

Lupión, M., Cruz, N. C., Sanjuan, J. F., Paechter, B., & Ortigosa, P. M. (2023). Accelerating neural network architecture search using multi-GPU high-performance computing. *The Journal of Supercomputing*, 79(7), 7609–7625. DOI: 10.1007/s11227-022-04960-z

Lupu, T., Marţiş, R. A., Nicu, A. I., & Marţiş, C. S. (2021). Open source software based design and optimization tool for electrical machines. In *2021 9th International Conference on Modern Power Systems (MPS)* (pp. 1–5). IEEE. DOI: 10.1109/MPS52805.2021.9492624

Lyu, C., Lin, N., & Dinavahi, V. (2021). Device-level parallel-in-time simulation of mmc-based energy system for electric vehicles. *IEEE Transactions on Vehicular Technology*, 70(6), 5669–5678. DOI: 10.1109/TVT.2021.3081534

Ma, X., Guo, F., Niu, W., Lin, X., Tang, J., Ma, K., Ren, B., & Wang, Y. (2019). *PCONV: The Missing but Desirable Sparsity in DNN Weight Pruning for Real-time Execution on Mobile Devices.*

Ma, X., Niu, W., Zhang, T., Liu, S., Guo, F., Lin, S., Li, H., Chen, X., Tang, J., Ma, K., Ren, B., & Wang, Y. (2020). *An Image Enhancing Pattern-based Sparsity for Real-time Inference on Mobile Devices.*

Maheswari, B. U., Imambi, S. S., Hasan, D., Meenakshi, S., Pratheep, V., & Boopathi, S. (2023). Internet of things and machine learning-integrated smart robotics. In *Global Perspectives on Robotics and Autonomous Systems: Development and Applications* (pp. 240–258). IGI Global. DOI: 10.4018/978-1-6684-7791-5.ch010

Maheswari, M. U., & Sathiaseelan, J. G. R. (2017). Text mining: Survey on techniques and applications. *International Journal of Scientific Research*, 6(6), 1660–1664.

Mahmoud, M. M. E., Rodrigues, J. J. P. C., Ahmed, S. H., Shah, S. C., Al-Muhtadi, J. F., Korotaev, V. V., & De Albuquerque, V. H. C. (2018). Enabling technologies on cloud of things for smart healthcare. *IEEE Access: Practical Innovations, Open Solutions*, 6, 31950–31967. DOI: 10.1109/ACCESS.2018.2845399

Mahmoud, M., & Slama, S. B. (2023). Peer-to-Peer Energy Trading Case Study Using an AI-Powered Community Energy Management System. *Applied Sciences (Basel, Switzerland)*, 13(13), 7838. DOI: 10.3390/app13137838

Malathi, J., Kusha, K., Isaac, S., Ramesh, A., Rajendiran, M., & Boopathi, S. (2024). IoT-Enabled Remote Patient Monitoring for Chronic Disease Management and Cost Savings: Transforming Healthcare. In *Advances in Explainable AI Applications for Smart Cities* (pp. 371–388). IGI Global.

Malița, M., Popescu, G. V., & Ștefan, G. M. (2020). Heterogeneous computing system for deep learning. *Deep Learning: Concepts and Architectures*, 287–319.

Malouche, I., Abbes, A. K., & Bouani, F. (2015). Automatic model predictive control implementation in a high-performance microcontroller. *2015 IEEE 12th International Multi-Conference on Systems, Signals & Devices (SSD15)*, 1–6.

Mann, B., Ryder, N., Subbiah, M., Kaplan, J., Dhariwal, P., Neelakantan, A., Shyam, P., Sastry, G., Askell, A., Agarwal, S., Herbert-Voss, A., Krueger, G., Henighan, T., Child, R., Ramesh, A., Ziegler, D. M., Wu, J., Winter, C., . . . Amodei, D. (2020). Language models are few-shot learners. *arXiv preprint arXiv:2005.14165, 1*.

Marozzi, M., Mukherjee, A., & Kalina, J. (2020). Interpoint distance tests for high-dimensional comparison studies. *Journal of Applied Statistics*, 47(4), 653–665. DOI: 10.1080/02664763.2019.1649374 PMID: 35707487

Marquez, M. (2022, Dec. 18). *What is information extraction?* [Available online] https://www.ontotext.com/knowledgehub/fundamentals/information-extraction/

Martinez, W. L., Martinez, A. R., & Solka, J. L. (2017). *Exploratory data analysis with MATLAB* (3rd ed.). Chapman & Hall/CRC.

Maturi, M. H., Satish, S., Gonaygunta, H., & Meduri, K. (2022). The Intersection of Artificial Intelligence and Neuroscience: Unlocking the Mysteries of the Brain. *International Journal of Creative Research In Computer Technology and Design*, 4(4), 1–21.

Mayer, R., Mayer, C., & Laich, L. (2017). The TensorFlow Partitioning and Scheduling Problem: It's the Critical Path! *Proceedings of the 1st Workshop on Distributed Infrastructures for Deep Learning*, 1–6. DOI: 10.1145/3154842.3154843

McIntosh-Smith, S., Price, J., Deakin, T., & Poenaru, A. (2019). A performance analysis of the first generation of HPC-optimized Arm processors. *Concurrency and Computation*, 31(16), e5110. DOI: 10.1002/cpe.5110

Meintz, A., Slezak, L., Thurston, S., Carlson, B., Thurlbeck, A., Kisacikoglu, J., Kandula, P., Rowden, B., Chinthavali, M., Wojda, R., & Associates. (2023). *Electric vehicles at scale (EVs@ Scale) laboratory consortium deep-dive technical meetings: High power charging (HPC) summary report*. National Renewable Energy Laboratory (NREL), Golden, CO (United States).

Meng, R., Chen, W., Yang, S., Song, J., Lin, L., Xie, D., Pu, S., Wang, X., Song, M., & Zhuang, Y. (2022). Slimmable domain adaptation. *Proceedings of the IEEE/CVF Conference on Computer Vision and Pattern Recognition*, 7141–7150.

Merenda, M., Porcaro, C., & Iero, D. (2020). Edge Machine Learning for AI-Enabled IoT Devices: A Review. *Sensors (Basel)*, 20(9), 2533. DOI: 10.3390/s20092533 PMID: 32365645

Microsoft. (2021). *Cheat sheet: How to choose a MicrosoftML algorithm*. https://docs.microsoft.com/en-us/machine-learning-server/r/how-to-choose-microsoftml-algorithms-cheatsheet

Microsoft. (2022). *What is Azure Machine Learning studio?* https://docs.microsoft.com/en-us/azure/machine-learning/overview-what-is-machine-learning-studio

Mikolov, T., Sutskever, I., Chen, K., Corrado, G. S., & Dean, J. (2013). Distributed representations of words and phrases and their compositionality. *Advances in Neural Information Processing Systems*, •••, 26.

Miles, R., & Mikolajczyk, K. (2020). *Compression of convolutional neural networks for high performance imagematching tasks on mobile devices. c*.

Miljanovic, M. (2012). Comparative analysis of recurrent and finite impulse response neural networks in time series prediction. *Indian Journal of Computer Science and Engineering*, 3(1), 180–191.

Miller, T. J., & Staton, D. A. (2013). *Electric Machine Design using SPEED and Motor-CAD*. Motor Design.

Miloslavskaya, N., & Tolstoy, A. (2016). Big Data, Fast Data and Data Lake Concepts. *Procedia Computer Science*, 88, 300–305. DOI: 10.1016/j.procs.2016.07.439

Mira, D., Pérez-Sánchez, E. J., Borrell, R., & Houzeaux, G. (2023). HPC-enabling technologies for high-fidelity combustion simulations. *Proceedings of the Combustion Institute*, 39(4), 5091–5125. DOI: 10.1016/j.proci.2022.07.222

Mirhoseini, A., Pham, H., Le, Q. V., Steiner, B., Larsen, R., Zhou, Y., Kumar, N., Norouzi, M., Bengio, S., & Dean, J. (2017). Device Placement Optimization with Reinforcement Learning. *ArXiv:1706.04972[Cs]*. http://arxiv.org/abs/1706.04972

Miri, I., Fotouhi, A., & Ewin, N. (2021). Electric vehicle energy consumption modelling and estimation—A case study. *International Journal of Energy Research*, 45(1), 501–520. DOI: 10.1002/er.5700

Mishkin, D., Sergievskiy, N., & Matas, J. (2017). Systematic evaluation of convolution neural network advances on the Imagenet. *Computer Vision and Image Understanding*, 161, 11–19. Advance online publication. DOI: 10.1016/j.cviu.2017.05.007

MOH. (2020). www.moh.gov.sa. https://www.moh.gov.sa/Ministry/About/Health (accessed Mar. 22, 2022).

Mohammad, A., & Mahjabeen, F. (2023). Revolutionizing Solar Energy with AI-Driven Enhancements in Photovoltaic Technology. *BULLET: Jurnal Multidisiplin Ilmu*, 2(4), 1174–1187.

Mohanraj, G., Krishna, K. S., Lakshmi, B. S., Vijayalakshmi, A., Pramila, P. V., & Boopathi, S. (2024). Optimizing Trust and Security in Healthcare 4.0: Human Factors in Lightweight Secured IoMT Ecosystems. In *Lightweight Digital Trust Architectures in the Internet of Medical Things (IoMT)* (pp. 52–72). IGI Global. DOI: 10.4018/979-8-3693-2109-6.ch004

Mohanty, A., Venkateswaran, N., Ranjit, P., Tripathi, M. A., & Boopathi, S. (2023). Innovative Strategy for Profitable Automobile Industries: Working Capital Management. In *Handbook of Research on Designing Sustainable Supply Chains to Achieve a Circular Economy* (pp. 412–428). IGI Global.

Mohanty, S. K., Premsankar, G., & di Francesco, M. (2018). An Evaluation of Open Source Serverless Computing Frameworks. *2018 IEEE International Conference on Cloud Computing Technology and Science (CloudCom)*, 115–120. DOI: 10.1109/CloudCom2018.2018.00033

Molakatala, N., Kumar, D. A., Patil, U., Mhatre, P. J., Sambathkumar, M., & Boopathi, S. (2024). Integrating 5G and IoT Technologies in Developing Smart City Communication Networks. In *Blockchain-Based Solutions for Accessibility in Smart Cities* (pp. 147–170). IGI Global. DOI: 10.4018/979-8-3693-3402-7.ch006

Morales-Hernández, M., Sharif, M. B., Gangrade, S., Dullo, T. T., Kao, S.-C., Kalyanapu, A., Ghafoor, S., Evans, K., Madadi-Kandjani, E., & Hodges, B. R. (2020). High-performance computing in water resources hydrodynamics. *Journal of Hydroinformatics*, 22(5), 1217–1235. DOI: 10.2166/hydro.2020.163

Mozafari, M., Farahbakhsh, R., & Crespi, N. (2020). A BERT-based transfer learning approach for hate speech detection in online social media. In *Complex Networks and Their Applications VIII: Volume 1 Proceedings of the Eighth International Conference on Complex Networks and Their Applications COMPLEX NETWORKS 2019 8* (pp. 928-940). Springer International Publishing. DOI: 10.1007/978-3-030-36687-2_77

Mrázek, V., Sarwar, S. S., Sekanina, L., Vašíček, Z., & Roy, K. (2016). Design of power-efficient approximate multipliers for approximate artificial neural networks. *2016 IEEE/ACM International Conference on Computer-Aided Design (ICCAD)*, 1-7. DOI: 10.1145/2966986.2967021

Muhammed, T., Mehmood, R., Albeshri, A., & Alsolami, F. (2020). HPC-smart infrastructures: A review and outlook on performance analysis methods and tools. *Smart Infrastructure and Applications: Foundations for Smarter Cities and Societies*, 427–451.

Mukerji, S. K., Khan, A. S., & Singh, Y. P. (2018). *Electromagnetics for Electrical Machines*. CRC Press., DOI: 10.1201/9781315222523

Müller, A. C., & Guido, S. (2016). *Introduction to Machine Learning with Python: a Guide for Data Scientists*. O'Reilly Media, Inc.

Muneer, A., Alwadain, A., Ragab, M. G., & Alqushaibi, A. (2023). Cyberbullying detection on social media using stacking ensemble learning and enhanced BERT. *Information (Basel)*, 14(8), 467. DOI: 10.3390/info14080467

Murach, J., & Urban, M. (2015). *Murach's Beginning Java with NetBeans*. Mike Murach & Associates.

Muralidhar, R., Borovica-Gajic, R., & Buyya, R. (2022). Energy efficient computing systems: Architectures, abstractions and modeling to techniques and standards. *ACM Computing Surveys*, 54(11s), 1–37. DOI: 10.1145/3511094

Murarka, U., Banerjee, K., Malik, T., & Providência, C. (2022). The neutron star outer crust equation of state: A machine learning approach. *Journal of Cosmology and Astroparticle Physics*, 045(01), 045. DOI: 10.1088/1475-7516/2022/01/045

Muthukumar, R., & Pratheep, G. V. G., S. J., S., Kunduru, K. R., Kumar, P., & Boopathi, S. (2024). Leveraging Fuel Cell Technology With AI and ML Integration for Next-Generation Vehicles: Empowering Electric Mobility. In *Advances in Mechatronics and Mechanical Engineering* (pp. 312–337). IGI Global. DOI: 10.4018/979-8-3693-5247-2.ch016

Mutlu, O. (2021). Intelligent architectures for intelligent computing systems. *2021 Design, Automation & Test in Europe Conference & Exhibition (DATE)*, 318–323.

Nakagawa, M., Kasagi, A., Liu, E., Ekawa, H., Yoshida, J., Dou, W., He, Y., Muneem, A., Nakazawa, K., Rappold, C., Saito, N., Saito, T. R., Sugimoto, S., Taki, M., Tanaka, Y. K., Wang, H., Gao, Y., Yanai, A., & Yoshimoto, M. (2022). Unique approach for precise determination of binding energies of hypernuclei with nuclear emulsion and machine learning. *EPJ Web of Conferences*, 271, 11006. DOI: 10.1051/epjconf/202227111006

Narayanan, D., Harlap, A., Phanishayee, A., Seshadri, V., Devanur, N. R., Ganger, G. R., Gibbons, P. B., & Zaharia, M. (2019). PipeDream: Generalized pipeline parallelism for DNN training. *Proceedings of the 27th ACM Symposium on Operating Systems Principles*, 1–15. DOI: 10.1145/3341301.3359646

Naresh, M., Subhahan, D. A., Narula, V. N., Roslin, D. K., Narula, S., & Boopathi, S. (2024). Edge Computing and Machine Learning Integration for Autonomous Electrical Vehicles. In *Solving Fundamental Challenges of Electric Vehicles* (pp. 99–127). IGI Global., DOI: 10.4018/979-8-3693-4314-2.ch005

Navaz, A. N., Serhani, M. A., El Kassabi, H. T., Al-Qirim, N., & Ismail, H. (2021). Trends, technologies, and key challenges in smart and connected healthcare. *IEEE Access : Practical Innovations, Open Solutions*, 9, 74044–74067. DOI: 10.1109/ACCESS.2021.3079217 PMID: 34812394

Nguyen, D. C., Pham, Q.-V., Pathirana, P. N., Ding, M., Seneviratne, A., Lin, Z., Dobre, O., & Hwang, W.-J. (2022). Federated learning for smart healthcare: A survey. *ACM Computing Surveys*, 55(3), 1–37. DOI: 10.1145/3501296

Niu, W., Ma, X., Lin, S., Wang, S., Qian, X., Lin, X., Wang, Y., & Ren, B. (2019). *PatDNN: Achieving Real-Time DNN Execution on Mobile Devices with Pattern-based Weight Pruning*. DOI: 10.1145/3373376.3378534

Niu, W., Ma, X., Wang, Y., & Ren, B. (2019). 26ms Inference [*Towards Real-Time Execution of all DNNs on Smartphone.*]. *Time*, ●●●, ResNet–50.

Okhrimenko, V., & Zbitnieva, M. (2021). Mathematical model of tubular linear induction motor. *Mathematical Modelling of Engineering Problems*, 8(1), 103–109. DOI: 10.18280/mmep.080113

Olson, D. L. (2017). *Descriptive data mining*. Springer. DOI: 10.1007/978-981-10-3340-7

Ono, J., Utiyama, M., & Sumita, E. (2019). Hybrid Data-Model Parallel Training for Sequence-to-Sequence Recurrent Neural Network Machine Translation. *ArXiv:1909.00562[Cs]*. http://arxiv.org/abs/1909.00562

Onoufriou, G., Bickerton, R., Pearson, S., & Leontidis, G. (2019). Nemesyst: A hybrid parallelism deep learning-based framework applied for internet of things enabled food retailing refrigeration systems. *Computers in Industry*, 113, 103133. DOI: 10.1016/j.compind.2019.103133

Othman, E., Bazi, Y., Melgani, F., Alhichri, H., Alajlan, N., & Zuair, M. (2017). Domain Adaptation Network for Cross-Scene Classification. *IEEE Transactions on Geoscience and Remote Sensing*, 55(8), 4441–4456. DOI: 10.1109/TGRS.2017.2692281

Owatchaiphong, S., & Fuengwarodsakul, N. H. (2009). Multi-objective based optimization for switched reluctance machines using fuzzy and genetic algorithms. In *2009 International Conference on Power Electronics and Drive Systems (PEDS)* (pp. 1530–1533). IEEE. DOI: 10.1109/PEDS.2009.5385926

Oyama, Y., Maruyama, N., Dryden, N., McCarthy, E., Harrington, P., Balewski, J., Matsuoka, S., Nugent, P., & Van Essen, B. (2020). The Case for Strong Scaling in Deep Learning: Training Large 3D CNNs with Hybrid Parallelism. *ArXiv:2007.12856[Cs]*. http://arxiv.org/abs/2007.12856

Palaniappan, M., Tirlangi, S., Mohamed, M. J. S., Moorthy, R. S., Valeti, S. V., & Boopathi, S. (2023). Fused Deposition Modelling of Polylactic Acid (PLA)-Based Polymer Composites: A Case Study. In *Development, Properties, and Industrial Applications of 3D Printed Polymer Composites* (pp. 66–85). IGI Global.

Pang, L.-G. (2021). Machine learning for high energy heavy ion collisions. *Nuclear Physics. A.*, 1005, 121972. DOI: 10.1016/j.nuclphysa.2020.121972

Pant, K., & Dadu, T. (2020). Cross-lingual inductive transfer to detect offensive language. *arXiv preprint arXiv:2007.03771*.

Papalambros, P. Y., & Wilde, D. J. (2017). *Principles of Optimal Design: Modeling and Computation* (3rd ed.). Cambridge University Press., DOI: 10.1017/9781316451038

Partee, S., Ellis, M., Rigazzi, A., Shao, A. E., Bachman, S., Marques, G., & Robbins, B. (2022). Using machine learning at scale in numerical simulations with SmartSim: An application to ocean climate modeling. *Journal of Computational Science*, 62, 101707. DOI: 10.1016/j.jocs.2022.101707

Paul, A. K., Karimi, A. M., & Wang, F. (2021). Characterizing machine learning i/o workloads on leadership scale hpc systems. *2021 29th International Symposium on Modeling, Analysis, and Simulation of Computer and Telecommunication Systems (MASCOTS)*, 1–8.

Pavlopoulos, J., Malakasiotis, P., & Androutsopoulos, I. (2017). Deep learning for user comment moderation. *arXiv preprint arXiv:1705.09993*. DOI: 10.18653/v1/W17-3004

Pavlopoulos, J., Thain, N., Dixon, L., & Androutsopoulos, I. (2019, June). Convai at semeval-2019 task 6: Offensive language identification and categorization with perspective and bert. In *Proceedings of the 13th international Workshop on Semantic Evaluation* (pp. 571-576). DOI: 10.18653/v1/S19-2102

Penney, D. D., & Chen, L. (2019). A survey of machine learning applied to computer architecture design. *arXiv Preprint arXiv:1909.12373*.

Perren, S., Dooley, J., Shaw, T., & Cross, D. (2010). Bullying in school and cyberspace: Associations with depressive symptoms in Swiss and Australian adolescents. *Child and Adolescent Psychiatry and Mental Health*, 4(1), 1–10. DOI: 10.1186/1753-2000-4-28 PMID: 21092266

Peterson, J. L., Bay, B., Koning, J., Robinson, P., Semler, J., White, J., Anirudh, R., Athey, K., Bremer, P.-T., Di Natale, F., Fox, D., Gaffney, J. A., Jacobs, S. A., Kailkhura, B., Kustowski, B., Langer, S., Spears, B., Thiagarajan, J., Van Essen, B., & Yeom, J.-S. (2022). Enabling machine learning-ready HPC ensembles with Merlin. *Future Generation Computer Systems*, 131, 255–268. DOI: 10.1016/j.future.2022.01.024

Petrushin, V. S., & Yenoktaiev, R. N. (2019). Modification of the criterion of the present expenses for the design of energy-saving induction motors. *Technical Electrodynamics*, 2019(2), 19–22. DOI: 10.15407/techned2019.02.019

Pires de Lima, R., & Marfurt, K. (2019). Convolutional neural network for remote-sensing scene classification: Transfer learning analysis. *Remote Sensing (Basel)*, 12(1), 86. DOI: 10.3390/rs12010086

Pitchai, R., Guru, K. V., Gandhi, J. N., Komala, C. R., Kumar, J. R. D., & Boopathi, S. (2024). Fog Computing-Integrated ML-Based Framework and Solutions for Intelligent Systems: Digital Healthcare Applications. In *Technological Advancements in Data Processing for Next Generation Intelligent Systems* (pp. 196–224). IGI Global. DOI: 10.4018/979-8-3693-0968-1.ch008

Pitsilis, G. K., Ramampiaro, H., & Langseth, H. (2018). Detecting offensive language in tweets using deep learning. *arXiv preprint arXiv:1801.04433*.

Pliugin, V., Shilkova, L., Lettl, J., Buhr, K., & Fajtl, R. (2015). Analysis of the electromagnetic field of electric machines based on object-oriented design principles. In *Progress in Electromagnetics Research Symposium Proceedings* (pp. 2522–2527). https://ssrn.com/abstract=3201920

Pliuhin, V., Sukhonos, M., & Bileckiy, I. (2020). Object oriented mathematical modeling of electrical machines. In *2020 IEEE 4th International Conference on Intelligent Energy and Power Systems (IEPS)* (pp. 267-272). IEEE. DOI: 10.1109/IEPS51250.2020.9263158

Pliuhin, V., Aksonov, O., Tsegelnyk, Y., Plankovskyy, S., Kombarov, V., & Piddubna, L. (2021). Design and simulation of a servo-drive motor using ANSYS Electromagnetics. *Lighting Engineering & Power Engineering*, 60(3), 112–123. DOI: 10.33042/2079-424X.2021.60.3.04

Pliuhin, V., Korobka, V., Karyuk, A., Pan, M., & Sukhonos, M. (2019a). Using Azure Machine Learning Studio with python scripts for induction motors optimization web-deploy project. In *2019 IEEE International Scientific-Practical Conference Problems of Infocommunications, Science and Technology (PIC S&T)* (pp. 631–634). IEEE. DOI: 10.1109/PICST47496.2019.9061447

Pliuhin, V., Pan, M., Yesina, V., & Sukhonos, M. (2018). Using Azure maching learning cloud technology for electric machines optimization. In *2018 International Scientific-Practical Conference Problems of Infocommunications. Science and Technology (PIC S&T)* (pp. 55–58). IEEE. DOI: 10.1109/INFO-COMMST.2018.8632093

Pliuhin, V., Plankovskyy, S., Zablodskiy, M., Biletskyi, I., Tsegelnyk, Y., & Kombarov, V. (2023). Novel features of special purpose induction electrical machines object-oriented design. In Cioboată, D.D. (Eds.) *International Conference on Reliable Systems Engineering (ICoRSE) – 2022* (pp. 265–283). Springer. DOI: 10.1007/978-3-031-15944-2_25

Pliuhin, V., Sukhonos, M., Pan, M., Petrenko, O., & Petrenko, M. (2019b). Implementing of Microsoft Azure machine learning technology for electric machines optimization. *Electrical Engineering & Electromechanics*, 0(1), 23–28. DOI: 10.20998/2074-272X.2019.1.04

Plum, A., Ranasinghe, T., Orasan, C., & Mitkov, R. (2019). Offensive language detection with deep learning. In *Proceedings of 15th conference on natural language processing* (KONVENS) (pp. 421-426).

Pozzato, G., Allam, A., Pulvirenti, L., Negoita, G. A., Paxton, W. A., & Onori, S. (2023). Analysis and key findings from real-world electric vehicle field data. *Joule*, 7(9), 2035–2053. DOI: 10.1016/j.joule.2023.07.018

Pramila, P., Amudha, S., Saravanan, T., Sankar, S. R., Poongothai, E., & Boopathi, S. (2023). Design and Development of Robots for Medical Assistance: An Architectural Approach. In *Contemporary Applications of Data Fusion for Advanced Healthcare Informatics* (pp. 260–282). IGI Global.

Prasad, M. S. C., Dhanalakshmi, M., Mohan, M., Somasundaram, B., Valarmathi, R., & Boopathi, S. (2024). Machine Learning-Integrated Sustainable Engineering and Energy Systems: Innovations at the Nexus. In *Harnessing High-Performance Computing and AI for Environmental Sustainability* (pp. 74–98). IGI Global. DOI: 10.4018/979-8-3693-1794-5.ch004

Prud'homme, R., & Koning, M. (2012). Electric vehicles: A tentative economic and environmental evaluation. *Transport Policy*, 23, 60–69. DOI: 10.1016/j.tranpol.2012.06.001

Puranik, T. A., Shaik, N., Vankudoth, R., Kolhe, M. R., Yadav, N., & Boopathi, S. (2024). Study on Harmonizing Human-Robot (Drone) Collaboration: Navigating Seamless Interactions in Collaborative Environments. In *Cybersecurity Issues and Challenges in the Drone Industry* (pp. 1–26). IGI Global.

Pusztai, T., Morichetta, A., Pujol, V. C., Dustdar, S., Nastic, S., Ding, X., Vij, D., & Xiong, Y. (2021). SLO Script: A Novel Language for Implementing Complex Cloud-Native Elasticity-Driven SLOs. *2021 IEEE International Conference on Web Services (ICWS)*, 21–31. DOI: 10.1109/ICWS53863.2021.00017

Pyrhönen, J., Jokinen, T., & Hrabovcová, V. (2014). *Design of Rotating Electrical Machines* (2nd ed.). John Wiley & Sons., DOI: 10.1002/9780470740095

Python (2019), "Welcome to Python.org," Python.org, May 29, 2019. https://www.python.org/

Qualcomm. (2018). *Qualcomm Snapdragon 855 Plus Mobile Platform | Snapdragon 855+ Processor for Mobile Gaming*. https://www.qualcomm.com/products/snapdragon-855-plus-mobile-platform

Quarteroni, A. (2018). The role of statistics in the era of big data: A computational scientist' perspective. *Statistics & Probability Letters*, 136, 63–67. DOI: 10.1016/j.spl.2018.02.047

Quiza, R., & Davim, J. P. (2011). Computational methods and optimization. In Davim, J. P. (Ed.), *Machining of hard materials* (pp. 177–208). Springer Science & Business Media. DOI: 10.1007/978-1-84996-450-0_6

Ramachandran, S., Jayalal, M., Vasudevan, M., Das, S., & Jehadeesan, R. (2024). Combining machine learning techniques and genetic algorithm for predicting run times of high performance computing jobs. *Applied Soft Computing*, 165, 112053. DOI: 10.1016/j.asoc.2024.112053

Ramaprasad, A. S. E., Smith, M. T., McCoy, D., Hubbard, A. E., La Merrill, M. A., & Durkin, K. A. (2022). Predicting the binding of small molecules to nuclear receptors using machine learning. *Briefings in Bioinformatics*, 23(3), bbac114. DOI: 10.1093/bib/bbac114 PMID: 35383362

Ramaswamy, S. (2015, April). *How micro-moments are changing the rules*. Think with Google. https://www.thinkwithgoogle.com/marketing-resources/micro-moments/how-micromoments-are-changing-rules/

Ramesh, R. S. (2024). Scalable Systems and Software Architectures for High-Performance Computing on cloud platforms. *arXiv Preprint arXiv:2408.10281*.

Ramudu, K., Mohan, V. M., Jyothirmai, D., Prasad, D., Agrawal, R., & Boopathi, S. (2023). Machine Learning and Artificial Intelligence in Disease Prediction: Applications, Challenges, Limitations, Case Studies, and Future Directions. In *Contemporary Applications of Data Fusion for Advanced Healthcare Informatics* (pp. 297–318). IGI Global.

Ranasinghe, T., Zampieri, M., & Hettiarachchi, H. (2019, December). Deep learning models for multilingual hate speech and offensive language identification. In *Proceedings of forum for information retrieval evaluation* (FIRE) (pp. 199-207).

Rapson, D. S., & Muehlegger, E. (2023). The economics of electric vehicles. *Review of Environmental Economics and Policy*, 17(2), 274–294. DOI: 10.1086/725484

Raschka, S., Patterson, J., & Nolet, C. (2020). Machine learning in python: Main developments and technology trends in data science, machine learning, and artificial intelligence. *Information (Basel)*, 11(4), 193. DOI: 10.3390/info11040193

Ravikumar, A. (2021). Non-relational multi-level caching for mitigation of staleness & stragglers in distributed deep learning. *Proceedings of the 22nd International Middleware Conference: Doctoral Symposium*, 15–16. DOI: 10.1145/3491087.3493678

Ravikumar, A., & Sriraman, H. (2021). Staleness and Stagglers in Distibuted Deep Image Analytics. *2021 International Conference on Artificial Intelligence and Smart Systems (ICAIS)*, 848–852. DOI: 10.1109/ICAIS50930.2021.9395782

Ravikumar, A., Sriraman, H., Saketh, P. M. S., Lokesh, S., & Karanam, A. (2022). Effect of neural network structure in accelerating performance and accuracy of a convolutional neural network with GPU/TPU for image analytics. *PeerJ. Computer Science*, 8, e909. DOI: 10.7717/peerj-cs.909 PMID: 35494877

Raza, M. O., Memon, M., Bhatti, S., & Bux, R. (2020). Detecting cyberbullying in social commentary using supervised machine learning. In *Advances in Information and Communication:Proceedings of the 2020 Future of Information and Communication Conference (FICC),* Volume 2 (pp. 621-630). Springer International Publishing. DOI: 10.1007/978-3-030-39442-4_45

Rebecca, B., Kumar, K. P. M., Padmini, S., Srivastava, B. K., Halder, S., & Boopathi, S. (2024). Convergence of Data Science-AI-Green Chemistry-Affordable Medicine: Transforming Drug Discovery. In *Handbook of Research on AI and ML for Intelligent Machines and Systems* (pp. 348–373). IGI Global.

Redmon, J., Divvala, S., Girshick, R., & Farhadi, A. (2016). You only look once: Unified, real-time object detection. *Proceedings of the IEEE Computer Society Conference on Computer Vision and Pattern Recognition*. DOI: 10.1109/CVPR.2016.91

Revathi, S., Babu, M., Rajkumar, N., Meti, V. K. V., Kandavalli, S. R., & Boopathi, S. (2024). Unleashing the Future Potential of 4D Printing: Exploring Applications in Wearable Technology, Robotics, Energy, Transportation, and Fashion. In *Human-Centered Approaches in Industry 5.0: Human-Machine Interaction, Virtual Reality Training, and Customer Sentiment Analysis* (pp. 131–153). IGI Global.

Rivière, N., Stokmaier, M., & Goss, J. (2020). An innovative multi-objective optimization approach for the multiphysics design of electrical machines. In *2020 IEEE Transportation Electrification Conference & Expo (ITEC)* (pp. 691–696). IEEE. DOI: 10.1109/ITEC48692.2020.9161650

Robertson, J., Fossaceca, J. M., & Bennett, K. W. (2021). A Cloud-Based Computing Framework for Artificial Intelligence Innovation in Support of Multidomain Operations. *IEEE Transactions on Engineering Management*, ●●●, 1–10. DOI: 10.1109/TEM.2021.3088382

Robey, R., & Zamora, Y. (2021). *Parallel and high performance computing*. Simon and Schuster.

Romeo, L., Loncarski, J., Paolanti, M., Bocchini, G., Mancini, A., & Frontoni, E. (2020). Machine learning-based design support system for the prediction of heterogeneous machine parameters in Industry 4.0. *Expert Systems with Applications*, 140, 112869. DOI: 10.1016/j.eswa.2019.112869

Rosu, M., Zhou, P., Lin, D., Ionel, D. M., Popescu, M., Blaabjerg, F., & Staton, D. (2018). *Multiphysics Simulation by Design for Electrical Machines, Power Electronics, and Drives*. John Wiley & Sons., DOI: 10.1002/9781119103462

Rousseeuw, P. J., & Leroy, A. M. (1987). *Robust regression and outlier detection*. Wiley. DOI: 10.1002/0471725382

Rousseeuw, P. J., & Van Driessen, K. (2006). Computing LTS regression for large data sets. *Data Mining and Knowledge Discovery*, 12(1), 29–45. DOI: 10.1007/s10618-005-0024-4

Roy, S. G., Narayan, U., Raha, T., Abid, Z., & Varma, V. (2021). Leveraging multilingual transformers for hate speech detection. *arXiv preprint arXiv:2101.03207*.

Rusiecki, A. (2013). Robust learning algorithm based on LTA estimator. *Neurocomputing*, 120, 624–632. DOI: 10.1016/j.neucom.2013.04.008

Sadiq, M. T., Yu, X., & Yuan, Z. (2021). Exploiting dimensionality reduction and neural network techniques for the development of expert brain-computer interfaces. *Expert Systems with Applications*, 164, 114031. DOI: 10.1016/j.eswa.2020.114031

Sadraey, M. H. (2017). Microcontroller. In *Unmanned Aircraft Design: A Review of Fundamentals* (pp. 123–137). Springer. DOI: 10.1007/978-3-031-79582-4_7

Saeedi, R., S. Norgaard, and A. Gebremedhin, (2022), "A Closed-loop Deep Learning Architec-ture for Robust Activity Recognition using Wearable Sensors." Accessed: Mar. 28, 2022.

Sak, H., Senior, A., & Beaufays, F. (2014). Long short-term memory recurrent neural network architectures for large scale acoustic modeling. In *Fifteenth annual conference of the international speech communication association*. DOI: 10.21437/Interspeech.2014-80

Salama, A., Ostapenko, O., Klein, T., & Nabi, M. (2019). *Pruning at a Glance: Global Neural Pruning for Model Compression.*

Salama, A. K., & Abdellatif, M. M. (2022). AIoT-based Smart Home Energy Management System. *2022 IEEE Global Conference on Artificial Intelligence and Internet of Things (GCAIoT)*, 177–181.

Saldaña, G., San Martín, J. I., Zamora, I., Asensio, F. J., & Oñederra, O. (2019). Analysis of the current electric battery models for electric vehicle simulation. *Energies*, 12(14), 2750. DOI: 10.3390/en12142750

Saleem, R. A., Radaideh, M. I., & Kozlowski, T. (2020). Application of deep neural networks for high-dimensional large BWR core neutronics. *Nuclear Engineering and Technology*, 52(12), 2709–2716. DOI: 10.1016/j.net.2020.05.010

Saravanan, S., Khare, R., Umamaheswari, K., Khare, S., Krishne Gowda, B. S., & Boopathi, S. (2024). AI and ML Adaptive Smart-Grid Energy Management Systems: Exploring Advanced Innovations. In *Principles and Applications in Speed Sensing and Energy Harvesting for Smart Roads* (pp. 166–196). IGI Global. DOI: 10.4018/978-1-6684-9214-7.ch006

Sarishma, D., Sangwan, S., Tomar, R., & Srivastava, R. (2022). A review on cognitive computational neuroscience: Overview, models, and applications. *Innovative Trends in Computational Intelligence*, 217–234.

Sarker, I. H. (2021). Machine learning: Algorithms, real-world applications and research directions. *SN Computer Science*, 2(3), 160. DOI: 10.1007/s42979-021-00592-x PMID: 33778771

Sarma, R., Inanc, E., Aach, M., & Lintermann, A. (2024). Parallel and scalable AI in HPC systems for CFD applications and beyond. *Frontiers in High Performance Computing*, 2, 1444337. DOI: 10.3389/fhpcp.2024.1444337

Sathupadi, K. (2023). Ai-driven energy optimization in sdn-based cloud computing for balancing cost, energy efficiency, and network performance. *International Journal of Applied Machine Learning and Computational Intelligence*, 13(7), 11–37.

Sawadogo, P., & Darmont, J. (2021). On data lake architectures and metadata management. *Journal of Intelligent Information Systems*, 56(1), 97–120. DOI: 10.1007/s10844-020-00608-7

Sax, S. (2016). *Flame wars: Automatic insult detection.* Technical Report, Stanford University, California, USA.

Schmidhuber, J., & Hochreiter, S. (1997). Long short-term memory. *Neural Computation*, 9(8), 1735–1780. DOI: 10.1162/neco.1997.9.8.1735 PMID: 9377276

Schwarz, P., & Moeckel, A. (2019). Electric machine design automation with Python and ANSYS Maxwell. In IKMT *2019: Innovative Small Drives and Micro-Motor Systems – 12. ETG/GMM-Fachtagung* (pp. 46–52). VDE.

Sefen, B., Baumbach, S., Dengel, A., & Abdennadher, S. (2016), "Human Activity Recognition - Using Sensor Data of Smartphones and Smartwatches," *Proceedings of the 8th International Conference on Agents and Artificial Intelligence*, 2016, DOI: 10.5220/0005816004880493

Sen, S. K. (2006). *Principles of Electrical Machine Design with Computer Programs* (2nd ed.). Oxford and IBH Publishing.

Senthil, T., Puviyarasan, M., Babu, S. R., Surakasi, R., Sampath, B., & Associates. (2023). Industrial Robot-Integrated Fused Deposition Modelling for the 3D Printing Process. In *Development, Properties, and Industrial Applications of 3D Printed Polymer Composites* (pp. 188–210). IGI Global.

Shams, S., Platania, R., Lee, K., & Park, S.-J. (2017). Evaluation of deep learning frameworks over different HPC architectures. *2017 IEEE 37th International Conference on Distributed Computing Systems (ICDCS)*, 1389–1396.

Sharma, T., Glynn, J., Panos, E., Deane, P., Gargiulo, M., Rogan, F., & Gallachóir, B. Ó. (2019). High performance computing for energy system optimization models: Enhancing the energy policy tool kit. *Energy Policy*, 128, 66–74. DOI: 10.1016/j.enpol.2018.12.055

Shawahna, A., Sait, S. M., & El-Maleh, A. (2019). FPGA-Based accelerators of deep learning networks for learning and classification: A review. In *IEEEAccess*. DOI: 10.1109/ACCESS.2018.2890150

Sheng, T., Feng, C., Zhuo, S., Zhang, X., Shen, L., & Aleksic, M. (2018). A Quantization-Friendly Separable Convolution for MobileNets. *Proceedings - 1st Workshop on Energy Efficient Machine Learning and Cognitive Computing for Embedded Applications, EMC2 2018*, 14–18. DOI: 10.1109/EMC2.2018.00011

Shen, J., Qu, Y., Zhang, W., & Yu, Y. (2018). Wasserstein distance guided representation learning for domain adaptation. *32nd AAAI Conference on Artificial Intelligence, AAAI 2018*, 4058–4065. DOI: 10.1609/aaai.v32i1.11784

Shen, J., Yu, T., Yang, H., Wang, R., & Wang, Q. (2022). An Attention Cascade Global–Local Network for Remote Sensing Scene Classification. *Remote Sensing (Basel)*, 14(9), 2042. DOI: 10.3390/rs14092042

Shevkunova, A.V. (2021). Optimization algorithms in the design of switched-reluctance machines. *E3S Web of Conferences, 258*, 11007. DOI: 10.1051/e3sconf/202125811007

Shevlyakov, G. L., & Oja, H. (2016). *Robust correlation. Theory and applications.* Wiley. DOI: 10.1002/9781119264507

Shi, C., Zhang, X., Sun, J., & Wang, L. (2022). Remote sensing scene image classification based on self-compensating convolution neural network. *Remote Sensing (Basel)*, 14(3), 545. DOI: 10.3390/rs14030545

Shoaib, M., Bosch, S., Incel, O., Scholten, H., & Havinga, P. (2014, June). Fusion of Smartphone Motion Sensors for Physical Activity Recognition. *Sensors (Basel)*, 14(6), 10146–10176. DOI: 10.3390/s140610146 PMID: 24919015

Shrestha, A., & Mahmood, A. (2019). Review of deep learning algorithms and architectures. In *IEEE Access* (Vol. 7, pp. 53040–53065). DOI: 10.1109/ACCESS.2019.2912200

Simonyan, K., & Zisserman, A. (2015). Very deep convolutional networks for large-scale image recognition. *3rd International Conference on Learning Representations, ICLR 2015 - Conference Track Proceedings.*

Singh, S., Rathore, S., Alfarraj, O., Tolba, A., & Yoon, B. (2022). A framework for privacy-preservation of IoT healthcare data using Federated Learning and blockchain technology. *Future Generation Computer Systems*, 129, 380–388. DOI: 10.1016/j.future.2021.11.028

Sittón-Candanedo, I., Alonso, R. S., García, Ó., Gil, A. B., & Rodríguez-González, S. (2020). A Review on Edge Computing in Smart Energy by means of a Systematic Mapping Study. *Electronics (Basel)*, 9(1), 48. DOI: 10.3390/electronics9010048

Skansi, S. (2018). *Introduction to Deep Learning: from logical calculus to artificial intelligence.* Springer. DOI: 10.1007/978-3-319-73004-2

Slominski, P. C. Vatche Ishakian, Vinod Muthusamy, Aleksander. (n.d.). *The Rise of Serverless Computing.* Retrieved April 19, 2022, from https://cacm.acm.org/magazines/2019/12/241054-the-rise-of-serverless-computing/fulltext

Sodhro, A. H., Sennersten, C., & Ahmad, A. (2022). Towards cognitive authentication for smart healthcare applications. *Sensors (Basel)*, 22(6), 2101. DOI: 10.3390/s22062101 PMID: 35336276

Sonia, R., Gupta, N., Manikandan, K., Hemalatha, R., Kumar, M. J., & Boopathi, S. (2024). Strengthening Security, Privacy, and Trust in Artificial Intelligence Drones for Smart Cities. In *Analyzing and Mitigating Security Risks in Cloud Computing* (pp. 214–242). IGI Global. DOI: 10.4018/979-8-3693-3249-8.ch011

Sreedhar, P. S. S., Sujay, V., Rani, M. R., Melita, L., Reshma, S., & Boopathi, S. (2024). Impacts of 5G Machine Learning Techniques on Telemedicine and Social Media Professional Connection in Healthcare. In *Advances in Medical Technologies and Clinical Practice* (pp. 209–234). IGI Global. DOI: 10.4018/979-8-3693-1934-5.ch012

Srinivas, B., Maguluri, L. P., Naidu, K. V., Reddy, L. C. S., Deivakani, M., & Boopathi, S. (2023). Architecture and Framework for Interfacing Cloud-Enabled Robots. In *Handbook of Research on Data Science and Cybersecurity Innovations in Industry 4.0 Technologies* (pp. 542–560). IGI Global. DOI: 10.4018/978-1-6684-8145-5.ch027

Srivani, M., Murugappan, A., & Mala, T. (2023). Cognitive computing technological trends and future research directions in healthcare—A systematic literature review. *Artificial Intelligence in Medicine*, 138, 102513. DOI: 10.1016/j.artmed.2023.102513 PMID: 36990590

Statti, F., Sued, M., & Yohai, V. J. (2018). High breakdown point robust estimators with missing data. *Communications in Statistics. Theory and Methods*, 47(21), 5145–5162. DOI: 10.1080/03610926.2017.1388396

Steinheimer, J., Pang, L.-G., Zhou, K., Koch, V., Randrup, J., & Stoecker, H. (2019). A machine learning study to identify spinodal clumping in high energy nuclear collisions. *The Journal of High Energy Physics*, 2019(12), 1–26. DOI: 10.1007/JHEP12(2019)122

Sterling, T., Brodowicz, M., & Anderson, M. (2017). *High performance computing: Modern systems and practices*. Morgan Kaufmann.

Stevens, R., Galloway, T., & Willemsen-Dunlap, A. (2019). Advancing our understandings of healthcare team dynamics from the simulation room to the operating room: A neurodynamic perspective. *Frontiers in Psychology*, 10, 1660. DOI: 10.3389/fpsyg.2019.01660 PMID: 31456706

Stojkovic, Z. (2012). *Computer-Aided Design in Power Engineering: Application of Software Tools*. Springer., DOI: 10.1007/978-3-642-30206-0

Subha, S., Inbamalar, T., Komala, C., Suresh, L. R., Boopathi, S., & Alaskar, K. (2023). A Remote Health Care Monitoring system using internet of medical things (IoMT). *IEEE Explore*, 1–6.

Sultana, F., Sufian, A., & Dutta, P. (2018). Advancements in image classification using convolutional neural network. *2018 Fourth International Conference on Research in Computational Intelligence and Communication Networks (ICRCICN)*, 122–129. DOI: 10.1109/ICRCICN.2018.8718718

Sundar, R., Srikaanth, P. B., Naik, D. A., Murugan, V. P., Karumudi, M., & Boopathi, S. (2024). Achieving Balance Between Innovation and Security in the Cloud With Artificial Intelligence of Things: Semantic Web Control Models. In *Advances in Web Technologies and Engineering* (pp. 1–26). IGI Global. DOI: 10.4018/979-8-3693-1487-6.ch001

Sun, L., Sun, H., Wang, J., Wu, S., Zhao, Y., & Xu, Y. (2021). Breast mass detection in mammography based on image template matching and CNN. *Sensors (Basel)*, 2021(8), 2855. DOI: 10.3390/s21082855 PMID: 33919623

Sun, L., & Wu, J. (2022). A scalable and transferable federated learning system for classifying healthcare sensor data. *IEEE Journal of Biomedical and Health Informatics*, 27(2), 866–877. DOI: 10.1109/JBHI.2022.3171402 PMID: 35486556

Su, X., Tong, H., & Ji, P. (2014, June). Activity recognition with smartphone sensors. *Tsinghua Science and Technology*, 19(3), 235–249. DOI: 10.1109/TST.2014.6838194

Swathi, K., Sandeep, T. U., & Ramani, A. R. (2018). Performance Analysis of Microcontrollers Used In IoT Technology. *International Journal of Scientific Research in Science, Engineering and Technology*, 4(4), 1268–1273.

Syamala, M., Komala, C., Pramila, P., Dash, S., Meenakshi, S., & Boopathi, S. (2023). Machine Learning-Integrated IoT-Based Smart Home Energy Management System. In *Handbook of Research on Deep Learning Techniques for Cloud-Based Industrial IoT* (pp. 219–235). IGI Global. DOI: 10.4018/978-1-6684-8098-4.ch013

Taghavipour, A., Vajedi, M., & Azad, N. L. (2019). *Intelligent control of connected plug-in hybrid electric vehicles*. Springer. DOI: 10.1007/978-3-030-00314-2

Tan, M., & Le, Q. (2019). EfficientNet: Rethinking Model Scaling for Convolutional Neural Networks. *International Conference on Machine Learning*, 6105–6114. http://proceedings.mlr.press/v97/tan19a.html

Tanash, M., Yang, H., Andresen, D., & Hsu, W. (2021). Ensemble prediction of job resources to improve system performance for slurm-based hpc systems. In *Practice and experience in advanced research computing* (pp. 1–8). DOI: 10.1145/3437359.3465574

Tan, L., & Yuan, Y. (2022). Computational fluid dynamics simulation and performance optimization of an electrical vehicle Air-conditioning system. *Alexandria Engineering Journal*, 61(1), 315–328. DOI: 10.1016/j.aej.2021.05.001

Tan, M., & Le, Q. V. (2019). *EfficientNet: Rethinking Model Scaling for Convolutional Neural Networks*. https://arxiv.org/abs/1905.11946v5

Tegmark, M. (2017). *Life 3.0: Being human in the age of artificial intelligence*. Alfred A. Knopf.

Teja, N. B., Kannagi, V., Chandrashekhar, A., Senthilnathan, T., Pal, T. K., & Boopathi, S. (2024). Impacts of Nano-Materials and Nano Fluids on the Robot Industry and Environments. In *Advances in Computational Intelligence and Robotics* (pp. 171–194). IGI Global. DOI: 10.4018/979-8-3693-5767-5.ch012

TensorFlow Lite Model Maker. (n.d.). TensorFlow. Retrieved December 27, 2021, from https://www.tensorflow.org/lite/guide/model_maker

TensorFlow. (2019), "TensorFlow," TensorFlow, 2019. https://www.tensorflow.org/

Tessier, R., Pocek, K., & DeHon, A. (2015). Reconfigurable computing architectures. *Proceedings of the IEEE*. DOI: 10.1109/JPROC.2014.2386883

Thilagam, K., Beno, A., Lakshmi, M. V., Wilfred, C. B., George, S. M., Karthikeyan, M., Peroumal, V., Ramesh, C., & Karunakaran, P. (2022). Secure IoT Healthcare Architecture with Deep Learning-Based Access Control System. *Journal of Nanomaterials*, 2022(1), 2638613. DOI: 10.1155/2022/2638613

Tian, Y., Fan, B., & Wu, F. (2017). L2-Net: Deep learning of discriminative patch descriptor in Euclidean space. *Proceedings - 30th IEEE Conference on Computer Vision and Pattern Recognition, CVPR 2017, 2017-Janua*, 6128–6136. DOI: 10.1109/CVPR.2017.649

Tirlangi, S., Teotia, S., Padmapriya, G., Senthil Kumar, S., Dhotre, S., & Boopathi, S. (2024). Cloud Computing and Machine Learning in the Green Power Sector: Data Management and Analysis for Sustainable Energy. In *Developments Towards Next Generation Intelligent Systems for Sustainable Development* (pp. 148–179). IGI Global. DOI: 10.4018/979-8-3693-5643-2.ch006

Tovazzi, D., Faticanti, F., Siracusa, D., Peroni, C., Cretti, S., & Gazzini, T. (2020). GEM-Analytics: Cloud-to-Edge AI-Powered Energy Management. *Economics of Grids, Clouds, Systems, and Services:17th International Conference, GECON 2020,Izola, Slovenia,September 15–17, 2020, Revised Selected Papers 17*, 57–66.

Tran, D.-D., Vafaeipour, M., El Baghdadi, M., Barrero, R., Van Mierlo, J., & Hegazy, O. (2020). Thorough state-of-the-art analysis of electric and hybrid vehicle powertrains: Topologies and integrated energy management strategies. *Renewable & Sustainable Energy Reviews*, 119, 109596. DOI: 10.1016/j.rser.2019.109596

Trindade, M. G., Coelho, A., Valadares, C., Viera, R. A., Rey, S., Cheymol, B., Baylac, M., Velazco, R., & Bastos, R. P. (2019). Assessment of a hardware-implemented machine learning technique under neutron irradiation. *IEEE Transactions on Nuclear Science*, 66(7), 1441–1448. DOI: 10.1109/TNS.2019.2920747

Tripathi, U., Chamola, V., Jolfaei, A., & Chintanpalli, A. (2021). Advancing remote healthcare using humanoid and affective systems. *IEEE Sensors Journal*, 22(18), 17606–17614. DOI: 10.1109/JSEN.2021.3049247

Troisi, O., Maione, G., Grimaldi, M., & Loia, F. (2020). Growth hacking: Insights on data-driven decision-making from three firms. *Industrial Marketing Management*, 90, 538–557. DOI: 10.1016/j.indmarman.2019.08.005

Tsai, M. C., Wu, Y. C., Chan, C. T., Cai, P. Y., Huang, P. W., & Tsai, M. H. (2016). Integrated design of magnetic gear and electric motor for electric vehicles. In *2016 International Conference of Asian Union of Magnetics Societies (ICAUMS)* (pp. 1–4). IEEE. DOI: 10.1109/ICAUMS.2016.8479780

Tsegelnyk, Y., Kombarov, V., Plankovskyy, S., Aksonov, Y., Pliuhin, V., & Aksonov, O. (2022). Investigation of the portal-type machine tool gear-belt gearbox. *International Journal of Mechatronics and Applied Mechanics*, 2022(11), 295–302. DOI: 10.17683/ijomam/issue11.41

Tuli, S., Gill, S. S., Xu, M., Garraghan, P., Bahsoon, R., Dustdar, S., Sakellariou, R., Rana, O., Buyya, R., Casale, G., & Jennings, N. R. (2022). HUNTER: AI-based Holistic Resource Management for Sustainable Cloud Computing. *Journal of Systems and Software*, 184, 111124. DOI: 10.1016/j.jss.2021.111124

Tuncer, O., Ates, E., Zhang, Y., Turk, A., Brandt, J. M., Leung, V. J., Egele, M., & Coskun, A. K. (2017). Diagnosing Performance Variations in HPC Architectures Using Machine Learning. Sandia National Lab.(SNL-NM), Albuquerque, NM (United States).

Tung, F., & Mori, G. (2018). Deep Neural Network Compression by In-Parallel Pruning-Quantization. *IEEE Transactions on Pattern Analysis and Machine Intelligence*, PP(c), 1. DOI: 10.1109/TPAMI.2018.2886192

Tzeng, E., Hoffman, J., Saenko, K., & Darrell, T. (2017). Adversarial discriminative domain adaptation. *Proceedings of the IEEE Conference on Computer Vision and Pattern Recognition*, 7167–7176.

Ugandar, R., Rahamathunnisa, U., Sajithra, S., Christiana, M. B. V., Palai, B. K., & Boopathi, S. (2023). Hospital Waste Management Using Internet of Things and Deep Learning: Enhanced Efficiency and Sustainability. In *Applications of Synthetic Biology in Health, Energy, and Environment* (pp. 317–343). IGI Global.

Ullrich, K., Welling, M., & Meeds, E. (2019). Soft weight-sharing for neural network compression. *5th International Conference on Learning Representations, ICLR 2017 - Conference Track Proceedings.*

Ulu, C., Korman, O., & Kömürgöz, G. (2019). Electromagnetic and thermal design/analysis of an induction motor for electric vehicles. *International Journal of Mechanical Engineering and Robotics Research*, 8(2), 239–245. DOI: 10.18178/ijmerr.8.2.239-245

UNICEF. (2022, Jan. 24). *Cyberbullying: What is it and how to stop it.* [Available online] https://www .unicef.org/end-violence/how-to-stop-cyberbullying

Upadhyaya, A. N., Saqib, A., Devi, J. V., Rallapalli, S., Sudha, S., & Boopathi, S. (2024). Implementation of the Internet of Things (IoT) in Remote Healthcare. In *Advances in Medical Technologies and Clinical Practice* (pp. 104–124). IGI Global. DOI: 10.4018/979-8-3693-1934-5.ch006

Upadhyay, K. G. (2011). *Design of Electrical Machines.* New Age International Ltd.

Usman, S., Mehmood, R., Katib, I., & Albeshri, A. (2022). Data locality in high performance computing, big data, and converged systems: An analysis of the cutting edge and a future system architecture. *Electronics (Basel)*, 12(1), 53. DOI: 10.3390/electronics12010053

Vaithianathan, V., Subbulakshmi, N., Boopathi, S., & Mohanraj, M. (2024). Integrating Project-Based and Skills-Based Learning for Enhanced Student Engagement and Success: Transforming Higher Education. In *Adaptive Learning Technologies for Higher Education* (pp. 345–372). IGI Global. DOI: 10.4018/979-8-3693-3641-0.ch015

Valueva, M. V., Nagornov, N. N., Lyakhov, P. A., Valuev, G. V., & Chervyakov, N. I. (2020). Application of the residue number system to reduce hardware costs of the convolutional neural network implementation. *Mathematics and Computers in Simulation*, 177, 232–243. DOI: 10.1016/j.matcom.2020.04.031

Vangeri, A. K., Bathrinath, S., Anand, M. C. J., Shanmugathai, M., Meenatchi, N., & Boopathi, S. (2024). Green Supply Chain Management in Eco-Friendly Sustainable Manufacturing Industries. In *Environmental Applications of Carbon-Based Materials* (pp. 253–287). IGI Global., DOI: 10.4018/979-8-3693-3625-0.ch010

Vapnik, V. N. (2000). *The nature of statistical learning theory* (2nd ed.). Springer. DOI: 10.1007/978-1-4757-3264-1

Vasilache, N., Zinenko, O., Theodoridis, T., Goyal, P., DeVito, Z., Moses, W. S., Verdoolaege, S., Adams, A., & Cohen, A. (2018). Tensor comprehensions: Framework-agnostic high-performance machine learning abstractions. *arXiv Preprint arXiv:1802.04730.*

Vaswani, A., Shazeer, N., Parmar, N., Uszkoreit, J., Jones, L., Gomez, A. N., Kaiser, L., & Polosukhin, I. (2017). Attention is all you need. *Advances in Neural Information Processing Systems*, ●●●, 30.

Venkateswaran, N., Vidhya, K., Ayyannan, M., Chavan, S. M., Sekar, K., & Boopathi, S. (2023). A Study on Smart Energy Management Framework Using Cloud Computing. In *5G, Artificial Intelligence, and Next Generation Internet of Things: Digital Innovation for Green and Sustainable Economies* (pp. 189–212). IGI Global. DOI: 10.4018/978-1-6684-8634-4.ch009

Venkateswaran, N., Kiran Kumar, K., Maheswari, K., Kumar Reddy, R. V., & Boopathi, S. (2024). Optimizing IoT Data Aggregation: Hybrid Firefly-Artificial Bee Colony Algorithm for Enhanced Efficiency in Agriculture. *AGRIS On-Line Papers in Economics and Informatics*, 16(1), 117–130. DOI: 10.7160/aol.2024.160110

Vennila, T., Karuna, M., Srivastava, B. K., Venugopal, J., Surakasi, R., & Sampath, B. (2022). New Strategies in Treatment and Enzymatic Processes: Ethanol Production From Sugarcane Bagasse. In *Human Agro-Energy Optimization for Business and Industry* (pp. 219–240). IGI Global.

Verma, R., Christiana, M. B. V., Maheswari, M., Srinivasan, V., Patro, P., Dari, S. S., & Boopathi, S. (2024). Intelligent Physarum Solver for Profit Maximization in Oligopolistic Supply Chain Networks. In *AI and Machine Learning Impacts in Intelligent Supply Chain* (pp. 156–179). IGI Global. DOI: 10.4018/979-8-3693-1347-3.ch011

Villa, O., Lustig, D., Yan, Z., Bolotin, E., Fu, Y., Chatterjee, N., Jiang, N., & Nellans, D. (2021). Need for speed: Experiences building a trustworthy system-level gpu simulator. *2021 IEEE International Symposium on High-Performance Computer Architecture (HPCA)*, 868–880. DOI: 10.1109/HPCA51647.2021.00077

Víšek, J. Á. (2011). Consistency of the least weighted squares under heteroscedasticity. *Kybernetika*, 47, 179–206.

Voicu, R.-A., Dobre, C., Bajenaru, L., & Ciobanu, R.-I. (2019, January). Human Physical Activity Recognition Using Smartphone Sensors. *Sensors (Basel)*, 19(3), 458. DOI: 10.3390/s19030458 PMID: 30678039

Wang, G., Luo, Z., Desta, H. G., Chen, M., Dong, Y., & Lin, B. (2024). AI-driven development of high-performance solid-state hydrogen storage. *Energy Reviews*, 100106.

Wang, K., Lu, D., Han, S. C., Long, S., & Poon, J. (2020). Detect all abuse! toward universal abusive language detection models. *arXiv preprint arXiv:2010.03776*. DOI: 10.18653/v1/2020.coling-main.560

Wang, S., Liu, J., Ouyang, X., & Sun, Y. (2020). Galileo at SemEval-2020 task 12: Multi-lingual learning for offensive language identification using pre-trained language models. *arXiv preprint arXiv:2010.03542*. DOI: 10.18653/v1/2020.semeval-1.189

Wang, S., Zheng, H., Wen, X., & Fu, S. (2024). Distributed high-performance computing methods for accelerating deep learning training. *Journal of Knowledge Learning and Science Technology ISSN: 2959-6386 (Online), 3*(3), 108–126.

Wang, S., Zheng, H., Wen, X., & Fu, S. (2024a). Distributed high-performance computing methods for accelerating deep learning training. *Journal of Knowledge Learning and Science Technology ISSN: 2959-6386 (Online), 3*(3), 108–126.

Wang, S., Zheng, H., Wen, X., & Fu, S. (2024b). Distributed high-performance computing methods for accelerating deep learning training. *Journal of Knowledge Learning and Science Technology ISSN: 2959-6386 (Online), 3*(3), 108–126.

Wang, Y., Gao, Z., Lü, H., & Li, Q. (2022). Decoding the nuclear symmetry energy event-by-event in heavy-ion collisions with machine learning. *Physics Letters. [Part B]*, 835, 137508. DOI: 10.1016/j.physletb.2022.137508

Ward, L., Sivaraman, G., Pauloski, J. G., Babuji, Y., Chard, R., Dandu, N., Redfern, P. C., Assary, R. S., Chard, K., & Curtiss, L. A. (2021). Colmena: Scalable machine-learning-based steering of ensemble simulations for high performance computing. *2021 IEEE/ACM Workshop on Machine Learning in High Performance Computing Environments (MLHPC)*, 9–20. DOI: 10.1109/MLHPC54614.2021.00007

Waseem, Z., Davidson, T., Warmsley, D., & Weber, I. (2017). Understanding abuse: A typology of abusive language detection subtasks. *arXiv preprint arXiv:1705.09899*. DOI: 10.18653/v1/W17-3012

Wei, J., & Zou, K. (2019). Eda: Easy data augmentation techniques for boosting performance on text classification tasks. *arXiv preprint arXiv:1901.11196*. DOI: 10.18653/v1/D19-1670

Wei, G., Li, G., Zhao, J., & He, A. (2019). Development of a LeNet-5 gas identification CNN structure for electronic noses. *Sensors (Basel)*, 19(1), 217. DOI: 10.3390/s19010217 PMID: 30626158

Wiedemann, G., Yimam, S. M., & Biemann, C. (2020). UHH-LT at SemEval-2020 task 12: Fine-tuning of pre-trained transformer networks for offensive language detection. *arXiv preprint arXiv:2004.11493*. DOI: 10.18653/v1/2020.semeval-1.213

Wilson, J. (2019). *Machine learning for nuclear fission systems: Preliminary investigation of an autonomous control system for the MGEP* [PhD Thesis]. Massachusetts Institute of Technology.

Wilson, P. W. (2018). Dimension reduction in nonparametric models of production. *European Journal of Operational Research*, 267(1), 349–367. DOI: 10.1016/j.ejor.2017.11.020

Wood, D., Cole, J., & Booth, T. (2019). NEURO-DRAM: a 3D recurrent visual attention model for interpretable neuroimaging classification. *arXiv Preprint arXiv:1910.04721*.

Wu, C.-J., Raghavendra, R., Gupta, U., Acun, B., Ardalani, N., Maeng, K., Chang, G., Aga, F., Huang, J., & Bai, C. (2022). Sustainable ai: Environmental implications, challenges and opportunities. *Proceedings of Machine Learning and Systems*, 4, 795–813.

Wu, N., & Xie, Y. (2022). A survey of machine learning for computer architecture and systems. *ACM Computing Surveys*, 55(3), 1–39. DOI: 10.1145/3494523

Xia, G.-S., Hu, J., Hu, F., Shi, B., Bai, X., Zhong, Y., Zhang, L., & Lu, X. (2017). AID: A Benchmark Data Set for Performance Evaluation of Aerial Scene Classification. *IEEE Transactions on Geoscience and Remote Sensing*, 55(7), 3965–3981. DOI: 10.1109/TGRS.2017.2685945

Xu, H., Song, S., & Mao, Z. (2024). Characterizing the performance of emerging deep learning, graph, and high performance computing workloads under interference. *2024 IEEE International Parallel and Distributed Processing Symposium Workshops (IPDPSW)*, 468–477. DOI: 10.1109/IPDPSW63119.2024.00098

Xu, J., Zhou, W., Fu, Z., Zhou, H., & Li, L. (2021). A survey on green deep learning. ArXiv:2111.05193.

Xu, X., Han, T., Huang, J., Kruger, A. A., Kumar, A., & Goel, A. (2021). Machine learning enabled models to predict sulfur solubility in nuclear waste glasses. *ACS Applied Materials & Interfaces*, 13(45), 53375–53387. DOI: 10.1021/acsami.1c10359 PMID: 34516090

Yadav, D. (2004). *Microcontroller: Features and applications*. New Age International.

Yang, C.-L., Chen, Z.-X., & Yang, C.-Y. (2020). Sensor Classification Using Convolutional Neural Network by Encoding Multivariate Time Series as Two-Dimensional Colored Images. *Sensors (Basel)*, 20(1), 168. DOI: 10.3390/s20010168 PMID: 31892141

Yang, F., Ma, Z., & Xie, M. (2021). Image classification with superpixels and feature fusion method. *Journal of Electronic Science and Technology*, 19(1), 100096. DOI: 10.1016/j.jnlest.2021.100096

Yao, S., Zhao, Y., Shao, H., Liu, S. Z., Liu, D., Su, L., & Abdelzaher, T. (2018). FastDeepIoT: Towards understanding and optimizing neural network execution time on mobile and embedded devices. *SenSys 2018 - Proceedings of the 16th Conference on Embedded Networked Sensor Systems*, 278–291. DOI: 10.1145/3274783.3274840

Yao, H. M., Jiang, L., Zhang, H. H., & Wei, E. I. (2019). Machine learning methodology review for computational electromagnetics. In *2019 International Applied Computational Electromagnetics Society Symposium-China (ACES)* (Vol. 1, pp. 1–4). IEEE. DOI: 10.23919/ACES48530.2019.9060439

Yao, M., Gan, Y., Liang, J., Dong, D., Ma, L., Liu, J., Luo, Q., & Li, Y. (2021). Performance simulation of a heat pipe and refrigerant-based lithium-ion battery thermal management system coupled with electric vehicle air-conditioning. *Applied Thermal Engineering*, 191, 116878. DOI: 10.1016/j.applthermaleng.2021.116878

Yi, H., Deng, C., Gong, X., Deng, X., & Blatnik, M. (2021). 1D-3D Online Coupled Transient Analysis for Powertrain-Control Integrated Thermal Management in an Electric Vehicle. *SAE International Journal of Advances and Current Practices in Mobility*, 3(2021-01–0237), 2410–2420.

Yi, H., Li, A., Sun, R., Hu, Y., Zhou, A., Zan, J., & Peng, Q. (2022). *1D-3D Coupled Analysis for Motor Thermal Management in an Electric Vehicle*. SAE Technical Paper.

Yi, L., Deng, X., Yang, L. T., Wu, H., Wang, M., & Situ, Y. (2020). Reinforcement-learning-enabled partial confident information coverage for IoT-based bridge structural health monitoring. *IEEE Internet of Things Journal*, 8(5), 3108–3119. DOI: 10.1109/JIOT.2020.3028325

Yin, S., Ouyang, P., Yang, J., Lu, T., Li, X., Liu, L., & Wei, S. (2019). An Energy-Efficient Reconfigurable Processor for Binary-and Ternary-Weight Neural Networks with Flexible Data Bit Width. *IEEE Journal of Solid-State Circuits*, 54(4), 1120–1136. Advance online publication. DOI: 10.1109/JSSC.2018.2881913

Yin, Y., Yang, Z., Hu, H., & Wu, X. (2022). Universal multi-Source domain adaptation for image classification. *Pattern Recognition*, 121, 108238. DOI: 10.1016/j.patcog.2021.108238

Younas, M., Jawawi, D. N. A., Shah, M. A., Mustafa, A., Awais, M., Ishfaq, M. K., & Wakil, K. (2020). Elicitation of Nonfunctional Requirements in Agile Development Using Cloud Computing Environment. *IEEE Access : Practical Innovations, Open Solutions*, 8, 209153–209162. DOI: 10.1109/ACCESS.2020.3014381

Yüksel, E., Soydaner, D., & Bahtiyar, H. (2021). Nuclear binding energy predictions using neural networks: Application of the multilayer perceptron. *International Journal of Modern Physics E*, 30(03), 2150017. DOI: 10.1142/S0218301321500178

Yu, W., Liu, Y., Dillon, T. S., & Rahayu, W. (2022). Edge computing-assisted IoT framework with an autoencoder for fault detection in manufacturing predictive maintenance. *IEEE Transactions on Industrial Informatics*, ●●●, 1–1. DOI: 10.1109/TII.2022.3178732

Yu, Z., Liu, J. K., Jia, S., Zhang, Y., Zheng, Y., Tian, Y., & Huang, T. (2020). Toward the next generation of retinal neuroprosthesis: Visual computation with spikes. *Engineering (Beijing)*, 6(4), 449–461. DOI: 10.1016/j.eng.2020.02.004

Zablodskiy, M., Pliuhin, V., & Chuenko, R. (2018). Simulation of induction machines with common solid rotor. *Technical Electrodynamics*, 2018(6), 42–45. DOI: 10.15407/techned2018.06.042

Zablodskiy, N., Lettl, J., Pliugin, V., Buhr, K., & Khomitskiy, S. (2013a). Induction motor optimal design by use of cartesian product. *Transactions on Electrical Engineering*, 2(2), 54–58.

Zablodskiy, N., Lettl, J., Pliugin, V., Buhr, K., & Khomitskiy, S. (2013b). Induction motor design by use of genetic optimization algorithms. *Transactions on Electrical Engineering*, 2(3), 65–69.

Zaheri, S., Leath, J., & Stroud, D. (2020). Toxic comment classification. *SMU Data Science Review*, 3(1), 13.

Zampieri, M. (2021, August 4). *OLID* [Data set]. https://sites.google.com/site/offensevalsharedtask/olid

Zampieri, M., Malmasi, S., Nakov, P., Rosenthal, S., Farra, N., & Kumar, R. (2019). Predicting the type and target of offensive posts in social media. *arXiv preprint arXiv:1902.09666*. DOI: 10.18653/v1/N19-1144

Zeng, G., He, Y., Yu, Z., Yang, X., Yang, R., & Zhang, L. (2016). *InceptionNet/GoogLeNet - Going Deeper with Convolutions*. Cvpr., DOI: 10.1002/jctb.4820

Zhang, H., Mahata, D., Shahid, S., Mehnaz, L., Anand, S., Singla, Y., Shah, R. R., & Uppal, K. (2019). Identifying offensive posts and targeted offense from twitter. *arXiv preprint arXiv:1904.09072*.

Zhang, Y., Gao, J., Tan, Z., Zhou, L., Ding, K., Zhou, M., Zhang, S., & Wang, D. (2024). Data-centric foundation models in computational healthcare: A survey. *arXiv Preprint arXiv:2401.02458*.

Zhang, A., Lipton, Z. C., Li, M., & Smola, A. J. (2021). *Dive into Deep Learning*. https://arxiv.org/abs/2106.11342v2

Zhang, J., Liu, J., Pan, B., & Shi, Z. (2020). Domain Adaptation Based on Correlation Subspace Dynamic Distribution Alignment for Remote Sensing Image Scene Classification. *IEEE Transactions on Geoscience and Remote Sensing*, 58(11), 7920–7930. DOI: 10.1109/TGRS.2020.2985072

Zhang, Y., & Davison, B. D. (2021). Deep spherical manifold gaussian kernel for unsupervised domain adaptation. *Proceedings of the IEEE/CVF Conference on Computer Vision and Pattern Recognition*, 4443–4452. DOI: 10.1109/CVPRW53098.2021.00501

Zhang, Y., Huang, T., & Bompard, E. F. (2018). Big data analytics in smart grids: A review. *Energy Informatics*, 1(1), 8. DOI: 10.1186/s42162-018-0007-5

Zhang, Y., Li, B., & Tan, Y. (2021). Making AI available for everyone at anywhere: A Survey about Edge Intelligence. *Journal of Physics: Conference Series*, 1757(1), 012076. DOI: 10.1088/1742-6596/1757/1/012076

Zhang, Z., Liu, S., Zhang, Y., & Chen, W. (2021). RS-DARTS: A convolutional neural architecture search for remote sensing image scene classification. *Remote Sensing (Basel)*, 14(1), 141. DOI: 10.3390/rs14010141

Zhou, V. (2021, Dec. 11). *A simple explanation of the bag-of-words model.* [Available online] https://towardsdatascience.com/a-simple-explanation-of-the-bag-of-words-model-b88fc4f4971

Zhou, W., Newsam, S., Li, C., & Shao, Z. (2018). PatternNet: A benchmark dataset for performance evaluation of remote sensing image retrieval. *ISPRS Journal of Photogrammetry and Remote Sensing*, 145, 197–209. DOI: 10.1016/j.isprsjprs.2018.01.004

Zhu, S., Ota, K., & Dong, M. (2022). Green AI for IIoT: Energy Efficient Intelligent Edge Computing for Industrial Internet of Things. *IEEE Transactions on Green Communications and Networking*, 6(1), 79–88. DOI: 10.1109/TGCN.2021.3100622

Zinovyeva, E., Härdle, W. K., & Lessmann, S. (2020). Antisocial online behavior detection using deep learning. *Decision Support Systems*, 138, 113362. DOI: 10.1016/j.dss.2020.113362

About the Contributors

Belgacem Ben Youssef holds the post of Associate Professor in the Department of Computer Engineering, College of Computer & Information Sciences at King Saud University, Riyadh, Saudi Arabia. He received his PhD from the Department of Electrical & Computer Engineering, Cullen College of Engineering, University of Houston, Texas, USA. He was previously an Assistant Professor in both the School of Interactive Arts & Technology and the TechOne Program at Simon Fraser University, British Columbia, Canada. His research interests include high-performance computing, machine learning, biological computing, image processing, and spatial thinking in learning and design. He has two years of industrial experience in software development and technical project management. He is a member of the IEEE, IEEE Computer Society, and the ACM.

Mohamed Maher Ben Ismail is an associate professor at the computer science department of the College of Computer and Information Sciences at King Saud University. He received his PhD. degree in Computer Science from the University of Louisville in 2011. His research interests include Pattern Recognition, Machine Learning, Data Mining and Image Processing.

* * *

Haikel S. Alhichri (M'02) received the B.Sc. (High Hons.) and M.Sc. degrees in computer science from the University of Saskatchewan, Saskatoon, SK, Canada, and the Ph.D. degree in systems' design engineering from the University of Waterloo, Waterloo, ON, Canada. He has more than 20 years of academic and industrial experience in computer science field in Canada, the United Arab Emirates, and the Kingdom of Saudi Arabia. He has worked briefly in a research capacity for Hypercore systems now bought by Sierra systems, Saskatoon, SK, Canada, and Intelligent Mechatronic Systems Inc., Waterloo, ON, Canada. From 2003 to 2007, he joined the American University in Dubai, Dubai, United Arab Emirates, as an Assistant Professor of Information Technology. From 2007 to 2010, he worked with Sharesoft Solutions FZ LLC in Dubai, UAE as a Product Manager and Business Development Director. Between 2010 and 2022, he joined the College of Computer and Information Sciences, King Saud University (KSU), Riyadh, KSA, as faculty of Computer Engineering and a member of the Advanced Lab for Intelligent Systems Research. He also acted as a Scientific Advisor to the Innovation Center at KSU from 2010 to 2013. His research interests include pattern recognition, machine intelligence, and remote sensing.

Abdullah Alsalemi received the B.S. degree in electrical engineering from Qatar University. From June 2016 to May 2017, he worked at the Qatar Mobility Innovations Center (QMIC) as an intern Mobile Application Developer. He is currently a PhD student at De Montfort University. He has authored over

70 research papers in refereed journals and international conference proceedings. His current research interests include energy saving behavior and medical simulator design.

Abbes Amira (S99-M01-SM07) received his Ph.D degree in 2001 from Queen's University Belfast, United Kingdom. Since then, he has taken many academic and consultancy positions in the United Kingdom, Europe, Asia, and the Middleast. He is currently the Dean of the College of Computing and Informatics at the University of Sharjah, UAE. During his career to date, Prof. Amira has been successful in securing substantial funding from government agencies and industry; he has supervised more than 25 PhD students and has over 400 publications in top journals and conferences in the area of embedded systems, IoT, image and signal processing. He obtained many international awards, including the 2008 VARIAN prize offered by the Swiss Society of Radiobiology and Medical Physics, CAST award, DELL-EM Envision the future (2018), IET premium award (2017) and many best paper and recognition awards in IEEE international conferences and events. Prof. Amira has participated as guest editor and member of the editorial board in many international journals including recent special issues in IEEE IoT Journal and Elsevier Pattern Recognition. He has taken visiting professor positions at the University of Tun Hussein Onn, Malaysia and the University of Nancy, Henri Poincare, France. Prof. Amira has also conducted consultancy services for several government agencies and companies in the private sector. He is a Fellow of IET, Fellow of the Higher Education Academy, Senior member of the IEEE, and Senior member of ACM. His research interests include artificial intelligence, embedded systems, high-performance computing, big data and IoT, connected health, image and vision systems, biometric and security.

Samir Brahim Belhaouri received a master's degree in telecommunications and Network from the Institut Nationale Polytechnique of Toulouse, France, in 2000, and the Ph.D. degree from the Federal Polytechnic School of Lausanne-Switzerland, in 2006. He is currently an associate professor in the Division of Information and Communication Technologies, College of Science and Engineering, HBKU. He also holds several positions at the University of Sharjah, Innopolis University, Petronas University, and EPFL Federal Swiss School.

Ihor Biletskyi is a Rector at the O.M. Beketov National University of Urban Economy in Kharkiv (Ukraine). He received his Ph.D. degree in Project Management from O.M. Beketov National University of Urban Economy in Kharkiv (Ukraine) in 2016 and a D.Sc. degree in Economics from Odesa National University of Technology (Ukraine) in 2023. He is an expert of the Ministry of Education and Science of Ukraine for examining research and development projects of the thematic direct "Energy and energy efficiency", and a Member of the Expert Council of the Sikorsky Challenge Startup Competition. His research activities mainly focus on Energy Efficiency, BIM Technologies, Smart Services, and Project Management.

Sampath Boopathi is an accomplished individual with a strong academic background and extensive research experience. He completed his undergraduate studies in Mechanical Engineering and pursued his postgraduate studies in the field of Computer-Aided Design. Dr. Boopathi obtained his Ph.D. from Anna University, focusing his research on Manufacturing and optimization. Throughout his career, Dr. Boopathi has made significant contributions to the field of engineering. He has authored and published over 300 research articles in internationally peer-reviewed journals, highlighting his expertise and dedication to advancing knowledge in his area of specialization. His research output demonstrates his commitment to conducting rigorous and impactful research. In addition to his research publications, Dr. Boopathi has also been granted one patent and has three published patents to his name. This indicates his innovative thinking and ability to develop practical solutions to real-world engineering challenges. With 17 years of academic and research experience, Dr. Boopathi has enriched the engineering community through his teaching and mentorship roles.

Soumaya Chaffar graduated from the University of Montreal, where she received in 2006 and 2009, respectively, her Master and her PhD in Computer Science. Then, she has been employed as a postdoctoral researcher at the School of Electrical Engineering and Computer Science of the University of Ottawa, her main concern was to propose and experiment promising ideas and approaches related to analysis and generation of emotion in textual data. After that, as a postdoctoral researcher in Nuance Communications, she worked on industrial projects related to sentiment analysis for speech technologies. She joined Prince Sultan University as an assistant professor and then University of Prince Mugrin as an associate professor. She received several excellence-based awards in Canada.

Saurabh Chandra is an accomplished legal scholar and currently serves as an Associate Professor at the School of Law, Bennett University, India. With a robust academic foundation, he earned his Bachelor of Arts and Bachelor of Laws (B.A. LL.B.) from the prestigious Aligarh Muslim University (AMU). He further specialized in Business Laws, completing his Master of Laws (LL.M.) at the renowned National Law School of India University (NLSIU), Bangalore. Dr. Chandra's academic journey culminated in a Doctorate in Law (Ph.D.) from the esteemed National Law University. In addition to his impressive legal education from some of India's most prestigious institutions, Dr. Saurabh Chandra also holds a master's degree in Management with specialization in Human Resources in Management and another in Journalism and Mass Communication. With 16 years of teaching experience, he has established himself as an expert in Business and Corporate Laws, with numerous publications to his credit. Dr. Saurabh Chandra is a distinguished expert in Business and Corporate Laws, with a profound understanding of the intricate legal frameworks that govern the business world. His expertise is complemented by a robust portfolio of scholarly publications, which underscores his commitment to advancing knowledge in his field. Throughout his career, Dr. Chandra has consistently produced high-impact research that addresses critical issues in business and corporate law. His publications are widely recognized for their depth of analysis, innovative perspectives, and practical relevance. He has contributed extensively to leading journals, where his work has often set new standards for legal scholarship. His publications not only reflect his scholarly rigor but also his dedication to addressing contemporary challenges faced by businesses and policymakers. By bridging the gap between theoretical insights and real-world applications, Dr. Chandra's work serves as a valuable resource for academics, legal practitioners, and industry professionals alike. Dr. Chandra brings a wealth of experience in Academic Administration, having successfully held various key administrative positions. His diverse qualifications and extensive experience make him a distinguished figure in the academic and legal communities.

Kegong Diao is a VC2020 lecturer in engineering and sustainable development, and a researcher specializing in development of complexity science-based method for urban infrastructure system analysis, with emphasis on urban water systems. Kegong has significantly contributed to 14 research and consulting projects, including 5 UK and EU funded projects. His research outcomes include 6 patents, 20+ peer-reviewed publications in well-renowned journals.

Ibtihal Ferwana received her B.S. degree in Computer Science from Prince Sultan University. She recieved her Master's degree from the University of Illinois at Urbana-Champaign, USA and currently she is involved in the PhD program of Computer Science at the University of Illinois at Urbana-Champaign. During her undergraduate, she was involved in several research and industrial projects in the area of machine learning and data science. In 2018, she was awarded the Google's Women Techmakers Award based on academic achievements.

Tariq Lasloum is a computer engineer. He received his M.Sc. degree in computer science from King Saud University, Riyadh, Saudi Arabia. Currently, he is studying for a PHD degree in computer engineering at King Saud University in Saudi Arabia. Presently, he works as director of technical support at the Ministry of Communications and Information Technology.

Hossein Malekmohamadi is a Senior Lecturer in Game Programming in the School of Computer Science and Informatics at De Montfort University. His research areas include Computer Vision, Computer Graphics, Deep Learning, Multimedia Signal Processing, Smart Systems, and Quality of Experience (QoE).

Sergiy Plankovskyy is originally from Volodymyr-Volynsky, Ukraine. He has 35 years of international experience in the research and development of processing with intense energy fluxes (mainly technologies using plasma, laser, and detonation sources). After being Head of the Faculty of Aircraft Engineering at the National Aerospace University "Kharkiv Aviation Institute", he is now Head of the School of Energy, Information and Transport Infrastructure at the O.M. Beketov National University of Urban Economy in Kharkiv, Ukraine. He has over 200 refereed publications and has supervised 11 Ph.D. students to successful completion. His research interests cover innovation technologies, including the methods of manufacturing for the digital industry. He is a member of the Expert Council on Mechanical Engineering of the National Agency for Higher Education Quality Assurance (NAQA), Ukraine.

Vladyslav Pliuhin is the Head of the Department of Urban Electrical Energy Supply and Consumption Systems at the O.M. Beketov National University of Urban Economy in Kharkiv (Ukraine). He received his Ph.D. degree in Electrical Machines and Apparatus from Donetsk National University (Ukraine) in 2004 and a D.Sc. degree in Electrical Machines and Apparatus from National Technical University "Kharkiv Polytechnic Institute" (Ukraine) in 2016. He had an international traineeship as a Post-Doctorate at the Czech Technical University in Prague (Czech Republic) in 2012. He is an expert of the Ministry of Education and Science of Ukraine for examining research and development projects of the thematic direct "Energy and Energy Efficiency", and a member of the Ministry of Education and Science of Ukraine Council for examining Ph.D. and D.Sc. thesis. His research activities are mainly focused on Electrical Machines Design and Optimization, CAD Software Development, Energy Efficiency, Machine Learning, and Digital Twins.

Dhivakar Poosapadi, a distinguished oil and gas research engineer, specializes in the design, development, and commissioning of advanced drilling systems, including subsea completion systems, well access systems, and riser gas handling systems. He has held critical roles at globally renowned organizations such as Keppel Offshore and Marine Technology, TechnipFMC, and Halliburton. With a Master's in Mechanical Engineering from Nanyang Technological University, Dhivakar has pioneered industry-transforming products like the Riser Drilling Device and Reservoir Downhole Condition Monitoring Systems, which operate under extreme high-pressure and high-temperatures (HPHT). These innovations that include patent contributions have redefined safety and efficiency in offshore drilling, meeting stringent API and ASME standards. Dhivakar has also contributed as a peer reviewer for leading organizations, including the Offshore Technology Conference and the Society of Petroleum Engineers, shaping advancements in the field. His groundbreaking work has earned him prestigious accolades, including the ASME Woelfel Best Mechanical Engineering Achievement Award and Hart's Meritorious Engineering Awards, solidifying his position as a leader in the oil and gas industry.

Aswathy Ravikumar is a Research Associate at the Vellore Institute of Technology. A passionate educator with over eight years of teaching experience at graduate and postgraduate levels as Assistant Professor of Computer Science and Engineering, Mar Baselios College of Engineering and Technology. An enthusiast in the domains of artificial intelligence and data science, with numerous publications and projects and an excellent academic track record. Her research interest includes Distributed Deep Learning, Big Data and Accelerating Deep Learning performance using an HPC environment.

Harini Sriraman is an Associate Professor with Vellore Institute of Technology. She has more than 13 years of teaching experience. Her research interest includes Distributed and Parallel computing, Accelerating Deep Learning performance using HPC environment, Hardware based Domain Specific Acceleration and Energy efficient and sustainable computing Web of Science ResearcherID: AAB-4513-2019.

Maria Sukhonos is a Vice-Rector for Research at the O.M. Beketov National University of Urban Economy in Kharkiv (Ukraine). She received her Ph.D. degree in Project Management from Prydniprovska State Academy of Civil Engineering and Architecture (Ukraine) in 2007 and a D.Sc. degree in Project Management from the National Aerospace University "Kharkiv Aviation Institute" (Ukraine) in 2013. She is the Curator of the "Energy Innovation Hub" implemented by Deutsche Geselschaft für Internationale Zusammenarbeit (GIZ) GmbH and funded by the Federal Ministry of Economic Cooperation and Development of Germany (BMZ) in the O.M. Beketov National University of Urban Economy in Kharkiv (Ukraine). Her research activities are mainly focused on Energy Efficiency, Sustainable Electrical Energy Systems, Smart Services for Smart Cities, Digital Project Management.

Vitaliy Tietieriev is a Postgraduate Student at the O.M. Beketov National University of Urban Economy in Kharkiv (Ukraine). He received his master's degree in Electrical Power Engineering, Electrical Engineering and Electromechanics from O.M. Beketov National University of Urban Economy in Kharkiv (Ukraine) in 2019. He had an international traineeship as Postgraduate at the University of Helsinki (Finland) within the Erasmus+ KA2 project ClimEd in 2022. His research activities are mainly focused on Engineering Software Development, Energy Efficiency, Smart Technologies, IoT and Machine Learning.

Yevgen Tsegelnyk is a Deputy Head (Research) at the School of Energy, Information and Transport Infrastructure of the O.M. Beketov National University of Urban Economy in Kharkiv (Ukraine). He received his Ph.D. degree in Aerospace Engineering from the National Aerospace University "Kharkiv Aviation Institute" (Ukraine) in 2010. He has more than 15 years of international experience in research and development. He had an international traineeship as a Post-Doctorate at the Czech Technical University in Prague (Czech Republic) in 2014. His research interests cover innovation technologies, including the methods of manufacturing for the digital industry, processing with intense energy fluxes (technologies using plasma, laser, and detonation sources), additive and subtractive manufacturing technologies, and applied computing techniques.

Index

A

AI-Powered Energy Management 279, 299
Anomaly Detection 224, 232, 368, 383, 384, 385, 388, 392, 393, 394, 395, 399, 402, 403
Apache Spark 213, 214, 215, 216, 435, 437, 440, 444, 445, 446, 447, 454, 460
Artificial Intelligence 4, 6, 30, 33, 35, 37, 38, 55, 58, 59, 60, 63, 84, 86, 90, 91, 103, 105, 122, 123, 127, 128, 143, 145, 146, 151, 165, 175, 181, 183, 186, 188, 219, 224, 225, 226, 227, 251, 271, 274, 276, 277, 278, 280, 282, 283, 285, 290, 291, 298, 299, 300, 325, 326, 327, 328, 341, 350, 351, 352, 353, 376, 377, 380, 384, 387, 405, 406, 407, 408, 428, 432, 434, 435, 436, 455, 456, 457, 459

B

Battery Management 255, 256, 268, 271, 276, 409, 411, 412, 426, 429, 434
Brain Activity 329, 338, 339

C

Cartesian Product 148, 150, 154, 187, 188
Cloud Computing 127, 128, 188, 189, 218, 219, 221, 222, 223, 224, 225, 226, 227, 248, 275, 276, 282, 298, 299, 300, 365, 385, 396, 397, 407, 433, 434, 437, 459
Complexity Reduction 38, 235
Comprehensibility 39
compression rate 107, 111, 113, 116, 118, 119, 120
Computational Neuroscience 329, 330, 331, 332, 333, 335, 336, 338, 339, 346, 347, 348, 351
Computer Vision 7, 67, 84, 85, 86, 87, 105, 106, 121, 122, 123, 124, 134, 189, 310, 312, 329, 351, 459
Computing Performance 128

D

Data Analytics 187, 197, 216, 219, 233, 248, 297, 342, 356, 373, 403, 459
Data Contamination 37
Data Integration 322, 340, 345, 371, 383, 385, 396, 397, 403
Data Lake 127, 128, 130, 132, 133, 134, 141, 143, 221
Data Parallel 225
Data Privacy 128, 139, 243, 294, 300, 301, 303, 304, 306, 323, 329

Deep Learning 1, 2, 3, 6, 8, 10, 11, 12, 13, 14, 15, 28, 30, 31, 32, 33, 34, 35, 54, 55, 56, 57, 59, 61, 62, 63, 64, 67, 84, 85, 87, 88, 89, 90, 92, 93, 94, 102, 103, 104, 105, 108, 119, 121, 124, 127, 128, 142, 143, 183, 188, 189, 197, 198, 201, 205, 207, 213, 214, 215, 216, 218, 219, 220, 221, 223, 225, 226, 227, 230, 232, 233, 238, 241, 243, 249, 250, 284, 288, 298, 299, 300, 326, 327, 329, 330, 331, 333, 339, 341, 344, 346, 348, 354, 379, 385, 388, 391, 395, 397, 399, 402, 405, 407, 435, 436, 437, 439, 440, 441, 442, 443, 444, 446, 450, 451, 453, 456, 457, 458, 459, 460
Deep Neural Networks 54, 58, 61, 84, 85, 92, 107, 108, 121, 122, 125, 225, 227, 243, 388, 406, 441, 451
Design 2, 47, 59, 62, 63, 73, 89, 90, 111, 112, 114, 119, 128, 145, 147, 148, 149, 150, 151, 152, 154, 156, 160, 164, 166, 167, 168, 175, 176, 181, 182, 183, 184, 185, 186, 187, 188, 202, 207, 214, 215, 221, 222, 232, 235, 237, 239, 240, 241, 242, 243, 245, 246, 254, 255, 256, 257, 260, 262, 263, 264, 265, 267, 268, 269, 270, 271, 272, 273, 315, 342, 345, 348, 351, 359, 360, 362, 371, 377, 378, 400, 409, 410, 411, 412, 413, 415, 416, 418, 419, 420, 421, 424, 425, 426, 427, 429, 430, 431, 442, 443, 451, 452, 454, 456, 457
Distributed Computing 206, 213, 214, 224, 233, 435, 437, 438, 444, 445, 446, 447, 449, 453, 454, 455, 457
DNN based mobile applications 107

E

EfficientNet-B3 75, 78, 87, 88
Electric Machines 145, 154, 176, 181, 182, 186
Energy Efficiency 54, 128, 129, 139, 141, 143, 254, 255, 257, 258, 259, 260, 263, 267, 272, 278, 279, 282, 283, 284, 285, 286, 287, 288, 290, 291, 292, 295, 298, 299, 359, 360, 409, 410, 411, 413, 414, 415, 416, 419, 425, 430, 437, 443, 444, 450, 452, 453, 455
Energy Harvesting 253, 299, 350, 380
Energy Optimization 277, 278, 279, 281, 282, 284, 292, 294, 295, 296, 297, 298, 299, 300
Entropy 69, 72, 74, 75, 76, 77, 78, 82, 83, 88
Environmental Monitoring 62, 236, 253, 366, 372

F

Federated Learning 84, 295, 296, 303, 304, 305, 306, 308, 309, 313, 315, 316, 317, 318, 319, 320, 321,

Printed in the United States
by Baker & Taylor Publisher Services